Date Due			

A HISTORY OF IDEAS IN BRAZIL

A
HISTORY OF IDEAS
IN BRAZIL

The Development
of Philosophy in Brazil
and the Evolution
of National History

By JOÃO CRUZ COSTA

TRANSLATED FROM THE PORTUGUESE BY SUZETTE MACEDO

1964
UNIVERSITY OF CALIFORNIA PRESS
Berkeley and Los Angeles

UNIVERSITY OF CALIFORNIA PRESS
BERKELEY AND LOS ANGELES, CALIFORNIA
CAMBRIDGE UNIVERSITY PRESS
LONDON, ENGLAND

Original title: *Contríbuição à História das Idéias no Brasil:
O desenvolvimento da filosofia no Brasil e a evolução histórica nacional,*
published by José Olympio, Rio de Janeiro, 1956,
as No. 86 of the collection *Documentos Brasileiros,*
edited by Octavio Tarquínio de Sousa

PUBLISHED WITH THE ASSISTANCE OF A GRANT
FROM THE ROCKEFELLER FOUNDATION

PRINTED IN THE UNITED STATES OF AMERICA

To the Memory of

ARMANDO DE SALLES OLIVEIRA

Preface

This work, originally published in a limited edition, was
the dissertation I presented in support of my candidature for the
chair of philosophy in the Faculty of Philosophy, Science, and Arts
of the University of São Paulo. It has been revised and expanded
for this edition. Since 1937, when I became assistant to the professor of philosophy, at that time my esteemed friend Professor Jean
Maugüé, I have felt that I should call the attention of students to
the changes which foreign philosophical currents in our own country underwent, and especially to the curious meanings they have
acquired in the evolution of our history. This has been ever since
one of my preoccupations as a teacher.

If thought is to be more than "idle fantasy"—to use the words
of King Duarte—it must not lose its contact with history or the real
problems of life. Of what value is a culture that is not aimed at an
understanding of what we are, is removed from the conditions of
this world, and ignores the fascinating lines of our destiny? Rather
than reject the foreign cultures that express a historic experience
richer than our own—a precious inheritance to receive—we should
absorb from them the lessons enabling us first of all to understand
what we are. We should be more than futile, we should be ridicu-

lous, if after learning from these cultures we still held ourselves aloof from the fascinating problems that concern us more directly.

What are we, the peoples of the Americas? We are mostly the descendants of humble folk who suffered in Europe. We are the fruit, almost all of us, of the adventure which led them to seek a better life in the New World. We spring from the Renaissance, from a new concept of humanity. Our origins, the conditions that have shaped us, and our historic experience combine to turn us from the summits of metaphysics to the hard realities of life, to invite us to contemplate the absorbing, contradictory adventures of our growth.

It was not my intention, at first, to undertake a study of so vast and thorny a subject. This work grew out of the notes I compiled on the way; and although it is neither profound nor original, it may perhaps be useful to those who seek to understand the mind of our people. I trust it will serve this purpose.

I take this opportunity to thank my friend and colleague, Professor Simões de Paula, who kindly undertook to correct my spelling. For the loan of books I wish to thank Professors Plinio Ayrosa, Alfredo Ellis Jr., Fernando Furquim de Almeida, Laerte Ramos de Carvalho, Fidelino de Figueiredo, and Antônio Candido; also Sérgio Milliet, Drs. Aquiles Raspantini, Estevão José de Almeida Prado; and my friends Guilherme Deveza, Amândio Sampaio, and Lineu Schützer. I wish further to thank Dr. Lewis Hanke of the Library of Congress and Drs. Geonisio Curvello de Mendonça and Paulo Duarte. I should like to record my sincere gratitude to Professor Jean Maugüé for the confidence he has always shown in me. I am indebted, too, to Professors Fernand Braudel, Emile Coornaert, Leopoldo Zea, Arturo Ardão, Joaquim de Carvalho, Herbert W. Schneider, and Paul Arbousse-Bastide for the interest they have shown in my work.

I am obliged to Professors Fernando de Azevedo, Milton da Silva Rodrigues, Arthur Versiani Velloso, and Fr. Orlando de Oliveira Villela for their many kindnesses. Here, too, I want to pay tribute to the late Professor Arnulf Konrad Ansorge, whose passing I so much regret. Lastly, I wish to thank the eminent historian, Dr. Octavio Tarquínio de Sousa, and José Olympio, for their interest in this work.

São Paulo, February, 1955.   CRUZ COSTA

Contents

x   *Contents*

"If we are some day to make a philosophical
contribution of significance, I am convinced
that it will not emerge from the heights of
metaphysics."—CLÓVIS BEVILÁQUA,
Esboços e Fragmentos

Introduction

In the opening chapters of his interesting study of American philosophy, Professor Herbert Schneider of Columbia University writes as follows:

The reader of the story that follows will note that American philosophy has continually been given new life and new directions by waves of immigration. In America, at least, it is useless to seek a "native tradition," for even our most genteel traditions are saturated with foreign inspirations. Spanish Franciscans, French Jesuits, English Puritans, Dutch Pietists, Scottish Calvinists, cosmopolitan "philosophes," German transcendentalists, Russian revolutionaries, and Oriental theosophists have all shared in giving to so-called American Philosophy its continuities as well as its shocks.

A little further on, he continues: "America was intellectually colonial long after it gained political independence and has been intellectually provincial long after it ceased being intellectually colonial. We still live intellectually on the fringe of European culture." [1]

I

This assertion by Schneider applies not only to the United States but to the whole of America. "Up to the present time," writes the Argentinian Professor Risieri Frondizi, "Spanish-American philosophy parallels the vicissitudes of European thought in Latin America." "No doubt," he goes on to say, "we have overcome many limitations and made great progress, but we are still under the powerful influence of European concepts." [2]

"Led by the hand of Europe," I myself recently wrote,

we made our entrance on the stage of history at a critical moment for Western culture. Europe imposed on us her languages, her religion, her ways of life—in short, her civilization. We of the Americas cannot speak of a truly American civilization. We are an extension, a new branch perhaps, of Western civilization. We can, however, speak of an American experience, the experience which has slowly taken shape during the four centuries of dramatic effort leading to the birth of nations and to the adaptation of Western civilization to the conditions of our continent. But the scene was set against quite another background; and our actors came from all divisions of mankind. In this setting time passed, history was made, and from this history a common human experience can be distilled, a "philosophy" in outline, which is of the greatest value to us.[3]

Thought is always the product of the activities of a people, and we should therefore turn to our own history and its interaction with world history to apprehend our own significance, the meaning of our spirit. In this way we can understand better the shades of meaning within the modulations of the ideas that influenced us. Many ideas were changed and many theories were born on the other side of the Atlantic that found expression in this part of the world—one that seems to be not altogether in agreement with the original premises. This is so because there is a style, peculiar to different conditions and subject to the historical evolution of a people, which determines or influences the transformation of the systems which our intelligence evolves to explain life.

In order to study the transformations or deformations of European doctrines in Brazil and the influence these doctrines exercised, particularly in the latter half of the nineteenth century, I think it would be useful to examine the origins of Brazilian intellectual life, since this would permit an analysis of the meaning particular to each of these doctrines or systems.

Thought is affected by the conditions of life. The deformation or molding which thought undergoes expresses the desires and intentions, if not of the people as a whole, at least of the groups which govern it and which exercise the greatest influence on its destiny. It is true that, as claimed by Sérgio Buarque de Holanda, "any comprehensive study of the Brazilian social structure must emphasize the basic fact that it is the only successful large-scale effort of a transplantation of European culture to a tropical or subtropical zone"; it is likewise true that "we are living *an unparalleled experience*"; that "having brought from distant countries our ways of life, our institutions, and our vision of the world" we pride ourselves on "maintaining all in an environment which is often unfavorable and hostile"; that "we are exiles in our own land"; that we share a "style and an evolution which belongs to another climate, another landscape."[4] It is equally true, however, that this complex suffers considerably from its contact with the new American environment, which exercises a transforming or modifying influence and alters the more outstanding features of this foreign civilization. It is for this reason that we are living through an experience without precedent. "Faced with the demands of the new environment, the foreign civilization can accept, assimilate, and produce new ways of life, becoming up to a point creative and not merely preserving a traditional but foreign legacy."[5]

Today's intellectuals, therefore, do not feel as exiled as Sérgio Buarque de Holanda suggested, because they are actively construing and interpreting the experiences of our eventful history—an activity which may sometimes be difficult and thankless, but is nevertheless vital and dynamic.

Thanks to the efforts of the people, who are the basis of our condition as a nation and the essential factor in all our progress, a new nation emerged, slowly but surely, a nation which gradually defined itself and—through a series of the most disappointing, as well as the most promising, adventures—began to assume an awareness of its intelligence and its destiny.

The Brazilian intelligence was formed by the same process which molded the Brazilian people. That is to say, both evolved as the result of foreign contributions. Eduardo Praz states: "to write the history of Brazil is to write the history of the immigrations to this country."[6]

Similarly, to write the history of its ideas is to describe the modifications of foreign ideas imported into Brazil. In this slow process of intellectual formation it is natural that there should have been some imitation, as there still is. It is understandable that we should have imitated the colonists. But the colonists themselves were subjected to the influences of the new conditions they encountered, and in this situation the first modifications to the original European form are already found. Some authors, who prize originality above all else, denounced "imitation" as the source of our errors and defects. But it is important not to forget that imitation is a natural and universal social phenomenon.[7] Our country has no monopoly on imitation. Besides, as Adrian Delpech correctly states: "imitation goes hand in hand with deformation, and this constitutes an originality."[8]

All American countries were the fruits of European economic expansion, which began in the sixteenth century and reached its heyday in the nineteenth, and they are therefore directly linked to European civilization and culture. "As a Daughter of Europe, America cannot be studied outside the European context. A correlation as sensitive as that between the equinoxes and the tides dominates the history of the two continents."[9]

Some of our compatriots, however, forget their own surroundings, fascinated by the continent whence the caravels set sail, a continent which continues to bewitch them with its ancient culture. Others insist that it is possible to create a civilization, an *ex nihilo* culture, based on a purely Brazilian reality. They forget that before a historic reality can be specifically Brazilian it must be common to mankind. It is therefore necessary for the understanding of our own characteristics to remember the mutual relationships between peoples.

In this study, in which I shall attempt to analyze one aspect of the history of our ideas, I wish to avoid, if possible, either of these two extreme positions and to consider the problem of the vicissitudes of European philosophy in Brazil in relation to the conditions of our history.

In Brazil, from colonial times, philosophy was the luxury of a handful of rich and cultured men. Determined to create the rudiments of a materially settled life, the men who immigrated to Brazil in the sixteenth century were inspired by a spirit of adventure and a desire for gain. The adventurer—and to risk one's life on the vast oceans was already an adventure—was impelled by a sense of the useful and the immediately effective.[10]

The fortunate few, who attended the Jesuit colleges at the end of the sixteenth and the beginning of the seventeenth centuries, were taught the Coimbran Scholasticism by their Jesuit tutors[11] and received the humanistic education which, together with the ownership of land and slaves, was a class distinction. In the seminaries and religious orders the philosophy of the Middle Ages continued to be expounded, with all its interminable logical and metaphysical controversies.

Philosophy was, therefore, from the first considered a bookish discipline. It arrived ready-made from Europe, but it was a sign of great culture to be able to reproduce simply the most recently arrived ideas. Desire for novelty took the place of an analytical spirit, and instead of criticism there was merely curiosity. The love of innovation is therefore an old characteristic of our intellectual life. There is another curious feature of our intelligence: an utter and unqualified admiration for all things foreign, which possibly springs from an inferiority complex traceable, perhaps, to the gulf between the problems of our "elites" and the immediate problems of the people of the land, and also to our condition as a colony.

We suspected our own enterprises and interpretations, and constantly preferred to depend on foreign thought. In the growth of our intellectual life from colonial times to the beginning of the twentieth century, our men of letters seemed to have become so completely identified with European thinking that they frequently give the impression of being "genuine exiles," in the words of Sérgio Buarque de Holanda. We must remember, however, as do the psychoanalysts, that all processes of identification (and, in the development of our history, philosophy became involved in such a process) are only partial, and that they take on individual forms which characterize the person or the nation engaged in this process. This seems to have happened to us. Although our culture went through a series of identification processes, they all reveal interesting aspects of a national thought taking shape. In the same way that a personality defines itself, having passed through a series of identifications, so the personality of a nation like ours—and the same can be said for the other American nations—is characterized by the elements which escape total identification. There are in the personalities of nations, as in those of people, developments and conditions which are purely individual and do not allow a total identification process to occur.

For a long time, like the sorcerer's apprentice referred to by Theodor Reik, we considered philosophy or "philosophies" simply as molds. The sorcerer's apprentice, says Reik, considers the master solely as the teacher: he sees the model, but does not see the example.[12] The example is experience interpreted, and is only apprehended by a personal effort. The individual and the nation must therefore realize their own experiences through continuous efforts. These experiences are written in the individual histories. The interest which Brazilian intellectuals today show in reëxamination of our historic experience clearly indicates that a profound change in our way of considering national problems is taking place.[13]

But where should we start in the attempt to reach an understanding of these problems? Naturally, from the rich fabric of our Portuguese background. It is there that we find some of the threads of the colorful design we have been embroidering during four centuries. But from there we must follow other, newer trails, because the meaning of our ideas is complex and not limited to its Portuguese ancestry, which, although of incomparable importance, is not the only influence on the vicissitudes of national thought.

I know only too well how dangerous is the attempt to make a synthesis of anything Brazilian. "In this disorder which is Brazil," the critics of cultural phenomena are

forced to make a link between unrelated creative personalities and works, in the mistaken need to establish a unity which does not yet exist. We have a criticism which is prematurely synthetic and which contents itself with generalizations often overly hasty and sometimes entirely false. These critics proclaim our individuality but socialize everything. Instead of analyzing either the individual personalities or even each individual work as the situation required, they attempt to achieve a synthetic vision of the main currents, in the mistaken conviction that a knowledge of Brazil could only be gained from such a synthesis. But it was impossible to achieve this panoramic vision, especially in relation to cultural phenomena, because, like the growth of other American nations, our own growth was not natural or spontaneous; or, to put it another way: it was not logical. Hence the bundle of contradictions we typify. The time has not yet come when the Brazilian soul can be understood by any attempt at a synthetic vision.[14]

In spite of the fact, however, that we are "a melting pot for conflicting elements," [15] a "mixture," [16] we can and should sound the depths of our nature, to coin a nautical phrase. To do this without

attempting any synthesis which could be interpreted as a formula
(a formula which, given the nature of things Brazilian, would in
any event be imperfect and oversimplified), we must consider the
facts provided by our past, the historic facts of a destiny covering
four centuries. A consideration of these facts would have no value
other than that of simple enumeration.

It can be objected, of course, that this is the task of a historian
rather than of a student of philosophy. But I fail to find it strange
that a man who has devoted much of his life to the study of philosophy should now decide to turn his attention to the fascinating
problem of ideas in his own country. Is it so odd that this person
should dedicate himself to attempting an understanding of the currents which make up the long stream of ideas opened up by the
various influences of European thought in Brazil? I do not think
so. It can still be maintained, however, that this is really the work
of a historian, as indeed it is. But such a historian would have to
follow the infinite meanderings of the *Geistesgeschichte* of the
German essayists or the more subtle paths of the study of sensibili-
ties: the rich and powerful thought of Lucien Febvre, which constitutes a study of different intellectual and cultural levels. He
would also have to apply to his studies the methods of analysis of
Marcel Mauss, attentive to the constant cosmic bombardment of
civilizations by their neighbor civilizations. He would have to reconstruct, from inside the thrilling and disturbing history of his
country, the painful labor involved in its formation and the struggles of conscience constituting its adventure of spiritual growth.
Further, he would have to try to understand the meaning of these
adventures in this constantly changing pattern and to place them
in their historical context in the manner of a river confined between
its banks. Finally he would have to discover what survives of these
adventures of the past.

But the past . . .

Il n'y a pas le Passé, ce donné [writes Lucien Febvre] le Passé, cette
collection de cadavres dont l'historien aurait pour fonction de retrouver
tous les numéros pour les photographier un á un et les identifier. Il n'y a
pas le passé qui engendre l'historien. Il y a l'historien qui fait naître
l'Histoire. Le Passé, chaque génération, à sa date, dans son climat, à
l'intérieur de sa civilisation, particulière, le recrée. Et c'est pourquoi, fait
de main d'ouvrier, un livre d'histoire est 'définitif'—mais pour quatre ou
cinq ans. Après quoi, il commence à dater. Ce qui n'arriverait pas si le

Passé était un donné. Au vrai, c'est une reconstitution des societés et des êtres humains d'autrefois par des hommes et pour des hommes engagés dans le réseau des realités humaines d'aujourd'hui.[17]

We cannot achieve such a reconstruction of past Brazilian society or of the men and ideas of bygone times. In this modest work, I have attempted merely to illuminate some of the signposts which stand out in the destiny of Brazilian ideas, and this I have done, as Lucien Febvre says should be done, as a man caught up in this curious web of contradictions that constitutes the contemporary human situation.

Philosophy is neither merely speculation in a vacuum, nor is it simply a game of abstract concepts. It is solidly based on real experience and cannot afford to lose that sense of the concrete which Professor Charles Morazé calls "cette sagesse qui naît de l'expérience."[18]

"History," writes that great master Léon Brunschvicg, "is the laboratory of the philosopher."[19] In the past, philosophy tended to be contemplative: it lost contact with men of flesh and blood. Today's philosophic inquiry has been reintroduced into the frame of reality through a study of history—philosophy has become more human. However, although it is the laboratory of the philosopher, history is not, as Meinecke claimed, simply "a pedagogical showcase."[20] It is the necessary condition for any perfect scientific investigation of the development of culture. The demands of the historical point of view insure a truer and fuller understanding of reality. Students of philosophy are naturally interested in understanding the material conditions in which man lives. It is impossible to abstract philosophy from the complex historical conditioning to which the human personality is subject and from the dynamics of the social relationships which all generations find as a basic condition.[21] There is therefore a vital relationship between history and philosophy. Is this a new idea?

It was during the classical age of science, the seventeenth century, that the importance of historical considerations for all philosophical inquiry first became apparent. Spinoza was the first to outline this new concept of philosophic criticism, which was to have such profound significance for the development of modern philosophy. Unlike the philosophers who opposed reason to nature, Spinoza considered that in the unity of reason and nature can be found the truth which governs the destined development of life. For Spinoza, therefore, history is at the same time a technical and an intellectual progression. A continual interaction takes place between these two forms of progress. As an instrument for technical progress, intelligence increases man's powers over material things, which, used and transformed by their use, create new conditions of life that will in their turn influence man's effective moral progress. In affirming the infinite possibilities for intellectual and material progress, Spinoza's theory expresses the confident optimism of youth in its own intellectual powers.[22]

Writers opposed to the historical viewpoint tried to find an anti-historical attitude in Cartesianism. This does not seem justified.

True history [writes Émile Bréhier], is a counterpart of rationalism; the age of Descartes is an age of great scholars; the historical criticism of Pierre Bayle in his *Dictionnaire Historique et Critique* is closely related to Descartes's methodical doubt. Just as Cartesian doubt seeks to establish the truth beyond all prejudices and beliefs, so historical criticism seeks to discover what was really thought, beyond all interpretations, traditions, and commentaries. Descartes was not the enemy of history but of commentary, which gives to the past those rights over the present that history rightly refuses.[23]

The importance of history for the study of philosophy was more strongly attested by the Encyclopedists of the eighteenth century. After Spinoza numerous currents of thought affirmed the value of history for a true comprehension of philosophical ideas.

Philosophy, therefore, is not outside the real world. It is not simply an adventure of the mind, but a total human adventure which, although it often finds a subtle form of expression, has its roots in the ground. Idealism—above all, the German idealism of the nineteenth century—tried to reduce the whole drama of history to an adventure of the mind. Concrete problems were ignored in favor of abstract ones. But the progress of the spirit or, to be more exact, of the mind is intimately related to the conditions of human activity.

A knowledge of history is therefore a gnostic necessity which cannot be ignored, and any theoretical knowledge which does not take into account the relevant historical conditions is invalid.

But we must not forget that this concept of history precludes certain reënactments.[24] History is not made to repeat the past, but to free us from it. Philosophy finds its truth only in relation to reality. "This reality is not fixed, but historical. It is therefore not possible to leap the barrier of history. When history changes, philosophy must perforce change with it."[25]

PART ONE

CHAPTER 1

The Portuguese Inheritance

The starting point for an understanding of our thought is our colonial origin. Here begins the rosary of contradictions which is our intellectual experience.

Some antinomies in our mode of being derive from the Indians: they can still be detected in the feelings of obduracy and resignation found in our half-breeds, in the blend of fascination and mistrust with which they regard foreigners. These traits may be survivals of the clash which occurred when two opposed civilizations came face to face—traits which neither time nor the development of the new civilization, which arose from this clash, has managed to obliterate. The contradictory and dramatic history of sensuality and abnegation, which was to mark the psychology of our people, was tinged by the importation of the hosts of Negroes into our country to lay the foundations of our economy. The most decisive influence on our intellectual life, however, was the white element, the conqueror—the Lusitanian. It was the Portuguese who linked us to Western culture. "Not even the contact and mingling with native inhabitants," writes Sérgio Buarque de Holanda,

made us as different from our European forefathers as we would have liked to be. As for Brazil, however unattractive it may seem to some of our patriots, the truth is that we are still linked to the Iberian peninsula, and especially to Portugal, by a long and living tradition, a tradition still vital enough to nurture a common soul in spite of all the factors separating us. We can say that the present *form* of our culture is derived from the peninsula; the rest was a plastic material molded for good or ill by that form.[1]

The pattern of thought, however, imposed on the colony by the conquerors and preserved by tradition, was itself not free from contradictions. In the troubled Iberian peninsula, which provided the mold for our equally restless continent, peoples of diverse tendencies had coexisted in the past, as they still do today, and had evolved an intellectual form very different from the classic patterns of thought beyond the Pyrenees.[2] Christian, Jew, and Arab living in the peninsula had mingled, traded, and married, and their thinking and their actions were orientated by the way of life evolved from these contacts. Their thinking is characterized by a deeply humanistic attitude and has the advantages and disadvantages which arise from the interaction of different races. Professor Altamira describes the Islamic domination of the peninsula in the following terms:

The subordination of Christian kingdoms by the Moslems, resulting from the weakness of the former and the inevitable recognition of the superiority of the latter, led to the growth of very intimate relations between the two groups, in spite of the frequent wars which flared up. During the intervals of peace, or in those areas where there were respites from battle, Christians and Moslems exchanged frequent visits, traded with each other, and intermarried. The upper classes—even the kings— set the example, as can be seen, for instance, in the marriage of the daughter of Count Aznar Golindo of Aragon to the Moor Mohammed Atawil; their son subsequently married a daughter of the King of Navarre. . . . Christians abounded in the Moslem towns, not only as Mozarabs but as temporary immigrants, principally as soldiers in the service of the caliphs or as high-ranking public servants.[3]

Fernando de Los Rios relates that in the eighteenth century a "temple," the Mosque of Santa Maria la Blanca in Toledo, was used by worshipers of all three religions—Christianity, Mohammedanism, and Judaism.[4]

The Iberian concept of culture derives from a pragmatic valuation of existence. The commercial, cosmopolitan, and bourgeois character of Portuguese life in the fifteenth and early sixteenth centuries served to accentuate this pragmatic way of thinking. Devotion to "the Faith and the Empire"—and perhaps more to the latter than to the former—was inseparable from the extraordinary progress of Portuguese science and the art of navigation, which took place in the fifteenth century under the guidance of Prince Henry the Navigator and the cosmopolitan group of scholars he had gathered around him.[5]

The activities of the Portuguese were increasingly orientated in a positive direction arising from a concrete form of thought steadily differentiated and separated from the intellectual forms of the other European countries. From the Middle Ages onward, the prevalence of an empirical or pragmatic position in Portuguese thought can be easily discerned.[6]

In the movement which preceded the maritime discoveries—to which the Franciscans made such a notable contribution—we can perceive this pragmatic turn of mind which so profoundly marked Portuguese culture. "By bringing man closer to nature and substituting a loving and pragmatic form of Christianity for the ideals of contemplation and unworldly aspiration, the Franciscans dispelled the shadow of malediction and terror which hung over life and opened the way for man's progress on earth," writes Jaime Cortezão.[7] From the thirteenth century to the sixteenth, Portuguese thought was intimately linked to action. King Duarte's reference to "useless fantasy" in his *Leal Conselheiro* is typical of this dynamic attitude.[8]

"In the writings of the princes of the House of Aviz," writes Costa Marques, "we discern a spirit alien to the transports of the imagination and to the purely artificial creations of the mind." [9] Their preference for the practical, the useful, and the immediate is evident.

Early Portuguese thought was characterized by the realization of the significance of human activity. In Gil Vicente we can already perceive the impassioned tenderness for life and nature, the "earthly love for human realities, the profound realistic feeling for existence." [10]

After the sixteenth century, however, Portugal entered a phase of decadence. Jaime Cortezão, in his commentary on this period of Portuguese history, remarks that it was the policy of monopoly, "when it became a purely royal prerogative instead of a national one, and, in the person of King João III, took the form of an honest but narrow-minded spirit, a nationalism zealous but mediocre, which led to the diffuse theocracy resulting in a monopoly of thought." [11] The "monopoly of thought" contributed to a great extent to the decadence of Portugal, but was itself perhaps a result of the maritime enterprise. "At the smell of cinnamon," to quote Sá de Miranda, the whole kingdom was deserted. The easy wealth and the luxury, which the conquests brought about, only resulted in misery for the people and the nation. Portugal did not have the economic stability to cope with the enterprise she had undertaken. The bankers of northern Europe were to reap the benefits of Portugal's imperial adventures.[12]

2

I have already had occasion to remark that it is difficult to undertake any serious study of the history of our land—and consequently of our thought—without considering the history of the Society of Jesus.[13] Capistrano de Abreu has observed that anyone who tried to write a history of Brazil before the history of the Jesuits had been written would be guilty of a serious presumption.[14] In fact, it would be extremely difficult, if not impossible, to examine the history of the Iberian nations—and that of their heirs in the Americas—without considering the influence exercised in those countries by the disciples of Saint Ignatius.[15]

During the reign of João III, at exactly the same time that Brazil was beginning to be colonized, the Jesuits, in the vanguard of the Counter Reformation, were called to the University of Coimbra.[16] This action was to lead Portugal away from the scientific movement which was gaining ground throughout the seventeenth century. It was to break the tradition of a positive culture and, as a consequence, Portuguese thought was to become, as Gonçalves da Câmara told Father Mirão, "less Latin but staunchly Catholic." [17]

Teaching, which up to then had been inspired by the same spirit that launched the maritime enterprise and was merely the continuation of the scientific tradition handed down by Prince Henry the Navigator,[18] was to become, in the hands of the Jesuits, a discipline with "neither a national nor a natural foundation." [19]

As Teófilo Braga puts it:

Knowledge was transformed into a bookish erudition and artistic expression was debased by a servile imitation of the classics. In the realm of speculation, the doctrines of Aristotle were propagated in an authoritarian manner and rendered sterile by an excess of canonical inflexibility. . . . The masters imposed the authority of the past and historians tried to trace the origins of each modern state from the wandering heroes of Troy or the garrisons of the Roman conquest. In the schools the vernacu-

lar was abandoned, and pupils spoke Greek and Latin even among themselves, producing the comedies of Aristophanes and Plautus for their
diversion. The contempt for the Middle Ages halted the progress of
European intelligence, which was seeking new methods in the negativism
of Sanches and in the works of Bacon and Descartes without realizing
that it lacked a sense of solidarity with the past. The Jesuits appropriated
the humanist tradition and have propagated it right up to the present
day with the same lack of intelligence with which they received it half-
way through the sixteenth century.[20]

Renaissance humanism, which opened up possibilities for the development of new concepts in natural and experimental philosophy
and had already borne fruit in the works of such writers as D. João
de Castro, Duarte Pacheco Pereira, and Garcia da Orta, was quickly
stifled by the classical humanities.

Portuguese philosophic development was lulled to sleep by the
mass of theological commentaries. "Doctrines were imposed on
thought by the cult of orthodoxy," writes Professor Fidelino de
Figueiredo. "This literature (the Portuguese) is not disturbed by
doubt or anxiety; it is soothed by certainty, and in it the tranquil
spirit glosses at length the eternal religious motives, indulges in self-
catechism, and falls asleep in the hand of God—the right hand of
God." [21]

The influence of the Jesuits cut Portugal off from the scientific
renewal which had taken place in the Renaissance and to which
Portugal had contributed the magnificent movement of the maritime
discoveries. The extraordinary upsurge born of the pertinacity of
Prince Henry fell into a decline, and Portuguese scientific and
philosophic culture will not easily find again the means to further
development.[22]

The artificial humanism which was inflicted on Portugal marked
the Portuguese intellect so deeply that some of its traces can still be
detected in ours: the formalism in which it continues to express
itself comes, I think, from this source. The love of rhetoric, gram-
maticism, and bookish erudition we have inherited from the so-called
humanist education derives from sixteenth-century Portugal.

Because of this anachronistic humanism, Portuguese culture
moved away from the true significance of its historical direction.[23]

The discoveries had had their origin in a truly scientific culture
and caused a transformation of the world. Its most fruitful consequence was "the formation of a new culture with a critical and ex-

perimental basis which we can call 'universalism.'" We designate
the culture by this word in contrast both to an earlier culture, which
was strictly Western and founded on classical authority, and to the
literary renaissance of Graeco-Latin inspiration, which made the
flow of thought and artistic expression revert to the same ancient
sources—both, although in different measure, founded on erudition
and tending to dogma, both sterilizing and regressive.[24]

It was this universalism which politically led Portugal to stem the
"torrent of Moslem power, thus liberating the West from the threat
of Islam."

In the art of navigation Portugal created what we may call a nautical
theory of latitude opposed to the previous one of longitude—the only
one which permitted the achievement of the geographic unification of
the planet. In addition to resolving the problem of international trade,
the Portuguese powerfully contributed to the creation of a world economy by the dissemination (in both senses) of edible plants and the distribution of animals throughout the world—a gigantic achievement,
which has hitherto received only little attention from historians. At the
same time, the Portuguese universalized the natural sciences by giving
them almost the whole planet as a field of study. In all the sciences of
observation, including geography, oceanography, meteorology, and medicine, the Portuguese mark an epoch, in contradistinction to Antiquity
and the Middle Ages. Although they were acute and understanding observers, they were also responsible for the introduction of a universal
exoticism into literature and the plastic arts. And, if the Graeco-Latin
Renaissance culminated in Erasmian humanism, Portuguese universalism
achieved in its totality a humanism more ample, more profoundly renovating and critical, both in the realm of morals and in that of ideas.[25]

From the fifteenth century on, Portugal had thrown herself with
feverish intensity into the maritime enterprise which was the fruit
of the energies of the sons of King João I. As early as the fourteenth
century—but even more so in the sixteenth—interest in navigation
had attracted to Lisbon the most varied groups of people. "Foreigners from many lands elbowed each other in the streets: Englishmen,
Germans, Flemings, Swiss, Frenchmen, Italians, and Castilians,
seeking at the best fountainhead more detailed news of oriental
matters." [26]

The mystery of the East with all its fabulous wealth attracted
to Portugal people of various backgrounds and cultures. "In the
Rua Nova dos Mercadores (Merchants' Row), wider than any other

in the city and adorned on both sides with beautiful buildings," wrote Damião de Góis, "merchants from nearly every land and from the four corners of the earth would daily meet, thronging the street because of the ease of trade and the commercial facilities offered by the port." [27]

In this setting, with a populace made up of adventurers, there was a great show of finery and sumptuousness. The discoveries, with the easy wealth they brought or promised, fostered this display, and with it came a laxity of manners. The monarchs tried in vain to correct the excesses of luxury with their rules for court etiquette. Some of these excesses would seem to have been mere ostentation, as we learn from an interesting letter written by Nicolau Clenardo to his friend Tiago Látomo. He says that the Portuguese had begun to care only for external show in the illusion of easy wealth—behavior highly symptomatic of the spirit engendered by the discoveries.[28]

A general lack of moral scruples accompanied this appetite for luxury, and not even the clergy showed much respect for their oaths of celibacy.[29] The gaudy façade hid the misery and robbery behind it. The situation can be explained, of course, in terms of the profound economic revolution which the discoveries had initiated in Portugal. Roberto Simonsen writes:

> The social repercussions of this economic revolution were extremely corrosive. The kingdom slowly became depopulated since, of those who left, only slightly more than 10 per cent ever returned. The publications of the period, setting out the statistics of widows left in the areas from which all the able-bodied men had departed, are truly alarming. Most of the fields were deserted, and, since Portugal had neither industries nor the articles in demand for bartering with India, most of the goods she exported had first to be imported from other countries.[30]

The prosperity and luxury derived from the profitable Asian trade was succeeded by one economic crisis after another and successively redeemed by borrowing. In Portugal, "the convulsive state of society, the internal and frontier wars, and finally the maritime epic, had created in the people a taste for adventure, which led them to abandon regular work and to compete with the growing hosts of parasitic beggars which the law was attempting to hold in check." [31] Agriculture withered, but "why should you waste time growing and harvesting these things of little worth, when you need only cross the ocean to garner a store of treasure?" [32]

This was the atmosphere of Portuguese society at the time of the discovery of Brazil.

3

It is not the aim of this work to consider the merits and demerits of the colonists who are inextricably rooted in Brazil—the Portuguese.

They may have, as Gilberto Freyre has stated, the admirable capacity for adaptation, which he so well described, and this would be a subject of obvious interest to me, but it would be idle to enlarge on it, especially after the publication of Freyre's remarkable work and all the criticism and commentary which followed. It is interesting to note, however, that the discovery of Brazil coincided exactly with the beginning of Portugal's decadence, already evident in certain blots which darken the picture of her African conquests. A dark shadow was cast over the destiny of Portugal after the death of the last Aviz. And the highly complex contradictions, pointed out with such profundity by Antônio Sérgio in his preface to Freyre's book *O Mundo que o Português Criou . . .*[33] became increasingly evident.

The seventeenth century had opened up new directions for mankind. Portugal had played a vital role in this widening of horizons. Yet, in spite of this, she was on the decline. The second half of the sixteenth century boded ill for her destiny.

In the Middle Ages, free from extraneous influences, the peninsula gloried in the full flowering of its genius and its natural qualities. The political instinct for decentralization and federation manifested itself in the number of kingdoms and sovereign countries into which the peninsula was divided, as though in protest against any standard, overwhelming, and ultimately artificial unity—a protest which represented the victory of local energies and interests over uniformity. Within each unit the communes and the chartered boroughs took over more and more rights, expressing and affirming, through myriad institutions, the autonomous and independent spirit of the people. And this spirit was not merely independent; it was, as far as the age allowed, remarkably democratic.[34]

Toward the end of the sixteenth and during the early years of the seventeenth centuries, Portugal, and with it the whole of the Iberian peninsula, passed from the state which had rendered possible the maritime discoveries into a "state of darkness, inertia, poverty, and stupidity." [35] Antero de Quental writes: "We forsook the society of living men, who moved with freedom in the open air, to enter a narrow, almost sepulchral enclosure, in which the air is thick with the dust of old books and haunted by the ghosts of scholars." [36]

The maritime discoveries were, as we know, the most fruitful source for the growth of modern capitalism. Portugal and Spain were the great sea powers of the age.[37] We have already seen that the discoveries had a depressing effect on the Portuguese people. Trade with the colonies was, by royal decree, a monopoly granted to those who produced most profit for the royal house. Already in 1503, King Manuel had signed an agreement conceding the authority to establish trading stations in Lisbon to some German merchants.[38] The Fuggers were among the first of these. In 1504 their first agent, Mark Zimmermann, arrived in Portugal. The Welsers of Augsburg soon followed to play their role in the trade with India. Trade was carried out indirectly, chiefly by foreigners, and, as we learn from the work of Henri Sée, especially by the maritime powers of northern Europe, which had begun to emerge at the end of the sixteenth century and were to develop at the cost of Spain and Portugal, by then incorporated into Spain through the wealth, power, and legitimate claims of Philipp II. Gold poured into the northern coffers. The Portuguese and Spanish were merely the carriers (*rouliers*) [39] in the colonial trade, since it was the rest of Europe that provided the manufactures needed for barter in the Iberian colonies.

The heavy losses suffered by the Portuguese and Spanish led to an outburst of religious fanaticism. The Jews, expelled from the peninsula at this time, took with them to Holland their zeal for trade, their commercial ability, and their wealth. Holland, with England close behind, was the true inheritor of the peninsula's colonial patrimony.

Naturalistic humanism began to gain ground in Europe, but Portugal was unable to adapt herself to the new spirit of the age. Up to the eighteenth century the ruling elite continued to have an anachronistic mentality: the suspicion that the "evil of Luther" was spreading sprang up everywhere in the peninsula, but the confirmed enemies of this new sect maintained a constant vigilance in defense of the faith. The Inquisition was ever watchful. In August, 1550, by order of the Holy Office, the principal and two of the most distinguished masters of the famous College of Arts founded by King João

III with the intention of modernizing the university, were arrested on charges of heterodoxy.[40] Diogo de Teive and Buchanan were the masters suspected of misinterpreting the faith.[41]

With the loss of independence the situation in Portugal became worse. Heretics were discovered everywhere. While the rest of Europe embarked on the revolution which was to lead to the renewal of scientific method and to the development of the critical spirit, Portugal remained static, and men were terrified at the prospect of the abyss which the scientific revolution might reveal!

The feature distinguishing philosophy in Portugal in the seventeenth century is the complete preoccupation with a renewal of Scholasticism.

As we have seen, pure speculation was never the essential feature of Portuguese thought. On the contrary, it was a thought dominated by "continued experience" and experimentalism.[42] The author of *Brasil Mental*, quoting Barthélemy de Saint-Hilaire, affirms: "This is the great calamity. We were still Scholastics in the sixteenth and seventeenth centuries." [43]

It is obvious, however, that the Portuguese do not suffer from an invincible mental incapacity, as Sant'Ana Dionisio has rightly pointed out.[44] The proof of their capacity is the colonial empire they built.

The renewal of Scholasticism was another form of reaction against the religious freedom preached by Protestantism. Scholasticism was to use humanistic studies to combat heresy. It also used them to fight the naturalism which was beginning to develop in various countries of Europe and which was in part the fruit of the movement which the Portuguese had initiated in the fifteenth century. Because of this Scholastic revival Portugal was of no great significance in the intellectual panorama of the seventeenth century. Her pedagogues remained aloof from the intellectual activities of the age and carried the country with them. To experimentation and to observation, to the work of Galileo and Descartes, they continued to oppose the "subtlety" of syllogism! Hernani Cidade writes:

The thin Aristotelian texts, preserved in the original Greek or in Latin translations, were all broken up, and the fragments were heavily encrusted with thousands of pages of commentary. The result was rather like the dump surrounding a mineshaft, a slagheap of reflection, comment, explanation, collation, adaptation of dogma—all that the subtle pickax of ingenuity could manage to extract from within.[45]

Everywhere, except in the peninsula, the philosophical revolution was in full swing. "While the cultured mind of Europe was engaged in these daring forays into the unknown, we remained static," adds Hernani Cidade, "as if we feared that the slightest movement would lead us toward the abyss." [46] Even Francisco Suarez, the famous author of *Disputationes Metaphysicae*, who managed to move furthest away from enslavement to the dogma and to the authority of Aristotle and St. Thomas Aquinas, failed to create a philosophical system.[47] Maurice de Wulf, for one, attaches little importance to the renewal of Spanish Scholasticism, of which Suarez was the most notable exponent. Wulf considers it (and this is worth stressing) "a local and ephemeral phenomenon," [48] incapable of establishing itself outside Portugal, Spain, or Italy. It was in the interest of the Counter Reformation that Suarez attempted to strengthen "the principles translated in the exaltation of papal theocracy and the diminution of the royal authority, which had become so powerful an ally of the ideas of the Reformation." [49]

From the time that King João III handed over the College of Arts to the Jesuits in 1555, they held their domination over Portuguese culture. Not until two hundred years later did this domination come to an end; and it was not without a struggle that liberty of mind and the liberty to criticize were once more able to reign in Portugal. The battle was not easy, for, as Newton de Macedo wrote: "the enemy sheltered at the core of our national consciousness, consubstantial with it, in the kind of mentality that only a slow and profound renewal of ideas could succeed in changing." [50]

The stream of Portuguese culture, which had formerly been oriented toward the experimentalism that, in the words of Duarte Pacheco, is the "mother of all things," was diverted. The practical, humanitarian, realistic sense faded into empty speculation and was lost in the commentation of texts. The brilliance had been extinguished, the impetus of the movement born in 1385 had been stilled, and the energies spent in the maritime discoveries had bled the nation dry. The conquests led to a weakening of the national economy, and finally the terror of heterodoxy changed Portugal, as it did Spain, into a veritable "island of purification." [51]

4

Europe, in discovering new lands, was to open up new vistas in philosophy, morals, politics, and economics. We Brazilians emerged on the scene at a moment of crisis in Europe's consciousness. The men who sailed in the caravels were no longer afraid to venture forth on the oceans, expanding the compass of the earth and spreading faith and commerce. Backed by science, and with a belief in learning from experience, the men who reached our shores in the sixteenth century were representatives of an age of restlessness and contradiction. "After the Middle Ages, which had been so essentially dogmatic," writes Fortunat Strowski, "one would suppose that scepticism would once more find the favor it enjoyed in antiquity. But anyone who believed this would be mistaken: the sixteenth century was no less confident in the power of reason and man's capacity for discovering the truth, than was the thirteenth." [52] The sixteenth century "worked in a half-light, knowing that the dawn was near and knowing exactly where lay the East but not yet able to distinguish the outline of things." [53] As Brunschvicg says, an "immense restlessness" characterizes this period.[54]

Our great Atlantic front was to open up to Western civilization at the moment when this civilization was passing through a profound crisis. We were to be the *trouvaille* of this moment of cultural change. Perhaps, from then onward, the contradictions of our destiny were outlined. Our history—and our culture—is linked to two broad lines. One is our "Atlantic vocation," accentuated by the great expanse of coast line, which compels our gaze toward the vast horizons of the ocean—toward what lies beyond. The other is the forests, the mountains, the wild undiscovered interior, the immense skyline stretching beyond the coastal mountains, which excited both the curiosity and the cupidity of the adventurers. The interior which, in the words of Alcantara Machado, "like the haunting insistence of an obsessive refrain or with the tyrannical persistence of a *leitmotiv*, appears again and again in our history, every time there is a profound crisis in our national life, every time we undergo some revolutionary transformation." It is toward the interior that "the collective soul must turn, as the needle of a compass is drawn magnetically toward the North." [55] This was to be the other broad line of our destiny. It was early recognized by a Franciscan friar, Father Vicente do Salvador—a member of that religious order which had given such impulse and momentum to the discoveries. "Far too long have men scuttled back and forth along the seashores," says the friar, "too long have they lingered on the beaches." It was time, he felt, to venture into the interior, to explore the jungle, and to continue, on land, the adventure which Prince Henry had dreamed of and planned.[56] In distinguishing these two lines, it has been my intention simply to name one of the principal antinomies of our history and our culture. Joaquim Nabuco, in his book *A Minha Formação*, points out this contrast to demonstrate the eternal instability with which we are afflicted.[57]

From European Portuguese culture we inherited our language, our customs, and our religion and mingled with many defects some of our virtues. Did we not also inherit a certain vision of the world and of man? And for an enterprise as great as that of the discoveries to have succeeded, must there not have been some basic idea or some conduit for ideas which permitted this success? Is it not possible that at the root of the maritime explorations of the fifteenth and sixteenth centuries there was a new conception of the world and of man, in other words, a philosophy?

The adventure of the discoveries does, in fact, follow from a certain concept of the value of life and of the dimensions of the world. Portuguese philosophy, as we have seen, is essentially pragmatic.

Philosophy in the golden age of maritime expansion and discovery could clearly be designated by the term "experimental pragmatism." It was not a theory or a concept that proved the reality of their knowledge of the world, until then unknown or only partly known. Their actual experience, in disproving ancient conclusions about the world and making them seem almost caricaturish, led to the belief in and enthusiasm for objective knowledge and a contempt for speculative fantasy.[58]

Contemplation was never a characteristic of the Iberian soul. Miguel de Unamuno admirably defines the spirit of peninsular philosophy when he says that "if a philosopher is not a man, he may be anything but a philosopher. He is above all a pedant, a mockery of a man." [59] And the malicious João Ribeiro penetrated the meaning of our thought when he said, ironically, that "our idealism is never very far from the ground, nor does it go beyond the nearest planets, and except in poetry or in Gongoric epithet, no one really cares about the infinite." [60]

CHAPTER 2

Vicissitudes of
Colonial Formation

The introduction of European culture in Brazil requires a brief examination of the economic history of the early years of the colony, which clearly reflects the situation not only of the colony itself but of the parent state. This has been done excellently by Caio Prado Júnior, and I shall draw on his work for the elements necessary to a more exact understanding of the adventurous implantation of European forms of life into a tropical land and of the changes that overtook the ideas we received from Western civilization.

All the great events of the age which has come to be known as the Age of the Discoveries can be seen as part of a movement which is no more than a chapter in the history of European commerce. All the events that took place were the outcome of the enormous commercial enterprise to which the countries of Europe had dedicated themselves from the fifteenth century onward, and which made them turn toward the oceans. This is the true impulse behind the exploration of the African coast, the discovery and colonization of the Atlantic islands by the Portuguese, the discovery of the sea route to India, the discovery of America and the exploration and occupation of its various parts.[1]

"The idea of populating these countries," adds Caio Prado Júnior (and these enlightening remarks help us to consider the problems bequeathed to American society),

did not at first occur to any nation. Commerce was their main concern; hence the relative contempt they felt for the primitive and empty territories which constituted America, and inversely the prestige of the East where there was an abundance of negotiable merchandise. The idea of occupation—not as had formerly been done, by merely sending out commercial agents, officials, or military garrisons to set up simple *feitorias* to serve as trading posts with the natives and links between the sea routes and the more coveted lands, but of establishing a permanent colony— this idea arose only as a contingency, a necessity imposed by new and unforeseen circumstances.[2]

The principal factor in the European expansion was economic. There was, however, veiling this imperialistic greed, a no less genuine need to spread the faith. "In the dawn of the great epoch of discovery and conquest, at once barbarous and magnificent, God was invoked to favor the enterprise and to crown it with success." This factor is mentioned and approved by all writers on the discoveries, who recommended that this religious spirit must be remembered by its heirs. They all seek to justify the inevitable violence, resulting from the custom of the times, in the name of some religious ideal which transcended all unrestrained egoisms. And it is no less significant that in the literature of the conquest and discoveries there is an insistence on these ulterior motives—the constant insinuation of an ideal, of a consciousness of the spiritual aims, behind even the most brutal expressions of instinct.[3]

There is, in the view of some Portuguese writers, an inner conflict,

particularly acute in the Hispanic personality [writes Sant'Ana Dionisio], between the religious tendency and the practical aspects of living. It is probably true that in most people one could find a religious streak warring with more practical interests. But it would perhaps be difficult to find an ethnic group which expresses this so clearly as do the people of this soil. The brilliant clairvoyance of Cervantes, when he created the idealized chivalry of Don Quixote in symbolic opposition to the belly-bound earthiness of Sancho Panza, is evidence of this conflict. With a nature compounded of extremes, the Hispanic personality sees the world either as a mere scenic reality of secondary importance (and in this he reveals the mentality of one whose face is turned toward infinity) or as a profitable estate to be colonized and exploited for immediate gain. Together with the bent for a formless universalism with mystical undertones, the people of the peninsula have a gross propensity for the over-cultivation of merely circumstantial matters.[4]

Even religion, for the Portuguese, is a kind of practical guide to morality.[5]

In Brazil, Portugal created an original form of society.

It was not [to quote Prado Júnior] the simple trading system, which we have already seen was not workable in America. But it nevertheless retained a decided mercantile character. It was the enterprise of the white colonist, which added to a nature bountiful in its supply of highly valuable commodities the work of slaves recruited from among the inferior races which he ruled, whether native Indian or imported Negro. The traditional commercial aims, which inspired the overseas expansion of Europe, were retained but adjusted to the new conditions in which the enterprise was carried out. These aims, which were relegated to a secondary plane in the more temperate colonies, were upheld in Brazil and were profoundly to mark the features of all colonies of our type, dictating their destiny.[6]

Brazil was really established to

furnish sugar, tobacco, and certain other commodities; later it was gold and diamonds; then cotton; and later still coffee for the European trade. This was all. And it was with this aim, an aim completely unconnected with the country itself and taking no account of problems other than those of trade, that the society and the economy of Brazil were organized. Everything was orientated in this direction: the social structure as well as all the activities of the country. The white European came to speculate and to do business, to invest capital, and to recruit the necessary labor force either from among the native population or by importing Negro slaves. It was from these elements, organized purely for productive and mercantile purposes, that the colony of Brazil was compounded.

This beginning, which retained the same essential character throughout the centuries of Brazil's formation, became deeply and lastingly engraved on the life and features of the community, and in particular on its economic structure. This impression has continued up to the present time; only now are we beginning to free ourselves from our long colonial past. To bear this in mind is to understand the essence of Brazil's economic evolution.[7]

In the enterprise of commercial speculation which was colonization, we find two types of "entrepreneur": the adventurer and the

Jesuit. However, it was the Negro who rendered possible the growth of the enterprise and laid the foundation of our economy.

The "first of the ships sent by the Brazil wood concessionaires, even those of the King, already brought their cargo of Negroes." [8] Slavery was organized by the Europeans after the first conquests. On this Negro labor were founded the sugar plantations—a capitalist form of agriculture *par excellence,* which rooted itself in the colony and, to quote again from Nélson Werneck Sodré's work,

condemned to perpetual poverty, and mercilessly crushed, the Indians and the Negroes who were turned into slaves and, even the white colonists who found themselves destitute, in bondage to the great owners of the plantations and sugar mills, eternally dependent on the latifundia and the work provided by the landowners, who from the outset held political power.[9]

In the society of adventurers, which evolved in the sixteenth century in this "neglected, lazy, and somewhat melancholy land," to use the words of Anchieta,[10] the Jesuits played a role still subject to much discussion.[11] With the pagan Indians the Jesuits employed a technique which smoothed their paths among them and enlisted their sympathy; toward the adventurers, although they sometimes showed understanding, they maintained an uncompromising stand against slavery and were intransigent—often for private ends—in defending the natives against enslavement.

As we know, this attitude bred conflict between Jesuits and colonists. In the early days, however, the Jesuits' activities helped the colonists considerably.

With their powers of infiltration, the Jesuits managed to bring the Indians into contact with the colonists. This approach, however, was promptly transformed into a bridge to be crossed by the settlers hungry for strong arms to perform the agricultural work. The catechism, as a prelude to submission, finally constituted a threat to private interests, since it drew the Indians—then the only labor force available to the colonist—away from their toil. The rupture was the inevitable result of the neutralization, which was the principal aim of the catechism and led to obvious losses for the foresters.[12]

In this way, the

rupture was as violent as the action of the Jesuits had been harmful to the interests of the colonists. In the areas of established wealth, where Negro slaves had been substituted for Indians, and where, as a rule, the labor problem had been solved, the clash between Jesuit and colonist was less violent. However, in the areas where Indians continued to be the only labor supply and where the available capital did not permit the general importation of African slaves, the conflict was from the outset radical and decisive.[13]

In the colony the man with the largest labor force succeeded in his venture. The privilege of saving souls granted to the Society of Jesus was, to quote Euclides da Cunha, "a casuistic euphemism to disguise their monopoly of the native labor supply." [14] This was the true source of the struggle between Jesuit and colonist, above all in the South in the early years of colonization and, in the seventeenth century, in Maranhão and Pará.[15]

Prado Júnior records:

The Jesuits, in their activities among the Indians and in the education they gave them, were often acting not only against the immediate and private interests of the colonists but against the interests of the parent state and its colonial policy. The regimen and organization of the missions was scarcely likely to make of the Indians active and integrated members of a colonial community. Segregation in the Jesuit villages, where they were not taught Portuguese in order to avoid any contact with the white colonists and the strict discipline to which they were subjected (and which made them into veritable automata controlled by the inexorable—and worse, irreplaceable—voices of their masters, the priests) locked them so fast in the routine of mission life that outside it they could not profit from the rudiments of civilization which they were taught. All this was not designed to create members of a community but to form collective groups embedded within the community and viscerally dependent on their organizers.[16]

2

In the seventeenth century the sugar industry had begun to enrich the colonists. The North was prosperous.[17] There the Society of Jesus inaugurated its first colleges. The same purpose—the making of the sons of well-to-do families into "good Catholics rather than Latin scholars"—had led the Jesuits to found in Bahia, as early as 1533, the first Latin classes.[18] The small elite of literates, all members of the families enriched by the cultivation of sugar cane, frequented the Jesuit colleges.[19] As a symbol of distinction and of superior "class," the wealth evidenced by ownership of land, sugar mills, and slaves, had to be combined with a humanistic education administered by one of the Jesuit colleges.[20] We must recognize, however, that the culture of the erudite elite, purely ornamental in purpose,[21] provided by the Jesuit colleges established the traditions of European culture in Brazil. The men of letters, educated by the Jesuits, assured the continuation of culture. But side by side with these men cast in the Jesuit mold, these literati forever leaning out of the casements of the Atlantic watching for the ships that brought them books and ideas from Europe, there were other men, men of the people, who continued the economic adventure which was the legacy of the vigorous mentality of the sixteenth century. These were the men who cut paths through the jungle, discovered rivers, founded villages, and traced the frontiers of Brazil. These two groups of men should be considered for the light they throw on the history of our thought.

In Rio de Janeiro, Bahia, and Pará, the Society of Jesus had its imitations of Coimbra's College of Arts, where philosophy, theology, and the humanities were taught. In 1572 the degrees of bachelor and master of arts were already being conferred in the colleges.[22] In all these colleges and in the seminaries, as was only to be expected, Scholastic philosophy was taught.[23]

The introduction of mining was an important element in the progress of the civilization of Brazil. In Minas Gerais the literati began to cherish the dream of independence and of a republic. The example of the American Revolution and, above all, of the political and philosophical ideas of eighteenth-century France affected our intellectuals. Despite all efforts by the Portuguese authorities to censor the entry of French ideas into the mother country and her colonies, the universities managed to propagate the philosophical and political ideas of the eighteenth century which reached Brazil. In 1790 Count Rezende was taking energetic measures against readers of the works of the Encyclopedists, and in 1794 people were being imprisoned in Brazil for the crime of "Encyclopedism." [24]

The influence of the ideas of the Encyclopedists on the intellectuals of Brazil created the outline of a political conscience before the true economic conscience had evolved. This may explain why our first attempts at independence were made by a handful of intellectuals who had, as Santa Rita says, "adopted France as a godmother." [25]

We must bear in mind, though, that from the reign of King João V onward, the "first premonitory symptoms of a new type of culture which had acquired city rights abroad began to be felt." [20] The open opposition to the culture represented by the Jesuits dates from this time. At the same time, modern culture began to be inroduced into Portugal. Convinced that "it was not from the Jesuit schools that the fountain of true instruction could flow," King João V established in Lisbon "in the manner of another Port-Royal des Champs, a seminary for scholars and ecclesiastics to undertake the instruction and education of youth." [27] In this way, writes Freire de Carvalho in his *História Literária de Portugal* "he most wisely provided competition for the exclusive schools which for two hundred years had been run by the Society called 'of Jesus,' " [28] by supporting the congregation of St. Philip Neri, also known as the Congregation of the Oratory, and the first to oppose the pedagogical and cultural domination of the Jesuits in Portugal.

Modern philosophy, Cartesianism, and the scientific revolution of the seventeenth century began to be apprehended in the peninsula.[29] The traditional influence of the Jesuits was counteracted by the new methods of study introduced by the Oratorians. While in Coimbra the last of the "Conimbricenses" spent their talent in the "useless task of saving Aristotle," to quote Newton de Macedo,[30] the Oratorians, with the support of João V, established themselves in Lisbon, where they substituted for the wooden logic and narrow tracts of the Jesuits books inspired by fresher doctrines. In books such as *Intrução sôbre a Lógica ou Nos Diálogos sôbre a Filosofia Racional* (*Instruction in Logic, or Dialogues on Rational Philosophy*) were popularized the ideas of "Francisco Bacão [sic], Renato Descartes, Pedro Gassendi, João Lockio's [sic] *Essay Concerning Human Understanding*, and Antônio Genovesi." [31] After 1730 Aristotelianism began to be criticized and attacked. Nonetheless, even as late as 1746, the Jesuits issued an edict prohibiting the teaching or discussing of the doctrines of Descartes, Gassendi, and Newton, philosophers whom they pronounced to be heretics.[32]

In 1746 *Verdadeiro Método de Estudar* (*The True Method of Study*), a book by Father Luís Antônio Verney of the Congregation of the Oratory, stirred up an enormous controversy. Although not himself a Cartesian, Verney felt a profound admiration for Descartes. "I am not," says Father Barbadinho in the book, "a Cartesian, because I am persuaded that this system is in many respects more ingenious than true; but I confess that I cannot mention the name of this philosopher without feeling the deepest veneration." [33]

This Portuguese illuminist was the pioneer of the Portuguese cultural renaissance.

His courage excited the execration of fanatics and fools. They attacked him for his audacity, tore him asunder for his innovations, slandered him. . . . The ideas he expressed in his well-considered commentaries were the seed from which flowered the mental revival of the eighteenth century. Pombal's educational reforms were based on these ideas.[34]

After signing the Methuen treaty, however, Portugal became a vassal of England.[35] The colonial conquests of the northern European states throughout the seventeenth and eighteenth centuries had allowed them to accumulate a vast amount of wealth.[36] England outstripped all the rest and after the Napoleonic wars gained complete mastery of the seas. For this reason, from the first quarter of the nineteenth century onward, it was England that tried to conduct the emancipation of the South American colonies, and it was by England that they were politically led. "The history of South America," writes a contemporary economist, "is inseparable from the history of England, and the public debts of these countries constitute a chapter in British economic history." [37] These events had a great influence on the history of our thought. With the liberation of the seas we were to enter into a long period of the free importation of ideas and doctrines, subject to the most curious and varied alternations.

Toward the end of the eighteenth century, then, Brazil entered in a decisive way into the economic struggles of the civilized world and thereafter came under the influences dictated by the contradictions of this complex game. Brazil owed the revival of its agriculture to cotton—a product which benefits from technical advances—after mining went into a decline. Thus our country played its role, and no minor one, in the boom the cotton trade enjoyed,[38] thereby demonstrating the growing importance of Portugal's American colony. On the other hand, "the Iberian colonies were already an anachronism in the eighteenth century." [39] The struggles in which the great powers were engaged during the eighteenth century and the early years of the nineteenth allowed the peninsula to retain its colonies for a time. But after this period the monopolistic trade between metropolis and colony began to decay.

England played a major role in this change. Little by little, through her colonial trading companies, she gained the monopoly of the sea trade.

The poor industrial development of Spain and Portugal did not permit them to retain their colonial dominions for long. It was impossible to keep up the old system, known as the "colonial pact," [40] by which the parent state "reserved unto herself, and hence to her own merchants, the privilege of all colonial transactions to the detriment of any foreign competitors." [41] These privileges hampered the free circulation of goods and the access to markets, and the ideal sought was the introduction of absolutely free trade, which would allow the maximum interchange between the producer and the world's markets, regardless of nationality. [42] This economic tendency is reflected in Sílvio Romero's statement that "From the end of the eighteenth century Portuguese thought ceased to be our master. We began to be interested in what went on in the rest of the world." [43]

The abolition of monopolies and privileges was a necessary condition for the development of capitalism. In the eighteenth century England was to take the lead since, "thanks to her dominion over Portugal arising from the Methuen treaty of 1703, she managed to take possession of the gold from Brazil, and the development of her industry provided her with better goods for barter than other nations." [44] On the other hand, Portugal in the eighteenth century had reached the limit of her colonizing capacity. "Her work in this field was done, and the kingdom had become simply a parasite of the colony." [45] Portugal had become a mere intermediary in the colony's transactions, since she was not even a consumer of its products. [46] The Portuguese merchant fleet no longer had the tonnage to cope with the transportation demands of the colonial traffic. Contraband, which Sombart called *Raub,* was on the increase, and Portugal, as Spain had done through the *Ordenanza del Comercio Libre* of 1778, [47] tried in vain to call a halt to it by imposing harsh penalties. The information revealed in the official document relating to the *Inconfidência* conspiracy is highly significant. João de Deus, one of the rebels of 1798, in reply to questioning said that he had hoped the planned revolt would "make this port (Bahia) free for all foreign nations to trade here, bringing cloth and other merchandise, for which they could take in exchange sugar, tobacco, and other products of the land without the intervention of Portugal." [48] Lucas Dantas also testified that what they had aimed at in the conspiracy was "to do away with the brazen robbery which the Prince practices in the market of this city, blatantly obvious from the convoy which lately sailed from here, leaving our merchants on the brink of beggary." [49]

At the end of the eighteenth century, then, Brazil had reached a stage of development which had outpaced the inefficient tutelage of the Portuguese, unable to serve the growth of the colony. The international conditions prevailing at the time were to hasten the disintegration of the old colonial system. When the monopoly of external trade has abolished, the colonial structure was shaken. Revitalizing forces were unleased, which progressively confirmed the change from a colony into an autonomous national community.[50] Thus in the nineteenth century a new group of nations emerged, which immediately became woven into the political destiny of Western civilization and which, in their development, were to be of the greatest economic significance.

In this group of American nations Brazil had a special place. The long years of the monarchical regime of the nineteenth century were to prove highly meaningful for her historical and cultural destiny.

3

The transfer of the Portuguese Court to Rio de Janeiro and the opening of the ports resulted in great economic and cultural development for the country.[51] Brazil welcomed the Portuguese Court with the greatest jubilation.

Mawe, who came from Rio da Prata and was in São Paulo when the Prince Regent landed in Bahia, records that the news of the Prince's arrival was greeted with intense joy, and that it occasioned processions, firework displays, and other more or less rowdy demonstrations.[52] Against the background of mediocre colonial scene events of the highest importance were to be played. A feverish activity began in the year of the royal family's arrival.

Immediately after his landing, the Regent promoted the foundation of Colleges of Surgery and Medicine in Rio and Bahia, and a Naval Academy. A Royal Press began to function. In 1810 and 1811 a School of Commerce and a Military Academy opened their doors. In 1814 a collection of books—the nucleus of our present National Library—was put at the disposal of the public. The National Museum was created in 1818, as was the School of Fine Arts. In this same year, with a view to improving agricultural methods, and the introduction and acclimatizing of new plants, the first steps were taken to create the Botanical Gardens we know today. Laws, regulations, and any other acts obstructing the industrial activities of the mining centers were revoked. Every endeavor was made to protect and develop the initial energies.[53]

The city, with its narrow streets "which reminded one of the ghettoes," [54] began to be built up.

A kind of generalized euphoria took hold of the nation. There was an enthusiasm for everything, especially for those things which promised material and spiritual progress. It was as if Brazil had awakened from a long sleep and was now on the way to conquer her freedom. Even the merchants, who found that business was thriving and that their social importance was growing, showed an interest in the development of culture and national education. Thus, when Brazil achieved the status of a kingdom, two years before the throne ascension of King João V, the merchants of Rio de Janeiro presented to the Prince Regent a large sum of money to be "used for general education, the best way to commemorate this auspicious occasion, so gratifying that even deputies from the provincial municipalities had come to the capital, all eager to express their gratitude for the great favor shown to the nation." [55] It was from this award that the project for an academic institute was born, the embryo of the university which King João VI wanted to create in Brazil.[56] What the colony had not managed to obtain in three centuries, it was now to achieve in a decade. However, this enthusiasm for intellectual activity did not always go unopposed. The old teachers of the Portuguese high schools were not favorably disposed toward these new departures, clearly symptomatic of Brazil's coming emancipation. Some stubborn members of the old guard were afraid to see the disappearance of one of the principal foundations on which rested the superiority of the metropolis. Already there were capable men in the colony, as was well known in the old kingdom; the intellectual life of eighteenth-century Portugal had been largely Brazilian. There were, however, men with greater foresight and a better understanding of the climate of the age, who could clearly see the meaning of these historic events. Silvestre Pinheiro Ferreira, a counselor at the Court of King João VI, was one of these.[57] In his *Memórias Políticas sôbre Abusos Gerais e o Modo de os Reformar e Prevenir a Revolução Popular* (*Political Memoirs on the General Abuses Practiced, and the Means Whereby These May Be Reformed to Prevent a Popular Revolution*), drawn up in 1813 at the request of the Prince Regent (later King João VI), he foresaw the emancipation of the colonies if the Court should return to Europe. He advised the future

king to delegate the powers of Regent of Portugal to the heir, the
Prince of Beira, and to assume the title of Emperor of Brazil, leaving
that of King of Portugal to the Prince.[58] Others who grasped the
historic situation were the Counts of Linhares and of Barca. The
former, nicknamed "Doctor Confusion" by Queen Carlota Joaquina,
was the power behind the new spirit in Brazil. The Count of Barca
—who was the "Cavalier of Araújo" so respected by Talleyrand—
succeeded Linhares and exercised in turn his influence in public
affairs. The good-natured Prince Regent, with his apparent skepticism, knew how to heed these two noblemen, especially "when
Tomás Antônio was in agreement." [59] Thanks, then, to a few intelligent men, useful measures were taken to insure the progress of the
country, which was to be for this unhappy Braganza a veritable
paradise of peace providing an interval of tranquility in his troubled
existence.

The nation began to progress. Everything was animated by the
spirit of the scientific renewal, which had been accelerated by the
French Revolution. The spirit behind the creation of so many scientific and technical establishments in Brazil was in marked contrast to
that which, not long before, had led to the prohibition of new printing presses and types. The reason for the change was that the men
now beginning to exercise their influence on the affairs of state had
lived through the tempestuous period of transition from the old
regime to the new one created by the bourgeoisie. Some of these
men were able to understand the inevitable shape of things to come.
The Count of Barca, for instance, reflected the mental attitude of
his age and showed the influence of his experiences as Portugal's
representative in the French republic. His interest in the arts,
sciences, and industry was that of an eighteenth-century nobleman
—it expressed the mental attitude of a century which concerned itself with the progress of science and which refused to entertain any
concepts not capable of proof.[60]

Thanks to his efforts and to King João VI's own inclination for
the arts a group of French artists was brought over to inaugurate the
Academy of the Arts. They were accompanied by a team of highly
skilled craftsmen who, in the words of the Decree of August 12,
1816, were to "improve and further the progress of other arts and
mechanical skills." [61]

Rio de Janeiro changed rapidly. "In a society which only yesterday
enjoyed the distinction of backwardness," writes Oliveira Lima,

"from one moment to the next even lectures in philosophy were heard." [62] These lectures were held at the Royal College of São Joaquim—from which was to evolve the future College of Dom Pedro II [63]—under the patronage of Silvestre Pinheiro Ferreira, the apostate Oratorian, friend of the Count of Barca and José Bonifácio. A proper course in philosophy was initiated on April 26, 1813, at the Royal College and conducted in the spirit of renewal so different from that which had hitherto reigned in Brazil.

The reform of the University of Coimbra undertaken by Pombal created, in effect, a new university, modern in spirit. Faculties, practical classes, syllabuses and methods of study, disciplinary measure and the penalties for infringement of the laws of academic conduct, buildings, textbooks—all were either established at this time or thoroughly revised and reshaped. To a great extent even the lecturers were selected and nominated by Pombal. This meant the destruction of the old university with its Jesuit colleges and its paralyzed and paralyzing teaching; and the creation of the Modern University, thrown open to all the light shed from the countries of Newton, Descartes, and Boerhaave—while for the first time devoting equal attention to national causes. [64] It was the men who frequented this university, inspired by Luís Antônio Verney's "new method of study," who were to live through the period which paved the way for independence. It was this new spirit, in spite of the reaction which followed the reign of King José, which helped to build modern Brazil. It is true, as we learn from João Lúcio de Azevedo, that Pombal's reforms turned out to be a failure. He writes:

The existence of certain shackles, intended to cause the nation to remain a nursery of intellectual eunuchs, was incompatible with the spirit of progress which the statesman tried to inculcate in the university. . . . Pombal only went through the motions of liberating the mind to aggravate the Jesuits. His own spirit was alien to the ideas which were exciting Europe at this period. With his approval, the official censors banned the works of Spinoza, Hobbes, La Mettrie, Voltaire, and Diderot. [65]

Azevedo recognizes, however, that, in the "abysmal pit of fanaticism and ignorance" [66] into which Portugal was sinking, there were some who managed to escape the "sea of superstition and ignorance" which, according to the sarcastic Alexandre de Gusmão, was flooding the country. The Marquis of Pombal, to quote further from João Lúcio de Azevedo, was not open to the ideas of intellectual and political liberty which were already predominant among the cultured classes of the rest of Europe. He had not had the good fortune to leave the country as a young man, as had Don Luís da Cunha and Alexandre de Gusmão, when the understanding is still malleable and can be easily conquered and subjugated. His was formed by that "Coimbran" teaching which he later so loudly condemned; it had hardened in the rigid mold imposed by the intellectual atmosphere of the university—a mixture of monkish stupidity and academic pedantry.[67]

In spite of this, the new European spirit was soon to penetrate even the most stubborn outposts of "traditionalism." The university reforms carried out by the Oratorians under the authority of the Marquis freed teaching and culture from its apostolic authority and its medieval Aristotelianism. The new character of the university was due to the complete reorganization of the old Faculties, the

creation of the Faculties of Mathematics and Philosophy, and the establishments intended for the pursuit of that strange novelty "practical studies." These were: the Botanical Garden, the Museum of Natural History, the Theater for Experimental Philosophy (the physics room), the Chemical Laboratory, the Astronomical Observatory, the Pharmaceutical Dispensary, and the Anatomy Theater. The existing hospital was remodeled on more scholarly lines, and placed under the direction of the university.[68]

Pombal did not "build a ruinous structure," as Antônio Ribeiro Sanches, the celebrated doctor, has claimed. He did, however, construct an edifice very difficult to balance on that site of ignorance and superstition. Ribeiro Sanches gives the just historical estimate of Pombal:

This minister wanted to achieve the politically impossible: he tried to civilize the nation while at the same time attempting to enslave it: to spread the light of the philosophical sciences while exalting royal power to a despotism; he inculcated the study of natural and common law and public universal law, and established chairs in these subjects at the university, but did not see that in this way he was giving the people enlightenment which would bring them to realize that sovereign power established only for the good of the nation as a whole, and not merely for that of its Prince, and was bound by certain limits which should not be transgressed.[69]

The despotic minister passed away, but his reforms lived after him. The men who arrived in Brazil knew how to profit from the spirit of the *Estatutos* (*Statutes*) of 1772. "It was in the university reformed by the passion for renewal of the Marquis of Pombal, the epitome of the enlightened despot, that José Bonifácio completed his higher studies." [70]

At that time, Silvestre Pinheiro Ferreira, the Oratorian who ended by revolting against his masters, was still teaching at the university. The congregation could not forgive this young man, who had already received minor orders for his refutation of the doctrines of Teodoro de Almeida. [71] Persecuted and suspected of Jacobinism Pinheiro Ferreira fled to England. He traveled widely, became a diplomat, and acquainted himself with other countries and with the new ideas then circulating in Europe.

In his work *Noções Elementares de Philosophia Geral*, published in Paris in 1838, [72] we can see how curious and how well-informed was the mind of this precursor of the new philosophical spirit in Brazil. On page vi he writes: "The author, educated in the principles of Aristotle and his successors, Bacon, Leibniz, Locke, and Condillac, regards with contempt the gloomy barbarism of the German Heraclitics and the brilliant phantasmagoria of the French Eclectics." [73]

Further on, he adds:

We often heard the most distinguished German philosophers, among them the two leading disciples, Fichte and Schelling, discourse on the intelligence of the system created by their master and oracle. We found not a single one who did not claim that only he truly understood Kant. It would seem, then, that the thing all were agreed on was that no one understood him. It was the same for Fichte and Schelling, and even the famous Hegel, who all ended by abandoning Kant and several times repudiating the systems they had once taught as heads of schools. We have noted similar behavior among the Eclectics of France. [74]

This quotation demonstrates the interest with which the initiator of the philosophy classes held at the College of São Joaquim followed the philosophy of his time. We cannot say, however, that the lectures given by Silvestre Pinheiro Ferreira changed the nature of what was taught under the heading of "philosophy" in this country.

Under the influence of the Oratorians, new compendiums were introduced into Brazil during the last years of the eighteenth century, above all those of Antônio Genovesi, the famous Genoan. [75] Professor Laerte Ramos de Carvalho, in an interesting study of the system of logic of Mont'Alverne, has demonstrated the existence of these "modern" books in our libraries at that time. In his work, this young professor gives a list of compendiums in the Coimbran tradition and of those in use after the Pombal reforms, which he found in the library of the Faculty of Law of São Paulo, evolved from the original Library of the Convent of São Francisco.

But for a long time philosophical studies in Brazil were ambivalent in their direction. For their lectures on rational and moral philosophy, some teachers used the old compendiums, some the new, as we can gather from the accusations made in 1737 by Professors João Marques Pinto and Manuel Inácio da Silva Alvarenga of Rio de Janeiro.[76]

Gradually, however, the use of "modern" compendiums—especially of Genovesi's—became widespread, as they were officially prescribed by the education authorities.[77] Newton de Macedo says that the authorities were imbued with an empirical spirit which encouraged the "attitude of hostility toward all speculation,"[78] then prevailing in the schools. What deserves to be stressed is the interesting fact that this eighteenth-century philosopher-priest understood the importance of the relationship between political economy and morals. Bartolomeu Intieri, having established a chair of commerce at the University of Naples, requested that the subject should be taught in Italian and that no friar should be appointed to the chair, probably—as Fiorentino records—at the instigation of Genovesi, who detested the friars and their Scholastic gibberish.[79] "Studiate il mondo, coltivate le lingue, le matematiche, pensate un poco meglio agli uomini che alle cose che sono sopra di noi, lasciate gli arzigogli metafisici ai frati," he counseled his friends and pupils,[80] advice which accorded well with the pragmatic tendencies of Portuguese thought. This was why Genovesi influenced Silvestre Pinheiro Ferreira, who disapproved both of the "gloomy barbarism of the German Heraclitics and of the phantasmagoria of the French Eclectics." Skeptical of philosophical systems, and even their declared enemy, Genovesi was cut out to serve the fundamental characteristic of the spirit behind Portuguese thought: an inclination toward the practical and a very mundane, earthbound notion of the meaning of philosophy.

This influence, as we can see from the defense of a project for the reform of public education presented to the Imperial Chamber in 1847 by Tôrres Homem, was still active in Brazil at that time. Tôrres

Homem, who later became Viscount of Inhomirim, deplored the condition of secondary education, saying:

After all the great revolutions that have taken place in modern philosophy, it is still taught in our schools with the aid of the Genoan Compendium, by order of the government. It would be better to teach nothing at all in this subject, perhaps the most important branch of human knowledge.[81]

The coming of the Portuguese Court to Brazil transformed the colony. In addition, this coming gave Brazil—whose political emancipation had been predicted since 1814—the

unique character which makes Brazil stand out in the historic process leading to the independence of the American colonies. All of them, more or less at the same time, broke the ties of dependence which bound them to the nations of the Old World. But, while in the other colonies the severance was violent and could only be achieved through open war, in Brazil it was paradoxically the metropolitan government which, under the compulsion of circumstance, had to turn the colony into the temporary seat of government and thus laid the foundations for Brazil's autonomy.[82]

The transfer of the Court to Brazil was, in fact, the last stage of Brazil's disintegration as a colony, a process which had spread over a lengthy period and which was merely accelerated by the armies of Napoleon and the economic interests of England.[83]

In this peaceful transition from colony to independence, the inevitable clashes—and there were clashes between the opposed "ideologies," if we can so call them—were attenuated. Just as independence was simply "a peaceful transfer of power from the metropolis to the new Brazilian government"—the responsibility for this being compounded of the extreme skill of José Bonifácio, the adventurous spirit of Pedro I, and the commercial interests of England—so there was little or no conflict between the partisans of the different doctrines current in Brazil. It was only when the necessity for the organization of the new nation arose during the Constituent Assembly and the political struggles which followed and continued up to 1840, that philosophical ideas once more began to declare themselves with greater intensity, translating the different shades of the ideological struggle which took place after the Napoleonic wars. The members of Brazil's Constituent Assembly also expressed, but in a much milder way, the contradictions then evident in the rest of the

world. The legacy of the French Revolution was still entangled with
the conditions created by the politics of the Restoration. "La France,"
writes Joseph de Maistre, in his *Considérations sur la France*, "a
reçu une mission qu'elle doit remplir. La France exerce sur l'Europe
une véritable magistrature qu'il serait inutile de contester et dont
elle a abusé de la manière la plus coupable." [84] It was from France
that we received the inspiration for the "constitutionalism" of 1823.
For, although the Portuguese and Spanish constitutions were also
imitated in Brazil, the inspiration was predominantly French.[85]
In its general outline, the draft of 1823 propitiated the interests
of the dominant classes, as did the Constitution granted on March
25, 1824. Brazil, through her dominating classes, was therefore
attuned to the rhythm of the European ideas of the time. It was
to become a constitutional monarchy and was to bypass the struggles which the other South American republics had to suffer.

Brazil was to become a peaceful empire, modeled on that of
Louis Philippe.

PART TWO

PART TWO

CHAPTER 3

Philosophy in Brazil during the First Half of the Nineteenth Century

Independence took the form of a simple and peaceful transfer of power, the achievement "more of a single class than of the nation as a whole." [1] Since the people did not participate in the independence movement, the class that assumed power was once again the class of rich property and mill owners, the heirs of the literati of the seventeenth century. This upper class, composed of university graduates and wealthy proprietors, was to lead Brazil during her imperial phase.

From the outset, the First Empire sought to create the civil servants necessary for its administration and for the regulation of public affairs. The idea of establishing an academic institute, or a university, had not, as we have seen, borne fruit in the reign of King João VI; and during the period of the Constituent Assembly it withered away altogether. In view of this, courses in jurisprudence and social science were introduced into the professional schools founded by King João VI—the School of the Convent of São

Francisco in São Paulo and the school attached to the Monastery of São Bento in Olinda. These two schools, founded in the shade of two convents, were for more than a century to take the place of an institution which provides a storehouse of information and coördinates the various branches of knowledge, as does a university. In these two establishments were heard the echoes of the literary and philosophical debates which resounded through distant lands. And in them arose important and widespread movements, which left their imprint on our national history. Castro Alves, in uniting the two faculties—those of São Paulo and of Recife—during the greatest of the nineteenth-century movements, proved that the two institutions did not produce merely obedient civil servants for the Empire. Literature, poetry, and philosophy were also cultivated. In these nurseries were bred the men of the imperial parliament, which, as Tristão de Ataíde says, was the true "forge of our literature." [2] However, at a time when the basic problems of the nation had not yet been solved, when living conditions in Brazil were worse even than those of China, when Brazil was "just beginning to submit to the paternal protection of Lombard Street," [3] our intellectual experience could only have been, as in fact it was, merely the expression of our colonial situation, which the sybaritism, cunning, and dilettantism of the rich and cultured classes represented in the parliament sought to disguise. What, in fact, did all these literary politicians express? They voiced their own interests, expressing a "culture" derived from the vicissitudes of the European importations.

From the eighteenth century onward, as I have pointed out, French influence began to make itself felt in Brazil. When we separated ourselves from Portugal we turned toward France, whose mission at that time was to "awaken, instruct, and guide other nations." [4] "In a Europe still almost entirely subject to the regimes and institutions of the past," France had, since the eighteenth century, but increasingly in the first half of the nineteenth, taken on "a mission of emancipation and education." [5] In seeking to liberate ourselves from the tutelage of the Portuguese, "we had acquired the habit of interesting ourselves in what went on in the world," writes Sílvio Romero significantly. [6]

From this time on, as heirs of Portuguese culture, we grafted on to the vine of the European intelligence implanted in Brazil our new visions of the world in an unremitting effort to produce new and varied strains. The history of the changes of the ideas and doctrines we imported throughout the nineteenth century is made up, therefore, of a curious series of contradictions, attended by the ceaseless drive to seek the meaning of our ideas. Strongly marked by its "Europeanization," the Brazilian mind turned toward the different European markets which supplied it. It was felt that within the tomes of European wisdom must lie concealed some ideal and miraculous formula! The surrounding reality was completely forgotten by the majority of the intellectuals of the early nineteenth century, to whom it seemed that the literary, artistic, and philosophical molds of Europe fitted Brazil perfectly. France provided literary and philosophical patterns; England, proud possessor of a model monarchy, furnished the ritual of parliamentary government; and Germany, especially after 1870, sent us not only her traditional metaphysics but also her new scientific orientation. After the proclamation of independence, the most varied doctrines began to circulate in Brazil. But it continued to be chiefly from, or by way of, Paris that our philosophical ideas reached us.

From Paris came doctrines and theories swallowed wholesale and ill-digested by the sybaritic intellectuals of the upper classes. "In the spiritual history of cultured nations," wrote Sílvio Romero in 1878, "each new phenomenon is but the latest link in a long chain." [7] In the intellectual history of Brazil—virtually a consumer market for European products—this was not true. "The reading of foreign authors and a preference for books from abroad shape the nature of the opinions of our own writers." [8]

Ideas in Brazil do not develop from each other; there is no historic link between them.

They are leaves blown about on the wind of our indifference, and the little or influence, if any, they exercised on Brazilian thought accounts for this anomaly. I cannot see what logical relationship exists between Dr. Tobias Barreto and Father Patricio Moniz; the one has read St. Thomas and Gioberti and has become a theologian and an a priori adherent of the Absolute; the other has read Schopenhauer and Hartmann, after having read Comte and Haeckel, and has become a critic. . . . What link is there between them? I do not know. Perhaps it is that, for both of them, the fountainhead which nurtured their ideas is extranational. [9]

2

The events of 1822 had inflamed the intellectuals in particular. Nevertheless, the break with Portugal, apparent rather than real, left them uncertain of the path they should follow. The advent of independence, and the fever of nationalistic enthusiasm it engendered, was to coincide with the importation of the new ideas of the Romantic movement. In his study of Gonçalves de Magalhães— one of the intellectuals most representative of the period following the successes of 1822—Sérgio Buarque de Holanda notes that, for the cultured men of the phase after independence, there was "a zone wherein politics and literature are closely allied, with no clear dividing line between them." [10] Politics and literature continued to be closely related during the first independent steps taken by the nation. It was this historical coincidence that led many of our writers to believe that Romanticism was a characteristic inherent in the national soul. The Romantic movement, however, in its philosophical, religious, and even social aspects, is a phenomenon characteristic of the beginning of the nineteenth century. "Lyricism, a philosophical spirit, a belief in the people, and a universal piety, are typical manifestations of the intellectual Romantic movement," [11] writes Roger Picard, who has made an exhaustive study of the subject.

For a great part of the nineteenth century, Romanticism was the guiding star. Throughout the century, European philosophy was steeped in Romanticism. Even Positivism displayed this Romantic tinge. In its Brazilian form, the Romantic influence on Positivism was not lost—on the contrary, it was heightened. It lost ground elsewhere, but in Brazil it was accentuated. It was under the influence of the Romantic revival, then, that Brazil initiated her independent intellectual and political career. Strongly influenced by European thinking, Brazilian intellectuals expressed the ideas which reached us from a Europe still in the throes of the struggle between traditional ideas and those derived from the philosophy of the eighteenth century. [12]

The transition between colonial philosophical thought and that of the Empire is marked by the "philosophy" of that vainglorious monk, Francisco de Mont'Alverne. Mont'Alverne still reflects the influence of the writers of 1770; the mark of Genovesi and his followers is still in evidence. [13] The ideas of Locke and Condillac, followed by Genovesi—and indicative of a rising bourgeoisie—appear in Mont'Alverne's only philosophical work, the *Compêndio de Filosofia* (*Compendium of Philosophy*), written in 1833 (or perhaps even earlier) but published after the death of this celebrated religious orator in 1859.[14]

Mont'Alverne's *Compendium* brings together, as we are told by its editor, Francisco Luís Pinto, the "lessons dictated both in the traditional seminars of the cloisters and in the Seminary of São José." [15] The doctrines expounded are those of Locke and Condillac. "Literary rather than philosophical, eloquent rather than profound, and lavishly embellished with classical citations," [16] the philosophy of Condillac seemed tailored to serve religious eloquence and, as we are told by Lenoir, "it met the needs of the Restoration bourgeoisie." [17] In addition to these sources, the *Compendium* echoed the new influence of the French Eclectics, particularly of Laromiguière and Victor Cousin. The oratorical tone of Cousin seems to have delighted the monk, and he made no attempt to restrain his doxological enthusiasm, going so far as to call Cousin's system "sublime"! The following excerpt is significant:

Exclusive systems were abolished by Victor Cousin. Sensualism and idealism, the school of Locke and Scottish philosophy, were brought together; and and the pure reason of Kant, taking the place of the reflection of Locke, gave us the true elements of the human spirit, the legitimate sources of ideas, and resolved the most difficult problems of psychology which had hitherto divided the philosophical world. Fortunately for me, the theories of power and of the activities of the soul, of sensations and attention, since they are based on idealistic elements, has somewhat repelled me from the sensualist school. But the theory of reflection and the origin of ideas demonstrate the vulnerable aspects of sensualism. This has been amply shown by Cousin in his analysis of Locke's *Essay Concerning Human Understanding* and in other works. The sublime system of Cousin is hardly known in Brazil, and unfortunately his philosophical works are not yet complete, nor are his later works published or known at all in this country. I shall, however, endeavor to take full advantage of what he has done and through him restore system to philosophy.[18]

For the effusive monk, Cousin is "one of those geniuses born to reveal the prodigies of human understanding," [19] a man who "arose like a god amidst chaos, in which all the philosophical elements crossed and conflicted, and, summoning his vast and sublime understanding, reconstructed philosophy, revealing those truths which the human reason had always perceived." [20]

Our great religious orator was certainly no thinker. We need only peruse some of the chapters of his *Compendium* to verify this. "Compelled by the energy of my nature," he writes, "and desirous of *winning all the laurels* (the italics are those of Father Leonel Franca), I abandoned myself with like ardor to rhetoric, philosophy, and theology, the chairs which I sometimes held simultaneously." He does not stop here, however. "The nation," he says, "has proudly declared that I was one of the glories she boasts of to this day!" [21] After 1836, when he succumbed to blindness, Mont'Alverne lost touch with modern philosophical movements. Nevertheless, his *Compendium* serves to mark the beginning of the influence of certain currents and writers on Brazilian intellectual life. Mont'Alverne

belongs to that generation which, young and robust in the time of King João VI, participated in the victory of independence and played its role in the First Empire . . . At that time, philosophical teaching in Brazil was an amalgam of Storkenau[22] and Genovesi, writers unknown in the public teaching of the civilized countries . . . A few mutilated fragments of Locke and Condillac, reduced to secondary importance by the work of their disciples and commentators, together with a few deceptive opinions, brilliant in style but weak in analysis.[23]

—this, in fact, in the words of Sílvio Romero, is what constituted the *Compendium* of Mont'Alverne and is all his "philosophy" amounts to.

It has been said that Mont'Alverne was responsible for the revival of philosophical studies in Brazil. We have seen, however, that, before the appearance of Mont'Alverne, Silvestre Pinheiro Ferreira had initiated in Brazil the exposition of the philosophical doctrines of the early nineteenth century. Mont'Alverne's fame was enhanced by his gift for oratory. As noted by Alcântara Machado, "it was not his knowledge, but his facility" [24] that delighted his pupils. "Since, even in ordinary conversation, he always declaimed," wrote his disciple Gonçalves de Magalhães, "his lessons were followed with much attention and some profit." [25]

Nevertheless, Mont'Alverne's influence was so small as to be almost nonexistent. Magalhães, considered by some to be Mont'-Alverne's "disciple," was in fact just one of the many listeners spellbound by the monk's sonorous rhetoric. And even Magalhães, although close to Mont'Alverne, felt that he "professed an Eclecticism in no way original," and merely modeled himself on "the compendiums of Genovesi, compensating for their deficiencies by the addition of copious marginal notes." [26]

However, Gonçalves de Magalhães himself became an adherent of Eclecticism in the philosophical works he later published. The success of this philosophical trend was due to the fact that, after 1830, it took a turn which satisfied the efforts to reconcile the various systems at a time of crisis for the old philosophical and political currents. Eclecticism offered a proposal of peace to all existing systems. "It reconciled the various doctrines, preserving what was worthwhile in each, just as a representative government is a mixed form of government representing all sections of the community." [27] This philosophical "solution" had the most important political consequences; and in our country it answered the needs of the agitated historical period extending from the abdication of Pedro I to the majority of Pedro II. It was a philosophy convenient to the interests of the moderates. "Let us have no excesses. We want a constitution, not a revolution," wrote Evaristo da Veiga.[28]

It was this mentality that held sway throughout the country, after the French Revolution and the adventures the bourgeoisie permitted itself during the Napoleonic period. There was an urgent need for peace and reconciliation. Eclectic philosophy, in spite of its ambiguities, offered a solution for the period.

Eclecticism, before 1830 a revolutionary doctrine, now became the official doctrine of the university during the reign of the peace-loving Louis Philippe. In 1840 Victor Cousin became Minister of Education in the Thiers cabinet.[29] "Eclecticism became the official philosophy and came to be known as 'Spiritualism.' " [30] Excesses were forgotten, as were words too reminiscent of the past. In the words of Taine, "philosophy came to be presented as the affectionate and indispensable ally of religion, and Eclecticism came to be regarded as a preparatory faith which allowed Christianity to retain its dogmas and its hold on humanity." [31]

Domingos Gonçalves Magalhães, the friend of Mont'Alverne, introduced this form of Eclecticism into Brazil.[32]

This doctrine suited the constitutional-monarchical ideals of the new South American aristocracy, the "slipper aristocracy" referred to by the future Viscount of Inhomirim, a new aristocracy composed of conservative rural landowners, freshly embarking on political careers modeled on the none-too-praiseworthy examples of Louis Philippe's France.

3

During the twenty years between 1830 and 1850, Brazil was engaged in a series of struggles reflecting, in a somewhat confused manner, the opposing interests and differences of opinion current at the time. The intellectual elites of Brazil were roughly divided into two groups—those favoring federalist republicanism and those in favor of a constitutional monarchy. The abdication of Pedro I was followed by a period of unrest and general disorder.[33] In Rio de Janeiro a society was formed for the "defense of national liberty and independence" (Sociedade Defensora da Liberdade e da Independência Nacional), which mustered the support of the most representative members of the conservative classes.[34]

From 1830 to 1850, then, many trends appeared on the political and social scene of the young empire. "The partisans of absolutism sought to restore the first sovereign. Dom Pedro I forbade any such enterprise; he multiplied affirmations of loyalty to his son, 'my Emperor,' as he fondly called him; he refused to receive the emissaries of the *Corcundas*, including Antônio Carlos, who sought an audience with him in 1833. In spite of this, there were numerous insurrections invoking as their aim the restoration of Pedro I." [35] Other upheavals were simply the reflection of the complete disorder engendered by the political unrest.

During this period, too, began to emerge the first signs of impending difficulties over the slave trade, which were to threaten the whole basis of Brazil's economy. "Slavery was fast losing its moral justifications, not only in the eyes of the general public but even in conservative circles. Shortly after independence slavery became the target of general criticism. It was accepted and justified only as a *necessity*, a temporary and inevitable evil. No one dared openly to defend it, and its disappearance in a not-too-distant future was recognized as inevitable." [36] On slavery depended the life of the country. The Father of our Independence (José Bonifácio) was fully aware of all the riot of evils which would befall us as the result of slave labor, "the miseries of this society we have evolved, a society of master and slave, which is inhuman, unjust, immoral, corrupt, and corrupting." [37] Slave labor was to maintain the Empire and was to be abolished with its downfall. The ending of the traffic in slaves is the true finale of the colonial phase of our history. From that point on, Brazil was impelled by a new rhythm.

The monarchy had survived in Brazil thanks to the support of the conservatives; it survived the storms of rebellion which raged from 1830 to 1840 thanks to that quality of "cordiality" or openheartedness which Ribeiro Couto noted in the Brazilian character. All the revolts of the period appealed against the "subterfuge of the minority, attacking the unpopular Regency and safeguarding the interests of the young Emperor, still lapped in the affection engendered by his childhood. For the sentimental Brazilians, there could be no enthusiasm for a cause which would rob a poor orphan of his rights, a defenseless little child who played in the gardens of São Cristovão." [38] The child-Emperor saved the monarchy; he was the talisman of the constitutional monarchists of the young empire. [39]

In 1850, the Empire found its proper balance in the stability of a bourgeois monarchy. [40] The gradual rise of the middle class, which reached its apex around 1870, [41] began around 1850, and was accompanied by the parallel growth of Eclecticism. We have already seen that Eclecticism proffered the olive branch to all philosophical systems. It sought also to coexist peacefully with the philosophical trends of the Church, hoping perhaps to replace it some day, as Taine had affirmed.

However, during the imperial period, our elites were, as Father Júlio Maria has pointed out, rationalists or skeptics, and their relations with the Church were characterized by their support of regalism—a regalism arising naturally from the progressive weakening of the religious orders and the growing discredit of the Brazilian clergy. [42]

To deny the influence of Catholicism in the formation of Brazil would be absurd. But to deny that Catholicism suffered some grave and compromising vicissitudes would likewise be impossible; and the effects of these changes were perceptible during the Second Empire. Father Júlio Maria, referring to the low standards of Catholicism in Brazil during the period of the Empire writes as follows: "ceremonies which fail to edify; devotions which fail to purify the spirit; novenas which reveal no fervor; processions which do naught but entertain; festivals which neither benefit the soul nor give glory unto God—this is what has befallen the glorious and majestic practices of Catholic worship in the parishes of Brazil." [43] In the words of Sérgio Buarque de Holanda, Brazilian Catholicism is always "more attentive to the outward pomp and splendor of the ceremonies than to their inner meaning." [44]

The clergy was decadent, and at the time of the famous "religious question" even Dom Vital (Bishop of Recife) declared that the affair "had been of immense benefit to the Faith among us. . . . The priests had realized the need to change their ways of life so that they could once more lift up their heads among the faithful and above the enemies of God." [45]

Relations between the Church and the "skeptical and rationalist" ruling classes of the Second Empire were not exactly happy,[46] particularly during the first phase of the Empire, when "bishops and parish priests were clearly considered and treated as agents of the executive power; this on the initiative of a priest, the celebrated Diogo Antônio Feijó." [47] On the other hand—and this was recognized by even the most ardent Catholics of the time—the want of prestige and the decline of the clergy were due to the errors committed by the clergy themselves and the abuses they had practiced. They had allowed themselves to become caught in a web of seriously compromising political intrigue. This contributed to the widening of the gap between the clergy and the more enlightened representatives of Brazilian culture. Nevertheless, more from habit and tradition than from conviction, the intellectual elite continued to respect Catholicism, which was the state religion.

Among the leaders of the Empire, however, as among their ancestors, who had flung themselves into the adventures of discovery and *Bandeirismo,* there was anticlerical caution. We could perhaps say that most of the intellectuals of the period can be identified with the portrait of Dom Pedro II drawn by Joaquim Nabuco in his book, *Um Estadista do Império (A Statesman of the Empire).*

The mind of Dom Pedro II [writes Nabuco], was steeped in anticlerical prejudice. He was not exactly anticlerical—he saw no real danger in the existence of the clergy; he rather failed to find attractive the actual religious vocation. For him, a tireless student of the sciences, the soldier and the priest were two social phenomena with no future, two temporary necessities which he would have liked to put to better use —the priest by adding to his functions those of schoolmaster or university professor; the soldier by replacing him by a mathematician, an astronomer, a chemist, or an engineer." [48]

Dom Pedro II, like his cultured contemporaries, was a Voltairean —a rationalist who somehow managed to reconcile a vague spiritualism with Catholicism.[49]

Félix Ravaisson, in his evaluation of the philosophy of France during the first half of the nineteenth century, concluded that "as Victor Cousin advanced in his career—although, according to his own affirmations, he continued to fly the flag of Eclecticism—he had in fact become increasingly reduced to a private system in which the ideas of Scottish philosophers and some of the ideas of Maine de Biran and Ampère provided the preliminary basis; it thus becomes possible to define Eclecticism as a brilliant development of the semi-spiritualism introduced by Royer-Collard."[50] In the richly varied and many-hued history of Eclecticism, which Taine examined with such penetrating irony, some curious transformations took place, owing to a great extent, to political circumstances. The doctrine of Victor Cousin (if this "fusion, lacking either method or critique"—to quote the words of Eisler, can be called a doctrine) revealed a certain daring in its first phase—the period extending to 1839.[51] However, the attitude of the Eclectics was to be quite different after Victor Cousin took over the Ministry of Education in the cabinet of Thiers. From then on, Eclecticism tended more and more toward a spiritualism which, because of its vagueness and imprecision, ended by satisfying no one. This doctrine, which had had its moment of success in the first half of the nineteenth century after winning over a number of scholars, thanks—to quote Ravaisson—to the "elevated tendency of its moral theories," ended by satisfying "neither the scientific mind nor the religious spirit."[52]

These "adventures" of European Eclecticism were to be repeated in Brazil, above all those of its last phase.[53] "Eclecticism in Brazil," wrote Clóvis Beviláqua, "was the philosophy which spread its roots most deeply into the Brazilian soul. In a fever of propaganda, numerous translations of the French masters appeared, such as that by A. P. Figueiredo of Victor Cousin's *History of Philosophy*."[54]

Even at the end of the nineteenth century, Eclecticism kept its hold on Brazil. "In those last few years," writes Clóvis Beviláqua, "when spiritualism has taken a new direction and acquired an apparently more solid foundation from the liberal, albeit fruitless, efforts of Paul Janet, whose sympathy with science is undeniable, the doctrine which has taken a hold on almost all the Brazilian teachers in Eclecticism."[55]

"The first decade of the Second Empire," writes Basílio de Magalhães, "was spent in consolidating the power of the Throne amid the wreckage of the last democratic energies, still attached to the interregnum of republican experimentation during the Regency." [56] From 1840 to 1850 the monarchy ensured its stability.[57] The prestige of Eclectic philosophy in Brazil is therefore linked to the advent of the establishment of the monarchy, to the long reign of Pedro II, the "Emperor-Professor"—a solidly bourgeois king, in tails, top hat, and bearing an umbrella in the manner of France's Louis Philippe. The monarchy naturally adopted a philosophy in tune with its ideals, and Eclecticism was just right. However, as Eclecticism was by its nature a philosophy of "compromise," it evolved with considerable ease and underwent several modifications.[58]

Eclecticism accepted Condillac's succession, although, as Lenoir points out, Royer-Collard attacked the doctrines of the author of the *Traité des Sensations* in his professional lectures. Nonetheless, Royer-Collard accepted the basic principles of Condillac's system.[59] It was thanks to Eclecticism that we did not experience the counter-revolutionary manifestation inspired by the doctrines of De Bonald and de Maistre. We did, however, have,

and this was an old story, some sincere adherents of theologism; but they were certainly neither linked to the philosophical reaction led by Bonald and Joseph de Maistre nor to the movement started by the Abbot Lamenais—that strange priest so deeply shaken by the chilling winds of disbelief. Our philosophers of the theologist school, both those who were content to be simply teachers in the secondary schools or seminaries and those who ventured into print, stem directly from St. Thomas, reinforced by the works of Gioberti, Rosmini, Balmes, and Ventura de Raulica.[60]

For this reason,

the French theologism of the beginning of this century (the nineteenth) did not produce a vibrant and responsive echo among our intellectuals. The main reason is that the pietist and malicious bent which it assumed in the *Soirées de Saint Petersbourg* was not of a nature to arouse the sympathies of an audience in Brazil, where benevolence melts into semi-apathy and where sincere or Pharisaic zeal only rarely achieves the manifestations of a militant sectarianism.[61]

In effect, the reactionary political situation created by the philosophical attitude of such writers as De Bonald and de Maistre did not find in our country a climate in which to flourish. This was due in part to the influence of the doctrines of French Eclecticism which continued, throughout the reign of Pedro II, to exert its dominance over the minds of our literati and "philosophists."

French Spiritualist Eclecticism already present in the work of Mont'Alverne in the first half of the nineteenth century, appeared with fresh vigor during the "crisis of renewal," undergone by the Brazilian intellect, immediately after what can be regarded as the major event in its evolution during the nineteenth century: the abolition of slavery.

In 1854 Eduardo Ferreira França published in Bahia two large volumes on questions of general psychology, entitled *Investigações de Psychologia* (*Investigations in Psychology*).[62] In the preface to this work, Ferreira França declares:

Steeped in the ideas of the so-called "sensualist" school and full of enthusiasm for Destutt de Tracy—to the point where I attempted to read and study only the works of the scholars he preferred—I became a disciple of materialism and was convinced that nothing existed beyond matter, that the spirit was simply the function of an organ. Many times I read and reread the works of the philosopher I had chosen as a master and felt pleasure only in reading works in which the doctrines expressed were similar to his, all others displeasing me as being unworthy of my attention. Obliged, however, to abandon these studies in favor of those which would qualify me for the profession of medicine, I ceased to read philosophy, but did not cease to ponder on the subjects with which philosophers occupy their minds. As a materialist, I felt an emptiness within myself, I was forever restless, even deeply disturbed. It was then that I began to reflect; and my reflections led me to question many things I had formerly accepted as proved truths; and gradually I came to realize that we are not merely composed of matter but indeed chiefly of something very different. I tried in my meditations to examine the true nature of my being and observed that many phenomena were not explicable solely in terms of the existence of matter: and thus, progressively, I examined all my opinions, until after some years I returned to the study of the philosophers, reading those who formerly had displeased me, only to experience an indefinable pleasure in their works and especially in those of the profound Maine de Biran who above all others contributed to the enlightenment of my mind.[63]

Ferreira França further confesses that he cannot help recognizing that

I owe a good deal to the profound philosopher who formerly served me as master, for, although he expounds a doctrine to which I cannot today subscribe, none more than he is endowed with so rigorous a power of logic, leading him on inevitably to certain ultimate conclusions from principles often admitted to be without much reason: it was he, above all, who taught me how to reason, and gave me the means to doubt even his own doctrines.[64]

Ideology, a doctrine which enlisted many followers in the Americas, represented from 1785 to 1830 the old spirit of eighteenth-century French philosophy. It experienced its moment of real glory during the Consulate, and at the time when Ferreira França was studying medicine in Paris it probably had still its adepts. For a time the "ideologists" ruled the Academy of Moral and Political Sciences of the Institute of France (Volney, Garat, Sieyès, Guinguené, Cabanis, Laromiguière—who was later to oppose them— Destutt de Tracy and the well-known historian of philosophy, Dégerando).[65] The ideologists who had at first approved of the coup of eighteenth Brumaire were disenchanted with Napoleon when they realized that he was no liberal and that he was not the heir to the Revolution they had imagined him to be. They expressed open hostility toward the proposed law against "crimes endangering the security of the state," and from then on Napoleon began to harass them. This led them to join the opposition against the Emperor; after his defeat they fought against the Restoration and, above all, against any religious restoration, being united in their resistance to the invading and engulfing spirit of Le Génie du Christianisme.[66]

The ideologists—and it is important to stress the assertion that follows for our consideration of the history of philosophy in America—constituted the link between eighteenth-century philosophy and Positivism. Many philosophers who later joined the Eclectic movement derived from the ideologists.[67] Ferreira França was one of those who moved away from this movement.[68] He does not seem to have gained much from his altered position. Although his work is of some interest to students of Brazil's intellectual history, he expresses some ridiculous ideas—as, for example, his proliferation of the "faculties" which he gives as more than twelve! Among them he lists the "faculty of foresight," "the faculty of faith," and others not quite so preposterous.[69] On instinct Ferreira França is equally detailed. On page 334 of his second volume, we find the instinct of "cunning"—"the secretiveness of phrenologists," he calls it.[70] We find also the instincts of "habitation," [71] "acquisitiveness," [72] "approvement," fantasy belief, recognition, subjection, and others. Nevertheless, some of his analyses are penetrating, showing that the author had the "secretiveness" he considers on page 334 of his work. But the work as a whole, with its cornerstones taken from the works of Jouffray, Garnier, Royer-Collard, and other Eclectics, does not have even that breadth of vision that Taine perceived among some disciples of the Eclectic school. Sílvio Romero, in spite of the customary pungency of his criticism, says of Ferreira França's work that it is "more worthy of a reading than that of Mont'Alverne and even that of Mr. Gonçalves de Magalhães." [73] And he is right.

Before we consider the not very original philosophical ideas of Viscount Araguaia, in order to arrive at some understanding of the position he occupies among Brazilian "philosophizers" we must first place him in his period and outline some of the features of his temperament. A figure of some importance in the history of Brazilian literature, he deserves a more detailed examination, since I believe he is a fair representative of Eclecticism in our country.

We must not lose sight of the fact that

from the beginning of the present century [as Sales Tôrres Homem wrote in 1836] a reaction has begun to shake the ancient foundations of the powerful kingdom of the muses. The shadowiness of the memories of the cradle of modern civilization, the sublime thoughts of Christianity, the simplicity of the natural scene providing such touching parallels to the misery of our hearts—all seemed to be a source of emotions more delicate and true than the ingenious dreams of antiquity. . . . Christianity, by banishing from the universe the elegant divinities who peopled the world of mythology, restored the majesty, the grandeur, and the gravity of creation, opening up new paths for poetry which hitherto had looked on nature only through the fictions consecrated by Hesiod and Homer. Today, from these new springs are drawn not only the most brilliant inspirations of poetry but of art and of *philosophy, sister of theology.*[74]

As we can see from this excerpt, the influence of *Le Génie du Christianisme* was felt by the Brazilians who lived in France at that time. Magalhães was to find in Paris the influences of the second generation of Romantics mentioned by Seillière.[75]

Domingos José Gonçalves de Magalhães was born in Rio de Janeiro in 1811. In his early twenties he participated in the disturbances which agitated the country, but there is no record of his having then manifested anything more than the patriotic enthusiasm which took hold of all and sundry after independence. At the age of fifteen he had begun to write verse.[76] In 1828 Magalhães matriculated at the Medical and Surgical College attached to the hospital of the Santa Casa de Misericórdia founded by King João VI. He seems to have had no vocation for the career he had chosen because, at a certain stage of his youth, he seriously contemplated entering a religious order, and the only reason he did not do so—we are told by Alcântara Machado—was that he met with opposition from his father and later "from the counsels of the man he had chosen as a model," [77] that is, his friend Mont'Alverne. In 1829 he began his studies of philosophy. He attended the courses given by Mont'-Alverne at the Seminary of São José and, in the same year, composed an ode in which all philosophers pass in procession, from the Greeks to Kant.[78] "Aboard, in an adventurous keel, my life exposing to the tragic waves," [79] he sailed for Europe in the middle of 1833, already as a qualified surgeon, "to cull the honeycombs of wisdom." [80]

This future Romantic, who claimed to be possessed of a "life-long melancholy," amused himself in Europe, while constantly declaring himself to be a "miserable exile." [81] The sighing and tearful sensibility of Klopstock—equally false—and the religious philosophism of Sousa Caldas[82] affected the young Magalhães. During his stay in Paris the poet became better acquainted with Romanticism and attended the lectures of Jouffroy. On his return to Brazil he was nominated to the chair of philosophy in the Pedro II College but occupied it only for a short period in 1842; in January, 1843, he was chosen secretary for Caxias in the government of the Province of Rio Grande do Sul, which he left to become a member of the imperial parliament.[83] He did not long remain a deputy, however, for in 1847 he was sent as consul to Naples. In 1854 he was transferred to Turin as Brazilian representative at the Court of Victor Emmanuel II. In 1855 he made a brisk trip to Brazil to publish his book *Confederação dos Tamoios*, a work which received poor critical notices and provoked a controversy in the newspapers, in which José de Alencar and the Emperor himself participated. The former did not mince his words in attacking the dullness of the conceits abused by the future Viscount Araguaia.[84] Ambitious but timid, dejected by the death of his children and the criticism of his latest work, Gonçalves de Magalhães sought consolation in the study of philosophy. If he had sought consolation only! But no: Magalhães wrote, too. Feverish with the desire for fame and not, as might be supposed, in a spirit of renunciation, the ambitious Magalhães, who had linked himself to Mont'Alverne, wrote a number of books on philosophy. The principal works are: *Os Fatos do Espírito Humano,*[85] *A Alma e o Cérebro,*[86] and *Comentários e Pensamentos*[87] written between 1858 and 1880. Magalhães remained faithful to the past. Just as "classical literature was of Catholic and monarchist inspiration and based on spiritualist concepts," [88] so also the philosophy of Magalhães was spiritualist and Catholic.

That illustrious historian of philosophical ideas in Brazil, Father Leonel Franca, records: "Magalhães had attended Jouffroy's lessons in Paris, had read Cousin and perhaps Malebranche, and from the ideas drawn from these divers sources, which he pondered with a certain originality, he concocted an amalgam of theories, for which none of these writers can be held exclusively responsible." [89] I feel, however, that Father Leonel, perhaps moved by his priestly charity, was too kind. That Magalhães had read Cousin is obvious—his style is much like that of Cousin, verbose and rhetorical. Besides, the most prevalent source of the Viscount's information is likewise Cousin. As for the ideas of Malebranche, I agree with the late lamented and brilliant Jesuit scholar that "Magalhães absorbed them from the works of Gioberti and Rosmini, the ontologists whom he must have met during his stay in Italy or through Lammenais's *Esquisse d'une philosophie.*" [90]

When we come to examine the philosophical books of Magalhães we become lost in a spate of words. Pages on pages are covered with rhetoric, used only to embellish style and not to convey any interesting point, a mere display of virtuosity, as in the opening passages of his book *Os Fatos do Espírito Humano.*[91]

And what are the philosophical trends expounded by Magalhães?

At the stage we have reached in the philosophical sciences [he writes], will it be needful for us to begin by supposing that all their truths require a new examination and new proofs? Should we, like Descartes, reject, albeit temporarily, all the ideas bequeathed us by so many centuries of reflection and seek, through our intelligence alone, to create a new basis for science? How often we permit our thoughts to roam at large through this vast field! And how often, guided by the demands of logic, do we find ourselves considering these questions! Why should we reject the truths we already know? Rather let us verify them. This skeptical method, so rightly employed by Descartes who is today called the "father of modern philosophy," deserves our approval when we consider the times and the circumstances in which this profound thinker lived, in the middle of the seventeenth century at the height of the general skepticism that followed the reforms of Luther, and the discrediting and downfall of Scholastic philosophy—a philosophy born and bred in the cloisters, where it had become narrow and constricted and had languished until at length it died, a philosophy in thrall to the faith and under the guardianship of theology. But, after Descartes had lifted philosophy from the benches of the schools and given it its emancipation by restoring to it its true method, the psychological, and its only true authority, reason—a service matching that rendered by Bacon of Verulam to the physical sciences when he counseled experiment and induction; and after the works of the illustrious heirs of Descartes, Malebranche, Locke, Leibniz, Reid, Kant, and many other modern philosophers who, with a complete independence of mind, walked in the footsteps of Plato and Aristotle, it would be a tremendous vanity to begin anew without considering the work of other writers, as though nothing had been achieved, as though no agreement had been reached between the different theories into which philosophy has been divided.[92]

In this way, Magalhães comes to the conclusion that all philosophical doctrines can be reduced to four systems: Sensualism, skepticism, spiritualism, and mysticism.[93] An amalgam of all these systems, together with a lengthy and detailed commentary, constitutes the "philosophy" of Gonçalves de Magalhães. In the introduction to the work he published in 1858, perhaps somewhat uncertain of the solution discoverable in this amalgam of widely opposed doctrines, he took the precaution of declaring: "I shall not anticipate myself by expounding the doctrine of this work in a shortened form. Surprise is one of the delights derived from reading." [94] It seems to me, however, that the technique of the detective story is not exactly suited to the traditions of philosophy. Magalhães was probably hesitating among the different doctrines—as we can, indeed, see from this work—and ended by introducing them all. From the outset of the work it is easy to perceive that all the doctrines lead to spiritualism. But Magalhães believed that he had to strengthen his position by buttressing it with historical and rhetorical argument. Thus, in *Os Fatos do Espírito Humano,* he examines in detail the doctrines of Locke providing a lengthy commentary and concluding that "sensualism in psychology is the negation of reason and liberty and of inevitable and absolute ideas" . . . and that "in the realm of morals it is the negation of any notion of duty or of justice"; and further that "in politics, it leads to the absolute despotism of Hobbes." [95] Next, he expounds and comments on Condillac presenting a series of considerations on his doctrines, examining skepticism and mysticism, and occasionally professing opinions of a banality equal only to that of his *Pensamentos*.[96] In the final chapters of the book, however, he states his position more clearly.

It is not with eyes glued to the exterior world and with senses open and attentive to perceptual phenomena that the human soul will learn to understand its true nature, its attributes, and its destiny; it is only by withdrawing to the sanctuary of its conscience, by reflecting on its actions, that it will come to penetrate the metaphysics of the spiritual world, of which it is but one of the inhabitants who travel through this external world, forgetful at times of that native land (!) from whence it comes.[97]

He cites Berkeley and ends by invoking, in the words of Sílvio Romero, "a shriveled vision in God," which is more or less Malebranchian.[98] He had previously studied matter and spirit. Basing himself on Flourens, he had said that "all matter, all material organs, all being, appears and disappears, makes and remakes itself with only one thing remaining constant, and that is the very thing which makes and unmakes, which creates and destroys, the force which resides in the midst of matter and governs it." [99]

The work of Magalhães is really one long, fastidious commentary on doctrines which tend to strengthen his position—a basic spiritualism in which are mingled ontology and idealism. The only useful aspect of his work, writes Leonel Franca, is the negative one, the pages in which he refutes Condillac and the materialism of his followers.[100] But not even this can be conceded. With a nice turn of wit, basing himself on one of the Viscount's *pensées* ("Human science is a voyage from the finite to the infinite across seas notorious for their wreckage"), Franca writes that the "voyage of the Viscount de Araguaia across those seas records yet another of those disasters," [101] but, in a spirit of charity, excuses him adding: "It was not easy for him to avoid disaster. The shoals of ontology and idealism had already proved dangerous to more powerful minds than his." [102]

Romanticism coincided with independence. "The nation embarked on its autonomous existence when other nations, emerging from medieval night and having undergone the severe trials of revolution, were beginning to evolve new forms for their institutions," writes Nélson Werneck Sodré. "Constitutionalism was replacing absolutism. The tradition of political charters was replacing the power of kings. The physiognomy of society was changing rapidly. Our country heard the echo of these changes, still in a convulsive stage in many countries as the result of the nature of their peculiarities, while in others they had already become fixed and fundamental." [103] Romanticism was to be "the means of expression," "the instrument of our mental autonomy." Magalhães was "a man of letters in a time of independence." [104] He was lucky to have lived at a time of national enthusiasm. He spoke from afar of the land of his birth, "depicting it in the colors of sentiment," [105] and never forgetting "the mainsprings which had given the nation its dominant characteristics, religious feeling and the prodigiousness of nature. No more was needed to endear him to our people and to transform him into the representative of a happy moment of our literature." [106] It is in these terms that the relative success of his "philosophy" can be explained.

CHAPTER 4

A Wave of New Ideas

In the "explanatory notes" to the posthumous *Vários Escritos (Collected Writings)* of Tobias Barreto, Sílvio Romero refers to the crisis of revival which occurred in Brazil about the middle of the nineteenth century as follows:

The most significant developments in our spiritual growth took place during the decade between 1868 and 1878. Only those who lived through this period could truly understand, through their experience of the profound disturbance it provoked, the deepest feelings of the national soul. Before 1868 Catholicism had reigned on these shores undisturbed by the least shock; spiritualist philosophy, Catholic and Eclectic by nature, had met with the most insignificant opposition; the authority of the monarchical institutions had hardly been subjected to attack by any of the classes; the institution of slavery and the traditional rights of the feudal plantation owners had encountered only the most indirect protest; Romanticism, full of the sweet enchantments of its delusory fantasies, had provoked only the faintest of reactions. Everything seemed to have fallen asleep under the shadows of the mantle of the happy prince who had put an end to the *caudillos* in the provinces and in South America as a whole, and had set the machinery in motion for the most cohesive centralization ever attempted in the history of a great nation. Suddenly some ancient subterranean agitation broke through to reveal the instability of

all things, and the sophistry of the Empire stood disclosed in all its naked-
ness.[1]

Soon a "wave of new ideas" flowed across Brazil, opening up new
directions. This crisis of renewal was directly linked to the rever-
berations set off by one of the most significant developments in the
country's economic life. We must not lose sight of the fact that

among the transformations suffered by Brazil in the nineteenth century,
none made so great a contribution to the nation's altered physiognomy
as the veritable revolution which took place in its agricultural production.
The first stirrings of this revolution were felt in the first half of the century, but in the second half it gathered momentum and revealed its true
nature . . . the decline of traditional cultivation—sugar cane, cotton,
and tobacco—and the parallel rise of a commodity hitherto relatively unimportant: coffee, which came to occupy a unique position in the economic balance of Brazil.

The agricultural revival inaugurated toward the end of the eighteenth
century, and tremendously stimulated by the opening of the ports and
the achievement of political emancipation, was, particularly at first, favorable to the older-established agricultural regions of the North: the coastal
provinces stretching from Maranhão to Bahia. They assumed once more
the leading position they had enjoyed in the past but had in part lost
to the mining areas. This renewal of prosperity did not, however, last
long; already in the first half of the nineteenth century the southern
centers were progressively taking the lead in the country's economic
activities. And by the second half of the century, a complete reversal
of former positions had taken place: the North came to a standstill
amounting to decadence; the South, now clearly ahead, continued to
flourish.[2]

Among the factors which contributed to the decadence of the North

we must include the cessation, in 1850, of the traffic in African slaves.
Already undermined by an unfavorable combination of events on the
international scene and the exhaustion of its natural resources, the
North suffered greatly from this new blow, which deprived it of easy
and relatively cheap labor. The South was less seriously hit by abolition
because it was in a stage of ascending development and could therefore
make a speedier recovery. It could even resolve its immediate labor
problem by importing slaves from the impoverished North, although
this aggravated the situation of the latter.[3]

It was the recently introduced cultivation of coffee[4] that permitted
the monarchy to recover during the last stages of the Empire. The

abolition of the slave trade had a further consequence, which must be emphasized for a proper understanding of Brazil's historical situation at this time. It freed a considerable amount of capital which had been invested in the slave traffic.

Up to that time [writes Joaquim Nabuco], the commercial and industrial spirit of the country seems to have been exercised only in the importation and sale of African slaves. With the prohibition of this traffic, a marvellous change took place. It is well known, reported the Commission of Inquiry into the system in 1860, that the abolition of the slave trade completely altered the face of agriculture, commerce, and industry. The capital which had hitherto been invested in this criminal trade flowed into the market, leading to a cut in the interest rate; money was freely available, and there was an extraordinary rise in the share prices of almost all companies.[5]

From 1850 to 1854 there was intense economic activity. Numerous commercial and industrial joint stock companies were incorporated, the Bank of Brazil became a bank of issue, an electric telegraph line was inaugurated, and finally the Central Railway Line of Brazil was opened to traffic.

In this series of events, all of an economic nature, the foundations were laid for the material development of the country, resumable under the following four heads: the organization of labor and production; the management of credit, circulation, and investment of capital in the form of currency; a new speed and ease in the transmission of news and ideas, allowing the number of transactions to be increased and speeding up the processes involved; the establishment of rapid means of transport between the commercial markets on the coast and the sources of production in the interior, which allowed of an increase in the circulation of commodities and a regular supply of goods for internal consumption and which gave an incentive to foreign trade by providing the possibility for the export of surpluses.[6]

After 1850 Brazil was on a completely new economic footing. Intellectually, we were also to seek new outlets.

2

"The contemporary cosmopolitanism in which we have a small share because of our commercial conquests has resulted in situations like the following: the lively minds in backward and uncouth nations, excited by the swift current of great ideas today revitalizing the cultured nations of the world, can, after transcending native prejudice, raise their heads above the reigning mediocrity and bask in a new light. I see in this phenomenon an exception to the rule which makes us subject to our social environment, often narrow and wanting in resources, an exception in favor of the civilization which flourishes abroad. The struggle for culture triumphs, after all, even among people as systematically backward as we." [7]

Thus wrote Sílvio Romero, to whom this departure from "the rule of the environment" seemed to account for the fact that "the reading of a foreign author or the predilection for books from abroad could determine the nature of the opinions of a Brazilian writer." [8] "For this reason," he adds, "Brazilian philosophers cannot be arranged in any logical classification springing from the laws which govern the development of philosophical systems, since here *these do not exist.*" [9]

Nevertheless, in his *Filosofia do Brasil* published in 1878, Sílvio Romero essayed a classification of our "philosophers." He sorted them into three groups: those educated in the French sensualism of the early nineteenth century; the neo-Catholics affiliated to the doctrines of Rosmini and Gioberti, or of Balmes and Ventura; and, finally, those who were beginning to emancipate themselves, under the tutelage of Comte and Darwin. [10] He seems to have overlooked the curious nature of an "emancipation" which is accomplished under "tutelage." Perhaps for this reason he revised the 1878 classification in 1905. [11]

We have already considered the writers who, according to Sílvio Romero, represented the currents which developed from Eclecticism. We must now examine the representatives of Catholic reaction. Before we do so, however, we must briefly consider the origins of this reaction, in order to place it in its national context.

The advent of Cartesianism and its subsequent propagation dealt a serious blow to Scholasticism. In 1787 Bossuet foresaw that more than one heresy would be born of the principles of the Cartesian doctrines. [12] Cartesianism led to enormous confusion among the ranks of the Church's traditional doctrines; its influence was felt throughout the ecclesiastical world, from the humblest monks to the highest prelates, as, for example, in Cardinal Gerdil, who failed to see why some doctors of the Church were so averse to this doctrine. [13] We cannot here study the curious history of Cartesianism in its struggle—and sometimes its seeming conformity—with the Church. As it developed, however, Cartesianism continually and more and more decidedly affirmed the scientific tendency of modern thought as opposed to the Scholastic tradition.[14]

The vague sentimental and aesthetic reaction attempted by the Romantics, despite the brilliance of some of its representatives, did not succeed in reconciling the modern ideas embodied in Cartesianism and its consequences with the traditional doctrines of the Church. The elegant weapons of Romanticism were equally unsuited to satisfy the Church, since they harbored grave dangers to orthodox doctrines. Besides, Romanticism had provided an opportunity for the idealism of modern German philosophy to penetrate into Catholic countries, undoing all the hard work put in by the Scholastics during the long years of the Counter Reformation. Nevertheless, after Encyclopedism and the revolution, the Church took advantage of political conditions to encourage the Restoration and the reconstruction of traditional spiritualist doctrines under the guidance of Ubaghs, in Belgium; Balmes, in Spain; Rosmini, Gioberti, and Ventura, in Italy.[15] Slowly, the Church took the path which led it to a revival of Thomism.

In Brazil the decadence of the clergy mirrored its decline, in process in Europe since the eighteenth century.[16] In a country like ours, only recently freed from its colonial subjection, the clergy retained the old habits of colonial days. "In certain areas in the interior of Pernambuco," writes Gilberto Freyre, "a malicious tradition attributed the useful, although hardly seraphic, profession of procurer to the sugar-mill chaplains."[17] "Everyone knows," Freyre goes on, "that whites of the finest stock—including priests, who were certainly among the most select and eugenic elements in the formation of Brazil—bred liberally on female slaves and half-castes."[18]

It is for this reason that Freyre rightly considers that the "patriarchal formation of Brazil can be explained, as much in its virtues as in its defects, less in terms of race or religion than in terms of simple economics, the experience, culture, and organization of the family, which was in Brazil the colonizing unit."[19] For our people, formed from such diverse elements, religion consisted precisely in those ceremonies which Father Júlio Maria said "failed to purify the spirit, the novenas which revealed no true fervor."[20]

The clergy, in addition to being intemperate, was generally ignorant. In fact, it was hardly to be differentiated from the bulk of the populace.

"The clergy of Brazil," wrote A. H. de Sousa Bandeira in 1881, was never distinguished for its learning. On the contrary, "its influence, when exercised, was based on an unworthy exploitation of fanaticism bred of ignorance." [21] This observation is not altogether true, since the Brazilian clergy has proved itself, with rare exceptions, to be both tolerant and understanding. In the history of our clergy there is, in general, little record of the aggressiveness and intolerance we find in that of other nations. They adapted themselves to life in a patriarchal society. Respected by all, enjoying the privileges they had been granted and which had never aroused any resentment, on excellent terms with the monarchy, the clergy lived in peace with the people, encouraging their superstitions because they themselves were profoundly steeped in them. To the Portuguese religious tradition—all Church feasts and gay pilgrimages—was added in Brazil the cult of Negro saints and the practice of fetishism in the frequent rites on the plantations, in the villages and settlements lost in the vast interior. Side by side with this popular Christianity, another, less primitive, "springing from a spiritual refinement, manifested itself among the 'elite,' discontented with the gross brutalization of religion demanded by the people." [22] This elite, generally educated in Europe or, if in Brazil, through study of foreign (chiefly French) books, was mostly skeptical or rationalist in outlook and hence falsely devout, as was remarked with some irritation by Saint-Hilaire, a naturalist who spent a Holy Week in São Paulo during 1822.[23]

It was as the result of Romanticism, Eclecticism, and finally of the neo-Catholic reaction—which sought to do away with religious ignorance and to halt the demoralization of the clergy—that spiritualism began to acquire new meaning for some members of our elite. The first signs of this reaction are visible in the works of two naturalized foreign priests—one Portuguese and one Italian: Father Patrício Muniz, and Monsignor Gregório Lipparoni.[24]

When studying the neo-Catholic philosophical reaction in Brazil, we must not overlook the fact that it was the reflection of a much wider general movement in the Church, which took place at this time. But this reaction is also related to problems specific to our history and was supported by national events. We must remember that shortly after the famous "religious question," one of the chief protagonists, Dom Vital de Oliveira, said, as we have seen, that it had "been of immense benefit to the Faith among us." [25]

There was therefore, about the middle of the nineteenth century, a constellation of circumstances favoring the revival in our country of philosophical studies with Catholic leanings.

3

We have already noted, in citing the work of Father Júlio Maria, the regalist nature of imperial politics. Even the clerics who participated in the early activities of the new Empire were markedly regalistic.[26]

For its part, the Holy See had recognized, after 1827,

that the Imperial Crown, like the Crown of Portugal from which it had splintered, was entitled to the right of advowson or patronage, that is, the right to present ecclesiastical benefices, and that it was further entitled to the right of sanctioning the acts of the ecclesiastical courts within its jurisdiction. This was the purpose of the diplomatic mission dispatched to Rome in the person of Monsignor Francisca Correa Vidigal to treat directly with the Pope, as well as to ensure disciplinary separation of the Brazilian and Portuguese religious orders, which were still attached to each other, and the exclusion of new foreign regular orders.[27]

Regalism proved to be, for the Church, a "gilded cage," in the words of Magalhães de Azeredo.[28] In this way

the statesmen who were the auxiliaries and advisers of our second and last Emperor in the business of government—either as ministers or as members of the Council of State—prayed, so to speak, from the same primer as Father Diogo Feijó [by treating the priests as agents of the executive power; see n. 47 to chap. 2—Trans.] The most famous constitutional jurists, such as José Antônio Pimenta Bueno (later Viscount and Marquis of São Vicente) and Judge Brás Florentino Henriques de Sousa, did not hesitate to uphold the doctrine that the state had judicial rights over religious worship as well as the right to regulate the discipline and to examine the spiritual activities of the clergy and, above all, that the nomination of bishops, like the presentation to ecclesiastical benefices, was exclusive to the national sovereignty, the Holy See being concerned merely with the confirmation of such appointments.[29]

In view of the decadence of the religious orders in Brazil, Senator Nabuco in 1854 "with the complete support of the monarch and the approval of the bishops," [30] took the measures necessary for a reform which would put a stop to the disorder of the convents where "there reigned a complete lack of discipline or proper administration, the squandering of their riches, the intrigues of shame-

less factions, and where simony was practiced for love of prefer-
ment." [31] The Bishop of São Paulo, to whom Nabuco had written
for advice, answered as follows: "I know full well that Your Excellency has deep insight and will therefore have noted that the
spirit of Catholicism is almost extinguished in Brazil." [32] The
Bishop of Pará, Dom José, in his turn bore witness to the "decadent
state of certain Orders." [33] The most penetrating and lively letter,
however, was written to Nabuco by the Bishop of Mariana, Dom
Antônio: "I am delighted to see how much attention you are giving
to questions of religion. May God grant you light to carry to its
conclusion this so promising beginning." [34] But Dom Viçoso felt
that the task would not be easy. "As for the regular orders, I almost
lose hope for them," he writes. "I was sent to reform the Carmelites
of Bahia and found almost no one to nominate as a prelate. Once
left on their own, they slid back into the same condition." [35] Homero
Pires, in his interesting study of Junqueira Freire, the poet, also
refers to the lamentable condition of the clergy in Brazil during the
poet's lifetime. There were friars who returned to the convent only
to spend the night. Others "were so far from their cloisters that
they had rented houses to live in. The most notorious was Brother
Antônio of the Order of the Virgin Mary Itaparica, who lived with
his illegitimate family in 'Barber's Alley.' " [36] It would seem, however, that this was a time-honored custom, for in 1764 the Archbishop of Bahia, Dom Manuel de Santa Inês, had written as follows
about the Convent of Santa Clara:

Although there are some nuns in this convent who lead a holy life,
nevertheless, as the result of the disregard for the rules of conduct proper
to their state and vocation shown by the majority, this same convent is
the scandal of the city, although many of its citizens encourage and
shield the nuns, whether through bonds of kinship or out of friendship,
licit or illicit. Never have the prelates, no matter how great their diligent
effort, succeeded in reforming it, for never has any of its members paid
heed to them or taken any note of precept and censure. [37]

In view of this decadent and disorderly plight of the clergy, it
seemed perfectly reasonable for the state to interfere in matters of
religion, and we have already seen the general approval evinced
by the bishops when official measures for reform were proposed.
Nevertheless, it was from this regalism—"the gilded cage of the
Church"—that many of the causes of ecclesiastical decadence in our
country derived. [38] Great harm was done the destiny of religion in

Brazil by having the clergy "closer to the temporal than to the spiritual," in the words of Oliveira Lima.[39] For this reason, the conflict which arose in 1873 between the bishops and the Empire politicians marked a new phase in the history of the Church in Brazil.

The leading protagonists in this conflict between Church and state were men who had spent their formative years in Europe and had returned with the intransigence which characterized the renewal of neo-Scholastic doctrines. Dom Antônio de Macedo Costa, Bishop of Pará, was a former pupil of Saint Sulpice, where he was admitted to Holy Orders before continuing his studies in Rome. Dom Vital de Oliveira was received into the Franciscan Order in Versailles and studied for the priesthood in Tolosa. These two prelates, together with Patrício Muniz, who had also studied in Paris and Rome, and Gregório Lipparoni and Cardoso Aires, former disciples of Rosmini, brought with them fresh from Rome the traces of the struggle in progress there between the Church and the rationalistic philosophies. Soriano de Sousa, who had studied philosophy in Louvain, also bore the imprint of this school.

The neo-Catholic reaction in Brazil [40] during the period under review produced only one figure worthy of note: Dr. José Soriano de Sousa (1833–1895),[41] professor of the University of Recife. Soriano de Sousa was from Paraiba, the province which gave Brazil another of her philosophers, Pedro Americo, better known as an artist.[42] Soriano de Sousa took a degree in medicine at the University of Rio de Janeiro, and in philosophy at the University of Louvain, the traditional Catholic university of Belgium. He competed with Tobias Barreto for a chair in the Pernambuco Gymnasium, and became his colleague in the Faculty of Law at Recife University. He was a deputy during the monarchy, and, later, a member of the Constituent Assembly.

Soriano's philosophical ideas are those of the Scholastic revival, that is, neo-Thomist. Of this movement, Soriano says that only in Brazil did this happy intent lack support. "The philosophy taught here is generally a mixture of Cartesianism and Eclecticism, dispatched to us by French authors, and even this is shrunk to such meager proportions that it could almost disappear from the school boards in the preparatory classes." [43] He adds:

The manuals used in lay schools abound in definitions, syllogistic rules, and a psychology that studies the faculties of the soul without the smallest regard for the organic part of man, as if he were compound of pure spirit. Because this philosophy's claim to glory is its emancipation from theology, nothing in these compendia serves to lift the spirit up to God.[44]

But it was not only the lay schools that lacked compendia serving to lift the spirit up to God. The same was true, says Soriano de Sousa, of the ecclesiastical schools—a situation far more grave! [45] Seeking to remedy this state of affairs, Soriano de Sousa gathered material from various authors and from this compiled his own compendium, designed to compensate for the failings of the others. He openly declares that he based himself largely on the *Summa Philosophia ad Mentem Angelici Doctoris S. Thomae Aquinitatis* by the Dominican Friar Salvador Maria Rosélio (published in Bologna in four volumes).[46]

In his book *Lições de Filosofia Elementar Racional e Moral* Soriano de Sousa declares:

Let us ignore the works of fools and rather base ourselves upon the judgments of wise men, for the greatest need of our time is the restoration of Christian metaphysics founded by St. Thomas in that marvellous accord between the two lights of the human spirit: reason and faith. Only thus can we find the true remedy for the ills we deplore in the realms of politics, morals and the intellect.

But it would seem that in his prescription the philosopher-physician gave much more importance to the second "light" than to the first. Influenced by the ideas of Liberatore, Taparelli, Sanseverino, and Kleutgen,[47] the works of Soriano de Sousa show no originality. They do not flow from a first-hand knowledge of the philosophers of the thirteenth century.[48] Thus, in the movement of Scholastic renewal, which took place in Brazil toward the middle of the last century, we can see the same characteristics that we noted in relation to other philosophical currents. It, too, was a mirror of fashion, a reflection of events in Europe in the philosophical circles related to the Church. It was yet another illusion, typical of our elite—religious or secular —removed from the problems of the land and the ordinary man.

4

About 1870 a new period opened in the history of Brazilian thought. A variety of new ideas, originating in the philosophy of the seventeenth and eighteenth centuries, began to permeate Brazilian intellectual life. Positivism, naturalism, evolutionism, in short, all the modalities of European thought of the nineteenth century, now found expression in Brazil and contributed to a remarkable advance of the critical spirit. This progress in criticism and understanding was accompanied by—perhaps even resulted from—an extraordinary economic advance, which made itself felt after 1860 in a perceptible rise in the living standards of some classes of the population and the beginnings of technical development in the country in the form of railroads, the mechanization of rural industries, and the establishment of its first manufacturing industries.[49] "We can rightly say," writes Caio Prado Júnior, "that at this time Brazil became aware of the meaning of modern progress and for the first time achieved some material well-being." [50] We have already seen that this economic progress was caused in part by the release of capital formerly sunk in the slave trade and now invested in new commercial and industrial enterprises. But this was not the only factor in the economic resurgence which took place after 1860. Factors of equal importance were the development of the coffee plantations and the reversion of English capital.[51] On the other hand, political events in the countries more representative of modern European culture continued to bear notably on our intellectual life. In 1871 France was defeated by Prussia, and the Third Republic was proclaimed. These events had immediate repercussions in Brazil. The *Manifesto Republicano* (*Republican Manifesto*) and the "Germanism" of the Recife school—which propagated the latest trends in German philosophy—are in part related to these changes in Europe. Members of the flourishing "coffee society" of São Paulo and the "philosophizers" of the Recife Law School opened up wider perspective for the Brazilian mind during the last quarter of the nineteenth century, the former through their economic initiative, the latter through their propagation of the new ideas for which the Northern Law School had become a center at that time.[52] It was during that period, too, as a result of the contradictions bred by these economic factors and the agitation of ideas, that the problem of slave labor began to come more clearly into focus. The War of Secession had also called attention to this problem. The Emperor himself, impressed by events in the United States, wrote to Zacarias de Vasconcelos in January of 1864:

The success of the American Unionists has led me to believe that we must seriously consider the future of slavery in Brazil to avoid a repetition of the events that followed the prohibitions of the African traffic. A measure which seems to me to offer advantages is the liberation of the offspring of all slave women a few years hence. I have given much thought to the means of carrying out this measure; but it is of the order that requires firm execution, the evils that will necessarily arise from it being dealt with as circumstances permit.[53]

Later, after the Paraguayan war, the problem, which had been shelved for the time being, became urgent once more. The Viscount of Rio Branco, addressed himself to parliament in the following words:

I found myself among at least fifty thousand Brazilians who came into contact with the neighboring people, and I know from my own experience and from the confessions of some of the most highly educated of my companions how frequently the continued existence in Brazil of this odious institution has been the cause of their vexation and humiliation among these foreigners.[54]

The situation of Brazil after the abolition of slavery in the United States was even more irksome.

Only in our own country and in Cuba did this hateful system linger on. In 1865 the French Council for Emancipation sent a message to the Emperor, signed by Guizot, the De Broglies, Laborlaye, Henri Martin, and Montalembert, urging him to take steps to liberate the slaves. But the slaves comprised one-fourth of the population of Brazil. They were, so to speak, the only source of agricultural labor in the country.[55]

The Council of State, composed almost entirely of great rural landowners, "did not dare contemplate a solution that would shake the foundations of the nation. All their efforts were engaged in an attempt to maintain the equilibrium of the two scales in the balance: agriculture on the one side, slavery on the other." [56] An atmosphere of panic was created around the question of emancipation. All feared that the "free womb" measure would provoke the most serious disorder throughout the country. Itaborai, a wealthy conservative landowner, spoke of "the threat of murder, widespread insurrection, and perhaps even civil war." [57] The Marquis of Olinda said in 1867 that "the least word containing even a hint of emancipation, no matter how much we adorned it, would throw open the door to a thousand disasters. . . . The publicists and statesmen of Europe (he was referring to the plea of the French Emancipation Council) can have no conception of the situation in countries where slavery still exists. Their ideas are useless to us." [58] A frank opponent of emancipation, he adds:

"And when should abolition take place? My answer is: only when it becomes possible to decree emancipation for all slaves indiscriminately, and for all at the same time. And when will this be possible? I say, only when the number of slaves is so reduced by enfranchisement and the natural course of death can this decree be carried out without causing a major shock to agriculture and the slaveholding landlords. . . . I tremble at the publication of these projects which, because of their very existence, can cause the piling up of things capable of causing a tremendous eruption in society.[59]

Eusébio de Queirós, who accepted the idea of the "free womb" measure, proposed that "foreign soldiers—white, of course—should be brought in to repress the continuation of slavery." [60]

Despite the terror of the rural landowners, the contradictions born of the existence of slavery were looming more plainly and menacingly.

After 1860 the pressure of events is strong enough to provoke a widespread defining of positions: the problem of slavery and its continuance was brought into the open and frankly discussed. All manner of publications on the subject began to appear: books, pamphlets, newspaper articles, and other writings. The question was analyzed and debated at length; different aspects of the problem—economic, social, and political —were minutely considered. The first to define their positions were groups of intellectuals, law graduates, advocates, and jurists who were chronologically, the first thinking class of the country.[61]

In the law schools and in the press, the opposition to the odious institution began to find open expression. Later, "clubs" were formed, "liberation leagues," and "centers"; "emancipation funds" and "societies" became the meeting grounds for intellectuals, artists, and some more progressive politicians.[62] The pressures against slavery became increasingly urgent. The Paraguayan war, which had for a time allowed the problem to remain in abeyance,

served to accentuate the organic weakness of a country in which the majority of the population was in bondage. . . . Brazil, although victorious, was humiliated by the war, not only in the eyes of her allies, but in those of the defeated nation, with its troops of recently freed slaves. The question of the abolition of slavery thenceforth became a point of national honor.[63]

The monarchy saw the portents of its doom in the abolitionist movement. Americanist and republican sentiments, stifled in 1831, were being revived. The principal stay of the monarchy, the landed aristocracy, was in the throes of the crisis resulting from the termination of the slave traffic, which had hitherto ensured a flow of cheap labor from the African coasts. The precariousness of a society based on slavery began to reveal itself to its full extent.[64]

The abolition of the slave trade had unleashed forces of renewal in Brazil, which had entered on a phase of economic prosperity after 1850. This rhythm of material progress was maintained despite the Paraguayan war, and the years from 1870 to 1880 were among the most prosperous in the nations history.[65]

Under the Empire, a most important stage in the economic history of the nation was reached. "The population rose to fourteen million; among the upper classes of this population there was wealth and material comfort almost equal to that of the corresponding classes in Europe, a situation unparalled in the past. There were considerable fortunes and a high standard of living, with all the contemporary refinements." [66] But, with all this progress, the Empire did not achieve financial stability and security. "What this represented, in the way of a hindrance to further development, it is difficult to estimate; but no one will deny that this instability is the principal factor responsible for the lack of consolidation in the social and economic life of Brazil, and for the chaotic nature of the future evolution of our economy." [67]

Coinciding with the economic development of the country was a remarkable renewal of national thought.

The Paraguayan war served also to show us the grave defects in our military organization [writes Sílvio Romero] and the backwardness of our social progress by unveiling in all its horror the festering sore of slavery. It was then that the problem of the slaves came to a head, followed almost immediately by the "religious question"; everything was thrown open to debate; the sophistry of the electoral system, the severity of the police system and the magistrature, and innumerable economic problems.[68]

It was at this period that the Liberal party, arbitrarily expelled from power, reorganized itself and produced a political program which was, in the opinion of Sílvio Romero—obviously a biased judge—"extremely democratic, almost true socialism." [69] The *Republican Manifesto* came out in 1870.

In politics it was a period of unrest. In the realm of abstract thought the struggle was even fiercer, since our backwardness was so alarming. A swarm of new ideas hovered over us from every point of the horizon . . . Positivism, evolutionism, Darwinism, religious criticism, naturalism, the cult of science in poetry and the novel, folklore, new methods of criticism and literary history, a change of direction in law and politics— everything was profoundly agitated, and the alarm call proceeded from the Recife Law School. Tobias Barreto was the most energetic of the combatants, with that quickness of perception with which he was naturally gifted.[70]

In the intellectual effervescence which took place in Brazil during the later nineteenth century, Pernambuco (Recife) played a major role.[71] The most important Pernambucan was undoubtedly Tobias Barreto de Menezes, whose vivacity and versatility of spirit left its mark on the young students of the Academy, both during the years he studied there and later, when he taught them as professor of the Faculty of Law. Sílvio Romero, ever careful to stress Pernambuco's leadership in the movement of renewal, attributes the pre-eminence of Recife to the successive revolutions which took place there between 1817 and 1848,[72] and he is not altogether wrong. Meanwhile, "the ideas which had begun to circulate in Europe before the end of the first half of the nineteenth century with Comtian Positivism, Darwinian transformism, Spencerian evolutionism, and the intellectualism of Taine and Renan"[73] spread throughout our country twenty years after their original appearance in Europe. Although Tobias Barreto "swept through the sleepy Academy of Recife like a cyclone,"[74] above all after he assumed the chair, the influence of European philosophical ideas was also felt in the other cultural centers of Brazil. The Recife school was merely the most brilliant example of the intellectual renewal, but this renewal did take pace throughout the country during this period, which was the most prosperous in its economic history. At the Recife school the figure of Tobias Barreto stands out. "His action was twofold: first, and perhaps foremost, he demolished our mental values, which had become stagnant and therefore a barrier to our spiritual progress; secondly, he acted as a stimulating and revitalizing impetus for that mentality."[75]

CHAPTER 5

The Advent of Positivism

The second half of the nineteenth century saw the greatest changes in Brazilian history.

A relative peace having been established between the political
"parties" of the Empire after 1850,[1] the country continued steadily
to progress in an atmosphere of security. In this second half of the
nineteenth century, despite the strongly conservative character of
the Empire, Brazil "modernized herself and made efforts to syn-
chronize her activities with those of the contemporary capitalist
world."[2] It is during this period that the "polyphony" of the new
European philosophical ideas echoed throughout Brazil. While
other currents were influencing the Brazilian elite, Positivism made
its appearance. It would be untrue to say, however, that the "flock
of new ideas" which, in the latter half of the nineteenth century,
left its imprint on the Brazilian intellect was represented by a
"brilliant lower class." The leaders of modern thought in Brazil,
although "brilliant" in the eyes of Gilberto Amado, were not on the
whole drawn from the lower classes or men of the people. Although
they were no longer sons of the lords of the sugar mills and coffee
plantations, they were still, for the most part, representatives and
heirs of the bourgeoisie, made up of merchants and bureaucrats,
that had arisen in the urban communities and that, as the result of

the economic changes of the second half of the nineteenth century, had found itself with a greater means of expression and greater significance. The lower classes were still not in an economic position to leap the barriers separating them from the country's elite. The representatives of the new nineteenth-century elite were the expression of a new form of bourgeoisie, opposed to the traditional one generally deriving from the aristocracy, which was a class of landowners possessed of the most important agricultural instrument of the time—the Negro.

It was, then, the sons of the modest and relatively unimportant commercial and bureaucratic middle class who, thanks to the similarly modest development of capitalism in Brazil, made their appearance on the political and intellectual scene of the second half of the nineteenth century. These members of the new bourgeoisie infiltrated into the generation then entering the country's law schools. They also sought outlets for their intellectual aspirations in the professional schools—the Central Technical and the Military —since they had not the means to embark on lengthy and costly studies. "Thus," explains Leontina Licínio Cardoso,

toward the end of the nineteenth century, a pleiad of forceful, self-educated men emerged from the Military School, almost all of them descendants of people of little means, men who had embarked on a military career in order to acquire the education their condition in life denied them. It was a generation formed under the influence of Benjamin Constant, with distinctly democratic ideals, and it contributed to the downfall of the monarchy and the establishment of the republic, inspired by the principles of Auguste Comte.[3]

In the Military School, and shortly afterward in the Central Technical School as well, the representatives of this nascent middle class sought the education and culture which would permit them to form a new elite, different in spirit from that formed by the law graduates of Coimbra, Recife, and São Paulo, where the sons of the rural patriciate continued to receive a higher education. The emergence of these representatives of the new bourgeoisie threw into relief the antagonism between the "agrarian latifundia and the nascent commercialism, already moving toward industrialization."[4] Thanks to the new spirit, the democratic ideals dormant under the domination of the great landowners, who had taken over power in 1837,[5] gained fresh vigor at the beginning of the second decade of the latter half of the nineteenth century. "There was a genuine awakening and a revaluation of the standards of culture." [6]

In the North, the upsurge of criticism by the Recife group "was paralleled by an increase in mathematical studies, partly related to Positivism; an intensification of natural-science studies; a transformation in the study of law under the influence of evolutionism; the founding of the School of Mines of Ouro Preto, etc." [7] And this movement, as Antônio Cândido aptly remarks,

> was not without its wider counterpart, nor was it merely by chance that it coincided with the first attempts of the bourgeoisie to take over the economic and political management of the nation. It was no coincidence that, in 1860, a great electoral victory was won for democratic liberalism, which counted among its supporters representatives of progressive capitalism such as Teofilo Otoni; nor was it a coincidence that the Liberal party split up in 1868 with the resultant formation of the Republican party in 1870.[8]

The elections of 1860 marked the first—and relatively decisive—triumph of the group that old Nabuco de Araújo called the "Reds." [9]

> With this victory [writes Joaquim Nabuco], the tide of republicanism, which had been ebbing since the monarchical reaction of 1837 and was at its lowest ebb after the majority, began to turn. In Rio de Janeiro the campaign was ardent, enthusiastic, popular—unlike anything ever seen before; the youth of the country took a hand in it; the commercial world contributed generously, as did the bulk of the people, under the leadership of Teófilo Otoni, whose white handkerchief was forever being referred to in the political epigrams of the period. The Liberal candidates were all successful—Teófilo Otoni, Otaviano, Saldanha Marinho; and the victory assumed the proportions of a peaceful revolution against the ruling oligarchy in their senatorial stronghold. It created a party; it meant, in fact, the resurrection of the Liberal party with new leaders and new ideas stronger than individuals or differences of opinion.[10]

"It was," wrote Euclides de Cunha, "the dawn of a new age." [11]

Thus, while economic antagonism grew between the traditional landowners—who governed the country as though they were administering their estates[12]—and the representatives of the new bourgeoisie, there was growing sympathy for the new ideas, which, as a result of the changes effected since the beginning of the century, had found wider circulation. After 1870 this "new bourgeoisie" began to play an important role, above all in the intellectual sphere.[13]

And it was from this middle class—composed of military men, doctors, and engineers, who tended to be more in touch with the positive sciences as a result of their professional activities—that the Positivist movement spread throughout Brazil.[14] Some of the adherents of the movement were men who had become disillusioned with the widely taught spiritualist Eclecticism, which had become indistinguishable from a verbose and useless rhetoric, meriting the disinterest and contempt felt for the philosophy of the period by someone like Miguel Lemos.[15] They were men who had turned to science and who believed that in it they had found a satisfactory answer and a definite solution for all problems. For others, an additional factor in their adherence to Positivism was the antagonism existing between traditional religious beliefs and the republicanism they supported.[16]

Others still found perhaps in the "Religion of Humanity" or orthodox Comtism, deriving from a concept of intellectual progress, a moral order that continued to be linked to traditional values, now merely in an altered form, or, to be more exact, that continued to be shaped in the interests of a class which had taken a step forward in the social scale. "At this time," wrote one of the orthodox Positivists, "there reigned in the religious orders a most complete anarchy."

The Catholic priesthood had early begun to share in the Western crime of enslaving the African race. This nefarious trade dragged the clergy into the disgraceful abuses which characterized the restoration of slavery in the West. Participation in this monstrous crime allied the representatives of spiritual power to the rich and the powerful for the common exploitation of the masses. Priests and landowners were alike influenced by ignoble material interests . . . Enmeshed in political intrigue, slack in the observance of their customs, and, among the higher orders, skeptical, the clergy exercised no direct influence on the ruling class, almost entirely imbued with the rationalism of Voltaire and Rousseau.[17]

And how could any influence be exercised over these exacting minds, avid for certainties, by the demoralized or skeptical clergy of the Second Empire? The republican ideal, which had grown more from revolt against the prevailing political hypocrisy than from a truly democratic spirit among the new bourgeoisie, eager to impose its own "order" and introduce its own concept of "progress," made innumerable converts and adherents for Positivism. [The motto on the Brazilian flag is "Order and Progress."—Trans.]

As for intellectual culture, our system of education continued, up to the middle of the nineteenth century, to perpetuate the "ornamental tradition" destined to produce "humanists" for the two Faculties of Law, whence they issued to enter the field of administration or imperial politics.[18]

This was the atmosphere in which Positivism made its bow.

The first manifestations of Positivist doctrines in Brazil began in 1850. In February of that year, Manuel Joaquim Perreira de Sá, a native of Maranhão, presented a thesis on statistical principles for his doctorate at the Military School in Rio de Janeiro.[19]

Shortly afterward, in April, 1851, Joaquim Alexandre Manso Sayão defended another thesis on physics—this one on the principles of floating bodies.[20] In 1853 Manuel Pinto Peixoto, in studying the principles of the differential calculus, was inspired by the ideas of Comte.[21] Augusto Dias Carneiro, also from Maranhão—curious the number of Maranhenses who were drawn to Positivism—"wrote a thesis on thermology supporting the views of Auguste Comte."[22] The fact that Positivism was introduced into Brazil thanks to the new bachelors of physical and mathematical sciences of the Central Technical and Military schools is understandable in view of the space dedicated to mathematics in its doctrines. This explains, in part, the success of Positivism in the South, where its adherents were drawn largely from among the mathematicians and engineers.

In 1858 Antônio Ferrão Muniz de Aragão published in Bahia *Elementos de Matemática.*

It was his intention [writes Clóvis Beviláqua], to publish a treatise on elementary mathematics which would serve, according to his introduction, as an intellectual discipline, and at the same time present a complete, albeit condensed, exposition of fundamental scientific ideas and the more important results of their application, thus serving as an introduction to a general study of the positive sciences. Only the first volume appeared, however, with the author's introduction, in which there is a résumé of the "law of the three stages" and the "hierarchical classification of the sciences" with certain modifications.[23]

—in fact, the first manifestation of a heterodoxical tendency which was to flourish in Brazil.[24] Muniz de Aragão divides biology into two categories: Phyto-biology and Zoo-biology; and sociology into sociology proper and teleology, or the science of final causes as a substitute for the science of morals.[25] In 1865 Francisco Bandão Júnior published in Brussels a booklet on slavery in Brazil, *A Escravatura no Brasil,* with an appendix on agriculture and the colonization of Maranhão, the author's native province; a work which, in the words of Teixeira Mendes, "despite the fact that it imperfectly interprets the teachings of Auguste Comte, constitutes the first sociological manifestation of Positivism among us." [26]

However, these early manifestations of Positivist doctrines had no appreciable influence on the political life of the country. Positivism was limited to the schools. It appeared in the North in 1868 in the brief references to Comte made by Tobias Barreto in his articles. When Benjamin Constant entered the Military School in 1852, he found a climate already affected by Positivist doctrines. In fact, it was for this officer and mathematician, a representative of the Brazilian lower middle class,[27] that an important role in the propagation of Positivist philosophy among the younger generations of the military schools was reserved.

Because of the prestige he enjoyed among his pupils, Benjamin Constant managed to enlist their support for the republican cause which he espoused, and these young men were to play a decisive role in the events which took place on November 15, 1889.[28]

In the letters which Benjamin Constant wrote to his wife from the battlefields of Paraguay in 1867 we find references to his religious Positivism. In a letter dated June 5, 1867, he wrote:

Remember that I am your best and truest friend, that I love you more than anyone or anything in this world, that you are my only happiness, my only fortune, my religion. You mean more to me—much more — than did Clotilde de Vaux to the wise and honored Auguste Comte. I am, as you know, a follower of his doctrines, I accept his principles and beliefs: the Religion of Humanity is my religion. I believe in it with all my heart, with only one difference—and that is that, for me, the preponderance of the family is supreme. It is a new religion, and rational withal, the most philosophical and the only one which flows naturally from the laws which govern human nature. It could not have been the first, because it depends on a knowledge of all the laws of nature and is a natural consequence of this knowledge, and therefore it could not have appeared in the infancy of human reason or even when the different sciences were still embryos: it would not yet have appeared, had it not been granted to the admirable genius of Auguste Comte, in the amplitude of his intelligence, to leap the centuries to come and, surprising the limits of science in his wise foresight, to give us the positive religion—the definitive Religion of Humanity. I must stop these ramblings, which may seem improper on this occasion but in fact are not so. By telling you that I hold Positivist beliefs, which I have in a measure done, I confirm all that I have ever said of the extreme love I bear you, and this is my purpose.[29]

In this letter we can clearly see one of the characteristics of Benjamin Constant, which is typical of those who, having climbed the social ladder on their intellectual merits, tend to assign to the intelligence a leading role in sentimental situations.[30] The "religious" Positivist ardor of Benjamin Constant, however, was later to cool. This will be demonstrated in the events we will later record.[31]

Before 1867, therefore, Benjamin Constant had accepted Positivist doctrines.[32] But it was when he competed for the post of lecturer in mathematics at the Military School in November, 1873, that he first openly affirmed his adherence to the doctrines of Comte.[33] During the years between this date and his death the principal changes in Positivist philosophy in Brazil were effected.

In 1874 the first volume of Dr. Luís Pereira Barreto's *As Três Filosofias* (*The Three Philosophies*) appeared with an introduction entitled "Uma Palavra aos Políticos" ("A Word to the Politicians"), in which the author wrote:

Brazil already harbors in her bosom a small group of Positivists, a group recruited mainly from the middle class and the profession of engineering which, far from diminishing in numbers, is growing apace and will tend increasingly to do so. We have hitherto scrupulously abstained from taking any part in the religious conflict now being dragged out (the "religious question" between the bishops and the imperial government); we were in no hurry; not to be too much ahead of one's time is also a condition of order and progress; we waited until society made its pronouncement, placing our entire confidence in the great mass of the nation; and only after it had manifested its opinion did we offer it the small stone of our contribution for building the edifice of the future, pointing out the opportunity for a further step forward.[34]

Pereira Barreto thought the moment had arrived when Brazilian society had ceased to be theological, as he said in a letter to Senators Jobim and J. F. de Godoy;[35] he also believed that in the government's attitude to the rebelliousness of the bishops the country's complete independence from an age-long guardianship had been affirmed.

Far from repeating the painful sarcasms which the author of the *City of God* hurled, as a reprisal, into the face of bloody Rome [wrote

Pereira Barreto], we, as Positivists, cannot fail to deliver a vote of praise for the dignified and noble behavior of our bishops. We unreservedly condemn their systematic pretensions as much as we admire sincerely their wholehearted dedication to the cause they had espoused. We are far from applauding their disrespect for the law, and we render profound homage to the judgment of our magistrature; but if we set aside this detail, we can discover in their behavior a great lesson to be learned for future use. Their vigorous resistance to the injunctions of temporal whims initiates a school of citizenship and virtue, fruitful for us in the salutary example it sets of the force of true convictions and the courage to uphold them. For the first time in our country, we saw a privileged class of exalted personages, great dignitaries of the Crown, recognized princes, set moral duty above material comfort. Instead of enjoying, in the serenity of leisure and under cover of the enervating indifference of our social environment, the legitimate advantages of their lucrative dioceses, they chose to lose all but honor.[36]

In revolt against the "enervating indifference of our social environment," Pereira Barreto, who maintained the same vivacity of spirit throughout his life,[37] saw in the religious conflict a chance for Brazil to liberate herself from the centuries-old tutelage of Catholic theology. He wrote:

Among the ruins of our Church and our Constitution, the bishops show us clearly which elements we should preserve and which we should reject. We feel that the moment has come to make the public realise that politics is an art—and undoubtedly the most difficult of all the arts—which springs basically from the science of humanity. And if it has hitherto been empirically cultivated, almost as a hobby, by the least able minds, henceforth it should march side by side, indissolubly linked to its corresponding philosophy.[38]

It is true that, from the philosophical point of view, Pereira Barreto's work shows no originality. He himself did not, we feel, pretend to achieve it.[39] What he wanted was to find, in the new doctrines expounded by modern philosophy, a new direction for our political life. Brazil is constantly present in his books. We must also recognize—and fortunately this recognition is at last forthcoming—that he did have the critical spirit which, until recently, certain authors denied him.[40]

Pereira Barreto, despite the fact that he had studied in Europe (and perhaps for this reason), did not fall victim to the enchantment of the "transoceanism" which had bewitched so many of our philosophizers, critics, and men of letters. On the contrary, his constant preoccupation was with Brazil. "We have no traditions," he would say, "we can only ape the European parties. Our national history begins yesterday: its first page is the emancipation of the proletarian womb; the clerical question its second; and the Paraguayan war its sombre preface." [41] Like the other men of his time, Pereira Barreto believed that a radical reform of public education would transform the country. Addressing himself to Senators Jobim and Godoy in his introduction to the first volume of *As Três Filosofias*, he expressed himself as follows:

Meanwhile, we have but one request to make of you and only one— the radical reform of our entire educational system, followed by suspension of any grant which would in future have been sanctioned for the Church. The Church and the Academy, these are everywhere the two great accomplices, both fully resolved to educate us—by turning us into brutes. It is the teaching emanating from these two "corporations" that is the true source of the corruption of our social customs. [42]

It is an old habit of ours to attribute all our defects to the weakness or bad organization of our educational system, when the latter merely reflects the defects or weaknesses of our social, political, and economic conditions. In this, Pereira Barreto did not escape the general rule. He did, however, understand that it was necessary to educate the masses and to give them a new and positive orientation. [43] Pereira Barreto called attention to a fact which had hitherto passed unnoticed by the men who made up the nation's elite. Citing Oliveira Martins, he emphasized that our economic development continued to be colonial in nature and that we had to intensify our intellectual culture in order to save ourselves from the tutelage of foreigners, to train men capable of taking over the administration of the country in complicated and difficult moments of struggle which the future held in store. [44] "We are sick of diplomas. What we need today is less glitter in our words and a more positive method in our doctrines," he wrote in 1874. [45]

The first work to expound Positivist doctrines, the book which initiated the Positivist trend in Brazil, was marked, therefore, by the desire for practical, efficacious, and active reform, a desire not expressed by any of the other Brazilian "philosophizers," all of whom simply repeated "pure doctrines," with no practical application to national life, which were mere adornments for those who toyed with the complicated game of philosophical ideas. Pereira Barreto's work, [46]

adapted from Positive philosophy, sought to present Positivist doctrines as a new guide for the intelligence of his time, a method or a
procedure for renovating the patterns of our culture. To liberate
the Brazilian intellect from its theological confines—or, more exactly,
from the tutelage of the Church, was his objective. Taking advantage
of the political-religious crisis in Brazil, Pereira Barreto did not propose the reform of "a fossil constitution";[47] he merely proposed the
liberation of education from its ecclesiastical tutelage. As late as
1901, in his book *O Século XX sob o Ponto de Vista brasileiro* (*The
Twentieth Century from the Brazilian Point of View*), he asserted
that

it is ideas that govern the world. But, to our misfortune, at this moment
attempts are being made to set on the throne of the supreme government of the spirit ideas of the other world. It is not enough for half a
dozen emancipated citizens to desire greatness for our country: all our
masses, united and of one mind, must work together to carry out this
intent. It seems obvious that, if the nation is divided, with the great
majority desiring only to tread the path to Heaven and not hesitating
to consign to Hell the few men of science who point out the path on
Earth, we shall inevitably end by laying ourselves wide open to Anglo-
Saxon domination and demonstrating once again the utter ineptitude
of the Latin race. Brazilian priests have ever been discreet, at no time
prone to that fury of ardent exhortation, inhuman and insensitive, which
sought to inhibit the mind; they can therefore do much to ease a mental
transition to a higher plane of thought, one which would prove more
fruitful and more adequate to our needs. At this moment they are threatened with extinction, overwhelmed by Jesuit rivalry. It is our duty to
support them and to refuse to allow them to be supplanted by those
insatiable vampires of ultramontanism.

And he added: "A national Church and the repudiation of Jesuitism,
this is the program I should like to see adopted throughout Brazil." [48]

These attitudes led to violent attacks on Luís Pereira Barreto by
the Catholics, such as Father Resende. "Every day," wrote Pereira
Barreto in February, 1880, "I am subjected to a torrent of invective
and abuse by the agents of ultramontanism . . . I understand perfectly their mission, but they do not understand mine." [49] And in
1874 he wrote: "To the self-styled apostles of morals I can say today quite openly and face to face that human morality on earth is
more noble and more elevated than revealed morality, the roots of
which are lost in a fictitious world." [50] "We must found a religion

stripped of fantasies and myths, in which the human ideal will be limited only by the good which it is possible to practice under the sun." "We must create a new aristocracy which will have as its only principles: civic virtue, intelligence, and wisdom," [51] a thought which reflects the desires of the new bourgeoisie in the middle of the nineteenth century.

Considering the "religious question" "as one would consider any scientific problem," Pereira Barreto reaches the same conclusion: the need for the suppression of theology. "Before we eliminate the idea, however, let us carefully consider the eminent service it has rendered to the popular cause." [52] The freethinkers in Brazil should not lose sight of this fact, since the Church played such a significant role in the Middle Ages. "Just as we can eliminate theology without offending the priests," he adds, "so can we eliminate royalty without individually offending the kings . . . rather, on the contrary, proclaiming without hesitation the great services which they rendered to the cause of humanity." [53] These ideas, which are in no way original, being merely reflections of the doctrines of Auguste Comte, are to some extent surprising, since Pereira Barreto was well aware of the nature of the environment in which he lived and knew that they would not easily be accepted. In a society in which, as he himself noted, "the tendency to suspect all the affirmations of our equals is very pronounced," and in which "the absence of any fellow-feeling is undoubtedly caused by the permanent atmosphere of distrust in which everyone lives—everyone suspecting and being suspect," [54] how could he have believed that it would be easy to steer a new course? Contrary to what he believed, theology still had the strength to muster the same influence on which it had counted in the past.

On the other hand, let not the conservatives among us delude themselves about the conditions necessary to guarantee the order they seek to discover in the past. The days in which we live are no longer like the days of yore. Today the social problem fights for precedence with the political, and there can be no order until this serious complaint of modern life has been put right. In the first French Revolution, the distinction between the social question and the political was not clearly understood, even by the most penetrating observers, in view of the tremendous precipitation of events that occurred at the time. But, although the secondary elements of the revolution—disorder, anarchy, the suppression of law, and the confusion of principles—have disappeared, the dominant principle has nevertheless survived and has become increasingly vigorous and pronounced. It is in the reign of Louis Philippe, during the years 1830 to 1848, that we must seek to clear symptoms of this profound distinction, which so radically separates modern from ancient times. The 1848 revolution was not such a paltry affair as some people would lightly have us believe, it was not a trivial parody of the great revolution. It is quite true that if we view it in a purely political light, in the strictest meaning of the word "political," the 1848 revolution is unquestionably less important than that of 1789. But for those who believe that from the dawn of history, and especially from the times of Copernicus and Galileo down to our own day, there has been but one revolution, and that 1848 marked the transition from the political to the social phase—for these, the last period will seem perhaps more momentous even than the first. It is true that the attempt of 1848 was frustrated, as was the explosion of 1789. But the history of the social revolution did not come to an end in 1848; it has continued ever since, and continues today, more threatening than ever, undermining both order and progress for lack of an enlightened policy.[55]

These ideas mark a new outlook on life in Brazil, in an environment at that time still patriarchal, where the genial Emperor and the secure old rural classes continued placidly to rule a colonial country.

We do not yet have in our midst those active, effervescent elements now agitating Europe [wrote Luís Pereira Barreto]. But already among us there is a good deal of discussion, too much even, about the needs of the people, the sovereignty of the people, and so forth. I do not here intend to reopen a question which, to the honor of the Brazilian Conservative party, is already on its way toward a solution; but I most solemnly declare that I do not even know what "people" to speak for. For me, the people is the sum of all those millions of nameless units that go to make up a complex which expresses the total of a nation's work. If the advantages of the proposed political reforms are directed only to certain classes in the nation, completely ignoring our "third estate," I believe it to be wiser and more suitable not to speak of reforms for the time being. Let us free from the shackles of the Church and the course of evolution in Brazil; this is the most opportune, even urgent, step.[56]

Convinced, then, of the decadence of the Catholic influence, Pereira Barreto felt that the moment had come to proclaim "the philosophic truths emanating from the positive sciences." [57] Only by drawing its inspiration from the principles of positive thought could Brazilian society "discover the art of taking from a condemned past the materials necessary for the building of the future. In the ruin of our Church and of our Constitution, the bishops clearly show us which elements should be preserved and which rejected." [58] As we can see, it was in political questions related to the problems which had accumulated as the result of the social and economic changes after 1850—and which had taken on new forms around 1870—that Pereira Barreto found the motive for a reform of the Brazilian intellect. When the bishops themselves affirmed, as did Dom Antônio in his letter to Nabuco de Araújo,[59] that the spirit of Catholicism was almost extinct in Brazil, it was hardly surprising that a man educated in the scientific spirit of the early nineteenth century should propose that traditional theological ideas be replaced by philosophical ideas emanating from the new scientific spirit.

A follower of Littré, Pereira Barreto sought in Positivism a method rather than a doctrine.

Those who believe that Positive philosophy denies or affirms anything in this respect (first and final causes) are mistaken; it neither denies nor affirms anything; since to deny or to affirm would be to declare that one possesses some knowledge of the origin of beings or of their end. What has been established at present is that these two extremes are inaccessible to us and that only the middle, what in the language of the school is called the relative, is ours.[60]

This statement of Littré's throws light on the position taken by Luís Pereira Barreto. Preoccupied more with political and social problems than with the Religion of Humanity, Pereira Barreto's position in the history of Brazilian Positivism—in which he occupies an important place as a precursor—is that of a relativist for whom formulae are of little importance and for whom facts, which are subject to mutation, are all-important.

In a letter written in 1881 to Pierre Lafitte, then still acknowledged as the leader of Positivism by Miguel Lemos, the latter said:

Il a paru hier dans un journal de Rio (*O Cruzeiro*) un article anonyme que tout porte à croire sans hesitation être écrit ou inspiré par M. Barreto. Dans cet article, on s'appuie sur le discours de M. Beesley pour nier, avec quelque vraisemblance, la necéssité d'une organisation positiviste et pour mettre de côté, jusqu'à nouvel ordre, le système politique et réligieux d'Auguste Comte, l'adhésion devant se borner à la philosophie positive.[61]

I was unable to ascertain whether the article was in fact written by Pereira Barreto. But the truth is that from his first contact with the

"Apostolate," Pereira Barreto's relationship with the new religious sect was not cordial. Miguel Lemos refers to Barreto's work *Positivismo e Teologia* as follows:

From the Positivist point of view, this pamphlet, within the philosophical limits which the author imposed on himself, leaves little to be desired, but we can already discern in it a fairly grave deviation which becomes patent in the second work we received (*As Coluções Positivas da Política brasileira*). In effect, Mr. Barreto, having at one point completely accepted the work of Auguste Comte, became further and further removed from the religious aspect and eventually fell into the vague "scientism" of our time.[62]

The antagonism between the Positivists and Pereira Barreto was already beginning to manifest itself.[63] Incapable of submitting to the systematic spirit of the Rio de Janeiro group, accused of heresy, Pereira Barreto remained faithful to scientific Positivist philosophy, completely abandoning the superficial religious aspirations he had for a moment entertained.

Miguel Lemos in his apostolic zeal declared that *As Três Filosofias* was a "patchwork quilt of ideas, scandalously plagiarized." [64] As seems inevitable with those who become fanatical about some theory or idea, Miguel Lemos was guilty of an injustice toward the forerunner of Positivism in Brazil. Contrary to his opinion, the second volume of *As Três Filosofias* reveals a scholarly erudition, an extremely modern outlook, and is a clear exposition of philosophical thought. It is plain from this work that, for Pereira Barreto, Positivism was no longer as exclusive as it had seemed to him in the first part of his work. Littré continues to be the preferred writer, but side by side with him Pereira Barreto studies Locke, Berkeley, Kant, and Hartmann. Of the older Brazilian works on philosophical problems, those of Pereira Barreto are the only ones that can still be read today with pleasure and profit. It is evident that the author attempted to assimilate the doctrines he studied and that he knows how to expound and to criticise them in a pleasant and simple style with no trace of the pedantry so rife in the style of later Brazilian "philosophizers." [65]

It is true, as I have previously remarked, that there is no doctrinal originality in the work of Pereira Barreto. He is a heterodox Positivist. But, above all, he is an anticlerical thinker who sees in Positivism a doctrine capable of replacing to advantage the tutelage that the Church exercized over the Brazilian intellect. He always fought the subordination of intellect to dogma. With a mind open to re search, he would never submit to any orthodox doctrine. "We must found a religion stripped of fantasies or myths in which the human ideal will be limited only by the good which it is possible to practice under the sun," wrote Luís Pereira Barreto in 1874. It was to be in this direction that the Brazilian Positivists would later orient themselves, when they founded, about 1881,[66] the Positivist Church of Brazil. At first, however, it was not the religious aspect of Positivism that attracted the enthusiastic adherents of Auguste Comte in Brazil, not even the two leaders of the Religion of Humanity, Miguel Lemos and Raimundo Teixeira Mendes.

At the time that the first volume of *As Três Filosofias* was published, Miguel Lemos, then a student at the Central School, was becoming acquainted with Comte's work. In the interesting testimony of the two leaders of the Comtist movement in Brazil, Miguel Lemos declared:

Toward the end of 1874, after I had sat for my second year examination in mathematics at the defunct Central School and had made up my mind to study general mechanics during the vacation to prepare myself for the March examination, a friend of the family, José de Magalhães, fellow-pupil at the school and today a distinguished architect in this city, recommended that I read, as a highly useful and to my new studies, the part concerning mechanics in the first volume of Auguste Comte's *System of Positive Philosophy*. I followed this recommendation, and my friend lent me his copy of our Master's fundamental work. As was only to be expected from one who had always subordinated his scientific preoccupations to his social aspirations, I began by reading the general part of the work, and I had the good fortune to discover in the introductory chapters what I had up to then sought in vain: a positive philosophy, that is, a philosophy endowed with the same certitude peculiar to the sciences already constituted and embracing in their coördination political and moral phenomena. It was then, toward the end of 1874 or at the beginning of 1875, that, for the first time, I made the acquaintance of the doctrines of Auguste Comte, having previously neither read nor heard anything on the subject. I recall only that, before this, disillusioned with the systems of philosophy I already knew, I had once seen on the shelves of a bookseller a work in a number of volumes with the title *Philosophie Positive*, by Comte. I remember I shrugged my shoulders on seeing such an adjective coupled with a word which was then for me synonymous with empty verbiage, and I did not even bother to leaf through the voluminous treatise. To my misfortune, the copy lent to me by José de Magalhães was one of those editions produced under the supervision of that pseudo-disciple Émile Littré, who had felt called upon to profane the work by prefacing it with one of his own efforts. The reading of this preface, in the condition in which I then found myself, ignorant of the history of Positivism and with all the defects and prejudices of the revolutionary phase, led me to reject, out of hand and without any direct examination, the later works of Auguste Comte, those concerned with religious Positivism. To add to my misfortune, my friend possessed Littré's biography of Auguste Comte. I went straight from the *System of Positive Philosophy* to reading that wicked libel on the life and religious organization of our Master, defenseless against the sophistry and treachery heaped up by the celebrated lexicologist. This is how I came to be led away from the last works of Auguste Comte at the same time as I initiated my reading of Positive philosophy and to reject, at that time, the Religion of Humanity.[67]

Up to then, Comte's doctrine had made itself felt in a diffused manner through the teachers of mathematics, who "introduced into their courses the philosophical views of Auguste Comte on that discipline; in particular, Mr. Benjamin Constant, who ceaselessly urged his pupils to read the *Analytical Geometry* and the section on mathematics in the first volume of the *Course on Positive Philosophy*." [68] Enthusiastic about the new doctrine, Miguel Lemos published in *A Idéia,* the organ of the academic press at the time (1875), an article on general mechanics in which he revealed his adherence to the philosophical ideas of Comte. With the speed of lightning, between January and March of 1875, "there occurred that mental evolvement which made of me an ardent disciple of the positive philosopher," wrote Miguel Lemos.[69] Also drawn to Positivism through mathematics, Teixeira Mendes relates that in 1874 he sought out Dr. Antônio Carlos de Oliveira Guimarães, lecturer in mathematics at the Pedro II College, to clarify some results at which he had arrived concerning the fundamental theories of geometry. On the advice of the doctor, or on his own initiative, he got in touch with Benjamin Constant, whom he had previously met.[70] On this occasion, Benjamin Constant advised him to "burn everything you have on analytic geometry; read only the *Analytical Geometry* of Auguste Comte." [71] Teixeira Mendes had become an adherent of Positivism by the time he sat for his examinations in April, 1875.

Toward the end of 1874, the ruin of my theological beliefs was complete. This was the result of various factors, pointless to enumerate here;

Suffice it to mention only two: In the first place, the antagonism between the Catholic Church and my republican aspirations was the dominating factor in my intellectual emancipation. Latent until my seventh year at the Pedro II College, this antagonism became clear to me on reading a book by the Jesuit Ramière, recommended by the present Bishop of Mariana who was at that time also vice rector of the college. Thereafter the inner conflict grew ever more acute. A second influence was the reading of a few pages of Herbert Spencer's *First Principles,* which I was moved to read by an incident in class during my first year at the Polytechnic. Dr. Joaquim Murtinho was in charge of my class, and in reply to some observations which I had elicited concerning "straight lines" and "directions," His Holiness asked me what I understood by the term "space." The bell saved me from the embarrassment of a reply. But, feeling the need to prepare myself for the question which might be put at any moment and recalling that His Highness was an admirer of Spencer, according to Mr. Francisco van Erven, I decided to read that sophist . . .

At that time the study of general mechanics was leading Miguel Lemos to meditate on the *System of Positive Philosophy* and to become subject to an equal admiration for

the Being who was to become our common spiritual father and the consecrator of our indissoluble friendship. Our school association, up to then determined and nourished by the similarity of our political aspirations, grew closer, and our mutual sympathy increased as the ties between us and our venerated sage grew stronger. Our conversations brought me a knowledge of certain aspects of the new philosophical synthesis, and, having accepted the tenets, I did not hesitate to declare myself a Positivist. The first joint work we planned was the translation of the *Analytical Geometry,*[72] and we made our appeal to the public for its publication on April 23, 1875. Only later did I manage to read the *System of Positive Philosophy,* and then only imperfectly, both through my want of scientific knowledge and because of an eye ailment which proved to be a forerunner of a far more serious affliction. The communion of ideas led me to read Littré and Stuart Mill and to become caught up, like my friend, in the web of sophistry and calumny they had spun to trap the incautious reader in his ignorance, presumption, and irreverence.[73]

Influenced by teachers of mathematics and by the republican ideas beginning to gain wider currency and to be propagated systematically[74] some young men of the Rio de Janeiro Polytechnic School began to read the *Course on Positive Philosophy*. Preoccupied with the reaction of science on politics, they managed in this work to assuage the civic ardor that revolutionary speech-making had failed to sate. As sincere republicans, they felt that in the new science founded by Auguste Comte there was a basis for rational politics, and they foresaw the final reconciliation of order and progress in his philosophic coördination. With the impetuosity of youth they began actively to spread propaganda, which had an enormous influence on their colleagues and made abundantly clear to the Brazilian public that Positive philosophy had arrived.[75]

There were, therefore, after 1874, two Positivist groups in Rio de Janeiro: one, the Littréists, "ardent and active, who wrote, made speeches, and won over the youth of the schools," [76] the others, who "remained apart and isolated, limiting themselves to recommending the scientific philosophy of Auguste Comte and having no political or social preoccupations—it was this group that accepted, or purported to accept with no essential divergences, the total work of the Master." [77] Oliveira Guimarães, a professor of mathematics, who belonged to the second group, attempted to unite all disciples of Comte, and from this attempt was born the first Positivist Association of Brazil. On April 1, 1876, was founded "a society composed of persons who confessed themselves to be Positivists in varying degrees, but all of whom accepted the Positive Philosophy. With no religious intent, the society proposed to organize a Positivist library on the lines suggested by Auguste Comte and to start courses in science at a later date." [78] The founders of the society were Antônio Carlos de Oliveira Guimarães, Benjamin Constant, Joaquim Ribeiro de Mendonça (who later in that year was to defend a thesis inspired by Positivist ideas, entitled *Da Nutrição (On Nutrition)*); Oscar de Araújo, Álvaro de Oliveira, Miguel Lemos, and Teixeira Mendes. Newsletters and journals were also started, and conferences were held to propagate the new philosophical ideas.[79] It was not long before opponents of the new ideas appeared on the scene, and soon

the din of the polemics in which the young men clashed their new weapons completely awakened the new generation, and in the light of the new radiance the flame of social enthusiasm was kindled in them. For the first time our country was witnessing an intellectual movement that sought to embrace the whole of human experience. The only general ideas and philosophical systems we had hitherto known were the puerile mixtures of theology and metaphysics taught in the colleges, for the most part no more than the literary meanderings with which a few pedants, singly or in groups, entertained their leisure, giving rein to their vanity or their envy. Apart from the host of scholars one finds in any country, who were occupied in the attempt to tack together the events of our history; apart from the scientific teaching of our Academy professors, which consisted in the unfaithful reproduction of bad foreign compendia or, at most, in the accumulation of isolated facts about our native works, all our intellectual activity was concentrated on pure literature, which invaded the realm of politics in the persons of the rhetorical lawyers, among whom emerged only rarely any statesmen guided by an enlightened empiricism. The Brazilian mind, as was only to be expected, confined itself to the exercise of its aesthetic faculties and eagerly assimilated the contemporary literary ideas. The Classics, the Romantics, and then the Realists fed our avid need to read or to write. Our intellectual life, with the minor exceptions cited earlier, was limited to the copying of French novels and the imitation of European poets, quite often compensated by flashes of local inspiration. In politics, the most enlightened among the monarchists were those who saw in England the model of a representative system; among the republicans those who fell into raptures about the democracy of the United States.[80]

Miguel Lemos is exaggerating when he attributes exclusively to Positivist ideas the enthusiasm for the intellectual revival which took place in Brazil at this period. From 1868 the Empire had been undergoing important changes. It had emerged from colonialism and, thanks to an incipient capitalism, had modernized itself. Its ideas, too, were brought up to date.

Up to 1871, the Empire had been one thing; from 1871 onward, it became something quite different—in its development, in its aims, in the new demands of the nation, even in the mentality of the statesmen who governed it. As in the history of other nations, it is an external war that marks the division between these two distinct periods, bound together by the Ministry of Rio Branco.[81]

In October, 1877, the two future apostles of Brazilian Positivism, Miguel Lemos and Teixeira Mendes, left for Paris.[82] A few months after their departure, Dr. Oliveira Guimarães, founder of the small Positivist nucleus of Rio de Janeiro, died, in January, 1878. In September of that year the four remaining members of the original society he had founded started a new society and recruited new adherents. This was the Sociedade Positivista do Rio de Janeiro, affiliated to the French school of Pierre Lafitte, with Dr. Joaquim Ribeiro de Mendonça as its first president.[83]

In the adventures through which Positivism passed in the nineteenth century, Auguste Comte was undoubtedly the moving spirit and the formulator of the principles underlying the Positive philosophical movement. But "other men and other currents, more or less independent of the direct influence of Comte, contributed powerfully to give Positivism its concrete form." [84] The legacy of Comte, therefore, took various forms. A number of different trends developed, although the basis remained the same. Each of the groups inspired by the doctrines of Comte adapted its ideas to different conditions and to its own especial needs. In this sense, Comte's successors varied the meaning of his doctrines to suit their own temperaments. Thus, in addition to the dissidence, which had already begun to appear during the philosopher's lifetime and which was to take shape under the leadership of Émile Littré, new forms of heterodoxy appeared, and, above all, quarrels sprang up among the different groups, each of which claimed to be the true representative of the thought of Auguste Comte, to represent the true spirit of his philosophy.[85] In this struggle, the Brazilian group represented by Miguel Lemos and the "Positivist Apostolate of Brazil" occupied a position which reveals a curious and significant orthodox sectarianism.

Miguel Lemos's voyage to Paris led to an alteration in the destiny of Positivist propaganda in Brazil.

Having left for Paris in 1877 [writes Miguel Lemos], still under the pedantocratic influence that made me persist in my resolution to qualify for some diplomaed profession, I suffered one of those transformations that permanently decide a man's vocation. In the capital of the West, I had the privilege of approaching my lips closer to that source whence had sprung the sacred new river, there to slake the thirst which had for so long consumed me: and as it had been the magical fountain of Eldorado, my lost vigor was restored, a vigor impaired by chasing after shadows to which an ineffectual science had sought in vain to give form and substance. I had failed to reconcile my emotions with an intellect broken by the rebelliousness of the modern spirit, and I found this in the religion which the Pharisees of science had taught me to believe was the raving of a madman. Like the great Saint Paul, I, a humble student, heard on the road to Damascus that voice of all redeemers: "My son, why persecutest thou Me?" [86]

From afar, Miguel Lemos had shared the ideas of the erudite Émile Littré, whom the Master himself had called his "eminent colleague." But in Paris, when he came closer to "that source whence had sprung the sacred new river," when he came to know the skeptical Littré, the young Brazilian student was deeply disappointed.

Soon after my arrival in the great city [he writes], I saw for myself that the man we had taken for the ardent leader of a school, tireless in his attempts to promote the universal regeneration propounded by the Master, was but a dried-up scholar, socially inactive, shut up in his study, and using the leisure of his later years to deny all he had learned from his intimacy with the great Builder. The renowned so-called leader of the Positivist school was merely a plodding investigator of words, empty of enthusiasm or faith, immersed in the minutiae of a sterile erudition. The disillusion of my first contact sowed the seed of doubt in my mind, which grew as I pursued my studies, and finally led me to decide that I should undertake a conscientious inquiry into the criticisms he had leveled against the complex of the Master's doctrines, into the accusations he made against the last stages of that incomparable life. I had felt for some time that there was in me an emptiness which Littréism was powerless to fill; I was sometimes on the point of giving way to the despair I felt when I contemplated the yawning gap between science and feeling. In vain I sought the link that would bind together the different aspects of human nature, combining them in relation to a common destiny. Where was the supreme principle that would give an aim to science, a direction to emotion, and a purpose to activity? What criterion would liberate me from the tyranny of my individual reason and offer to all men—great and small, learned and unlettered—the basis of all duty? [87]

Disillusioned by Littré's aridity, Miguel Lemos approached the group of Comte's faithful disciples that met in the Master's apartment at No. 10, Rue Monsieur-le-Prince.

I knew of the existence of this obscure nucleus of faithful disciples but had heard of it only by way of Émile Littré's bad faith and thought it was composed of minds constricted by a new liturgical formalism, the outcome of the so-called mental decadence of the Master. My first impression, however, was altogether different from my expectations after such forewarnings. M. Lafitte was then conducting a first course in philosophy. I had never seen a more charming, more learned, more luminous teacher;[88] his simple, intimate words sometimes became animated, to convey to the tiny audience which surrounded him enthusiasm for great causes. The lessons lasted two hours, sometimes more.

But I left with a foretaste of universal regeneration. We felt ourselves to be in the presence of a new world, a religion consecrated by the abnegation of its disciples and the martyrdom of its founder. I suspected immediately that the new Redeemer might have had his Judas and his cross; and began to judge Émile Littré within my heart. This resolution proved the more difficult in that I had personally had from him repeated proofs of literary goodwill. It was not a question of soothing my vanity, however, but of repairing my errors and my injustice.[89]

Impressed, therefore, by the simplicity of Lafitte—with whom, a few years later, he was vehemently to sever connections proclaiming him a "sophist"—the young Brazilian set out to read the *Politique Positive.*

The powerful aid rendered by the lessons of M. Lafitte made clear to me what, in another situation, might have appeared profoundly obscure [wrote Miguel Lemos]. I soon perceived the superiority of that monumental work, fruit of a mature genius, over the *Cours de Philosophie Positive.* These four volumes, far from revealing mental collapse, made it amply clear on every page that here was moral vigor such as to make me feel at once that it was the most marvelous synthesis ever achieved by human brain. Of a certainty, Littré was deceiving us; and, if he blundered in his intellectual estimation of the Master's last works, there was room for suspicion as to the exactitude with which he presented the corresponding phase of his private life.[90]

His communication with the faithful band of disciples in the Rue Monsieur-le-Prince, the charm of Lafitte's intelligence, and his meeting with another South American, the Chilean Jorge Lagarrigue —like Miguel Lemos, also a Littréist before his arrival in Paris but now converted to the Religion of Humanity—were factors which determined our young compatriot's complete adherence to religious Positivism. Once converted, he wrote at once to Dr. Ribeiro de Mendonça, apprising him of his "transformation" and of his adherence to the Positivist Society of Rio de Janeiro.[91] In this letter, he wrote:

Blessed be the day I decided to come to Paris! Although I left behind the support and joy of my heart,[92] and despite my exile, I bless the resolve which led me to make that sacrifice. Only thus could I visit the holy city, a pilgrim to Mecca, and enter into the first temple of the new religion, to hear the word of the Master's disciple and to become a convert.[93]

Miguel Lemos remained in Paris for some time. From there he wrote to his friends, exhorting them to follow his example, particu-

larly to his friend Teixeira Mendes, whom he advised to read the
complete works of the Master and to join the Positivist Society,
which he should provoke into energetic action, since hitherto it had
abstained from any activity. Teixeira Mendes, who took his friend's
advice, was not satisfied with the attitude of the Society. He even
feared that his "admission to the Society would restrict his civic activities. This, however, did not happen, and his entry, along with
that of some of his companions, impressed upon the Society entirely
new features, as Miguel Lemos had foreseen, transforming it into a
nucleus for the active promoting of propaganda." [94] From Paris
Miguel Lemos unremittingly urged his friends to extend their en-
deavors. Meanwhile it was still without the participation of the
Positivist Society of Rio de Janeiro that the first civic commemorations of Positivism took place. [95]

It was in Paris that Miguel Lemos initiated his career as a preacher
of Comtist doctrines. Up to then, as we have seen, he had written
several articles on subjects related to the Positive philosophy and had
given way to "pedantocracy," as the Positivists called it. In 1880 the
third centenary of the death of Camões was commemorated, and
Miguel Lemos felt that the Positivist group should pay homage to
the great figure of one of "the five peoples of the Western world"
(Comte had inscribed the name of the poet in the eighth month of
the Positivist calendar). Lafitte had entrusted him with this task,
which Miguel Lemos was by illness prevented from carrying out.
His work was nevertheless published in the *Revue Occidentale* and
later appeared in book form, dedicated to Pierre Lafitte and the author's fiancée. [96] Closely following Comte's doctrines, Miguel Lemos's
Luís de Camões is a tribute to the great figure of the Iberian group
of Latin nations; it aims to "extinguish, in the colonial descendants
of the European peoples, the hatreds which derived from their struggles for independence and to replace them with a profound feeling
for historical continuity." [97] The time had come to "forget the old
prejudices against the mother country. We must accept the fact
that the Brazilians are Portuguese: bonds of love and gratitude
should tie us to the historical womb from which we spring." [98]

Miguel Lemos' first work is based entirely on Comte's doctrines;
it draws heavily on the writers of the fifteenth and sixteenth centuries and on the seventeenth-century Portuguese historians; it is,
in short, an intelligent commentary on Portuguese development.
The conclusions he reaches are those of Comte: the people of Spain,

said the Master, have especially cultivated feeling and imagination. "This prejudice, which has long been handed on and is today deeply rooted among foreigners who do not really know these nations (as was the case with Auguste Comte, we may add), we ourselves have oft repeated," Lemos affirmed.

At the instigation of Miguel Lemos, aflame with the zeal of the neophyte, the first Positivist commemorations were initiated in Brazil. On June 10, 1880, Teixeira Mendes organized a conference at the Ginásio Theater, and a "civic procession" was staged, in which the bust of Camões was borne to the National Library. It was on this occasion that the Flag of Humanity was first unfurled, with its sacred motto, which was later partly used for the republican flag. In September of that year, the Positivist Society of Rio de Janeiro, invigorated by the zeal of Teixeira Mendes, commemorated at the Mozart Club the death of Auguste Comte. In October, Teixeira Mendes, together with Aníbal Falcão and Teixeira de Sousa, published in the *Gazeta da Tarde*[99] an article about the abolition of slavery with the subtitle *Apontamentos para a Solução do Problema Social no Brasil*[100] (*Annotations on the Solution of Brazil's Social Problems*). In this work Teixeira Mendes, after prolix doctrinaire generalizations and reference to Comte's curious ideas on economic problems,[101] traces the path that Brazilian statesmen must follow if they would solve the social problem in Brazil, namely, the problem of slavery.

Man cannot be any man's chattel, since the "producer of human capital can in no way be confused with the *product* of his work or, in other words, with his true and useful acting on the external world." [102] It was necessary, then, to liberate him, and, against this necessity for emancipation, considerations derived from allegations about "the possible ruination of a handful of slave owners" [103] could in no way be invoked. But, in the opinion of Teixeira Mendes, the state of the slave laborer in Brazil would not permit of a complete and immediate emancipation. This must be brought about with great care and in an organized manner. "If the mental and moral state of the slave were such that it would allow him to survive sudden transition to freedom, no statesman could, in the circumstances, hesitate to decree immediate emancipation, pure and simple." [104] If the national economy were not organized on the foundation of servile labor, abolition should be immediate. But it was not so. It was therefore necessary—and here Teixeira Mendes agreed with his cautious contemporaries—to find a solution that would ensure the "transformation of the slave laborer, by binding him to the soil and so assimilating him into Brazilian society under the direction of his former masters." The main points of the abolitionist program presented by the Positivists in 1880 were as follows:

Immediate suppression of the slave regime;
astriction of the former slaves to the land under the guidance of their present owners;
consequent suppression of corporal punishment and all special laws;
constitution of a moral code through the systematic adoption of monogamy;
consequent suppression of the "barracks" regime through the widespread development of family life;
fixing of the number of daily working hours; setting aside the seventh day for rest with no restrictions imposed;
establishment of primary schools, to be kept up in rural districts by the great rural landowners;
allocation of part of the profits for the provision of reasonable wages.[105]

This project showed an accurate sense of historical conditions, tending to promote order among the slave masses who, after the Lei Áurea (the law abolishing slavery), became dispersed and economically disorganized, their disorder affecting the country as a whole. Nevertheless, the project did not enjoy the approval of Miguel Lemos. This was, in fact, not the first time that partial emancipation of the slaves had been proposed, with the condition of astriction to the land and continuing obligations toward those who for so many years had exploited servile labor. I have already referred to the work of F. A. Brandão, another native of Maranhão, who proposed abolition in the same terms as those advocated by Teixeira Mendes and his companions and who was also inspired by Positivist doctrines. F. A. Brandão was equally afraid that total emancipation would completely disorganize the national economy and proposed, as a measure to avoid this, the change from slavery to serfdom by confining the slaves to the land. Later, Miguel Lemos, as head of the Apostolate and identified with the abolitionist movement, was to criticize this solution in the following terms:

This solution (the change from slave to worker), which at first sight appears very attractive by seeming to accord with historic precedent and which has of late been once more extolled, does not stand up to the most cursory examination. Indeed, those who preach such a reform forget that when it was first enacted, in the first centuries of the Middle

Ages, there was still an accredited and influential spiritual power, serving as the natural intermediary between serf and lord, supervising the actions of the latter and promoting final emancipation of the former. The complete absence of any like power in our contemporary situation precludes a similar transformation; and the new servitude would merely be another name for the real state of slavery, which would go on as before or, rather, be even more exposed to the greed and brutality of the owners.[106]

Thus, from its first manifestations, Brazilian Positivism played a part in the abolitionist movement, which once more became active after 1862[107] and which the *Gazeta de Tarde,* edited by Ferreira de Meneses, intensified in 1880.[108]

On January 1, 1881, the Positivist Society of Rio de Janeiro publicly celebrated the Festival of Humanity. In February of the same year Miguel Lemos came back from Paris, covered in glory after his consecration by Pierre Lafitte who, in November, 1880, had ordained him an "aspirant to the priesthood of humanity." [109] On March 20, the Positivist novice gave his first public lecture, to mark the centenary of Turgot.[110] The presence of Miguel Lemos invigorated the Comtian Society, which had been dragging itself along like so many of the societies founded in our country. The Positivist Society of Rio de Janeiro, which up to the date of Lemos's arrival had met only twice, now began to meet every Sunday, in the drawing room of the house No. 14 Rua do Carmo—a room soon to become, as we are told by Miguel Lemos, too small to contain the many who came to espouse the new religion.[111] Shortly after his arrival, the president of the Society, Dr. Ribeiro de Mendonça, a *fazendeiro* absorbed in the business of administering his mother-in-law's estate at Jacarei and obliged to absent himself frequently from Rio de Janeiro, felt that Miguel Lemos should become president of the Positivist Society. In fact, according to Miguel Lemos, Dr. Ribeiro de Mendonça[112] had only accepted the presidency in 1878 with the intention of resigning "the day someone came forward equipped to carry out the presidential duties in a more systematic fashion." [113] None better than the new "aspirant priest" of humanity—who had imbibed from the "source whence had sprung the sacred new river," the creed of the Master's true disciples—to take over the leadership of the small groups of Brazilian Positivists! Thus it was that, on May 11, 1881, in the familiar drawing room of No. 14, Rua do Carmo, Ribeiro de Mendonça handed over the presidency of the Positivist

Society of Rio de Janeiro to Miguel Lemos. Once in the saddle, Miguel Lemos set out at once to reorganize the group in a satisfactory manner. "Putting away the old regulations, still compiled under the influence of old habit, I tried to conceive and carry into effect a new organization, inspired by the general principles of our doctrine and the particular precepts we had been taught by Auguste Comte himself." [114] All was entrusted to the Positivist novice, then in his early twenties. He became responsible for all administrative and spiritual business of the new center.

Having organized itself along the lines set out by Auguste Comte in his *First Manifesto of the Positivist Society of Paris,* dated 1848, [115] the former Society, now transformed into the Positivist Church of Brazil, sought to attend to the immediate demands of its doctrine: to attract believers and to change opinion through timely intervention in public affairs. On July 11, 1881, having received from Pierre Lafitte the title of "temporary leader" of Positivism in Brazil, Miguel Lemos inaugurated in the front drawing room of No. 7, Travessa do Ouvidor (now Rua Sachet), the first Positivist Church of Brazil.

A new facet of European philosophical thought was to be seen in Brazil.

2

As Joaquim Nabuco has pointed out, the elections of 1860 marked the rising of the democratic tide in Brazil. With them, a new era opened in the history of the South American monarchy which, for many, had always been an exotic flower in the American continent. "We are of America," declared the signatories of the "Republican Manifesto" published in *A República* on December 3, 1870,

and we want to be American. Our form of government is both in essence and in practice an antinomy hostile to the rights and the interests of the American states. The continuance of this form, apart from being the origin of internal oppression, is of necessity the perpetual source of hostility and wars with the surrounding nations. [116]

After the 1860 elections,

representation for the minorities was demanded on all sides; the governing patriarchies of the unanimous chambers were condemned; and, in the Senate itself the historic statement—"the King reigns but does not govern"—echoed like a strange and threatening refrain. Finally, imperial policy which, as the result of popular manifestations, had recently lost one of its ministries, lost another in a parliamentary defeat. The Caxias cabinet fell (May 21, 1862) and with it the Conservatives, who had been in power since 1848. The Assembly, composed almost entirely of liberals and dissidents, once more acquired the right to govern after a usurpation of fourteen years.[117]

The economic developments which had been taking place since 1850 permitted these audacities on the part of the new elite which was now beginning to replace the old rural landowners in the government of the country. Liberal ideas were winning over the new governing class of Brazil. The Paraguayan war, however, for a time attenuated and retarded the political progress of the Empire. Deeply affected by the experiences of the *Farrapo* revolution, a legacy of the diplomatic complications over the River Plate which had already disturbed both the kingdom and the First Empire—and which had become further complicated after independence, by the struggles of the *caudillos* of the young and turbulent Spanish American republics—the Brazilian monarchy was threatened; and, with it, the territorial integrity of the country. The Empire thus became involved, compelled by force of circumstance, in the politics of the Uruguayan *caudillos*.[118] In fact, as Júlio de Mesquita Filho demonstrates, the dismemberment of the nation was being plotted in the sinister atmosphere of the southern *caudillos*, and in the process we lost an entire province, Rio Grande do Sul, and part of Matto Grosso. A revolution with separationist aims had recently taken place in the South, and the Empire had perforce to heed the machinations of men like Urquiza and Lopez.

The treaty of October 12, 1851 [wrote Euclides da Cunha], a unilateral contract, which turned us into passive protectors of Uruguay, requiring us to turn a neutral eye on the clashes between *blancos* and *colorados* in their perpetual disagreement, tied us to the feuds of the River Plate. On the sidelines of a chronic revolution, the treaty turned us into spectators of the scandals being constantly perpetrated among the different *caudillos* and excited the Gauchos of Rio Grande do Sul to indulge in the most sinful border raids—the so-called *califórnias* modeled on the *montaneras* of the River Plate, in which successive bands invaded the eastern encampments, fomenting the strife. Our neutrality was, then, purely official: we collaborated in the feuds of that disturbed regime, with our sorties of mounted lancers; and it is not surprising that we should have become seriously embroiled in the disorders.[119]

This involvement in the Southern feuds, linked to other economic and political problems related to free passage of the Paúna River,[120] and further complicated, as Euclides da Cunha notes, by the "interference and clash of two unjustifiable wills," [121] plunged us into the conflict with Paraguay, which was to bring in its train such grave consequences for the politics of Brazil in the last quarter of the nineteenth century.

The war gave the reactionaries, who had lost their position of authority, a chance to return to power with the support of the Emperor. In fact, the exacerbation of his "moderative power" dates from this period. Even among the reactionaries a revolt against Imperial tutelage began, as in the instance of Saião Lobato.[122] At that time, José Antônio Saraiva declared that "the dictatorial power of the Crown is a fact ignored only by the uninformed or those subservient to its illegal interests." [123]

Opposition to the monarchy revived after 1875. "In that turmoil of unrest, a patchwork of disappointments and setbacks, discouragement and rebelliousness, two liberals, still unknown, were, without the aid of inflammatory speeches—indeed, almost noiselessly—delineating the frontiers of the republic: Francisco Rangel Pestana and Henrique Limpo de Abreu." [124] Abolitionism, republicanism and federalism[125] were

rapidly gaining ground, and were moving steadily toward their final and triumphant fulfillment; to the old dynastic parties, Liberal and Conservative, was added the Republican party, which attracted to its ranks the dissidents of the former monarchist factions, and which was further swelled in 1888 by the considerable mass of aggrieved former slave owners, who had received no compensation for their losses and so were inevitably thrown into the avalanche against the Crown.[126]

We have already seen that in the decade between 1870 and 1880 the country reached a high point of economic development. Prominent in this development was immigration, which gave a new look to the country and a new concept of labor.[127] The Empire, then at its apex, began from this point on to decline. After 1875 the republic could no longer come as a surprise. The republican ideal, at first supplanted by the "basic need for political autonomy and later by the more urgent preoccupation with national unity—premature in 1822, inopportune in 1831, and abortive in 1848" [128]—began to gain ground, and the republic did not come into being sooner because "to favor its advent, a degree of social development was needed."[129]

To the republican movement, accelerated after 1870, the principal leaders of the future Positivist Church of Brazil had given their support even before they had completely embraced the doctrines of their Master.[130] In accord with the precepts of Comte's *First Manifesto of the Positivist Society of Paris*,[131] the Positivists were republicans, but

in their own way, in their own highly original manner. Although agreed on the superiority of the republican form of government, they differed profoundly on many essential points; on some points they disagreed radically with the signatories of the 1870 "Republican Manifesto." In effect, the latter were in the first place democrats, whereas the Positivists, in idealizing their republican organization, were not, or appeared not to be, in favor of the democratic element; at least in the form of government they conceived, democracy did not play a major role; we can even go so far as to say that it hardly came into the picture.[132]

To develop their cult, to organize education, and to intervene in public affairs when opportunity arose—this was the task Miguel Lemos set himself after taking over leadership of the Positivist Church of Brazil in 1881. Brazilian society, proclaimed the young apostle, provided the most favorable conditions for Positivist activities. Indeed the conditions must have seemed favorable at the time, for the Empire was undergoing an economic and intellectual revival. The elite was changing and anxious to revise old patterns of thought. "There was a genuine awakening, and a revaluation of the standards of culture."[133] It was the "flock of new ideas which hovered over Brazil." The country was fast modernizing itself, and the old institutions were falling into decay.

Auguste Comte, writing of the future of humanity in chapter v of his *System of Positive Philosophy*, believed—and his faithful Brazilian disciples followed suit—that the transition to the modern world would be made easier by American expansion. For, wrote Comte, in the American republics

the conditions especially favoring the political and religious growth of Positivism are both temporal and spiritual, spontaneously preserved from the parliamentary regime. Even before France has managed to rid herself of this regime, these republics will tend directly toward sociocracy as soon as their democratic dictatorships have been transformed into systematic triumvirates.[134]

Comte believed that his doctrines had a great future in America and that his religion would probably infiltrate with ease. But the reasons that led him to believe this were to hamper the influence of the true Positivist spirit and of Comtism in the "American extensions of the double Iberian branch." Since these offshoots had neither "a clergy as powerful as the European, an oppressive and uncontrolled industrialism, dominating scientific institutions, or any real parliamentary traditions," [135] Comte's prophecy was only partly realized, and then only for a short space, and except in Brazil and Chile met with only transitory success. "The descendants of the fervent votaries of the Virgin Mary," [136] pursuing their pragmatic tradition did not adhere to "a religion which establishes its cult of Woman and proclaims the supremacy of Love." [137] The "double Iberian branch," to quote Comte, passed through a series of curious vicissitudes. These illustrate how much foreign doctrines become deformed when they come into contact with needs arising from environments other than those which gave them birth. Unification around a new creed,[138] which would replace the old religious beliefs with scientific ideas, was perhaps one of the moments in the history of American ideas. Each of the "branches" of "The American extension" was to take the place apt to its own conditions and formation when faced with that particular moment of history in human thought. Their destinies were likewise to differ.[139]

The likenesses between "the American extensions of the double Iberian branch" are nevertheless striking. As Leopoldo Zea demonstrates in his excellent study of Positivism in his country, Mexican Positivists looked on the Positive philosophy and method as the only embodiment of truth, all else being, in their view, the product of unemancipated minds.[140] Brazilian Positivists, bound to the letter of their doctrines, believed that those who did not accept the whole Comtian system were mere "sophists," deserving of their pity.

A doctrine of action, Positivism began its activities through the teaching and propagation of its principles. To achieve the uniformity of opinion needed to achieve the "convergence of feeling" required for the propagation of Comtian ideas, the Apostolate intensified its civic commemorations. In May, 1881, Teixeira de Sousa gave a lecture to mark the second centenary of Calderon de la Barca;[141] in the same month Teixeira Mendes initiated a regular series of Sunday lectures on the doctrines of Positivism, and, in June, Miguel Lemos inaugurated a series dedicated to the life and works of Auguste Comte,[142] in which he sought to "put into perspective the early works of Auguste Comte, those in which he prematurely attempted a social reconstruction." [143] In July of the same year the Positivists had their first opportunity to intervene in public affairs—on the question of Chinese immigration.[144] In the spirit of the Positivist principle that "politics should be subordinate to morals," and in opposition to an alleged theory of racial superiority, they protested against a measure proposed by the Sinimbu cabinet, which was agitating political circles and the rural landowning class. During the imperial parliament's session of January 10, 1879, the question of the "Chinese mission" had arisen, and the president of the Council of Ministers, João Lins Vieira Cansanção de Sinimbu,[145] who was also minister of agriculture, had declared: "Let us tell the truth and be quite frank. The education and example we have received from our forebears, together with the habit we have acquired of giving orders to our slaves, will make it difficult for us to be in a position of authority over free laborers who enjoy the same rights as we do ourselves." [146] The intentions of the rural lords were therefore plain. They understood clearly the nature of their "education" and the situation that would confront them when the Negroes were emancipated.[147] Afonso Pena, an enemy of the liberals, indicated in his turn the government's intentions: to substitute slave labor by "semi-slave" labor.[148] As early as 1879 a brochure entitled *Trabalhadores Asiáticos (Asiatic Laborers)* [149] was published in New York on the direction of Sinimbu, written by Salvador de Mendonça, the Brazilian consul in New York. Salvador de Mendonça declared in this brochure—and in this he was no different from other publicists of his day—that

we can see today no immigration other than the Chinese capable of providing an immediate and ready labor supply for our agriculture and industry. As a transitory stage in our economic development it will provide for the replacement of slave labor by free labor; it will clear the field and open up the way for later European immigration to come and dispute the ownership of our country's soil, like the promised land of the century.

He added:

These are the people who seem to us the best instrument for forging our greatness. To use them for some fifty years, without creating any permanent conditions or allowing them to become attached to our soil, and to make provisions for a periodic renewal of contracts and personnel, seems to be the best step we can take to surmount the present difficulties and to prepare for an auspicious future.[150]

During his visit to Rio de Janeiro in 1881, Salvador de Mendonça delivered a lecture on the same subject. Miguel Lemos writes:

His lecture was a résumé of his doctrines. He did not hesitate to advocate anew man's systematic exploitation of man; and asked quite openly that the future colonists be subjected to special legislation sanctioning the new form of slavery. He attempted to vindicate the policy of the United States, which consists of systematic destruction of the so-called inferior races to ensure the exclusive domination of the white race. To the shame of our country these literary-industrial abominations, so repugnant to human morality and true material progress, were listened to by a minister of state and an audience of one hundred and fifty persons without provoking the slightest protest.[151]

The Positivists could not keep silent in face of this crime against humanity. They immediately protested in the press and sent a message to the Chinese ambassadors in Europe, which appeared as Publication No. 5 of the Positivist Church and Apostolate of Brazil.[152]

In August, 1881, the October elections began to be prepared, and the

Republican party of Rio de Janeiro decided to participate, in order to assess the strength of its supporters and to publicize its political aims; but it had no illusions about its candidates' chances. The Positivists of the Brazilian capital could not refrain from intervening, as citizens and electors, in the civic manifestation of the vote. Although opposed to any revolutionary metaphysic which attempts to base the political constitution of society on the superiority of numbers, we could not remain indifferent to the elections as long as these remained the only way to choose public functionaries. During this transition stage, to vote is to meet the obligations of a citizen, because on the way in which we exercise this function will depend, up to a point, the direction of political affairs. Positivism is, above all, a civic religion.[153]

The Positivists resolved, therefore, to support the Republican party, to whom they were linked by similar aspirations, and in whose progressive tendencies they saw possibilities for carrying out the ideas for which they were fighting.[154]

On his return from Europe Miguel Lemos had been enthusiastically received by Quintino Bocaiúva. This astute politician had known how to win the sympathies of the young apostle;[155] as a result, the members of the Positivist center of Rio de Janeiro supported his candidature. But they were giving their support to the candidature, not to the party.[156] In fact, Miguel Lemos—who consistently revealed himself to be a somewhat inept politician—delivered a lecture on August 15, 1881, in which he clearly defined the attitude of the Positivists toward Republican policies and the compromises which they would require of the Republicans. When Quintino declared that the party program was essentially that of the 1870 manifesto, Miguel Lemos insisted that "the Positivists can accept that document only as a statement of the problem of the political doctrines which inspired it." [157]

Senhor Quintino Bocaiúva [added Miguel Lemos], has come out in favor of evolution: the Positivists also believe in human progress; but they have worked out the direction of this progress and believe they have the means, based on the social science created by Auguste Comte, to achieve the political metaporphosis we all desire.[158]

On the same occasion, Miguel Lemos (who appeared to have little confidence in the impending advent of the republic), wondered whether Quintino Bocaiúva would, once elected to the Chamber, come to terms with Positive measures, restricting his program to urgent and necessary reforms, as in fact Saldanha Marinho was already doing; or whether he would fight for the "overnight" changeover from monarchy to republic.[159]

Liberty is not an end, it is a condition; but unless the conditions exist, the ends cannot be achieved—the Positivists therefore expect Sr. Quintino Bocaiúva to consider their request: to postpone what cannot be achieved immediately and to work gradually toward the desired end, fighting for those reforms which are of greater urgency at this moment.[160]

This courtship between the Republican party and the Positivist group did not last, however. Quintino Bocaiúva soon emerged as the "incurable" journalist he was, and this in itself was enough to disenchant the Positivists. Quintino accepted the editorship of *O Globo*—"a paper which, as everyone knows, has connections with certain business enterprises." [161] "The Positivists could in no way continue to express political solidarity with a representative of the monstrous and degrading union between the forces of industry and

the press, in which the latter is subordinated to the uncontrolled interests of the former." [162] Thus, on October 31, when the elections,
in the course of preparation since August, at last took place, the
Republican party, and especially its candidate Quintino Bocaiúva,
no longer enjoyed the collective support of the Positivist group. [163]

The year 1881 continued, after the political incident with the
Republicans, to be marked by civic commemorations. [164] In September Teixeira Mendes celebrated national independence with a "so-
cialatric"—in Positivist parlance—gathering. During this function,
Teixeira Mendes read the speech he later published under the title:
A Pátria brasileira. [165] Part Three of this speech contains the outline
of an interpretation of national history which is, incidentally, worthy
of note.

Brazil, declares Teixeira Mendes in his opening remarks on the
Brazilian "transition," had the good fortune to be preserved from
Protestantism. [166] Thanks to a combination of circumstances, Catholicism managed to preserve the intellectual integrity of the country
at the height of revolutionary anarchy. When Brazilian ports were
thrown open to friendly nations in 1808, the French Revolution had
already entered its period of retrogradation. Napoleon had become
a monarch and in the delirium of his ambition had plunged France
into war with the whole of Europe. This had been the cause of the
Portuguese Court's arrival in the former colony. In continual contact with England after this, it was from England that the inspiration came which would have altered the Brazilian mentality, "had
it not been for the feminine sentiment which preserved us from
Protestant aridity, which would have been aggravated by the purely
mercantile nature of the relations with Britain." [167] Influenced by
the Master's doctrines, Teixeira Mendes seems to be closing his
eyes to historical realities. The relations with Britain were not
purely mercantile, nor was feminine influence so strong that it
could preserve us from Protestantism. From Gilberto Freyre's account of women in *Casa Grande e Senzala* [translated into English
by Samuel Putnam as *The Masters and the Slaves* (Chicago: 1946)
—Trans.], their influence in Brazil will be seen to have been very
slight. Freyre relates that in the eighteenth century an English-
woman, Mrs. Kindersley, who visited the country, found the condition of Brazilian women deplorable. They were ignorant, bigoted,
and badly dressed: "they got themselves up like monkeys." [168]

They aged early, led an indolent indoor life deprived of normal intercourse, going out only to Mass, and under the constant vigilance of jealous, and much older, husbands. In our country, the tender feeling for women was never understood without that primitive trait of man's domination and the husband's superiority. It was a feeling of complete possession, excited by sexuality, but sometimes exalted to the point of deification.[169] However, once "passion" was satisfied, women, with few exceptions, exercised little influence. Hence the reason for the feeble influence of Protestantism in Brazil seems to me to lie elsewhere. In the conditions of the time, women could hardly have preserved the country from the influences exercised on men, since they were so utterly dependent.

Teixeira Mendes does not go into detail about the historic period between 1822 and 1830. He jumps to 1870. Up to then, he says, it was impossible to effect any profound transformation in the mental climate of Brazil. Political activity led youth to vie for places in the law schools which, devoid of any scientific basis, did not permit of the full emancipation of these future statesmen. On the other hand, the moral degradation of the European scholars—servile tools of princely power or bourgeois despotism—made this emancipation equally impossible for those who devoted themselves to the studies of the positive sciences: the doctors and the military engineers.[170]

Politically the Brazilian nation expanded "without knowing any subordination other than that deriving from royalty: without a tradition of nobility or of spiritual power distinct from the monarchy."[171] Colonial development was almost entirely in the economic field, for "Brazil had come to be regarded as a mine which to its rulers seemed inexhaustible." But among the generations born in America, there slowly emerged "that essentially fetishist love that ties a man to the land and the sky that his eyes first open to behold. They began to forget the faraway Portugal, which they had never seen, and whose caravels put in an appearance only to carry off the best part of their wealth and to bring the harshest of their oppressors."[172] From the *Inconfidência* conspiracy to independence, the ideas of the Encyclopedists predominated: Rousseau based his system on the existence of God and the immortality of the soul; Voltaire led to skepticism and to "the organic school of Diderot—who developed the scientific foundations of future order."[173] In the absence of a scientific basis for the new order, since up to then

there had been no positive theory of government,[174] empiricism—
the only sure guide in the absence of the positive science—had led
to the solution adopted by the 1822 patriots. Teixeira Mendes also
points out that Brazil went through a long period of internal struggles, because of the dissensions between those who felt that local
independence should prevail and those who believed that national
integrity was the next hurdle in the path of the young South
American nation.

But it is inevitable that in the future Brazil will break up into a
number of independent republics, bound in a moral confederacy by the
ties of faith and common sociological origin. But at present the needs
of our common progress make it necessary to give political sanction to
the homogeneity created by our historical antecedents. It was this spontaneous necessity for political unity, characterized by a central dictatorship, that made it possible for "parliamentarianism" to be effectively
annulled, and for personal power to become established, as is recognized
by all parties. Republic or monarchy, as long as our social conditions
demand a dictatorship, it will continue to be a central one, and never,
among us, a parliamentary one. For us this is a fate as inevitable as the
air we breathe. And when the "regime of opinion" at length emerges,
through recognition of the authority of the religion founded by Auguste
Comte, the dictatorship will have disappeared; but the federation then
will not be political—it will be, quite simply, moral.[175]

Party struggles, the memory of the provincial revolts, the example of America, the 1830 and 1848 revolutions in France, and
"the corrupting character assumed by imperial dictatorship" succeeded in nourishing the desire to eliminate the monarchy. Those
who shared this aspiration fell into two groups,

the first, made up of members of the old constitutional parties, who had
become alienated from the monarchy by political disappointment; the
second, constituted by the rising generation, in whose mind the ugly
spectacle of headless, mutilated corpses being dragged to their graves
at the tail of a horse and the memory of the civil strife, which had flared
up in our country during the First and Second empires, made it seem
as though the Braganzas had been involved in the martyrdom of our
country ever since 1792. Apart from all political maneuvers, the republic
appeared in the eyes of Brazil as the consummation of all the desires
of her Southern heart, a government of fraternity and peace without
its equal in the entire universe.[176]

Fired with enthusiasm, continues Teixeira Mendes, the younger generation[177] gave its support to the republican ideal, seeing in the declaration of a republic in France yet another stimulus for their ideas. The organization of the Republicans as a political party dates from this period, under the leadership of men holding positions of preëminence in the country.[178] Propaganda spread like wildfire "through all the schools, vigorous and disinterested, against the elements of the old order, including the academic institutions." [179] At the same time,

the study of the special sciences—principally of mathematics, under teachers of the moral worthiness of Benjamin Constant—led some of these young men to meditate on the works of Auguste Comte. The deep rift between the two republican groups became immediately apparent and widened after the last attempt at a theological restoration. While the old democrats repeated the themes of metaphysical criticism, supporting the subordination of religious authority or proclaiming the imprescriptible rights of the individual conscience, the younger generation was ordering its attack on all elements of the old constitutional regime, attacking official education policy, refuting the revolutionary dogma of sovereignty, demonstrating the bankruptcy of the democratic parties, propagating the law of progress discovered by Auguste Comte, and proclaiming regeneration through science and the moralization of the people.[180]

This was the situation at the time Teixeira Mendes delivered his speech on September 7. The country was organized as a constitutional monarchy, representative and hereditary, with a Republican party composed of democrats and Positivists nursed in its bosom. Almost all monarchical parties, oddly enough, expressed republican opinions too, and merely postponed the advent of a republic to some vague future date.[181] In these circumstances what, by Positivist reckoning, was the proper political direction to be taken? It should be the expression of custom and the result of historical antecedents, the maintenance of the nation's integrity, symbolized by the political preëminence of its capital city, and a series of concerted measures that would lead to civil emancipation and the removal of Church influence on public affairs.

All this [said Teixeira Mendes] could be summed up as follows: the preservation of order and the assurance of progress should result from free propagation of all theories, inevitably leading the country to adopt the only doctrine capable of fulfilling Brazilian aspirations, thus pro viding a scientific proof of the great social and moral qualities of our race. And when the victory is complete, the patriotic bond will have become a moral confederacy through the unity of beliefs, customs, and origin, which will be the immortal characteristic of all future republics into which Brazil will come to be divided.[182]

These were the conclusions of Teixeira Mendes in the first Positivist bid to interpret national history.

Still in line with the Positivist concept of our historic life, the second public intervention of Comte's disciples in Brazil came when the creation of a university in Rio de Janeiro was proposed.

As early as 1870, in a project for the reform of public education drafted by Paulino de Sousa, an attempt had been made to found a university, in the imperial capital. It was to consist of four faculties: Law, Medicine, Mathematical and Natural Sciences, and Theology.[183] The project came to nothing. Eleven years later, in 1881, it reappeared in a new guise. It was no longer only four faculties that the government proposed to open, but five—the fifth to be a Faculty of Letters.[184]

The Positivists immediately opposed the project. The same year, 1881, Miguel Lemos protested against this "absurd scheme"; it would, in his opinion, merely systematize our "pedantocracy" and result in "stifling the scientific development which should arise out of a regime of complete spiritual freedom." [185] The university was, in Positivist eyes, an attack on spiritual freedom. Stressing the fact that, in practice, all enterprises depended on the exclusive will of the Emperor,[186] the Positivists appealed to his patriotism, begging him "in the name of the most vital interests of our country and of your own glory" not to give his blessing "to so monstrous a project." "Universities had been true centers of freedom when Catholicism became oppressive in the eighteenth century," the Master had declared. They had then become decadent institutions, "major obstacles to any attempt at spiritual reorganization." [187] "The creation of a university," declared Lemos, "answered no real need in Brazil." It was a symptom of the unenlightened chauvinism of certain citizens who "want to drag us into an imitation of decrepit institutions for so long condemned by all enlightened minds of the old world." [188] The professional schools were enough for Brazil's needs; the university would merely "give a sharper edge to the deplorably pedantocratic pretensions of our bourgeoisie, whose sons are already forsaking honorable professions in order to acquire any kind of a diploma." [189] The university, by interfering with the care that should be given to public education, would benefit only the privileged few.[190]

Deep in more pressing problems, Miguel Lemos asked Teixeira Mendes to study public opinion and to undertake to enlighten it on this new project, a task which the latter performed through a series of articles, appearing between 1881 and 1882 in the *Gazeta de Notícias* of Rio de Janeiro.[191] These articles, besides enlightening us on the Positivist position on the problem of education, reveal other aspects of their stand on the political and social situation of Brazil.

Teixeira Mendes, like his friend and companion Miguel Lemos, regarded the founding of a Brazilian university as a "puerility." In his view, at this stage of national history an educational reform which would decisively enhance the nation's greatness was certainly called for, but it should be a reform taking into account the social needs of the country, and for these the foundation of a university represented—in the eyes of the Positivists—a merely negative aspect.

When we contemplate society [wrote Teixeira Mendes], one phenomenon immediately catches the eye, namely, that the population falls into two classes: on the one hand, those who till the soil, extract the ores, manipulate raw materials to turn them into useful objects, erect buildings—those, in short, in direct contact with nature, who make up the "proletariat." On the other hand, we find those who eat, dress, live, and amuse themselves—those who dispose of the capital accumulated by the proletariat from remotest times and who, without it, would be condemned to perish. In this second group we must also distinguish two categories: the first is composed of those who, freed by proletarian labor from the need to earn a living, devote their consequent leisure to the general good, directing industrial operations, controlling disturbing influences, inventing ways of facilitating work through their scientific and technical discoveries, ensuring the spread of altruism through aesthetic productions, broadening the intellectual sphere of all and sundry through free education, studying the conditions requisite for social and moral well-being, and, finally, educating man. This is the role of women, old men, industrial leaders, government officials, military forces subordinated to the public interest, corporative administrators, scholars who dedicate themselves to the study of the useful and do not try to inflate their pride by searching the skies, artists who pay tribute to all that is great and generous. The second category, like the first, is composed of those who are supported by the proletariat but who contribute nothing to the common good and are sunk to the level of "dung factories," in the vigorous words of the poet; this category includes a superabundance of militarists and functionaries, the poets of immorality, scandalmongers, critics with no idea but to destroy, windbags of every description, scholars whose researches have no demonstrable social interest.[192]

It is this group of "useless people" that stifles the proletariat.

The proletarian, throughout the West, lives homeless and almost deprived of his family. His home is a tent, from which he can be evicted at any moment by the owners of the wealth he has himself created. It is almost always impossible for him to have a family, because the wages he is conceded or the share of human wealth he is given seldom suffices for even a single man. His wife, exposed to every kind of privation, is forced to desert the home; the children, orphans with both father and mother, grow up in hunger, deprived of all the social benefits, which would not exist but for the sweat of their fathers and their companions in misery. In Brazil, the picture is even more heinous, for the mass of the agricultural and domestic proletariat is held in the most execrable slavery! [193]

In such terms, truly incendiary for this time, Teixeira Mendes described the social situation of the period.

It was necessary, then, to reduce the horde of parasites, keeping only the "useful individuals," to liberate the proletariat, raise its morale, and provide it with homes and the chance to raise a family. "For us, to work for the greatness of Brazil is to work for these three things," concludes Teixeira Mendes.[194] "Without recourse to violence or to the division of human capital," [195] but simply through propaganda and the "moralization of the present depositaries of the public wealth," [196] the Positivists believed they could achieve their ends. They were especially interested in primary education, since this was attained by all citizens indiscriminately. The two other levels, secondary and higher, were the privilege of the few.

This situation, maintained by the state, is aggravated by the moral disposition of our bourgeoisie, and the proletariat is already becoming contaminated. This moral disposition consists of the following: parents want their sons to earn a diploma, to become teachers or members of the administration, or at least to enter the scientific corps of the army and navy, looking on agricultural work and the industrial jobs to be beneath them.[197]

The result of this "moral disposition," in the view of Teixeira Mendes, was that it led to the triumph of mediocrity, since national education was conditioned by the opportunities for the bourgeoisie to rise in the scale, and its members were endowed with neither profound intelligence nor moral robustness.

The level of secondary and higher education tends therefore to be lowered to adjust itself to the incapacity of the bourgeois parasites swarming everywhere, in the places of pupils and teachers alike; new chairs are established for graduates in the name of progress and on the pretext of educational necessity, the class of social directors grows by leaps and bounds, and the humiliations of the proletariat increase. Society is the loser, as it witnesses the misappropriation of its human capital, diminished by the amount consumed by parasites who have ceased to contribute to that capital, not to mention the pernicious effects of their social and moral influence.[198]

The spread of "parasites," the rise of mediocrity, and an aggravation of the conditions of the proletariat—these were, according to Teixeira Mendes, the results of the educational policy in Brazil. Reform of public education was therefore imperative. But this reform should spring from a realistic political concept, which would take into account our "cosmological and social conditions" (related to the continent in which we live, the territorial extent of the country, the means of transport at our disposal, our economic, moral and intellectual condition). Teixeira Mendes further advises Brazilian statesmen not to take into account the "obstacle presented by parliament." It was, he said, "merely a scarecrow, a legislative specter with no real power." [199] In this way, he once more insinuated the nature of his beliefs into this early "Positivist intervention." These he shared with all orthodox Positivists, who were opposed to parliamentary government and openly in favor of a dictatorial policy.

We shall not detain ourselves with an examination of Teixeira Mendes's reflections on the political destiny of education, inspired, naturally, by Comte's doctrines, and which, paradoxically, for that philosophy of progress, tend to create a class which is the "trustee of a common doctrine and of the virtues already achieved; able to broaden the sphere of useful knowledge, to raise the standards of morality through the introduction of new virtues; dedicated to the spread of the doctrine through education and providing a model for individual existence through the example of their private and public conduct," [200] a class of priests who, like the class of "philosophers" in Plato's *Republic*, would be in charge of the spiritual education of the other classes, softened, in this case, by feminine influence.[201]

The project for the creation of a university, perhaps on the initiative of King Pedro, came to nothing. It is possible that Teixeira Mendes's criticism had something to do with this.[202] Although there are many just observations in his work, it is quite apparent that the apostle gave way to the resentment derived from the injustice he felt had been done to the founder of the Positivist doctrines, his Master, by the scholars of the early nineteenth century.[203] To conclude the series of articles in which he examined the project elaborated by Baron Homem de Melo, Teixeira Mendes wrote—and in this he was right—that he should not attempt to "disguise our tatters with the tinsel of a false grandeur." [204] It was not an educational reform, nor the creation of a university, that would alter the Brazilian situation. Only a political organization capable of reducing "parasitism," cutting to a minimum the number of "useful men" to be supported by the proletariat, and liberating the masses through education and instruction could effectively better the situation of the country.

It was about this time that the first differences of opinion among the Brazilian Positivist group began to emerge. The antagonism became more evident over the question of a subsidy for the Brazilian leader. This first divergence led to the alienations of Benjamin Constant from his former companions of the Positivist Society[205] and paved the way to some extent for the "divorce" which later split off the Brazilian group from the French group led by Pierre Lafitte.[206]

In December, 1881, Miguel Lemos sent out his *First Circular of the Positivist Apostolate of Brazil* to the members of the former Positivist Society of Rio de Janeiro.[207] He stressed in it the need for the provision of a subsidy which would guarantee the support of the Brazilian Positivist leader—in other words, himself. He had renounced "every kind of political and temporal ambition," [208] but, before considering the establishment of a fund to assure the satisfaction of his material needs, he had tried to earn a living in some "proletarian occupation in commerce or industry." [209] He said that the nature of his duties as leader of Brazilian Positivism "did not permit him to seek a living by teaching or in any post dependent on the civil power," [210] a condition imposed by the Master for those of his disciples dedicated to the spread of the new gospel.

After consulting Pierre Lafitte—supreme leader of orthodox Positivism and at that time still on good terms with the Brazilian group—Miguel Lemos fixed the amount of the subsidy at 300,000 reis per month—a sum "strictly necessary to live with his family in the modest style prescribed for members of the spiritual power," as he stated in his circular.[211] Consent came from all provinces. The disciples were ready to contribute, faithful to the precepts of the Master on what he considered incumbent on all adherents to his doctrines.[212] Some, however—and the first of these rebels was Dr. Álvaro de Oliveira, professor of the Polytechnic School—"refused to recognize the duty demonstrated by the Master." [213] Miguel Lemos replied to the indisciplined attitude of Álvaro de Oliveira in a letter which, besides demonstrating his sagacity in argument, provides a portrait of his personality as a convinced disciple of Comte and a most interesting proof of how much he prized his priestly dignity.[214]

Dr. Álvaro de Oliveira's break with the Positivist group of Rio led to that of Benjamin Constant. I believe—but unfortunately there is insufficient documentation on this question—that Miguel Lemos's orthodox intransigence and his headstrong nature must have been an early cause of the cooling-off of enthusiasm among the first adherents of Positivism in Brazil. We can read between the lines of the letters that passed between Miguel Lemos, Benjamin Constant, and Álvaro de Oliveira that these two Positivists, the first to abandon the "Apostolate," did not like the dictatorial line taken by Miguel Lemos with the former Positivist Society. In fact, from the start, Pierre Lafitte (considered by some a keen judge of character) counseled the young Brazilian aspirant to the priesthood of the Religion of Humanity to be more prudent in his propagation of Positivism in Brazil.[215] But Miguel Lemos was by nature intense and passionate. For him, the fourth volume of the *Politique Positive* is our scientific *Leviticus,* as definitive for us as geometry." [216] The motives of his orthodoxy—he wrote later, in 1889—

do not provoke in me the smallest despondency, nor do I feel the least doubt concerning the path I am treading, since I am wholly convinced that the service of humanity is my own personal happiness and is entirely dependent on these accepted canons of conduct. I despise all else and, like St. Paul, would rather be thought unreasonable and follow our Master's behests than be hailed a sage by the frivolous of the time.[217]

This was not the temperament of Benjamin Constant. This difference of opinion led to his alienation from the Brazilian Positivist leader. Benjamin Constant's feeling that the "spread of the doctrine should neither be imposed by force nor by remonstrances full of indignation and censure against the beliefs and acts of those who are ignorant of it," [218] leads us to believe that he had no sympathy for the fanatical attitude of Lemos, the "vehemence of passion" that enslaved the apostle.[219]

The question of a subsidy then, was the first serious difficulty of the Positivist group. Benjamin Constant thought the subsidy was justified and even modest. But he felt that it should be allotted to Miguel Lemos by the supreme leader of the orthodox group, Pierre Lafitte. It was not, however, the refusal to join in the granting of a subsidy that led Benjamin Constant to resign from the group. It was a remark made by Miguel Lemos in his letter to Álvaro de Oliveira that hurt Benjamin Constant and led to his resignation. Miguel Lemos had written, according to the letter Benjamin Constant wrote in reply,[220] that he "counted only on moral and material support, and not on intellectual coöperation, in order to prevent any difficulties"—a version that does not agree with the published letter included in the *First Circular*—so that it would seem that Benjamin Constant unconsciously distorted the actual remark because he wanted to break with the Comtist society, whose leader seemed to him to be too demanding and even inconvenient. When he dissociated himself from the Apostolate in January, 1822, Benjamin Constant used a phrase which seems to me both curious and revealing of his position in relation to the doctrine: nothing prevented him, he assured Lemos, "from working in favor of a doctrine like Positivism, provided I can continue to do so, as I have done hitherto, with the dignified propriety demanded by this doctrine.[221]

These opening hostilities were to be followed by the ostentatious "divorce" of the Brazilian orthodox group from the Parisian group under the leadership of the aging Lafitte.

In the foreword to the *Second Circular of the Positivist Apostolate of Brazil*,[222] Miguel Lemos refers to the "total insufficiency of M. Lafitte," who had up to then been regarded as the supreme leader of orthodox Positivism, and to whom the Brazilian group had shown complete obedience. "A series of disappointments has finally convinced us that this current (that of Lafitte) has deviated completely from the true spirit of the doctrine, and that it is in absolute contradiction to the traditions of our holy Founder." [223] Two decisive circumstances determined the secession of the Brazilian group, two circumstances which were merely "the undeniable symptoms of the religious insufficiency already suspected by all Positivists." [224] Thus, after the foreword to the *Second Circular,* the "Positivism-Lafittism" question became the obsession of the Apostolate, and especially of Miguel Lemos.

The history of this break—and its consequences—takes up nearly all the space of the Apostolate's publications in the nineteenth century. The causes of the rupture are, however, fully narrated in the *Third Circular of the Positivist Apostolate of Brazil,* dated 1883,[225] and in Miguel Lemos's interesting booklet, *Pour notre maître et pour notre foi—le positivisme et le sophiste Pierre Lafitte.*[226]

The conflict between the Brazilian Positivists under the leadership of Miguel Lemos, aged 29, "aspirant to the priesthood," and Pierre Lafitte, successor to Auguste Comte, the venerable supreme leader of Positivism, came to a head on December 3, 1883. The Brazilian Positivists had, it seems, forgotten the Master's dictum that the Positivist priesthood, more than the theological, required complete maturity, that veneration, of all social sentiments, was the one that formed the basis of all true discipline.[227]

Brusquely, the young Brazilian aspirant announced "to all true disciples of Auguste Comte," in his *Collective Circular* that he no longer recognized the spiritual leadership of Pierre Lafitte.[228] What were the causes of this extraordinary attitude? Two decisive circumstances had led Miguel Lemos and the other signatories of the *Collective Circular* to take this stand, so different from the submissive and docile manner they had hitherto displayed in their dealings with the Lafitte group. As we saw, the Master had forbidden Positivists to accept any political positions during the so-called transition phase. All members of the Positivist Society of Rio de Janeiro had undertaken to respect this disposition of Comte's. Further, they had undertaken not to own slaves; not to exercise academic functions either in the secondary schools, or in the Pedro II College, or any similar establishment; and not to become members of scientific or literary societies. Also, they were neither to engage

in journalism nor to receive any payments for their publications."[229]
Now, in 1822, the former president of the Positivist Society of Rio
de Janeiro, Dr. Joaquim Ribeiro de Mendonça, disagreed with the
ideas of Auguste Comte and held that "a Positivist could exercise
political functions during the transition phase," claiming further
that "in this matter each man should be judge of his own conduct." [230] We should point out that Dr. Ribeiro de Mondonça intended to stand for election as deputy for his province. This gave
rise to the break between the Brazilian Positivist group and the
"completely inadequate general leadership" of Pierre Lafitte, according to Miguel Lemos.[231]

   In view of Ribeiro de Mendonça's attitude Miguel Lemos wrote
to Lafitte, telling him that he was opposed to this proof of overt
rebellion, and that he would take energetic measures against this
"revolutionary pretension that each man may constitute himself
judge of his own public conduct, without taking into consideration
the discipline and deference due to their leaders." [232] In reply, Lafitte explained to his representative in Brazil that he felt uneasy
about the "extreme rigidity and lack of proportion" which seemed
to typify the leadership of the young Brazilian Positivist leader.[233]
Lafitte considered, in that skeptical manner of his so well described
by Anatole France, that, although he agreed in principle with
Miguel Lemos, he believed it to be possible, after maturer consideration of the circumstances, for the case not to be taken quite so seriously. After all, during the German occupation of 1870, Dr. Robinet,
an eminent Positivist, had become "maire d'arrondissement," and
this had occasioned no misunderstanding between him and Lafitte.
"There is no absolute rule, except in theory," continued Lafitte in
his letter,

for those who consecrate themselves absolutely to the priesthood. As
for your request for a form of vow renouncing political activities, I
think this is very premature and applicable only in pure theory. This
kind of action could lead to a "crystallization" of Positivism for want of
sufficient comprehension of the differences between theory and practice.
Your action would therefore be purely restrictive, instead of being
affirmative and positive. I cannot, therefore, in any way approve your
intention.[234]

In reply to this disapproving letter from Lafitte, Miguel Lemos reminded him of the special condition of Positivism in Brazil and the

reasons that made its propagation and expansion here more homogeneous and synthetic—reasons which should govern its leadership to avoid the risk of nullifying both the prestige of that leadership and the principles of the doctrine. Miguel Lemos pointed out that the public knew the prescriptions of the Comtian doctrines and, by way of example, related that when one of the deputies of the São Paulo Provincial Assembly voiced Positivist opinions on the incompetence of the temporal power in public education, one of his *confrères* had replied in the following terms: "If our fellow-deputy is in effect a Positivist, I am most surprised at his presence among us, since he should imitate his *confrère* for whom it is a duty not to aspire to public office and to be content only with their spiritual influence." [235] He felt it was therefore necessary, bearing in mind the spread of Positivist ideas, to make plain the disinterestedness and lack of ambition of the Positivists. It was important, he told Lafitte, "not to accuse Positivism of ignoring in practice the moral precepts it lays down in theory." [236] In short, it was necessary for Positivism not to be transformed into a kind of "scientific Jesuitism," which would ally itself to the governing classes, always at the cost of the proletariat, "whose integration into modern society is the supreme aim of our activity." [237] This was the reason for the intransigence of the Brazilian Positivist leader, his "extreme rigidity."

In addition to committing the first "heresy" by standing for election, Ribeiro de Mendonça also published, in the Rio de Janeiro newspaper *Jornal do Comércio* an advertisement, in which he offered 200,000 reis reward for the apprehension of a runaway slave from his plantation. This action, fairly commonplace at the time, was a serious matter for a Positivist. The *Gazeta da Tarde* alluded to it, and Miguel Lemos, after consultation with his coreligionists, resolved to point out to the member who had swerved from the precepts of the doctrine the embarrassing nature of his behavior. He wrote to Ribeiro de Mendonça on March 1, 1883:

But even if we can tolerate the fact that, in certain special instances, a Positivist may own slaves (which, as I have pointed out, I do not accept), it is not fitting that he should behave like any other master, resorting to violence, denouncement, and the offer of reward, as permitted by a monstrous legislation in order to force a slave to stay when clearly he would rather go. It is understandable that the ordinary man, bound only by the minimum moral obligations of his society, should claim such a "right" to repossess his "property," but a Positivist, a disciple of the purest moral doctrine that has ever appeared in the world, cannot do these things; his moral threshold is much higher, and he cannot tolerate such recourses. "Noblesse oblige." [238]

Miguel Lemos offered his erring fellow-Positivist three solutions: the renunciation of slave labor for his plantation or the choice of another career, in this case, medicine, since Ribeiro de Mendonça was a qualified doctor.

This is the path of abnegation and sacrifice, I know. But it is my duty to suggest it: the rest depends on individual altruistic strength. If this were addressed to a worldly skeptic, he would shrug his shoulders and call me a utopian or a dreamer. A Positivist, however, knows that social abnegation is not only the most beautiful of attitudes but also the most positive. If, my friend, you are capable of taking this resolution, a great thing will have been accomplished, and the blessing of posterity will be your reward.[239]

If this path proved impossible, there remained another solution: "If your personal life does not permit such a step, if you are not in agreement with us on the question of slavery—as already you are not as regards other matters—would it not be better, in these circumstances, to resign voluntarily from the Positivist center?" [240]

As Dr. Audiffrent was to say: "C'est un fort habile homme que M. Lemos"! [241] In fact, the young leader of Positivism in Brazil was such a man. Gradually, through his audacity, his forthrightness, and his firmness, he gained complete control over the diminished group of adherents to the Comtian doctrines. Few of the founding members of the first Positivist Society of Rio de Janeiro remained, and those who did submitted entirely to Miguel Lemos.

While he was settling the question of principles with Ribeiro de Mendonça, Miguel Lemos wrote to Lafitte, asking him to sanction the measures he had taken as Positivist leader in Brazil. He pointed out to the unconcerned Gascon who had succeeded Comte the dangers of any weakening of doctrine. "Just imagine," he wrote, in a letter dated March 24, 1883,

with what eagerness the restrictions and appeasements of your last letter would be gloated over, and how they would give rise to all manner of sophistries. We would be buried under an avalanche of hastily formed Positivists who, quite happy with this title, would not be prepared to make any sacrifices. This is the danger that threatens Positivism in

Brazil, where everyone wants to declare himself a Positivist so long as he can carry on as before.[242]

The local needs of the doctrine (and this in no way detracted from the relativism proper to it, Lemos hastened to add) obliged him (1) to reaffirm the considerations expounded in his previous letter, in which he had asked Lafitte to forbid Positivists to join in any partisan political activities, and (2) to ask him to withdraw the decisions he had then made. At the same time, he broached the subject of his dispute with Ribeiro de Mendonça over the question of slaveholding by Positivists, stressing the importance of this question in Brazil at that moment.[243] Lafitte replied in a letter dated June 8, 1883, again insisting on the need for "proportion" and asking him to reflect once more on the question of the participation of Positivists in politics, since it was his opinion that on this question Lemos was treading dangerous ground.[244]

Le sacerdoce [wrote Lafitte], bien loin de conquérir l'adhésion publique resterait sans action. Sa fonction est de se faire croire, et non pas de s'imposer. La règle est absolue pour le pouvoir spirituel et nul ne peut faire partie du sacerdoce, s'il ne renonce au pouvoir politique. Mais elle est de simple conseil, trés variable, pour les gens pratique.[245]

This letter, and particularly the excerpt, was the first hint of the separation soon to take place between Lafitte and the Brazilian group.

Upon reading this deplorable document, my conscience cried out that I had erred in trusting such a guide. The more I tried to calm my fears, the more vividly this conviction grew in my mind. In practical morality one small symptom is often enough to disillusion us and to reveal, suddenly, what had hitherto been concealed from our sight. This passage of M. Lafitte's letter plunged me into a truly distressing situation. In that document one could discern the confusion of a leader lacking in courage, who muddled everything to save himself with all speed from a situation in which he had been cornered.[246]

Miguel Lemos then became preoccupied with a number of details which neophyte zeal had prevented him from perceiving when he had been in Paris. He had heard much pass among the Parisian Positivists, which veneration for Lafitte had led him to interpret entirely as the skeptical spirit of most of his fellows and as their lack of respect[247]—a number of things, which could be summed up as the unfitness of Pierre Lafitte for the role of supreme leader of the Comtian doctrines. After the letter, Miguel Lemos had no more illusions. He realized that, sooner or later, he would have to break with a leader who showed himself so ready to "sophisticate certain questions and, above all, to deny consideration to the precepts of Auguste Comte." [248] Nevertheless, the young aspirant to the priesthood of humanity resolved to wait and be patient and, while adhering strictly to the precepts of the Master, continue to respect the general leadership of Lafitte. But this wavering of resolution did not suit his temperament. To ease the situation he resigned as Lafitte's deputy in Brazil but maintained—and this was more important—his position as president of the Positivist Society of Rio de Janeiro, since he thought the latter post had nothing to do with Lafitte's authority.[249] We must not forget that it was his rank as aspirant to the priesthood, conferred by Lafitte, that had led him to this post. In three years, Positivism in Brazil had come a long way.

A few months later, toward the end of 1883, Dr. Jorge Lagarrigue, the Chilean Positivist, passed through Rio de Janeiro on his way home and took advantage of the brief stay of little more than one day to contact his Brazilian fellow disciples. Lagarrigue also expressed doubt and concern about the future of Positivism under the "insufficiency" of Lafitte's leadership. He felt, nevertheless, that it would be better if they all continued to be associated with the Paris group. A few hours before his departure, however, he told his Brazilian fellows of a visit he had paid to the leader of the Religion of Humanity in Bordeaux and alluded to a legacy which had involved Lafitte in some legal dispute with a close relative.[250]

This startling revelation had on the Positivists the "effect of a thunderclap," leading to the complete severance of the ties that had bound the Rio group to the leadership of Lafitte. Henceforward Lafitte was no longer to be the recognized leader of the Brazilian group, no matter what scandal and anger resulted from their breakaway! Lafitte's leadership was demonstrably insufficient—contrary to the teachings, precepts, and traditions of Auguste Comte.[251] "Since I am convinced that my doctrine and my veneration for Auguste Comte demand certain things of me, I attempt to carry out these things, regardless of what others may say or of the criticisms leveled at me by the indifferent and the hostile, unmoved by the calumnies that may be spread about me." [252] The rupture between the two groups became complete by the letter Miguel Lemos sent to Pierre Lafitte on November 15, 1883; and was proclaimed *urbi et orbi* by the *Collective Circular Addressed to All True Disciples of Auguste Comte* of December 3.[253]

A score of Brazilian Positivists—the "elite of our group," according to Miguel Lemos—no longer were disposed to recognize the supremacy of the Parisian leader. They continued, however, to propagate the doctrine of the Master in a spirit of strict fidelity to the letter ("submission is the basis of all improvement"), until a worthy successor to Comte should emerge, in order to "recreate on a more solid foundation the fictitious and nominal unity which exists at present."[254] In this way, yet another adventure of European philosophy in Brazil had come to an end.

3

Freed from an "enervating and corrupting bond,"[255] Miguel Lemos went on to recall the varied series of "mystifications" indulged in by the leader now cast off by the Apostolate. Just as he had once found Littré an "insufficient" guide, so now he piled up fearful accusations of "insufficiency" against Lafitte. The divergences and the scandals on the question of succession that had followed the death of Comte now came to the surface. The precedents of Congreve and of Audiffrent were used to justify the national schism.[256] Charges of error, doubt, and deviation from orthodox Comtism were showered on Lafitte,[257] and an attitude of *mea culpa*—a curious form sometimes taken by self-criticism—pervaded the circulars of the "Positivist Apostolate of Brazil." To the heresies of Lafitte, Miguel Lemos had opposed his unshakable faith in the Master's doctrine. "The fourth volume of the *Politique Positive* is our *Leviticus*, a scientific *Leviticus* as definitive for us as geometry.[258] Old letters were brought to light to justify present attitudes. The long history of Comte's *Testament* was recalled, and the passages in which he had expressed his doubts concerning the disciple he had chosen as his successor[259] were cited. A flood of invective was let loose:

Growing daily in theoretic vanity and moral laxity, he (Lafitte) observed the practical precepts of our religion as a mere formality, while seeking at every favorable opportunity to reject them or demolish them with one blow after another. He pretended to respect in the mass what in the detail he destroyed. Hence the extraordinary growth of the casuistic spirit which is the very stamp of his moral physiognomy, so to speak. In his fundamentally skeptical nature he is a true son of Voltaire, out of place in a movement of religious reconstruction.[260]

Positivism in Brazil became increasingly religious. On December 3, 1883, the Brazilian Positivists issued their famous *Collective Circular,* signed by twenty-five "militant" Positivists, the elite of the group. "We hasten to make known," wrote the orthodox Comtists, addressing themselves to the Master's "true disciples,"

as we consider ourselves in duty bound to do, that we have ceased to acknowledge the spiritual leadership of M. Pierre Lafitte. A series of disappointments has finally convinced us that his leadership is completely alien to the true spirit of our doctrines and absolutely opposed to the traditions of our holy Founder.[261]

Miguel Lemos then related (for everything points to his authorship of the *Collective Circular)* the facts we have presented above. Entertaining no further illusions in view of the violation of their doctrine and in the face of so much "sophistry," it seemed to the twenty-odd Brazilian Positivists that Lafitte did not even fulfill the requirements for a simple aspirant to the priesthood.[262] The sincerity with which they professed the Positivist faith, the "limitless" veneration in which they held the sacred memory of the Founder, his example, his doctrine, and his traditions, could not—in the opinion of the votaries—suffer any correction, and for this reason they had not hesitated to perform the duty that constrained them to break with the man who was betraying their Master. To follow any other course of conduct, they affirmed, would be

to lie to our consciences, to betray our commitments, and to mystify a public familiar with the moral conditions which must be satisfied by the Positivist priesthood. . . . Suppressing our painful feelings, we firmly passed the resolution, knowing that we would be deserted by the apathetic and those of whom the great Italian poet wrote: "Che non furon rebelli né fur fedeli a Dio, ma per se foro." From that day onward, M. Lafitte ceased to be our chief. This is the grave event we wish to bring to your attention.[263]

This was the declaration of the rebellious, but highly orthodox, disciples of Auguste Comte in Brazil. They refused moral and material support for Lafitte and awaited the advent of a "worthy universal guide" [264]—a curious expression of the Messianism of our Positivists.

Nevertheless,

if M. Lafitte renounces his pretensions to the priesthood, and if he needs the material support of the Positivist group, we shall consider it a duty to join our efforts to those of all our brethren and help him to continue the undeniable services he has rendered, both as a propagandist for the faith and as president of the group of executors of Auguste Comte's testament; and also to ensure for him that dignified retirement to which he is entitled for all these services.[265]

Faithful to the doctrine and to the strict obedience to the Master's doctrines, but nevertheless considering themselves "henceforth freed from an enervating leadership that had produced in Positivism a profound degeneration," [266] making concessions neither to prejudice nor to any powerful group,[267] these faithful disciples of Comte vowed to submit to the true successor of the Master when he should emerge.

Until then, we shall work according to our own lights, since this is prescribed by him who is to us the inexhaustible and incorruptible fountainhead of teaching and example. Faithful to Auguste Comte, we cherish the deep-rooted hope that posterity, to which we appeal, will likewise be faithful to us and will approve our conduct.[268]

With these words, the Brazilian Positivists closed the circular, in which they accounted to their fellows for a rebellion born of the desire to reestablish the doctrine in its entire purity.

The rupture with the Paris group occasioned protests and resignations, as Miguel Lemos had foreseen. In 1882 the number of Brazilian adherents was 59. By 1883 it was down to 43, and in 1884 to 34.[269] In Paris, the president of the Sociological Study Circle of Proletarian Positivists, Keufer, rallied his associates and sent a message of solidarity to Lafitte, dated March 16, 1884, censuring the "insolence and brutality" of the attack by Miguel Lemos and his compatriots. This behavior, directed by "a proud and insubordinate man, as incapable of leadership as he is of obedience" —in the words of the motion proposed by Jeannolle, Lafitte's friend —"can only result in a slowing up of the evolution of Positivism in Brazil." [270] Pointing out that the words of Comte did not constitute articles of faith, that there should be no servile submission to the letter of the doctrine, and that the Master must certainly have trusted the intelligence of his disciples, the French Positivists gave Miguel Lemos—unshakable in his orthodoxy—cause to find in their motion reasons which seemed to more than justify the attitude he had adopted. "Lafittism," said Miguel Lemos, in reply to Jeannolle's motion,

has at last issued its manifesto, and taken off its mask. The true disciples of Auguste Comte now know how they must behave. In effect, gentlemen, you have just proclaimed, doubtless repeating the lessons you have been taught, that the work of Auguste Comte is subject to revision, is even revocable. You wish, therefore, to use your reason to control and interpret his doctrines. You do not admit the infallibility of Comte, just as you do not accept that of Aristotle or Descartes. You demand, in short, the right to correct his errors. In truth, one is amazed to read such revolutionary excesses from the pens of persons who call themselves Positivists.[271]

Is the social and political aspect of Comte's work not, then, scientific? Do the Lafittists place it on the same plane as the "provisional" systems of Descartes and Aristotle? Miguel Lemos was further scandalized by the fact that the Lafittists doubted that it was Comte who had founded positive, scientific, and definitive politics, completing the conjuncture of the branches of knowledge. "All these things," he said, "I had already heard from the mouth of the leader during conversations. But only now have they come fully to light, and you, gentlemen, were chosen as the editors." [272]

M. Lafitte, in his own way, openly carries on the work of Littré. He takes his place among the string of sophists who, in France and in England, have vainly attempted to adapt our doctrines to their ambitions and their foibles. I predict for him a similar success; but what has been learned from this—and that is what I sought to verify—is that those who accused Lafitte of having debased Positivism and of having ignored the traditions and precepts of Auguste Comte have been proved right, in the most unmistakable manner, by Mr. Lafitte himself and by his partisans.[273]

Pierre Lafitte, at the meeting convened by the Sociological Study Circle of Proletarian Positivists of Paris, thanked them for their proof of solidarity and said that Positivism would be "sterile and ridiculous if it consisted merely of reciting and paraphrasing Auguste Comte," as Miguel Lemos was doing. In reply, Miguel Lemos wondered what Lafitte, as a philosopher, had ever done but recite and paraphrase Comte.

Positivism becomes facile, sterile, and ridiculous when it attempts to bring our doctrines down to the level of a source of themes for the digressions of pedantry and ambition, when it introduces free examination of the work of the Master and excludes veneration for his person; when it fails to prescribe the duties of its followers, and recruits them everywhere; when it is subordinate to political leaders; when it is silent in order to please and, if called upon, provides politicians with scholarly dissertations to justify what our doctrine most plainly condemns.[274]

The South American Positivists, led by Miguel Lemos, Jorge Lagarrigue, and Teixeira Mendes, were convinced that what "the regeneration of the world" most needed was "saints, as well as scholars." [275] Oliveira Viana is right, therefore, when, in his consideration of Positivist influence on the preparations for a republic, he says that it had an insignificant effect since "in its dogmas, precepts, and rules, tough as the fibres of bastard hemp," there was something reminiscent of the rough hair shirts of the monks, and its disciples seemed more like severe Baptists clothed in skins and armed with prophetic staffs, macerated by the rude abstinences of the desert." [276]

The year 1883 [277] passed into the history of Brazilian Positivism as the year of the schism. From then on the battle with the heretical leader continued in a crescendo, monopolizing the attention of Brazilian Positivists, who became veritable crusaders, ready to try anything to wrest from the hands of the heretics the "sacred places" where the Master and those most dear to him had passed his life.

The period between 1884 and 1886, apart from problems of worship, has little interest for the student of Positivist history. In 1887 [278] Brazilian Positivists rejoiced in the march of political events in the "central nation"—France—where, since the previous year, parliamentary democracy had been in serious difficulties.

After his review of the troops on the Fourteenth of July, General Boulanger had been the focus of increasing popularity. The interests of the Northern industrialists, the great rural landowners, and the "revanchisme" of Déroulède had played their part in this.[279] To the strains of the famous song of the period—*En Revenant de la Revue*[280]—the general's fame spread rapidly, and the reactionaries trusted him to clear up all the difficulties of a grave moment in the democratic history of the French people. Miguel Lemos, ever alert to prophesy the forthcoming "definitive regime," wrote in his *Seventh Circular*:

The advent of a republican dictatorship, in doing away with all turbulent parliamentarians, will make the social situation as clear as possible. It will inevitably lead to the abolition of theological, metaphysical, and scientific budgets and, by reducing all doctrines to their own resources, will permit the ascendancy of the only doctrine capable of resolving the combination of problems arising from previous evolution.[281]

"Boulangism" was, curiously enough, the great dream of the Brazilian believers in the dictatorial republican ideas of Comte! [282] But this enthusiasm did not last long: "Le Boulangisme est fini," wrote Jean Jaurès in November, 1889. "Nous pouvons reprendre hardiment avec la démocratie, l'oeuvre de justice." [283] Another dream of the Brazilian Positivists had faded.

The year 1888—so important for our country—found the Positivists preoccupied with details of religious ceremony. On January 6 Teixeira Mendes was elevated to the post of Deputy Director of the Apostolate; on April 5 another feast was celebrated—that of Clothilde de Vaux, a touching demonstration of fidelity to the lessons of the Master and an affirmation of the significance of the feminine influence for Brazilian Positivists.

So much concern for the forms of worship diverted the Positivists from the more urgent problems then agitating the country. This is perhaps the reason why João Camilo de Oliveira Tôrres says in his interesting study that, on the matter of abolition, the Positivists did no more than record their presence,[284] a statement that appears to me unjust. Although not engaged in militant politics, the Positivists had concerned themselves with the problem of emancipation since the Society's foundation. It is known that, despite their poverty, Miguel Lemos and Teixeira Mendes were regular contributors to emancipation funds.[285] The episode involving Ribeiro de Mendonça—which led to the break with Lafitte—arose in part from the stand taken by the Positivists on the slave-owning problem. It is true, however, that after 1883 the Positivists had become almost entirely absorbed in the Lafitte case and the religious aspects of their doctrine.

Despite this, Comte's disciples seemed to show a proper appreciation of the major event of 1888. "We must recognize the fact that slavery would have been abolished some time ago," wrote Miguel Lemos in his *Eighth Circular,*

had not the present Emperor prevaricated with the slave owners instead of displaying the energy that his high political function required.

Realizing that monarchical privilege was intimately linked to the main-tenance of the privileges resulting from slavery, but impelled by public opinion, both at home and abroad, to take steps toward emancipation, his conduct was marked by chronic indecision, arousing in the abolition-ists great hopes, to be followed almost immediately by bitter disappoint-ments.[286]

"The institution of the monarchy could not be favorably disposed toward abolition, since this act would be the final blow to its remain-ing support among the conservative classes of our country, where such an institution has no real roots or traditions." [287] The Positiv-ists naturally took the opportunity of pointing out what they con-sidered an example of the preponderance of feeling, a theory of some importance to Positivism. Princess Isabel, they said, besides being unaware of the exact nature of the contradictions originating in the clash between the conservative classes, deprived of what they looked on as their rights, and the overwhelming tide of national opinion in favor of abolition, "suffered, as a woman, from the preponderating influence of the heart" [288] and was therefore not subject to the same doubts as the old Emperor, who had been so characteristically hesitant during the last years of his reign. The Positivist apostle, deeply imbued with his own philosophy, did not take into account, however, that even stronger than the "prepon-derating influence of the heart" was the increasingly sharp con-tradiction in a regime based on slavery, and that the army—a decisive element in our politics, particularly after the Paraguayan war—was even then refusing to take part in the recapture of slaves.

But what service did Positivism in fact render to the cause of emancipation? Miguel Lemos enumerates them in his *Eighth Cir-cular*.

Basing themselves on Comte's doctrines, the Positivists attempted to demonstrate the "affective superiority" of the Negro race. It was this Negro trait which, in their view, explained the resignation they had shown throughout the long years of oppression to which they had been subjected, a resignation which was, according to the Posi-tivists, a prerequisite for the country's progress. Reproducing the lessons of the "Master of Montpellier," they insisted on demonstrat-ing the differences between slavery in ancient times, considered by Comte to be a natural result of human evolution, and modern slavery, which the great maritime discoveries reëstablished in the fifteenth century. "We brought to the cause of emancipation," he added, "the powerful support of our Master's authority against the sophists who claimed an impossible and fallacious 'gradual transformation,' and supported the claims of the slave owners to monetary compensation."[289] In April, 1888 (although the work was perhaps only published after the edict of emancipation), Miguel Lemos and Teixeira Mendes had presented "a program of urgent political reforms, opening with the statement: 'slavery is in its death throes.'"[290]

With the abolition of slavery, the Positivist leaders felt that the preliminary stages of the social problem in Brazil had been passed: a problem the same for the whole of the West—"the integration of the proletariat into modern society."[291] For this integration to become effective—based on the twofold Comtian maxim: "dedication of the strong to the weak, veneration of the weak for the strong"—the former slave owners must guarantee the possession of an abode capable of supporting a family; allow the former slaves a wage adequate to keep up their homes; ensure that they developed altruistic sentiments; train them for the professions they wished to follow; and provide an education "allying theoretical knowledge with practical apprenticeship between the ages of fourteen and twenty-one,"[292] while demanding from them only six hours of actual work; and, finally, promote the "replacement of products which absorb our agricultural activities with products more useful and necessary for human existence."[293] If the slave owners proceeded along these lines, the two apostles concluded, they would avoid the fragmentation of the great estates empirically commended by the abolitionists.[294] The landlords should not allow themselves to become blinded by greed, for the surest means to greater and better productivity was to make the worker increasingly "honest, intelligent, and active." These were the true prerequisites for a revolution. Everything that had been done up to that point derived, according to Miguel Lemos and Teixeira Mendes, from a want of discipline; and to achieve discipline it was not enough to "simply replace present parliamentarianism with democratic parliamentarianism."[295] In their opinion this would be mere ingenuity.

Modern revolution has the highest aim: to establish the "republic" in the true sense of the word: a regime based exclusively on the overriding consideration of the public good and its supreme law, eliminating any pretensions to individual rights. In such a regime, only the duties of each toward all would be recognized: duties defined by the relation of the individual to the vast organism of which he is a part. This organism is humanity, to which we are successively linked by the bonds of patriotism and family.[296]

We must remember that "the integration of the proletariat into modern society" had been, since Comte's youth, one of his constant concerns, one to which, unfortunately, he was never able to give a form, perhaps as the result of his fundamentally conservative nature. In the organization of the old regime the worker had some degree of security, but with the growth of industry and economic freedom he became a mere pawn in the hands of fate. It was this insecurity that disturbed romantic and generous natures like that of Auguste Comte. Hence his declaration of the worker's need to be integrated into modern society where, in the words of Comte, he had hitherto been merely encamped. But for this end he did not wish in any way to disturb the balance of "the vital general economy." [297] "Comte's ideas," writes Roger Mauduit, "are inspired by generous thoughts and arise more or less indirectly from the positive philosophy; but in relation to the science of economics they are very superficial.[298] Comte's Brazilian disciples proved no more profound than their Master and did not enjoy a sufficiently exact vision of the landscape about them, as can be seen from reading the second part of the work of Miguel Lemos and Teixeira Mendes on spiritual freedom and the organization of labor in Brazil.

As has been pointed out, the Positivists were republicans in their own fashion.[299] They themselves confessed that they were republicans, but "Positivist republicans," [300] not to be confused with the metaphysical democrats. We have already briefly considered the delight with which the Positivists announced that the "central nation" was on the way to establishing a dictatorial republic. "But for all their self-proclaimed republicanism, if Brazilians had followed their advice (that of the Positivist Apostolate) we would still be enjoying the delights of the Fourth Reign," writes Ximeno de Villeroy.[301] It is true that, faithful to the precepts laid down by the Master, the Positivists were loyal and respectful to all forms of authority and did little to hasten the advent of a democratic republic, which they regarded as a paltry "imitation of French Empiricism." In September, 1888, in their postscript to a letter sent to the Bishop of Pará on the subject of religious freedom, they declared:

Faithful to our principles, we Positivists would like the chief of state to understand the political situation and to satisfy the just aspirations of the people, instead of waiting for it to find its mouthpiece in individuals who have shown themselves in heart, spirit, and character unworthy of so sublime a mission. If the sovereign were to make the move we have always so respectfully counseled, he could save the truly sociocratic elements of our present political institutions, which consist of a life term of office for the supreme functionary or for any other functionary. At the same time, such a move would give him the prestige needful to establish the succession along the lines set out during the Roman dictatorship, each chief designating his heir, either within or outside his family, subject to national approval. In this manner, instead of having a republic, a servile imitation of empirical and vicious constitutions, we would institute a republican form in accord with moral and scientific political prescriptions. If, however, the sovereign elects to turn a deaf ear to the demands of public opinion, upon his memory will, in great measure, weigh the responsibility for what eventuates in the transformation which he could have directed, but would not.[302]

In a letter to Joaquim Nabuco entitled "A Propósito da Agitação Republicana" ("On the Republican Agitation"), written in October, 1888, Teixeira Mendes develops more fully Positivist ideas on the regime which had been for so long awaited. He recalled that

the way in which we perceive the republic alienates us not only from neorepublicanism but even from those who styled themselves republicans before May 13. In 1881, when Positivist propaganda became systematized in Brazil, we believed, in the flush of our inexpert zeal, that we could work side by side with those who advocated abolition of the monarchy. Although aware even then of the profound antagonism between Positivism and democracy, we imagined that sincere concern for the public good would serve as a link between us and those who declared themselves republicans. The illusion, however, was short-lived: the events that transpired on the occasion of a simple choice of candidate for the Chamber of Deputies were enough to prove that it was our duty to go forward alone and in obscurity.[303]

In the light of modern events, and according to the letter of Positivist doctrine, Teixeira Mendes believed the political problem of Brazil to be analogous to that of the West as a whole. As for the institution of monarchy, it seemed to Comte's disciples to be completely exhausted, sterile, and inept.[304] Unfortunately, the republic was merely the replacement of the dynasty by an elected and temporary president. The theological absurdity was exchanged for a metaphysical one, in the words of the Apostolate's Deputy Director.[305]

The remedy for the country's ills could only be a "dictatorial republic," that is, a strong government with a national and popular chief who would dissolve parliament, since the dictatorship should limit itself to the maintenance of material order, guaranteeing complete spiritual and moral freedom.[306]

This was the dream of the Brazilian Positivists. "For all our efforts," continues Teixeira Mendes,

have hitherto gone into the attempt to transform the leader given us by our historical antecedents into such a dictator; and our attitude will remain unchanged to the last. Furthermore: if, through the political insufficiency of the present chief of state, the democratic republic should be implanted, as everything seems to indicate, our propaganda will continue to advocate for the present the transformation of the metaphysical president into the dictator demanded by our social situation. Just as for us the proletarian problem was not resolved by emancipation, so the republic will not have been achieved by the substitution of pure bourgeois parliamentarianism for monarchical bourgeois parliamentarianism.[307]

We have already noted in this work that around 1868 a veritable renewal of ideas occurred in Brazil. Nevertheless, as has been shown by José Maria Bello, the philosophical and literary ideas that emerged in this period did not lead the intellectuals toward the republican idea.[308] The indifference of Tobias Barreto toward republican propaganda was largely shared, as we find on probing deeper, by the intellectuals of the period. Many of them declared themselves republicans, rather than be thought retrograde, but basically they were indifferent to politics. They were almost certainly liberals, but this did not make republicans of them. In fact, curiously enough, almost everyone approved of the republic, believing it a better form of government than the monarchy, but with the addition that the change might not suit the country, in view of its backwardness.[309] "At heart, I am a republican," was said without much, if any, conviction. Republicanism was preached, but no active efforts were made to bring about any real changes. The only doctrine of any influence in this confused and amorphous scene was that of Auguste Comte. This did not, however, derive from the Positivist Apostolate, but from the prestige among the youth of the Military and Polytechnic schools enjoyed by Professor Benjamin Constant, who had resigned from the Positivist Society of Rio de Janeiro and was, therefore, not spared the criticism of the orthodox Positivists. This teacher of mathematics was the true source of republican ideas among the younger generation.

Benjamin Constant was a "molder of men." A descendant of humble folk and professor to young men who were not the sons of slave owners, he knew how to implant enthusiasm for the republican regime and how to sow the seeds of revolt against the monarchy. He had accepted Comte's philosophy but was not orthodox. "Alienated from the Apostolate, Benjamin did not make of Positivism a religious priesthood. He simply expounded it, being more interested in the teaching of Comte's Positivism as a philosophy." [310]

"The republic had to come"—not, however, because of the orthodoxy of the Apostolate or the simple philosophical teaching of Benjamin Constant. The republic, like emancipation, had more profound causes, longer antecedents. [311] José Maria Bello considers that two parallel forces, having equal effect, can be traced in the immediate causes of the republic:

The direct force was that of the republicans, the indirect that of the monarchists themselves, for whom the Empire had lost its last enchantment and who, especially after May 13, formed the large and dangerous party of defeatists. Among these theoretical monarchists who, wittingly or not, were working for a republic, there could be distinguished the liberals, the reformers, the abolitionists, the federalists (such as Joaquim Nabuco and Rui Barbosa and those of the lineage of Tavares Bastos), the disappointed, and the angry, such as those conservatives injured by abolition. Among the republicans, it is likewise possible to distinguish four separate streams: that of the historical 1870 republicans, principally Paulistas, who followed the lead of Quintino Bocaiúva, moderate but resolute and convincing political doctrinaries (as Olivier, in the days before he adhered, or Jules Favre, in their opposition to the Empire of Napoleon III), who at the last moment promoted the military conspiracy; that of the ardent youth of Silva Jardim believing in revolutionary action in the press and in the streets, reminding us of the old tradition of the French romantics of 1830 and 1848; that of the young military men imbued with the doctrines of Comte and fired by Benjamin Constant; and finally that of the older, military generation—typified by General Deodoro da Fonseca [leader of the republican revolt of November 15, 1889.—Trans.]—who favored the republic but had no definite ideological bent, through the spirit of their class and the intuition that the Empire was a page of our history turned forever. It is certainly to this latter group that the republic owes its proclamation in 1899. [312]

Beyond all doubt, Positivism had only the slightest influence on the advent of the republic. "The strength which has been attributed to the *religion of Positivism* in the political advent of the republic," writes Licínio Cardoso, "is grossly exaggerated. . . . The orthodox Positivists under Teixeira Mendes and Miguel Lemos always wanted the impossible, the unattainable." [313] They demanded saints for the reforms they had in mind; "they are like bastard descendants of historical saints, no longer in tune with modern social environments, of limited mysticism, shrinking religiosity; in short, as Renan said, to permit the emergence of new sects." [314] Paradoxically distant from the "possible" and the "attainable," these orthodox Positivists did little or nothing to hasten the advent of the republic. Nor could they have. They were few (fifty-three in 1889), and mainly preoccupied, as we have seen, with problems of religious worship and the question of Lafitte. Besides, politics had already caused them many disappointments. "Modern society," said one of the Positivists, "will cease to be the victim of anarchy only through a complete reform, freely understood and practiced, of feeling and thought, which is completely beyond the powers of temporal governments or what is commonly known as politics." [315] The leaders themselves confess their failure to act. In his work on Benjamin Constant, Teixeira Mendes, besides stating the situation of the Apostolate at that period, gives the opinion of the leaders: "We are alien to all that was being plotted. We did not advice, nor would we now advice, revolt, for it is contrary to the precepts of our Master." [316] His explanation of the Apostolate's abstention from the events of November 15, 1889, is curious:

As we have said, we were alien to the uprising; we did not advise it and we would not have advised it if we had been consulted beforehand. But once it had become an accomplished fact, many thought our conduct should have been otherwise; in other words, that we should have expressed an opinion on what had been done. No judgment could be more superficial. In effect, however critical the situation of the Empire had been, complete freedom of opinion was guaranteed; and freedom of association was violated only in respect to political meetings with more or less subversive tendencies. Despite its reactionary character, the Ministry was being forced to grant us freedom of public worship, civil marriage, and the secularization of cemeteries. These measures, taken as a whole, gave evidence of the political and moral exhaustion of the official church and brought to light the problem of its separation from the state. On the other hand, freedom of education would soon have put an end to academic privilege, which had in fact already been eliminated by popular custom. As for administrative decentralization, this was urgent. Republican agitation and the incorrigible lack of discipline of the public force, given the maneuvers of imperial politics, would have kept the government of the former monarch in a state of constant alarm and would have forced it to proclaim a republic, perhaps through the very parliament elected to crush it. Emancipation was put through by a Chamber favoring slavery. This evolution would probably have taken a number of years; but it was inevitable, whatever the tortuous and retrograde nature of the monarchist dictatorship.[317]

The essentially negative instinct of the Positivists, as Sérgio Buarque de Holanda observes, becomes apparent afresh in this passage.[318]

To hasten this outcome [added Teixeira Mendes], it would only have needed the growth of the social and moral influence of the Positivist Apostolate. Now we can all calculate the degree of prestige we would have had if Benjamin Constant, instead of promoting the movement of the 11th Frederick (November 15) had brought us the firm support of all those who enthusiastically followed him. Instead of an admirable military revolution, there would have been a surprising peaceful evolution through the voluntary transformation of the imperial dictatorship into a republican dictatorship, under pressure of strong public opinion.[319]

The Positivists were obviously not responsible for the advent of the republic and at once became its first critics. This, however, did not prevent Miguel Lemos from writing in his *Ninth Circular* for 1889 (dated May, 1890) that the culminating proof of Positivists evolution during the year under review was provided by the proclamation of a republic in Brazil and that in this "the influence of our doctrine made itself felt in such a favorable way that in this regard the event was not of a purely national order, but was of considerable importance to the general march of Positivism in the West." [320] Now the influence of Positivism was felt only through the medium of Benjamin Constant's prestige, and the Apostolate had taken no steps to promote the events of November 15. "At any rate, once the explosion had gone off, it only remained for us to guide the new government. This was, from the outset, our intention," wrote Teixeira Mendes.[321]

Once the republic was proclaimed, the Positivist leaders, who had until recently been unsparing in their criticism of Benjamin Constant for his heterodoxy, approached the man who had been the soul of the republican movement and who had done everything to turn an event which could have been merely a show of military strength aimed at the overthrow of a Ministry into a change in the country's political institutions.[322] But it was thanks to the collaboration of Demétrio Ribeiro, "true son of our propaganda, who came to power with the Positivist program in his hand," [323] that the influence of Positivism made itself felt in the new regime for almost two months. These two months gave Positivism its fame and gained for it the inexact reputation of having created the republic in Brazil.

Always high-flown in his enthusiasm, Miguel Lemos said that the Brazilian "revolution took the rest of the world by storm and occasioned great amazement." [324] It is an old custom of ours to give too much credit to the resonance of national events. The transformation that came about in 1889 did not cause any surprise in "the rest of the world," and we ourselves did not overlook the importance of slave labor as a prop of the monarchy and of imperial society. After emancipation it was accurately foreseen by all clear-thinking men (including Teixeira Mendes and Cotegipe) that the monarchical institutions would soon be abolished. Even that shallow journalist, Max Leclerc, of the *Journal des Débats,* who hastened to Brazil shortly after proclamation of the republic, had grasped the importance of this factor in determining the transformation that took place in our counry.[325]

Benjamin Constant's propaganda had recruited some fervent disciples of republican ideas among the younger generation. The orthodox Positivists in their turn claimed their share of glory for the spread of republican ideas. These young men, taught "by a master whom they dearly loved and revered" these Positivists said, "also hastened to join those who had consecrated themselves to the complete and faithful propagation of Positivism." [326] In this way,

the too-vague impulse emanating from Dr. Benjamin Constant was rendered more precise by our teaching, despite the grave divergences that separated our orthodoxy from the incomplete adherence of the remarkable professor. While he told his pupils of the advent of a new ideal, presenting this powerful creation of human ingenuity as a fund in the hands of the future, we showed these young men what this ideal consisted of and what were the steps to be taken now in preparation for that distant future.[327]

Nevertheless, the most powerful Positivist influence in the republican government was beyond any doubt that of the heterodox

Benjamin Constant. Demétrio Ribeiro—who later was also to move away from the influence of the Apostolate—mustered the sympathies of the orthodox Positivists. Benjamin Constant, although reconciled with them, did not heed them without reservations. In fact, when the financial reforms were discussed, that led to the "exoneration of Demétrio Ribeiro, Benjamin Constant agreed with Rui Barbosa," [328] who, in the opinion of the orthodox group, was one of those "ill-omened figures who soon polluted the new regime and extinguished all regenerative ardor." [329] The members of the Apostolate thought nothing of Rui Barbosa and had amiable reservations about Constant's capacity:

Unfortunately, let us admit quite frankly and with no hostile intent, Dr. Benjamin Constant was unprepared for this political role. Highly capable, through his outstanding moral and intellectual qualities and through the devotion he inspired in the young military men, of preparing and carrying out the revolution as it was conceived and executed, he lacked the theoretical enlightenment that the situation demanded. His insufficient adherence to Positivism did not permit him to endorse the views or to put into practice the political solutions indicated by Auguste Comte, which we had not ceased to propagate. On the other hand, he no longer believed in the revolution ontologically and therefore could not seek to orient himself from this base. Politics caught him unawares, and he found himself suddenly transported to a world almost unknown to him, for he had always lived outside the accompanying agitation and had had neither opportunity nor leisure to familiarize himself with the concepts that our Master put in place of the errors and fantasies of democratic theory.[330]

Once the republic had been proclaimed, the rough edges smoothed over, the frictions that had divided people more or less forgotten, the due compliments paid, and the necessary excuses made, the Comtists went back to their restrictions. They were, as Vicente Licínio Cardoso said, the eternal lovers of the "unattainable," hankering after the impossible. Manuel Bonfim observes that Positivism gave to its disciples "a tone of sovereign and absolute self-sufficiency . . . This gives them the privilege of infallibility; they have a solution for everything, an answer for every question." [331] Was there not perhaps in the Positivist inflexibility of the Apostolate an aspect symbolic of the anxiety that besets some Brazilians, who seek to cure by a simple formula the evils arising from a formation in which adventure is dominant? Was there not, beneath their fanaticism, the profound and ingenuous hope that, if new formulae were to be employed, the results would be splendid?

Quite recently, Georges Friedmann, in studying the optimism of Leibniz, wrote:

toute la subtile construction, si soigneusement ornée, polie, arrondie, de l'optimisme leibnizien rend, donc pour nous, dès l'origine, une resonance cachée, inquiète et douloureuse, qui ne fait que de préciser lorsqu'on avance dans la carrière intellectuelle de Leibniz, à travers ses efforts pour vulgariser et imposer socialment son 'Système nouveau'. Aussi les railleries de 'Candide' ne sont-elles pas moins superficielles que *l'optimisme* auquel elles s'attaquent: elles tombent, au vrai, sur un philosophe obsedé par une anxieté fondamentale, et resolu à tout faire, intellectuellement, pour s'aider et aider l'humanité a la surmonter. On ne se tromperait guère (et je crois même qu'on irait assez loin dans la caractéristique historique du leibnizianisme, surgi au seuil d'une longue période de crise des societés occidentales) en suggerant que l'optimisme leibnizien est en realité une des premières formes des philosophies de l'angoisse et du deséspoir.[332]

Might not a similar factor have been present in Brazilian Positivism? Behind the inflexibility and exaggerated intransigence of Brazilian Comtism, there was, perhaps, a painful conviction of the reigning general disorder in society and in the intellect and, at the same time, the hope that in the formula of the Master the miraculous remedy for this terrible disorder could be found. "Was there not," asks Sérgio Buarque de Holanda, "at the root of the belief held by the Positivists in the efficacy of the Master's formula, a secret horror of the national reality?" [333] Was it not as the result of a tragic and profound contradiction that our Positivists were always so terribly negative? Perhaps from this sprang the "excessive rigidity," "the lack of proportion," the fanaticism, in short, of the Religion of Humanity's Brazilian apostles. But woe to those who attempt to impose order on the uncertainty of adventure!

Positivism—as has been said and as was confessed by its leaders—gave its adherence to the republic only two day after its proclamation. In fact, "two days after the event, when we had ascertained the true nature of the change that had just been effected, we took a message of adherence to the Minister of War for him to transmit to the new head of state." [334] In this message the Positivists recalled their "incessantly reiterated warnings in an attempt to obtain from the Emperor himself the transformation demanded by the Brazilian situation, in order to avoid the dangerous consequences of all revolutionary processes, even those with the best motives." [335] It was not long before the Positivists addressed "urgent suggestions" to "the people and the government of the republic," expressing the ideals formulated by Auguste Comte: "Now that the republic has been proclaimed," they said, "we must organize it. All the care of true patriots should be directed to this end." [336] Until they were able to present a more developed work, they offered to the people and to the government the most urgent suggestions for this organization. On November 21, 1889, they published their political program, whose principal and most "urgent" points were as follows: (a) "The republican dictatorship should be maintained in a definitive form." (b) The present "provisional government" should evolve, with the aid of competent persons, a "projected constitution." (c) The draft constitution should be presented for public consideration so that it could be thoroughly discussed. (d) This draft constitution, after the "amendments considered acceptable by the government had been made," should be presented "for sanction to all municipalities" of the republic, and should be promulgated after a "plebiscite" in which would participate all citizens over twenty-one years of age, regardless of whether they could read and write. (e) This constitution should "combine the principle of a republican dictatorship with the widest spiritual freedom; the former characterized by the conciliation of the executive power and the legislative faculty through the perpetuity of its function and its transmission to a successor freely chosen by the dictator, subject to the sanction of public opinion"; the latter characterized by the "separation of Church and state"; the "suppression of all public education except at the primary level" and the subsequent "complete freedom for all professions and abolition of the privileges inherent in scientific or technical diplomas"; the new régime would be based on the "widest possible freedom of association and thought," and the only obligation on all citizens would be to take full responsibility for their writings by signing them." [337] (f) There should be, according to the "urgent suggestions," one single general Chamber, popularly elected, composed of only a few deputies, "dedicating itself only to financial problems," and intended for the control of public revenue. [338] The Positivists believed that only by this means could they stop the "rebirth of the evil system that had just expired, characterized by the irresponsible preponderance of idle talk and intrigue."

We must adopt a political organization that, based upon complete spiritual freedom, will institute a responsible government, opposed to rhetoric; to theological and metaphysical fictions; to the absurd process of taking decisions by a majority vote; to political brokerage; and, finally, to the exploitation of the proletarian masses, the productive basis of the nation, by the lawyers, graduates, scientists, and men of letters of all sorts—an exploitation which constitutes the worst of absolutisms because it is the most degrading of all. Let us not be led blindly to imitate the institutions of this or that country; let us remember that each nation has its own characteristic features resulting from the combination of its historical antecedents.[339]

After 1889 the Apostolate's intervention in public affairs became frequent—by means of leaflets, brochures, and abundant occasional literature.[340] It was always an intervention that demonstrated a true incompatibility of temperament between them and the democratic republic.

Nevertheless, as we have said, from December 5, 1889, when Demétrio Ribeiro arrived in Rio de Janeiro, to January 30, 1890, Positivism enjoyed an idyll with the republican regime. The new political life of the country was uncertain, and during this period the Comtists contributed to the reforms and transformations, some of them superficial, that are usually undertaken at such times. Their greatest contribution was the idea of a new national flag, the design being entrusted to Teixeira Mendes and Décio Vilares, the Positivist painter.[341]

Politically inexperienced, full of confidence in their faith, the Positivists were content with the minor contribution they were making to the republican government; they believed that this was on the path to fulfillment as a "dictatorial republic," the form envisaged by the Master in his *Politique,* and they regretted that this was not happening in other countries.

The results we have achieved in our country [wrote Miguel Lemos in May, 1890], make us feel all the more vividly the stagnation into which Positivism in France has for so long fallen. This state of affairs is as harmful for the great central nation as it is for the other Western countries which it serves as a guide. The more we develop here, the more we realize how much we depend on initiative from Paris. Unfortunately, despite the efforts of our fellow, Sr. Jorge Lagarrigue, Paris remains almost alien to the new faith developed in its midst, and the holy city knows only the Lafittist sophistications of Comte's doctrines. The Parisian proletariat, increasingly subjected to the influence of communist aberrations and anarchist hatreds, does not seem even to suspect that in Paris itself, in 1855, a French philosopher resolved all the great problems on which depend the integration of the working classes into modern society.[342]

One of the faults of those who have no doubts is the loss of a fine sense of perspective and proportion.

Submissive to the doctrines of the Master, convinced of the superiority of their position, solemnly pledged to consecrating all their devotion to the two related problems of the "advent of the new priesthood" and "the incorporation of the proletariat into modern society"[343] the Brazilian disciples of Auguste Comte continued doggedly to propagate their doctrines, their teaching, and their cult during the first years of the republic. The imposition of the new sacraments of the new religion, whose disciples had increased in number from fifty-nine in 1889 to one hundred fifty-nine in 1890, and intervention in matters related to the public cause were of equal concern. For our purposes, we are not interested, except so far as it is related to the problems of Positivism as a whole or to its implications, in a minute analysis of the cult. We shall only consider that aspect connected with the efforts of Comte's followers to establish a "new order" in the political and social life of the country. In this aspect the contrasts of the actions of Positivism interest us, as reflections of conditions at that time and also for the echoes that remained, not to mention their survival in our own time.

The last political intervention of the Positivist group, in 1889, came about because of Teixeira Mendes. It consisted of a series of deliberations meant to establish measures assuring basic guarantees for the workers. The result of these deliberations, dated December 25, 1889, was presented to the government in February, 1890.

After Demétrio Ribeiro's resignation from the Ministry, our reserve toward Benjamin Constant increased [wrote Teixeira Mendes], nevertheless, we sought him out in order to make representations on behalf of four hundred state factory workers. The aim of this representation was the establishment in these factories of a system permitting the integration into our society of the proletariat in the service of the republic. At the same time, it was felt that this example would soon have an effect on the private factories. Benjamin Constant received the delegation with sympathy; he left the Ministry of War, however, without having taken any steps in the required direction.[344]

Through Teixeira Mendes, the state factory workers had asked for measures to be taken which they felt were indispensable for the "regeneration of the Motherland." It was not solely a preoccupation with their own fortunes that prompted them, said Teixeira Mendes.

Their cause is the cause of the national proletariat, it is the cause of the whole of the proletariat throughout the West, it is the cause, even, of humanity itself. They demonstrate the justice of their claims by demanding for themselves exactly what they demand for all men in any part of the world which destiny has made them inhabit.[345]

The fate of the republic is linked to the fate of other nations, and at this moment the nations of America and Europe have their eyes fixed on us. Our example will inevitably influence them; therefore the trend of the social problem in our country will show the world the path it should tread for the definitive solution of this momentous problem on the face of the whole earth. On the other hand, the fate of the Brazilian republic depends on the elevation of the national character, the formation of true citizens. It would be useless to demonstrate to the founders of the republic in our country that almost everything still remains to be done in this sense. Only a little more than a year and a half ago, a great number of our fellow citizens groaned in slavery. Now the elevation of the Brazilian character consists essentially of the elevation of the proletariat, since it composes almost the whole nation; it constitutes the "people"; from it spring and to it revert almost all other social classes.[346]

It was therefore not possible to think of the "regeneration of the Motherland" without considering the miserable condition of the Brazilian working class, a condition in which workers the world over found themselves. Although suffering had taught them resignation, and "although they knew that death hovered at every moment above their heads, the Brazilian state factory workers still made some claims in consideration for future generations." "It is in the bosom of the proletarian family that is formed, and always will be formed, the mass of citizens—it is urgent, therefore, that the proletarian family should live in circumstances that permit the formation of true men." [347] It was necessary, then (and here the principal points of the Master's doctrine were set forth and applied), that women be freed from the work that enfeebled their bodies, coarsened their mind, and deprived them of the time needed to educate their children, comfort the old, and solace their husbands." [348] It was also necessary for the young to be given a suitable education, that is, an education that would form at one and the same time heart, mind, and character, since the

perfecting of man, even from the exclusively moral point of view, is more important than the improvement of industrial machinery; for, as the saying goes, there was never a good tool for a bad workman. The development of modern industry will increasingly demand a higher standard of education from the workman, to enable him to handle the machinery. On the other hand, since republican life demands that each citizen should spontaneously perform his duty, it imposes a higher degree of individual morality and education to carry out and recognize this duty.[349]

But how can this be achieved while the majority of the nation lives in misery and destitution? Teixeira Mendes writes:

The bourgeoisie, those who can already reap the benefits of humanity's evolution, reply to these just demands in a phrase whose immorality can be equaled only by the folly it characterizes: "Make money," they say, "work. All the comfort we enjoy is the result of our own will power and the efforts of our fathers." What deplorable mockery! Who has ever conceived of a society composed of the rich and the bourgeois? Whoever, in his right mind, did not see that it is in the natural order of society that there should always be rich and poor; the former in small, minute numbers, the latter making up the great majority, almost the total of the population? The problem therefore is not to enrich the poor; it is to dignify poverty, to remove from it the misery. Now the solution of this problem is possible, and it demands the moralization of both rich and poor, so that the former do not consume the superfluous at the expense of the latter's necessities and so that the poor claim only the necessary without casting envious eyes toward the superfluities of opulence! [350]

Comte's vague economic ideas are applied in this work: nothing need be altered in the traditional economy; generosity and moralization will accomplish all.

In this work, Teixeira Mendes further considers the meaning of the word "salary." It is

a subsidy liberally granted by society to each citizen so that he can maintain his family, the basis of all civic action. If this subsidy is given through the intermediacy of the rich they will indubitably be accomplishing a bounden duty, since the capital they possess, belonging in fact to society, must be applied for the benefit of that society. Modern civilization cannot retain, in relation to property, the principles that operated in the old society. The common good is the supreme law of nations, and all human institutions should be based on morality and reason.[351]

But if the duty of the rich is to provide salaries in consideration of their social and moral destiny, the poor, in their turn, must "limit their claims to what is required of them by their destiny. They must guarantee to carry out their duties, accepting for the regulation of work the rules resulting from an exact knowledge of human nature." [352] This manner of considering the problem, entirely based on the Master's economic ideas, led Teixeira Mendes to present a proposal for a law which, for that time and in view of local conditions, was truly revolutionary.[353]

Despite the supposed aptitude for moral problems of the nations of the Iberian branch and despite the influence exercised by the affectionate nature of the Negro on the Brazilian mentality (notions spread by the Positivists), it was easy to foresee that the proposal would not be accepted in a milieu so deeply marked by servile labor. These ideas, together with the Positivists' insistence on conducting the young republic toward the dictatorship envisaged by Auguste Comte, were doomed to failure.

"There was no lack of advice for the dictatorship that founded the republic in 1889," said Rui Barbosa in a speech to the Senate,

and insistence that it should prolong its existence for a number of years. There was even a proposal formulating this aspiration, favored by a radical school of philosophy. But the proposal was rejected without so much as a debate—the impulse of that revolutionary junta, general if not unanimous, being to renounce the responsibility that weighed so heavily upon it and to hand over to the nation the new regime. This dictatorship, composed of men who abhorred dictatorship, had come into being solely to fulfill the well-known and solemn mission of organizing a constitution, of substituting the republican form for the imperial. This mission was rapidly accomplished by Brazil with the formation, within fifteen months, of the federal union.[354]

Teixeira Mendes, in his work *A Incorporação do Proletariado na Sociedade Moderna* and in reply to Rui Barbosa's affirmations, attempts to explain the meaning attributed by the Positivists to the republican "dictatorship" in accordance with the Master's ideas. Republican dictatorship is not a "despotism" or an "absolute and arbitrary" form of government. In reply to Rui Barbosa's statement that the dictatorship which founded the republic abhorred dictatorship, Teixeira Mendes pointed out that Benjamin Constant not only did not abhor, but in fact admired dictatorship; and to prove this he invoked the fact that Constant used the *Positivist Calendar,* in which appear dictators such as Caesar, Trajan, Cromwell, Frederick.[355] He recognized, however, that Benjamin Constant

felt that Brazil was not yet ready for such an advanced form of government. The reasons contributing to this were: (1) the democratic prejudices of our ruling classes against the word "dictatorship" and in favor of maintaining the legislative assemblies and judicial bodies, guided by the metaphysical theory of the independence and supposed importance of the three powers: executive, legislative, and judiciary; (2) the didactic prejudices of Benjamin Constant himself, which prevented him from then accepting the suppression of public education, both secondary and higher, that is one of the characteristics of such a dictatorship.[356]

Modern nations, once the democratic and aristocratic fictions have been removed and the reality revealed, are all under dictatorial regimes, since a dictatorship is the political form of government resulting exclusively from the political supremacy of material power, the form which does not recognize the supremacy of an independent spiritual authority. In a theocracy the political supremacy was constituted by the dominance of intellectual authority.

It is this theocratic government, degraded by its disregard for social and moral duties, that the majority of Western intellectuals hopes to achieve for its own benefit after the Catholic priests have been disposed of, and which our Master characterized by the epithet "pedantocracy," a word invented by John Stuart Mill . . . Therefore, whether material power is concentrated, both actually and legally, in one man, as in a king, and termed absolute or is distributed among one or more assemblies, as in the so-called representative monarchies and republics, the true nature of the political regime remains unchanged; it is a dictatorship.[357]

Dictatorship does not depend on anybody's will; on the contrary, it results from a historical situation. Thus, the

temporal leaders, who are pure representatives of material power (the only power that continued to exist after the disintegration of universal faith toward the close of the Middle Ages) must, whether they like it or not, follow their wishes, inevitably based on one of the infinite number of factors into which contemporary public opinion has been divided. In these circumstances, means of convincing and persuading disappear in an increasing number of instances, and the only thing left to impose the orders of the government is the material power of the army or of money. In other words, the government inevitably becomes a dictatorship.[358]

For this reason, according to the Positivists, the government should be simply technical, not political.

The prerogative of making decisions on matters of opinion, and consequently on the beliefs of citizens, should be taken away from the temporal power; all possibilities of violence should be withheld from the government, in this way reduced to its basic function, which is the promotion of any general works of public utility not carried out spontaneously by private enterprise; the police force should be used only to prevent disorders of a material nature.[359]

In this way "supreme liberalism" would be the republican dictatorship envisaged by the Positivists.

This opinion was not shared by the republican politicians who had come through the struggles of the Empire. Many of them did not conceive of a republican dictatorship in Positivist terms—Rui Barbosa, for instance, whose power in the provisional government soon made itself felt. Most republican politicians were still inspired by eighteenth-century English and French rationalist ideas—the ideas that had formed the liberals of the classic nineteenth-century type, of whom Rui was an example. Positivist ideas did not exercise the influence the Comtists had hoped for on the course of politics during the early stages of the republic. On the contrary, they quickly declined, to be revived during the framing of the Constitution in 1891. But even then it was classical liberalism that prevailed. In spite of this, in spite of the "democratic prejudices" resulting from liberal ideas, Miguel Lemos and Teixeira Mendes published, in January, 1890, a work entitled *Bases de Uma Constituição Politica Ditatorial Federativa para a República brasileira* (*Basis for a Dictatorial Federative Political Constitution for the Brazilian Republic*). In the preface to this work, the apostles enthusiastically claimed that the Positivist movement had already caused great changes, at least among the republicans of Rio Grande do Sul and Pernambuco, the provinces in which the republican spirit was liveliest.[360] It is true that the Positivist influence was stronger in Rio Grande do Sul than in any other state. In a burst of enthusiasm—and we have already seen that the Positivist apostles were easy victims of these transports—they claimed that

Positivism today, after the proclamation of the republic, is a social and political force to be reckoned with in the conflicts that will inevitably arise when the different political schools begin to compete for the control of the government and of opinion. We need hardly say that we are convinced, not only that this influence will grow daily, as we can already see, but that it is finally destined to prevail. (!) . . . There can be no effective resistance against timely doctrines; neither material power, nor the sophistry employed by outworn creeds, can hold back, still less can they stop, the inevitable rise of new spirituality demanded by a combination of human needs. It is obvious, then, that the two most important factions of the Brazilian Republican party will very soon be dictatorial and democratic.[361]

The project for a dictatorship presented by the two apostles, although curious, does not hold sufficient interest to warrant consideration for the purposes of our study. The Positivists encountered, at the time, a strong federalist current in public opinion, represented by Rui Barbosa and Campos Sales. They conveniently preached "confederation," an idea in accord with the notion of small republics envisaged by the Master. The Apostolate was of the opinion that the new dictatorial organization of Brazil should unite "the systematically confederated Brazilian occidental states deriving from the fusion of the European, African, and native American elements" with "the empirically confederated Brazilian American states composed of the fetishistic hordes sparsely populating the territories of the republic," [362] with provision for the formation of new states, under certain conditions.

In the liberal atmosphere inherited from the Empire, the Positivists did not exercise the strong influence they had hoped for. They were unable to implant the dictatorial republic they had dreamed of and preached, despite their allies in the Army. "Positivism," wrote José Veríssimo, "accepted principally by military men, where it found its strongest support, increased its hold on this class, by nature prone to exaggerate the need for order and authority and lacking confidence in liberty and the liberal achievements characteristic of democracy." [363] But, as might have been foreseen, Positivist ideology did not succeed in altering the liberal temper of the time. From the outset, to the majority of politicians, including members of the military class, such as Deodoro, Positivist ideas seemed contrary to the national tradition. Nevertheless, although the Positivists did not manage to achieve the republic advocated by the

Master, they managed to have some of their points of view adopted when the Constitution was being drawn up. Although in a minority, they were organized, disciplined, knew what they wanted, and so managed to make themselves felt.[364] Having the support of certain officers (not that of the Army as a whole), they also attracted the interest of many of those who, as so often, take advantage of times of uncertainty to turn things to their own profit; and so it was that disciples of Comte sprouted rapidly in our midst, for, as José Veríssimo remarks, "at that time, to be a Positivist was a good recommendation." [365]

After 1890, however, Positivist influence declined. Nevertheless, it still made itself felt, in a diffuse manner, in the lengthy period of development of the first stage of the republic.

"Abandoning the hope of having the dictatorial organization elaborated by our Master immediately adopted," wrote Miguel Lemos in his *Tenth Circular,* published in April, 1891, "because it clashed with the democratic prejudices of most political leaders, we concentrated our efforts on the attempt to make the Constituent Assembly approve all clauses which, in our opinion, would help to establish in our country a regime of completely unfettered freedom." [366] Shortly after proclamation of the republic, the Positivists had proposed in their *Indicações Urgentes* a series of measures that, had they been adopted, would have made of our country the first Comtian dictatorial republic. In this work, Comte's disciples had already asked the government to set up a commission to draft a constitution, which was done on December 3, 1890. The members of the commission were: Saldanha Marinho (president), Américo Brasiliense (vice president), Antônio Luís dos Santos Werneck, Francisco Rangel Pestana, and José Antônio Pedreira de Magalhães Castro.[367] The Positivists had also suggested that once the Constitution had been framed, it should be "submitted to public scrutiny for an adequate length of time (and) promulgated by the government without resorting to the dangerous recourse of a Constituent Assembly." [368] In lectures given in the "physics amphitheater" of the Polytechnic School and later in the National Institute of Music, Teixeira Mendes had already expounded the "political program" of the national Positivists, and Miguel Lemos, in newspaper articles, had considered the question of a "constitution without a constituent assembly," which was then being widely discussed in republican circles, both in Rio de Janeiro and São Paulo. The *Correio Paulistano* of March 22, 1890, also contained a reference to what the Positivists considered the "dangerous recourse" of a constituent assembly. The republican contributors to the *Correio Paulistano* argued that the "procedure in framing the basic laws through a constituent assembly was too lengthy"[369] and that the framing of the Constitution should be speeded up by means of a plebiscite.

Time is of the essence in the life of nations [added the writer]; to fritter it away in fruitless deliberations of a doctrinal nature or in discussions that shake the confidence of the public, is to create a stumbling block for the progress of our country. Although the method of decreeing the Constitution by charter is not free of faults, we should accept it as the speediest, most adequate, and most suited to the principles of the democratic school.[370]

Comte's disciples in Brazil did not have the sympathies of Deodoro, who referred to them in the manifesto setting out the reasons for the *coup d'état* of November 3, 1891, as "an obscure philosophical sect."[371] Having lost, with the resignation of Demétrio Ribeiro, their chief government support, the Positivists made every effort to participate in the first republican constitutional project. Thus, in the "representations" they made to the National Congress in December, 1890, through Demétrio Ribeiro, the Positivist Apostolate of Brazil proposed modifications that "according to the teachings of Comte it considers indispensable to the Constitution proposed by the republican dictatorship," to make it "correspond sufficiently to the present needs of the Brazilian people,"[372] since the system proposed in the constitutional project presented by the government was not in accord with the needs of our situation "determined by scientific politics." Contaminated by democratic prejudice, the republicans had confined themselves to transplanting the characteristic elements of the North American Constitution to Brazil, a constitution which had evolved out of different moments of history and which was the expression of other conditions. These conditions were not present in Brazil at the end of the nineteenth century, at the moment when a new basic code for the country was under consideration. "If the backwardness of the masses is still considerable," said the Positivist leader—and it is worth stressing that this observation was made—"if the mental state of the masses is still what might be described as a Catholic fetishism,"[373] among "the active classes, we find every shade of intellectual emancipation. Among the older generation, the vague deism of Voltaire and Rousseau is still predominant; among the younger, we find a preponderance of materialism and Positivism, these being nevertheless quite different systems." [374] "Science has invaded everything and now dominates the world, society, and man. It is only natural, therefore, that this progress should be taken into account, and that the methods of the nineteenth century should not be those of the eighteenth." Today, "a politician abreast of the times has as little need to invoke God in order to vindicate a civic code of conduct as has an engineer in order to justify his plans or a doctor in order to support his diagnosis or his clinical intervention." [375] For Miguel Lemos and Teixeira Mendes, therefore, it was inadmissible to

want to establish officially in Brazil a so-called Christian spirit analogous to that of the United States. The separation of Church and state was a measure indispensable for the establishment of order and the assurance of progress. This separation would, in fact, facilitate the advent of a scientific doctrine and a scientific priesthood that would put an end to the modern revolution; but only complete spiritual freedom would safeguard society from the degradation of theoretical power, forcing it to rise to a level at which it would meet the moral, intellectual, and practical needs of humanity. [376]

In view of this, they continued,

we will not try to offer you, as a substitute for the Constitution proposed by the republican dictatorship, the project we have formulated according to the principles of Auguste Comte, which we here append. Accepting the basic proposed structure of the proposed Constitution as an inevitable consequence of the present moment, we will merely try to indicate the points which it would be impossible to retain without dire consequences for the vital interests of Brazilian society, if not for the world at large. [377]

Since it was not possible to adopt the standards of orthodox organization, they insisted that at least complete spiritual freedom should be allowed, "so that any doctrine destined to put an end to the anarchy of modern times will be given an opportunity to spread among us." [378] Similarly, complete industrial freedom should be allowed in order to reveal the urgent need for a universal scientific doctrine capable of regulating the relationship between the employers and the proletariat. [379] Further, the "dignity of local autonomy" should be respected in order to ensure the union of American nations of Portuguese origin until it becomes possible to transform the political tie into a religious one, at the same time preparing each state of the Brazilian federation for a completely independent existence in the future. Finally, we hope that our progress will have its effect on Paris, on whose regeneration depends the regeneration of the world.[380]

As we can see, the Positivists were prepared to allow complete freedom because they were convinced that, as a result of this freedom, the "new universal science and the politics of fraternity" would finally triumph, as the Master had predicted.

Besides the general considerations set out above, wherein numerous concessions are apparently made, the Positivists also supported federalist ideas, ascribing to them, however, what may be regarded as "religious" meanings. Believing that the "universal scientific faith" would shortly replace the disintegrating Catholic religion and still affirming their Master's ideas (that the population of a truly free nation should not exceed three million inhabitants), the Positivists wanted the form of the proposed Constitution presented to Congress, which provided for the perpetual and indissoluble union of the Brazilian states, to be replaced by a form permitting true freedom for the various provinces of the former Empire, with no binding obligations imposed. In this way the new states of the Brazilian republic would not be tied down to any obligations. This explains the odd phrase "Brazilian (or American) nations" so often used by the Brazilian Comtists. We must bear in mind, however, that the Positivists frequently affirmed that the federal regime should allow the widest possible local freedom, while insuring the fraternal alliance of the former provinces—an alliance which "results from the past evolution and our present interests and feelings." [381] For them, "political formulae should always, as the Master had shown, preclude any binding obligations which were daily shown to be socially and morally insufficient to assure order and progress." [382]

Since they favored completely unrestricted freedom, the Positivists were naturally opposed to any privileges and monopolies that would encroach upon it. As might be expected, they began to agitate for the revocation of Decree No. 165, promulgated on January 17, 1880, a decree providing for the organization of banks of issue, allowing them "the most scandalous privileges and monopolies." [383] The uproar caused by this decree,[384] framed by Rui Barbosa, is well known, and the crisis it occasioned in the provisional government led to the resignation of Demétrio Ribeiro from the first republican ministry.[385] Besides pointing out the disastrous effects that would follow the enormous issue of paper money provided for by the decree, they claimed in their work on the subject, *A Política Positiva e a Liberdade Bancária* (*Positive Politics and the Freedom of Banking*), that it was offensive to republican politics.[386] The Positivists, like most of the bourgeois citizens who had participated in politics during the Empire, were cautious men and could not give their approval to the series of audacious and risky blows that the imagination of Rui Barbosa aimed at the dragging economy of the country, still set in the narrow molds of the past. Following the ideas of their Master and prompted by their growing antipathy for Rui, the Positivists did not spare their criticism of the provisional government's Ministry of Finance. We know that Positivism, although opposed to anarchistic individualism, attempted to replace the faulty social science of the economists of the past with a new science based on systematic "connections"—the science of sociology—and to make of it the culmination of all human knowledge and the basis for social reorganization. But Comte and his faithful Brazilian disciples had found only one solution of this social reorganization: intellectual and moral regeneration. In fact, from his first writings Comte had claimed that his wish was to regenerate society and that the real reason for his disagreement with Saint-Simon was the latter's feeling that the reform of human society should begin with the material reorganization of that society. For Comte, as he said in a letter to Pierre Lafitte in 1849, all experiments undertaken by "phalansteries, mutual savings funds, nationalized factories, and all the measures that, in the minds of their authors, would provide an immediate and definitive solution of the social problem [were] premature attempts, which should have been preceded by a spiritual reform, because any efforts in those directions were but simple economic palliatives." [387] Thus, for the Positivists, the social question could not be resolved by political means, but only by intellectual and moral means. The "grave prejudice" that had given rise to the belief that "industrial" regulation could be obtained by political means—a prejudice that, "because it constitutes the basis of communist utopias, is a danger to society" [388]—should be replaced by the conviction that "only regeneration of opinion and custom can remedy the defects of the present industrial organization." [389] Comte's armchair vision of the practical problems of humanity, faithfully followed by his Brazilian disciples, led them, the last survivors of Romanticism, to a paradoxical "positive" conception wherein problems lost "reality" to gain in "abstraction." The vague concept of "regeneration," in Comte's system, is somewhat similar to "salvation" or the "remission of sins" in the theological tradition that the Positivists so strongly rejected.

Having accepted the fact that the dictatorial republican form they had advised would not be adopted, the Positivists, determined to ensure a regime of completely unrestricted freedom and suggested a number of amendments to the proposed Constitution framed by the commission nominated by the provisional government, which are both characteristic and indicative of their attitude toward national problems.

The Positivists objected to Article 26 of the proposed Constitution, which declared that all regular and secular members of religious orders, such as archbishops, bishops, vicars, parish priests,[390] were ineligible for public office, on the grounds that the prohibition should be extended "to all theorists," philosophers, scientists, artists, doctors —all who followed what they termed "theoretical professions" (?) "so that the Congress should be composed wholly of industrialists." [391] They argued that the law should not have the "odious characteristic" of permitting to "theologists" what it forbade to the "metaphysicians" and "scientists," saying: "The clause under consideration, which is purely a Swiss imitation, is based on a grave political error, fostering the illusion that Catholicism enjoys social prestige among us." [392] They added:

We must leave the Catholic priesthood, like all the others that sprang from it, in a position that makes it quite evident to the public that theology is politically, socially, and morally exhausted. Only thus can we hope to impress upon the masses the need to terminate the modern revolution through the free advent of a universal scientific doctrine and an equally scientific priesthood.[393]

In Article 33, dealing with the declaration of war, the Positivists pleaded for the following amendment, which does them great credit: "that no war may take place, except in the event of immediate aggression, unless arbitration has first been resorted to." [394] They considered that paragraph 24 of the Article referred to, establishing as the exclusive prerogative of the National Congress the codification of civil and criminal law and the law of procedure, should be reframed to take into account the different usages and customs of the various federal states.

The attempt to impose uniform legislation can only lead to one of the following two contingencies: either the stronger states will impose their backward or anarchistic opinions and customs on the weaker ones, even if the latter are more developed, in this way preventing them from exercising their moral and intellectual influence; or the stronger states will impose by violence the progress they have achieved, instead of trying to influence the weaker states morally and intellectually. We have already witnessed an example of this in the disastrous, absurd, and illusory law of naturalization, today completely torn to pieces, that was imposed on Brazil because the State of São Paulo so desired it. For the same reason, we are threatened by the prospect of having divorce set up as a law when one of the stronger states, more affected by Protestant immigration, decides that such a measure is necessary to material progress. Adequate freedom would result in confinement of such aberrations to the states concerned. The consequences of either of the two hypotheses outlined above would be to foster feelings of complete autonomy and of rivalry that would lead to the eventual severing of the federal ties. Thus, the empirical preoccupation with the preservation of Brazilian unity, by violating the natural laws of human organization, would only lead to disruption of that unity. It would be like losing one's life in order to save it.[395]

The Positivists also recommended that paragraph 34, which gave Congress the right to legislate on public education, should be simply deleted. "A civil government," wrote Miguel Lemos and Teixeira Mendes,

has none of the indispensable requisites for framing legislation on higher education. A congress is not composed of philosophers; it cannot reach decisions on matters of science. For the time being, the government should suppress all public education, whether secondary or higher, leaving it to private enterprise. We must wait until some doctrine springs from the core of the mental anarchy into which modern society is plunged, proving its efficacy for the active bulk of the nation. Only then can the government afford to undertake the inevitable expense of providing free public teaching of such a scientific doctrine, which will never, for all that, entitle those who have mastered it to the least privilege.[396]

Article 34, clause 1, was framed as follows: "It shall, moreover be the business of the Congress, but not exclusively (1) to encourage the development of public education, industry, and immigration . . ."[397] The Positivists suggested the deletion of the word "immigration," since they felt that this too should be left to private enterprise. The same applied to clause 2 of Article 34 (the creation of institutions for secondary and higher education in the different states), which they felt should be omitted for the same reasons as those given for clause 1.

The government project denied the vote to beggars, the illiterate, and common soldiers. "These exclusions," according to the two Positivist leaders, were "not only odious but false, since beggars were not the only 'dependent' citizens, nor were the illiterates the only citizens unable to exercise that political discernment presupposed by suffrage. It is even conceivable," they added, with a touch of malice, "that there is many a beggar and illiterate with higher moral and social criteria than certain capitalists and literates." [398] Article 72, paragraph 2 of the draft Constitution stated: "The republic does not acknowledge privileges of birth, nor recognize ennobled rank, and does not create titles of nobility or bestow decorations." [399] The Positivists subjoined to this clause: "The republic likewise does not acknowledge philosophical, scientific, artistic, medical, or technical privilege, the exercise of all professions being free in Brazil, regardless of scholastic or academic title of any description whatsoever" [400] —principles accepted by the State of Rio Grande do Sul in its Constitution of July 14, 1891, and promulgated in "the name of the family, the nation, and humanity." [401] In line with their aim of ensuring the "unfettered freedom," the Positivists further objected to clause 8 of Article 72 of the draft and managed to have it deleted. The clause read: "The Society of Jesus will continue to be proscribed from the country, and the founding of new convents or monastic orders will continue to be prohibited." [402] "It is inadmissible," wrote Miguel Lemos and Teixeira Mendes,

that old grudges and fears born of the conditions of the Occident at the close of the eighteenth century should be allowed to linger on at the end of the nineteenth. The Brazilian republic cannot establish a regime less free in spiritual matters than that gloriously instituted and maintained by a great king (Frederick II of Prussia) a century ago. If the social offices of Catholicism had not already been exhausted among the Portuguese race, it would have been impossible for the Marquis of Pombal to deal the blow which immortalized him. But, at the time of his movement, royal power was still effective, and it was indispensable to deprive it of all its retrograde supports, the chief of which was the Society of Jesus. But things are different now. We live in a time of freedom. The emancipation of the active mass of Brazilians, the current popular trends, provide enough proof that such oppressive measures against the last representatives of the religion of our forefathers constitute an unjustifiable act of ingratitude, besides being a grave political error. Instead of enlightening the people about the position of religion in modern society, such behavior can only lead to a belief in phantoms. Catholicism as a social force is as dead in the national soul as the monarchy, and if it has not yet followed the latter into oblivion it is only because the scientific priesthood has not yet come to power as heir to the glorious legacy of Hildebrand, Saint Bernard, Bossuet, and even of Saint Ignatius Loyola.[403]

During the Constituent period, the Positivists were the perfect defenders of the freedom of the Catholic Church, as César Zama affirmed in a speech to Congress on January 29, 1891.[404] By that time, however, the influence of Positivism was already on the wane. Not even Benjamin Constant hearkened to the appeals of the Apostolate. As we know, in April, 1890, the provisional government created the Ministry of Public Education, and Benjamin Constant, who had hitherto held the Ministry of War, was appointed Minister of Education. While still at the Ministry of War, Benjamin Constant had set about reform of military education, introducing into its syllabus biology, sociology, and the science of morals in order to round off the scientific training of the future officers.

Led astray by this Positivist mirage [contended Miguel Lemos], which resulted from imperfect assimilation of our doctrines, Benjamin Constant failed to realize the inconsistency of his attempt to establish official Positivist teaching before arrival of the favorable opportunity determined by Auguste Comte and did not allow for the fact that no competent teachers were available for such a measure—a condition of such importance that our Master had decreed that no Positive schools should be founded until there were philosophers capable of undertaking the teaching of an encyclopedic program.[405]

Benjamin Constant's reform was a grave mistake in the eyes of the Positivists; more, it was "a mistake that revealed a tendency in direct opposition to a true republican program." [406] In this, they were partly right.

Teixeira Mendes lost no time in publishing a criticism of Benjamin Constant's reforms of military education—*A Política Positiva e o Regulamento das Escolas do Exército* (*Positive Politics and the Military School Regulations*), April, 1890. Benjamin Constant's reform, aimed to "galvanize militarism through its relationship to science," [407] was not only a grave error in itself, it was opposed to true republican policies as understood by the Positivists. Thus, the Apostolate, ever faithful to its Master's doctrines, was not in favor of the reform. Some writers claim that Positivism "horribly corrupted teaching in our military schools, distorting their essential character as centers of military education and intellectual and moral preparation for war." [408] However, Positivism was not responsible for this distortion, which originated neither in the republic, nor from the supposed Positivist influence. If our Military School was, for some time, a simple engineering school where "those with a vocation for mathematics quickly lost any bellicose spirit they might have had," [409] the true causes of this much-discussed "civilianization of our military class, and particularly of the Army, went much deeper, some of these having already been indicated in this work. Positivism, ever opposed to privilege and titles, was not the inventor of the crop of "scholar-majors" and "scholar-colonels" so sharply criticized by Lima Barreto. Even Eduardo Prado, who has little sympathy for the republic and still less for Positivism, recognizes that "the monarchy made a great mistake in allowing military education to retain its exclusively theoretical character. King Pedro II, who was so preoccupied with science, did nothing but 'scholarize' the Army officers who now (1890) naturally display such a bent for politics, debates, and manifestations." [410] It was not the Positivists who corrupted the bellicosity of the young officers of the late nineteenth century. It was the monarchy itself, today regarded by so many as purely beneficent, and Benjamin Constant was the perfect product of that "scientism" so beloved of the Emperor.

The position of orthodox Comtism in relation to the reform of military education could not, of course, have been other than that dictated by the Master. From the first page of his *Regulamento das Escolas do Exército*, Teixeira Mendes stresses the repugnance of the Apostolate for "an educational program that violates the most vital interests not only of the nation, but of humanity." [411] We do not say that the Positivists desired suppression of the Army, as their Master had recommended; or, more exactly, its transformation into a *gendarmerie*, although even Benjamin Constant shared this notion. In reply to a manifest presented to the founder of the republic by the pupils of the Military School, he said that

he would not be able to witness what was in store for youth . . . that for him the fraternity of America was a true dream . . . the laying down of arms so that future generations, seeing them in museums, could feel all the horror of that long period of barbarism that had lasted from the origins of humanity, transmuting the elements of progress into the elements of destruction.[412]

But "falling into the dangerous aberration from which the citizen Minister of War would have been saved had he but possessed sufficient knowledge of Positivism," [413] Benjamin Constant added

that he wished to see the Army fully respected and respectful, as a guarantor of security and the maintenance of order and public peace, working in a manner worthy of it for the aggrandizement of the nation, honoring public authority so long as it carried out the law, and, if need be, taking action in the public square if the abuses of the government led to disrespect for the law to the point of conspiring against the rights and the honor of the Army incompatible with the dignity of a patriotic class which loves the Motherland in the highest degree.[414]

This was not the lesson of Auguste Comte. In his *Système de Politique Positive*, Comte counseled reduction of the armed forces to the status of a veritable police force (which could, in the event of external aggression, form the nucleus of a patriotic army), and preached the suppression of military schools.[415] For the Positivists, then, Benjamin Constant's reforms were "a violation of the policy counseled by our Master." [416] "At any rate," they declared, "if the Army must be retained, for the moment, with its present organization, the duty of the republican dictatorship is solely to prepare it *to fulfill its purpose. A* soldier is not naturally destined to become an administrator, professor, engineer, scholar, and so on." [417] As we can see, for the Positivists, if the measures counseled by their Master and believed by them to be timely, were not to be integrally adopted, the only solution was to preserve the status quo, or, as the italics used by Teixeira Mendes indicate, to continue to prepare the armed forces for the traditional duties of their station. But what had happened, according to Teixeira Mendes, was that "military education had become nothing but a pretext for organizing a new pedantocratic class, turning Army officers into leaders of civilian society, which had long since been irrevocably industrialized as the result of our historical evolution." [418] The Positivists were, therefore, far from approving the "civilianization" of the Army.

To give the finishing touch, making it abundantly clear that the aim is simply to put into uniform a contingent of pedantocrats [added Teixeira Mendes], the reform confers the title of "bachelor of science" on those who pass the course with full marks and the title of "surveyor" to those who scrape through. . . . It would appear that our military citizens, tired of the rule of the frock-coated bachelors, elected to replace it with the prepotency of bachelors in uniform.[419]

To the Positivists, the "regulation" reforming military education signified yet another stage in the development of

the system by which the bourgeoisie seeks to perpetuate its domination over us. Since the coup of November 15 handed over to the military men of letters the political influence formerly exercised by the civilian bachelors and doctors of the Empire, the military men are now making great efforts to attract the bourgeois ambitions hitherto directed toward the juridical, medical, and technical professions, in order to keep their new-found supremacy. This is the hidden motive for the favoring of academic institutions which, under military titles, profess to prepare their pupils for military careers, in a century and in a continent which abhors war and desires peace.[420]

The Positivists, jealous guardians and defenders of spiritual freedom, continued to "intervene" every time they sensed a threat to this freedom. The Minister of Justice, Campos Sales, was inundated, especially during the period of the provisional government, with protests from the Apostolate, always accompanied by the inevitable explanatory leaflets.[421]

On October 12, 1890, Comte's disciples laid the foundation stone of the Positivist Chapel of Rio de Janeiro. Summarizing the Apostolate's activities up to then, Miguel Lemos emphasized that its aim was "to reform the ideas and customs of a skeptical and materialistic society." A new faith would lead Brazil to the achievement of that great Western world of which Auguste Comte dreamed. The foundations of a new life for our country were being laid in that church.

The following year, 1891, found the Brazilian Positivists, by now numbering one hundred seventy-four members, confident of the possibility of a truly republican, or dictatorial, revolution in France. And France was, as the Master had said, the Occident. "Boulangism," which had come to an end with the suicide of the general who had given the movement its name, still held out to them the hope of the advent of the dreamed-of dictatorial republic in the "central nation." Positivism must ultimately triumph.

Only the adoption, without delay, of the dictatorial policy counseled by Auguste Comte as early as 1847, could forestall the terrible social struggles in store, only the timely rise of Positivism, facilitated by this policy, would have strength to prevent them in a decisive manner. Unfortunately, on the one hand the blindness of statesmen is so extreme, on the other the egoism of the bourgeoisie so invincible, that it is to be feared that the regenerating doctrine will not spread soon enough to forestall the proletarian revolution, and the only task left for it to perform will be to clear away the ruins and rebuild the social structure after the terrible conflict. This is the awful prospect before us that we foresee, undeceived by vain illusions, for we cannot take seriously the puerile attempt at socialist intervention that the dying Catholic Church is trying to bring to a happy conclusion. The sight of this futility and impotence merely adds to these painful forebodings.[422]

Thus, although they were convinced that "terrible conflict" menaced society, the Positivists believed they would be able to rebuild the edifice of society after that conflict.[423] The regenerative doctrine of their Master, the new faith of which they were the apostles, would find after the disruption its opportunity for the "scientific" reconstruction of a new world—the fruit of the religious and scientific thought of the man who, for them, was the greatest genius of mankind.

Ever on the *qui vive* for any infringement of the republican principles designed to ensure "true spiritual freedom," the Positivists protested against retention of the embassy at the Vatican,[424] against proclamation of state constitutions in the name of "God Almighty," against the presence of crucifixes in jury rooms—all of which they considered violations of the fundamental law and spirit of the republic.[425] They also posed as defenders of freedom at the time of the *coup d'état* of November 3, 1890. Lacking all sympathy with Deodoro, they recorded their "emphatic disapproval of this ill-considered and criminal act, the fruit of egotistical and foolish counsels." [426] Warned of the "disastrous plan" by Naval Lieutenant Tancredo Jauffret, at that time working with Justo Chermont in the Ministry of External Affairs, they hastily drew up, on the night of November 3, an appeal to the President of the Republic,[427] in an attempt to dissuade him from his condemnable project, pointing out the lamentable consequences such an act would bring upon the country. Miguel Lemos relates that the appeal was sent to the *Jornal do Comércio* to be published in the next day's issue, but arrived too late for inclusion.[428]

"The egotistical and retrograde causes of the *coup d'état* were obvious. It was enough to read the President's Manifesto to realize that their illegal action offered no recompense, and that, on the contrary, it would lead our country to the horror of civil war and the shame of despotism." The passage in the document containing a hostile allusion to Positivism[429] was "sufficient to illustrate the true intentions of the authors of that criminal adventure." [430] Explaining the apparently inconsistent position they had taken in condemning an action they had earlier desired, since they themselves had proposed that Deodoro institute a republican dictatorship, Miguel Lemos wrote:

For us, of course, the real gravity of this violent action resided in its egotistical and retrograde nature. The reason for our disapproval was no Pharisaic concern for legality, nor any zealous concern for the metaphysical prerogatives of the national Congress. The principal question for us was the suppression of freedom, without the excuse of any real public interest to legitimize so extreme a measure, since the alleged monarchist conspiracy with which the Chief of State attempted to justify his action was nothing but a gross imposture.[431]

Unconcerned, therefore, with the "metaphysical prerogatives" of Congress which had, as the Positivists said with a touch of irony, protested "in secret" by means of a "mediocre" manifesto, they published, at the end of our first republican crisis which had lasted twenty days, a new manifesto which sheds an interesting light on the Positivist position in national politics.

"In order to arrive at a sure and clear appraisal of the events of November 3," wrote Miguel Lemos and Teixeira Mendes in *A Última Crise*, published on November 24, 1890,

it is essential to have a scientific understanding of politics. It is not enough to know that the leader of the executive power violated legality to condemn his conduct, for the violation of legality has often proved of great benefit and has been rewarded by the approval of posterity. This means that the infringement of legal order only becomes criminal when it violates the conditions for "order and progress" in a society. In the present situation, therefore, it must be proved that for maintenance of order and the assurance of progress in the Brazilian nations the federal Constitution should have been respected at this junction.[432]

Those outside Positivism,

imbued with more or less extravagant notions [they continued], want to establish an eternal form of government; but scientific politics, established after the creation of sociology, demonstrates that it is not possible in our time to establish any but a provisional form of government destined to permit the peaceful advent of the definitive regime. This regime, the aim of the age-old efforts of humanity, consists in the establishment of scientific-industrial republics; in other words, nations completely free of theology and militarism. In these republics, faith will be the science, not supported by privilege but by its own prestige; industry will not be in the hands of monopolies; universal brotherhood will permit armies and navies to be dispensed with, so that all the militia of the world will be reduced to police rank.[433]

For the Positivists there was not the faintest air of fantasy in any of this.

Deodoro had attacked "material order," he had created obstacles to "progress." From the struggles that ensued in the Constituent Assembly between the retrogrades, the revolutionaries, and the Positivists, a Constitution was framed which, although imperfect, sufficed to guarantee order and permitted the assurance of progress. Spiritual freedom had been achieved, and the duty imposed on all citizens was to respect the Constitution, since its defects could be remedied by complementary measures.[434] In short, while they did not share the "metaphysical prejudices" of the democrats, the Positivists felt that the Constitution created no obstacle of any significance to the possible and much-desired "regeneration of humanity" for which they were fighting, and this was, in their opinion, the greatest merit of the 1891 Statute.[435] The violation of its provisions, therefore, was "purely the manifestation of a power unable to adduce in its own favor any altruistic motive." [436] All "patriotic hearts" would be moved to protest against an act that, by violating the Constitution, would give rise to a veritable material disorder, a proliferation of hatred, and many other threats to both public and private order.

Once the crisis had been overcome, following the resignation of Deodoro, the Positivists drew the "conclusions" demanded by their doctrine from the events of November 3.

Recent events in Brazil [they said], constitute a simple, albeit grave, incident in the struggle that agitates all Latin nations and for which Auguste Comte had provided, as early as 1847, the only solution. It consists, as we indicated at the outset of this work, in the organization of what he called the "republican dictatorship." [437]

In view of this lesson,

we do not hesitate to call once more the attention of all true patriots to the political solutions proposed and counseled by our Master. We are certain that our republican statesmen, backed by the active masses of the nation and inspired by altruistic motives (since, failing these, the best doctrines are worthless in their application) will manage to avoid a repetition of this crisis, if they learn the lessons of the Master, and so save our country from anarchy and despotism.[438]

For the Positivists, as Richard Congreve was to say of the Brazilian events of November, 1890, "Liberty is the indispensable condition inherent in the Positivist concept of dictatorship . . . since one should not lose sight of the distinction between a reactionary dictatorship and a progressive one." [439]

Despite their active intervention in national politics, which produced doubtful results, the Positivists did not cease to devote their energies to the essential aspect of their doctrine: their religious organization. Thus, on May 3, 1892, Miguel Lemos for the first time wore the "vestments" he had designed for the solemnity of the occasion. He was officiating at a marriage.[440]

The religious aspect was by this time in the ascendant. It had always been of great importance to the "Apostolate," but, after the inauguration of the chapel and the growing number of conversions, its importance grew apace. On Sundays, the "catechism" was preached and commented on by Teixeira Mendes, and the "sacraments" were administered by Miguel Lemos. Later he himself suspended them until he should reach his forty-second year, the age he considered the beginning of full maturity. Since 1891 Teixeira Mendes had become Miguel Lemos's acolyte in the Apostolate, having to this end abandoned his apprenticeship in watchmaking, a trade which he had hoped would make him self-supporting. This recruitment of Teixeira Mendes to the "priestly" life strengthened the Apostolate because his scientific culture, recognized by all with whom he came into contact, his modesty, and his obvious apostolic vocation made him ideally suited to share the leadership of orthodox national Comtism.

The personalities of these two apostles are curious, their brotherly mutual friendship being another example of their noble spirit of abnegation and altruism. But although they had much in common, the temperaments of these two friends were different. It is in their writings that we find the most marked traces of these differences: in the writings of Miguel Lemos we feel the anguished and violent passion of a combative temperament; in those of Raimundo Teixeira Mendes the serenity of the profoundly religious soul.

"We continue to insist," wrote the latter in 1903, "on the need to transform political preoccupations into religious ones, amid principally and directly, but not exclusively, at the conversion of the female sex." [441] Later, in 1908, he continued to assert that "the first step in the regeneration of society is the recognition of the need for the coming of a true universal religion, after the failure of the theological syntheses which pave the way for its advent." [442] Among these "theological syntheses" the Positivists always showed an especial preference for Catholicism[443] (the Master himself had furnished the example), as marked as was their dislike for Protestantism. Nevertheless, contrary to the expectations of the Count of Montesquieu and to what he counseled as a good policy for France, there was never an understanding between the Catholic clergy and the Brazilian Positivists. Thus, however great their care and attentions to the Church, one can detect a critical and reticent attitude. "The Catholic clergy of our country," wrote Miguel Lemos,

does not see in Positivism either a worthy rival or a simple competitor, like Protestantism. They look on us as a usurping rival, growing in strength and influence among those destined to predominate in a more or less near future, and feel for us only those sentiments corresponding to hatred and envy. To hear their complaints and invective, one would suspect that they are afraid they will shortly be reduced to a situation like that of the old polytheistic priests when Catholicism prevailed among the upper classes of the Roman world, or that they recall the term *sacerdotum pagani,* which was applied to the few remaining official priests reduced to numbering among the faithful only members of the lower classes or the rural population. We regret such an attitude, all the more since it is so contrary to the generous hopes that our Teacher cherished in regard to the Catholic priests of Latin America. All we can do is to take due note of this attitude and resign ourselves to it. Nevertheless, we cannot avoid taking, against the religion of our mothers and the fetishistic faith of the popular masses, all the cares and precautions compatible with the great republican achievement—the abolition of any official Church. Likewise, we shall not cease to fight against any violation of spiritual freedom, such as that established in our federal Constitution, the most flagrant in this respect. By so proceeding we are, in fact, only conforming to the spirit and the precepts of our doctrine and the explicit counsels of our Founder.[444]

CHAPTER 6

Ideas during the Last Years
of the Nineteenth Century

The Positivists could not remain indifferent to the naval revolt of 1893. In the *Thirteenth Circular* of the Apostolate for the year 1893 (published on October 15, 1894), Miguel Lemos referred to the revolt of the Armada as that "ignominious moral rebellion." This description (perhaps unjust) is sufficient indication of the importance the Positivists attached to the events of September 6, 1893.

The revolt aroused the passionate protest of the Positivists.

This movement [wrote Miguel Lemos], which is completely unjustifiable, was due solely to the criminal and vulgar ambitions of former Admiral Melo, who managed to gather about him a group of the rowdy and disruptive elements in our society. Joining the rebels of Rio Grande do Sul and accepting the coöperation of all malcontents, no matter how demoralized or divergent, he did not hesitate to subject our country to one of the cruelest trials she has yet had to face.[1]

It was not usual for the Positivists, not even for Miguel Lemos, the most passionate of them (except when he referred to "that sophist, Laffitte"), to use such violent language.

But the passion for politics, which gripped so many people at that time, also swayed the Positivists. The revolt, "which began with the hypocritical pretext of restoring the supremacy of the Constitution, very soon . . . threatened the existence of the republic, particularly after another admiral, already renowned for his rational neutrality, openly joined the movement without attempting to disguise his monarchical tendencies." [2] Saldanha da Gama, the admiral referred to by Lemos, had in the "manifesto" he published when he joined the naval revolt,[3] referred to Comte's doctrines and their influence in Brazil as one of the chief causes of the country's current misfortunes.[4] This was the reason for the strongly hostile attitude of the Positivists to the rebel admiral, an attitude which they consistently maintained, not even sparing his memory. Even before Saldanha da Gama's adherence to the revolt, however, the Positivists had come out in favor of Marshal Floriano Peixoto, successor to Marshal Deodoro da Fonseca. As usual, they were on the side of "material order," a condition for "progress." Saldanha da Gama's declaration that "the government of Brazil should be restored to what it was before November 15, 1889" and the opposition of the rebels to Castilhos, who was sympathetic toward the Positivists, naturally ranged them on the side of Marshal Floriano, in whom they perhaps still hoped to find the dictator for the republic they so ardently desired.[5]

The revolt of September 6 proved to be just another of the series of conflicts resulting from the clashes of personal ambitions and the greed for power born of the confusion into which the country was plunged after November 15. As the historian of the September revolt records: "On the white flag the rebels bore, they could have inscribed the motto, which was in effect their program: 'ôte-toi de là que je m'y mette.' " [6] There was "not a single principle at stake in the revolt." [7] It was just another demonstration of the "caudillism" which the long tradition of legality in the Empire had only with difficulty managed to smoother. It exploded anew in the initial period of the republic, and was to make more than one appearance in its later history. It does not seem to me, however, that the revolt had any real intention of restoring the monarchy. In the last stages of the republic no real supporters of the monarchy existed any longer, and the only manifest protest had been the shot fired by Baron de Ladário in the early hours of the morning of November 15, 1889. The clash of ambitions openly expressed in the September revolt led paradoxically to a consolidation of the nascent republican institutions. Paradoxically too, the consolidation of the republic, which gave rise to a wave of fanaticism and Jacobinism, was aided by the foreign fleets anchored in the Bay of Guanabara, which, in the interests of their trade, prevented any more decisive action by the rebel army against Floriano.[8] The naval revolt was therefore yet another aspect of the confusion that reigned among the holders of power—although they went on affirming that they "fraternized with the people" or that the people fraternized with them—after the proclamation of the republic. Not until December, 1893, when Saldanha's "manifesto" was published, was an attempt made to seek a restoration, disguised by the "hypocritical pretext," as the Positivists called it, of restoring the supremacy of the Constitution. It was then that the rebels appealed for a decision by plebiscite, a means which in France had helped to consolidate the monarchy.[9] As we had always imitated France, it is easy to conjecture that the idea of a plebiscite, a feature of the restoration of monarchical institutions, probably occurred to Saldanha da Gama, who had never in his heart accepted the republic.[10] In fact, if we investigate the composition of the officer ranks of the imperial armed forces, we discover that the naval officers were recruited above all from aristocratic circles.

From the Empire, when no attempts were made to overcome or diminish them, date the rivalries between Army and Navy [writes José Maria Bello]. Of a profoundly "civilian" disposition, Pedro II had no special sympathy for the armed forces; if it had been possible to discover in him any sympathy, it would have been for the Navy. An admiral's uniform seemed to him more attractive than that of a marshal. . . . Members of the imperial aristocracy willingly allowed, and even encouraged, their sons to choose naval careers. The glories of the Paraguayan war, the preëminence of the Brazilian Armada in South America, the constant voyages abroad, the taste for a worldly life, all these gave the Navy an aristocratic appeal. Admiral Luís Filipe de Saldanha da Gama, for instance, of noble descent, highly esteemed at the Court of São Cristovão, brave, cultured, widely traveled, elegant and worldly, was the eminent representative of this class. Republican propaganda had aroused little enthusiasm in the Navy and had hardly an effect on the students of the Naval School. The Navy accepted the republic as an accomplished fact, in a spirit of discipline and patriotism, but at bottom was discontented with the preëminence of the Army in the implantation of the new regime.[11]

The Army, however, was as a rule composed of members of the lower middle class.

There were families of officers who succeeded each other for a number of generations; for example, the Fonsecas, the Mena Barretos, the Fontouras, the Câmaras. The modest pay of the officers, who in general had no private means, obliged them to lead strictly frugal lives. Abolitionist and republican ideas of equality and freedom, therefore, found a more favorable climate in the Army than in the Navy.[12]

It was principally in the Army that the ideas of Comte were propagated. The Navy was always more closely attached to the Throne and to the traditions preserved by the Empire. Hence the Army's defense of the republican principle which, they claimed, was threatened by the naval revolt.

In the conflict that had started in 1891 with Júlio de Castilhos's resignation on November 12, followed by the proclamation of a governing junta for Rio Grande do Sul, the so-called "little government"—"the repulsive and criminal little government of Cassul and Demétrio," as Júlio de Casthilhos called it in a letter to Aparício Mariante da Silva[13]—the Positivists had already expressed themselves in favor of the group of Júlio de Castilhos, who was later to be honored by Floriano. Among those who followed "a former imperialist chief," Silveira Martins, was Demétrio Ribeiro, a coreligionist who had the sympathies of the Apostolate and who, both in the provisional government and in the Constituent Assembly, defended the ideas of the Brazilian Positivist group! Nevertheless, despite his Positivist convictions, Demétrio Ribeiro allied himself to those who opposed the Constitution, which for Miguel Lemos was "the most advanced step yet taken in the direction of reaching our solutions." [14] Demétrio Ribeiro joined the "União Nacional," a political organization under the command of Counselor Silveira Martins. In *Rio Grande,* the newspaper opposed to Castilhos, he expressed himself against the current situation and adopted an attitude not in accord with his recent past in the federal Constituent Assembly.[15] In some respects the members of the Apostolate were more tolerant than Demétrio Ribeiro, whose personal enmity for Castilhos perhaps prevented him from giving calmer consideration to political events. The attachment to "Gasparism" was therefore to lose the Apostolate one of its important members.

How much confidence can be inspired by a man who, at this very moment, is arming a public force for the oppression of citizens?" telegraphed Demétrio Ribeiro to Miguel Lemos. To which Lemos replied:

As much as, or even more than, by the "Gasparists" and other old political meddlers with whom you have allied yourself in the electoral struggle. You cannot expect me to be moved by the familiar declamations of the opposition against the intervention of authority in the elections—interventions invariably copied by the opposition when it comes to power itself. In this respect I merely relate an anecdote published in the newspapers here. During the last elections in Rio de Janeiro, an opposition leader complained to Deodoro that there had been violations of electoral procedure on the part of the governor. "Come, come, my dear doctor," answered Deodoro, "you know that this business of elections has always been a bit of a farce." In its brutality, this reply summarizes all the feelings of Positivism toward the electoral system.[16]

Demétrio Ribeiro's acceptance of Comte's doctrines now revealed itself to be "too incomplete," for him to escape "the revolutionary suggestions still too much alive in him"—in the words of Miguel Lemos—"and be raised to the religious point of view, the only one able to subordinate the multiple aspects of our activities, domestic, civic, and planetary."[17] The man who had for a moment been the idol of the Positivists was thus transformed.[18] There is one further passage in Lemos's letter to Ribeiro that must be pointed out for the light it throw on the evolution of Comte's doctrines in our country. It reads:

It is very painful for us to witness your political discredit and to see our hopes fade! You will remember that I often warned you, with all the frankness of sincere friendship and with the foresight that comes from constant contact with the Master's words, that you either abandon militant politics, accepting the role of propagandist for our political solutions, or end a victim of the vices and corruption that typify other politicians.[19]

Miguel Lemos pleaded with Demétrio Ribeiro to "leave to the crows flesh unfit for the mouths of heroes" and to "shake from his feet the verminous dust" which had settled on him in "the pestilent arena of parliamentary democracy" he had entered in the company of the liberal chief Silveira Martins. Demétrio Ribeiro never replied to this letter.

Positivism had lost another valuable coreligionist on the republican political scene. In the drama that unfolded in the South, the Positivist position was quite clear: the Positivists were on the side of the legal forces. Unlike those who had applauded Deodoro's *coup d'état* and then become ardent defenders of "legality," to quote Tobias Monteiro,[20] the Positivists maintained their position, although they were the group that least respected, as we have seen above, the formality of the legal tradition. Without any connection with Júlio de Castilhos, whom they did not consider free of error and defect, the orthodox Positivists placed above all else the republic and "the conditions for order and progress." [21]

From 1894 to 1898, the year in which the last circular of the Apostolate appeared over the name of Miguel Lemos, the decline of Positivism can easily be traced. Henceforth Positivism was to become more restricted to the religious sphere. Its expansion during these years, the "astonishing development" claimed for it by one of its faithful followers, is simply the illusion of a believer.

In the last years of the nineteenth century, the Positivists continued their tireless efforts to do away completely with privileges and monopolies.[23] But already cracks were beginning to show in the structure that the Positivist disciples, in their zeal and misled by ephemeral success, had taken to be far more solid than it really was. In 1881, following the counsels of the Master, Miguel Lemos founded the Religious League—"an association spontaneously formed by the support of people who sympathize with the Apostolate's mission or who are already inclined to accept Positivist solutions; or who, although affiliated to other creeds, recognize the social usefulness of our efforts to establish the general conditions needful for the realization of religious reform." [24] In spite of this, in a circular addressed to his fellow members, the leader of the Apostolate referred to the progress made by their doctrine in the twelve years of his leadership, but recognized "the lack of preparation and the slender religious preoccupation of most of the Positivists"—deficiencies, as he said, caused by "my office, which weakens my authority and leaves it without the prestige it needs to make any effective decision on the constant self-command which must be exercised by each Positivist and the pains he must take with those about him in order to carry out the manifold exacting duties of our sacraments." [25]

The annunciator, the apostle, doubted the future of his doctrines. He doubted himself. Soon afterward, the leadership of Positivism passed into firmer hands. Nevertheless, in spite of the change, the doctrine did not develop, nor did it achieve greater importance.

"The history of Positivism is not yet at an end," wrote Oto Maria Carpeaux[26] recently with no paradoxical intent. He was right.

Brazilian Positivism, which was in the main religious—and which perhaps for this reason did not produce a greater effect on us—has been a great myth running through our spiritual and political history, and one for which I can find no clear or cogent justification. Perhaps this justification does exist, although the influence of Comte's doctrine contributed little to the successes associated with the development of ideas in Brazil. As Oto Maria Carpeaux has rightly said, Brazilian Positivism is "a symbol of deeper realities," [27] a symbol perhaps of the profound contradictions inherent in our destiny. Although it was a doctrine impressing only the narrow group of the Apostolate, Positivism may well have a significance greater than appearances suggest.

Although the other doctrines imported after the first half of the nineteenth century seem to me mere intellectual games—typical of erudite elites, no more than embellishments for curious intellects—about Positivism, I nevertheless have the impression (paradoxical, to be sure) that some deeper relationship exists between the nature of this doctrine and the nexus of contradictory factors which gave rise to our national life and which still govern it. Although Positivism, like the other doctrines, is an importation, it contains elements that reveal its compatibility with our formative influences and the most profound verities of our spirit.

Although the Positivist republic dreamed of by Miguel Lemos and Teixeira Mendes was never realized, it is possible that the desire to achieve it in a more modern form has not yet entirely disappeared.

2

After Hegel's death philosophy in Germany entered a state of crisis. With this great thinker speculation had conquered the realm of the intellect, and his influence had also extended to French Eclecticism. Some of the new philosophers, educated in the school of positive science, began to question the conclusions the Romantics were seeking to draw from Hegelian thought. Even Hegel's immediate successors resorted to experience. Schelling, for instance, was among the first to proclaim a "new philosophy," in which harmony was created between speculation, experience, and religion.[28] From this crisis in nineteenth-century German philosophy derive many of the currents of contemporary thought, and some of these currents were to find a reflection—in a vague, imprecise, and highly artificial manner—in the famous Recife School. From the philosophical vicissitudes originating in the struggle between the Hegelian "left" and "right" wings (as these trends were called by David Frederick Strauss) emerged "powerful levers for energizing the old Brazilian mentality."[29] A *mestizo,* the Germanist Tobias Barreto of Sergipe, flung open windows in the North, through which blew "a gust of free thought and modern culture that quickened many minds." [30]

The two great systems, however, that characterize the spiritual life of the nineteenth century, Romanticism and Positivism, are to some extent related. The contrast between them is more apparent than real. To study the past and to find in that past the germ of the future—this was the "task that Romanticism and Positivism sought to perform." [31] Each in its own way, we may add. "It would not be accurate," writes Harald Höffding,

to consider Positivism as a simple reaction against Romantic philosophy. Even in chronological terms, this would be false, since the origin of Positivism precedes the development of Romanticism. It was not the exhaustion of one trend that led to the other, although Positivism met with better conditions for its growth when Romanticism began to lose its hold.[32]

Romanticism, "in its enthusiasm for unity of thought, neglected the diversity of the Real and, in its firm conviction of the truth of the Ideal, ignored the strict mechanical connections to which all that is, in the form of reality, must be submitted." [33] Positivism, on the contrary, "has its point of departure in the given fact and is open to the diversities and contradictions of reality, seeking those laws that govern the appearance and development of phenomena in the real world." [34] Positivism and Romanticism took different paths to achieve unity of thought.

Around 1860 evolutionism,[35] a philosophical current connected with the positive philosophy, came to accentuate in its turn the progressive importance and influence of the natural sciences on European thought.

The publication of Darwin's *Origin of Species* in 1859 [writes Sorley], marks a turning-point in the history of thought. It had a revolutionary effect on the world vision of cultured men, similar to the lesser effect produced three centuries earlier by the work of Copernicus; in philosophical thought its influence can be likened to Galileo's effect on mechanical theory. Galileo's contribution to philosophy was the viewing of nature as a mechanical system; Darwin propounded a theory of evolution, and as a result of this theory, biological concepts held greater sway in philosophical constructions than mathematical ones.[36]

The evolutionist doctrine of Herbert Spencer, outlined in two articles, one published in 1852 ("The Development Hypothesis") and the other in 1857 ("Progress: Its Law and Cause"), was developed until the publication in 1887 of *Factors of Organic Evolution*.[37] Rejecting metaphysics and asserting that all knowledge is contained in the positive sciences, evolutionism, like Positivism, declared that man can investigate only the world of phenomena. Beyond this is the unknowable, the absolute mystery. This positive, naturalist philosophy suited the mentality of the Brazilian elite, made up as it was, according to Clóvis Beviláqua, of "intellects indisposed to sustained effort and lofty abstractions."[38] Or, in the words of Sérgio Buarque de Holanda: "Whatever spares us continuing, tiring mental effort—ideas that are clear, lucid, and definitive—seems to us to constitute the true essence of knowledge."[39] The love of a set form, of the definitive, of "the general laws that confine a complex and difficulty reality within the ambit of our desires" is "one of the most constant and significant traits in the Brazilian character."[40]

We must point out, however, that it was not only in Brazil that philosophies founded on the natural sciences prevailed. Naturalism enslaved cultured circles in the second half of the nineteenth century. This was an anti-idealist age, says Oesterreich, an age opposed to metaphysics.[41]

Evolutionism, then—immediately following or, we might say, at the same time as Positivism—was one of the most emphatic expressions of the naturalist and antimetaphysical attitude of the nineteenth century. Our men of letters and "philosophizers" were affected by it, as were most Europeans of the time. The surprising element was the speed with which Brazilian intellectuals were caught up in the contemporary European currents. This is noteworthy, for it reveals our curiosity and our thirst for knowledge. We knew more of Europe than we did of events in the different parts of the Empire. Our importers of ideas, the cultural elites concentrated in the coastal areas, were avid for news of the doings in the great European cultural centers, often neglecting to find out what was going on at home. Around 1870 this eagerness to learn of changes taking place in the intellectual life of Europe became more pronounced. The period of unusual intellectual activity between 1868 and 1878 was also marked, as we have seen, by an unusual development of Brazilian economic life. Gilberto Freyre observes that during the Second Empire the old nobility, with its Portuguese coats of arms and its families rooted in the Lusitanian tradition, was gradually replaced by a new nobility deriving from the lords of the sugar mills, the coffee growers, and the Portuguese merchants of the cities, whose European university degrees or bachelor diplomas of the new Faculties created by the Empire, constituted veritable titles of nobility.[42] The "liberal professions" became a new sort of noble privilege.[43]

Spencerianism, which presents the widest theory of progress and affirms the "law of progressive differentiation," perfectly corresponded to the aspirations of this new nobility. The concept of the infinite perfectibility of the individual contained in evolutionist philosophy suited the interests of this new class of bachelors and doctors and at the same time freed them from theological beliefs without obliging them to become adherents of the Religion of Humanity. The bourgeois Brazilian elite found in evolutionism a philosophical synthesis that justified its political, social, and even religious position for, as Engels said, even agnosticism was a way of indirectly accepting materialism while publicly denying it.[44]

A kind of idolatry of science, wanting in the requisite critical sense,[45] marks this reaction of "vulgar materialism," as it was called, of the middle years of the nineteenth century. In a country like Germany, where the philosophical tradition was idealistic, the materialist reaction sparked off a burst of indignation, particularly in the universities. Writers contributing to this "scandal" were Jakob Moleschott, with his book *Kreislauf des Lebens* (1852), Karl Vogt, with *Köhlerglaube und Wissenschaft* (1855), and Ludwig Büchner, whose great work of popularization, *Kraft und Stoff*, was one of those most widely read in the nineteenth century. At that time everyone seemed to expect science to be an instrument with the power to bring men together, as religion had done in the past. German materialism was, however, paradoxically idealistic, animated by a purifying love for humanity and impregnated with the notion of progress. This ingenuous materialism, artlessly dogmatic, rendered some service, however: it was opposed to "ecclesiastical dogmatism" and so led to reflection on "problems that had been forgotten after the disintegration of Romantic philosophy."[46] The materialism of Moleschott, Vogt, and Büchner lent itself to just and severe criticism, and "toward the end of the century, freethinkers oriented themselves toward 'naturalistic monism' for preference, above all, those of the settled and cultured classes." [47] Thus, by the end of the century, Büchner was replaced by Haeckel, and Büchner's book, which had enjoyed such a widespread reputation, was replaced by *Das Welträtsel* (*The Riddle of the Universe*).[48]

"The spread of Haeckel's ideas is readily understandable," wrote August Messer. A book like *The Riddle of the Universe* could "satisfy the philosophical needs of many." "Because Haeckel's philosophy does not have a backbone of historical-philosophical erudition, it holds a certain easy attraction.

His rudimentary philosophizing, with its mythological animation of matter, recalls the first stages of Greek philosophy—the helotism of the Ionians and the poetic doctrine of Empedocles on the love and hatred between the elements. For this reason, those who begin to philosophize on their own account sympathize with the style of Haeckel. Besides, he refers at great length to the great questions that captivate nascent philosophical interest: the question of God, of immortality, of freedom —themes that for most professional philosophers matter less than specific analysis of the particular problems that occupy them. And Haeckel resolves the "riddles of the universe" with firmness, along the ingenuous lines that for every rational question there is an irrefutable answer, at least on the part of science, and above all of natural sciences.[49]

One philosophy in particular, then, was destined to ensnare self-taught and venturesome minds of uncertain historico-philosophical formation, who sought sure and precise answers to problems which are forever open: to an activity which must continually be starting afresh, such as philosophy. These characteristics in themselves show the reasons for the influence of monism on our elite. Without an adequate hitorical and philosophical formation, self-taught Brazilian intellectuals filled with curiosity and avid for precise answers, turned toward the new ideas sent to us from Germany. While in the South the Positivist current was carried on by Spencerianism, in the North the German ideas influenced a group of Recife intellectuals, among them a number from Sergipe. It was principally the latter who made up the Pernambuco "Germanist" group or the "Teuto-Sergipan School," as it was ironically called by Carlos de Laet. Tobias Barreto, Sílvio Romero, and Farias Brito were, in different ways and from different points of view, the chief representatives of the nineteenth-century German intellectual importation. It was in this group that Germanism was most active, although German ideas were not solely confined to it.[50]

It was not, however, the materialism of Büchner, Vogt, and Haeckel that influenced the group, nor yet was it the philosophy of Kant,[51] Schelling, Fichte, or Hegel. What chiefly roused the enthusiasm of the Germanists of the Teuto-Sergipan School and its disciples was, as João Ribeiro has said, "a second-rate Germanism" in which a prominent position was occupied by Ludwig Noiré, a writer destined to be completely forgotten by the younger generation. "This Noiré," writes João Ribeiro, "a notable expositor of monism, posed as the oracle of contemporary philosophy. They spoke of Noiré as of Homer or of Shakespeare."[52] The chief influences on the last member of the Recife Germanist group, Raimundo de Farias Brito, were Schopenhauer and von Hartmann. Von Hartmann, in fact, represented the neo-Romantic movement, the metaphysical "resurrection," or, as it was known here, the "spiritualist reaction"[53] against the exaggerations of naturalism. A pessimistic philosopher for whom the redemption of the world consists in its extinction, von Hartmann influenced Tobias Barreto and, more intensively, Farias Brito, especially in his early philosophical works, the series *A Finalidade do Mundo*.

In Brazil, writes Sérgio Buarque de Holanda, "each individual asserts himself among his peers, heedless of community law, concerning himself exclusively with what distinguishes him from the others."[54] Among the figures of the second half of the nineteenth century, Tobias Barreto is certainly a man of this sort. He still shares a characteristic, or various characteristics, of the community, such as love of novelty, versatility, and perhaps a certain intellectual irresponsibility.

Tobias Barreto came from the "brilliant lower classes, the group of men of humble background and mixed racial origin, who thanks to the academies had invaded public and intellectual life in Brazil, proclaiming the new society in the making."[55] Young and indigent, Tobias Barreto left Itabaiana, where he had taught Latin, to enter a seminary in Bahia. For members of the lower classes without means to pursue higher studies, the seminary was—like the Military School—the gateway to a liberal profession or the life of an intellectual.

The seminary of Salvador did not, however, succeed in housing for more than one night this young backlander who was to sweep "like a cyclone" through the sleepy Pernambucan Academy, shaking it out of its lethargy. In Bahia the first steps of this highly intelligent mestizo seem to symbolize his own destiny. On leaving the seminary[56] he walked headlong into a fire! His whole life was to follow the same pattern: a never-ending whirl of confusion and challenge, of enmities, mutability, bohemianism.

As one of his most distinguished and enthusiastic disciples, Graça Aranha, was later to say:

[Tobias Barreto] had the exuberance, vigor, and the heedlessness that made him completely uncalculating and careless even of his reputation for posterity; he had the gift of fantasy, the fabulosity of the creative artist, the impatience and the alarming capacity for flaming into revolt that was one of the liveliest traits of his character. He refused to fit into any mold; he recognized only the limitless freedom of irresponsibility. Like his fellow settlers of the *sertão,* he lived among the people; he was neglected, poor, unhappy.[57]

A group of young men gathered about him from 1882 onward, to hear a language far different from that with which the old professors of Recife Academy had bored and sickened the younger generation of students. These young men were delighted with the novelty of the latest philosophies and, on inadequate grounds, began to style themselves "philosophers." "In the South, you are poets," they told Pardal Mallet, fresh from Rio, "here in the North, we are philosophers." [58] Monism, ontogenesis, phylogenesis, monadology, "all the windy rhetoric of the 'history of creation,' a rich but indigestible diet, nourished the 'school' of the professor who could laugh with his pupils and for whom humanity was divided into three groups: himself, who was good; those who liked him, whom he ignored; and the rest, who were butts for the surpassing verve of his attack." [59] These young men, enchanted by his unconcern for scandal, were faithful to him throughout their lives, perhaps more in tribute to the memory of their lost youth than to the ideas spread by their master, which he later came largely to disown.

Tobias Barreto's first philosophy teacher was Father Itaparica, who initiated him into "an eclectic spiritualism *à la* Cousin, tenuous and shallow." [60] From 1861 to 1868 this was the philosophical school followed by Tobias. His first philosophical article—"Guizot e a Escola Espiritualista do Século XIX"—still relies on the writers of the French spiritualist eclectic school. "In spite of the different distinct trends followed by free thought in our time," writes Tobias Barreto, "the general tendency of the century is toward spiritualism. The sense of infinity and of the divine has broadened the sphere of the human intellect in all its aspirations." [61] Laromiguière, he added, had recoiled at the words of Royer-Collard! This is a sample of Tobias Barreto's style and ideas. Maine de Biran and Royer-Collard were still his masters in March, 1868.

But although he was an Eclectic in March, by April of that same year he was boldly affirming, in his article, "A Proposito de Una Teoria de S. Tomas de Aquino": "Positivism is right when it declares that the question of a first cause is both inaccessible and intractable." [62] In his writings of 1870—*Moisés e Laplace* and *A Religião Perante a Psicologia*—Tobias Barreto cited extracts from Comte's work[63] and considered Cousin "superficial," voicing "serious doubts about spiritualist psychology." [64] In 1871, in *A Ciência da Alma, Ainda e Sempre Contestada,* in which he criticized Charles Levèque's work *La Science de l'invisible,* he wrote: "The torpor— not to say, total inanition—of the old Cartesian-Catholic spiritualism, is blatant. Any attempt to deny it would be the result of fatuous superficiality or a blind rebellion against the sovereign authority of fact. The doctrines of Cousin and Jouffroy are worn out." [65] In this article the incipient influence of German philosophy on Tobias Barreto can already be seen. Here we find the first signs of what he was later to call "that same old Germanic obsession" which, as he says in the preface to *Questões Vigentes de Filosofia e de Direito,* "acts for me as a kind of isolator, cutting me off from a more intimate communication with the general spirit of national culture" [66]—a strange manifestation by a man of culture who sought to isolate himself from the spirit of his country!

Tobias Barreto was beyond all doubt the first to propagate German philosophical ideas in Brazil.[67] He got to know German philosophy through the works of the French writers, who were at that time great admirers of German culture. In the articles he wrote between 1868 and 1871 this influence is easily detected.

In 1870 [wrote Sílvio Romero], Tobias Barreto cast his vote for the Germanic philosophers. With the ardor he brought to everything he did and the enormous facility for learning that distinguished him, he walked into Laillacard's bookshop in the *Rua do Imperador* in Recife, bought a German dictionary and a German grammar, and asked the bookseller to order from Europe Ewald's *Geschichte des Volkes Israel*. This was the first German book the poet from Sergipe ever owned.[68]

We must bear in mind that the spread of German ideas was a general phenomenon in the nineteenth century—the century in which that country appears to have experienced a certain amount of happiness, for, as Nietzsche said, all great cataclysms of civilization had afflicted it.[69]

It was not only in Brazil that German ideas exercised their influence. Edmond Scherer, a French writer who may have moved Tobias Barreto in his inclination toward German philosophy, wrote in his *Mélanges d'histoire réligieuse*:

Germany is of a nature excellently rich. She unites those qualities that appear to be most opposed. She is both religious and wise, delightfully visionary and tremendously critical . . . When the future historian comes to consider the social development of our time, he will discover that nothing has contributed more to the transformation of ideas in the nineteenth century than German science or has exercised a greater influence on the modern mind in its ultimate notions, and consequently has more decisively, if indirectly, led to the renaissance which has just put an end to the Middle Ages.[70]

Reading this, we are no longer surprised that there were Brazilians who waxed enthusiastic over the excellences of German culture.

Tobias Barreto and Sílvio Romero—"the St. Paul to whom Tobias played Christ," in the malicious phrase of José Veríssimo—were the leading exponents of German ideas; and if they dedicated themselves to the propagation of German philosophy and German literature, they did so, according to Sílvio Romero, "as a tonic for our spirits." [71] They recommended this strong German tonic principally for criticism. Using the mold of German ideas, these two intellectuals believed, once again, that with its aid they could reform Brazil!

German ideas, at first recommended by Tobias Barreto as capable of putting us on the path of truth, were soon to grip him to such an extent that he conceived, as he himself later acknowledged, a veritable "mania for Germany." His enthusiasm and Teutonic faith led him to the ridiculous extreme of publishing, in a tiny city with a presumably high proportion of illiterates, a periodical in German titled *Deutscher Kämpfer*, written and edited by himself, and doubtless read solely by himself as well; and this in a city where justice took its orders from the rural lords and was the tool of their arbitrary decisions—facts even denounced by Tobias Barreto, which revealed the lamentable backwardness of the country. This is what befalls those who believe they can isolate themselves from their environment and nourish their minds on exotic fantasies.[72]

My admiration for Tobias Barreto—and his value as a renovator and invigorator of the Brazilian intellect is undeniable—does not go so far as to permit me to appreciate his writings with the same sympathetic spirit. I believe that his influence was purely personal, justified by the charm of his enthusiasm and his vivacity. His work bears the lively imprint of a strong, brilliant, and darting personality, lacking in true culture. But if we examine his writings carefully, we find that he was merely another "philosophizer" in love with the new songs that Europe was beginning to sing, the far-off melody which, in Recife, he composed anew with noise enough for the ears of those still intoning the old plain song or the arias from romantic opera. In the words of Father Leonel Franca, Tobias Barreto, in his mental excursions, culled "enough erudition to captivate the simple-minded," [73] but it is equally fair to say that he also brought back some truths that satisfied healthier intellects. His exuberance, his recklessness, his gift for fantasy, and his hastiness prevented him from building a more orderly edifice, in which the ideas from Europe, which he knew to assimilate and artfully to popularize, could be housed together. His books are all long articles by a powerful polemicist, in which crudity and jesting take the place of irony. Tobias, however, did not escape that particular misfortune that afflicts Brazilian culture—of merely "recording and commenting echoes of foreign schools and currents," as Hermes Lima has said.[74]

The reason [writes Hermes Lima], is that the task in our country is to rethink, to propagate, and to win respect. The same philosophy at once takes on a proselytizing air. It is for this reason that the philosophical position occupied by Tobias was one of the most active, pugnacious, and influential that Brazil has known. This is the explanation for the propagandist tone distinguishable in his work.[75]

In fact, this "proselytizing" character of philosophical doctrines in our country, where ideas and principles are, in the words of Hermes Lima, "like munitions for war," is in my opinion the result of the cleavage between imported intellectual doctrines and our own historical conditions.

A monist, although not in complete agreement with Haeckel's ideas, Tobias Barreto was also influenced by the currents that in Germany, after 1870, were the forerunners of the resurrection of metaphysics and criticism, returning to the Kantian source. The writers who inspired this "return to Kant" were those who influenced Tobias in the last phase of his writings. Referring to their philosophy in *Questões Vigentes,* he wrote:

The materialistic tendency of the times, with its corresponding taste for mechanical explanations, has led many minds to the extremes of categorical affirmations and negations that have no real basis in fact. Fortunately, there is already more than one example of scientific sobriety on the part of naturalists, once intoxicated with their own wine but now convinced that science has limits beyond which something still exists that cannot be submitted to its processes of observation and explanation. The first and most valuable example of this change was given by Du Bois Raymond.[76]

The monism followed by Tobias Barreto was that of Ludwig Noiré,[77] or what the latter called "philosophical monism," not to be confounded with that of Haeckel. "The great professor of Jena, who is one of the most illustrious savants of modern science," wrote Tobias Barreto,

seems to me to allow himself to be misled by one of the prejudices of our time when he identifies the mechanistic with the monistic vision of the world. The one is not exactly like the other. Philosophical monism can be reconciled with teleology, and is undaunted by final causes, the concept of which is not, as systematic materialists claim, an easy way for lazy minds to evade research into efficient causes; naturalistic monism, on the other hand, accepts only the latter, believing that with them it can build a scientific explanation.[78]

For philosophical monism, since "movement and sentiment are inseparable, it is merely a question of degree between them: where movement is dominant, the 'causa efficiens' preponderates; where sentiment is uppermost, the 'causa finalis' takes first place." [79] The world is not, "as narrow materialism would have it, merely a chain of 'why's,' it *is* a chain, but a chain of 'what for's,' of ends or aims which support, limit, or proceed from each other." [80] These ideas of

Noiré, linked to others taken from von Hartmann, made up the philosophical arsenal of Tobias Barreto.

Tobias Barreto was certainly not an original philosopher. He could not have been. He was, however, as Tristão de Ataíde perceived, a man of his time. Tristão de Ataíde also states that Tobias had no national spirit. I am none too sure what this illustrious critic means by "national spirit," but for my part, I believe that the defects and the qualities of his contemporaries are clearly marked in Tobias. That he believed himself infinitely superior to his environment, convinced that in Germany he had discovered a kind of "dictionary of truth," [81] is undeniable, but this type of discovery has been almost a constant for our elite. Intellectual modesty, or the just assessment of one's own intellectual capacity, is not frequent among the Brazilian literati. They do not have an exact perception of the "ages of the intellect." Similarly, it does not seem to be true to say that Tobias "died convinced that he had pointed out a definitive path for the Brazilian intellect." [82] I think that Tobias Barreto died as skeptical, even in this, as he had always in fact lived.[83] He could not have deluded himself, and in this respect the letters he wrote to Sílvio Romero are significant.[84] If, however, he did not open up definitive paths for the Brazilian intellect (and there is nothing definitive in the realm of the intellect), he did succeed in gathering about him a sufficient number of intellectuals who knew how to follow new paths.

Tobias Barreto was not a thinker. He was, like others of our literati, a commentator of European thought, especially of German thought. His influence was refreshing for his time, but was limited only to his time and did not survive the lifetimes of those who had known him and been his disciples. "The generation that followed," wrote Tristão de Ataíde,

the generation alive at the end of the last century and the beginning of this one, accepted the philosophical and religious demolition that Tobias had undertaken, but rejected his naturalistic and Germanic reconstruction. They remained relativists, skeptics, and dilettantes. It was the age of Anatole France of philosophical aestheticism; of mental sybaritism.[85]

And, he adds, the age in which we learned to think.

Linked to the name of Tobias Barreto is that of Sílvio Romero,[86] that indefatigable and enthusiastic worker who, in a constant and remarkable effort—never since equaled—spent his life studying our country, eager to understand and interpret it. The linking of his name with that of Tobias has frequently caused his work to be forgotten or belittled in favor of that of Tobias, although it is of greater reach and significance. I believe, however, that no one can withhold his admiration for this man who, in the history of national ideas, marks a turning point for the Brazilian intellect. With Sílvio Romero, the "intellectual merchandise" we imported is relegated to a secondary plane, and national problems, above all those related to the history of culture, become the preoccupation of our intellectuals. Sílvio Romero was the precursor of the effort to interpret Brazil that has gained ground since the publication of his first works in 1871.[87] When we study our history of the second half of the nineteenth century, Sílvio Romero figures dominantly in the widest range of subjects, opening up new paths, experimenting with new ideas, constantly aware of the Brazilian problems to which he devoted such zealous care. Almeida Magalhães, moved by the memory of the master he so sadly missed, wrote recently:

To continue work on certain political, economic, social, ethnographic, educational, and critical problems, is to bring him back to life and to see him again in the throes of the struggle, with the battle in full swing, with his wide gestures, prevailing as the victor. Here, he routs his enemies and convinces them; there, he surprises with the novelty of his doctrines, ever supported by robust arguments and sound authorities; everywhere, he arrests the imagination with his vigor, his impetuosity, his sincerity. He has been accused of partiality and unfairness. In fact he was partial and unfair, although his sincerity is unquestionable, in the case of Machado de Assis, as he himself has admitted. But his accusers forget the partiality and injustice of his critics and that he had continually to defend himself against aggressive presumptions, lack of wisdom, and hasty judgments, which often went beyond reasonable limits, "forcing the tone," to use the expressive phrase of Nélson Romero. His exaggerated severity toward the Brazilian spiritualists of the last century . . . can be explained by the nature of the book in which he demolishes them, a book both refreshing and combative, that could not have been written in any other way, given his temperament, the time of its writing, and the end it had in view . . . This book was an outcome of the critico-philosophical period of Recife. It was his visiting card to the Court, after his *Cantos do Fim do Século*. He had need to be strong. There were enough reasons to "force the tone." And Sílvio forced it, as he was later to do against the Positivists.[88]

In his *Estudos,* Tristão de Ataíde says that to speak of Tobias Barreto means to write too much or too little. I believe this is truer of Sílvio Romero. We always end by confusing Romero with Brazil. He is so like things Brazilian—he is a hotchpotch of contrasts, hopes and disillusions, simplicity and complexity, enormous errors and the desire to hit the nail on the head. In my opinion, Sílvio Romero reflects the somewhat complicated ingenuousness of our elites. This is the reason for his attraction. What makes him great is his tireless effort to understand Brazil, not his "philosophy."

In replying to Garcia de Merou, who, writing of Tobias Barreto, said that he had expected something more original, more indigenous in Tobias, Sílvio Romero throws light upon his own "philosophy." In the preface to Tobias Barreto's *Polémicas,* Sílvio Romero writes:

The worthy diplomat seems to be making the error of supposing that one can give the name of "philosophy" only to one of those monstrous constructions of the fancy, abstract and arbitrary, that bear the name of system and presume to provide the key to the riddle of things, and that one can count among the philosophers only the authors of such Cyclopian works and their professed disciples.[89]

In this reply to the Argentinian intellectual, Sílvio Romero expressed his own views on philosophy, which show the influence of a philosophical orientation opposed to metaphysics and also demonstrate an aspect of his temperament in which true "idealism" was never far removed from worldly problems, as João Ribeiro was later to say.

Sílvio Rabelo justly observes that

Sílvio Romero was not prone to discussing ideas on a purely abstract level. He applied his critical intelligence only to philosophical systems dealing with a particular problem. And he considered them with the care of a naturalist taking up some strange creature between his forceps. Science could only lose by linking itself to the whims of philosophy.[90]

For Sílvio Romero, "philosophical systems and the old speculations concerning essence were an uncomfortable memory—merely a moment in the human intellect." [91]

I do not, however, agree with the intelligent Pernambucan writer in his opinion that "Sílvio Romero was condemned to the shackles of Positivism all his life," [92] since his mind was not of the sort that allowed itself to be constricted in any way whatsoever and would have thrown off any shackles with ease. We must remember that

what he objected to in Positivism was precisely what he opposed
in other metaphysical systems—the inflexibility and doctrinaire
austerity that to him seemed fantasies unrelated to experience with
little bearing on real life. Ready answers and solutions to all problems did not suit his temperament.

We must demonstrate [he wrote], that it is the wholeness and inflexibility of Positivism that is at once its strength and its weakness, the advantage that will further its progress and the handicap that will make it
lose ground. Its advantage lies in its logical and unbending totality, providing an answer and a solution for the most disquieting questions that
have troubled humanity; such answers and solutions, although merely
apparent, are easily apprehended and taken in. Hence the favor it finds
in the eyes of uninventive nations, more or less intellectually lazy, such
as our own. Its defect is that, in order to remain whole, it must become
a "stationary doctrine," crystallized in its immobility, at odds with scientific progress and the spirit of modern times.[93]

Sílvio Romero, with his acute and critical intelligence, his curiosity,
and his enthusiasm, was aware that the true concept of philosophy
attempts to maintain close contact with experience. He did not ask
for doctrines, but for a method. In philosophy he saw a spiritual
orientation that perpetually remakes itself, is perpetually renewable,
and is not a bundle of dogmatic theses. Philosophy is only fruitful
when it liberates and develops the mind. It is sterile when it provides formulae in lieu of a spiritual life.[94]

It does not seem to me true to say that Sílvio Romero was a "ship
with neither helm nor compass." The philosopher's compass is the
combination of circumstances thrown up by life itself. It is true that
Sílvio Romero wavered—to a considerable extent, in fact—but then
so do all those who are buffeted by the salutary winds of doubt, all
who feel that uneasiness is a sign of life. Concerned with the practical problems of life, Sílvio Romero did not waste time in the quest
for abstraction. If he had done so, he would not have had the great
work he left us.

For him, philosophy was a method, not a mass of formulae, because formulae are the real shackles of the mind, which hinder the
revelation of wider and newer horizons. It is true that his work suffers from the defects of self-education, but this is true of all our
"philosophizers." What is surprising is the harshness some critics
show toward Sílvio Romero compared with the benevolence they
show toward Farias Brito. What possible link can be made between

the wonderful work bequeathed us by Sílvio Romero and the philosophy of Farias Brito? Sílvio is Brazil—disorderly, blundering, but very much alive. Farias is the commentator of a commentator, the promise of a metaphysical philosophy that was never fulfilled.

Raimundo de Farias Brito belonged by education to the Germanist group of Recife but occupied a solitary position. Farias Brito's destiny was a curious one. After a number of political setbacks in his youth,[95] he dedicated nearly all his time to teaching and philosophy. With an obstinacy matched only by that of his fellow Cearenses, who refuse to abandon their native land even during the worst droughts, Farias Brito, in an environment in which philosophy aroused hardly any interest and had little effect, dedicated his life to the building of a philosophical system which he never managed to complete and for which he did not even lay the foundations. Having been affected by the Germanism[96] of Recife and the influence of Tobias Barreto,[97] like the other young students of the Recife Faculty of Law, Farias Brito earned a reputation as a philosopher partly through his fidelity and dedication to philosophical studies, partly because in his work—somewhat confused, monotonous, and wordy—he preached the resurrection of metaphysics, a theme announced by European philosophers which, in Brazil, attracted the sympathies of the generations following Positivism and Spencerianism.

The philosophical work of Farias Brito, essentially moral in intent,[98] is, then, what I may call an eternal re-beginning, a never-ending commentary on nineteenth-century European philosophical doctrines. It lacked sufficient connection, and, like other studies of philosophical subjects in our country, it was the fruit of suggestions emanating from the works read by Farias Brito during the last quarter of the nineteenth century and the first decade of the twentieth. Farias Brito's work is another expression of the vicissitudes of cultural importation—of the European novelties that appeared in the bookshops and often made the philosopher from Ceará change course, although it is important to point out that it never made him deviate from his preoccupation with reform and moral regeneration.

From Schopenhauer and von Hartmann to Bergson—by way of Lange, Kuno, Fischer, Vacherot, Gratry, Renouvier, and Spencer—all philosophical trends of the last century left their mark on Farias Brito's "philosophy." The objectives of his work—and even the method—varied according to suggestions or influences. In this way his work, melancholy and somber, never follows a direct course. It fluctuates considerably—closely following the oscillations of our cultural importations. His books repeat foreign ideas; they are tedious melodies in which one can distinguish a vague naturalistic *leitmotiv* mingled with a hesitant spiritualism. In the dense undergrowth of his interminable commentary on the history of philosophy it is not easy to find the main thread of his thought. It wanders continually. He repeats himself over and over again, recapitulating ideas and commentaries on all philosophers connected with the problems he proposes to consider. In one book he promises what he does not fulfill in the next. He opens up gigantic perspectives, but they are immediately lost in the thickets of commentary on the philosophizing of others. It is true that Farias Brito's "philosophy" never swerves from history, but for him the history of men and ideas is pure abstraction, a mere "adventure of the mind." Sílvio Rabelo wrote: "Farias Brito's philosophy has no windows opening on the natural or the human scene." [99] The dominant note in his work is the note of pessimism that echoes through the German philosophy of the nineteenth century. Schopenhauer and von Hartmann profoundly influenced his thought. The first volume of *Estudos de Filosofia e Teleologia Naturalista (Studies of Naturalist Philosophy and Teleology)*, which he called *Finalidade do Mundo* (published in 1895), opened with the following extract from F. A. Lange:

When a new age dawns and another dies, two great factors combine: a moral idea able to inflame the world and a social direction powerful enough to raise the oppressed masses to some considerable extent. This cannot be done through cool reasoning or artificial systems. Victory over destructive and isolating egotism and over the ice that kills living hearts can only be won by some great ideal that will appear like a *stranger from another world,* demanding the impossible and so forcing reality off its hinges.[100]

From such a promise, leading one to expect a passionate and vital result, Lange reaches a pessimistic conclusion: "to live is to be a slave to necessity, it is to want, to suffer. The first cry of a newborn babe is a cry of pain; and all life, even the happiest and most successful, is a tragedy." [101] From *Finalidade do Mundo* to *Mundo Interior* (1914), the *leitmotiv* of Farias Brito's thought was to be the theme of pain and tragedy.[102] For him, everything in the contemporary world was crisis and suffering.

In the present state of the world [he wrote in 1905, in part iii of *Finalidade do Mundo* ("O Mundo como Atividade Intelectual")], everyone feels an indefinable unhappiness, a tremendous anguish. It is not only in the lower classes of society that this occurs. The leaders, those who are at the head of the political movements of nations, are also suffering. This is not a characteristic of our country alone. The disease is general. It is true that we are suffering; but all other nations are suffering in the same way. It is therefore unfair to attribute our part in the crisis to local causes. It is unfair to attribute to the political change, effected by the fall of the Empire, the abnormal situation to which we find ourselves reduced. On the contrary, the republic was an outcome of the general crisis which was already making itself powerfully felt among us; it came as the hope of relief from the crisis; it came as the dream of renewal.[103]

From this pessimistic concept, a thirst for order naturally derives—order for its own sake. Farias Brito's attitude, like that of the Positivists to whom he was so bitterly opposed,[104] was also "regenerating": "The truth is that in the midst of the profound doubt that assails us, in the midst of the general incertitude that surrounds us, only one thing can give us strength: virtue." [105]

Comte's disciples also appealed to virtue. They aimed, however, at reorganizing society with "neither God nor king." [106] In his commentary on this Positivist attitude, Farias Brito said that "it faithfully reflects the present state of the human mind," dominated and corrupted by "modern impiety." [107] For "to deny God is to deny moral order, to suppress the reason for the world." [108] This position of Farias Brito's immediately attracted the sympathy of the Church and gave his name greater prominence. The so-called spiritualist tendencies and currents, that had met with a temporary setback during the last years of the Empire and the first years of the republic, seemed to have found in the assertions of Farias Brito support for their steady and progressive organization. But among those who, in my opinion, always had a clear perception of the meaning of our history and the complex movement of the forces that direct it, were some who were immediately aware of the weakness and hesitancy of the Ceará philosopher's "spiritualism." In 1917 João Ribeiro pointed out in the *Revista do Brasil* that Farias Brito "was an irresolute and unbelieving spiritualist who took the path of faith." [109] Farias Brito's approach to Catholicism, brought about by Jackson de Figueiredo, may have given him in the last years of his life the illusory impression of the success of his philosophy,[110] the belief that it had attracted a number of disciples.[111] But a prudent reserve quickly replaced the lukewarm sympathy that had for a moment enveloped Farias Brito. And his disciples—if it can be said that he ever had any—quickly abandoned their master to integrate themselves in the traditional thinking of the Church.[112]

Although a tenacious adversary of Positivism, Farias Brito was affected by the Brazilian environment of his time, impregnated by Comtist, Littréist, and Spencerian ideas. His concept of science— that of a man who has no real contact with scientific disciplines —was based on Herbert Spencer, as we can see from his assertion that philosophy is "knowledge *in fieri,* knowledge about to be organized; while science is knowledge already gained, knowledge organized." [113] In the work from which the previous statement is quoted —an interesting history of psychology—he wrote: "Science must serve as the foundation for the erection of the philosophical monument. One cannot imagine any serious philosophical construction that is not based upon a complete synthesis of the general conclusions of science." [114] These ideas are the ideas of Spencer, ideas much criticized by Farias Brito but which he nevertheless approached.[115]

I said above that Farias Brito's destiny was a curious one. When, in 1924, a questionnaire worked over by writers of the generation born with the republic was published in Rio de Janeiro, one of these writers, Tasso da Silveira, declared that Farias Brito "gave the first genuine expression to our metaphysical desires." [116] Tasso da Silveira added:

He was, so to say, the first voice in which we heard the sonority of our soul. The fact that it was not yet he who left to Brazil a work whole and original is unimportant; what he assimilated or repeated from the great universal philosophers, he instinctively adapted to our history and our spirit. He adapted, combined, and, above all, reconsidered, giving eloquent expression to what he felt—from the doctrines he knew and thus adapted, reconsidered, and restated—would find an echo in our collective consciousness. In this way he was, as far as it is possible to be, the interpreter of our thirst for the infinite, the word we lacked to identify for us our hitherto vague conception of the world. . . . A man like Farias Brito . . . signified the true awakening of our conscience.[117]

Apart from the eloquent and enthusiastic tone of Tasso da Silveira, everything in his ardent affirmations seems to me inexact. Philosophy is an expression of life. Farias Brito lived—as so many men have lived before and still do—shut in a world of abstractions, quarreling with life. To repeat the phrase of Sílvio Rabelo: Farias Brito's thought "has no windows opening on the natural or the human scene." [118]

How could one who "always lived remote from the problems of the land and the people surrounding him" have expressed our consciousness? "Except for his poems in favor of the emancipation of the slaves, and occasional references to the mistakes of Positivist politics at the beginning of the republic, there is, in the work of Farias Brito, no mention of Brazil or anything that could distinguish him as a genuinely Brazilian thinker." [119]

A curious paradox: Farias Brito considered the interpreter of the national conscience! And a strange and equally paradoxical symptom is the consideration of Farias Brito as the spiritual leader of the vague ideology that the reactionary doctrines of the "integralists" attempted to impose on the country! [120] There may, however, have been reasons for this. As Gilberto Freyre says:

Having failed in republican politics, Farias Brito, with his black tail coat and mournful moustache, took refuge in philosophical inquiry. Like a kind of slave who had escaped from the conventions and routines of the common life of his country and his time, to install himself adventurously but with dignity, in the heights of Palmares [a village where a rebellion of runaway slaves took place.—Trans.], not only to attain an "inner life," but also to achieve ideas of the moral and even the social reform of the plain. A plain which his reformer's eye never quite abandoned. Which he always hoped to dominate. Or, at least, to reform: to subject it to the results of his own intellectual adventure, impregnated by Messianism. [121]

This silent Juvenal [122] may, however, have cherished the profound hope that he might, through sublimation, become the leader of a philosophical and sociological school. [123] In the famous letter to Jackson de Figueiredo in which he expressed his hopes and disillusionments, he ended in the following terms:

I am now convinced: we shall succeed. A man alone would represent nothing and would inevitably disappear. But if one man joins himself to another because he shares the same ideas, a chain is formed, an irresistible center of attraction. Others will give us their support: this will not be long in coming. If this bond of ideas that unites us is not a mere banal convention but a sincere and unshakable conviction, it will suffice. For sincerity is already truth, or at least one of its essential aspects, and for truth is reserved universal dominion and empire over the mind.[124]

But what "truth" did he present in his long and hesitant divanations? Was it not Farias Brito himself who affirmed that "philosophy is a permanent activity of mind," a constant search for truth? "What we must do," he said,

cannot yet be determined. But we will certainly go far. And our work remains extremely difficult: but it already has deep roots and cannot be destroyed. Consequently we have faith. The truth is that we shall succeed. There is no more reason to waver. We shall see. Therefore let no-one doubt. Quasimodo will take effective action against evil. Don Quixote will succeed, with those who will achieve the spiritual renaissance of the world. And let the multitude tremble: for it will have to be subjugated; its obscure and uncertain representations must be guided, its blindness enlightened, its savage instincts vanquished.[125]

These statements, as Gilberto Freyre has rightly observed, express less Farias Brito's desire to be "the leader of a philosophical school than the leader of a political or religious sect."[126]

Farias Brito was neither "the genuine expression of our metaphysical desires," nor "the first voice in which we heard the sonority of our soul," nor yet "the interpreter of our thirst for the infinite," for, in our country, as João Ribeiro said, "no one cares about the infinite." Farias Brito was, therefore, not the interpreter of our conscience—unless it corresponds to that state described by Gregório de Matos:

> that neither chooses Good nor Ill reproves,
> but dazzled and uncertain, suffers all.

What his philosophy may have translated—although in this his thought was no different from that of other Brazilian intellectuals —was the hesitation and the sudden contrasts that seemed to characterize the behavior of the national elite. His philosophical work is fragile—despite all the enthusiasm of the few and ungrateful disciples he at first attracted and of those others, merely interested in the "justification," if I may use the word, of his reactionary politics. It echoes the pessimistic melody of German philosophy as its main theme. And although Farias Brito was not, as so many others in Brazil, a mere "improviser in philosophy," the rest of the work is a tedious commentary of the philosophical systems he examined, "dazzled and uncertain." [127]

PART THREE

PART THREE

CHAPTER 7

Ideas in the Twentieth Century

The monarchy, an exotic growth in America, as we have seen represented at the moment of independence the most viable solution in the historical circumstances. The adoption of the monarchical regime was once more the result of the improvisation that seems to characterize our actions.[1]

Thanks to the monarchy—which had marked a decisive phase of our formation as a nation—our political history constitutes a special chapter of the agitated history of the young South American nations in the nineteenth century. We did not, however, escape disturbances, which, carefully considered, reveal the same trace of rebelliousness and disorganized individualism found in the other American countries of Iberian origin and which are perhaps the outcome of the adventurous spirit that presided over our common historic destiny.

During the monarchy, however, a relative calm prevailed, interrupted only by the natural misunderstandings between the parties, the cabinets, and the Houses—all very much part of the regime—but the life of the country managed to remain unaffected. The system worked in such a way that any discord ended up in the *Quinta da Boa Vista* [the imperial residence.—Trans.] and did not survive the "ominous pencil" of the moderative power: no serious agitation, no incident disturbed the tranquility of Dom Pedro II's partriarchalism.[2]

It was against this "perfect civil servant," the Emperor, holding moderative power in his hands, it was against his personal power, that the Empire politicians were soon to revolt.[3]

The fall of the Zacarias cabinet in 1868 was a blow "to the prestige of the monarchical institutions in our country. We can say that the process of disintegration of the monarchy dates from this time."[4] The fall of this cabinet accentuated the latent irritation with the Emperor's personal power. Thus, the *Radical Manifesto* published in 1869, called for the immediate suppression of the moderative power.[5]

We are not concerned here with an analysis of events during the last twenty years of the monarchy. But we must not forget the influence of the international political and social events of the time which, coupled with emancipation, had powerful repercussions in the last years of Empire. Examples are the Paraguayan war, with the resulting familiarity between Brazilian officers and their Uruguayan and Argentinian allies; the Civil War in the United States; Emperor Maximilian's Mexican adventure; and, finally, the fall of Napoleon III's Empire and the installation of the Third Republic in France. All these factors hastened the fall of the monarchy. We must also recognize, as did the first republican Minister of Justice, that it was the Army that was immediately responsible for the proclamation of the republic in Brazil on November 15, 1889. "The revolt was due to them and to them alone, the civilians having contributed practically nothing. The people witnessed the events stupefied, astounded, surprised, not realizing the significance of what was taking place."[6]

The republic was not brought about by the effects of propaganda. It was the Army that, having exhausted its patience with the ineptitude of the last few governments of the monarchy, finally decided "between luncheon and dinner," in the words of a contemporary commentator, to overthrow the regime. Republican propaganda had been "vague and indecisive, insisting on the need to replace the monarchy by a republic but giving no indication of the new regime's essential characteristics, the new features that were to replace those to be destroyed, or the practical steps to be taken."[7] The republic—like many other events in our history, as though to confirm the pragmatical nature of our spirit—was yet another improvisation.

"The republic had passed from dream to reality. How was it to survive? How was the highly centralized parliamentary monarchy to be transformed into a predominantly presidentialist republic?"[8] This was the task of the provisional government, and principally of the man who was to occupy a prominent position on the Brazilian scene for many years to come—Rui Barbosa. A "republican of the moment," as he himself was to declare,[9] it devolved upon this Bahian intellectual to undertake not only the most difficult work of the early days of the republic,[10] but also, during the thirty-odd remaining years of his life, the most thankless apostolizing for the regime at whose birth he presided.

The statement that "in the week following the proclamation of the republic only one mind was active—that of Rui Barbosa,"[11] was made by a man who had never nurtured any sympathy for Rui. Rui was in fact an improvisor, an organizer, who revealed himself with the proclamation of the republican regime in Brazil. "His vigilance and his desire for renovation and construction"[12] encompassed everything. He was, however, a classic nineteenth-century liberal, for whom the most perfect form of government was the constitutional monarchy. Twenty-two years after the proclamation and consolidation of the republic he had organized—and to which he had linked his own destiny—he was to confess in the Senate: "I fought against the monarchy never having ceased to be a monarchist. I became a republican in the last few days of the monarchy when its situation made me bear the responsibility that I had assumed by my agitation in the press."[13] Rui had neither promoted nor desired the republic. He had opposed the monarchy and had ended up a republican, because the imperial regime had shown itself averse to the reforms the country so badly needed.[14]

This studious man, a voracious reader, did not, however, have a speculative turn of mind. "The immense work of Rui Barbosa," writes Batista Pereira, "suffers from the lack of a synthesis summarizing the main points of his *organum,* or the doctrinal body of his ideas."[15] As Luís Delgado observes,

even Rui's expression of ideas was, to a large extent, the outcome of the position of the problems he presented at the moment of expression. It is not merely a question of coördinating excerpts or organizing definitions —one must know in what circumstances, under the influence of what factors, impelled by what social needs, these words were uttered. They can be explained in terms of an environment—the complex environment of a society that had not yet succeeded in devising its spiritual discipline or in making its institutions reflect the fundamental principles of its life, of all life.[16]

Thus, Rui Barbosa was neither "exclusively erudite and artistic nor exclusively critical; he was a lively realist." [17] Involved in political struggle,[18] Rui was not "a contemplative, intent on abstract thought and philosophical speculation, nor did he take pleasure in the art of subtle debate or the finesse of specious argument." [19] In fact, on the layer of humanism was superimposed the lawyer and jurist,[20] the active politician. For this reason Rui did not "withdraw from the whirlpool of humanity to contemplate it from afar." [21] With a temperament that was "distant, grave, and proud," [22] he was insensitive to irony. In the writings of this man—whom Capistrano de Abreu described to João Lúcio de Azevedo[23] as "simple and well educated [with] a dislike of too many words [who] seems to possess no philosophical culture, since for him philosophy is reduced to logic and dialectics"—there once is a note that perhaps expresses his *"earthly love for reality."* It occurs in his welcome to Anatole France on the occasion of the latter's visit to the Brazilian Academy of Letters. Rui recalled the words of Jerôme Coignard: "Les verités découvertes par l'intelligence démeurent stériles. Le coeur est seul capable de féconder les rêves. Il verse la vie dans tout ce qu'il aime." And Rui concludes indignantly: "N'est ce pas, du moins ici, la philosophie la plus humainement vrai?" [24] Perhaps in this speech, the active fighter having been laid to rest, Rui was making a confession.

It is now widely recognized that the method of dividing history into periods is both arbitrary and of uncertain worth. The current of events bursts the banks of any system, and only the need for clear exposition at times seems to demand or to justify them. To determine the dates of origin of certain veins, threads, or currents of ideas is "very difficult and the historian of ideas is in this respect at a greater disadvantage than even the historian of political events." [25] The study of ideas in Brazil during the republican period presents this difficulty.

It would be absurd to pretend [writes Gilberto Freyre], that political forms are unrelated to an institution, a way of life, or an economic production of the extent and strength of the old agricultural and slaveholding patriarchy. Officially this had come to an end in Brazil, once and for all, a year before the beginning of the republican period. Sociologically it had not died; mortally wounded by emancipation, it adapted itself to the republic and for years a semi-slaveholding patriarchy and the federal republic continued to live almost as symbiotically as the slaveholding patriarchy and the centralized Empire had done. Even today, a number of patriarchal survivals are familiar to the Brazilians of the areas most marked by the long dominion of the slaveholding rural and even pastoral patriarchy—less affected by the neo-European (Italian, German, Polish, and so on) or Japanese imagination, or by industrialization of national life.[26]

A similar phenomenon occurs in the history of ideas in Brazil. In the foregoing pages we have referred to some of the names linked to certain currents of thought that provoked an echo in our country —names that bestride two periods, active not only during the last years of the Empire but also in the period of the republic. Among these, that of Rui Barbosa stands out from the beginning, his action being intimately linked to the first phase of our republican life or the phase that, after the 1930 revolution, is normally referred to as the "First Republic" or the "Old Republic."

It was, then, a monarchist, a counselor of the Empire, who organized and directed the first steps of the new regime. This was not the first time—nor will it be the last—that political events take such a paradoxical turn.

During the Empire's last years, Rui Barbosa had fought against monarchical centralization in favor of the federal principle.[27] Once the republic had been proclaimed, he followed the example of the United States and, in the republic's First Decree, fixed the new form of government for the nation: federalism, the form that "best corresponds to the needs of that vast archipelago of human islands"[28] that is Brazil.

From the earliest days of the republic the "government's action was clearly influenced by democratic liberal aspirations, in which the old French and English doctrines were juxtaposed with the new republican and federalist models of the United States of America."[29] This was what justified the initial reserve of the Positivists toward Rui and the republican regime, and their later criticism and opposition.[30] Republicans "in their own manner," the dictatorial manner outlined by Auguste Comte, the Positivists, as we have seen, were opposed to "democracy"[31] and were not prepared to forgive the liberal "deviations" of the Empire politicians converted to the new order by the republic.[32]

Rui Barbosa, who was chiefly responsible for the new direction taken by government policy, had been, from the days of his adolescence, an admirer of eighteenth-century ideas and principally of English culture. The *Social Contract* and *The Rights of Man* had already inspired his father, João Barbosa, who after the revolutionary adventures of his youth had never given up his reading of English and French writers.[33] No one, at the time of the proclamation of the republic, was as well-versed as Rui in North American institutions.[34] Thus, the ideas followed by the republicans who, to quote José Maria dos Santos, "had transformed a military conspiracy into a republican revolt," [35] were those derived from a tradition as peculiar to its native country as is the Anglo-Saxon.

As at all times of improvisation, the practical sense was predominant. Thus, the leaders of the First Republic, as Gilberto Freyre observed, "nearly all wanted to be *essentially practical* men, opposed to poetic fantasies." They managed to achieve their ambition in the organization of higher education as an almost entirely professional training. To such an extent that Bryce, who visited Brazil, expressed surprise at the strictly practical nature of our higher education. "We were more Papist than the Pope; more practical than the English." [36]

It might seem that the old ideas were being as quickly disposed of as the antique jacaranda wood tables and Portuguese *paliteiros* [beautifully worked toothpick stands or cases.—Trans.] that were, as we are told by Gilberto Freyre,[37] being rapidly auctioned off. However, the same pragmatic spirit apparent in our historic formation survived in the republic. If the Portuguese, as Sant'Ana Dionísio feels, "have a gross propensity for the overcultivation of merely circumstantial matters," [38] we Brazilians, according to a contemporary writer, "are like men of other countries in conditions similar to ours, very poor in ideological aspirations. Our greatest achievements always have a flavor of empiricism, of an improvisation imposed by the circumstances of the moment." [39] It was therefore not without reason that Clóvis Beviláqua said that "if we are some day to make a philosophical contribution of significance, I am convinced that it will not emerge from the heights of metaphysics." [40]

Our spirit leads us, like our colonizing ancestors, who gave Brazil its form, toward earthly realities. In the republic the same trait continued to prevail. This pragmatic nature, the propensity for the essentially practical, of our republican leaders can be understood—and perhaps explained—in terms of an environment such as ours, one that had not yet succeeded in devising its "spiritual discipline or in making its institutions reflect the fundamental principles of its life." [41]

This practical bent still characterized our intelligence after the proclamation of the republic. Professor Miguel Reale, in writing of Rui Barbosa, justly observed that he "was dominated by the beliefs of the liberal state and accustomed to the game of the juridical abstractions of British parliamentarianism or Yankee presidentialist federalism, but concerned himself with these abstractions with a practical aim in view, that is, in an active sense." [42] I believe, like this writer, that Rui Barbosa was almost certainly interested in abstractions "as tools, or as the traditional means of interference sanctioned by precedent, or when they came within the field of actual human experience, but not in abstraction for its own sake." [43] Rui Barbosa, then, is another example of that "realistic spirit, with precise, defined, and concrete objectives" [44] referred to by Professor Joaquim de Carvalho in his study of Portuguese culture, that seems to have left its mark on our own intelligence. Sérgio Buarque de Holanda is also right when he says that "in Brazil, however unattractive it may seem to some of our patriots, the truth is that we are still linked to the Iberian peninsula, and especially to Portugal, by a long and living tradition, a tradition still vital enough even now to nurture a common soul, despite all the factors that separate us." [45] Ideas, as reflections of historical conditions and shaped by national circumstances, are always an instrument for action. It is with this practical stamp that they express themselves in Brazil, a stamp that corresponds, as we have seen, to the traditional Portuguese mold.

The ideas that resounded in our country after the proclamation of the republic are the same ideas that predominated in the last twenty years of the imperial regime, but now enlivened by a new feeling for the destinies of nations.

"The revolution is over, and no one seems minded to protest. But it so happens that those who made the revolution had not entertained the least intention of doing so. And hence there is, in America, a 'President of the Republic' by force." [46] It is in these words (which confirm Aristides Lôbo's observation that "the people witnessed with stupefaction the proclamation of the republic") that Max Leclerc, correspondent of the *Journal des Débats*, refers to the political atmosphere of the capital a little more than a month after the advent of the republican regime. This also explains what José Maria dos Santos writes in his *Política Geral do Brasil*: "It devolved upon Benjamin Constant to transform the military rebellion into a republican revolution." [47] A revolution or, as Sérgio Milliet rightly preferred to call it, *"the coup d'état"* or "revolt," "since the word revolution implies a change of customs and habits, institutions and philosophy of life," and the republic simply changed the form of government, not making itself felt to any extent in the daily lives, customs, and preoccupations of the people." [48]

We must not forget, however—and this factor did not escape Sérgio Milliet—that great changes had taken place at the end of the nineteenth century.

What had previously been impossible because of the slowness of communication became a commonplace, within reach of even modest purses. The big French and English newspapers began to send correspondents wherever important events occurred and instructed them to send back detailed despatches written not only to inform readers but also to prepare the ground for less immediate objectives. In the case of Max Leclerc, the newspaper's interest in the launching of future enterprises requiring capital investment was immediately apparent. Capitalist expansion was already in full swing, and keen competition between England and the continental powers had already begun. The fall of the Empire had widespread repercussions in Europe, where the Emperor had always enjoyed considerable prestige. In the eyes of French politicians a possibility for penetration had been thwarted. It had become necessary to acquire a more intimate knowledge of the battlefield: to become friendly with members of the government, to discover their affiliations with conservative elements, and to find ways of turning these things to advantage. [49]

During the second half of the nineteenth century, and particularly after 1870, there was an expansion of new productive forces in Brazil, and from this expansion, as we have already had occasion to note, the country entered a new phase of material and spiritual life. In the last years of the Empire, Brazil was already taking the first steps on "the transitional path from commercial capitalism to industrial capitalism," writes Afonso Arinos de Mello Franco. [50]

We must also bear in mind that the last three decades of the last century were a period of relative peace, hitherto unknown in Europe, although it was an armed peace. It is in these periods of armed vigilance that the rhythm of economic development in countries like Brazil is accelerated. In our situation, this acceleration was achieved in large measure through immigration[51] and progressive industrialization.

> After modest beginnings [writes Caio Prado Júnior], Brazilian industry experienced its first considerable leap forward during the last decade of the Empire (1880-1889) . . . This phase of industrial progress continued during the republic and corresponded to the feverish spate of new undertakings in the early years of the new regime. The sharp fall in the exchange rate reinforced industrial prosperity, and the disruption of the Empire's conservative equilibrium opened the doors for a policy more openly protective toward the country's production.[52]

"Economic organization developed with the expansion of commercial enterprises. Capital was invested with increasing boldness and led to a rise in the value of the new countries." [53]

The republic took advantage of this "bold" investment of capital in new countries, and it was around coffee, the product that had come to monopolize national economy, that its application revolved.[54]

It is not easy to attempt a study of the penetration and development of capital in Brazil. In this field, as in others of our history, we suffer from a lack of reliable monographs that would serve as guides over such rough terrain.[55]

Summing up the situation of the Second Empire, during which production of sugar, one of the main export crops of colonial times, had already begun to decrease, we can say that the decline of the monarchy is marked by the first crisis in coffee, the cultivation of which was threatened by abolition. In the republican period "coffee gave us our favorable balances in international trade. It built São Paulo, supported Brazil, and, when it could dispense with slave labor, conspired for the republican federation, abandoning the Empire to its melancholy fate." [56] Coffee, then, was up to the 1930 revolution—and even afterward—the support of Brazilian economy. "Brazil," said Silveira Martins in the imperial Senate, "is coffee, and coffee is the Negro." "General Coffee," as it has been called, is therefore intimately linked to the political vicissitudes of our history, principally those of the republican period.[57]

The model of the United States of America was the example set before Brazil already during the last years of the imperial regime and later during the republic when it became a *leitmotiv* of propaganda. Even the statesmen of the Empire had been impressed by the development of the United States and were preparing to reorganize the nation's economy. Thus, with the republic, new prospects were opened up for the economic life of the country. The federal republic, in "liberating the provinces, awakened in them a spirit of initiative. The extraordinary growth of São Paulo and, later, that of Minas and Rio Grande do Sul, was in large measure the cause of this." [58] Just as the abolition of the slave trade had done previously, the abolition of slavery provoked a veritable flurry of business that, in the last days of the monarchy and the first days of the republic, became a fantastic and fabulous race. This period, which has not yet been sufficiently studied, was the period of the *"encilhamento"* [59] or wave of speculation.

"The cause of this crisis can be found in the functioning of the monetary system, although it was complicated by other factors," writes Caio Prado, Júnior, "and in the ever-recurrent recourse to uncontrollable and more or less arbitrary issues of currency, of which the past offers . . . so many examples." [60] This crisis, carried over from the Empire, was aggravated during the republican transition. The imperial government had already been forced to issue currency in order to

satisfy the important class of former slave owners, who had been dealt a severe blow by abolition without monetary compensation. Nevertheless, the facilities for issuing money, which had been granted to several banks (backed only by existing gold reserves and legal tender notes for the internal public debt), had not been used, since the republican *coup d'état* quickly ensued. But the new regime was faced with an unchanged financial situation and could not, therefore, abandon the banking scheme bequeathed by the Empire. Added to this was the fact that it would not have been prudent for a newly established regime, not yet sure of its reception by the nation, to refuse to sanction a measure so eagerly awaited.[61]

Rui Barbosa, the republic's first Minister of Finance, who had formerly opposed the financial scheme of the monarchy's last cabinet, was now compelled by political circumstance—and perhaps, too, by his ardent desire that the country should be provided with new industries—to continue the policy of his predecessor, extending the issuing capacity of the banks.

The republic had received from the Empire a "kind of seigniorial plantation, modest and well-regulated. It was only natural that the republicans should attempt to enlarge and beautify it, fighting the old routines that they themselves had criticized." [62] The republicans —among them Rui Barbosa, that recent convert to republicanism— became actively engaged in this attempt to liberate "the new forces, pulsing in the bosom of society, that were to substitute for the agrarian and feudal structure of the Empire a more diversified economic structure." [63] We can understand Rui's enthusiasm when we learn that the single-crop and slave-holding state vibrated [64] with intense and unorganized industrialization. "About three hundred companies registered their articles of association with the Board of Trade in the republic's capital during 1890, and this business boom rose in crescendo from month to month." [65] This "policy of widening horizons," to quote the significant expression of the *Jornal do Comércio's* commercial commentator at that period,[66] could not last long. Soon the fabulous enterprises of the *encilhamento* crumbled noisily into ruin—

the great period of enterprises and companies of every description . . . Sonorous and spectacular cascades of ideas, inventions, and concessions poured forth daily, to make a thousand reis, a hundred thousand reis, a thousand thousand reis, thousands upon thousands of reis. Paper and shares issued crisp and unceasingly from the presses. There were railroads, banks, factories, mines, shipyards . . .[67]

The intense activity of the *encilhamento* was succeeded by the disorder in public finance that afflicted the early years of the First Republic. Those responsible for the new regime felt that a "return to reality" and experience was needed. Thus the republic came once again to the counselors of the Empire. Thus, "soon afterward the republic went back to being governed by the landed class, which imposed on the republic its own representatives . . . and, with the irresistible expansion of the coffee economy, the greatness of the Santos market was established and the foundations laid for the true industrialization of Brazil." [68]

The immigration of foreign colonists and the development of the coffee industry assisted and determined, as Roberto Simonsen has observed, "the formation of a considerable internal market for industrial products. Progress in electric power and the construction of large electric power plants, principally in São Paulo and the Federal District, were among the essential factors in industrial growth." [69]

The new growth of industry, the influx of immigrants, and the

direct or indirect influence of the ideals that had begun to predominate in the country after 1870, were paralleled by the historical
growth of the First Republic. It was in São Paulo, "given the internal
relationship of economic factors and the movement of ideas"[70] that
the republic found, in my opinion, the best basis for its consolidation.

A new phase in the country's history emerged, in a somewhat
confused manner, during the first three decades of the twentieth
century. During this phase, many of the currents we have previously
briefly examined in the first part of this work still survived. But
while these nineteenth-century ideas continued to flourish, new
ideas arising from new forms of universal thought began, thanks
to the rapid economic development of the country, to ripen into
new "ideologies."

After 1914, or perhaps a little later, "our books became increasingly redolent of the jungle, of wet earth, and of fresh sea breezes.
Brazilian themes and the landscape that surrounds us were to give
to our literature a greater spontaneity," writes Tristão de Ataíde.[71]

2

In the second part of this work I attempted to indicate the Brazilian
representatives of the principal European currents of thought that
made themselves felt in the second half of the nineteenth century—
those who followed in the wake of the new ideas that agitated Brazil
after 1868, when important transformations in the destiny of the
country were effected. These currents were, as we have seen: that
of the orthodox Positivists of the "Apostolate"; that of the heterodox
or, better, "scientific" Positivists, like Luís Pereira Barreto; that of the
evolutionist naturalism of Sílvio Romero and others; and that of
Farias Brito, who, "perplexed and uncertain," struck the most varied
notes of the philosophy of the second half of the nineteenth century.

The ideas that echoed in the first years of the republic were still
European. In the course of their expression in practice and in action
—for, in Brazil, ideas were always chiefly instruments of action—as
they were measured against the other ideas that kept appearing in
the intellectual centers of Europe and from whence they were ex-
ported to us (easily managing to pass our extremely liberal customs
barrier of criticism and judgment), they began to suffer the effects of
wear and tear and went out of fashion quickly or slowly, according
to the amount of their "use," so to speak. It is, then, still the ideas

of the second half of the nineteenth century—and it could not have been otherwise—that we find at the time of the Constitution of the new political regime. It was during the first phase of the republic, with the new conditions of the civilized world and all the local changes, that we witness the appearance of new interpretations resulting from the changes effected in European thought.

Fernando de Azevedo observes that we can distinguish three phases in the history of sociology in Brazil, the first stretching from the second half of the nineteenth century to the year 1928.

During this period . . . appear, at wide intervals, studies and books which reveal, in their interpretation of general or literary history, sociological ideas and trends displaying a greater or lesser, but generally superficial, understanding of the spirit of the ideas current in social science—then still in its nascent state—in the middle years of the nineteenth century.[72]

All these interpretations were still inspired by Positivist or evolutionist ideas,[73] and it must be stressed that this was still going on up to 1928, or the eve of the 1930 revolution.

Gradually, and mainly during the early years of the twentieth century under the influence of a diffuse Positivism and Spencerian evolutionism, sociological preoccupations began to impose themselves on the Brazilian intellect, ever eager for novelty and synthesis. Comte's philosophy already offered one such synthesis, or *summa,* as did the philosophy of Herbert Spencer, which, based on positive science, is, as Sorley says, "a scheme with a place for everything." [74]

We must also bear in mind that philosophy suffered a profound crisis at the end of the nineteenth century. The symptoms of this crisis were

the appearance of movements opposed to the most important doctrines of modern thought, materialist mechanicism and subjectivism. This transformation spread beyond the borders of philosophy and can be compared to the great crisis that gave birth to modern culture at the time of the Renaissance. It is difficult to trace the numerous and intricate causes of this crisis, but the facts are clear: at this period, Europe was gripped by a widespread movement of social thinking.[75]

The spiritual atmosphere of the civilized world underwent a profound change. It corresponded to changes in the social structure and was at the same time a necessary consequence of these changes.[76] Philosophy is influenced by sociological contributions and, like other forms of spiritual life, acquired a new attitude and a new spirit. A phenomenon similar to that imagined in the eighteenth century took place, when "what had before lurked in the shade was now growing day by day: what had been the speculation of a few rare spirits was spreading among the multitude; what had been timid, grew bold." [77] In this way were born the "sociological syntheses" referred to by Léon Brunschvicg[78] that appeared in a diffident form with Montesquieu, broke out powerfully in the nineteenth century, and became like *reginae scientiarum* or new *summae* for our time at the beginning of the twentieth century, falling into the errors and vices that Marcel Mauss pointed out in sociology thirty years ago: the tendencies toward the philosophy of history and the philosophy of society.[79]

Thus, the "philosophism" of imperial times was succeeded by "sociologism" marked by traces of Positivism, Spencerianism, or evolutionism, at times timidly or brazenly materialistic but always considered scientific, finished, and definitive "when sociology was still in its initial stage and struggling to assert itself." [80] The same boldness and love of novelty—together with the belief in the immediate redemptive power of ideas—characteried the advent of "sociologism" in Brazil.[81] "As we know," wrote Sílvio Romero significantly in 1904, "the old uproar that was raised over the intrinsic nature of history and gave rise to a number of systems is now being repeated, with even greater fervor, over the nature and character of society and sociology." [82]

The crisis in philosophy at the beginning of the twentieth century, a reflection of the change in spiritual life that had been going on since the previous century as a result of important social movements, was also felt in Brazil, and, once again, it was in terms of the tradition of cultural importation rather than in terms of the local conditions of the social problem. Only later, after the First World War, became the social problem in Brazil more apparent and came to preoccupy a greater number of Brazilian intellectuals. Thus, at the time of the 1891 Constituent Assembly, which laid the foundations for the federative republican regime, we still find the old currents of nineteenth-century ideas.

The opinions that have been held concerning this Constituent Assembly and the Constitution that was somewhat hastily drawn up by it, are contradictory. The Constitution was always belittled during our youth and was held responsible for all the ills that befell

Brazil. It was said that the Constitution was the work of utopian idealists, "good fellows who had grown accustomed to throwing stones at the government" and who, "taken by surprise when they found themselves entrusted with the solemn mission of statesmanship, hastily improvised a program for development." [83] It seems true that the republicans—both the "historical" ones and the later "adherents"—except for the Army which was to play a major role from the first moments of the republic—did not represent "a strongly coherent nucleus of opinion or a social class with any real prestige." [84] The group of republicans was nothing but "a tiny group of dreamers, acting in an intermittent and dispersive way amidst the lack of curiosity and indifference of an immense country." [85] Martinho Prado, one of the members of the Constituent Assembly, compared it to a sphinx:

This Congress is a mystery; it nurses in its bosom natures so diverse and opposed that I do not know how to describe it. Nevertheless, it is more than was expected and is above the anomalous circumstances in which the country finds itself. It is a sphinx whose riddle we shall decipher in future legislative sessions.[86]

In fact, the Constituent Assembly did harbor diverse and opposed natures: Positivists following Comte and Littré, Catholics, Spencerians, some liberal monarchists, and numerous military republicans. In the bitter description of Lúcio Pestana (the pseudonym of Dunschee de Abranches), the Congress was "a heteromorphous assembly, wherein political passions boil over and the majority of members make no attempt to hide their terror and the memory of the annihilation of their political ambitions by the enmity of the second oligarchy surrounding Deodoro." [87]

The committee initially nominated—a committe of five, appointed to draft a constitutional project—was composed of older republicans: Saldanha Marinho, Rangel Pestana, Santos Werneck, Américo Brasiliense, and Magalhães Castro. They drafted three projects,[88] finally replaced by the definitive project handed to the provisional government on May 30, 1890. It fell to Rui Barbosa to touch it up before it was published as a decree "ad referendum" of the Constituent Assembly.

The Constituent Assembly was installed on November 15, 1890. Luís Viana Filho recorded that it was an assembly "to frighten even the most cautious." In fact, the fall of the Empire, by sweeping away the country's old political hierarchy, had aroused new and great ambitions. Once the old idols had fallen, a pleiad of bachelors and military men, greedy for power, emerged, each more eager than his rivals to get to the top. There were clashes between veteran propagandists and opportunists determined to take the lion's share. And even among the propagandists themselves, Positivists, Jacobins, and pure democrats fought each other for the privilege of ensuring the spiritual domination of their sect.[89]

Thus, heated discussions were soon in full swing and also, on occasion, those tournaments of loquacity that seem so much to our taste (bad taste), the lengthy speeches[90] that led Prudente de Morais to declare, on one occasion, that "in the name of order the deputies were creating the greatest disorder." [91]

Once the members of the Constituent Assembly had been elected by the Cesário Alvim Regulation—a regulation that permitted, in the words of César Zama, "a veritable assault on the ballot boxes" [92] —the deputies, above all the Republicans, made a display of Jacobinism forcing the recent converts, or "adesistas besieged by mistrust, to allay suspicion by displaying ideas even more radical than those of the 'historical' republicans." [93]

Politicians of the time, such as Dunschee de Abranches, did not see in the 1891 Constitution a document worthy of "advanced liberal ideas." They even denied that it consecrated the republican spirit! They considered it "an iron hoop devised by a man whose intentions toward the Constituent Assembly were well known." [94] The moderns—those who were born with the republic—such as Oliveira Viana, saw in it "a work beautiful from the doctrinal point of view, but doomed to immediate failure," [95] a code in which were epitomized "the most liberal aspect of the idealistic currents of the time." [96] Nevertheless, although the Constituent Assembly was composed, as many thought, of inexperienced soldiers and "violent and demagogic young men," and was "inspired by divergent aims, it managed to produce a praiseworthy work, thanks to the calm and methodic action of its president," [97] despite the fact that it was divided, according to the deputy from Alagoas, into four groups: the "malcontents," the "restless and the revolutionaries," the "lovers of order," and the "disillusioned." [98] As the product of a handful of "greedy bachelors of law and military men," it translated, I feel, the legal formalism of the Law School's "bacheloristic" tradition and the military love of regulations. It offers a good example of the superstitious belief in the power of written formulae.[99] The grave error which Oliveira Viana condemns in the Constituent Assembly is the conviction of its members that "a political reform is possible only by political means," when, in fact, this is "only the auxiliary of greater reforms of a social and economic nature."[100] Nevertheless, despite their chastisement as "constitutional aesthetes" by the author of *Ocaso do Império* and despite their disagreements and the clashes[101] that took place—those arising in the Assembly itself or those that echoed external arguments—the members of the 1891 Assembly managed to construct a new framework for the country's political powers.

It has also been often repeated that the new regime was implanted by the assault of the military class.[102]

It is true that the republic was chiefly the work of military men and that it gave them a position that they had never enjoyed under the Empire. But it seems to me inadmissible to assume that the Army should remain aloof from political struggles.

The liberal sentiment dominant in our political formation was never alien to the armed forces [writes José Maria dos Santos]. If the officers had remained indifferent to the popular agitation of 1831, the revolution of April 7 that led to the abdication of Pedro I would never have gone beyond a simple riot, easily put down by a few fusillades and rounded off by a number of summary executions. But our armed forces were no longer the Army and Navy intermingled with foreigners that had smothered the Pará mutiny in the holds of the brig *Palhaço* in 1823 under a cloud of lime hurled down through the hatches and that had placed Frei Caneca before a firing squad in Pernambuco after the republican revolution of 1824. It was only natural that the intense public life of the Second Empire should have left a profound mark on the spirit of the troops, predisposing them to accept the political transformations that were effective without any resistance.[103]

The creation of the soldier citizen, which some believe was due to the influence of Positivism, antedates this: it was a creation of the Empire itself.

The responsibility for the ruin of military education is often attributed to Positivism, accused of having taken away from the military schools "their essential character as centers of military education and moral and intellectual preparation for war"[104]—and so of having "civilized" the soldiers.

Positivism—as we have seen, always opposed to titles and privilege—was not responsible for the appearance of the "doctor" or "scholar" majors and colonels of the early days of the republic.[105] The progressive accentuation of the Army's political activities dates from the Paraguayan war, the struggles of emancipation, and the series of misunderstandings that had arisen from 1883 onward; these misunderstandings, to which the designation "military question" has been given, involved military opposition to the various imperial cabinets and led the Army gradually to accept a new political regime more in accord with the other American nations.[106]

The "military question" was the "most direct cause" [107] of the fall of the monarchy.

"Toward the middle of the nineteenth century, because of a number of factors, the Brazilian bourgeoisie found itself able to make a bid for the power that swung in the tremulous hands of the sugar aristocracy." [108] The bourgeoisie, or, as San Tiago Dantas prefers to call it, "that rudiment of a bourgeoisie," was

unable to change the structure of society. The nascent middle class, incorporating civil servants and "white collar" workers, crystallized itself around a new power that drew nearly all its members from this class, the national Army . . . Although it is true that among us the middle class did not emerge with that economic strength that gave it so much power in other societies, it is likewise true that this deficiency was compensated by the concentration of political power permitted by the emergence of power in the military class.[109]

We must not forget, however, that

among our armed classes there was never that "esprit" that constitutes militarism or its logical consequence, military politics. Our Army may possess "esprit de corps"—which is, in any case, less active than in older militarized nations; but it has not, and has never had, the pretension to any political mission in opposition to the nation's political classes. It is true that it has played a decisive role in many national political movements, beginning with independence; but it has never, in all these movements, acted on its own impulse originating from within the core of the Army and embodying political thinking in class terms. It has often shown a capacity for responding to the idealism of the civilian classes, as in the case of independence or abolition, but one can also say that the idealist attitudes it displayed often served merely to disguise its extreme awareness of the exploitation and intrigue of our frock-coated politicians.[110]

In the confusion following the hesitations[111] that overtook the "astounding deed" [112] of November 15, in the verbose vagueness of the historical republicans who did not know how to organize a concrete program for action—since they limited themselves to criticism of the imperial regime—the military class, for all its defects, was the essential prop of the new regime and constituted its power. This explains its preponderance in the history of the most difficult moments of the first republican governments and perhaps even of those of today. The significant declaration by a politician that "the rupture between the armed forces and the government in a country where the populace is unarmed is that government's irremissible condemnation" [113] is of recent date. It was, then, the "frivolousness" of the masses and the "unarmed populace" that favored and explained the Army's intervention in politics in 1889 and made it on a number of occasions party to the political game of the republic. The monarchists, however, all affirmed for a considerable time, following in the steps of Américo Werneck, "that militarism is the cancer of the republic, the most virulent ulcer currently (1893) poisoning the body of the nation." [114] Militarism, however, in its true sense, never existed in Brazil. The Army was composed, principally during the last years of the republic, of young men of humble origin who sought in the Military School—as others did in the Catholic seminaries— the education that their slender resources would not otherwise permit. "At that time the young men of the Military School found in the philosophy of Auguste Comte guiding principles for their conduct and discipline for their minds," [115] and for this reason became estranged from Catholicism. On the other hand, the Paraguayan war gave the Army the "stability and internal cohesion that thenceforth made it the most resistant point of our political organism." [116] It was therefore not only understandable but natural that it should have played such an important role in the fall of the monarchy and the early days of the republic.

If we read a work that purports to give us a general view of the literary situation in Brazil during the early years of the twentieth century, such as *O Momento Literário,* written by Paulo Barretto under the pseudonym João do Rio,[117] we note even then the same ideas that we have previously attempted to outline. Besides a vague and eclectic aestheticism, the following currents were still in vogue: Positivism;

evolutionism in its Darwinistic form, which was gaining ground because of a growing "scientific" orientation; eclecticism, that "in the Brazilian soul had found the deepest and most widespread radiation," according to Clóvis Beviláqua;[118] and ideas originating in Catholic trends. It is therefore possible, I feel, to affirm that this was the intellectual situation in Brazil up to 1914.

Once the Constitution had been accepted, a revolutionary phase, foreshadowed during the period of the Constituent Assembly, was initiated. The Constituent Assembly "managed to reconcile itself to the country's conservative elements, which had at first looked upon it with suspicion, afraid of its lack of experience and its Positivist and radical tendencies," [119] but no reconciliation was achieved for the executive power or, rather, for the loyal and ingenuous Marshal Deodoro. From the outset, he was engaged in a running quarrel with the politicians of the Constituent Assembly, who had elected him president and whose ambitions had been aroused by the new situation. He soon resigned in favor of his vice president, Marshal Floriano Peixoto, who was largely responsible for the military pronouncement that resulted in the republic.

It is still difficult to judge with any degree of calmness this man composed of apparently contradictory elements—and hence so profoundly Brazilian—who was Floriano Peixoto.

> He inspired in his contemporaries the most ardent enthusiasms and the most violent hatreds . . . In this gift for kindling the passions of those who lived in his own time and even of those who attempt to consider him from a historical viewpoint, we detect the first sign, not of his greatness but certainly of his originality.[120]

Euclides da Cunha called him a "sphinx," who lived, in the early days of republican Brazil, "amidst a play of unfortunate contrasts—senators armed to the teeth quarreling with Platonic military men crying out for peace, a legality that triumphed by the suspension of law, and a Constitution strangled by the tight embraces of its adorers." [121]

Floriano had inherited a somewhat difficult situation. The quarrels that had culminated in Deodoro's resignation on November 23, 1891, after the *coup d'état* of November 3 (or the "closing down of the Stock Exchange," as it was called by some) [122] abated for a while only to break out afresh shortly afterward as the result of the "vaulting ambition" that raged in the congressmen. [The Constituent Assembly, which had appointed Deodoro as first president under the new constitution and continued itself as the first congress, reached an impasse with him and was dissolved by him on this date. —Trans.] Throughout the country passions were kindled, provoked by individual interests. But a grave situation for the new regime had developed in the South, where "republicans" with Positivist tendencies, led by Júlio de Castilhos, were engaged in fighting their former political enemies. "The caudillism of the frontiers, almost forgotten in Brazil since the 'War of the *Farrapos*,' was once more sparked now, "at the service of the embattled parties." [123] The country was in a state of ferment, and the republic that had been "proclaimed by a bloodless revolution began to pay its arrears in the caudillism that chronically afflicted the continent." [124] Floriano Peixoto, as a soldier of the old school, believed that the regime of *pronunciamentos* was the worst calamity that could befall the nation. He decided to quash it, but in a veiled manner, and this he was able to do because of the "legality that triumphed by the suspension of law and of a Constitution strangled by the tight embraces of its adorers."

"The republic," wrote Tristão de Ataíde (when it had survived thirty-five years of struggles, compromises, scandals and had lived through a chapter of miseries with some moments of grandeur)—

results from two contradictory forces: Caesarism and caudillism. The former is a central authority that becomes increasingly absorbent; the latter, the latent or active forces of opposition that become increasingly dissolving. Between these two forces are the indifferent populace, the great unseen forces of labor, intelligence, egoism and sacrifice that silently weave the life of the nation and in whose name the two contradictory forces battle each other.[125]

In the opinion of Tristão de Ataíde these two contradictory forces were embodied in two personalities: Rui Barbosa and Pinheiro Machado. Pinheiro was the incarnation of caudillism—or "the transplantation to a broader scene of municipal colonelism" with a pyramid-like structure in which the anonymous electorate of the interior groups itself around local leaders, these forming the basis for the election of state leaders who in their turn support the national leaders." [126] Pinheiro was a *caudillo* (a "Southern colonel"—in fact, most generals were from the South), who had kept alive the feeling—or what Tristão de Ataíde[127] prefers to call the "instinct"—for freedom, the "love of adventure" tempered by the "comfort of social order," which maintained the link between "the natural anarchy of a wild people, not yet fully adapted to a collective sense, and the authority needed to develop this as yet amorphous feeling." [128] He was an adventurer who despised theories and would have nothing to do with systems. He was a general of the pampas with a love of battle and power. He was "a political realist possessed only of the culture of experience, of intuition, and of courage." [129]

Rui Barbosa, his opposite—who exercised in the republic what we may term the "function" that had formerly devolved upon the Bahian literati, that of fixing culture—was "an idealist, a romantic . . . The political liberalism of nineteenth-century parliamentarianism had molded his spirit. He was a man of law, a believer in precedent, in the example of England and the United States . . . He had no intuition, no sense of the immediate, no culture of experience," [130] he was a man of the city, of the library. Both Pinheiro Machado and Rui Barbosa, therefore, are facets of an adventure that was to continue in Brazil.

Tristão de Ataíde believed that neither the personality of Rui nor that of Pinheiro was attuned to their environment. To me this does not seem to be true: they both simply express the contrast that Nabuco indicated in one of the most beautiful passages of his book *A Minha Formação,* a contrast that still exists in Brazil. Rui represented "European culture," striving to adjust itself to the environment but lacking the requisite intuition; the stubborn preference for the adaptation of a model rather than reflection on an example; he represented also "the passion for liberty through a political idealism." [131] Pinheiro, on the other hand, represented the "American feeling," the passion for liberty "that strives to adjust itself to the human need for authority (and hence the power), the Machiavellian political blows, the realistic spirit of Brazilian formation." [132] Each embodies two threads of the historic destiny of ideas in Brazil. Hence the contrasting, and opposed, but significant action of both these men: "Pinheiro, reining in the ever resurgent Southern caudillism; Rui, giving a juridical cast to the coastal passion for 'governmentalism'; Rui embodying the spirit of authority, Pinheiro the spirit of anarchy. They met, having come from opposite directions." [133]

It is not easy to accept the simple lines of the scheme delineated by Tristão de Ataíde as an explanation—or rather as a suggestion—for the underlying meaning of political life in the first phase of our republican history. Tristão de Ataíde gives a shrewd, but perhaps insufficient, view. I am convinced that he must now consider his scheme a just but incomplete one, as I have said. Caesarism and caudillism mingle and take on strange and diverse guises in the unfolding of republican history. Costa Pôrto is probably right when he says that "the roots of 'colonelism,' caudillism, and political chieftainship are steeped in a kind of determinism in our formation" [134] —but we need not on this account go to the extreme of undertaking an "apology for the colonel," as Costa Pôrto proceeds to do.[135]

"If we analyze the elements of contemporary Brazilian life," Caio Prado justly observes, "elements in their widest sense, geographical, economic, social, and political, we find that the past, the colonial past . . . is still present, it still stands out conspicuously; it has, of course, been partly modified, but it is present in unmistakable traces." [136] It is true, however, that in the unfolding of republican history—which was, in its early years, "a series of gropings in the dark, fumbling steps, hesitations, and uncertainties" [137]—the various currents that, for lack of anything better, were used by Tristão de Ataíde as the two opposing forces of his scheme, were to confront one another throughout the evolution of the First Republic and to break out in a confused way in the 1930 revolution.

With Prudente de Morais, the first civilian president, Brazilian politics entered a new phase. The nine years preceding his presidency had been troubled and disturbed.[138] The agitation in the South continued, and a new struggle—a strange and profoundly significant movement—broke out in the backlands of Bahia: the revolt of the *Canudos*, which republicans such as Euclides da Cunha called the "Vendée of the republic." [In 1897 the revolt, or "war," of the *Canudos*, under the leadership of Antônio Conselheiro, the mystical and fanatical prophet of the half-savage mestizos of the interior of Bahia, presented a new threat to the maintenance of order.—Trans.]

In the realm of philosophical ideas, Brazil continued to be, with only slight modifications, what it had been in the days of Empire. Nevertheless, after 1891, the enthusiasm aroused by Positivism began to wane. Its influence became gradually restricted to the members of the Apostolate.[139] At this time, other forms of European philosophical thought represented in Brazil began to compete more seriously with the hitherto influentital philosophy of Auguste Comte. Even the Positivist leader recognized a "fatal waning" of the doctrine. In

1898 Miguel Lemos, that quick-tempered preacher of Cumto's ideas, relinquished the direction of the Apostolate. Teixeira Mendes, his successor, was probably more closely attached to the religious aspect of Comtism, which did not inhibit the continued "interventions" of the Apostolate in the political life of the republic, but tended increasingly to prevail. Nevertheless, because of the nature of Comte's philosophy, the Positivists always showed a special interest in the social aspect[140] of national events—and to this day still do. It was the Positivists who, in their writings, indicated to the younger generation the growing importance of social studies.[141]

The appearance of studies showing sociological preoccupations dates from the time that Positivism began to affect the Brazilian intellectual elite. Being closer to concrete problems, sociological studies were, and are, more in accord with the national temperament and our cultural conditions. It is interesting to note the influence of "positive" thinkers on the young Capistrano de Abreu, for instance. In the series of lectures on Brazilian literature, which he gave in 1875 at the Escola Popular of Fortaleza, he already showed traces of positive influence and sociological preoccupations, both in the authors he cited and in the general trend of the lectures.[142] In 1880 appeared Luís Pereira Barreto's book *Solucões Positivas da Política brasileira*; in 1901 his *O Século XX sob o Ponto de Vista brasileiro*; in 1887 Tito Lívio de Castro's *A Mulher e a Sociogenia*.

It was Positivism, then, that guided the Brazilian intellect toward the preoccupation with sociology that seems most suited to its nature. We verify once more that the Brazilian intellect is at its best when dealing with concrete problems. This is so because the more general questions are contained in concrete and actual problems, because for us the task of dealing with these problems is more urgent than the branching out into broader and deeper lucubrations. And let it not be said that this task is wanting in glory or that those who attempt it are vanquished in what some call the spirit. Brunschvicg says, in one of his writings:

Idéaliste vaincu, j'enregistre l'empuissance de l'homme quand il veut, selon l'expression de Pascal, faire le dieu. Considerons maintenant l'homme faisant l'homme, l'homo hominans, suivons le développement des normes de relativité et de réciprocité qui faisaient apercevoir aux Pythagoriciens la possibilité du mouvement de la Terre, comme elles ont suggéré à Einstein la solution du paradoxe de Michelson. Alors nous n'avons plus affaire au schématisme illusoire d'un universel concret qui marquera sa limite de la synthèse proprement philosophique, la synthèse scientifique tend a nous donner l'univers concret. Et ce qui est curieux, admirable, et qui à mes yeux du moins justifie toute la peine que la philosophe doit se donner pour prendre contact avec la réalité de la science, c'est que passant de l'universel concret à l'univers concret, l'esprit humain a gagné, non pas seulement au point de vue de l'objectivité, mais encore au point de vue de l'intelligibilité.[143]

I shall not go so far as to affirm that it was a sociological preoccupation that led Euclides da Cunha to write his great work *Os Sertões*. A young man of the republican generation, inconsistent and fanciful, like all highly strung people, "a very advanced writer for the Brazil of 1900, a writer strengthened by his scientific pursuits, enriched by his knowledge of sociology, sharpened by his specialization in geography,"[144] Euclides, a man of the coast, found himself during the Canudos campaign face to face with the *sertão*, which appears in our history at moments of crisis and revolutionary change and toward which, in the words of Alcântara Machado, "the national soul turns like the magnetized needle toward the magnetic pole."[145] The sertão has been the obsession of the adventurer—the salvation sung by the elites that "sympathized" with it,[146] but forgot its existence.

In the intellectual environment of the time, full of "writers who were far too French and far too English—and these were the best of them—others who were Greek or Hellenic, still others purely Portuguese, their ears plugged with cotton to escape adulteration by harsh Brazilian sounds,"[147] Euclides da Cunha, writing not as a geologist, geographer, botanist, or anthropologist—roles in which he was not always reliable—was the artist who "interpreted in words strong enough to pierce the ears and shake the souls of the pale bachelors of the coast with the sound of a young, and sometimes harsh, voice crying out on behalf of the misunderstood desert, the abandoned sertão, the forgotten 'sertanejos.' "[148]

In the dawn of the republic the sertão made its dramatic appearance on the scene of Brazilian life, revealing tragic aspects of our formation. And we,

who had lived four hundred years on the vast coastland on which reflections of civilized life glimmered palely were suddenly handed an unforeseen improvisation, like an unexpected legacy: the republic. We arose, carried along through shock on the torrent of modern ideals, leaving a third of our population, in the heart of the country, to the semidarkness in which they had hidden for centuries. Deluded by a borrowed civilization; gleaning odds and ends from all that is best of the organic codes of other nations in our blind toiling as copyists; refusing to come to terms with the demands of our own nationality, as revolutionaries we deepened the cleavage between our way of life and that of our primitive countrymen, more foreign in this country than the European immigrants. It is not the sea that separates us from them, it is three long centuries . . .

And when, through our undeniable improvidence, we let a nucleus of madmen form itself among them, we failed to perceive the higher aspect of this event. We diminished the spirit of that narrow concept of partisan preoccupation. We betrayed a compromising astonishment at these monstrous aberrations; and, with a daring worthy of greater causes, we beat them down with our bayonet charges, in our turn recreating the past in an inglorious "entrance," reopening in those unhappy places the faded tracks of the *bandeiras*. [The *bandeiras*, or flags, were borne by semimilitary groups of *bandeirantes* of São Paulo, who colonized the interior.—Trans.] We saw in the agitators of the sertão, whose revolt was only one aspect of their rebelliousness against the natural order itself, a serious enemy, a brave paladin of the extinct regime, able to wreck our nascent institutions.[149]

The "fanatics," as they were called by the men of the coast—and as they continue to be called, despite the admirable passage of Euclides da Cunha just cited—the fanatics were beaten by our regular troops. While this was going on, the literati of the coast were still engaged in the task of building a European façade for the country. Only Euclides da Cunha had the courage to defend the men of the sertão. The literati, far from the land, turned toward Europe, still listening to the lullabies that came from afar, from a past that offered them the most refined products of sensibility and thought. They all turned their backs on the mystery of the land. One man, however—and one of the greatest—made the nostalgic intellectuals of the coast realize the full significance of the fact that the people who had retreated to the sertão—incorporating in their fanaticism (made up of misery and suffering) the sacred cause of justice—were now engaged in a jungle revolt to demand a reform: a reform of the Brazilian intellect. It was Euclides da Cunha who sounded the alarm that preceded and heralded this reform. It is not, then, as a "philosopher"—which would be absurd—that he occupies a prominent position in the history of ideas in twentieth-century Brazil; but as the initiator of the reaction against intellectual sybari-

tism,[150] against the "blind toil of the copyists" and borrowed thinking. He competed for the chair of logic at the Pedro II College (in
which, incidentally, Farias Brito was one of the competitors). But
he gave only ten lectures at the College, from July 21 to August 13,
1909. On August 15, he was assassinated.

After the death of Dr. Vicente de Sousa,[151] the chair of logic in
the Pedro II College fell vacant. Forced to compete for the post
because of private circumstances,[152] Euclides da Cunha, who had
never undertaken any formal study of the subject, "shut himself up
at home, recapitulated everything he knew, read ceaselessly, devour-
ing book after book, compendia, and magazines. He resumed his
intimacy with philosophical systems and doctrines neglected almost
since the far-off days of the *Praia Vemelha,* the days when he had
been a pupil at that Military School.[153]

He was not, however, a man who could take seriously "the interminable brawls of the philosophers and the irritating echoes of
the clamor set up by theories." [154] "The engineer in him, accustomed to the positive sciences, could hardly find a balance in the
confusion of opposed doctrines and concepts of the so-called pure
philosophers." [155] He did not know them; he judged them as one
who could not fully grasp their ideas or who did not quite catch
their meaning. "Kant especially," he wrote to Oliveira Lima, "fills
me with amazement, not only for his incoherence (for he is the
most flagrant example of a philosopher destroying his own system),
but for the a-priori exaggerations that diminish him. My untutored
opinion," he went on,

is that that famous hermit of Königsberg to whom, even today, half
thinking Europe bends the knee is merely an Aristotle gone wrong.
Comte (whom I knew and admired only through mathematics) revealed
himself to me in his ability to shake up preconceived ideas and notions
and principles, as an ideologist capable of keeping his end up with the
most demented scholastics without taking into account any nuances in
the whole restless line stretching from Roscelin to St. Thomas Aquinas.
As for Spinoza, I am surprised that humanity has for so long taken
seriously a man who discovered the art of being crazy in an orderly
and methodical fashion, making hallucinations into syllogisms!

And he ended: "I could go on forever if I gave way to the wave of
anger that overwhelms me when I think of those names, formerly
so dear." [156] Which goes to show that it is not enough merely to
shut oneself up indoors and pore over one's books, if one would

grasp the exact meaning of philosophical ideas and systems. They must be conquered daily, reflection slowly giving them greater clarity and form. Euclides da Cunha's intellect, sensitive and impressionable though it was, was not gifted with the perseverance that the growth of consciousness seems to demand. Euclides was not, then, a philosopher. His significance in the history of ideas in Brazil lies elsewhere.

Floriana Peixoto and Prudente de Morais had consolidated the republican regime. The latter had managed, as Pedro Calmon said, "to spare the republican evolution the 'mystique' of revolution," to this end using "the confidence of the conservative classes, terrified by Florianism, and the sympathy of the former rebels, won over by his generous pardon," instituting and imposing "civil order with no trace of timidity." [157] But all of this was not accomplished without serious disagreements and bitter disillusionments in the ranks of the republicans.[158]

Campos Salles, like Prudente, one of the historical republicans, was the second civilian president and was faced with a chaotic financial and economic situation. The treasury had been gutted by the struggles and economic mystifications of the *encilhamento*. Nevertheless, foreign capital began to flow into Brazil in considerable quantities. This permitted not only restoration of the balance in the country's external accounts, so seriously affected by the financial crisis of the preceding years, but also a financial recovery that led to widespread material reconstruction and to a notable increase in the country's standards of living.[159]

While Campos Salles was engaged in the difficult task of repairing the financial chaos of the country, he was faced with another problem demanding solution: the normalization of political life. The pacification that had taken place in the last years of Prudente de Morais's term was more apparent than real. The position of Campos Salles, therefore, was somewhat difficult.

He does not have the Army to give him prestige, he does not have the "brigades" or even the "civilianist" warmth and peacemaking qualities of Prudente; he cannot nominate and dismiss presidents, nor can he remove governors from office; and he needs Congress to avoid the alarms and crises that have beset his predecessors. Lacking what had so greatly helped them, some kind of mystique—of legality, Jacobinism, pacification—he was obliged to resort to other means, and outstanding among these was the appeal for a political life based on the party system.[160]

But Campos Salles, as a historical republican, still retained the vivid memory of the discredited imperial parties and was against party politics. "This hostility toward the national parties is evident in the men who are most representative of the First Republican generation." [161] In his interesting book *Da Propaganda à Presidência* published in São Paulo in 1908, Campos Salles defended himself against the accusations leveled against him of being hostile toward the parties and of dissolving them:

One cannot dissolve something that does not exist. I never showed myself hostile toward the organization of political parties, and it would be necessary to know nothing whatsoever about the nature of democratic institutions to seek to impose in principle such a paradox under the aegis of these institutions. It would be tantamount to promoting the paralysis of the whole social organism. I always recognized, and declared in unequivocal terms, the necessity for parties to ensure a political balance, through the succession, in government, of contrasting opinions. What I declared an evil that must be removed because it impeded the efficiency of the government's actions, above all at a time of crisis, such as in that period when the most serious administrative problems were crying out for solution, was the partisan spirit, with its passions and its violence, which disturbed the beneficial growth of ideas and obstructed the peaceful development of governmental action.[162]

Further, he adds:

Among us, the only association that had been formed with the aim of influencing the administration was that which called itself the "Republican Federal party." But this party, with no specific program and undefined aims, did not fulfill any of the conditions essential for the high ends to which a well-constituted party is destined. To start with, one cannot conceive of a party that has no antagonism in its aspirations, no contradictions in its ideas and sentiments, no disagreement on basic principles, and no disputes about the best way to prepare for the needs that might arise in the spheres of politics and administration. It is obvious, therefore, that the existence of one party inevitably presupposes the existence of another which will set up different aims from those of the first. The Republican Federal party tried to stand on its own, without opponents, attempting to coördinate all ideas, even the most contradictory, so that there would be no room for any other party.[163]

José Maria dos Santos would seem to be right, therefore, when he writes that "the Brazilian republicans greeted Comte's ideas on the organization of the government and the state with the most enthusiastic and joyful surprise. It fitted in marvellously with the idea of a *strong government* of which they had begun to dream." [164]

Since there were no political parties and no atmosphere in which they could be born and flourish—with the exception, perhaps, of Rio Grande do Sul where Assis Brasil and Pedro Moacyr expressed themselves in favor of the formation of parties[165]—Campos Salles was obliged to cling to some power, but

he did not want to become involved in partisan exclusivism or in party politics, which meant politics for the party, so as to avoid aggravating existing hatreds or running the risk of becoming the prisoner of groups. On the other hand, even though it was subject to these evils, the existence of parties was preferable to their absence. This is why he ended by falling headlong into a new solution that turned out to be harmful, but seemed inevitable: the politics of governors, or, as he preferred it to be called, the "politics of the states." [166]

This resulted in the transformation of the state governors into "great electors" of the republic or, as José Maria Bello has justly said, in the "consolidation of the state oligarchies," which became one of the targets for the opposition of the "Aliança Liberal," or Liberal Alliance, on the eve of the 1930 revolution. We must point out that these oligarchies were largely composed of elements descended from the old monarchical parties.[167] Thus, the advent of the "politics of governors" coincided with the "republic of counselors."

Not all republicans, however, accepted this orientation. Adolfo Gordo, also a historical republican, was one of the first to stress "the radical differences bound to arise between the declared orientation and the republican faith." [168] His opinion was shared by Paulo Sousa, Bueno de Andrada, Miranda Azevedo—who labeled the new orientation "the shameless venture of self-seeking apostates"— and Cincinato Braga, who "recalled the promises of propaganda and the doctrines of liberty preached to the people." He added that he entertained no doubts about the great evils that would befall Brazil if what he termed the autocratic plan carried the day in that assembly (where the political leaders of the time were foregathered)." [169]

From then on, national politics became the politics of

a group of feuds, large and small . . . With their demographic and economic superiority, São Paulo and Minas became the leading centers of republican politics. Rio Grande do Sul, under the governorship of Borges de Medeiros but still under the powerful discipline imposed by the caudillo chief, Júlio de Castilhos, was another decisive center, represented in federal politics by a figure of growing prestige, Pinheiro Machado.[170]

In this way, a course of action and certain political customs and patterns of thought were established in the country, which came to an end only with the 1930 revolution. It is alleged that Campos Salles needed order and peace and that he cared little about means used to gain his ends. It is also said that he needed "a Congress that would give him, with no obstacles or struggles, the financial laws he required in order to govern. Others, in the future, could undertake to clean up the vote." [171]

Since the old political parties had been wiped out by the advent of the republic, the administration of the states devolved upon Army officers and historical republicans. But the existing

accumulation of adherents made their task more difficult. The survival of the old parties, now transformed into groups of common interests, permitted only an imperfect separation. . . . The young men in their red waistcoats, the propagandists, and the liberals found their guiding star in Floriano. . . . But the "Florianists" won the day and lost the morrow. Treated with hostility by the Florianists, Prudente de Morais won the confidence of the defeated. His pacification exasperated the irreconcilables. His firmness controlled them.[172]

Now it became clear that "the presidential regime could not easily be harmonized with national parties: its foundation rested on the states, and the states are their governors." [173] Campos Salles consecrated the formula. "Nothing was more convenient or more accommodating for the central power," observed Rui Barbosa,

that depended for the consummation and perpetuating of its oligarchization on the consolidating of the state oligarchies. From then on, intervention in state matters took on its conciliatory tone, in deference to a tacit agreement between the states and the union. An exchange of attributions and a mutual conceding of guarantees smoothed out any differences. The federal government handed over each of the states to the first faction that came to power. So long as it put itself in the president's hands, this group of privileged exploiters received unlimited concessions from him.[174]

Such was the magic formula for political authority.

A figure who dominated Brazilian politics to the outbreak of the First World War was soon to emerge: "General" Pinheiro Machado.

Less than fifteen years after the fall of the monarchy, the highest post in the republic was held successively by two imperial "counselors": Rodrigues Alves of São Paulo and Afonso Pena of Minas Gerais. Both were experienced, energetic, and endowed with insight into economic and political affairs. This does not show merely that the powerful political axis of São Paulo and Minas was becoming increasingly important and beginning to find expression; it shows, too, that there was an absence of genuine political and administrative form in the republican ranks. The former counselors, both experienced and moderate, could also count on the confidence of the conservative classes.[175]

Referring to an event that seems to have been ever troublesome in republican history, Campos Salles said: "The election of a president of the republic is the great hinge of national politics, although the agitation this event provokes is not always governed by an influx of principle." [176] This was so during the elections for his successor and has in general always been so.

No one will withhold his preference for a "historical" republican [said Campos Salles], when it comes to nominating a candidate for the most responsible post in the republic, the presidency. But although this quality is of great importance, it is not the only one: on the contrary, it will go for nothing if not accompanied by others which I deem essential. The situation of the republic is such that it needs an administrator rather than a politician. It is not the strong pulse of the lively republican that we need, but essentially the competence of a calm and wise administrator.[177]

In fact, the presidency of counselor Rodrigues Alves was a period of calm and wise administration.[178] He transformed the "pestilent" Brazil that he found into a "disinfected" Brazil. Credit improved, and Rodrigues Alves, surrounded by such capable men as Oswaldo Cruz, Pereira Bastos, Saturnino de Brito, and Frontin, transformed the nation's capital from a colonial Portuguese town into a modern, spacious city. In 1906 the Third Pan-American Conference was held in Brazil, and the Barão do Rio Branco, a baron of the Empire, now Minister of External Affairs, "had an unmatched opportunity for enlarging the republic's social prestige." [179]

The presidency of Dr. Rodrigues Alves determined—or coincided with—a period of euphoria in republican history. Between 1887 and 1897 more than a million immigrants had landed in Brazil. Slavery, one of the impediments to the inflow of immigrants, had come to an end.[180] International capital began to flow into the country. "The establishment of subsidiaries of the great foreign banks (English, French, North American, and others) and the impetus given to business were symptoms of this entirely novel situation." [181] The flow of capital and the introduction of free labor, now in process of rapid expansion, were the causes of this euphoria. Brazil was held to be the best-administered state in South America.[182] São Paulo, thanks to the growth of the coffee industry, flourished and new industries began to spring up.

It was during Rodrigues Alves's term of office that Pinheiro Machado asserted himself, determining the presidential succession and giving a dexterous new twist to the notorious "politics of governors" with his regime of the "Morro da Graça."

Rodrigues Alves was succeeded by another Empire politician, Counselor Afonso Pena. The "more brightly colored" republicans, to use the words of Sertório de Castro, were becoming rare. It was at this time that the so-called *Bloco* was founded, in 1905, "an alliance contracted between the republican chiefs to put an end to the president's power, hitherto recognized, to designate his successor." [183] Skillful maneuvers on the part of Pinheiro made him a political arbiter. Afonso Pena tried in his turn to nominate his successor, David Campista. But Pinheiro Machado had not forgiven him for permitting "personal politics," chiefly personified by Carlos Peixoto, the young leader from Minas Gerais. Pinheiro permitted only his own "personal politics." Thus, when everyone expected that "Afonso Pena's successor would be João Pinheiro,[184] who governed Minas Gerais with a new spirit—guided by sociology, practical economics, and the good sense of the highlander, and filled with exemplary energy," [185] Pinheiro Machado, for the Republican party of Rio Grande do Sul, a *caudillo* tamed by "social and political expediency," appealed for the nomination of Afonso Pena's Minister of War, Marshal Hermes Rodrigues da Fonseca. This was "his candidate," and he was duly elected.

Was this a return to republican purity? It might have seemed so, but it was in fact merely the outcome of domination by one group. A "renovation" was essayed by a group of the new members of parliament and ministers—the so-called kindergarten group (*Jardin da Infância*), but Pinheiro's astute political maneuvering finally triumphed.

A web of contradictions[186] was at the bottom of Rui Barbosa's candidature in opposition to that of Marshal. São Paulo, the most powerful state in the federation, nominated Rui. The latter, who had previously contested a Paulista candidature, now joined with São Paulo against Pinheiro and thus, for the first time in the republic's history, "a gigantic electoral campaign was to agitate the country," [187] the "civilianist campaign." Despite the importance that Rui's opposition of "civilian" to "military" assumed—although Rui himself did not altogether endorse this opposition[188]—Pinheiro Machado's politics gained the upper hand and came to be the dominant force in the government. In fact, the presidency of Hermes da Fonseca, promoted by Pinheiro, did not prove very constructive: it was tormented, unequal, and at times tragic. He had meant to do away with the oligarchies that dated from the beginning of the century; he replaced them with the *salvações* (salvations),[189] interventions and states of emergency that occurred throughout his term of office.

In August, 1914, three months before the expiration of Marshal Hermes's disastrous term, the First World War broke out.

During the first months of the war, no one supposed that it would last very long, still less that it would bring in its train such dire and far-reaching consequences. Brazil pursued her destiny with little apprehension and few cares. Coffee continued to be the mainstay of the national economy. Industry had developed considerably and, as the result of the war and the difficulties of transportation, its growth was accelerated. There had been a severe crisis in the rubber industry, but in spite of this the accelerating rhythm of national prosperity remained unaffected.

During part of the period we have briefly reviewed, the figures that stand out in literature were still those that originated in the days of Empire, the greatest being the mestizo Machado de Assis, in whom, as José Osório de Oliveira observes, "gaiety and melancholy were blended," "a contrast which perhaps still expresses today one of the aspects most genuine and profound in the Brazilian intellect." [190] Joaquim Nabuco, Luís Guimarães, Olavo Bilac, and Raimundo Correa also belong to this period and are still European in spirit, continuing so until they "verified the existence, on the

American continent, of strong elements of individual culture, adapted from the European." [191] Coelho Neto, Afonso Arinus, Aluísio de Azevedo, Raul Pompéia, and others introduce themes in which the problems of the land and the people of Brazil are expressed. Another half-caste, Lima Barreto, with less art than Machado de Assis but with deep feeling, wrote of the social aspects of the country's "bourgeois comedy." [192] In Lima Barreto, as in Euclides da Cunha, the socialist currents that were to become influential after 1919,[193] begin to appear.

In historical studies, Capistrano de Abreu, Oliveira Lima, João Ribeiro, and Teodoro Sampaio were active during this period. In jurisprudence, Rui Barbosa, Pedro Lessa, and Clóvis Beviláqua are prominent. It was, however, in the sciences that the most notable strides were made. In 1901 was founded the Instituto de Manguinhos, one of the country's great scientific institutions.[194]

3

The São Paulo-Minas Gerais axis—which some see as a system of political balance lasting until 1929 [195]—was reëstablished in the succession to Marshal Hermes da Fonseca. The Mineiro candidate, Dr. Wenceslau Brás Pereira Gomes, vice president in the previous government, a cautious politician whose career had been quiet and undistinguished, became president on November 15, 1914. Skeptical, disenchanted with politicians, and "absorbed in the great world tragedy, the nation accepted with indifference the government of Wenceslau Brás." [196] But he had not come to power without creating some trouble. It was generally believed that the next president would be the man whose prestige stood highest in the country at that time: "General" Pinheiro Machado, "a kind of supreme 'colonel' of colonels in the country," [197] sought after and obeyed by all— or nearly all. But

the politicians, even those who seemed to be faithful to him, were at bottom against his assumption of the presidency. In Rui Barbosa, on another level and for completely different motives, the old *caudillo* of Rio Grande do Sul was admired and feared rather than loved. Although the old Northern politicians and the small Southern states came round to accepting his candidature, the Paulistas were openly hostile and the *Mineiros* opposed him surreptitiously. The movement of the *salvações* created obstacles by putting at the head of some of the large Northern states, such as Pernambuco and Bahia, a number of the Gaucho chief's most tenacious enemies.[198] The reëstablishment of the alliance between São Paulo and Minas defeated the "caudillesque democratic" empire of the "Morro da Graça."

Gradually the conviction that the war would not last long began to fade. After the initial panic created by the first intimations of war —disturbing trade relations, causing a drop in exports, and increasing the difficulties of a government landed with an awkward legacy —business began to boom, as always in the countries of other continents when Europe is at war. Commerce thrived, industries sprang up, and everything Brazil produced found a market. As a result the war aroused ambition and alerted those who had hitherto been ingenuous and had believed in international agreements.[199]

Soon the excitement engendered by the war, enthusiasm for the Allied cause—especially among the bulk of the country's intellectuals—and fear of a German victory that would endanger the nation's future, led to the formation of the Liga de Defesa Nacional, in which Bilac played a prominent role. Thus, "in 1917, Brazil was the antithesis of what it had been in 1910," writes Pedro Calmon. "In 1910 'civilianism' excited men's minds against militarism as a policy. Now a lyrically militant mentality aroused men's consciences against civil indifference as something alien to the national interest." [200] In April, 1917, the United States entered the war. In October of the same year we joined them in the struggle against the Central empires. At the same time, the revolution broke out in Russia.

If, even before the outbreak of the First World War, the slow but progressive decline of the currents of ideas that had predominated since the end of the previous century was apparent, it was likewise apparent that, from then on, as we have already seen, interest in sociological problems grew. Side by side with these preoccupations, some intellectuals—many of them the same as those concerned with "sociologism"—showed some interest in philosophical subjects.[201] James's pragmatism, and later that of John Dewey, Bergsonian intuitionism, and neo-Thomism were the currents that seem to stand out in this period.[202] We must note, however, that in the period between the proclamation of the republic and the First World War, the number of persons in Brazil showing an interest in philosophy was very small. Farias Brito, one of the few students of philosophy, wrote in 1899:

Brazil has not yet produced a philosopher; but if we take into account our special circumstances, this is not surprising, and, if we broaden our gaze, this statement is seen to be true of America as a whole . . . We are a nation born yesterday, and for the development of great philosophical constructions the passage of time is essential.[203]

Whoever dedicated himself to, or wrote about, philosophical matters became an object of curiosity and was considered somewhat strange. Referring to Farias Brito, José Veríssimo wrote in 1912: "The only Brazilian I know who is preoccupied with philosophy and has a philosophical vocation, proved by a long, permanent, accurate, and mature study of philosophy, the only true philosopher we have is Senhor Farias Brito. I confess that the case of this man has always seemed to me singular and strange." [204] Later, writing on Farias Brito's *O Mundo Interior*, José Veríssimo says:

O Mundo Interior, an essay on the general principles of the philosophy of the spirit, testifies to the repercussion caused among us by the spiritualist reaction against the scientific or purely rationalist philosophies that have hitherto been paramount. This is all the more noteworthy since, whether through the influence of Comtian Positivism or through our intellectual indolence, our country, among all those that call themselves civilized, was the one in which the death, not only of metaphysics but of all philosophy, appeared certain.[205] [But] notwithstanding my legitimate appreciation of Sr. Farias Brito and his work, I am not sure whether I can consider him a philosopher endowed with the constructive capacity of the true philosopher, with his own doctrines and the scientific culture that modern philosophical speculation presumes and demands.[206]

João Ribeiro was therefore quite right when he said that our idealism is never very far from the ground.

The spectacle of war and its tragic aftermath, the disillusionment with "transoceanism," the country's new way of life—and perhaps a new and more robust sense of responsibility forced on us by the war—led us in new directions after 1919.

The 1914 war confirmed the inferiority of nations dependent on others for the necessities of life. On the other hand, it proved that we were able to improvise a number of industries. Economic nationalism was born then with the war, opening up new prospects for labor. The preoccupation with economic autarchy went hand in hand with the desire for intellectual emancipation.[207]

This desire was the first and most important result of the war for the Brazilian intelligentsia, hitherto in bondage to European culture. "The war," says Tristão de Ataíde in an article written in 1919, "has freed us from many a prejudice." [208] The First World War, one of the gravest moments of crisis in modern history, lighted the torch of the liberation movement which has continued to our own time. And the new generations turned, as always, toward the sertão. "They felt more curious about their own country, its economy, its sufferings, its miseries, in short, about all that affected it." [209] Years before, Euclides da Cunha, with the coastal literati in mind, had said:

We are alienating ourselves from this land. We are creating the absurdity of a subjective exile, which makes us withdraw from the land while we wander like sleepwalkers through its unknown heart. This is largely the reason for our weaknesses of action and of spirit. The true Brazil terrifies us; we would gladly exchange it for the withered civilization that elbows us in "Listener's" Street; of the sertão, we know little more than its curious etymology, *desertus*; and, aping the medieval cartographers in their imaginings of powerful Africa, we might well inscribe on certain areas of our maps our ignorance and our wonder: *hic abeunt leones* . . . No need to wonder at the want of color, expression, and character, the lameness and impracticality of our art and our enterprises; they lack the maternal sap.[210]

In the Americas, disappointment was followed by the "warning" referred to by Theodore Roosevelt (see n. 199).

The first works of Alberto Tôrres appeared shortly before the outbreak of the war. At the time neglected, he became "suddenly and by chance, the Duc de Guise of national idealism." [211]

Alberto de Seixas Martins Tôrres was born in 1865 in the State of Rio. He was the son of Dr. Manuel Monteiro Tôrres, the Empire politician who had later become a Republican Senator. For a time Alberto Tôrres frequented the Faculty of Medicine in Rio de Janeiro, but, abandoning his medical studies, he graduated in law at São Paulo where, in company with Luís Murat, João Ribeiro, and Xavier da Silveiro, he founded the republican and abolitionist magazine *Ça Ira*. As a historical republican, then, he was integrated in the regime which he served as deputy, minister of state, president of the State of Rio de Janeiro, and, later, minister of the Federal Supreme Court.

Unlike so many, he was not disenchanted with the republic. "My life," he said once, "is, like that of the generation now entering maturity, simply an episode of the crisis in the last few decades of our history." [212] From this crisis he drew inspiration for the second part of his work, completed by the publication, in 1914 and 1915, of *A Organização Nacional, O Problema Nacional brasileiro,* and *Fontes de Vida no Brasil.* Earlier, Alberto Tôrres had published a work in French—*Vers le paix* (1909)—studies on the establishment of peace and international organization and, in 1913, still in French, *Le Problème Mondial,* studies in international politics. Completely mistaken about the historical direction of his own time, in my opinion, at the very moment when the European situation warned of the approaching horror, he referred, in 1913, to the "pacific feelings" of Wilhelm II;[213] he declared that war had "had its day" and that the "visible proof of this assertion was modern life"! [214] Undaunted, he declared in 1916 that "the European war came as the greatest surprise in history, a prodigious example of the lack of logic, explicable only in terms of the persistence of the imperialist illusion." [215] As a pacifist, he was prey to conflicting feelings. But occasionally, it would seem, he understood the complexity of certain events.[216] He frequently demonstrated his sympathy for Germany—an attitude uncommon among the intellectuals of his time and one which may partly explain some results of his "pedagogy." He shows similar contradictions in his appreciation of Brazilian problems.

In the introduction to *O Problema Nacional brasileiro,* Alberto Tôrres wrote: "If one lives through a revolutionary crisis without the revolutionary temperament, one is a victim of all its shocks. This was my fate during the twenty-four years in which the republic has attempted to adopt the borrowed form in which it was conceived." [217] And further:

Unorganized studies had made me dimly perceive the tremendous confusion of ideas in our time. Insubmissive to the mental despotism of authority, to form my own opinion on the problems that interested me as a man and as a Brazilian, this was the ardent desire that burned in me; and, abandoning systems, categories, and divisions of knowledge, making no attempt to be a philosopher, sociologist, economist, or cultivator of any science, I opened the way for my political and social researches, guiding myself by the first ideals of my life.[218]

In this, the practical and improvising tendencies of the Brazilian are once more revealed. This was the attitude which Alberto Tôrres called the "essentially humanist preparation . . . , but humanist in one of the contemporary meanings of the word, as an expression of a philosophy of life and facts, able to open the eyes and illuminate them with all the light of clarity, for the beholding of future horizons." [219] In this way, armed with a philosophy "of life and facts," he turned to the problems of the country he considered "not merely threatened by social and political anarchy and the imprudent financial adventures that are being practiced in South America, but perhaps already being effectually attacked." [220] Both his manner of dealing with facts and the facts he selected for consideration—economic facts—could have given Alberto Tôrres (and on occasion certainly did so) an almost exact view of conditions in Brazil at the time. But this realist looked at Brazilian realities through very particular spectacles. He simply considered—for preference—those aspects which were closest to him. In his immediate environment he noted the "dilettantism, the superficiality, the dialectic, the florid language, the taste for ornamental phrases" of the elites, the way in which some "prepared for heaven" and others "for glory," still others "for applause" [221]—it was all easy to note in his own world, his own class. We may say that his criticism is a curious and paradoxical libel on the men of letters, the lovers of fine phrases and speeches and of worthless glories, a libel, in short, on the irresponsibility of the so-called elites. But Alberto Tôrres did not himself escape the taste that characterized the elites of his time, the love of fine speeches and oratory.[222]

"Philosophy, science, art, and politics," he wrote, "are systems of abstraction and concepts that mean nothing and achieve nothing unless they adapt and vitalize themselves as motors of real life— the nerves, blood, and will of a people." Tôrres does not seem to have noticed the contradiction that this affirmation presents to the one immediately following, in which he says that "in practice, each land and each people has its own philosophy, its own science, art, and politics that do not alter the general ideas of human knowledge, which are in fact extremely limited, but establish and help to develop autonomous forms and processes of life." [223] Now we had the "philosophy," science, art, and politics that had arisen from the nature of things at that historical moment. It would be useless to desire others that would not correspond to the nerves, blood, and will of the people that Alberto Tôrres hoped in his idealism to cure. Plínio Barreto says that Alberto Tôrres's "sociological pharmacy" was opulent, but that politically the medicine prescribed by this acute clinician was not the most suitable, since "Alberto Tôrres's plan . . . would be the point of arrival of our political activity. It is not, and cannot be, the point of departure." [224]

Unfortunately, Alberto Tôrres's ideas have not been critically studied, as they should be.[225] Oliveira Viana, who has been considered the "reviser" of Tôrres,[226] said in 1932 that "Tôrres's ideas are slowly beginning to have their effect on the minds of our elites, and one can feel that minds with innovating inclinations—and all the young minds of the present seem to show this tendency—are insensibly moving in his direction, as if attracted by some invisible center of gravity." [227] This did in fact come about, especially around 1930–1937, immediately after the triumph of the October revolution, which, I may say in passing, triumphed with a very poor, not to say nonexistent, ideological program.[228] Thus, if I am not mistaken, it was between 1931 and 1933, in the midst of the reigning confusion, that Ronald de Carvalho had occasion to say that

our generation, with its magnificent flowering of writers, sociologists, and journalists, all oriented in the direction of the supreme policy on which depends the life of a nation, is the generation of which Alberto Tôrres dreamed. It has come and knows that Brazil needs the collaboration of all its human contingents in one great party, with a *raison d'être* arising, not from vulgar politics, but from the study and resolution of administrative, economic, financial, and social problems— a movement uniting all economic forces of the nation.[229]

Tôrres, the man who, at the end of his life, confessed himself disillusioned and misunderstood, would have found, it seemed, the "generation foreseen by Farias Brito," [230] the "spiritualist and nationalist" generation with

a political program based on our national realities. It started the only movement of nationalist character in the republic, reconciling all its "human contingents." Among other things, it accomplished the destruction of the liberal taboo, laid the foundations of a strong state, saved youth from materialism and skepticism, unmasked the maneuvers of international finance, and fought against the Communist movement.[231]

Alberto Tôrres would have found, in fact, the "Integralist" group that, from 1932 to 1937, aped Fascist and Nazi attitudes in the wake of Mussolini and Hitler and enjoyed the goodwill of President Getúlio Vargas, who took advantage of the connivance or the ingenuity of this group to carry out his own coup of November 10, 1937.

Although Alberto Tôrres has sometimes been cited by the Integralists,[232] the movement that in 1937 attempted, unsuccessfully, to take over power using his ideas was more affected by the political ideas of right-wing movements then gaining sway in Europe than by the Brazilian thinker. And because this right-wing movement, an *ersatz* of foreign ideas, lacked the "motors of real life—the nerves, blood, and will of the people"—the Fascist movement in Brazil failed, fortunately, lost behind the smokescreen of an ideology as vague as it was confused, which the real people never accepted or followed.

The First World War brought prosperity to the country and created, in consequence, a climate of optimism, above all in the business world, which flourished under the presidency of Epitácio Pessoa. During this period a new direction in intellectual, political, and social life began to provoke repercussions in Brazil.

Among the younger generation [writes Gilberto Freyre], discontent with theories increased, above all with the political practices of the republican administration and with the academic literature and art represented by someone like Coelho Neto or the School of Fine Arts, against which the "modernist movement" broke out in São Paulo and Rio.[233]

When, therefore, in 1921, long before the end of President Epitácio Pessoa's term, politicians began to agitate about presidential succession—a problem which flared up (and still does) every four years in our political history—the person indicated to take over the *Catete* [The presidential palace.—Trans.] from Epitácio Pessoa was the president of the State of Minas Gerais, Artur Bernardes. He was accepted by all, with the exception of Borges de Medeiros of Rio Grande do Sul, who alleged that it was "indispensable to know beforehand the candidate's program."[234] This led to a division in national politics. Against Artur Bernardes's candidature, that of the "republican reaction" was proposed, consisting of the two veteran politicians Nilo Peçanha and J. J. Seabra. "Once again, therefore, the small group of men who, through the governments of the larger states, dominated Brazil was divided, not through divergences of ideas, plans, or administrative programs, but through vanities, great and small, wounded susceptibilities, and the desires to perpetuate themselves in their government machines."[235] But times had changed. The war had given rise to other ideas and other ways of looking at things. Revolutionary agitation, even agitation serving the same old groups, was risky since, although it bred the desired participation, could so easily take an unforseen direction. The masses, still largely unconscious, were beginning to move and to participate in a slow and confused manner in political life. In 1917 there had already been a serious strike in São Paulo—which had begun to become the great industrial center it is today—more significant than the previous strikes of cigarette makers and railwaymen in 1891 and of the employees of the São Paulo railway company in 1906.[236] In 1917 Lima Barreto had already referred to "maximalism" and had protested against the expulsion of foreigners accused of being agitators.[237] In 1918 the Maximalist Union was founded in Pôrto Alegre. In 1921 an anarchist majority under the leadership of Astrogildo Pereira formed the initial nucleus of the Communist party founded in March, 1922, in the presence of delegates from Rio, Niterói, São Paulo, Cruzeiro, Juiz de Fora, Recife, and Pôrto Alegre.[238] Bourgeois liberal agitation facilitated the political organization of the masses, although "during the first years of its existence the Communist party was a party of intellectuals, having little contact with the proletarian masses."[239]

At this point a new "military question" arose, as during the years preceding the fall of the Empire. Nilo Peçanha, a historical republican of humble origins, an orator "who understood the impulses of the multitude," as Sertório de Castro said, managed to capture the sympathy of the people. In Brazil—and I am quoting one of our most intelligent men, Barbosa Lima Sobrinho—the men who come to ephemeral power seem to live out the famous metaphor of the Marapata island in the mouth of the Rio Negro, "where, it was said, the traveler abandoned his conscience in order to survive or surmount the adventures and hazards of the rubber forests."[240] In the same way, "it is possible that the occupants of the governors' palaces leave in the vestibules, if not their conscience, at least a large part of their personalities, exchanging them for the qualities they find hanging on the hooks of power."[241] Among these qualities are arrogance, the sense of infallibility, the assuredness of omnipotence. Before this possession of power all else fades. Sometimes, as we had occasion to see, disillusionment leads to tragic endings. From 1922 to 1930, then, "the old tendency of our rudimentary democracy to split into opposing camps the government and the people"[242]

was accentuated. The "republican reaction" campaign attempted
to throw into relief this sad opposition.

Nilo Peçanha and those who supported him against the candidature of Artur Bernardes were prepared to revive for their own benefit the old formula to which the opposition sometimes resorts for
victory: an appeal to the armed forces, a phenomenon that seems
all too common in the South American countries. Nilo Peçanha,
bred in "the generation that made the republic, had not yet lost . . .
the habit of counting on the Army as a decisive factor in political
campaigns." [243]

Marshal Hermes da Fonseca, after the end of his highly unpopular and disastrous term, had retired to Europe in voluntary exile.
He wandered abroad for a number of years. On his return to Brazil
this man, who had left it slandered and demoralized by public
opinion, found himself almost consecrated. A halo of prestige gathered about the old soldier, which was to be used in the ensuing
struggle for succession. The question of the presidency had already
become a burning issue

when, in order to serve the ambitions of a group of the friends and exploiters of Marshal Hermes, two well-known forgers forged some letters,
imbecile in form and content, alleged to have been written by Artur
Bernardes to Raul Soares. There were alleged to be five letters, each
more compromising for Senhor Artur Bernardes than the last, in which
he was supposed to have rudely insulted the national Army.[244]

During this period the country lived in constant fear of a *coup
d'état* or of the revolution hourly expected. Once the elections were
held, Artur Bernardes won by a majority of votes.

In July, 1922, the Copacabana garrison revolted against the government. Together with the "modernist movement" this revolt was
the sign that something was about to change. In September, the first
centenary of independence was celebrated, with galas, visits by European heads of state, naval reviews in Guanabara, and so forth.
The celebrations did not, however, manage to still the apprehension
felt, with good reason, by many. Finally, in November, the new
president was installed, and his presidency proved as unpopular as
that of the Marshal, years earlier. Throughout his term, opposition
to the government increased.

The country's finances, which had seemed promising at the beginning of Epitácio Pessoa's presidency, were shown by the end to

be in a bad state. Partisan struggles and spending aggravated the country's financial condition. "Political cases" were multiplying by leaps and bounds. The regime of "interventions" and declarations of states of emergency of the days of Pinheiro Machado was back. In Rio Grande do Sul struggles broke out afresh, ending only with the *Pacto de Pedras Altas,* a pact reforming (by prohibiting reëlections) the state constitution, which was Positivist in nature and dated from the first days of the republic. In 1924, exactly two years after the revolt of the Copacabana garrison, a revolution broke out in São Paulo, and the revolutionaries held the capital of the state for almost a month. At the same time in Rio Grande do Sul "the revolutionary movement was given fresh impetus, the tradition of fighting columns and guerrilla warfare that had so often laid it waste in the past being renewed." [245] One of these fighting columns took the name of its chief, the young Army captain Luís Carlos Prestes,[246] calling itself the "Coluna Prestes," and won fame by its audacious and extraordinary march from north to south through the interior of Brazil.[247] Many of the young officers who made up the Coluna Prestes are today prominent generals in our country. The Brazilian revolution was marching forward. The question of the 1929–1930 presidential election unleashed it. And at the head of the armed movement that overthrew the last government of the Old Republic marched the lieutenants of the Coluna Prestes.[248]

4

"The transformation of the world," wrote Mário de Andrade in 1942,

with the gradual weakening of the great empires, the practice of new political ideals in Europe, the speed of transport, and a thousand and one other international causes, together with the development of an American and Brazilian consciousness and local progress in technology and education, demanded the creation or remodeling of the national intelligence.[249]

Mário de Andrade thus indicated the causes of the "modernist" movement of which he was a leader. "It was the 'modernists' and the 'futurists,' " writes Andrade Muricy, "who, during these difficult times, for good or ill, had sufficient strength of spirit and (what to many seemed paradoxical), disinterested love for the great tradition of art, to make the effort to give it a transfusion of fresh blood." [250]

The modernist movement, with the *Semana da Arte Moderna* (*Week of Modern Art*) as its principal collective manifestation,[251] acted then as the "loudspeaker of a universal and national force, much more complex than we were"—"it was the result of the heightened rhythm of an evolution which, retarded and colonial up to a certain point of time, had suddenly been transformed by the rise of the coffee industry into a high civilization along the coastal strip," [252] as another leader of the movement, Menotti de Picchia, says.

In this coastal area, immigration and wealth swept away the colonial residues glued to the old mentality spread by the São Paulo Academy where, although a number of "liberationist" poets had declaimed their verses and various golden-voiced orators had delivered their addresses, there had never been anyone like Tobias Barreto, that thunderous and bold renewer of values, to enliven its staff. The need was felt to furnish Brazil with its real ways of life, and Monteiro Lobato, an intuitive and imaginative writer, brought into literature the tragic problem of the peasants of the interior and later called attention to the activities of the oil prospectors.[253]

The modernist movement helped give a form to a direction new in the history of Brazilian thought. It was an "alarum. Everyone awoke, and saw the dawn in the sky. The dawn held the promise of day, but it was not yet broad daylight." [254]

Great importance is attributed to Graça Aranha as the initiator of the modernist movement. "The truth is that, with or without Graça Aranha, modernism would have developed in Brazil as the result of the influence of a universal state of mind." [255] It initiated an important, albeit short-lived phase[256] of criticism, research, and experiment,

a creative, pragmatic task, provoking a hitherto nonexistent spirit of revolutionary and liberating tendencies. Good or not in their revolutionary orientation, the books of His Excellency Plinio Salgado, such as *Bagaceira* (*Cane Trash*), already announced a social direction and propagated ideas. Graça Aranha, in his essays, reached the conclusion that modernism should not confine itself to aesthetic preoccupations but should complete itself by intervening in politics, too.[257]

It is interesting to note that the movement arose in São Paulo, since São Paulo was

culturally much more up to date . . . as the inevitable consequence of the coffee industry and its attendant industrialization. A brash hillbilly, still smelling of the servile provincialism so blatant in its politics [this was written in 1942], São Paulo was at the same time, in its smart commercialism and industrialization, in closer contact, spiritual and technical, with the present-day world.[258]

Added to this was the

clearly aristocratic nature of the modernist movement. In its character of a dangerous game, in its wildly venturesome spirit, its modernistic internationalism, its militant nationalism, its antipopular gratuitousness, its ruthless dogmatism it exhibited an aristocracy of the mind. It was only natural then that the bourgeoisie should fear it. Paulo Prado was at the same time one of the representatives of the Paulista intellectual aristocracy and one of the leading personalities of our traditional nobility. Not from the improvised aristocracy of Empire but from a more ancient aristocracy, justified by centuries-old toil on the land and derived from some European brigand, its concubinage with genealogy was recognized by the monarchical pronouncement of the "Deus-Rei." [259]

The upper middle class could neither understand nor support

a movement destined to destroy its conservative and conformist spirit. The bourgeoisie never knows how to lose, and this is what brings its loss about. If Paulo Prado, with his intellectual and traditional authority, took to heart the organization of the *Week* . . . and carried with him his aristocratic peers and others dominated by his personality, the bourgeoisie protested and mocked.[260]

It is this contradictory character of the 1922 movement of intellectuals and aristocrats that explains both its scandalous and rapid influence and its liquidation in 1930, when the country realized that, "although it had not yet found a definite course to steer, something had been profoundly altered. The year 1930 was the clear demarcation of the end of a culture. It was the busy crossroads that marked the end of the reign of the elite of pure literati, of the dilettantes of knowledge, of vague and dispersive amateurism." [261] The 1922 movement was not, then—and even Mário de Andrade recognizes this—the cause of the political and social changes that later took place in Brazil.[262] It was an "alarm signal," an expression of the disintegration of a state of mind that no longer applied. The reform was soon to follow. Or rather: the wished-for reform was soon to initiate a new phase in our history that has continued through the years and has not yet come to an end. This explains the touch of pessimism—an expression of all the contradictions of this apparently joyful movement—found in the later works of Mário de Andrade, Paulo Prado, Oswald Andrade, and others. "I don't feel that the intelligence of the new generation is much superior to my own," said Mário de Andrade.

It is true that, from the cultural point of view, we have made much progress. Although some traditional schools remain backward, in the centers of some new faculties of philosophy, science, letters, medicine, economics, and politics, new generations are being formed, far more technical, far more humanistic . . . This appreciable improvement in technical achievement is evidenced chiefly in the schools that had the good sense to recruit teachers from abroad, or even Brazilians educated in other countries, who brought with them their cultural habits and contributed a healthier mentality to the progress of teachings . . .[263]

But "despite our up-to-dateness, our nationhood, and our universality, we did not really contribute to one thing or further its progress: we did not participate in the social and economic improvement of man." [264] This was because many intellectuals of the new generation, the generation formed after 1914 and even that of 1930, continued to "flirt with ideologies by telegram," in the delightful phrase of Mário de Andrade.

Graça Aranha, considered by many the leader of the modernist movement, was, as it were, the point of balance between intelligence of the recent past and the "spirit of youth" of the movement that to many represented "a complete break with all cultural compromise, rousing anger in the mature and the old in spirit, which appealed to certain young men desirous of entering literature in this way through a kind of examination by decree." [265] Graça Aranha had come under the influence of Tobias Barreto in Recife, which, although it did not determine his pupil's destiny—so different from that of Tobias himself—certainly left a strong trace. Tobias, at the end of the century, "had opened up a new epoch for the Brazilian intellect, and we got from him the new seed without knowing how it would germinate in our minds but knowing that it would transform us." [266] Thus, much later: "After more than forty years had passed since I received that mental shock," wrote Graça Aranha, "I still felt its ineffable vibrations. Through him I penetrated the fog of a false understanding of the universe and of life." [267]

In 1902 Graça Aranha published his famous novel *Canaã* (*Canaan*). Agripino Grieco says that the novel has not become dated, but, with more justification, Olivio Montenegro says that it is the "prototype of the medallion novel." [268] In this "emphatic" novel Graça Aranha poses the problem that had begun to attract the attention of the intellectuals: the problem of immigration and the immigrant settlements. The novel, uninteresting from a literary point of view, reveals more of the somewhat confused philosophical tendencies of the writer than of the country that is supposedly its central theme. It still mirrors the contradictions of the "Europeanism" of the Brazilian literati, although it does give some indication of an attempt to overcome this situation.

It has been said that the basic characteristic of Graça Aranha's thought was its attempt to base philosophy on Brazilian experience.[269] It is true that from the publication of *Canaã*, in its repetition, *Viagem Maravilhosa*, and in *Espírito Moderno* (published after the *Week of Modern Art*), this seems to have been Graça Aranha's attempt. "All our culture," he writes in *Espírito Moderno*,

came to us from the European founders. But civilization here found itself in a melting pot that produced a "civilization" which is not exclusively European, having undergone the transformations of the environment and the effects of the mixed races that populated it. This civilization is still in mere outline, with no definite character. It is a point of departure for the creation of true nationality. European culture should serve, not to prolong Europe, not as a pattern to imitate, but as a tool to build something new out of the elements of the land, the people, the primitive wildness that still persists. The desire for liberation is a sign that this new thing is already present in us.[270]

Thus we will not make of Brazil the "mortuary of Portugal," [271] "we will break up the continental uniformity with which we are threatened," [272] since

to be Brazilian is to see all and to feel all as a Brazilian, whether it be our lives, foreign civilization, the present, or the past. National emancipation is a state of mind, a spirit with which we can conquer nature. This is our metaphysics and our intelligence and will transfigure our creative energy, making it free and fit to build the nation . . . There is a burning need for a philosophical, social, and artistic transformation. It is the thrust of a conscience in search of the universal beyond the scientific relativism that has fragmented the infinite whole.[273]

This was Graça Aranha's position when the modernist movement reached its peak. This attitude, which he tries to justify in his

Estética da Vida, reflects, as Sanchez Reulet says, an original meta-physical intuition, although it does not seem a vigorous one but rather somewhat contradictory.[274] It is in the *Estética da Vida,* pub-lished in 1920 ("We used to laugh at it," recalls Mário de Andrade), that we find the principal *motifs* of Graça Aranha's orientation. This was, however, not the first time he had dealt with philosophical problems. In 1894 he had written the preface to Fausto Cardoso's book *A Concepção Monística do Universo,* in which we can see that Graça Aranha did not accept, as did his contemporary Farias Brito, the philosophy of Auguste Comte, whom he nevertheless called "a modern Aristotle." [275] The writers he cites are Hartmann, Scho-penhauer, Lange, and Haeckel, the "brilliant precursors of a future Newton who has not yet been produced by the accumulated forces of heredity and adaptation, but who will inevitably appear." [276] He also refers to Ludwig Noiré, so often cited by the master, Tobias Barreto.[277]

In *Estética da Vida* we still find as a "philosophical background," woven of embroideries taken from the philosophies of Schopenhauer, Nietzsche, and other late-nineteenth-century thinkers, the "monism" of the Recife school, which had so strongly marked Graça Aranha. The aesthetic concept, the "spectacular view of the world," was, for him, the core of perfection.

Since an inexorable causality does not permit of any freedom; since one cannot find in ideal space the fulcrum for a lever capable of having initiated phenomenal life; since it is impossible to discover first and last causes—any rigorously materialistic or spiritualist concept of the uni-verse is absurd. The only thing left of this universe in the mind is a pure ideality, and a feeling of its infinite unity forces itself upon our consciousness as our true raison d'être. It links us to all universal phenomena and explains our being as a phenomenal appearance of matter. The universe is projected on our minds as an image, a spectacle. Thus, any notion one has of the universe, whether scientific, mathe-matical or biological, idealistic or religious, is spectacular. It can be affirmed that the essential function of the human mind is the aesthetic function, and that through this we can explain the universe to our-selves.[278]

Tobias Barreto proffers somewhat similar ideas in his book *Questões Vigentes,* and similar *motifs* appear in *Finalidade do Mundo.* In fact, in their youth all had drunk from the same fountain.

The aesthetic vision, the "spectacular view of the world," suffered, however, from the defect that afflicts all thoughts "so light that they cannot be thought," as Graça Aranha himself put it.[279] This was perhaps understood by the younger modernists, who soon abandoned the "philosopher" of the *Estética da Vida.* His thoughts were, in fact, too light to be thought.

In the chapter entitled "Metáfisica brasileira," Graça Aranha asserts that the characteristic collective trait of the Brazilian mentality is imagination,

that magical state in which reality fades and is transformed into the image . . . The distant roots of this imaginative faculty are in the souls of the different races and in the prodigy of tropical nature. Each race brought its peculiar melancholy. Each man carried in his heart the dread of different gods, the anguish of memories of a past forever lost, and each was filled with an infinite anxiety in the foreign land.[280]

The theme of the "three sad races," as Paulo Prado was later to call them, makes its entrance in this chapter:[281] The Portuguese, oscillating between his realism and the mirage, unable to create, to give the world a new sensibility, the perfect executor of the ideas of others; the Negro, shrouded in the mists of his eternal illusions, reacting with lies to a false representation of things, deluding, inventing, and imagining, that reality is the voluptuousness of gross spirits, but being in reality weak and terrified; the savage, transmitting to his descendants the terror that "lies at the root of the relationship between man and the universe." [282] For Graça Aranha, these are the characters in the "Brazilian adventure," on whom a Brazilian metaphysics is based. To these he added the land itself, which the Brazilian "fought and martyrized," but which had become for him "an object of veneration and love." The grandeur of the land is, for the Brazilian,

a source of delight and exultation. He prides himself on being the man of a great land, in the knowledge that she is beautiful. And in the seduction and domination of nature lies the source of the providentialism that for the Brazilian spirit is the motive power of action but leads also to soft negligence.[283]

Sebastião da Rocha Pitta left behind him innumerable continuators in Brazil. They still exist today. "Of the New World," he wrote at the beginning of the eighteenth century,

hidden for so many centuries and slandered by so many scholars—whose native shores never witnessed the coming of Hannon with his ships, the Libyan Hercules with his battle columns, or the Theban Hercules with his exploits—of this New World the best part is Brazil, a vast region of fertile land, its surface covered with fruit, its interior bursting with treasures, its mountains and coasts laden with aromas.[284]

This note is struck by Graça Aranha, too. But he feels as well the sadness, "the insuperable lack of correlation between the physical environment and man," [285] who, "transplanted, languishes in lonely nostalgia." [286] Although, as we can see, contradictorily, Graça Aranha's "metaphysics" spring from the country's historical and cultural conditions.

The history of civilization in Brazil could be written in four lines, so simple and so insignificant has been its contribution to the luminous history of the human spirit. All efforts of culture in the immense territory in which we have encamped, can be reduced to three essential facts: the discovery, which excited European greed and was the accident leading to the fusion of races that first peopled the country; the foundation of the nation on servile labor; the transformation of this economic foundation that gave way to free labor, which was developed by European immigration and resulted in a modification of the established bases of the nation. Only three great historic successes hold any interest for humanity: discovery, national independence, and the abolition of slavery. Like the rest of America, Brazil had a simple economic destiny.[287]

Thus, Brazil "in its origin, was a nation of masters and slaves." [288] In 1822, with independence,

at the joyful birth of the motherland, nationalism was an affirmation of the Brazilian will. At that time of nationalist incandescence, we did not draw back from the compromises necessary to populate the land, which is the destiny of the country in need of foreign collaboration. In the dawn of nationhood Brazilians labored under the shining delusion that they were self-sufficient. It soon began to fade. And the history of Brazil ceases to be the elaboration of an elite, to become propelled by the movement of the masses.[289]

Despite the interest provoked by his curious fantasies on the "Brazilian metaphysics," I do not believe that Graça Aranha exercised a permanent or effective influence. Tristão de Ataíde says that Aranha was the "strongest and most vital link" [290] between the old and new generations, the "new generation" being the one to which he himself belonged. But, like his contemporary Farias Brito, Graça

Aranha was a master without disciples. Like Farias Brito, he had his day, thanks to the support of youth. But he too was soon forgotten. No one considered him a philosopher, and it would seem that no one troubled much with his "cosmic terror," the foundation of his "metaphysics."

It is not easy, even today, more than one generation after his death, to study Jackson de Figueiredo, the curious renovator of the Brazilian Catholic movement in the twentieth century. It is with a degree of hesitation, therefore, and a fear of being mistaken, that I shall try to integrate him in the confused current of ideas that corresponds to the moral, intellectual, social, and political climate of the phase immediately preceding the 1930 revolution.

Jackson de Figueiredo (1891–1928) belongs to the generation born after the advent of the republic. Although from a Catholic family, he was educated for a time at a Protestant college.[291] In Bahia, where he went to study law, he found that in education the ideas disseminated by the Recife school were still in force. "[In my youth I plunged into] all the monisms, evolutionisms, and mechanisms that appeared in cheap editions. I was a materialist, evolutionist, mechanist, a candidate for the class of scientific 'mandarins,' and, after all, I can today forgive myself all this," he wrote in the first pages of *Algumas Reflexões sôbre a Filosofia de Farias Brito*.[292] But, as a student, it was not exactly to philosophy that the future Catholic leader devoted his time. In Bahia,

He flung himself wholeheartedly into Bohemian life. His companions were of all sorts—ranging from ill-famed braggarts to fine and luminous spirits, such as Xavier Marques, who was so well portrayed by Jackson de Figueiredo's vivid pen. He chose companions for all occasions: the wild car parties that terrified and amazed quiet suburban residents . . . the brawls with fellow students in cafes and confectioneries when the cups, glasses, and bottles flew; at other times, he would be embroiled in grimmer fights in cinemas and theaters, emerging from them on occasion wounded or having inflicted wounds; he was always in the forefront, always with the voice of leadership.[293]

During this period he was a "stoner of friars," [294] and the avowed enemy of the priests.[295] "Dionysius was perhaps my only adolescent ideal," he wrote in 1915 in a letter to Mário de Alencar.[296]

In 1914 while still a very young man, he moved to Rio de Janeiro. In 1908 he had brought out in his native state, like so many other

Brazilians, a book of sonnets entitled *Bater de Asas* (*The Beating of Wings*). In 1915 he began a series of articles on the work of Farias Brito, which were published in *Revista Americana,* and in 1916 he published *Algumas Reflexões sôbre a Filosofia de Farias Brito,*" subtitled *Profissão de Fé Espiritualista* (*A Profession of Spiritualist Faith*). Jonathas Serano considers that in this book his spiritualism is still as hesitant as it is vague.[297] The fact that he studied Farias Brito with affection has led some writers to consider him a disciple of Farias Brito. He was simply an admirer.

He has a special place in my heart, and in this work I shall reveal myself as one of his most intransigent admirers. What matter our difference of temperament, what matter my lack of principles and faith, or, at least, the unhappy complexity of my spirit, unable to strengthen itself through belief in some system? [298]

In the early years of his stay in Rio de Janeiro, then, he was gripped by "an endless dryness, a sterility, a cruel skepticism," which dragged him into "a terrible, paralyzing pessimism that for a time crippled the energy of the tireless fighter innate in him." [299] His most salient characteristic was precisely this "fighting" nature. "An unquiet and restless soul," [300] Jackson de Figueiredo belonged to "that caste of men full of noble heroism, naturally chosen to guide, command, and fight." [301] He had, wrote Nestor Vitor, "the capacity to gather people round him and join them in association, dominating those he gathered and so associated. He dominated above all through his affection, which was all but hidden behind his somewhat fascist exterior, but which could be felt as a current, arousing irresistible enthusiasm." [302] "Gifted with fine sensibility, his was nevertheless the temperament of a warrior, a man of a terrible violence of soul, aggravated by his evangelical vocation. . . . A wise but orthodox thinker, he felt that he knew the reasons for the gloomy crisis we are going through, and wanted to supply the remedies." [303] Historical events of our time and the spread of socialist ideas caused him considerable apprehension.

Disruptive socialism and iconoclastic bolshevism, he told me, are slowly eating away, like leprosy, the body of Europe; but Europe is prepared to defend herself. What will happen to us, he asked me, when we have to defend our poor carcass from the onslaught of the disease? It will not be the armed forces, armed only in name, cruelly and irremediably divided, that will come to our aid. Our cross-eyed statesmen, unaware of modern anxiety and of the most simple and banal problems, are not to be taken seriously in this grave moment.[304]

In Jackson de Figueiredo's opinion, amid the general ruin there would remain standing the Church alone. And it is to the Church "that we must cry, it is upon the Church that we must lean." [305]

Jackson de Figueiredo was, then, the first layman in Brazil to voice the Catholic reaction against the socialist ideas beginning to spread after the First World War. With his fighter's temperament, however, he was neither a philosopher nor a disciple of Farias Brito's vague spiritualism. He became a Catholic convert in 1918.

His entry into the Church was for him a struggle, a conquest, a peace-bringing victory. Disturbed by his philosophical objectives, dissatisfied with his social individualism, the encounter with Catholicism was a revelation to his brilliant intellect, the discovery of a new thing. It was the unexpected vision of truth, order, peace, the complete valorization of man.[306]

In his book *Pascal e a Inquietação Moderna*, published in 1922, Jackson de Figueiredo declared that he was

publishing this work on Pascal and modern anxiety to use what I could save of a bolder work written years ago, when I did not yet feel, in the realm of philosophy and belief, what today, thanks to God, I feel that I am, and that is: a Catholic in the most rigorous sense of this noble term, a man who has consciously abdicated his intellectual individualism into the most loving hands of the Catholic Church.[307]

In turning to "the most loving hands of the Church," Jackson de Figueiredo no longer felt "the need to meditate upon systems or even the need to propose new solutions, more or less fantastic, for the great fundamental problems of thought. The perennial philosophy represented by neo-Thomism offered him all that was needful to slake his spirit." [308]

As an evolutionist, he was shocked to read in Farias Brito that the theory of evolution was false. He had put the book aside, considering this affirmation a monstrosity.[309] "But time passed . . . I began to understand that I too suffered from a prejudice against religion, that I was wandering blindly hither and thither, and that I needed to hear other voices besides those of my blessed materialists. And I sought to heed these voices." [310] Farias was merely the cause of the first step on Jackson's path to conversion.

Jackson de Figueiredo, writes Tristão de Ataíde, condensed three tendencies that had been growing in Brazil from the nineteenth century to the twentieth: materialism, spiritualism, and skepticism. "Each contributed something to his thought. But he repudiated all three, going beyond them by means of the 'Catholic synthesis.' " [311] In fact, "he reposed his heart in the hand of God," [312] and all his activities were directed toward Catholic action. After his conversion, his preoccupation became the political action of Catholicism. His attitude was inspired by Joseph de Maistre, Pascal, and Charles Maurras, "from whom he was opportunely liberated by the serene voice of Rome, coming to recognize the error of (Maurras's) orientation on a number of points." [313]

Jackson de Figueiredo initiated the intellectual and political renewal of Catholicism in contemporary Brazil. He closely followed the vicissitudes of Western Catholic thinking, but in some instances he was marked by the national stamp, which led him to support nearly all reactionary political tendencies.

We cannot add more detail to this brief examination of the part played by Jackson de Figueiredo in the history of ideas in Brazil. But I would not like to end without noting that I have doubtless failed to convey all the wealth to be found in this personality—and in this historic circumstance. As Ronald de Carvalho says:

> The personality of Jackson de Figueiredo is a sum of values so concrete that it still escapes the generalizations of a perfect analysis; there is still an insufficient distance of time . . . What is amazing in this extraordinary man is the utter simplicity he achieved in his moral being after the most various and most unlikely weldings.

We must also bear in mind that

> the whole drama of his life can be summed up in this axiom: Jackson de Figueiredo was a man in search of the truth. His tendency toward extremes, the complete negativism of the formative phase of his intelligence, or the absolute dogmatism of the balance struck in his maturity, these are clear proof of the truth of this assertion. He had a basic horror of relativism. For this reason, none of his contemporaries showed in the same degree his qualities as a party leader, his energy in command, his faculty of promptly seizing obstacles the better to overcome them.[314]

His death at the age of thirty-seven, shortly before the outbreak of the 1930 revolution, leads us to wonder whether new and contradictory historical circumstances might not have led to a different orientation for this man, subject as he was to "such varied and unlikely weldings." He confessed to Augusto Frederico Schmidt on their journey together to Friburgo to participate in a retreat at the Anchieta College: "My temperament is not one of the most Catholic, on the contrary. I am like a runaway slave of the Middle Ages, with chains on my feet." "I realized," writes Schmidt, "that this was not just another phrase. There was a limpid gravity in his penetrating glance. . . . One of the penitents began to recite the rosary. It grew completely dark. And Jackson prayed with the others. His voice was lost among all the other voices." [315]

I omitted to point out the nationalistic orientation of Jackson de Figueiredo's work, which is, naturally, a Catholic nationalism. "From the early days of the colony," he writes, "despite repression by the metropolis, the Brazilian tradition was evidently Catholic and anti-Lusitanian, that is, it contained an element of faith that created the formal unity of our character and made of it a political force based on the constant aspiration toward autonomy." [316]

The problem of Brazilian Catholicism has been constantly posed, but it remains difficult of solution. Jackson de Figueiredo himself, a few days before his death, had prepared an article for the magazine *Ordem,* in which the following words appear at the outset: "No matter how much we try to deceive ourselves, we cannot help feeling how lukewarm and inexpressive is the moral atmosphere of Catholicism in Brazil." [317] It is evidently not such a simple matter, then, to assert the Catholicism of a nation in which even the leader of Catholicism feels its "lukewarm and inexpressive" atmosphere.[318]

This nationalist note or "intention," Catholic or otherwise, will be found in the movements of ideas and in the works of Brazilian intellectuals, particularly those writing after the First World War. Among modern Brazilian thinkers, there is a common faith in the future,

that warms the heart and lights up the imagination; an identical intention of resolving the destiny of Brazil outside the vicious circle of empiricism and, independent of exotic systems and methods, to direct research and reflection . . . The predilection for sociological studies, the rebirth of a humanistic curiosity about philosophy, and the attention with which each political experience of the American and European nations is followed and commented upon, indicate an almost unanimous movement of cultivated minds. We can see the preoccupation with a rebuilding of Brazilian culture on more solid foundations, and the desire to recover, through profitable and methodical work, the time lost in futile literary diversions.[319]

This was the attitude of the Brazilian intelligentsia after 1922. It was hoped that this attitude would give a new direction to national culture and permit a better understanding and interpretation of the nation's soul. This "intention," however, was nothing new. It appears and renews itself every now and then, almost always with the sertão as its basic theme.[320] The problems of Brazil—prominent among them that of the inhabitants of the sertão (the *sertanejos*)—tend to preoccupy the Brazilian intellectual whenever we are faced with a serious crisis. As our history unfolds, we gradually find examples of men clearly conscious of these problems; men like Tavares Bastos during the Empire and Euclides da Cunha, Alberto Tôrres, and Capistrano de Abreu during the republic.[321]

A few months after the outbreak of the First World War, Afonso Arinos said, in one of the lectures he gave at the Artistic Cultural Society of São Paulo:

During these days of eclipse of the great civilization of the twentieth century, it has been proved that the greatest, the most beautiful, and the most magnificent monuments on the face of the earth can be wrecked and crumbled to dust like the sand castles of children at play in a garden. In the cataclysm only one thing manages to keep afloat; one art alone defies the iconoclasts; only one treasure is fearless of plunder: I mean the wealth of tradition, ideas, and poetry, which is the soul of a race and the only proof of its identity among the fellow inhabitants of this planet. The adversity of others brings us nearer to each other. Let us use this moment to get to know ourselves. For a century we have been gazing outward, toward foreign lands; let us now look at ourselves. How often does capricious Fortune hide close at hand what, with such persistent eagerness, we have sought in distant lands! [322]

This aim reappears in 1924, in Ronald de Carvalho's first series of *Estudos brasileiros*:

Our duty is to destroy the bias in favor of Europe, the worst and most noxious of all our ills. We must give to the history of the American peoples that preeminence in our thoughts which we now give to the nations of other countries. We must stop thinking "European." We must think American . . . Our duty is to fight all these deviations, crowning the work of our political independence by achieving independence of thought.[323]

This literary "Creolism"—to quote Eduardo Frieiro, "an ingenuous fear of influence, as if a literature in process of formation, like ours, could possibly isolate itself from the world" [324]—was in vogue during the second decade of this century, giving rise to the most varied forms of "Brazilianism," which sometimes invoked the return of the legendary savage, something sought its inspiration in the Negro element, sometimes plunged into the shining waters of primeval ignorance.[325] There was in all this, we must agree, "a sincere desire to create something new, truly our own, truly Brazilian." [326] Something positive resulted from this movement of ideas in which, as José Osório de Oliveira justly realized, modernism was one of the highlights: our final liberation from the inferiority complex, our national "Bovarism." [327] In this movement Euclides da Cunha was "the first to equate the problems of land and people." [328] Others followed in his wake.

The radical transformation of standards wrought by the social disequilibrium bred of the European strife had its repercussions among us in the wider search for simplicity of style, the shift toward clarity of argument, the trend toward placing thought uppermost and putting it in a clear light. There was a sudden surge of nationalism. Jacobin groups appeared. This type of extremism, polished by time, had its advantages. In Brazilians an enormous curiosity was aroused about Brazil.[329]

It was this interest—and perhaps, at least initially, also the amazement created among the literati of the coast when they learned the true conditions in the country they had been regarding "as if its head were in Europe" [330]—it was this interest that was felt by such writers as Vicente Licínio Cardoso, Ronald de Carvalho, Paulo Prado, Oliveira Viana, Manuel Bonfim, and Azevedo Amaral to mention but a few.

Vicente Licínio Cardoso, an engineer like his father, Professor Licínio Cardoso of the Rio de Janeiro Polytechnic School, received much of his education in the bosom of a Positivist family. But he, like his father before him, was not an orthodox Positivist. "The orthodox Positivists under Teixeira Mendes and Miguel Lemos always demand the impossible, the unattainable." He added: "I admire these men, who exchange the realities of life for the fervent contemplation of impossible things." [331] But, while admiring them, he did not follow them. His thought was directed toward the positive sciences.

The first works of Vicente Licínio Cardoso date from 1916, when he published the report *North American Architecture* as the result of a voyage he had won as a prize at the Polytechnic. In 1917 he presented as his thesis for the chair of fine arts in Rio de Janeiro, *Prefácio à Filosofia da Arte*. In 1918 his book *Filosofia da Arte* was published in Rio. Most of his other books, *Pensamentos brasileiros* (1924), *Vultos e Idéias* (1924), *Figuras e Conceitos* (1924), *Afirmações e Comentários* (1925), as well as his posthumous works, *A Margem de História do Brasil* (1934), *Pensamentos Americanos* (1937), and *Maracás* (1934), deal with subjects directly or indirectly related to Brazil. "When the history of aesthetics or the philosophy of art in Brazil comes to be written," wrote Alcides Bezerra, "the point of departure will be the work of Licínio Cardoso, the initiator of these studies among us, and hitherto the only writer to bring to the field of aesthetic problems an original and praiseworthy solution." [332]

For Cardoso, there were three "principal and fundamental notions for the establishment of a philosophy of art: art as a function of the environment; the variation of degree of the ideal in art; and art as an expression of civilizations." [333] In this, the Comtian influences of his education are still present.

I do not believe, however, the most stimulating aspect of Vicente Licínio Cardoso's work to be his philosophy or his aesthetics. His principal contribution as a thinker is to be found in his concern to know his country. He turned his attention to the sertão. "We must penetrate into the sertão," he wrote in 1924,

to reinvigorate ourselves in the new *bandeira* of nationalism of our century, but we must sound our rivers and scour our land with the educated spirit of cultured men like Martius, Spix, Saint-Hilaire, Eschwege, Reclus, and Agassiz; and, as Euclides realized: "we must learn to know our land in order to build for the future the destiny of our nation." Here I would like to recall the sonorous voice of Euclides da Cunha and the utterly honest judgments of this brilliant personality, among the finest representatives of the mentality of my generation, not omitting to recall, too, what Tristão de Ataíde said some years ago, when he refused to let himself be lulled by the songs sung here and "beyond the seas" (João do Rio and João de Barros) at a time when we were being lured by the siren "call of the sea."

The conquest of the land, the settlement of the race, the problem of the interior—these are the preoccupations of Licínio Cardoso.

All our efforts should be centered on this. The siren voices that preach historic greatness or future glory in the "call of the sea" speak falsely, for it is not toward the sea that our natural evolution leads us. Another ideal must animate our collective conscience—the call of the land. "We must not deceive ourselves. We must face the dark truth that torments us, no matter how much we try to evade it. We must confess. Brazil itself is the concrete symbol of all our potential wealth in the future. It is also the living symbol of all our grave and gloomy difficulties in the present. To discover it is to know ourselves.[334]

The illustrious thinker paid dearly for his love of Brazil, for,

in descending the São Francisco River, the most Brazilian of all our rivers, "the river of national unity," the "path of Brazilian civilization," the river which has wielded the greatest influence on our history, he contracted the disease that led him to the grave, trypanosomiasis. It seems like predestination that the Brazilian thinker suffered, in the very heart of the nation, close to the shining waters that bathed its birth, the common fate of the inhabitants of the interior whom, a few years before, Euclides da Cunha had found in such a deplorable state of mental backwardness, almost three centuries removed from us.[335]

Paulo Prado belonged to one of São Paulo's traditional families. He was twenty-odd years older than Ronald de Carvalho,[336] Vicente Licínio Cardoso, and his fellow contributors to the São Paulo *Week of Modern Art* initiating the "modernist movement." Since 1887 he had been working on problems of immigration. I believe that it was this contact with the country's concrete problems that led him to undertake his study of our land. A friend of Capistrano de Abreu, who must have helped to accentuate his bent for historical studies,[337] Paulo Prado published only two books: *Paulística* (*A History of São Paulo*), 1925, which, as he himself declared, "owed all to the affectionate care of Capistrano de Abreu, even its title," and *Retrato do Brasil: Ensaio sôbre a Tristeza brasileira* (*Portrait of Brazil: an Essay on Brazilian Melancholy*), 1928. The first lines of the latter work are in themselves a confession of pessimism much to the taste of his age: "In a radiant country lives a sad people. This melancholy was bequeathed them by the discoverers who revealed the country to the world and who peopled it." [338] "Lechery," "Greed," "Sadness," and "Romanticism"—these are the chapter headings of Paulo Prado's significant meditation on Brazil, which ends on the following note:

Humanity, awakening from the false calm of prewar days, is gradually moving toward radical changes that will transform not only the political and financial establishment but its mental essence. In this great crisis—certainly the greatest in man's memory—we are moving toward a revision of the old material and spiritual values hitherto consecrated —a revision for which East and West have for centuries done battle. An undreamed-of life-and-death struggle will take place among the most varied "isms" in human philosophy: capitalism, communism, Fordism, Leninism. A new force is emerging to destroy the old civilizations and chimerae of the past. It is the revolution. In the midst of the cataclysm that is preparing, what role will be played by Brazil? A role of complete ignorance of all that passes in the world. Brazil sleeps on in its colonial sleep. It still believes in the lullabies of the speech makers, in the theories of doctrinarians, and in the misleading security provided by those who, even though weak and uncommitted, monopolize positions of power and profit. It does not see the imminent disaster; it does not realize the danger of being on the margin of the great world paths in navigaton and aeronautics; it does not see that the world has become too small for imperialisms, peaceful or warlike, and that it is a paradox to have orange trees laden with sweet oranges growing alongside the roads. . . . For all our semblance of civilization, we live isolated, blind, and immobile in the mediocrity complacently accepted by the governors and the governed. In this rotting apathy everything will have to be razed to the ground before a complete renewal can be undertaken. We are all moving toward the new ideal with the limitation of our contingencies, consciously or unconsciously, involved in a thousand ties, traditions, friendships, money, the bad habits of my thinking and my life—and of yours. . . . These words are certain to be misunderstood. For some, they are mere phrase-making; for others, simply a political maneuver disguised by going off at a tangent of philosophical dissertation. The idea of revolution, while not confusing, is at least complex. It expresses the synthesis of two opposing tendencies: hope and revolt. For the man who revolts, the present state of affairs is intolerable, and the efforts of his possible action will go as far as the violent destruction of all that he condemns. The revolutionary, however, as the builder of a new order, is an optimist, who still believes, through the natural progress of man, in a better state than the present. This is what makes me conclude on a note of renewal: confidence in a future that cannot be worse than the past. [339]

During Oliveira Viana's youth the influences of Comtism, evolutionist Spencerianism, and the monist and materialist ideas of
Haeckel and Büchner were still current in Brazil. His teacher in the
Rio de Janeiro Faculty of Law was Sílvio Romero, who opened up
new horizons for his intelligence.[340] Later Oliveira Viana became
acquainted with the works of Le Play and Demolins, which established 'the bases of his thinking in social research and in the dif-
ferentiations he made when he came to study the life and evolution
of the great rural areas of Brazil." [341] Once he heard a man talking
about the usual political conflicts between factions in the small cities,
concluding his remarks by saying "they are going to appeal to the
government of Bahia."

Oliveira Viana thought this over. And he remembered that a century
and a half ago, the government of Bahia had ruled the captaincy of Rio
de Janeiro, since it was the seat of the general government of Brazil.
He understood, suddenly and vividly, the importance of social psychology through the eloquent reality of this curious episode. He realized
the value of the historic element in the psychological formation of a
people.[342]

"From then on I undertook a work, sometimes arid, sometimes
full of inexpressible enchantment: the investigation, in the dust of
the past, of the germs of our present ideals, the dawn of our national
psyche," he writes in the preface to *Populações Meridionais do
Brasil,* published in November, 1918. In this work he indicates the
writers on whom he then based his work:

There is today a group of new sciences of inestimable value for the
scientific comprehension of the historical phenomenon. They are: an-
thropo-geography, the foundations of which were laid by the great
Ratzel; anthropo-sociology, a recent and comely science on the sub-
structure of which have labored such vigorous, fertile, and original
geniuses as Gobineau, Lapouge, and Ammon; the psycho-physiology of
men like Ribot, Sergi, Lange, and James; the collective psychology of
Le Bon, Sighele, and principally Tarde; the admirable social science
founded by the genius of Le Play and remodeled by Henri de Tour-
ville, aided by a select group of brilliant investigators: Demolins, Poin-
sard, Descamps, Rousiers, Préville, whose minute analyses of the physi-
ology and structure of human societies, all done with the most perfect
scientific rigor, give to even the most obscure historical texts a Mediter-
ranean clarity.[343]

There is no space to examine in detail the work of Oliveira Viana, who is no longer so important as he was at the time Capistrano de Abreu said: "Oliveira Viana spreads like an epidemic." Nevertheless, although it has dated, Oliveira Viana's work is still stimulating. Many young men gathered from his ideas elements of sociological science which led them, unfortunately, to practice vague right-wing politics; a kind of fascism. Oliveira Viana's ideas show three main aspects: the sertão, which must be integrated in the country; the Aryanization of miscegenated groups; and political centralization.

Manuel Bonfim, a doctor who devoted himself to teaching, published two books of interest for the history of pedagogical studies in Brazil: *Noções de Psicologia* and *Lições de Pedagogia*. He also attempted an interpretative study of Brazil in a series of works such as *O Brasil na América*, *O Brasil na História*, and *O Brasil Nação*, in which he attempted to appreciate the conditions of Brazil's formation. In the preface to *O Brasil na América* he indicates the object of his research: "to study the causes that interfered with the progress of the Brazilian nation, among them: systematic attacks on tradition . . . the effects of the degradation and degeneration of the metropolis, which acted on the colony in the form of direct lesions and putrid contamination." [344] Manuel Bonfim's books develop around this *leitmotiv*, the theme of the "degeneration" produced by Portuguese colonialization and the subsequent political "degradation" of Brazil.

The first work of Azevedo Amaral is *Ensaios brasileiros* (1930). This book, declares Nélson Werneck Sodré, marked

the turning point in the Brazilian mentality—subconsciously shocked by the world crisis initiated in Wall Street in 1929, with its repercussions in the political and military subversion that took place in Brazil the ensuing year—which began to awaken from its long sleep, its inertia, and its lethargy, to feel reality and to realize that it needed a true political conscience for the new directions and new paths, a pragmatic direction and objective; that it needed to abandon the old formulae and the sonorous verbalism with which it had been lulled and deluded.[345]

Azevedo Amaral's works (*Ensaios brasileiros*, 1930; *O Brasil na Crise Atual*, 1934; *A Aventura Política do Brasil*, 1935; and, later, already during the "Estado Novo" or Vargas regime, *O Estado Autoritário e a Realidade Nacional*, 1938), despite the serious criticism that can be leveled against them, bring an important contribution to the interpretation of Brazil, if only for their opposition. They display, however, that old fault, pointed out by Mário de Andrade when he said that "sociology was the art of rapidly saving Brazil." And Azevedo Amaral, who was, in fact, a doctor, seems to have suffered from this professional impulse, particularly after the advent of the *Estado Novo*. He did not see (or did not want to see) the ridiculous contradiction contained in the affirmation: "The *Estado Novo* . . . has achieved an immediate and radical transformation. The nation is no longer an enormous herd, whose destiny was simply to pay taxes and take to the polls the illustrious names of the republican dynasts." [346]

All writers who, at the height of their spiritual maturity, were writing at the time of the revolutionary movement of October, 1930, shared the preoccupation with Brazilian problems. The 1930 revolution was sparked in part by the political tinder which is the presidential succession, but it was aggravated by the Wall Street crash. Thus, while literary subversion continued to seek the true paths and began to have its effect, an economic crisis, occasioned by the collapse of international trade during the great depression of 1929–1930, came to a head, breaking through the line of least resistance toward the end of 1930. The rebellion which, at first, seriously threatened the foundations of the nation because of the absence of direction and the divergence of aims, absorbed in its torrent the gods themselves and led to a political centralization forecast by the progressive development of the executive power—a centralization which sought to organize itself along distinctly nationalist lines, although it never established its doctrines and did not in fact possess even the embryo of a precise ideology.[347]

Although no path or orientation had yet been found for the country's future—and the proof of this is the abundant, varied, and contradictory literature on "Brazilian problems" that followed the 1930 revolution—anyone who could understand, realized that something had been profoundly altered in Brazil. Thus 1930, with all its contradictions, was, if not the end of a culture, as Nélson Werneck Sodré thought, at least "a busy crossroads marking the end of the domination of an elite of pure literati, of dilettantes of knowledge, and of a vague and dispersive amateurism." [348]

We are still too much caught up in the web of contradictions which is the present to be able to consider and examine with the justice they merit the events that succeeded the 1930 revolution. After almost a quarter of a century (in which there were important adventures in our history), the events of 1930 still influence the present. Many of the leading figures who participated in this adventure are still alive and active. Some, however, are already missing, and perhaps among them the most curious figure of all. But he passed quickly. These personalities daily diminish, giving way to a personality that grows apace (a fact which political personalities appear not to grasp)—I mean, the Brazilian people, ignorant of all ideologies and all cultures.

The political-military revolution of October, 1939;[349] the Constitutionalist revolution of São Paulo;[350] the emergence of the Integralist movement[351] and its transformation into national fascism in view of international political circumstances; the development of communism;[352] the advent of the *Estado Novo;*[353] the war;[354] "Getulism," [355] the cult of President Getúlio Vargas; the reinstatement of democracy in 1945;[356] and the present state of profound crisis we have now reached—all are events too complicated to be dispassionately examined, since in them is reflected the confusion and restlessness characteristic of the period following the First World War, which was further accentuated by the most recent struggle among the civilized nations.

About ten years ago, two Paulista writers collected testimonies, which are curious symptoms of the state of ideas at that time. Time has gone by, and many things have changed since then, which makes one feel that the value of testimonies is relative, as is the meaning of the notion "generation." Edgard Cavalheiro, in his *Testamento de Uma Geração,* published twenty-six replies from representatives of the Brazilian intelligentsia, men who are today in their fifties. Mário Néme, in his turn, published in *Plataforma da Nova Geração,* twenty-nine testimonies from members of the generation that has not yet reached its fiftieth year.[357]

What historical events and what ideas impressed the members of the Brazilian intelligentsia now in their fifties, and what solutions did they present in the first of these collections? All point to the First World War, as one of the most decisive historical events; all, or nearly all, express an interest in Brazil and Brazilian studies, although opinions vary on Brazil's probable destiny.

For members of the "new generation"—the generation now in its forties—the *consequences* of the First World War are the principal preoccupation, and they show a clearer understanding of the *results* of events. As for Brazil, the interest is still the same, perhaps greater, but without the exaggerated nationalism of the first generation. The new generation shows a more scientific but no less affectionate understanding. There is, says one of its more enlightened representatives, "a deperate anxiety to understand the confusion," [358] and, for this reason, there is restlessness (which might be the result of their youth) among the generation of 1945. To sum up the ideas of this new generation, I will quote, as a conclusion to this work, the words of a young Brazilian scientist:

To get some idea of the tasks awaiting youth we must carefully examine the total Brazilian situation. But this is not subject to a purely logical understanding. Many aspects of the situation, which are in marked contrast to the others, are survivors from a remote past. Hence the need for a careful study of historical conditions of time past and the work of precursors. A study of the past and of contemporary facts is not enough. There are also the seeds of the future. No matter how minute they may seem, they are already opposed to everything that already exists or has existed and constitute one of the motive powers of the historical process. If we did not take tomorrow into account, we would fall into the fatal error of impotent historicism, which ignores the creative originality of the moment represented by these seeds. The work of the intellectual is only truly significant when it has the power to fertilize, when it contains the embryo of things to come.[359]

Such, then, in imperfect view, is the history of ideas in Brazil. We could not have understood it unless we had taken the care to examine the past. As Vicente Licínio Cardoso has said: "To commemorate the past should imply planning for the future." [360]

CHAPTER 8

Conclusions

What immediately impressed me when I undertook the study of the evolution of philosophy in Brazil, was the long and varied importation of apparently contradictory ideas and doctrines that continued throughout our history. What significance do these ideas have for us? What meaning did these doctrines take on in our country? I was led in this way to reflect on the vicissitudes of ideas and doctrines once they have crossed the ocean. But another problem presented itself: in what measure did we assimilate the Western thought to which we are linked? How much imitation, how much deformation is present? This was another problem and, I must confess, it is still difficult to provide a satisfactory solution.

In our process of identification with the philosophical problems posed by European thought, on the fringes of which we live—the universal problems of man's destiny—one part seems to have escaped total identification. Despite the clear lines of the model, historical conditions of the intellect proper to the destiny of the American peoples exist and lead us to attribute to philosophy a significance that, I believe, we have not yet clearly understood. Evidently, "philosophy, like any other branch of investigation, aspires to truth and consequently to universal validity. It cannot, therefore, present itself as national. On the other hand, it is impossible to escape the influence of the national," writes Ralph Barton Perry,[1] who adds, referring to the philosophic thought of his own country:

Although in the United States there is no body of doctrines or school of philosophy that can be considered North-American, there is, nevertheless, an intellectual mould created in the United States as the result of its history, its ethnic origin and its natural environment, which is reflected in the type of philosophy that tended to predominate and to prevail.[2]

This is perhaps equally true of what goes on in our own country.

"A society," writes Toynbee, "faces in the course of its existence a succession of problems to be resolved individually by each one of its members in the best possible way. The presentation of these problems takes the form of a challenge which must be considered a test." [3] This challenge and this test must be, I believe, studied in the evolution of our own history.

For this reason, I was immediately committed to the historical position which is, in fact, the position taken even by the writers who criticize it in America.

"Ideas," wrote Professor Schneider not long ago,

suffer a strange and different fate when they disembark on the American shore. The new circumstances automatically serve as a testing ground for the old ideas: some take on a new meaning, others are soon lost. . . . For this reason, historians of culture and ideas should not consider America as a mere province, for even when they represent "frontiers" of European culture which were and still are relatively uncultivated, these wild regions are highly significant as centers of new interpretations.[4]

In the enterprise of commercial speculation that was colonization, we find two types engaged in this undertaking: the adventurer and the Jesuit.

For the adventurer, a man of his time—that of the agitated Renaissance—Brazil unfolded like "a field favorable to free endeavor, to possibility, and to hope." [5]

The easy wealth which the conquests permitted attracted the Portuguese, always characterized by a practical view of existence. In Portugal philosophy had never appeared as pure speculation. Even before the great age of the discoveries and expansion, philosophy was, as Joaquim de Carvalho and Vieira de Almeida have said, of a pragmatic nature.[6]

From earliest times Portuguese thought had a practical end in view. It gravitated around realistic problems, with limited, precise, and concrete objects. The sense of the useful, the immediate, is what by preference appears in this thought. It was, in the words of the poet João de Barros, "an earthly love for human realities, the profoundly realistic sense of existence."[7] The Jesuits themselves did not escape this practical sense of existence.

Two types, then, apparently opposed but integrated in an identical notion of action, faced each other in the colony. On the one hand the Jesuit, pledged, in the widest sense of the word, to spiritual conquest; and on the other the adventurer, bent on the conquest of the land and of material wealth. It was with a cast composed of these two characters that our broad Atlantic front was to make its debut in history. In this there is already latent, perhaps one of the contradictions of our history and also the antagonism between the two aspects of culture in Brazil.

The fixation of European culture in our land fell to the adventurer and the Jesuit. One opened up paths in the jungle, built villages, and planted cities; the other molded the Brazilian intellect.

If we consider the meaning of ideas in Brazil, we will see that they are like tools of action, principally of social and political action. Philosophy was in Brazil to a considerable extent in the service of this action, just as in the medieval Portuguese past it had been in the service of theology and its ethical and political reflections.

After the eighteenth century, we began to take an interest in "what went on in the world," in the words of Sílvio Romero. The break with the metropolis accentuated our intellectual links with France, which thenceforth became our principal market for importing ideas and doctrines.

Eclecticism set the tone—the "Louis Philippard" tone—of our Second Empire.

It was in the second half of the nineteenth century, however, that philosophical ideas were more widely divulged, when Brazil went through a phase of complete material remodeling. New paths were also opened up for the Brazilian intelligence.

In a Brazil dulled by the humanities, which in certain respects provoke a genuine cultural inertia, the campaign for cultural and philosophical revision (which began in 1868–1870) appeared like a force for mental renewal. The criticism of Sílvio Romero so profoundly linked to this movement was paralleled by an increase in mathematical studies

. . . and the intensification of the study of the natural sciences . . . Such a movement was not without its parallels, nor was it mere accident that it coincided with the first attempts of the bourgeoisie to take over the economic and political management of the nation.[8]

Positivism, Spencerianism, and evolutionism corresponded to and served this situation.

Alberdi rightly expressed the meaning of philosophy in the American countries when he said in 1841 that "the direction of our studies will not be in the line of speculative philosophy or philosophy *per se,* but in the line of applied philosophy, real and positive philosophy—philosophy applied to the social, political, religious, and moral institutions of these countries. The people will be the great Being whose impressions, laws of life, movement, thought, and progress will be studied and determined." [9] "Pure abstraction," he added, "metaphysics *per se,* will not put down roots in America." [10] All this seems true.

In Brazil, from independence to the republic, we have witnessed a parade of doctrines in which the practical use of philosophy is a constant factor. Eclecticism corresponds to the political needs and conditions of the moderates and even more to the traditional orientation of spiritualism. The Scholastic revival is linked to a political question, that of the bishops, and to the need to raise the moral and cultural level of the clergy. The Littréist Positivism of Pereira Barreto is linked to the rise of the bourgeoisie in Brazil; the religious Positivism of the Apostolate from the beginning subordinated its scientific preoccupations to social aspirations and corresponds to the need for a rule for individual, political, and administrative morality. After 1870 the Germanism of Tobias Barreto is a gust of free thought opening up new directions in a variety of intellectual fields. Even the work of Farias Brito is involved in the search for a criterion that would lead to moral regeneration. For Sílvio Romero—who, reflecting the destiny of his own country, passed through all the shades of nineteenth-century thought—philosophy was not one of those fantastic and arbitrary constructions that bear the name of "systems" and claim to provide the key to the riddle of things.

After the First World War, Brazilian thought became more independent. Ears hitherto closed to Brazilian stridency were now unstopped. Basing itself on a reality nearer at hand, the Brazilian intellect entered another phase of renewal. "Our books became increasingly redolent of the jungle, of wet earth, and of fresh sea breezes. Brazilian themes and the landscape that surrounds us were to give to our literature a greater spontaneity," writes Tristão de Ataíde. "National inspiration will not lead us as high, but it will lead us, with greater security, toward a remote future of creativity and independence." [11]

The social question begins to become a preoccupation. The spread of industrialization determined new changes in the attitude of the Brazilian intelligentsia.

The "European spirits," as they were called by José Osório de Oliveira, were followed by other generations who, although not entirely free from "transoceanism," applied their intelligence to concrete studies, relating to their own country and their own environment. The nostalgic transoceanism of one and the bold but ingenuous nationalism of others was succeeded by a generation which included some men endowed with a new kind of formation and an intellectual equipment more adequate for the comprehension of the problems of culture and perhaps, for this reason, gifted with a more exact understanding of our country and our history. Nevertheless, despite the considerable progress of consciousness verifiable in some, the history of ideas in Brazil—and their philosophic aspect—continues to display some of the traits indicated by Mário de Andrade in the curious figure of Macunaíma, a character in the "chanson de geste" of Brazil. "Macunaíma does all he can to sate himself on copious meals and every kind of fruit. He talks about the art of dressing but does not bother to dress much . . . he sings all the songs and dances to all the tunes. He is the cunning but ignorant heir of all cultures and all instincts." [12]

It would be rash to examine the contrasts and confusions that are revealed in our thinking during the last thirty years, and the time is not yet ripe to do so. We still lack the perspective for such an undertaking and find ourselves, as I have said, in a web of contradictions far from overcome. Our economic life—and with it our thought—presents phases which still reproduce different stages of history. From 1922 to the present day, however, many things have changed.

In the early days of the republican regime, the descendants of the adventurers who had traced the frontiers of our land—the people who were scattered through the sertão—made their tragic appearance on the national scene, disturbing and amazing the coastal intelligentsia. Other aspects of our situation, no less tragic, began to reveal themselves to our coastal intellectuals, showing them their responsibilities and demonstrating how far they had hitherto lived from the problems of their country. The anxiety which today possesses Brazil's intelligentsia—which will not be resolved simply by the solutions of an imported anguish or the juggling tricks of a neophilosophism—will find its salvation only if we have eyes to see, ears to hear, and, above all, the wisdom to take action. Wisdom in the sense the Greeks gave to this word, signifying both "knowledge" and "virtue."

Brazil is a country of contrasts. In its economic life, as Normano has pointed out, exist side by side "the primitive world of the sertão, a medieval economy in the towns of the interior, and a modern civilization in the cities." [13] The same holds true in the realm of the intellect. It is Brazil's historical conditioning that gives meaning to its thought. This life, this experience, should constitute in an initial stage the interest of those who, devoid of the ingenuous pretension of creating a Brazilian philosophy, simply want to create philosophy.

The intelligentsia of the American nations, as Alfonso Reyes has said, has not had time to "break with the incentives of action, as has happened in countries of older civilizations, where ivory towers and extravagant theories can be built, according to which any thinking man who participates in the life of his century is condemned as a traitor." [14]

For us, genuine philosophy was always linked to action. Clóvis Beviláqua was therefore right when he said that "if we are some day to make a philosophical contribution of greater significance, I am convinced that it will not emerge from the heights of metaphysics."

SUPPLEMENTARY
NOTES

Supplementary Notes

To the materialist orientation of philosophy in the nineteenth century in Brazil belongs the work of Domingos Guedes Cabral: *As Funções do Cérebro* (*The Functions of the Brain*), Bahia: Imprensa Econômica, 1876), 2 XXXVIII. Domingos Guedes Cabral (1852–1883) wrote this work as a thesis for a doctorate in medicine at the Bahia Faculty of Medicine. It was refused by the authorities because it was considered harmful to the state religion (cf. Sacramento Blake, *Dicionário Bibliográfico brasileiro*, II, 207). In view of this attitude, Guedes Cabral's colleagues paid for the publication of his work in protest against the "coercion of freedom of thought, which all around us we see curtailed even in the Statutes of our Faculty" (Cabral, *op. cit.* p. vii). Acknowledging in the first pages of his book his gratitude to his colleagues, Guedes Cabral gives an explanation of some significance in the history of the vicissitudes of philosophical currents in Brazil, which also reveals some aspects of the Brazilian situation at that time. "It is almost two years," he writes, "since, stimulated by my readings in medical literature, I undertook the study of a delicate subject, a subject arising out of the *positive philosophy*, a philosophy which is no more than logic applied to facts, and which differs from other philosophies in that, unlike these, it is based on the natural sciences and experimentation" (pp. xii–xiii). Imbued with the naturalist ideas of his age, Guedes Cabral examines in detail the different functions of the brain. The authors he follows are Darwin, Huxley, Broca, Longet, and other naturalists and doctors of his time. In the conclusions to his work Cabral makes some affirmations which modern science, and science in his own day, had put aside; for instance: "man is, therefore, a perfected monkey. A terrible blow to our pride, but, although it seems to humiliate us, it is really ennobling for, by showing us our place in nature, it indicates what it is lawful to aspire to scientifically" (p. 218).

Büchner, Moleschott, Darwin—even on occasion Le Bon—are used to support the ideas of the young doctor from Bahia intoxicated by naturalism. The book provoked a scandal in Bahia. The clergy were up in arms, and an episcopal journal, *Crônica Religiosa,* violently opposed the work of Guedes Cabral. Belarmino Barreto, the publicist, and Canon Romualdo Maria de Seixas also wrote against Guedes Cabral. He defended himself in articles published in *Diário da Bahia* in February, 1876, entitled "A Ciência e os Padres" and "A Propósito das Funções do Cérebro."

A book which appeared anonymously in 1875, written by José de Araújo Ribeiro, Viscount of Rio Grande (1800–1879), has little value for philosophy in Brazil, although its author concerned himself with Brazilian subjects, particularly geology. The Viscount of Rio Grande, who was a diplomat and politician, wrote the curious work on geology which is, in part, on philosophy as well: *O Fim da Criação ou a Natureza Interpretada pelo Senso Comum* (Rio de Janeiro: Tip. Perseverança, 1875). The Viscount believes that one of the means by which the human spirit arrived at important results in science seems to have been the generalization of partial ideas, applying to many things what was known only of a few (p. 3). He attempts to "demonstrate that the earth is endowed with a life of its own and nourishes itself as do organized beings, growing in volume like these and gathering in the regions of space by means of its atmosphere, the matter needed for its nutrition and growth" (p. 4). Despite the curious intent, there are some interesting observations in this book, and there is certainly a knowledge of geological and palaeographic matters. The Viscount of Rio Grande says in one part of the book: "As to the human species, its members likewise are born and grow, but to die and thicken to the quaternary layer, and all their intelligence will not shield them from this inexorable law"

(p. 553), which is self-evident and leads to most melancholy conclusions. All life is nothing more significant than the swift race toward the thickening of the earth's crust. A sad destiny for humanity to serve as a material for sedimentation!

Our moral and spiritual life, which may appear to us the reason for our existence, disappears entirely with death, and usually even before death, as though it had been but a dream, nothing real or positive remaining but our corpses, those portions of condensed air that the earth immediately claims and which nature constrains us to give up without delay. All this is present in the minds of thoughtful men, but it would be better if it were present in all, since the knowledge of our real power in the economy of nature should not prove less profitable to us. It will save us from many illusions which are ever the cause of ills [p. 553].

As we can see, the Viscount of Rio Grande is a pessimist, who bases his moral concepts on conclusions resulting from geological studies.

The Viscount's work, curiously enough, makes pleasant reading despite its gloom. His tendencies are obviously materialistic. But it did not befit a Viscount to confess these ideas publicly during the Empire (and perhaps not even afterward), and hence he never scandalized the few people who read him.

One of the most important names in the history of Catholic ideas in Brazil is missing from this work: that of the illustrious Jesuit, Father Leonel Franca. There was no ill intention in that omission, for, as we have seen, he was often cited in the pages of this work, principally in references to his study of philosophy in Brazil *Noções de Historia da Filosofia.*

This Jesuit priest, who was also one of our country's most cultured intellectuals, was, I feel, also concerned with action. Father Luís Gonzaga da Silveira d'Elboux, in a book which seems to be the best study to date of Leonel Franca (*O Padre Leonel Franca*, S.J., Rio de Janeiro: Agir, 1953), indicates the principal spheres in which he exercised his action or his apostolate. Three centers owe much to his work: the Centro D. Vital, the Sociedade Jurídica Santo Ivo, and the Açao Universitário Catolica.

His action was further evident in his opposition to the secularization of education established by the 1891 constitution, and in his opposition to divorce reform. To him also we owe the establishment of the Catholic University of Rio de Janeiro, where he was principal. "Leonel Franca," writes Tristão de Ataíde, "was on the theological and philosophical level what Rui Barbosa was on the political and juridical. The sword of an invincible analyst in the hands of a fighter whose culture was profound and invincible. . . . At first sight, he did not create the impression that he knew a great deal. . . . He knew how to be silent. He knew how to listen. He was an exceptionally good listener! He was not out to impress. On the contrary. He was silent as often as possible. But as we penetrated the core of his knowledge, we were overcome by a feeling of respect until we could advance no more, for the deeper we went into a subject, the more solid we discovered the ground, the more difficult it became to oppose any contradiction, the more convincing his arguments became, his dialectics as solid as a rock" (Tristão de Ataíde: *Father Leonel Franca*, apud Father Luís Gonzaga da Silveira d'Elboux, *op. cit.*, p. 350). His life was wholly devoted to the service of the religious ideas he professed.

NOTES

Notes

Notes to Introduction
(Pages 1–9)

[1] Herbert W. Schneider, *A History of American Philosophy*, pp. vii–viii.

[2] Risieri Frondizi, "Hay una Filosofía ibero-americana?" *Realidad*, No. 8, p. 11.

[3] Cruz Costa, "A Situacão da Filosofia no Brasil e em Outros Paises da América," in *A Medicina Modena*, I: 2 (April–June, 1948), p. 194.

[4] Sérgio Buarque de Holanda, *Raizes do Brasil*, p. 3.

[5] Sérgio Buarque de Holanda, *Monções*, p. 7.

[6] Eduardo Prado, "Immigration" in *Le Brésil en 1889* (ed. Santa-Ana Nery), p. 473.

[7] René Maunier, *Introduction à la sociologie*, p. 14.

[8] Adrien Delpech, "Da Influência Estrangeira em Nossas Letras" in *Anais do Congresso Internacional de História da América* (1922) pub. *Revista do Instituto Histórico e Geográfico Brasileiro*, IX, 215. See also: Vitorino Magalhães Godinho, *História Ecônomica e Social da Expansão Portuguêsa*, pp. 7–9.

[9] Batista Pereira, "A Formação Espiritual do Brasil" in *Pelo Brasil Maior*, p. 375.

[10] "In all forms of collective life," writes Sérgio Buarque de Holanda, "we can distinguish two principles, perpetually at war with each other, which in their different ways control men's activities and regulate their lives. These two principles are incarnated in the prototypes of the adventurer and the worker. In primitive societies they are manifest in the fundamental distinction between a hunting community and an agricultural one. For the adven-

turer, the final aim, the crown of all his efforts, the moment of arrival—the word 'adventure' comes from the Latin *ad-ventura, advenire*—is of such paramount importance that all intermediate steps are relegated to second place, and seem almost superfluous. He would like to pluck the fruit without having to plant the tree. This type knows no boundaries. The whole world is spread before him, and if he finds any obstacle to his ambition, he soon turns it into a springboard. He needs the limitless freedom of the wide open spaces, grandiose plans for the future, distant horizons forever in the background. The worker, on the contrary, thinks first of the difficulties to be overcome, not of the triumph to be achieved. . . . There exists an ethic of work, and an ethic of adventure. Thus, the man of the worker type will attribute a positive moral value only to those actions which he resolves to practice, and, inversely, he will regard as immoral and abominable all qualities of the adventurer—audacity, improvidence, irresponsibility . . . and everything related to that *spacious* vision of the world which characterizes the adventurer. On the other hand, the energy and effort spent for immediate recompense is exalted by the adventurer, and attempts to preserve peace, to consolidate stability and personal security, or the activities necessary for material profit, are regarded as vicious and despicable. Nothing seems to him meaner or more stupid than the ideals of the worker. *Between these two types there is not so much an absolute opposition as a complete misunderstanding.* Both types are subject, in greater or lesser degree, to a number of variations, and it is obvious that neither exists in reality outside the world of ideas. But as prototypes they are invaluable for the study of the formation and evolution of any society" (Buarque de Holanda, *Raizes do Brasil*, 1st ed., pp. 20–22).

[11] Cf. Fernando de Azevedo, *A Cultura brasileira*, Pt. III, Chap. 1. Also pp. 83 and 174f.

[12] Theodor Reik, *Treinta años con Freud*, p. 62.

[13] In this respect, we must point out the importance of collections such as *Brasiliana*, published under the general editorship of Fernando de Azevedo and *Documentos brasileiros* at present edited by Octávio Tarquínio de Sousa.

[14] Mário de Andrade, *Aspectos da Literatura brasileira*, pp. 16–17.

[15] Afonso Arinos de Melo Franco, *Conceito da Civilização brasileira*, p. 8.

[16] Álvaro Lins, *Notas de um Diário de Crítica*, I, 74.

[17] Lucien Febvre, "Avant-propos" in Charles Morazé, *Trois essais sur histoire et culture*, p. viii.

[18] "C'est une forme de l'intelligence capable de se mouvoir à l'aise (et comme accoutumée) dans les situations les plus variées. Ce sens"—adds the distinguished French professor—"s'acquiert peut-être dans l'étude et les livres. Il s'acquiert bien plus sûrement dans le grand livre du monde" (cf. Morazé, *Trois essais sur histoire et culture*, p. 7).

[19] Léon Brunschvicg, "Vie Intérieure et Vie Spirituelle," apud A. Etcheverry, *L'Idéalisme français contemporain*, p. 105.

[20] Friedrich Meinecke, *El Historicismo y Su Genesis*, p. 12.

[21] "Ainsi le fait . . . apparait comme le suprême, manifestation d'un ensemble social et économique complexe. Ce n'est pas un fait historique, c'est un fait de condition humaine commendé par de larges évolutions encore sensi-

bles de nos jours. Je n'ai cure des étiquettes de matérialisme qu'on pourrait en cet état du raisonnement attacher à cette méthode" (Morazé, *op. cit.* p. 10).

22 Cf. Rodolfo Mondolfo, *En las Origenes de la Filosofia de la Cultura,* p. 157.

23 Émile Bréhier, *La Philosophie et son passé,* pp. 28–29.

24 Cf. Benedetto Croce, "Antihistoricisme" in *Revue de Métaphysique et Morale* (1931), p. 2.

25 Leopoldo Zea, *El Positivismo en México,* pp. 19–20.

NOTES TO CHAPTER 1
(Pages 13–25)
The Portuguese Inheritance

1 Sérgio Buarque de Holanda, *Raízes do Brasil,* p. 15.

2 "Spain and Portugal," writes Gilberto Freyre, "although conventionally regarded as European states, are not orthodox European and Christian in all their qualities, feelings, and ways of life. In many respects they are a compound of Europe and Africa, of Christianity and Mohammedanism. The Iberian Peninsula is, geographically, a zone of transition between two continents: and we have all heard the popular saying that 'Africa begins at the Pyrenees,' a saying Northerners often use with sarcastic intent" (Freyre, *Interpretación del Brasil,* pp. 7–8. Cf. E. Simões de Paula, *Marrocos e Suas Relações com a Ibéria na Antiguidade,* pp. 260f.).

3 Rafael Altamira, *Historia de la Civilización Española,* pp. 82–83. Cf. also pp. 84–88.

4 Fernando de Los Rios, "Spain in the Epoch of American Civilization" in *Concerning Latin American Culture,* apud Freyre, *op. cit.* p. 10 and p. 191. A region in which peoples of such diverse tendencies could coëxist must have been a region where the greatest tolerance was exercised. It seems to me that the humanism and realism which characterizes Portuguese culture can be explained, in part, by the influence on it of Arab culture and the necessities which arose from the intercourse of these widely differing peoples. From the Arabs, the Iberians acquired a knowledge of Greek philosophy and above all the "physical" interpretation which the Arabs had placed on it. It was under Arab influence, and also under the influence of the practical sense of the Jews, that in the dawn of the Renaissance the Portuguese initiated their maritime expansion. The isolation of Portuguese secular science—which was of a profoundly empirical tendency—from the philosophical movements of a more truly Continental inspiration, is another symptom, suggestive of the influence of Arab culture in Portugal. "The Arab philosophers of Spain," writes Ingenieros, "on a much wider scale than those of the East, introduced Aristotelianism into Europe, thus preparing the way for renewal of Christian

Scholasticism. The enormous progress we find from St. Augustine to St. Thomas Aquinas was, to a great extent, the result of the work of these philosophers, combined with that of the Jews. Their civilization had other merits which place it much higher than that of the Christian Europe of their time. Two important branches of the natural sciences, mathematics and astronomy, were carefully studied, as was the science of medicine, and the Arab scholars attained considerable achievements in these fields. This scientific movement assumes even greater importance when we consider the confusion which then reigned in the Christian world. Moslem culture drew its inspiration from the twin fountainheads of *man* and *nature,* the true bases of any philosophy, and their achievement overflowed the narrow limits of dogma imposed by the theologians and fanatics of Islam" (José Ingenieros, *La Cultura Filosófica en España,* p. 27).

Arab culture, influenced "those scholars who were becoming progressively alienated from the dogmaticism of the Scholastic method and, when there was a revival of Christian Scholasticism as a result of Arab teaching, these scholars continued to study applied science, turning their backs on the maze of theological and philosophical argumentation. A deep division between secular and ecclesiastical science was soon apparent, the latter almost wholly concerned with subtle commentary on philosophers; the former, the true precursor of the Renaissance vision of the world, concerned with the study of the different sciences. Moors and Christians maintained in spite of their wars a close cultural contact. One could almost say, as did a German writer, Erdmann, that 'during a considerable period the struggles between Christians and Moors in the Peninsula had the character of a civil war, and that only through the influence of the Crusades did they take on the nature of a proselytizing extermination'" (Hernani Cidade, *Lições sôbre a Cultura e a Literatura portuguêsas,* I, 67).

[5] According to Zurara, "Prince Henry desired in all things that certitudes should be made manifest, as is necessary with all the works of man and all his judgments, in which doubt and certainty do forever mingle." Apud Cidade, *op. cit.,* I, 80. Cf. Antônio Sérgio, *História de Portugal,* pp. 48f. Cf. also the important work by Jaime Cortezão, "Influência dos Descobrimentos dos portuguêses na História da Civilização" in *História de Portugal,* IV, 179–240. It was neither as the originator of systems nor as a subtle commentator of theological texts that St. Anthony, the saint who has lived on in the popular imagination, distinguished himself in the history of medieval Portuguese culture. It was through the intense concern for social justice that inspired his actions and the battles he waged against clericalism that he was elevated to the special position he occupies in Portuguese thought. "In the conflicts which harassed the Franciscan order after the death of its founder, St. Anthony openly took the part of the 'zelanti' and was the eloquent champion of the ideal of poverty as the sum of Christian perfection, opposed in this to the views of Father Elias." Cf. Joaquim de Carvalho, *Desenvolvimento da Filosofia em Portugal durante a Idade Média,* p. 7. Cf. also Fr. René de Nantes, *Histoire des spirituels de l'Ordre de Saint François,* p. 63f., apud Carvalho, *op. cit.,* p. 22. Another representative of this practical orientation

in Portuguese thought is the famous Pedro Julião Rebêlo, Petrus Hispanus, otherwise known as Pope John XXI. Of the medieval doctors, Petrus Hispanus was immortalized by Dante in the *Divina Commedia* (Canto XII, 132–134): "Ugo da San Vittore è qui con elli/e Pietro Mangiadore e Pietro Hispano/lo qual giù luce in dodici libelli." Here Dante is referring to the "Summaries" famous in all medieval schools. The *Summulae Logicales* is a clear summary of Aristotle's *Organon,* and Hauréau considers it a most and intelligent work. Forty-eight editions were printed in the first century of the printing press, and the work was still current in the fifteenth and even in the sixteenth centuries. Some writers, among them Karl Prantl, in his *Geschichte der Logik im Abendland,* attributed the authorship of the "Summaries" to Michael Psellos, the Byzantine scholar. The arguments collected by Joaquim de Carvalho in his interesting work "Cultura Filosófica e Científica" in *História de Portugal,* IV, 475–528, clearly summarize the doubts which still exist on the subject and indicate how difficult research has proved. "It would not be too bold to claim," writes Joaquim de Carvalho, "that for Petrus Hispanus the fundamental problem in logic was the meaning of words: indeed, it was the emphasis placed on this problem that made of the "Summaries" an indispensable source for the history of nominalism and terminism. This is quite understandable. The *Summulae Logicales* was the most famous and most widely expounded compendium of the *New Logic* (the Logica Moderna), the term used in the twelfth century to designate the sudden enrichment of logic after the diffusion of the complete *Organon.* The *logica vetus,* or logic of Boethius, included only two of the *Organon* treatises of Aristotle—the *Categoriae* and *De Interpretatione,* Porphyry's *Isagoge* and the writings of Boethius *De Divisione* and *De Differentis Topicis,* whereas the Logica Moderna was based, in addition to these texts, on the *Analytica priora* and *posteriora* the *Tropica* and *De Sophisticis elenchis,* that is, on the whole *Organon.* The work of Petrus Hispanus carries on the work of Aristotle, summarizing almost all his logical thought" (Carvalho, *ibid.,* pp. 511–512). See João Ferreira, O.F.M., "As Súmulas Logicais de Pedro Hispano e os Seus Comentadores" in *Coletânea de Estudos,* 2d ser. III, No. 3 (1952) and, by the same writer, "Temas de Cultura Filosófica portuguêsa" in *Coletânea de Estudos,* V, No. 1 (1954). There is nothing truly original in Petrus Hispanus' compendium of the logic of the period. Like the similar works of William of Shyreswood and Lambert d'Auxerre, the principal aim is to train the student in the dialectic arguments of university debate. "All these works," writes Michalski, "stem from the confrontation of propositions, almost invariably lifted textually from Lambert d'Auxerre's *Summa.* This becomes evident if we compare the work of Petrus Hispanus with the Latin manuscripts in the Bibliothèque National (MSS 7392 and 13966) which contain the work of Lambert" (Michalski, *Les Courants philosophiques à Oxford et à Paris pendant le XIV*ᵉ *siècle,* cited in Carvalho, *op. cit.,* p. 512). Petrus Hispanus is also the author of *Thesaurum Pauperum.* Thanks to the discoveries of Monsignor Martin Grabmann, who visited the libraries of the Iberian Peninsula in 1927, we know today that this Portuguese philosopher did write the *Thesaurum,* probably first published in 1462. A marked

Arab influence can be detected in the book (cf. Maximiano de Lemos, *História da Medicina em Portugal*). *De Oculis* by Petrus Hispanus is of great interest for the history of science and especially for ophthalmology (cf. Carvalho, *op. cit.*, p. 508, and Egas Moniz, "O Papa João XXI" in *Ao Lado da Medicina*, pp. 153–174). Among the works on medicine by Petrus Hispanus is a treatise on the Galenic art of Huanim ibn Ishâg; commentaries on Galen's *Microtechne* and *De Crisibus*, Hippocrates' *Prognosticon* on diet, and Isaac Israeli's *De Urinus*. Besides these works, Monsignor Gravmann found in the Biblioteca Nacional of Madrid a compendium on psychology by Petrus Hispanus, which has not yet been published. Cf. "Ein ungedrucktes Lehrbuch der Psychologie des Petrus Hispanus (Papst Johannes XXI) in Cod. 3314 der Biblioteca Nacional zu Madrid," by M. Grabmann, in *Spanische Forschung der Gorresgesellschaft*, I. Reihe. *Gesammelte Aufsätze zur Kulturgeschichte Spaniens*, pp. 163–173; apud Carvalho, *op. cit.* Cf. also P. Janet and G. Seailles, *Histoire de la philosophie*, pp. 508f.

[6] Lothar Thomas, *Contribuição para a História da Filosofia portuguêsa*, p. 390.

[7] Jaime Cortezão, "A Influência dos Descobrimentos portuguêses na História da Civilização" in *História de Portugal*, IV, 180.

[8] Rodrigues Lapa, *Dom Duarte e os Prosadores da Casa de Aviz*, p. viii.

[9] Costa Marques, *D. Duarte-Leal-Conselheiro*, p. 7.

[10] João de Barros, *Pequena História da Poesia portuguêsa*, pp. 40–41 and p. 96.

[11] Jaime Cortezão, *Teoria Geral dos Descobrimentos portuguêses*, p. 51.

[12] Cf. Bento Carqueja, *O Capitalismo Moderno e as suas Origens em Portugal*, Chap. VIII, and Henri Sée, *Les Origines du capitalisme moderne*, Chap. III.

[13] Cruz Costa, "O Pensamento brasileiro" in *Boletim da Faculdade de Filosofia, Ciência e Letras da Universidade de S. Paulo*, No. LXVII (1946), p. 11.

[14] Capistrano de Abreu, *Capítulos da História Colonial*, p. 278.

[15] Cf. Herbert Schneider, *A History of American Philosophy*, p. 144f; Samuel Ramos, *Historia de la Filosofia en Mexico*, pp. 27–40; Guillermo Francovich, *La Filosofia en Bolivia*, p. 25f; Arturo Ardão, *Filosofia Pre-universitaria en el Uruguay*, p. 17f; José Ingenieros, *La Evolución de las Ideas argentinas*, I, 46; Alejandro Korn, *Influencias Filosóficas en la Evolución Nacional*, in *Obras Completas*, pp. 45–79.

[16] Cf. Teófilo Braga, *História da Universidade de Coimbra*, II, pp. 275f, and Mario Brandão, *O Colégio das Artes*, p. 501. See also Dr. Manuel Eduardo da Motta Veiga, *Esboço Histórico-Literário da Faculdade de Teologia da Universidade de Coimbra*, pp. 75f.

[17] Hernani Cidade, "A Literatura: O Seiscentismo" in *História de Portugal*, VII, 450. Cf. Cidade, *Lições sôbre a Cultura e a Literatura portuguêsas*, I, 187; Motta Veiga, *op. cit.*

[18] Prince Henry tried to expand and to improve the organization of the University of Lisbon. He became patron of the University, and introduced several reforms. Of the prince's role in the history of the University, Joaquim

de Carvalho writes as follows: "The task he had undertaken required the collaboration of minds oriented in a modern direction and concerned with the study of nature. In turning to the University, Prince Henry must have recognized its inability to equip the kind of minds he needed, since the studies it provided were still based on antiquated doctrines" ("Instituições de Cultura" in *História de Portugal*, IV, 243).

[19] Braga, *op. cit.*, I, 170.

[20] *Ibid.*, pp. 170–171.

[21] Fidelino de Figueiredo, *Estudos de Literatura*, 4th ser., p. 112.

[22] Cf. Antônio Sérgio, "O Reino Cadaveroso ou o Problema da Cultura em Portugal" in *Ensaios*, II, 17f.

[23] "The University of the Counter-Reformation," writes Joaquim de Carvalho, "was an organism in the service of the ethical and religious ends of the state, a moral tendency thus supplanting learning—or, at least, the discursive and dialectical capacity of the mind" (cf. Carvalho, "Instituições de Cultura" in *História de Portugal*, V, 563).

Antônio Sérgio, in his critique of the work of Dr. Manuel Murias, *O Seiscentismo em Portugal*, writes as follows: "Neither the Jesuits, nor the Inquisition, nor the Index, proved incompatible with the *intellectual flowering* which then took place—if we may use this term to describe what in fact we then had: an elegant style of rhetoric. But it is not of this that we complain; the problem lies elsewhere. What we do complain of is that we did not share in the progress of much more important things, the fruitful renewal of science and philosophy. Even Dr. Murias recognizes this when he says: 'The philosophy of the seventeenth century was confined to the Scholasticism so dear to the universities of Coimbra and Évora, and the colleges and seminaries of the Jesuits, at a time when it was being impugned all over Europe by the disciples of Bacon and Descartes. We can harbor no doubt that the philosophical thought of the seventeenth century stayed aloof from the modern currents which, in France and England, were ousting Thomism'" (Antônio Sérgio, "Crítica do Trabalho do Dr. M. Murias, O Seiscentismo em Portugal" in *Lusitânia* [June, 1924], p. 443).

By chaneling the energies which had led to the success of the maritime enterprise, into a humanism which in Portugal was transformed into the cult of a refined Latinity, the Jesuits managed to achieve in their colleges (the College of Arts and the College of St. Anthony) and in their universities (of Coimbra and Évora) an "elegant style of rhetoric," to quote Antônio Sérgio; but they diverted the intellect from higher and more important problems—the renewal of that very intellect. During the Renaissance, Portugal had made a notable contribution. In the seventeenth century her brilliance was extinguished.

The seventeenth century is also the period of her political decadence and the period of sterile university teaching. The sterility of the universities was largely owing to the excessive ecclesiastical influence, and perhaps even more to the stagnation into which the old methods of study had fallen. Students were bound to the texts, compelled to limit themselves slavishly to what was already known; the masters' duties were subject to the strictest surveillance—

all these limitations prevented any pedagogical renewal, and, in consequence, isolated Portuguese culture from the modern currents of thought. The authority of the ancients was evoked against these present-day currents. With the reinvocation of Aristotle in the university, philosophy diverged ever further from scientific investigation. It was against this anachronistic state of affairs that exceptional men like Amato Lusitano and Garcia da Orta raised their protest. (Cf. Joaquim de Carvalho, *Estudos sôbre a Cultura portuguêsa do Século* XVI, pp. 10–11.)

[24] Jaime Cortezão, *Teoria Geral dos Descobrimentos portuguêses*, pp. 48–49. Cf. Carvalho, *op. cit.*, pp. 51f.

[25] Cortezão, *op. cit.*, pp. 49–50.

[26] Dr. Fortunato de Almeida, "O Século XVI: Aspectos Gerais—a Sociedade, o Rei" in *História da Literatura portuguêsa*, by Albino Forjaz de Sampaio, I, 266.

[27] Damião de Góis, *Lisboa de Quinhentos*, tran. R. Machado, p. 48.

[28] "If I wished to comply with the customs of this land, I should straightway get me a mule and four lackeys. But how could I bring this about? By fasting at home, while I shone abroad like a conqueror, and I would needs swallow the bitter pill—that of owing more than I could ever pay. This is how the accomplished courtier lives, in this land! Which calls to mind a certain gentleman, from whose description you may imagine the others. This gentleman, whose portrait I am about to paint for you, had quarreled with a foreigner, a Frenchman, I believe, who had come to Portugal in the days of King Manuel, as a member of Queen Leonor's household. In the display of outward pomp, our Portuguese friend bore the palm, but the Frenchman kept a better table. Acquainted with the local practices, and consumed with curiosity, the Frenchman contrived most skillfully to gain possession of his rival's book of household accounts.

"At once his eyes lighted on a page most droll, and typically Portuguese. He perceived the following entry of the daily expense:

Water 4   ceitis [A ceitil is an old Portuguese farthing]
Bread 2   reais [Real is an old Portuguese monetary unit]
Radishes .... 4-½ reais

"Since these prodigalities continued throughout the week, he fancied that on Sundays, at least, the household would be treated to a sumptuous banquet . . . but for that day, what was his astonishment to find the simple inscription: 'Today nothing, as there were no radishes in the market.'

"This land, my dear Látoma, abounds in such splendid radish eaters who, in the streets, are attended by a train of servants far exceeding in number the amount of reais they spend at home. And I am even persuaded that there are many whose income is lower than my own, but who nonetheless maintain a household of eight servants, God knows how—if not by abundantly feeding them, then certainly by the power of hunger, or by some other means which I am too stupid to learn in my alloted span on earth. Withal it is not easy to recruit a gang of useless servitors, since these people will bear anything rather than study some profession" (Cardeal Cerejeira, *Clendardo—O Humanismo em Portugal*, pp. 279–280).

[29] "D. Jorge de Almeida, Bishop of Coimbra, provides a curious testimony to the liberties permitted at this time. It had often come to his ears that clerics in holy orders and beneficiaries, both in the city and in the villages of the bishopric, would go to the rivers and other public places to speak dishonestly to the women, *more than if they had been laymen*. For this reason, he forbade them to go to the rivers or to the gate of Belcouce, or to other public places to engage in talk with women of doubtful virtue, under pain of penalties to the sum of 500 reis for each infringement, the monies to be used on the cathedral works and the parish" (apud Almeida, *op. cit.*, p. 270).

[30] Roberto C. Simonsen, *História Econômica do Brasil*, I, 63.

[31] João Lúcio de Azevedo, *Épocas de Portugal Econômico*, p. 19.

[32] *Ibid.*, p. 21. Between the cultured classes of the nation, grown soft by the humanism of gallantry, and the bold men who went to challenge fortune on the seas in search of a new life, there exists a tremendous gap. Hernani Cidade rightly records: "Beyond the seas and on the oceans there was a heroic life; but in the drawing rooms of the palace, the order of the day was gallantry and diversion. This is the theme of one of the best poets in the 'Cancioneiro,' João Ruiz Castelo Branco:

> The barriers of the Moors you break,
> And all their frontiers you raze,
> While we fight bulls and feasts do make
> To celebrate the sweet May days.
>
> We never pause to think of strife,
> Of assegais and shining arms,
> On fine array we spend our life,
> And all our thoughts are women's charms (124—III).

An echo of the economic revolution through which Portugal was passing can be heard in the verses sent to his friends by Luiz da Silveira, serving in the Armada. They are symptomatic of the time:

> Live well—all you whom Fortune loves,
> And hold the reins of Fortune
> Already in your hand;
>
> The rest of us are called,
> From one fate to the next,
> And know not what may be (322—III).

Apud Cidade, *Lições sôbre a Cultura e a Literatura portuguêsas*, I, 63–64.

[33] Gilberto Freyre, *O Mundo que o português criou*. Cf. the extremely interesting "Introductory Notes" by Antônio Sérgio in *Antologia dos Economistas Portuguêses*.

[34] Antero de Quental, "Causas da Decadência dos Povos Peninsulares" in *Prosas*, pp. 95–96.

[35] *Ibid.*, p. 101.

[36] *Ibid.*, p. 103.

[37] Sée, *op. cit.*, p. 49.

[38] Bento Carqueja, *O Capitalismo Moderno e as Suas Origens em Portugal*, p. 98.

[39] Sée, *op. cit.*, p. 57.

[40] Mario Brandão, *O Colégio das Artes*, p. 123.

[41] T. Braga, *op. cit.*, I, 485.

[42] "And more than any words, experience, which is the mother of all things, disabuses our minds of misconception and resolves all our doubts," wrote Duarte Pacheco Pereira in *Esmeraldo de Situ Orbis* (critical and annotated edition, ed. Epifanio de Silva Dias), p. 23.

[43] Cf. Álvaro Ribeiro, *O Problema da Filosofia portuguêsa*, p. 17.

[44] Sant'Ana Dionisio, *A Não Cooperação da Inteligência ibérica na Criação das Ciências*, pp. 39–50. Despite the odd title, this is a most interesting work.

[45] Cidade, *Lições sôbre a Cultura* . . . , I, 190.

[46] *Ibid.*, p. 189.

[47] Cf. Joaquim de Carvalho, "A Teoria da Verdade e do Êrro nas 'Disputationes Metaphysicae' de F. Suarez" in *Revista da Universidade de Coimbia*, Vol. VI (1917); Manuel Carvillo, "Francisco Suarez (La Filosofia Juridica, El Derecho de Propriedad)" in *Jornadas*, No. 43.

[48] Maurice de Wulf, *Histoire de la philosophie médiévale*, II, 288.

[49] Giuseppe Saitta, *La Scolastica del Secolo XVI e la Politica dei Gesuiti*, pp. 155–156.

[50] Newton de Macedo, "A Renovação das Idéias e das Instituições de Cultura" in *Historia de Portugal*, VI, 421–422.

[51] Cf. Hernani Cidade, *Lições de Cultura e Literatura portuguêsas*, II, 22.

[52] Fortunat Strowski, *Montaigne*, pp. 120–121.

[53] *Ibid.*, p. 124.

[54] Léon Brunschvicg, *Le Progrés de la conscience dans la philosophie occidentale*, I, 121.

[55] Alcântara Machado, *Vida e Morte do Bandeirante*, 2d ed., p. 245.

[56] Cf. Júlio de Mesquita Filho, *Ensaios sul americanos*, p. 144.

[57] Joaquim Nabuco, *A Minha Formação*, pp. 40–41.

[58] Vieira de Almeida, "Dispersão no Pensamento Filosófico português" in *Revista da Faculdade de Letras de Lisboa*, IX, 176.

[59] Miguel de Unamuno, *Del Sentimento Tragico de la Vida*, 1st ed., p. 19.

[60] João Ribeiro, "A Filosofia no Brasil" in *Revista do Brasil*, No. 22, 2d year, VI (1917), 255.

NOTES TO CHAPTER 2
(Pages 26–43)
Vicissitudes of Colonial Formation

[1] Caio Prado Júnior, *História Econômica do Brasil*, pp. 22–23.

[2] *Ibid.*, p. 24.

[8] Hernani Cidade, *A Literatura Portuguêsa e a Expansão Ultramarina,* pp. 18–19.

[4] Sant'Ana Dionísio, *A Não Cooperação da Inteligência ibérica na Criação da Ciência,* pp. 37–38.

[5] "The constitutional mysticism of the Spaniard [and the concepts which follow can be applied equally to the Portuguese] is not metaphysical, it is moral. St. Theresa or St. Ignatius did not achieve the visionary state through the philosophical speculation that brought the Alexandrians to this state. There is nothing in common between the disciples of Plotinus and those of St. Ignatius. Spanish mysticism is repelled by philosophy—hence neither scientific investigations nor metaphysical meditations illuminate the pages of its history. The Spaniard has neither systems nor schools nor erudite traditions; he cannot resolve a problem by means of subtle combinations without at the same time denying himself and his heroic soul, and committing suicide in God" (Oliveira Martins, *História da Civilização ibérica,* 6th ed., pp. 243–245).

[6] Prado Júnior, *op. cit.,* p. 31.

[7] *Ibid.*

[8] Nélson Werneck Sodré, *Formação da Sociedade brasileira,* p. 109.

[9] *Ibid.,* pp. 78–79. Cf. Fernando de Azevedo, *Canaviais e Engenhos na Vida Política do Brasil.*

[10] "Informação de 1585" in *Materiais e Achegas para a História e a Geografia do Brasil,* apud Eduardo Prado, "O catolicismo, a Companhia de Jesus e a Colonização do Brasil" in *O III Centenário do Venerável Joseph de Anchieta,* p. 50.

[11] Sodré, *op. cit.,* pp. 105–106. Cf. Sérgio Buarque de Holanda, *Cobra de Vidro,* pp. 90f.

[12] Sodré, *op. cit.,* p. 106.

[13] *Ibid.*

[14] Euclides da Cunha, *Os Sertões,* p. 84.

[15] "The most significant consequence of the conflict, in which the Jesuits were inevitably defeated, was the neutralization of their work, intrinsically opposed to all that characterizes the modern state—lay colonization being a part or one of its fundamental aspects. The essentially political tendency of Jesuitism and its theocratic application was not strongly influential in the development of Brazil. It was never allowed to elaborate the structure to which were devoted most of the energies of its practitioners in the colony. Even the theocratic cordon which the Jesuits managed to establish around what were later to become our geographic frontiers, was subject to the attack of the forces truly dominating the Brazilian scene. We must bear in mind the economic part played by the members of the Society of Jesus. They played a leading role among other religious orders, and in the colony this role grew in importance. Anyone who was possessed of wealth but showed no regard for the Church—records one of the chroniclers—risked the denial of the sacraments and the refusal of burial in hallowed ground. During their stay in the colony, the Jesuits did not remain the poor Order of the early days of the College of St. Paul. Over the years, the Order amassed a fortune

—it became a wealthy and powerful landowner, receiving either through inheritance, donations, or government concessions extensive lands, numerous slaves, and all those assets which constituted the marks of distinction, thus aligning the Jesuits with the wealthy landowners in the social structure of the time."

[16] Caio Prado Júnior, *Formação do Brasil Contemporâneo*, pp. 86–87. José Bonifacio noted that the "aim of the Jesuits was to turn the Indians into monks and docile pupils. They were despots, albeit just ones, but they banished anything likely to give the neophytes any ideas about the dignity of man, or intellectual culture" (Octavio Tarquínio de Sousa, *O Pensamento Vivo de José Bonifacio*, p. 118).

[17] Gilberto Freyre, *O Mundo que o português Criou*, pp. 112–124.

[18] Serafim Leite, S.J., *História da Companhia de Jesus no Brasil*, I, 74.

[19] Fernando de Azevedo, *A Cultura brasileira*, p. 178.

[20] *Ibid.*

[21] *Viano Moog, Uma Interpretação da Literatura brasileira*, p. 35.

During the seventeenth century we were the world's largest sugar suppliers. It was only natural that we should, for this reason, attract the attention of foreigners. And this is precisely what did happen. The struggle for the sugar monopoly which Holland initiated aroused a new interest in Brazil. But it was not only the foreigners who showed interest in our country. We ourselves began to manifest a renewed interest in our land. We began to care for it. Even the literati turned their eyes toward our native scenery. They began to write our history—"a history of slippers," in the words of Capistrano; but at least when one begins to write the history of something, it must be because one feels a certain love for that thing. The literati went as far as to write:

> Brazilians are such stupid geese,
> That all their lives they work in vain
> For all their toil is to maintain
> Some lazy rogue of a Portuguese . . .

already an indication of the rebellious attitude toward their colonial condition. Their interest in the faraway laurels, sycamores, and cypresses of the Hellenes began to wane. Now they wrote of coconut, cashew, and palm trees. (Cruz Costa, "Alguns Aspectos do Pensamento brasileiro" in *Boletim da Faculdade de Filosofia, Ciência e Letras da Universidade de S. Paulo*, No. LXVII (1946), p. 25.

[22] Leite, *op. cit.*, p. 96.

[23] Alcides Bezerra, in his book *Achegas à História de Filosofia*, reproduces a paper he presented to the Brazilian Philosophical Society entitled: "A Filosofia na fase colonial" ("Philosophy in the Colonial Phase"), in which he enumerates, without examining their doctrines, the following Brazilian "philosophers": In the seventeenth century—Antônio Vieira, S.J. (1608–1697); Dr. Diogo Gomes Carneiro (1618–1676); Friar Manuel do Destêrro (1652–1706), author of a *Scholastic Philosophy*; Mateus da Encarnação Pina (1687), a member of the Benedictine Order responsible for treatise

Dogmatic and Scholastic Theology. In the eighteenth century, he records the name of Nuno Marques Pereira (1652–1728), author of *Peregrino da América*. He adds Matias Aires to this list. However, the latter writer spent almost all his life in Europe, and it would be inappropriate to study his work in relation to the philosophy of Brazil merely because he happened to be born a Brazilian. (Cf. E. Ennes, *Dois Paulistas Insignes.*) Gaspar da Madre de Deus (1715–1800), of the Benedictine Order, the historian of the captaincy of St. Vincent, wrote a treatise of philosophy, summarizing his lessons in the Benedictine convent of Rio de Janeiro during 1748. The title of this treatise, according to Afonso d'Escragnolle Taunay, in "Fr. Gaspar da Madre de Deus," *Memórias para a História da Capitania de S. Vincente,* pp. 94–99, is the following: *Philosophia platonica seu rationalem, transnaturalem, philosophiam sive logicam, phisicam et metaphysicam complectens* (apud Bezerra, *op. cit.,* pp. 80–96). None of these writers is worthy of more than cursory interest, since they are all ecclesiastics limiting themselves to the reproduction of Scholastic philosophy.

²⁴ Adrien Delpech, "Da Influência Estrangeira em Nossas Letras" in *Revista do Instituto Histórico e Geográfico brasileiro,* International Congress on the History of America, IX, 205.

The care taken to guard against so-called "French ideas" was such that "it was no longer sufficient to have books inspected by the Board of Censors; booksellers had to present their catalogues for approval by the government and declare any books which they dispatched to any part of the kingdom or Brazil. Books were examined by officials at the Customs, and, if the author was suspect, they were burned in the public square by the public executioner, after due proclamation" (Teófilo Braga, *História da Universidade de Coimbra,* III, 15). Silva Bastos mentions that he came across a document in the Tôrre de Tombo (Archives), in which the Marquis of Penalva begs the king for permission to retain Beyle's *Dictionary* in his library. The monarch granted him the permission he pleaded for, but only on condition that he keep the "set of that work under lock and key in a bookcase with a sheet of wire netting to cover it, so that no person may handle these books, subject to the penalties imposed by the law" (J. T. da Silva Bastos, *História da Censura Intelectual em Portugal,* p. 208). See also: Eduardo Frieiro, *O Diabo na Livraria do Cônego.*

²⁵ Delpech, *op. cit.,* p. 27.

²⁶ Newton de Macedo, "A Renovação das Idéias e das Instituições de Cultura" in *História de Portugal,* VI, 423.

²⁷ *Ibid.*

²⁸ Freire de Carvalho, *História Literária de Portugal,* apud *ibid.*

²⁹ Cf. M. Menendez y Pelayo, *História de los Heterodoxos Españoles,* VI, 86f. and 148f.

³⁰ Newton de Macedo, *op. cit.,* p. 424.

³¹ T. Braga, *op. cit.,* III, 19. See the important study by Professor Joaquim de Carvalho in *John Locke, Ensaio Philosophico sôbre o Entendimento Humano: Resumo dos Livros I e II, Recusado pela Real Mesa Censoria* (Coimbra: 1950).

[32] *Ibid.*

[33] Joaquim Ferreira, *O Verdadeiro Método de Estudar, por Luís Antônio Verney*, p. 152. See also the edition of the *Verdadeiro Método de Estudar*, ed. by Professor Antônio Salgado Júnior.

[34] Ferreira, *op. cit.*, p. 7. Cf. L. Cabral de Moncada, *Um "Iluminista" português do Século XVIII: Luís Antônio Verney* and Hernani Cidade, *Ensaio sôbre a Crise Mental do Século XVIII.*

[35] Nélson Werneck Sodré, "O Tratado de Methuen" in *Digesto Econômico* (June 1949), p. 97f.

[36] Max Weber, *Historia Económica General*, p. 315.

[37] J. F. Normano, *Evolução Econômica do Brasil*, pp. 197–198.

[38] Prado Júnior, *História Econômica do Brasil*, p. 89.

[39] *Ibid.*, p. 131.

[40] *Ibid.*

[41] *Ibid.*, p. 132.

[42] *Ibid.*

[43] Sílvio Romero, *História da Literatura brasileira*, II, 151; cf. p. 50.

[44] Henri Sée, *Les Origines du capitalisme moderne*, p. 116.

[45] Prado Júnior, *op. cit.*, p. 133.

[46] *Ibid.*

[47] Sée, *op. cit.*

[48] *Autos da Inconfidência de 1798* in Public Archives of Bahia (Testimony of J. J. Sant'Ana) apud Luís Viana Filho, *A Sabinada*, pp. 26–27.

[49] *Ibid.*

[50] Prado Júnior, *História Econômica do Brasil*, p. 134.

[51] *Ibid.*, p. 140, note 30. The following statistics for the years 1812, 1816 and 1822 are quoted. (The figures are given in pounds sterling.)

	Imports £	Exports £
1812	770,000	1,233,000
1816	2,500,000	2,330,000
1822	4,590,000	4,030,000

[52] John Mawe, *Viagens ao Interior do Brasil*, pp. 93–94.

[53] João Pandia Calógeras, *A Formação Historica do Brasil*, p. 105.

[54] Oliveira Lima.

[55] "With the intention of providing a solid foundation for the study of medicine, he issued a Royal Charter in 1810 which provided for three of the most able students in the hospital of Rio to go and practice in Edinburgh and London in order to acquire greater skill and improve their knowledge in their particular fields of study so that later, as professors in the Faculty, they could help Brazilian medical science to develop along the right lines" (cf. Oliveira Lima, *D. João VI no Brasil*, I, 233).

[56] *Ibid.*, p. 238. Cf. José Silvestre Ribeiro, *História dos Estabelecimentos Scientíficos Litterarios e Artísticos de Portugal*, IX, 374. It was for this university that Dom João VI invited José Bonifácio, on his return from Europe,

to become the future principal; cf. *ibid.*, p. 412. See also: Oliveira Lima, *op. cit.*, p. 242.

⁵⁷ For information about the remarkable personality of Silvestre Pinheiro Ferreira, see Innocencio Francisco da Silva, *Diccionario Bibliográphico*, VII, 259f.; *Anais da Biblioteca Nacional do Rio de Janeiro*, II (1876–1877); Fidelino de Figueiredo, *Estudos de Literatura*, IV, 145, 146, 147, and 153, and the work already cited by Figueiredo in *Estudos de Literatura*: J. J. Louzada de Magalhães "Silvestre Pinheiro Ferreira, Sein Leben und seine Philosophie" (thesis presented to the University of Bonn, 1881). Cf. J. J. Lopes Praça, *História da Philosophia em Portugal*, Terceiro Periodo, Section I, X, 213. Cf. also Newton de Macedo, *op. cit.*, VI and Delfim Santos, "Silvestre Pinheiro Ferreira" in *Perspectivas da Literatura portuguêsa no Século XIX.*

⁵⁸ Silvestre Pinheiro Ferreira, "Memórias Politicas sôbre os abusos gerais e o modo de os reformar e prevenir a revolução popular" in *Revista do Instituto Histórico e Geográfico brasileiro*, XLVIII (1884), 3.

⁵⁹ Tobias Monteiro, *História do Império: A Elaboração da Independência* (Rio de Janeiro: 1939), p. 235.

⁶⁰ Oliveira Lima writes that "in his house [that of the Count of Barcas] there was always to be found some professional man; whether it was the Cavalier Neukomm, Haydn's favorite disciple and composer to the Royal Chapel, or some Italian painter, clinging on God knows how, or one of the numerous mechanics, engravers, or other artisans for whom he managed to obtain Royal pensions to enable them to perfect their talents and cultivate their natural aptitudes. Debret records that in the patio of this highly intelligent minister's house, there was a small porcelain factory; in one of the out buildings there was a chemical laboratory where research was being carried on in the improvement of cane-spirit distilling, among other things; in a store lay the unassembled parts of a steam engine ordered from London" (Oliveira Lima, *op. cit.*, p. 244).

⁶¹ Cf. José Silvestre Ribeiro, *op. cit.*, p. 237. Ribeiro records: "On the 6th day of April of the year 1816, the American ship 'Calphe' which sailed from Havre de Grâce, brought to Rio de Janeiro the following craftsmen: Joachim Le Breton, permanent secretary of the Fine Arts Course of the Institute of France, Knight of the Legion of Honor; Taunay, the sculptor, and his disciple Debret, historical and ornamental painter; Grandjean de Montigny, architect, together with his family and two disciples; Pradier, engraver, Ovide, machinist"; and also "João Batista Fevel, master smith; Nicolau Magliore Enout, locksmith and ironworker; Pilite, currier and tanner; Fabre, leatherworker; Luís José Roy, coachbuilder, together with his son, Hipólito Roy, who followed his father's trade" (p. 240).

⁶² Oliveira Lima, *Dom João VI no Brasil*, 1st ed., I, 240.

⁶³ José Maria Rapôsa de Almeida, "Origens do Colégio Pedro II" in *Revista do Instituto Histórico e Geográfico brasileiro*, XIX, 528f. Cf. José Silvestre Ribeiro, *op. cit.*, p. 232.

⁶⁴ Hernani Cidade, *Ensaio sôbre a Crise Mental do Século XVIII*, pp. 53–54.

[65] João Lúcio de Azevedo, *O Marquês de Pombal e a Sua Época*, p. 341.

[66] *Ibid.*, p. 87.

[67] *Ibid.*, p. 89.

[68] Cidade, *op. cit.*, pp. 69–70.

[69] Teófilo Braga, *História da Universidade de Coimbra*, III, 569.

[70] Octavio Tarquinio de Sousa, *José Bonifácio* (1763–1838), p. 23.

[71] Cf. Inocêncio F. da Silva, *Diccionario Bibliográfico*, VII, 259.

[72] Silvestre Pinheiro Ferreira, *Noções Elementares de Philosophia e Suas aplicações às Sciências Morais e Políticas* (Paris: 1839).

[73] *Ibid.*, p. vi.

[74] *Ibid.*, p. vii.

[75] Laerte Ramos de Carvalho, "A Lógica de Mont'Alverne" in *Boletim da Faculdade de Filosofia, Ciência e Letras da Universidade de S. Paulo*," No. LXII (1946), p. 49. "The Genoese compendium," wrote Silvestre Pinheiro Ferreira, "is the insignificant work which for more than half a century has been blunting or perverting rather than stimulating the nascent intelligence of Portugal's youth" apud Delfim Santos, *op. cit.*, p. 22. Cf. Silvestre Pinheiro Ferreira, *Preleções Filosóficas sôbre a Teoria do Discurso e da Linguagem, a Estética, a Diceosina e a Cosmologia* (Rio de Janeiro: Imprensa Régia, 1813). The edition includes a translation from the Greek of Aristotle's *Categories*.

[76] According to D. Antônio da Costa, the title given to primary school teachers after the reforms of November 6, 1772, was "Mestre Régio" (Royal Master) "in order to put an end to the contempt in which the profession had been held, hitherto regarded as purely mechanical" (Antônio da Costa, *História da Instrução Popular em Portugal*, p. 106). For information on teaching during the period of the Kingdom of Brazil, see "A Memória de Martim Francisco sôbre a Reforma dos Estudos na Capitania de S. Paulo" in *Boletim da Faculdade de Filosofia, Ciência e Letras da Universidade de S. Paulo*, No. LIII. The work is the thesis presented by Dr. José Querino Ribeiro for his doctorate. The chartered teachers of Rio de Janeiro claimed that "the prohibited philosophy which the priests teach to the public (it should be taught only to their students of divinity) consists of a series of peripatetic apostils, full of obscure and useless argument, which serve only to ruin the appetite for worthy studies." (Cf. *Revista do Instituto Histórico e Geográfico brasileiro*, LXV (1902), Part I, p. 220. Cf. also Octávio Tarquínio de Sousa, "Frades e Professôres" in *Estado de São Paulo* of September 4, 1947.

[77] Newton de Macedo, *op. cit.*, p. 441.

[78] *Ibid.*, p. 442.

[79] F. Fiorentino, *Compendio di Storia della Filosofia*, II, 317.

[80] *Ibid.*

[81] Primitivo Moacyr, *A Instrução e o Império*, p. 254.

[82] Caio Prado Júnior, *Evolução Política do Brasil*, p. 81.

[83] Cf. C. K. Webster, *Gran Bretanha y la Independência de la America Latina*, I, 231f.

[84] Apud J. P. Mayer, *Trajectória del Pensamiento Politico*, p. 230.

85 "On April 24, 1840, during the sitting of the Chamber of Deputies, Antônio Carlos related how the project (for the constitution of 1823) had been drawn up. They had elected him president of the Commission. The members soon presented their work, and I, said the great Brazilian, told them quite unceremoniously that it was all no good; one had copied the Portuguese constitution, others had taken bits from the Spanish; in view of these poor examples, the Commission did me the honor of appointing me to draw up the new constitution: and what did I do? After deciding on the fundamental clauses, I gathered together all the best clauses from all the other constitutions, taking advantage of those which proved most applicable to our state" (Aurelino Leal, *História Constitucional do Brasil*, p. 63).

NOTES TO CHAPTER 3
(Pages 47–66)
Philosophy in Brazil during the First Half
of the Nineteenth Century

1 Caio Prado Júnior, *A Evolução do Brasil*, p. 93. Cf. Octávio Tarquínio de Sousa, "A Diplomacia inglêsa e a Independência" in *Digesto Econômico*, June, 1949, pp. 102f.

2 Tristão de Ataíde, "Políticas e Letras" in *À Margem da História da República*, p. 272.

3 Rui Barbosa, *Discursos e Escritos*, p. 232.

4 Roger Picard, *Le Romantisme social*, p. 282.

5 *Ibid.*

6 Sílvio Romero, *História da Literatura brasileira*, 3d ed., II, 151.

7 Sílvio Romero, *A Filosofia no Brasil*, p. 15.

8 *Ibid.*

9 *Ibid.*, p. 36.

10 Sérgio Buarque de Holanda, "Prefácio Literário" in J. G. Magalhães, *Obras Completas*, II, xii.

11 Picard, *op. cit.*, p. 261. Buarque de Holanda writes: "Side by side with our Romanticism and inseparable from it, there existed in Brazil a host of forms and ideas that must be borne in mind if this movement is to be properly understood. Although they do not really belong to the history of literature. Politics, society, the clergy—all were influenced by the same inspiration that animated this school of poets (*op. cit.* p. ix). Romanticism corresponds to a historic *moment* in Brazil which reflects the French influence in the history of ideas. Magalhães, for instance, who frequented the works of the French writers, attempted to justify in this way the literary break with Portugal (*op. cit.*, p. x). The extremes to which Magalhães resorted are often ridiculous (cf. *op. cit.*, pp. xiii, xiv, xv). Romanticism is, then, a *moment* and not a *constant* in the spiritual history of Brazil. Like the Portuguese, we usually

manage not to lose ourselves in mystic anguish or metaphysical extravagance" (Buarque de Holanda, *op. cit.*, p. xxiv).

[12] Freyre writes "The Portuguese colony in America had attained qualities and conditions of life so exotic—from the European point of view—that the nineteenth century, in renewing Brazil's contact with Europe—a Europe now considerably changed: industrial, commercial, mechanized, and thoroughly bourgeois—was characterized by a re-Europeanization of our country. In a certain sense, it was a reconquest . . . In Brazil during the early years of the nineteenth and the end of the eighteenth centuries, re-Europeanization was evident in the assimilation of a few and the imitativeness of the majority of Brazilian literati ("imitation" in the sociological sense defined by Tarde), and also in coercion—the English, for instance, imposed on the Portuguese American colony through the Methuen treaty—Portugal, which was almost a colony of the English, reigning in name only—and later they imposed on the empire a series of moral attitudes and ways of life that would not have been spontaneously adopted, or at least not quite so soon" (Gilberto Freyre, *Sobrados e Mucambos*, p. 259).

[13] Professor Laerte Ramos de Carvalho, in "A Logica de Mont'Alverne" in *Boletim de Faculdade de Filosofia, Ciência e Letras da Universidade de S. Paulo*, No. LXII, p. 48, writes: "There is more than one reason to believe that Mont'Alverne had become acquainted with the works of Genovesi in São Paulo while studying at the College of the Convent of St. Francis at the beginning of the nineteenth century." He also demonstrates the influence exercised on Mont'Alverne's *Compendium* by the works of an old writer who seems to be relatively unknown—François Para du Phanjas, *Institutiones Philosophicae ad usum seminariorum et collegiorum* (Paris: 1782), a work on which, according to Ramos de Carvalho, Mont'Alverne based part of his "logic." Cf. D. Mornet: *Les Origines intellectuelles de la révolution française*, p. 542.

[14] Laerte Ramos de Carvalho, *op. cit.*, p. 39.

[15] Friar Francisco de Mont'Alverne, *Compêndio de Filosofia*. Note to the Reader.

[16] Raymond Lenoir, *Condillac*, p. 155.

[17] *Ibid.*

[18] Mont'Alverne, *op. cit.*, p. 105n.

[19] *Ibid.*, p. 104n.

[20] *Ibid.*

[21] Apud Leonel Franca, S.J., *Noções de História de Filosofia*, 9th ed., p. 418, n. 273. Cf. Sílvio Romero, *A Filosofia no Brasil*, p. 2.

[22] Sigismund Storkenau (1751–1797), the Austrian Jesuit who published *Institutiones logicae et metaphysicae* which, according to Leonel Franca, S.J., had "a great vogue." "The author expresses himself with clarity, but the book suffers from the fault that besets nearly all writers of this period: superficiality." "His scholasticism is spineless, with no metaphysical nerve center, and is contaminated by foreign doctrines that disturb the harmony of the synthesis." Apud Franca, *op. cit.*, p. 429, n. 290.

[23] Sílvio Romero, *op. cit.*, p. 8.

[24] Alcântara Machado, *Gonçalves de Magalhães ou o Romântico Arrependido*, p. 26.

[25] Gonçalves de Magalhães, *Opúsculos Históricos Literários*, apud Machado, *op. cit.*

[26] *Ibid.*

[27] Émile Bréhier, *Histoire de la Philosophie*, II, 657–658.

[28] *A Aurora Fluminense*, No. 59, June 25, 1828, apud Octávio Tarquínio de Sousa, *Evaristo da Veiga*, p. 88.

[29] Jules Simon, *Victor Cousin*, p. 28.

[30] H. Taine, *Les Philosophes classiques du XIXᵉ siècle*, p. 306.

[31] I quote the section referred to in order to place the problem of eclecticism in a clearer perspective. He writes: ". . . l'éclectisme devint la philosophie officielle et prescrite, et s'appela désormais le spiritualisme. Rien de plus aisé qu'un nom à faire ou à défaire; le dictionnaire est riche, et le dictionnaire manquant on peut inventer. Refaire des doctrines est plus difficile, et il fallait en refaire. On s'était trouvé panthéiste en 1828, très mauvais chrétien jusqu'à considérer le christianisme comme un symbole dont la philosophie démêle le sens bon pour le peuple, simple préparation à une doctrine plus claire et plus haute. Tout cela était à propos dans l'opposition de la part d'un homme isolé, écrivain indépendant, et qui portait seul le faix de ses opinions. Rien de tout celà n'était plus à propos, maintenant que l'enseignement descendu d'en haut, officiel et public, devait convenir aux pères de famille et au clergé. Sous cette pression, et grâce à la lecture assidue du XVIIᵉ siècle, on prit le panthéisme en horreur et le christianisme en vénération. On retrancha, dans les écrits publiés, quelques phrases mal sonnantes et trop nettes. On essaya de donner un sens tolérable à celles qui n'étaient pas douteuses. On devint à peu près cartésien, plus volontiers encore partisan de Leibnitz par cette raison excellente que Leibnitz est le plus loin possible de Spinoza. On oublia d'autre paroles très expressives, trop expressives qu'on avait autrefois jetées contre le christianisme, que les critiques n'osent citer, et dont tous les contemporains se souviennent. On finit par faire des avances au clergé, présenter la philosophie comme l'alliée affectueuse et indispensable de la religion, offrir le dieu de l'éclectisme comme une base qui peut porter la trinité chrétienne, et l'éclectisme tout entier une foi préparatoire qui laisse au christianisme la place de ses dogmes, et toutes ses prises sur l'humanité" (Taine, *op. cit.*, pp. 306–307).

[32] To the French spiritualist, Eclectic current is linked Manuel de Morais Vale, professor of the Faculty of Medicine of Rio de Janeiro, author of books on chemistry which were well known during the empire. Morais Vale also wrote a compendium, *Elementos de Filosofia* (Rio de Janeiro: 1851), which was designed or, as the author says, "is suitable for the new examinations of the Rio de Janeiro Medical School." There is nothing of interest in this little compendium designed for facilitating the Faculty's entrance examinations. This was nothing new. As Tobias Barreto said: "Philosophy in Brazil was never more than a preparation."

[33] Pereira da Silva refers to the successes following the abdication of April 7 in the following terms: "After the first few days, which were given over

to outbursts of delight and enthusiasm, the atmosphere became overcast and storms threatened. In the capital, hostile intentions were openly expressed against disaffected politicians and former servants of state who had become highly unpopular, and more particularly against the Portuguese who had become the butt of the ill-feeling of the lower classes, who believed them dedicated to the cause of Dom Pedro I. Riots, disorders, and constant disturbances broke out in the city squares, and it became dangerous to venture out at night, especially for those suspected of harboring sympathies for the former emperor. Authority proved powerless, and the police were unable to suppress or punish the rioters or to take any preventive measures. These criminal movements grew in intensity, terrorizing industrious and law-abiding citizens and turning the city into a focal point for anarchy. Both in Rio de Janeiro and in the provinces, therefore, the situation became threatening" (Pereira da Silva, *História do Brasil durante a Minoridade de D. Pedro,* II, 18–19).

[34] The League was organized by Evaristo da Veiga, one of the most bitter opponents of Dom Pedro I. "The Society for the Defense of National Liberty," writes Prado Júnior, "aimed to consolidate the political situation created by the events of April 7, both against the reaction of the Portuguese party, which despite its defeat had not completely disappeared, and, chiefly, against the revolutionary extremism which had emerged" (cf. Caio Prado Júnior, *Evolução Política do Brasil,* p. 122).

[35] João Pandiá Calógeras, "O Brasil en 1840" in *Revista do Instituto Histórico e Geográfico brasileiro,* t. 98, CLII, 229.

[36] Caio Prado Júnior: *História Econômica do Brasil,* p. 151.

[37] Octávio Tarquínio de Sousa, *José Bonifácio,* p. 207. 'In October, 1822, during the period in which his detractors claim that he was exclusively preoccupied with preparations for the downfall of Ledo and the Masonic group, José Bonifácio wrote to Caldeira Brant in London, asking him to recruit English rural workers for Brazil. On December 26, taking staps to carry out the mission entrusted to him, the future Marquis of Barbacena wrote to Antônio V. Meireles Sobrinho, resident in Liverpool, saying: "Since Sr. José Bonifácio de Andrade wishes to convince his compatriots by practical example that the work of free men offers greater advantages than that of African slaves, he has commissioned me to send him at least 600 English farm laborers as soon as possible . . .' " (p. 208).

[38] Luís Viana Filho, *A Sabinada,* pp. 116–117.

[39] In all the convulsive movements of these years, the "Sabinada," the Pará movement, and the Rio Grande rebellion, opinion always rallied behind the child emperor. In Pará, a president was acclaimed who would "reign while Dom Pedro continues a minor." In Rio Grande do Sul, "the first manifesto" issued by Berto Gonçalves on September 20, 1835, promised to "support the throne of our young monarch . . . and to respect the vows made to our sacred code in support of a constitutional throne" (Viana Filho, *ibid.,* p. 117).

[40] Caio Prado Júnior, *Evolução Política do Brasil,* p. 158.

[41] Antônio Cândido de Melo e Sousa, *Introdução ao Método Crítico de Sílvio Romero*, p. 181.

[42] Father Júlio Maria, "A Religião" in *Livro do Centenário* (1500–1900), I, 3. Cf. also the informative study of Basílio de Magalhães, "D. Pedro II e a Igreja Católica" in *Estudos de História do Brasil*, pp. 89–155.

[43] Júlio Maria, *op. cit.*, p. 88.

[44] Buarque de Holanda, *Raízes do Brasil*, p. 108. "The popularity among us of St. Thérèse of Lisieux—our little 'Santa Teresa'—is in large measure due to the intimate character acquired by her amiable cult, almost fraternal in tone, ill at ease with ceremony and averse to distance" (Buarque de Holanda, *ibid.*, pp. 105–106).

[45] "The Empire," writes Júlio Maria, "asked the Church for its blessing. Hardly three years had passed, however, before the state began to show a tendency to overrule the Church, to invade its sphere of action, to ignore its rights and trample on its privileges" (Júlio Maria, *op. cit.*, p. 66).

[46] *Ibid.*, p. 70.

[47] Cf. Cândido Mendes, *Direito Civil Eclesiástico*, apud Júlio Maria, *op. cit.*, p. 75.

[48] Joaquim Nabuco, *Um Estadista do Império*, III, 389.

[49] *Ibid.*, n.1.

[50] Félix Ravaisson, *La Philosophie en France au XIXᵉ siécle*, p. 21.

[51] Cf. "Observações" by M. V. Egger in A. Lalande, *Vocabulaire Technique et critique de la philosophie*, I, 185–186.

[52] Ravaisson, *op. cit.*, p. 33.

[53] It was not merely in Brazil that Eclecticism exercised its influence. It made itself felt equally in other Latin American countries. "After 1830," writes Samuel Ramos, "the ideas of German Romanticism became known in Mexico, albeit in a vague way, through the writings of Victor Cousin. In the works of this French thinker was initiated in Mexico the study of the history of philosophy. In the historical summaries of Cousin were found the first references to the philosophy of Kant" (Samuel Ramos, *História de la Filosofia en Mexico*, p. 113). Francovich, in his turn, in his study of the philosophy of his country refers to Eclecticism in the following terms: "In Bolivia, Eclecticism was the movement that gained most widespread diffusion. Not only were various translations published of the works of Cousin, Damiron, Delavigne, Bernard, but some original works were written inspired by the Electicism of these authors . . ." (Guilhermo Francovich, *La Filosofia en Bolivia*, p. 95). Ardao, in his study of philosophy in Uruguay, also mentions the influence of Eclectic ideas in this country: "Ideology, the last form of eighteenth-century philosophy, the form faithful to which the Chair of Buenos Aires remained had gone into a decline after the last years of the First Empire. It was supplanted, in the favor of fashion, first by the counter-revolutionary current of Bonald and de Maistre and then by the Eclectic current of Cousin, Royer-Collard, and Jouffroy. The latter current was in great favor after 1830, taking over public education" (Arturo Ardao, *Filosofia pre-Universitária en el Uruguay*, p. 87). José Ingenieros in his study of Alberdi's social

philosophy in _Evolución de las Ideas argentinas,_ Book III (_La Restauración_) expresses himself as follows: "The dedication to philosophical studies revealed in Alberdi's preface to the _Fragmento Preliminar,_ confirmed in his autobiography and illustrated by the polemics in which he engaged, revealing himself to be exceptionally well-informed, continued throughout his stay in Montevidéo. One of his works, which has never been cited, has an especial value from our point of view. It is: _Ideas para Presidir a la Confección del Curso de Filosofia Contemporanea_ (Montevidéo: 1842). The essential inspiration for this program was provided by Jouffroy, who had already broken with Cousin's Eclecticism to make his own reflections on the Scottish psychology of Reich and Stewart. We must point out that Alberdi did not choose Cousin because he considered him more important than the others, but because, after 1830, he was more in vogue than the others" (p. 667).

[54] Clóvis Beviláqua, _Escoços e Fragmentos,_ p. 24.

[55] _Ibid._

[56] Basílio de Magalhães, _Estudos de História do Brasil,_ pp. 40–41.

[57] "Justiniano José da Rocha, discerning, quite rightly, in the period 1840–1852, 'the growing dominance of the monarchical principle, reacting against the social work of the democratic domination which could not defend itself except through violence and so was crushed,' observes in another part of his admirable work: _Ação, Reação, Transação,_ that what robbed the liberals of the sympathy of the bulk of the nation was 'the constant appeal to arms to which they resorted'" (Basílio de Magalhães, _op. cit.,_ p. 44).

[58] Professor Sousa, in his analysis of one of the most interesting periods of the history of ideas in Brazil—that immediately following the period now under consideration—writes as follows on his excellent study of the critical method of Sílvio Romero: "In a Brazil deadened by the study of the humanities, which in certain respects lead to cultural inertia, the campaign for culture and philosophical revision (which was to take place around 1868–1870) appeared as a force of mental renewal. Sílvio's criticism, which was so closely linked to this campaign, runs parallel to the growth of methematical studies related in part to positivism, to the intensification of studies of the natural sciences, the creation of Brazilian ethnography and ethnology, the transformation of law under the influx of evolutionism, the foundation of the School of Mines, etc. A true movement of awakening through the patterns of culture. I believe that this movement was not without its correspondence, nor was it a coincidence that it was accompanied by the first attempts of the bourgeoisie to take over the economic and political administration of the country. It was not merely by chance that in 1860 a great electoral victory was won for democratic liberalism, to which was linked someone like Teófilo Otoni with the mentality of a typically progressive capitalist; nor was it by chance that, in 1868, the Liberal party collapsed with the subsequent formation of the Republican party in 1870. In this year, when Limpo de Abreu and Rangel Pestana founded their newspaper, the development of the Mauá undertaking was at its height, the Positivism was spreading among the military class. Abolitionism received its consecration in the following year. The intellectual and scientific movement signified, in the realm of culture, the

same process of breaking with traditional authority and the same desire for a new and free affirmation. The critical movement of Recife which flourished from 1868 to 1869 and which had immediate repercussions in Ceará and was quickly followed by similar movements in the South, was the first organic and flagrant manifestation of the growth of the bourgeoisie reflecting itself in the mental spheres. It was the first coherent expression in the literary and philosophical fields, of a bourgeois ideology in Brazil" (Antônio Cândido de Melo e Sousa, *Introdução ao Método Crítico de Sílvio Romero*, pp. 179–181).

[59] Raymond Lenoir, *Condillac*, p. 154.

[60] Clóvis Beviláqua, *Esboços e Fragmentos*, pp. 19–20.

[61] *Ibid.*, pp. 20–21.

[62] Eduardo Ferreira França *Investigações de Psychologia* (Bahia: 1854). Dr. Eduardo Ferreira França (1809–1857) was the son of Dr. Antônio Ferreira França, physician to Pedro I and Deputy in the 1823 Constituent Assembly. He took his medical degree in Paris where, according to Sacramento Blake (*Dicionário Bibliográfio brasileiro*, II, 247), he was singled out as the best student of his year. On his return to Brazil he became professor of medical chemistry and principles of mineralogy at the Faculty of Medicine of Bahia. He was also a deputy in the 1848 and 1851 legislatures. He was—still according to Sacramento Blake who had been one of his pupils—very popular with the students. His doctored thesis in medicine dealt with the influence of food and drink on man's morale, a subject which indicated his philosophical preferences ("Essai sur l'influence des aliments et des boissons sur le moral d l'homme," 1834). This work was translated into Portuguese by Dr. João Ferreira de Bittencourt e Sá and published in 1851 (cf. Blake, *op. cit.*, p. 247).

[63] Ferreira França, *op. cit.*, I, vi.

[64] *Ibid.*

[65] Émile Bréhier, *Histoire de la Philosophie*, II, 599. Cf. F. Picavet, *Les Idéologues, passim.*

[66] Bréhier, *op. cit.*, pp. 599–600. When the decrees founding the Imperial University were drawn up, the ideologists were excluded from the university. Cf. P. Alfaric, *Laromiguière et son école.*

[67] E. Spuller, *Royer-Collard*, pp. 75f.

[68] "As a disciple of the sensualist school, I presented myself as a candidate for a doctorate in medicine; today I once more present myself in public, but belonging to another school" (Ferreira França, *op. cit.*, I, viii).

[69] The "faculty of the future" (Chap. 16, II, 246) is "presentiment," a cross between the association of ideas and induction! The "faculty of faith" must surely exist. To use the words of Ferreira França: "There must be some faculty different from those we have already discussed (external perception, reason, generalization, judgment) through which we apprehend indirect knowledge and accept it as though it had been acquired through our own efforts. It is to this faculty that I give the name of 'faith'" (*op. cit.*, II, 274).

[70] *Ibid.*, p. 334.

[71] *Ibid.*

[72] *Ibid.*, p. 337.

[73] Sílvio Romero, *A Filosofia no Brasil*, p. 16.

[74] F. S. Tôrres Homen in an article published in *Revista brasiliense* (Paris: 1836) apud *Obras Completas* of Domingos José Gonçalves de Magalhães, II, 1–2.

[75] Cf. F. Seillière, *Le Romantisme*, pp. 61–62.

[76] Magalhães's earliest verses were written in 1827, *Uma Epístola a Marília*, an obvious subproduct of the reigning sub-Arcadianism. In them was already evident the first trace of the philosophical tendency, impregnated with religiosity, that was to be one of the most characteristic features of Magalhães's poetical work. Love was enkindled in his heart, in his pubescent flesh,

> Not by the tender son of Cytherea . . .

but by

> The wise Architect of Nature,
> This Supreme God who reigns o'er all

(Alcântara Machado, *Gonçalves de Magalhães ou o Romântico Arrependido*, pp. 10–11).

[77] Machado, *op. cit.*, p. 24.

[78] D. J. G. de Magalhães, *Poesias Avulsas*, p. 55, apud Machado, *op. cit.*, p. 25.

[79] Magalhães, *op. cit.*, p. 75, apud Machado, *op. cit.*, p. 30.

[80] Magalhães, *op. cit.*, p. 358 apud Machado, *ibid.* This voyage was described with significant realism by the future Romantic, an indication of his psychological makeup. Machado, in the work cited, records in minute detail the seasickness of the first few days which led to "complete anarchy of the digestive system"; the discomfort of the berth which was "like a shelf with a neighbor on top," and the poor quality of the water and the food, which worsened as the provisions grew staler; the malodorous liquid "with the smell and taste of rotten wood" which made him long for "the tasty water of Carioca"; the "brick-colored bread, petrified to the core"; the suspect and watery coffee; the "brown" tea served in a teapot made of an old tin with a dirty spout; the "salt meat with its accompaniment of lumpy mashed potatoes" (Machado, *op. cit.*, p. 30).

[81] *Ibid.*, p. 43.

[82] Magalhães fell ill during the course of his studies and spent the time reading Young, Hervey, Sousa Caldas, and Klopstock. Cf. Machado, *op. cit.*, pp. 15, 47, 49. "The sum total of the religious philosophy of the author of *Suspiros*," says Machado, "is expressed in the following inexecrable verses:

> Though we lament our cruel fate
> Let us our lives not desecrate,
> We must live in faith not impious hate.

[83] Sales Tôrres Homen and Magalhães were the deputies who in 1847 presented the project for the reform of public education referred to in a previous footnote.

[84] The "Confederação dos Tamoios" which it is alleged took seven years

to polish up, was coolly received in Rio de Janeiro. José de Alencar under the pseudonym "Ig," harshly attacked the diplomat-poet. Pedro II, under the pseudonym "Another friend of the poet," contradicted Alencar. Alcântara Machado confesses that he did not have the patience to read through this work of Magalhães, as it was so boring. I cannot resist transcribing one of Antônio de Alcântara Machado's pages, full of the humor so typical of the author of *Brás, Bexiga e Barra Funda*. Machado, in reproducing a page from his son's work, writes: "Antônio de Alcântara Machado had the patience I lacked. The result was this page I here transcribe. There are three lines in the poem, among innumerable others, that Paulo Prado never tires of savoring. He is quite right. They occur in Canto V. Jagoanharo goes by canoe to São Vicente on the instruction of his father to seek his uncle Tibiriçá. He discovers Tibiriçá only to find him Catholic and Portuguese. A miles-long dialogue ensues, which is one of the funniest things I have encountered in literature. Tibiriçá shows his nephew around the village. Magalhães puts the following fantastic verses into his mouth:

> Do you see that house? There dwells
> Ramalho, the Portuguese, who is my son-in-law.
> You will meet him, and his wife,
> and my little grandchildren.

. . . And what about the episode in Canto VI? Aimberé and Parabuçu set fire to the house of Brás Cubas. Brás Cubas flees through the window. Aimberé rapidly wounds him and is about to kill him when:

> Enveloped in a snowy nightgown (!)

the victim's daughter appears, pleading for her father's life. This incident is most moving. Aimberé wavers before the lovely maiden. Then:

> Grateful memory enkindles in his soul
> Like a flash of light in a thundery sky.

He drops his war club. And, what is worse, he drops the following words: " 'Maria,' he exclaims, 'poor Maria, is it you?' " (Machado, *op. cit.*, pp. 72–73). Cf. José Aderaldo Castello, *A Polémica sôbre a "Confederação dos Tamoios."*

[85] *Os Fatos do Espírito Humano* (X, 401). The date of the preface is June 5, 1858. I have the second edition, published in 1865, at Garnier, Rio de Janeiro, printed in Vienna. This work, according to its author, was first published in Paris toward the end of 1858 and was translated into French by M. N. P. Chancelle in the following year. Chancelle's translation was published by the Librairie Auguste Fontaine in 1859. The author does not describe the flattering note written by the translator because he does not wish to seem vain.

[86] *A Alma e o Cérebro* (XII, 422) printed in Rome, constitutes Volume IX of the *Complete Works of Magalhães* (Rio de Janeiro: B. L. Garnier, 1876). It is dedicated to Dom Pedro II, "zealous patron of the sciences and of letters," who had kindly consented "to hear the reading of certain chapters."

[87] *Comentários e Pensamentos* also printed in Rome (Rio de Janeiro: B. L. Garnier, 1880) is dedicated to his son, Dr. Amadeus, M. J. G. de Magalhães Araguaia (IV, 165).

[88] Alcântara Machado, *op. cit.*, p. 48.

[89] Leonel Franca, S.J., *Noções de História de Filosofia*, 9th ed., p. 422.

[90] *Ibid.*, p. 424, n. 281.

[91] "And what does man seek in the infinite space of the heavens, weighing stars, measuring in millions upon millions of leagues their grandeur, their orbits, and the immeasurable distances that separate them? What does he seek in calculating the parallax of the stars, those suns of so many other planetary systems, or the ellipses described by that numberless shoal of comets, some of which takes millions of years to complete their periodic revolution while remaining with the sphere of influence of the sun's attractive force notwithstanding the enormous distance of their aphelia? What does he seek in computing the speed with which light travels from the sun to the earth, or from the sun to Uranus, or the number of years taken by a bullet to cover an equal distance, as though he were contemplating the conquest of the heavens? What does he seek among those hundreds of pale nebulae, embryos of new stars which forever form and reform in the depths of the heavenly abyss? Why does he descend from the heights of the sideral regions and what does he seek in the volcanic craters of Etna and Chimborazo, the summits of the Andes, the virgin forests of America, the different layers of the earth's crust, the fossiliferous beds holding fragments of extinct families of animals and plants, in all those pages of geology traced by the hand of the centuries, and, finally, in those microscopic worlds of organic existence of instantaneous life that peoples the rivers, the lakes, the ocean, and the polar ice and, gathered in their hundreds, can rival in size only a grain of sand? Does he perhaps seek new nourishment for his body, a way of prolonging his fleeting existence, which slips away hour by hour or is suddenly extinguished in the midst of his toils and uncompleted triumphs? No! In these sublime flights of intelligence man does not even remember that he possesses a body of precarious duration, composed of those inorganic elements that make him a son of the earth, those elements he analyzes in his chemical laboratories. He seeks perhaps, in these transports of his soul, new objects for his wonder, to fill him with admiration and to enkindle the ethereal wings of his creative imagination, so that he may sing an immortal hymn to the ineffable perfection of the Eternal Creator? No: he does not believe himself a poet. What then, does man seek with such ardor and such constancy? What? The truth, for the sake of the truth" (*Os Fatos do Espírito Humano*, pp. 4–6). Most of the chapters in this work are written in this style. Lengthy, tiresome, oratorical, useless. In justifying his reply, he takes up an equal number of pages in the same vein. This renders the reading of Magalhães a veritable torment for those who wish to acquaint themselves with the "ideas" of the baron, who later, with greatness, became a viscount, and who was the author of the *Confederação dos Tamoios*.

[92] D. J. G. de Magalhães, *Os Fatos do Espírito Humano*, pp. 32–33.

[93] *Ibid.*, p. 34.

⁹⁴ *Ibid.*, p. x.

⁹⁵ *Ibid.*, p. 46.

⁹⁶ In the *Comentários e Pensamentos*, the banality reaches the same pitch of absurdity earlier demonstrated in the citation from Antônio de Alcântara Machado. Alcântara Machado (Senior) found his letters equally boring. Cf. Machado, *op. cit.*, p. 89, n. 3.

⁹⁷ D. J. G. de Magalhães, *Os Fatos do Espírito Humano*, p. 291.

⁹⁸ Sílvio Romero, *A Filosofia no Brasil*, p. 34.

⁹⁹ Flourens, *De La Vie et de l'intelligence*, apud D. J. G. de Magalhães, *op. cit.*, p. 60.

¹⁰⁰ Leonel Franca, *op. cit.*, p. 424.

¹⁰¹ *Ibid.*

¹⁰² *Ibid.*

¹⁰³ Nélson Werneck Sodré, *História da Literatura brasileira*, p. 110.

¹⁰⁴ *Ibid.*, p. 111.

¹⁰⁵ *Ibid.*

¹⁰⁶ *Ibid.*, pp. 111–112.

NOTES TO CHAPTER 4
(Pages 67–81)
A Wave of New Ideas

¹ Sílvio Romero, "Explicações Indispensáveis" in Tobias Barreto, *Vários Escritos*, p. 23.

² Caio Prado Júnior, *História Econômica do Brasil*, p. 167. He comments on this transformation in the following terms: "The general explanation of these phenomena can be found mainly in the decline of traditional crops in the north which was not compensated, as in the south, by the development of a substitute such as coffee. This decline was the result of an unfavorable combination of circumstances on the international scale. In the nineteenth century, a successor was found for sugar cane in the production of sugar, which was to become the chief source: beet root. Europe and the United States, the great sugar consumers and chief markets for the products of the American tropics, with the utilization of sugar beet, became producers rather than consumers, and produced quantities not only sufficient for their own internal needs but for export purposes as well. Prizes and bonuses were awarded to the producers to ensure disposal of these excess quantities, and the governments compensated themselves for this expenditure by placing heavy taxes on the importation of sugar cane. There was enormous competition, the history of which is well known, leading to the first international trade agreements on economic production: agreements which were not, in fact, always carried out. The crisis for the sugar-producing countries was general. Colonies continued to enjoy certain privileges in the markets of their

metropoles. But independent producers could count only on their own efforts. Brazil was particularly affected. Its awkward geographical situation placed it at a disadvantage, but the rudimentary level of production technique was an even greater handicap. Its contribution to the international market declined steeply; by the middle of the century it was fifth among the world's sugar producers, with less than 8 per cent of the total production. Its total decline occurred toward the end of the century" (Prado Júnior, *op. cit.*, pp. 167–168). See Alice Piffer Canabrava, "Máquinas Agricolas" in *Estado de São Paulo* for July 6, 1949.

   [3] Prado Júnior, *op. cit.*, p. 169.

   [4] Cf. Sérgio Millet, *Roteiro de Café, passim.*

   [5] Joaquim Nabuco, *Um Estadista do Império*, I, 255.

   [6] Ramalho Ortigão, "Surto do Cooperativismo" in *Contribuições para a Biografía de D. Pedro II*, Part 1, special edition of the *Revista do Instituto Histórico e Geográfico*, p. 289.

   [7] Sílvio Romero, *A Filosofia no Brasil*, p. 36.

   [8] *Ibid.*

   [9] *Ibid* (italics mine).

   [10] *Ibid.*

   [11] In *Evolução da Literatura brasileira (Vista Sintética)*, published in 1905 with a biographical note by Dunshee de Abranches, Sílvio himself revised his first classification. In this revised scheme he divided Brazilian "philosophers" as follows:

   I. Spirits educated toward the end of the eighteenth and beginning of the nineteenth centuries in the doctrines of the French *sensualism* of Destutt de Tracy and Larominguière that later went over to the spiritualist "eclecticism" of Cousin and Jouffroy (1820–1850), the most notorious of these being Mont'Alverne and Eduardo Ferreira França.

   II. Pure adherents of *eclecticism*, the chief of these being Domingos J. Gonçalves de Magalhães and Morais Vale (1850–1870).

   III. The *Catholic reaction*, with Patrício Muniz and Soriano de Sousa, during the same period as Phase II and later.

   IV. A reaction, at first through critical *agnosticism* and later through the *evolutionist monism* of Haeckel and Noiré with Tobias Barreto (1870–1889).

   V. The *Positivist* current of Littré, with Luís Pereira Barreto, who was joined by Martins Júnior and Sousa Pinto, the latter later joining the movement of "orthodox Positivism" as did Aníbal Falcão and others (1880–1904).

   VI. The *orthodox Positivist* current, with Miguel Lemos, Teixeira Mendes, and several other adherents, among whom it would not be unreasonable to include, despite their differences, Benjamin Constant Botelho de Magalhães and his son-in-law Álvaro Joaquim de Oliveira (1880–1904).

   VII. *Spencerian branch of evolutionism*, with Sílvio Romero, who was joined by Artur Orlando, Clóvis Beviláqua, Samuel de Oliveira, Liberato Bittencourt, João Bandeira, França Pereira, and a few others (1870–1904).

   VIII. *Haeckelian branch of evolutionism*, with Domingos Guedes Cabral, Miranda Azevedo, Lívio de Castro, Fausto Cardoso, Oliveira Fausto, and Marcolino Fragoso (1874–1904). Various independent attempts by Estilita

Tapajós and R. Farias Brito preceded in a certain sense and without the same effort by those of J. de Araújo Ribeiro (Sílvio Romero, *Evolução da Literatura brasileira*, pp. 93–94).

[12] Letter dated May 21, 1787, in *Oeuvres*, XI, 109–110, apud Giuseppe Saitta, *Le Origini del Neo-tomismo*, p. 13.

[13] Saitta, *op. cit.*, p. 37. Ramon Ceñal, S.J., "Juan Caramuel, Su Epistolario con Anastasio Kircher" in *Revista de Filosofia*, No. 44 (1953), and "La Filosofia de E. Maignan" in the same journal, No. 48 (1954).

[14] Cf. Saitta, *op. cit.*, particularly Chaps. 2, 3, and 4. Also Francisque Bouiller, *Histoire de la philosophie cartésienne*, particularly Vol. II. "Through his method and his criteria," wrote Soriano de Sousa in 1867, "which constitute the whole of his philosophy, Descartes is the father of the anarchy that today lays waste the province of philosophy, and also of the majority of modern errors and heresies" (Soriano de Sousa, *Compêndio de Filosophia Ordenado Segundo os Princípios e Methodo do Doutor Angélico S. Tourás de Aquino*, p. xxx).

[15] Cf. Leonel Franca, *op. cit.*, pp. 337, 339–340, 341, and 348. The encyclical "Aeterni Patris" August 4, 1879) exhorted all Christian philosophers to return to the study of the great medieval masters, chief among whom was St. Thomas Aquinas. "Leo XIII, in pointing out the dire consequences of modern intellectual anarchy, set out in the pontifical document, with admirable knowledge, the rules that should govern the delicate task of rejuvenating medieval ideas. The act of Leo XIII produced the desired effect in Catholic circles. Everywhere, a philosophy that was dragging itself along, anemic and crippled, was replaced in the seminaries by the direct and profound study of the Thomist synthesis" (Leonel Franca, *Noções de Historia de Filosofia*, 3d ed., p. 230).

[16] Prosper de Martigné, *La Scolastique et les traditions françaises*, p. 458, apud Saitta, *op. cit.*, p. 22. Cf. F. Picavet, *Esquisse d'une histoire générale et comparée des philosophies médiévales*, pp. 216f.

[17] Gilberto Freyre, *Casa Grande e Senzala*, I, 323.

[18] *Ibid.*, II, 671–672. (Cf. Alfredo Ellis Júnior, *Raca de Gigantes*, pp. 153–154.)

[19] Freyre, *op. cit.*, p. 22.

[20] Father Júlio Maria, "A Religião" in *Livro do Centenário*, I, 88.

[21] Antônio Herculano de Sousa Bandeira, "Rosmini e a Sociedade brasileira" in *Revista Brasileira*, VIII (1881), 44. Soriano de Sousa in his *Compêndio de Filosofia*, (1867) said the same things of our clergy.

[22] Lídia Besouchet, *José Maria Paranhos, Visconde do Rio Branco*, p. 162.

[23] Apud Sérgio Buarque de Holanda, *Raízes do Brasil*, p. 109.

[24] Father Patrício Muniz (1820–1871) was born in Funchal (Madeira), studied law in Paris and theology in Rome. He came to Brazil as a very young man and became a naturalized Brazilian. In 1863 he published *Theoria da Affirmação Pura* (*Theory of Pure Affirmation*), (Rio de Janeiro: 1863).

According to Sílvio Romero, Patrício Muniz was one of the first students of philosophy in Brazil who fought against Eclecticism. He was also one of those who followed German philosophy, referring in his book to various German writers, particularly Krause. "Father Patrício Muniz concerned himself with combating sensualism and pantheism, and for this twofold task he sought his weapons in the Middle Ages. In his hands, Catholic theology wears an overcoat lent by modern metaphysics" (Sílvio Romero, *op. cit.*, p. 38). Leonel Franca is equally unkind toward Muniz. He confirms the concern expressed by Sílvio Romero and refers to the philosopher-priest's body of "doctrines" in the following terms: "Unfortunately the main body of the edifice does not correspond to this deceptive frontispiece." Muniz had written on pages 10 and 11 of his book that he wanted to proceed with Scholastics, "treated with disdainful contempt by modern writers but with a robustness of criteria and an elevation of ideas that will reduce to silence its rash detractors" (apud Franca, *op. cit.*, p. 425). Franca adds: "Of Scholastics, the good priest understands not one jot." The study of Kant, Fichte, Schelling, and Hegel fogged his mind. (In footnote 285, p. 425, *op. cit.*, Franca says that he went so far as to write: "The German school . . . has the incontestable merit of having provided the most complete doctrine on the intimate nature of thought without, however, ignoring its form," which, as Franca observes, one cannot conceive of as having issued from the pen of a Scholastic.) In the conclusion to his brief study of this curious priest, Franca writes: "No. Father Patrício is an original thinker in all senses of the word. The transcendental philosophy of pure affirmation was born with his book and with it died. This was only right. Justice was done" (*op. cit.*, p. 428).

In the "charadist" philosophy of this priest we find such statements as the following: "The relative is the deductibility of the positive"; "the absolute is the discrete affirmation of the definite and the indefinite"; "the limitative is the discrete affirmation of the multiple," and others of the same meaninglessness. (see Sílvio Romero, *A Filosofia no Brasil*, pp. 39–40). We must not forget that Father Patrício Muniz was also a poet, and that he wrote a book with the significant title *Meditações Nocturnas* (*Nocturnal Meditations*); cf. Sacramento Blake, *Dicionário Bibliográfio brasileiro*, VI, 352. If Patrício Muniz holds little interest for us, Gregório Lipparoni holds even less, since he came to Brazil fully formed. Monsignor Lipparoni was rector of the Seminary of Olinda and a friend of that fervent disciple of Rosmini, Bishop D. Cardoso Aires. Later, claiming that he was persecuted by the Jesuits for not having taken part in the religious question, we find Lipparoni teaching Italian at the Pedro II College. In 1880 he published *Filosofia Conforme a Mente de S. Tomás de Aquino, Exposta por António Rosmini em Harmonia com a Ciência e com a Religião* (*Philosophy according to the Mind of St. Thomas Aquinas Expounded by Antonio Rosmini in Harmony with Science and Religion*) which, as the title indicates, is a work greatly influenced by Rosmini. Thanks to the kindness of Dr. Aquiles Raspantini, the illustrious librarian of the Faculty of Philosophy, Science, and Letters, I was able to examine this work. It is composed of three fascicles published by the industrial Press of João Paulo Ferreira Dias in 1880. The first of these fascicles, *O Princípio Supremo Filosófico e o Seu Sistema* (72 pp.) is dedicated to Dom Pedro II. In it, Monsignor Lipparoni offers Rosminian philosophy to the emperor so that with it Brazil may initiate its own "national" philosophy (p. 7). The second part (82 pp.) deals with the "harmony between the supreme philosophical principle of the Rosminian system and science." It is dedicated to Counsellor Baron Homem de Melo, minister of the empire. In it Lipparoni once more insists that Rosmini should be the guide for national thought. The third part is dedicated to Manuel de S. Caetano Pinto, abbot of the S. Bento Monastery and to the Benedictine Order of Brazil. In this dedication, Monsignor Lipparoni refers to "the indescribable persecution instigated against the Rosminian system and in which I found myself involved for having professed and defended this system" (p. 5), a persecution for which the motives are not made clear, but which it would be interesting to know.

Lipparoni's works are based on Rosmini's ideas and have no originality, except for the desire to initiate "national philosophy" with ideas alien to our history. A. H. de Sousa Bandeira, in an article published in *Revista brasileira*, VIII (1881), 31, entitled "Rosmini e a Sociedade brasileira" refers in the following terms to the work of Monsignor Lipparoni: "It is propaganda, and bad propaganda at that, for the author proposes to popularize Rosmini and to make him the foundation of a national philosophy." "Monsignor Lipparoni must despise national development, to wish to inculcate a philosophical system without taking into account the laws that govern the formation of the nation." He adds: "Although we do not have a national philosophy, no one denies that eclecticism has taken over our schools and has been taught in them, providing us, at least, with the precious advantage of a philosophical criterion which is not dogmatic" (*ibid.*, p. 43).

[25] Apud Júlio Maria, "A Religião" in *O Livro do Centenário*, p. 101.

[26] The Júlio Maria writes: "All the following priests were Gallicans, some more than others: Father Romualdo de Seixas, later Archbishop of Bahia, Father Marcos de Sousa, later Bishop of Maranhão, Father D. José Caetano, later Bishop of Rio de Janeiro, Monsignor Vidigal, Canon Vieira Soledade, Father Diogo Antônio Feijó, Father Miguel Reinaut, Monsignor Pizarro, Canon Januário Cunha Barbosa, Fathers Rocha Franco, José Custódio Dias, José Bento Leite Ferreira" (*ibid.*, p. 86).

[27] Oliveira Lima, *O Império brasileiro*, p. 162. Cf. Basílio de Magalhães, *Estudos de História do Brasil*, p. 91.

[28] Apud João Dornas Filho, *O Padroado e a Igreja brasileira*, p. 16.

[29] Basílio de Magalhães, *Estudos de Historia do Brasil*, pp. 103–104. See Renato de Mendonça, *O Barão de Penedo e a Sua Época*, Chaps. 13, 20, and 21.

[30] Basílio de Magalhães, *op. cit.*, p. 108. "The Bishop of São Paulo, D. Antônio, wrote to Nabuco in October, 1853: 'Having been on a visit to Paraibuna, I had the honor to receive your Excellency's confidential letter dated the 4th of this month, in which you indicate the need to adopt providential measures in order to reëstablish lost discipline among the religious orders. Your Excellency, I praise Divine Providence for the light of inspiration that has been granted you' " (Joaquim Nabuco, *Um Estadista do Império*, I, 308).

[31] Basílio de Magalhães, *op. cit.*, pp. 108–109.

[32] Nabuco, *op. cit.*, I, 308.

[33] *Ibid.*, p. 309.

[34] *Ibid.*

[35] *Ibid.*

[36] Homero Pires, *Junqueira Freire*, p. 105.

[37] Cf. *Anais da Biblioteca Nacional*, XXXII, 66, apud Pires, *op. cit.*, p. 100.

[38] Basílio de Magalhães, in reply to a contention by E. Vilhena de Morais that the nation had manifested itself in favor of the two bishop martyrs of the "religious question," writes as follows: "If there had been in Brazil a sincere and fervent Christian faith, not merely a flow of stylized words, a faith that had really inflamed the hearts and minds of those who had received the shining waters of the Church—the question of the bishops and the freemasons would inevitably have produced an armed revolt throughout the country in defense of the two martyred bishops. But I will take advantage of this opportunity to point out that, in Brazil, partisan politics and economic interests have always prevailed over religious beliefs. Simply because the temporary Chamber of 1842 was dissolved, the liberals of São Paulo and Minas Gerais took to arms; and, because of the legal adoption of the decimal metric system in 1874 there was in the following year an insurrection known as the 'kilo breaking' insurrection in the northern provinces. And yet, at the same time, there was no one to brandish a sword or handle a firearm in defense of the fundamental principles of the Catholic Church, preached and propounded by two intrepid and cultured prelates who were imprisoned for having made a public and self-abnegating testimony of their faith. This, however, was nothing to be surprised at; even the name 'Brazil,' which had replaced that of 'Santa Cruz' (despite the heavy censure of the sixteenth-century soldier João de Barros), indicated the domination of material interests over the spiritual." (Basílio de Magalhães, *op. cit.*, p. 133n.) The "Collective Pastoral" of the Brazilian bishops published on March 19, 1890, is also symptomatic of their attitude (cf. Júlio Maria, *op. cit.*, p. 108). On the "religious question," see also: Bishop of Pará; *O Barão de Penedo e a Sua Missão a Roma* (1888) and *Processo e Julgamento do Bispo do Pará pelo Supremo Tribunal de Justiça* (1874). Cf. Besouchet, *op. cit.*, particularly the chapter "Freemasonry in Brazil and the Religious Question." Also: Viveiros de Castro, "A Questão Religiosa" in *Contribuições para a Biografia de D. Pedro II* (*Revista do Instituto Histórico a Geográfico brasileiro*, Part I, pp. 477f.).

[39] Oliveira Lima, *op. cit.*, p. 162.

[40] In the period 1850 to 1878, in which the renewal of the Brazilian intelligence was being prepared and the ideas of the eighteenth century were beginning to decline, we find another representative of Scholastic thinking, the Bishop of Pará, Dom José Afonso de Morais Tôrres (1805–1865), whose philosophic work, *Compêndio de Filosofia Racional*, I was unable to obtain in the São Paulo libraries. Morais Tôrres, who was educated in Caraça, taught philosophy in Congonhas do Campo. In 1852 he published a highly condensed compendium of 144 pages, according to Leonel Franca. In this work, he attempts to present "a pure and expurgated doctrine of the princi-

ples of the Eclectic system." "The doctrines of Morais Tôrres are of a spiritualism which I would hesitate to call Scholastic, so distant are they from the profundity and coherence of the great thirteenth-century masters" (Franca, *op. cit.*, p. 429). Cf. Sacramento Blake, *op. cit.*, IV, 266).

[41] I only managed to find the following works by Soriano de Sousa: *Compêndio de Filosofia Ordenado Segundo os Princípios e o Metodo do Doutor Angélico S. Tomás de Aquino* (Recife: 1867) and *Licões de Filosofia Elementar Racional e Moral* (Pernambuco: 1871). His other works, *Princípios Sociais e Politicos de S. Agostinho* (1866); *Princípios Sociais e Politicos de S. Tomás de Aquino* (1866); *O Liberalismo nas Constituições e a Reforma Eleitoral* (1873); *Considerações sôbre a Igreja e o Estado* (1874); *Apontamentos sôbre Direito Constitucional* (1883); and *Pontos de Direito Romano* (1880) were unobtainable in São Paulo.

[42] Since I was unable to consult the work of this Brazilian painter, as it was unobtainable in our libraries, I drew on the information supplied by Sílvio Romero in his book, *A Filosofia no Brasil*.

Pedro Américo's book *Le Science et les systèmes,* is the republication of his doctoral dissertation in the physical and natural sciences, presented to the free University of Brussels in 1869. It had previously been entitled *De La Liberté, de la méthode et de l'ésprit de système dans l'étude de la nature: Questions d'histoire et de philosophie naturelle."* Sílvio Romero says that Pedro Américo's work is still inspired by Eclectic doctrines. He may also have suffered the influence of Tiberghien, one of Krause's followers (Sílvio Romero, *A Filosofia no Brasil,* pp. 49–65).

[43] Soriano de Sousa, *Compêndio de Filosofia Ordenado . . .* , p. vii.

[44] *Ibid.*

[45] *Ibid.,* pp. vii–viii.

[46] *Ibid.,* p. xxxix.

[47] Leonel Franca, *op. cit.,* p. 431.

[48] *Ibid.*

[49] Caio Prado Júnior, *História Econômica do Brasil,* p. 179.

[50] *Ibid.*

[51] "This was not the only effect of the development of the coffee industry," writes Prado Júnior. "It also had the effect of reinforcing the traditional structure of the Brazilian economy, entirely geared to the intensive production of a few commodities destined for export. Thanks to the support of coffee, which was easily produced in the country and had considerable commercial importance in world markets, this structure, temporarily shaken by the setbacks of the first part of the century, was rebuilt and even prospered considerably for some time. And with it, the different economic elements to which it was linked, were likewise reinforced . . . principally the great monocultural estate worked by slaves. Despite the contradictions inherent in this system, it once more became possible during the period under consideration to reëstablish the life of the country on this basis (Prado Júnior, *op. cit.,* pp. 179–180).

[51] *Ibid.,* p. 180.

[52] "Thanks to the divulgence of the new philosophical and literary ideas,

a generation was formed in Brazil, in the seventies, with eminently critical tendencies and the desire to investigate national culture and give it a new direction. It was, as José Veríssimo called it, a true 'modernism' with its focal point in the Pernambucan capital. One of Sílvio's chief manias was the revindication of Recife's priority and importance in the history of post-Romantic Brazilian thought, and he sometimes went to almost grotesque lengths to establish this. José Veríssimo, exaggerating in his turn, was led to belittle the role of the Pernambucan group. It is established beyond doubt that the divulgence of Positivism, evolutionism, and modern criticism in Brazil spread from Recife, if not initially at least intensely. The first signs of the new criticism were provided by Sílvio Romero, Celso de Magalhães, Rocha Lima, Capistrano de Abreu, and Araripe Júnior, the last three belonging to the group that was formed in Ceará, but had studied in Recife" (Antônio Cândido de Melo e Sousa, *Introdução ao Método Crítico de Sílvio Romero*, pp. 39–40). Cf. José Veríssimo, *História da Literatura brasileira*, Chap. 15.

[53] Memorandum dated January 1, 1864 in the archives of the imperial family apud Heitor Lyra, *História de Dom Pedro II*, II, 236. Wherever the slave regime was abolished, the first step was the liberation of the slave womb. Ferreira França, father of the philosopher, had presented a project for the liberation of children born of slaves in July, 1837 (cf. Sacramento Blake, *Dicionário Bibliográfico brasileiro*, I, 162). The Law Society of Rio de Janeiro had been fighting for an improvement in the conditions of the slaves since 1845 (cf. Evaristo de Morais, *A Escravidão Africana no Brasil*, p. 105), and Perdigão Malheiros, who became celebrated for his excellent work *A Escravidão no Brasil*, had been systematically demonstrating since 1862 the illegitimacy of slave ownership. The slave womb had been liberated in Portugal in 1773, but the American and African possessions had been excluded from this decree.

[54] Speech delivered on June 14, 1871, apud Lyra, *op. cit.*, pp. 245–246.

[55] Lyra, *op. cit.*, p. 246.

[56] *Ibid.*

[57] *Ibid.*, p. 247, n. 216.

[58] Joaquim Nabuco, *Um Estadista do Império*, III, 45.

[59] *Ibid.*, p. 44.

[60] *Ibid.*

[61] Prado Júnior, *op. cit.*, p. 187.

[62] Osório Duque Estrada, *A Abolição* (*Esboço Histórico, 1831–1888*), p. 93.

[63] Prado Júnior, *op. cit.*, p. 189.

[64] "The slaves were beginning to weigh heavily on national economy. They constituted a mass to be fed, clothed, and sheltered. The slave owner, as the proprietor of productive 'machines' had to keep them in good repair. He had to feed them, ensure that they enjoyed a minimum of health to carry out their labors. The mass of slaves was enormous, precisely in the area afflicted by the economic setbacks" (Nélson Werneck Sodré, *História da Literatura brasileira*, p. 146).

[65] Prado Júnior, *op. cit.*, p. 205. "During the decade preceding 1850, there are already indications of this growth: 62 industrial undertakings were established, 14 banks, 3 savings banks, 20 steamship companies, 23 insurance companies, 4 colonization companies, 8 mining companies, 3 urban transport companies, 2 gas companies and, finally, 8 railroad companies" (p. 203).

[66] Prado Júnior, *op. cit.*, pp. 206–207.

[67] "All enterprises, had an aleatory existence; production was always risky; all activities had a decidedly speculative character and could as easily lead to sudden and unexpected fortunes as to total ruin, with no margin for immediately secure provisions to be made. The result of this can be observed in the singular instability of private fortunes and the financial situation of individuals. Brazilian patrimonies lasting more than a generation were rare, and cases of financial extremes in the life of one man were almost the rule. Naturally, other social and political factors contributed to this; but the role of the country's financial instability was always one of the most decisive in this panorama of insecurity that characterizes Brazilian life in the second half of the nineteenth century" (*ibid.*, p. 212).

[68] Sílvio Romero, "Explicações Indispensaveis" in Tobias Barreto, *Vários Escritos,* 1st ed., p. xxiv.

[69] *Ibid.* Cf. Américo Brasiliense, *Os Programas dos Partidos e o Segundo Império*, pp. 23–59 and xxxi. See also: José Maria dos Santos, *A Política Geral do Brasil*, Chaps. 5 and 6.

[70] Sílvio Romero, *op. cit.*

[71] Cf. Sílvio Romero, "A Prioridade de Pernambuco no Movimento Espiritual brasileiro" in *Revista brasileira* (1879), p. 486.

[72] *Ibid.*

[73] Veríssimo, *op. cit.*, p. 341.

[74] Graça Aranha, "Discurso na Academia brasileira" in *Revista da Academia Brasileira*, January, 1911, apud Veríssimo, *op. cit.*, p. 343.

[75] Veríssimo, *op. cit.*, p. 351.

Notes to Chapter 5
(Pages 82–175)
The Advent of Positivism

[1] "The alternation of the two parties, Liberal and Conservative, with which the Second Empire, having established the pattern, sought to disguise the closed nature of the national organism, unable to tolerate any real and clear division of ideas expressible in terms of truly opposed parties, was never more than an illusion, since both parties were merely associations of clans organized for the common exploitation of the advantages of power" (Nélson Werneck Sodré, *A Formação da Sociedade brasileira*, p. 301).

[2] Caio Prado Júnior, *História Econômica do Brasil*, p. 206. In addition to

the crises of 1857 and 1864 which were caused by "the sudden liberation of capital previously invested in the slave trade, the inflation of credit, and the emission of paper currency" Brazil suffered its most serious international crisis from 1865 to 1870—the Paraguayan war. The economic, political, and intellectual consequences of the war are of prime importance for an understanding of the period 1870–1889. The crisis of the monarchical regime in Brazil can be said to have begun then. (Cf. *ibid.*, p. 203, and Teixeira Mendes, *Benjamin Constant,* particularly Vol. II, in which he transcribes letters from Benjamin Constant commenting on the war.)

³ Leontina Licínio Cardoso, *Licínio Cardoso, Seu Pensamento, Sua Obra, Sua Vida,* p. 22.

⁴ Lídia Besouchet, *Mauá e o Seu Tempo,* p. 78. "On one side was ranged the nascent commercial bourgeoisie, composed of bankers, financiers, businessmen, importers, all linked to England by ties of liberal politics; radical parliamentarians, protectionists, partisans of a more advanced legislation, inflationists; defenders of immigration as a solution of the labor problem; industrialists who clamored for the replacement of the old dispersive agriculture by centralized factories. On the other side were the representatives of the agrarian bourgeoisie, the great landowners, believers in free trade, slave owners, demanding the removal of customs barriers and the free export to England of cotton, tobacco, sugar, and coffee, intransigent enemies of any immigration policy" (pp. 78–79). "The empire," writes Prado Júnior, "was always a conservative force, often reactionary, which only cautiously accompanied the surge of renewal that was taking place in Brazilian life. When it did give in to the pressure of events, it soon settled back into determined immobility. This can be seen in slavery. The empire did not show itself any more progressive in relation to the other economic and social reforms demanded by the circumstances of the time. And this, perhaps, was the chief cause of its downfall" (*op. cit.,* p. 206n. 67).

⁵ Cf. Basílio de Magalhães, *Estudos de História do Brasil,* p. 38.

⁶ António Cândido de Melo e Sousa, *Introdução ao Método Crítico de Sílvio Romero,* p. 180.

⁷ *Ibid.*

⁸ *Ibid.*

⁹ Joaquim Nabuco, *Um Estadista do Império,* II, 71.

¹⁰ *Ibid.,* p. 74. Cf. Paulo Pinheiro Chagas, *Teófilo Otoni,* pp. 263–275, and Basílio de Magalhães, *op. cit.,* pp. 40–75.

¹¹ Euclides da Cunha, *À Margem da História,* p. 346.

¹² "The Brazilian monarchy, was the empire of the landowner, the only element accustomed to giving orders, to command. And he began to rule the country as though he were governing his estates" (J. F. Normano, *Evolução Econômica do Brasil,* p. 97).

¹³ It is not easy to make a clear distinction between the class divisions in Brazil. The main groups into which imperial society was divided are roughly as follows: the landowner, the functionary, the artisan, the shopkeeper in the few urban centers, the mestizo, and the Negro. But, as in all new coun-

tries, "the class structure was flexible" (Sodré, *op. cit.*, p. 292). One could move from one class to another, or, as the old proverb said, "innkeeper father, gentleman son, and beggar grandson." "In Brazil all activities had a speculative character and could as easily lead to sudden and unexpected fortune as to total ruin" (Prado Júnior, *op. cit.*, p. 212). Economic and financial fluidity makes it impossible to speak of a bourgeoisie and an aristocracy. The problem of miscegenation, too, had considerable importance in the formation of our society and the difficult fixation of class barriers. "The intense growth of miscegenation was the result more of the social position of the individual than of his physical characteristics" (Sodré, *op. cit.*, p. 292). Thus, "from earliest times, we created a social organisation that, in its very immaturity, was always plastic, flexible, easily adaptable" (*ibid.*).

[14] Miguel Lemos (1854–1917) was the son of a naval officer; Teixeira Mendes (1855–1927) was born into a well-to-do family; his father had taken an engineering degree at the Paris École Centrale. Luís Pereira Barreto (1842–1924), who studied in Belgium, was the son of Commendador Fabiano Barreto and belonged to "one of the many illustrious Minas families who emigrated to the Paraíba Valley at the beginning of the great coffee boom" (João Camilo de Oliveira Tôrres, *O Positivismo no Brasil*, p. 182 and Alberto Pizarro Jacobina, *Dias Carneiro*, p. 10). Silva Jardim (1860–1891) was the son of a farmer who made up for the "deficiencies of agriculture with a primary school" (João Dornas Filho, *Silva Jardim*, p. 25).

[15] "It was then, toward the end of 1874 or the beginning of 1875, that I made the acquaintance of the doctrines of Auguste Comte, having previously read or heard nothing on the subject. I recall only that, before this, disillusioned with the systems of philosophy I already knew, I had once seen on the shelves of a bookseller a work in a number of volumes with the title *Philosophie Positive* by Comte. I remember shrugging my shoulders on seeing such an adjective coupled with a word which was then for me synonymous with empty verbiage, and I did not even bother to leaf through the voluminous treatise" (Miguel Lemos and R. Teixeira Mendes, *A Nossa Iniciação no Positivismo*, pp. 7–8).

[16] "Toward the end of 1874, the ruin of my theological beliefs was complete. Several factors contributed to this end which it would be pointless to enumerate here. It will be sufficient to mention only two. In the first place, the antagonism between the Catholic Church and my republican aspirations was the preponderant factor in my intellectual emancipation. Latent until I reached my seventh year at the Pedro II College, this antagonism revealed itself when I read a book written by the Jesuit Ramière, a book recommended by the present Bishop of Mariana, who was at that time vice-principal of the College. From then on, the conflict became more pronounced, and ever more deeply felt. Secondly, the reading of a few pages of Herbert Spencer's *First Principles* contributed to the same end" (Miguel Lemos and Teixeira Mendes, *op. cit.*, pp. 18–19).

[17] R. Teixeira Mendes, *Benjamin Constant*, I, 21.

[18] "As for intellectual culture, it was at this time more literary than scien-

tific, because of the aesthetic rather than theoretic predisposition of the Brazilian people, as of their historic antecedents. The ruling classes usually entered the legal professions. Only the military classes of the army and navy on the one hand, and the engineers and doctors on the other, made any attempt to undertake scientific studies. Nearly all competed to draw near to the monarch, and began to form about him that pedantic atmosphere that was the greatest delight of his life" (*ibid.*, p. 22).

¹⁹ *Ibid.*, p. 49, and Teixeira Mendes, *Resumo Cronológico da Evolução do Positivismo,* p. 17.

²⁰ Teixeira Mendes, *Benjamin Constant,* I, 49.

²¹ *Ibid.*

²² *Ibid.*

²³ Clóvis Beviláqua, *Esboços e Fragmentos,* pp. 70–71.

²⁴ We must not forget that in a letter to Hutton, Auguste Comte had written: "I can only recognize as true disciples those who, renouncing the foundation of their own syntheses, consider the one that I have constructed as essentially sufficient and radically preferable to any other. Their duty is then to propagate it and apply it without any attempt to criticise or even perfect it" (apud 1st *Circular Anual do Apostolado Positivista no Brasil,* 2d ed., 1900).

²⁵ Cf. Beviláqua, *op. cit.,* pp. 70–71.

²⁶ Teixeira Mendes, *Benjamin Constant,* 1st ed., 175.

²⁷ Benjamin Constant was the son of a Portuguese immigrant, Leopoldo Henrique Botelho de Magalhães, of Tôrre de Moncorvo, who had been in the army up to 1843. When Benjamin Constant was born, his father was running a private school, where he taught the three R's, Portuguese grammar, and Latin. With scanty resources and finding it difficult to live from these lessons, he moved to Macaé with his family where, thanks to the protection of the Viscountess of Macaé, he established a new school. Here he baptized his first son, to whom he gave the name of the French politician he so much admired. From Macaé the family moved to Magé, where Benjamin Constant acquired the rudiments of learning from the vicar, and later moved to Petropolis, where Magalhães opened a bakery (cf. Teixeira Mendes, *Benjamin Constant,* pp. 29–32). Teixeira Mendes says that Magalhães was in the services up to 1848 (*ibid.,* p. 29). After 1833, he belonged to the class of the noncommissioned officers.

²⁸ Cf. A. Ximeno de Villeroy, *Benjamin Constant e a Política Republicana,* Chap. III.

²⁹ Apud Teixeira Mendes, *Benjamin Constant,* pp. 205–206.

³⁰ "It was not long, however, before the charms of a young girl not quite fifteen years of age, daughter of an illustrious citizen (Dr. Cláudio Luís da Costa, director of the Institute for Blind Children where Benjamin Constant had been nominated professor) captured his imagination" (Teixeira Mendes, *Benjamin Constant,* p. 81).

³¹ Ximeno de Villeroy, who was a pupil of Benjamin Constant's at the Military School, in his interesting study of his former professor and the

latter's political activities during the republic, expresses himself as follows on Constant's religious Positivism: "Contrary to what the Positivist Apostolate affirms, and to what many coreligionists of good faith have accepted, particularly those who had never come into contact with the learned professor, Benjamin Constant was thoroughly familiar with the works of Auguste Comte. I frequently heard him cite the *Politique*, and as for the powerful *Syntèse subjective*, he constantly referred to it in his memorable lectures. He was not, however, a fanatic, nor was he convinced that humanity should immobilize itself before Comte like the Dark Ages before Aristotle. As far as possible, he followed the program of the great reformer, but was never dominated by that puerile terror of 'algebraic materialism.' In his lectures on the theory of elimination, for instance, he recommended the reading of Cauchy and called this algebraist's exposition of the theory, 'a chapter of pure gold.' Benjamin Constant had the greatest veneration for the incomparable genius of the Philosopher of Montpellier, whose learning he considered unequaled, and never took the liberty of criticizing his mathematics, as was stated by the egregious Teixeira Mendes, who had it 'on hearsay'—a lapse which cannot be forgiven in someone who proposed to reform the world. Whenever he disagreed with the supreme legislator of mathematical philosophy on some minor point, he always attributed his disagreement to his own lack of understanding. This was his attitude on purely scientific questions, especially mathematical ones; as for religion, my impression is that Benjamin Constant was completely emancipated, and had many reservations about the religion of humanity. I think that he did not see the need for a religion with its dogmas, its complicated and numerous sacraments (nine in the Religion of Humanity) ministered by a sovereign and infallible priesthood. He often referred to the religion of duty. I am recording here my impressions, arising from the number of my recollections of him, and not making any definite assertions because I never heard him expatiate on this subject" (Ximeno de Villcroy, *op. cit.*, pp. 28–30).

[32] Teixeira Mendes, *Benjamin Constant*, p. 210. "Before he began the oral examinations," writes Teixeira Mendes, *ibid.*, "he [Benjamin Constant] declared that he accepted Positivism and that his lessons would be guided by its principles, and he consulted the board of examiners. The story goes that the examiners, after an imperial gesture, allowed Benjamin Constant to proceed with the examination. Some have added that Constant's conference with the examiners included reference to his republican sympathies. But we heard this addition only after the death of the illustrious Brazilian. During his lifetime, the only incident that came to our knowledge was the one we have just related." Benjamin Constant was already known to the emperor. As is well known, the emperor had a weakness for schools and spent his time attending examinations. He felt that he had been born to be a professor. In his *Diary*, under November 28, 1862, there is an entry referring to the examinations he had attended at the Institute for the Blind, in which he mentions Benjamin Constant (cf. Heitor Lyra, *História de Dom Pedro II*, II, 136). See also, on this subject, the interesting article by Tobias

Monteiro, "A Tolerância do Imperadui" in *Revista do Instituto Histórico e Geográfico brasileiro* (*Contribuições para a Biografia de Pedro II*, Part II), CLII, t. 98, pp. 150ff.

[33] Teixeira Mendes, *Benjamin Constant*, p. 210. Cf. Teixeira Mendes, *Resumo Cronológico da Evolução do Positivismo no Brasil*, p. 19.

[34] Luís Pereira Barreto, *As Três Filosofias*, Part I: *Filosofia Teológica*, with a preface written in the form of a letter to Senators Jobim and J. F. Godoy (Rio de Janeiro: 1874), p. lxxv.

[35] Pereira Barreto, *op. cit.*, p. v.

[36] *Ibid.*, pp. v–vi.

[37] I was fortunate enough to meet, in 1917, the charming old gentleman who was Dr. Pereira Barreto. I remember the enthusiasm with which he spoke to my father on the great future that was in store for viticulture in the region stretching from Jundiaí to Campinas. He believed that in this region, so close to the capital, a kind of huge granary could be created, to serve the needs of the metropolis.

[38] Pereira Barreto, *op. cit.*, pp. xiii–xix.

[39] "The author, it seems, wished to produce a work of popularization; the volumes we have are a summary of Positivist doctrines; they are clear and well-ordered" (Sílvio Romero, *A Filosofia no Brasil*, pp. 67–68).

[40] "His work is interspersed with references to Brazilian life, considered in the light of Comtism. The two volumes published display his learning and, what is more important, a critical spirit." (João Camilo de Oliveira Tôrres, *op. cit.*, pp. 183–184). Cf. Leonel Franca, *Noções de História da Filosofia*, pp. 443–452.

[41] Pereira Barreto, *op. cit.*, p. xvii.

[42] *Ibid.*, p. xviii.

[43] "We must educate and revolutionize the masses," wrote Pereira Barreto in an article entitled, "O Século XX sob o Ponto de Vista brasileiro," published in the *Estado de São Paulo* for April 23, 1901. Barreto's friends published the article as a separate work with the same title (São Paulo: 1901).

[44] Luís Pereira Barreto, *O Século XX sob o Ponto de Vista brasileiro*, p. 33.

[45] Luís Pereira Barreto, *As Três Filosofias*, Part I, p. xx.

[46] Pereira Barreto wrote the second volume of *As Três Filosofias* in Jacarei, where he practiced medicine. It was entitled *A Filosofia Metafísica* (Jacarei: 1876), and was dedicated to Counsellor Nabuco. The date appearing on p. iii of the work is January 11, 1877. In addition, he published, *As Soluções Positivas da Política brasileira* (São Paulo: 1880), which I was unable to obtain; *Positivismo e Teologia*, a polemic with G. Nash Morton, an American professor who was principal of a Protestant college in Campinas (São Paulo: 1880), and the work above referred to, *O Século XX sob o Ponto de Vista brasileiro*. In addition to the polemic with Morton, he conducted others: with Eduardo Prado and with the former Abbot of the Monastery of St. Benedict, D. Miguel Kruse. See also: Father José Severino de Rezende, *Eduardo Prado* (*A Vingança do Percevejo*) (São Paulo: n.d.) and Lorobadel, *O Sábio Dr. Barreto e o Sr. Kruse* (São Paulo: April, 1901).

[47] Pereira Barreto, *As Três Filosofias,* Part I, p. xviii.

[48] Pereira Barreto, *O Século XX sob o Ponto de Vista brasileiro,* p. 19.

[49] Pereira Barreto, *Positivismo e Teologia,* p. 21.

[50] Pereira Barreto, *As Três Filosofias,* Part I, p. xxxvii.

[51] *Ibid.,* p. xxxix.

[52] *Ibid.,* p. li.

[53] *Ibid.,* p. liv.

[54] *Ibid.,* pp. liv–lv.

[55] *Ibid.,* pp. lv–lvii.

[56] *Ibid.*

[57] *Ibid.,* p. xxv.

[58] *Ibid.,* p. viii.

[59] Apud Joaquim Nabuco, *Um Estadista do Império,* I, 308.

[60] Littré, *Paroles de philosophie positive,* p. 33 apud R. P. Gruber, S.J., *Le Positivisme depuis Comte jusqu'à nos jours,* pp. 25–26.

[61] Miguel Lemos, *Le Positivisme et le sophiste Pierre Lafitte,* p. 20.

[62] Miguel Lemos, 1st *Circular Anual* (1881), Annex D., p. 149.

[63] *Ibid.,* Annex D, pp. 151–154. Cf. Miguel Lemos and R. Teixeira Mendes, *A Política Positiva e a Grande Naturalização,* Note B.

[64] In the 1881 circular of the Apostolate, Miguel Lemos referred to the work of Pereira Barreto. In the second edition of this circular, he added a footnote, reading: "*As Três Filosofias,* Part II: *Filosofia Metafísica* (Jacarei: 1876). This volume, like its predecessor, is a hotchpotch of plagiarisms, scandalously culled from various sources." Miguel Lemos, 1st *Circular Anual* (1881; 2d ed., 1900), p. 15.

[65] "Dr. Pereira Barreto is undoubtedly the most important offspring of Positivism in Brazil. His name has been inscribed among those of the country's most distinguished men of letters since the publication of the two volumes of *As Três Filosofias.* This work, which remains incomplete (1883) aims to popularize Comte's doctrines since the central ideas on which it hinges are taken from the leaders of the French school. There are, however, a fair number of fertile ideas sprinkled here and there throughout the two volumes, whenever the author turns his eyes toward the motherland" (Beviláqua, *op. cit.,* p. 126).

[66] "The year that has just ended" (1881), writes Miguel Lemos, "marks the formal organization of Positivist propaganda in Brazil, and the normal intervention of the regenerating doctrine in the business of the Brazilian homeland." Miguel Lemos, 1st *Circular Anual* (2d ed., 1900), p. 11.

[67] Miguel Lemos and R. Teixeira Mendes, *A Nossa Iniciação* . . . (a corrective note to *Resumo Histórico do Movimento Positivista no Brasil,* published in 1882), 1889, pp. 7–8.

[68] Miguel Lemos, 1st *Circular Anual,* 2d ed., 1900, p. 12.

[69] Miguel Lemos and R. Teixeira Mendes, *A Nossa Iniciação* . . . , p. 9.

[70] "It was not the first time that I was to meet the famous professor [B. Constant]. Dr. Oliveira Guimarães had introduced me to him when I attended the examinations at the Institute for the Blind. He spoke to me with

indulgence, alluding good-humoredly to my progress in geometry, which left me somewhat embarrassed. I cannot recall with exactitude the date of this first encounter. When I sought him out to show him the mathematical attempts to which I have referred (*"refusão"* of the fundamental theories of geometry), I met with the warmest welcome. His judgment of the work was unfavorable to me; but at the same time he spoke with praise of a demonstration I had given in my fourth year at the Pedro II College. This spontaneous college exercise had been brought to the attention of the Polytechnic Institute, without my knowledge, by Dr. Aarão Reis, during its session of June 9, 1874. It was concerned with the relations discovered by theocracy between the sides of a right-angled triangle and which, up to the time of Comte, had been attributed, in the West, to Pythagoras. Dr. Benjamin Constant had pronounced his opinion on my demonstration, in his capacity as mathematical correspondent of the said society, on August 11, 1874" (*ibid.*, p. 16).

[71] *Ibid.*, p. 17.

[72] Cf. Miguel Lemos, 1st *Circular Anual*, p. 14, n. 2.

[73] Miguel Lemos and Teixeira Mendes, *A Nossa Iniciação* . . . , pp. 18–20.

[74] Cf. José Maria dos Santos, *Os Republicanos Paulistas e a Abolição*; José Maria Bello, *História da República*, Chaps. I and II, and Cristiano B. Ottoni, *O Advento da República no Brasil*, Part II. In 1876 Teixeira Mendes was absent from Rio de Janeiro. At this time he was excluded, together with Miguel Lemos, from the Polytechnic School. Not yet converted to religious Positivism, Teixeira Mendes, gripped by "political fervor," transmitted to the public "that mixture of Positivism and revolutionarism" in which, up to then, he was involved, as he himself declared (Miguel Lemos and Teixeira Mendes, *A Nossa Iniciação* . . . , p. 23). In that same year, Teixeira Mendes accompanied Miguel Lemos to Montevideo, where Lemos's family was at that time residing. On his return, Teixeira Mendes matriculated at the Faculty of Medicine, "preoccupied," he relates, "with the thought of completing my philosophic preparation in accord with the plan of Auguste Comte" (*ibid.*, p. 21). Thanks to the support of Godofredo Furtado and Manuel Pereira Reis, Teixeira Mendes left for Paris with Miguel Lemos, shortly afterward (*ibid.*).

[75] Miguel Lemos, 1st *Circular Anual*, p. 13.

[76] *Ibid.*, p. 14.

[77] *Ibid.*, p. 15.

[78] Teixeira Mendes, *Resumo Cronológico da Evolução do Positivismo no Brasil*, p. 20. Cf. Teixeira Mendes, *Benjamin Constant*, I, 238–239.

[79] Miguel Lemos mentions the following periodicals which appeared during this time: *A Idéia*, monthly; *O Rebate*, weekly; *A Crença*, weekly; *A Crónica do Império*, fortnightly. Cf. Miguel Lemos, 1st *Circular Anual*, p. 16, note.

[80] Miguel Lemos, 1st *Circular Anual*, pp. 16–17.

[81] Heitor Lyra, *História de Dom Pedro II*, II, 11–12.

[82] Miguel Lemos and Teixeira Mendes had been barred from attending

the Polytechnic School's examinations for two years from November 28, 1876, as the result of an article they had written criticizing the director, the Viscount of Rio Branco. (Cf. Miguel Lemos and Teixeira Mendes, *A Nossa Iniciação* . . . , p. ii.)

[83] Teixeira Mendes, *Resumo Cronólogico* . . . , p. 23.

I will transcribe the text of the minutes of the first meeting of the Positivist Society of Rio de Janeiro, because it is interesting from more than one point of view for the comprehension of the origins of Positivism in Brazil. It reads as follows:

"On the 24th Gutenberg 90 (September 5, 1878), the 21st anniversary of the death of Auguste Comte, founder of Positivism. Present: Drs. J. Mendonça, Benjamin Constant, Álvaro de Oliveira, and Oscar de Araújo, Sr. Joaquim Mendonça being elected president. The latter member declared that he was empowered to represent Drs. Pereira Barreto and França Leite. The following resolutions were passed during the meeting: (1) to found a society to propagate and develop the Positive Doctrine by all means within the powers of the members; (2) to note in these minutes that this association is the continuation of the association founded on 7th Archimedes 88 (April 1, 1876) by Dr. Oliveira Guimarães, who died on 2d Homer of the current year (January 30, 1878), and who is gratefully remembered by all true Positivists; (3) to use the sum of 481,000 reis, collected through the efforts of Dr. Oliveira Guimarães and now in the hands of the treasurer, for the purchase of the books which constitute the Positive Library of Auguste Comte and for a subscription to the *Revue Occidental*; (4) to accept any donations whether of money or of books provided the latter appear in the Positivist Library of Auguste Comte or are publications of the Positivist School; (5) that each member contribute from the outset the sum of 2,000 reis at least, payable at the beginning of each month; (6) that these monthly contributions and the donations collected by the treasurer shall be used as follows: (i) half toward the purchase of the books of the Positivist Library of Auguste Comte if the sum mentioned in point 3 above should prove insufficient for the acquisition of all the volumes needed, and the publications of the Positivist School; (ii) a fourth for the sacerdotal subsidy to be sent in the most convenient form to the Director of Positivism in France; (iii) another fourth for the establishment of a reserve fund to be used as the Society decides at future meetings; (7) that the sums referred to in the preceding articles be entrusted to a treasurer; to be duly instructed by the director; (8) that the members present and represented at this meeting solemnly undertake to propagate Positivism by means of articles published in the press not later than the month of Archimedes (March and April), dedicating themselves to the demonstration of this doctrine's capacity for educating and moralizing society; (9) that members undertake to propagate Positivism in the periodical press, whenever possible; (10) that their writings be submitted for approval to two fellow members before publication, in order to assure the perfect agreement of other members with the opinions expressed by the writers; (11) that the author of such articles send one copy of the periodicals in which the articles appear to each fellow member, (12) that in order to be admitted to membership, prospective members be recommended by three members and approved by the director; (13) that the director convoke meetings by means of letters or circulars addressed to members, notifying the date, time, and venue, and setting out an agenda of matters for discussion. Agreed that Dr. Joaquim Mendonça be appointed director. The director nominated Dr. Álvaro de Oliveira as treasurer and Dr. Benjamin Constant as librarian. I, Oscar Araújo, acting as secretary, drew up the foregoing minutes, which are signed by each and every member present. Director: Dr. Joaquim Ribeiro de Mendonça; treasurer: Álvaro de Oliviera; librarian: Benjamin Constant; secretary: Oscar Araújo. Members: Drs. Pereira Barreto, França Leite (signed in their absence by Dr. Joaquim Ribeiro de Mendonça). (1st *Circular Anual*, Annex A, pp. 79–81.)

[84] Gruber, *op. cit.*, p. 2.

[85] Professor Paul Arbousse-Bastide, in a work presented as a dissertation for a doctorate at the Sorbonne, expressed the belief that the true thought of Auguste Comte, his true intentions, were only truly understood and carried out by the Brazilian Positivists of the "Apostolate." It has not yet been published, but I am looking forward to reading the work of my friend, Professor Arbousse-Bastide.

[86] Miguel Lemos, 1st *Circular Anual*, pp. 19–20.

[87] *Ibid.*, pp. 20–21.

[88] Both friends and enemies of Pierre Lafitte are unanimous in their praise of his vast erudition, the ease with which he propounded subjects, the clarity of his syntheses. Gay and somewhat Bohemian, he was endowed with "a subtle and insinuating charm that seemed miraculous" (*Le XIX*e *Siècle*, September 7, 1887, apud Gruber, *op. cit.*, pp. 91–92). Cf. Anatole France, *Oeuvres Complètes*, XVII. The strict Positivists criticized his lack of "religious fervor." (Cf. Dr. Audiffrent, *Circulaire exceptionelle addressée aux vrais disciples d'Auguste Comte*, p. 8, apud Gruber, *op. cit.*, p. 92.) Miguel Lemos wrote: "Par ses dispositions foncièrement railleuses et sceptiques, il [Lafitte] est un fils de Voltaire fourvoyé dans un mouvement de reconstruction religieuse. Sa robe de Pontife l'embarasse, comme l'a dit spirituellement M. Sémérie, et l'on peut eroire qu'il serait bien aisé de pouvoir jeter de froc aux orties" (Miguel Lemos, *Le Positivisme et le sophiste Pierre Lafitte*, p. 41).

[89] Miguel Lemos, 1st *Circular Anual*, pp. 21–22.

[90] *Ibid.*, p. 22.

[91] Teixeira Mendes, *Resumo Cronológico* . . . , p. 22 and Miguel Lemos, 1st *Circular Anual*, p. 24.

[92] Miguel Lemos was at the time engaged to Albertina Tôrres de Carvalho, who was perhaps the first Brazilian woman to become converted to the Religion of Humanity.

[93] Miguel Lemos, 1st *Circular Anual*, p. 24, n. 1. According to Dr. C. Tôrres Gonçalves, the Executive Delegation of the Positivist Church of Brazil intends to publish shortly the correspondence between Miguel Lemos and Teixeira Mendes before their conversion to Positivism.

94 João Pernetta, *Os Dois Apóstolos,* I, 36.

95 Cf. Teixeira Mendes, *Resumo Cronológico* . . . , p. 23. A public exhibition of the Religion of Humanity was held in the Escola do Clube Republicano de S. Cristóvão of Rio de Janeiro in April, 1880. On June 10 the first of the "social occasions" was organized for the commemoration of the third centenary of Camões (*ibid.*).

96 Miguel Lemos, *Luís de Camões* (Paris: Central Headquarters of Positivism, 1880).

97 *Ibid.,* p. iii.

98 *Ibid.,* pp. iii–iv.

99 *Gazeta da Tarde,* October 8, 1880.

100 In *O Positivismo e a Escravidão Moderna,* excerpts from the works of Auguste Comte, followed by Positivist documents relating to the problem of slavery in Brazil, with an introduction by Miguel Lemos (1884; 2d ed., 1934), pp. 29–36.

101 "To sum up, the full understanding of a political problem demands (1) knowledge of social laws as a basis for the measures to be adopted in the abstract; (2) examination of the conditions of each specific case in order to determine the legitimate, or opportune, measures to be taken; (3) patience, in order to allow for the time element, indispensable for all arts, but above all for politics. Having stated which, let us briefly examine the economic problem in modern societies, that is, in the "industrial régime," summarizing as far as possible the views of Auguste Comte . . . All activity depends on the nature of the environment and on individual organization. If our solid nutrition were subject to as little care as our gaseous and liquid nutrition, our egoistic instincts would lose, for want of stimulation, the necessary energy, and the solution of the economic problem would be found in an altruistic sense. The spontaneous economic solution would be 'to live for others' . . . But our nature and the nature of the cosmological world, demand a continual activity if we are to assure our survival. In this way, under pressure of egoistical impulses, industrial efforts are initially contrary to the altruistic solution of the human problem." (Teixeira Mendes, "Apontamentos para a Solução do Problema Social no Brasil" in *O Positivismo e a Escravidão Moderna,* p. 32). In what way, then, does an egoistical existence become transformed into an altruistic one? According to Teixeira Mendes, this transformation is based on two laws, formulated by Auguste Comte. The first of these is subjective: "Each man is able to produce more than he consumes." The second law is objective: "Materials can be kept longer than the time needed for their renewal." The possibility of an excess in production, and the conservation of stocks of consumer products, these are the laws devised by the "genius of Auguste Comte" (*ibid.,* p. 33). From these laws results the "theory of accumulations" in which each generation reserves for the generation to follow the excess of its production, and thus "human capital" will be formed, "a name happily chosen by the universal language to designate the indispensable basis of collective existence" (*ibid.*). It is this possibility of "accumulation" that ensures the altruistic development of man's

activities. Although these laws render accumulation possible, they are not in themselves sufficient to assure it. "Thus, as with the laws of geometry, which permit the measurement of the area of a circle, but require someone to do the measuring, so with the laws I have cited, which permit of accumulation but require some means of transforming the 'possible' into the 'reality.' Hence the need for appropriation and transmission. But once these have been assured by society in view of its collective interest, they cannot acquire the absolute character that the egoism of landowners and the immorality of present-day economists would attempt to impose. The origin of capital is social; its conservation demands social coöperation; hence its distribution must likewise be social. Now the social distribution of capital demands that those who possess it should allocate wages for the maintenance of the agents who produce this capital, and for the acquisition of production tools, keeping for themselves only a sum which has been wisely determined. Only in these conditions can society permit some of its members to administer the capital of humanity" (ibid.). Positivism elevates respect for property into a moral law. And further: it demands that the distribution of property be moralized. Comte believed that an important agent for this moralization was "the pressure of strongly organized public opinion or, in other words, the existence of a universally accepted doctrine, with power entrusted in the name of this doctrine and no material means of coercion" (ibid., p. 34). Cf. Roger Mauduit, Auguste Comte et la science économique, passim and Ivan Lins, "Augusto Comte e o Liberalismo Econômico," Digesto Econômico (June, 1949), pp. 106ff.

[102] Teixeira Mendes, Resumo Cronológico . . . , p. 34.

[103] Ibid., p. 35.

[104] Ibid.

[105] Ibid., p. 36.

[106] Miguel Lemos, introduction to O Positivismo e a Escravidão Moderna, p. 8.

[107] "In 1862, Tavares Bastos, a young man of considerable talent and noble sentiment, published a series of articles expressing the need for abolition in the Correio Mercantil. They are so well written that, since they were published anonymously, they were attributed to the Viscount of Jequitinhonha, a former parliamentarian and eminent jurist" (C. B. Ottoni, O Advento da República no Brasil, p. 9).

[108] Osório Duque Estrada, A Abolição, p. 85. Cf. Joaquim Nabuco, A Minha Formação, pp. 226–250 and Lyra, op. cit., Vol. II, Chap. VI.

[109] Cf. Miguel Lemos, 1st Circular Anual, p. 29 and Miguel Lemos, 4e Circulaire Annuelle de l'Apostolat Positiviste du Brésil (1884; 2d ed., 1895), pp. 14–18.

On December 31, 1879, just before his return to Brazil, Miguel Lemos solemnly vowed to dedicate himself entirely to the Religion of Humanity in a speech pronounced at the tomb of Auguste Comte. The following excerpts from this speech are particularly relevant for an understanding of Positivism in our country: "To you [Comte] we owe the reattachment of the past, to the future, through the anarchy of the present; we owe the revelation of the sacred principle that subordinates the mind to the heart, without which scientific culture would have effectively stanched in us the fountains of feeling in the soul, and on which is based the religious edifice destined to shelter future humanity. . . . As sons of the two nations that you have just joined, in your historical theory, under the name of Spain, we owe you a special debt of gratitude. When, misled by the fallacious scientific concepts of our age, all were speaking with disdain of these two nations—one of which is epitomized in the incomparable ingenuity of Cervantes, and the other in the daring deeds of her navigators, sung by the immortal Camões—you alone pointed out their role in the evolution of the West, you alone did them justice, attributing to these two nations, above all, the cultivation of sentiments of fraternity and human dignity. As Americans, for the same reason, we owe you the ability to reconstruct the feeling for historical continuity with our mother countries, despite the hatreds bred of the struggles for national independence. But thanks are not enough: we must continue to propagate your work. Humanity is crying out for a new balance, able to put an end, at last, to the dissolving anarchy that has been loosed upon the world since the end of the Middle Ages. For us all, great or small, who in these times of skepticism have had the remarkable good fortune to know and accept the universal religion, our duty is clear: we must spread the glad tidings and repeat, like St. Paul, to hearts torn by conflict between a dying dogma and one about to be born: 'Our unknown God is here: we bring Him to you.' For this reason, today, on the edge of your tomb, we take the solemn vow to dedicate all our devotion, all the energy of our being, to the propagation of your regenerating doctrine. It is an apostolate full of bitterness in the present, which will expose us to all forms of injustice, public and private, which will make us misunderstood and misjudged even by those we love. No matter. In this apostolate, in the conviction that a religion cannot be founded without complete sacrifice by those who sow the first seeds, in the contemplation of the ideal we follow, we shall draw strength not to falter on this stony path. As someone has said: Saints are needed for this task! May your doctrine and your example, O Master of Masters, bring each of us, according to his strength, closer to that complete abnegation, and may the memory of this corner of sacred earth to which future world pilgrims will flock, support us in our hours of anguish when we return to our native countries, and fill our souls with veneration for your sacred memory. So be it!" (Miguel Lemos, 1st *Circular Anual*, Annex C, pp. 142–143).

[110] Ferreira de Araújo, at that time editor of the *Gazeta de Notícias*, gave space in his newspaper to the Positivist group from the time of Miguel Lemos's first public lecture (Miguel Lemos, 1st *Circular Anual*, Annex C, pp. 81–83).

[111] In the *11ᵉ Circulaire Annuelle de l'Apostolat Positiviste du Brésil* (1891), Miguel Lemos gives the table on the following page of the growth in the number of subscribers to the Brazilian Positivist subsidy, from 1878.

The fluctuations are indicative of the vicissitudes of the doctrine in Brazil in its relations to national political life. (Cf. Miguel Lemos, *11ᵉ Circulaire Annuelle de l'Apostolat Positiviste du Brésil*, p. 61.)

YEAR	NUMBER OF SUBSCRIBERS
1878	5
1879	6
1880	13
1881	55
1882	59
1883	43
1884	34
1885	54
1886	48
1887	49
1888	52
1889	53
1890	159
1891	174

[112] Dr. Joaquim Ribeiro de Mendonça later broke away from the Positivist Church over a question on the acceptance of Positivist practice in relation to the problem of slavery. Cf. Miguel Lemos, *Circulares do Apostolado Positivista do Brasil* (1883 and 1884). See also: *O Positivismo e a Escravidão Moderna*, pp. 37–55.

[113] Miguel Lemos, 1st *Circular Anual*, p. 32.

[114] *Ibid.*, p. 33.

[115] Augusto [sic] Comte, *Manifesto Inicial da Sociedade Positivista de Paris*, trans. by Miguel Lemos.

[116] "Manifesto Republicano" in Americo Brasiliense, *Os Programas dos Partidos e o Segundo Império*, Part II, p. 85.

[117] Euclides da Cunha, *À Margem da História*, p. 348.

[118] Cf. Júlio de Mesquita Filho, *Ensaios Sul-Americanos*, pp. 21–113.

[119] Cunha, *op. cit.*, p. 354.

[120] "The determining factors in the empire's external politics, had their roots in the geographical configuration of the Plata basin or, rather, in the dangerous anomaly constituted by the fact that two and a half million square kilometers of Brazilian territory—an area almost equal to that of the Argentine Republic—are only accessible through the Plata, Paraguay, and Paraná rivers. This difficulty inevitably conditioned all actions of the Brazilian Foreign Affairs Department, whether under the monarchy or under the republic. While access to such a considerable area of our territory remained totally dependent on a means of communication spread entirely through non-Brazilian territory, the efforts of our statesmen were naturally centered on ways and means, if not to assume entire control of this route, at least to ensure that the possibility of its eventual interruption be reduced to a minimum. To the pressure of this delicate situation was further added the fact that the Brazilian provinces bordering on the Plata were largely composed of territories still not subject to complete agreement as to ownership. And to add to these complications, rendering almost insoluble the

grave problem with which destiny amused itself by testing our diplomatic astuteness, was the fact that nine-tenths of our population were concentrated in the Atlantic coast, whereas almost the entire Spanish populations were packed tightly along the margins of the Plata and Uruguay rivers, that is, virtually along the frontiers of the empire. Summarizing the delicacy of our situation, Alberdi writes that 'in its geographical position, the Republic of Paraguay is, so to speak, driven like a wedge into the heart of Brazil.' " (Júlio de Mesquita Filho, *Ensaios Sul-Americanos,* pp. 37–38).

[121] "On the one hand, the delusions of grandeur of a despot too small for his own ambitions, on the other the rash diversion of a constitutional emperor probably affected by the internal political scene of his country" (Cunha, *op. cit.,* p. 356).

[122] *Ibid.,* p. 360.

[123] *Ibid.*

[124] *Ibid.,* p. 316.

[125] Cf. Brasiliense, *op. cit.,* pp. 76–80.

[126] Basílio de Magalhães, *Estudos de História do Brasil,* p. 58.

[127] Cf. Eduardo Prado, "Immigration," an excellent study appearing in *Le Brésil en 1889,* a work edited by M. F. J. de Santa-Anna Nery for the World Exhibition of Paris. The following statistical table of immigrants landing in Rio de Janeiro appears on p. 495:

NATIONALITY	1864–1872 (9 years)	1873–1880 (14 years)	1887
Portuguese	56,351	110,891	10,205
Italian	9,307	112,279	17,115
French	5,862	3,475	241
English	5,252	2,215	72
Spanish	3,229	15,684	1,766
North American	3,515	316	31
German	3,119	23,469	717
Austrian	. . .	9,022	274
Swiss	. . .	479	. . .
Russian	. . .	417	889
Various	2,188	26,549	. . .
TOTAL	88,823	304,796	31,310
Yearly average	9,869	21,771	

[128] Cunha, *op. cit.,* p. 376.

[129] *Ibid.*

[130] Cf. Miguel Lemos and Teixeira Mendes, *A Nossa Iniciação* . . ., pp. 18–19.

[131] Auguste Comte, *Manifesto Inicial da Sociedade Positivista de Paris,* trans. by Miguel Lemos. In this work, written in 1848, the time of the proclamation of the Second Republic in France, Auguste Comte wrote: "The henceforth irrevocable proclamation of the French Republic [a few years

later, Napoleon III proclaimed himself Emperor of the French] is in all respects the greatest event since the fall of Bonaparte. It clearly sums up the negative aspect of the Revolution, radically destroying the reactionary hopes and illusions that, from the second half of Louis XIV's reign, were attached to the name of royalty alone—whatever the form in which it was maintained. On the other hand, the name 'republic' represents in its happy organic connotations the universal program, sentimental rather than rational, of the true social future. It thus announces the continual subordination of politics to morals, admirably essayed in the Middle Ages under the Catholic principle, but only fully realizable under a better spiritual regime and in a favorable environment" (p. 8).

[132] Oliviera Viana, *O Ocaso do Império*, p. 120.

[133] Antônio Cândido de Melo e Sousa, *Introdução ao Método Crítico de Sílvio Romero*, p. 180.

[134] Auguste Comte, *Système de politique positive*, IV, 488–489.

[135] Miguel Lemos, 1st *Circular Anual*, p. 36.

[136] *Ibid.*

[137] *Ibid.*

[138] In Mexico, for instance, Gabino Barreda felt that "after the bloody struggles that had divided Mexico after independence, leading to the most complete anarchy, it was indispensable to find the unification of the Mexican spirit around some new creed, a creed in harmony with the scientific progress of the age, to replace religious ideas" (Samuel Ramos, *História de la Filosofia en México*, p. 119).

[139] Cf. Richmond Laurin Hawkins, *Positivism in the United States*, Chaps. I and II, and *Auguste Comte and the United States*, Chap. 2; A. P. Peabody, *The Positive Philosophy*; Guillermo Francovich, *La Filosofia en Bolivia*, p. 117; *El Pensamiento universitário de Charcas*, p. 229; Artur Ardao, *Filosofia pre-universitária en el Uruguay*, p. 115; Medardo Vitier, *La Filosofia en Cuba*, p. 140. See also Francisco Romero, *Filosofia de la Persona*, pp. 123ff and Leopoldo Zea, *Ensayos sobre Filosofia en la História*, Chaps. VI and VII; José Gaos, *El Pensamiento Hispanoamericano, passim*. Also Alejandro Korn, "Influencias filosoficas en la evolucion nacional" in *Obras Completas*, p. 43.

[140] Leopoldo Zea, *El Positivismo en México*, p. 26.

[141] The lecture was given on May 25, 1881, in the hall of the Congresso Brasileiro, by Teixeira de Sousa, an early collaborator of Miguel Lemos and Teixeira Mendes in the propagation of Positivism. Teixeira de Sousa dropped out of the Positivist group when it broke away from Pierre Lafitte. (See Teixeira de Sousa, *Calderon de la Barca*, 2d ed., 1936, and Miguel Lemos, 1st *Circular Anual*, pp. 38–39.)

[142] Miguel Lemos, *ibid.*

[143] *Ibid.*, p. 40. This series of lectures was also destined to combat the "habitual ineptitudes and calumnies" of Littréism (*ibid.*, p. 39).

[144] Chinese immigration was not exactly a novelty. Rodrigues de Brito had already referred to it in a report on the economic situation of Bahia in 1807. "If, instead of these [the Negroes], we attracted the Chinese and Oriental Indians, as we have done in the past . . ." (cf. Rodrigues de

Brito, *A Economia Brasileira no Alvorecer do Século XIX*, p. 94). Sinimbu's liberal cabinet had taken steps to import "coolies" for working the plantations. Farming, especially in the north, seriously felt the growing threat of the abolitionist wave. Attempts had to be made to think of a substitute for slave labor. "Since the fountain of slavery had been quenched by the Paranhos law, and an abolitionist movement had arisen demanding the complete extinction of the slave regime, a number of estate-owner staesmen, aided by paid journalists, attempted to present the Chinese colonist as the best transition toward free labor. The Ministry of Sr. Sinimbu, organized these attempts by sending a special mission to China, which was a veritable international crime since, under the cloak of a treaty of trade and friendship with the Celestial Empire, it attempted to establish a new slave traffic. A new form of slavery was, in effect, the secret aim of the egoistical landowners, who covered this up with inconsistent sophistries. The Ministry of Sr. Saraiva accepted this part of its predecessor's legacy, for diplomatic negotiations continued to be made with the Court at Peking, which managed, with its proverbial tact, to elude the unconfessed aims of these negotiations" (Miguel Lemos, 1st *Circular Anual*, pp. 44–45).

[145] Cf. Max Fleiuss, *História Administrativa do Brasil*, p. 334, and Gaveiro Costa, *O Visconde de Sinimbu*, Chap. XI.

[146] Apud Miguel Lemos, *Imigração Chinesa*, 2d ed., p. 8.

[147] During the session of September 3, 1879, Deputy Martin Francisco expressed himself as follows: "We must import Chinamen as laborers as a substitute for slave labor, as an immediate measure to save agriculture from ruin" (*ibid.*, p. 9). See also other passages on pp. 9 and 10 and *Anais do Parlamento brasileiro*, 17th legislature (1878 session, Vol. I; 1879 session, Vol. V).

[148] See Miguel Lemos, *Imigração Chinesa*, pp. 11–13.

[149] Salvador de Mendonça, *Trabalhadores Asiáticos* (New York: 1879).

[150] *Ibid.*, pp. 19 and 25. Miguel Lemos, *Imigração Chinesa*, pp. 13–14.

[151] Miguel Lemos, 1st *Circular Anual*, pp. 45–46.

[152] "Chinese Immigration: A message to Their Excellencies the Ambassadors of the Celestial Empire at the Governments of France and England." On July 21, 1881, the following Positivists signed a protest against the theories expressed by Salvador de Mendonça: Miguel Lemos, Generino dos Santos, Teixeira Mendes, Honorino Pinheiro, Teixeira de Sousa, and Calisto de Paulo Sousa. This protest was published in all newspapers of Rio de Janeiro. (Cf. 1st *Circular Anual*, Annex, pp. 83–85.)

[153] Miguel Lemos, 1st *Circular Anual*, p. 47.

[154] *Ibid.* The minimal program for the transition period drawn up by Miguel Lemos included the following points: (1) change to the republican form; (2) statement of the minimum necessary and opportune reforms, to wit: civil registration of births; civil marriage, secularization of cemeteries— all measures preparing the way for the complete separation of Church and state; (3) decree of providential measures to complete the law of September 28, 1871 (*ibid.*, p. 48).

[155] "On my return from Europe," writes Miguel Lemos, "I was warmly

welcomed by Sr. Quintino Bocaiúva. During the course of our interviews, I understood, despite the Sibylline nature of his conversation, that he was disillusioned with militant politics, above all with his journalistic profession; and that he was contemplating a purely practical activity. In my view, these indications, which I considered symptomatic of mental regeneration, were a source of joy, and I attempted to nourish these aspirations. I believed that the excellence of his organization had after all managed to overcome the damages wrought by his career as a journalist and as a democratic orator; and that, convinced at last of the frivolity and unseemliness of such pursuits, he was aspiring to an intellectual and moral renewal, which he had sought in vain in democracy and in the rhetoric of the press and the orator's pulpit. He showed curiosity concerning the new religion, and went so far as to ask me for a list of books that would help initiate him into Positivism." In short, concludes Miguel Lemos, with apostolic ingenuousness, "I believe that the orator and the journalist are in their death throes in his person, and that I shall witness the first glimmerings of a new dawn in his spirit" (Miguel Lemos, 1st *Circular Anual*, p. 49).

[156] In a letter to the editor of the *Gazeta da Tarde*, the Positivist leader wrote: "We do not, and could not, adhere to any Republican directorate because we have an organization of our own, our own ideas and methods; we have our own political system, discipline, and even our own hierarchy, all founded on doctrines entirely different from those adopted by the majority of the Republican party. Our aim (in supporting the Republican political directorate of Rio de Janeiro) was based only on the community of aspirations that links us to other republicans . . ." "Republicans like you, but, with different methods and a different doctrine, the Positivists hope that their just request will be accepted," wrote Miguel Lemos in a request sent to the president of the directorate of the Republican party of Rio de Janeiro and Niterói (1st *Circular Anual*, Annex G, pp. 85–86).

[157] Miguel Lemos, *ibid.*, Annex H, p. 86.

[158] *Ibid.*, pp. 86, 87.

[159] *Ibid.*, p. 87.

[160] *Ibid.*, p. 88.

[161] *Ibid.*, p. 50.

[162] *Ibid.*

[163] Since it was impossible to choose another candidate at the last moment, the Positivists voted according to their personal convictions. We must not forget that at the time they numbered only 53! (Miguel Lemos, *ibid.*, Annex J, pp. 90–91. See also: 11th *Circular Anual*, p. 61.) Miguel Lemos later regretted his intervention during the elections in which Quintino Bocaiúva was a candidate, attributing it to a deviation caused by the direction of Lafitte. After this election the Positivists abstained from voting (cf. 1st *Circular Anual*, p. 47, footnote).

[164] The Positivists commemorated the 24th anniversary of Comte's death on September 5, 1881. At first, like the Lafittist group, the Positivists gave fraternal banquets like those of the Freemasons. Later, Miguel Lemos records,

the banquets were replaced by "family" reunions at the home of the Apostolate leader.

[165] Teixeira Mendes, *A Pátria brasileira,* 2d ed. (1902).

[166] *Ibid.,* p. 43.

[167] *Ibid.,* p. 44.

[168] Gilberto Freyre, *Casa Grande e Senzala,* II, 551.

[169] On Comte's attitude to women, see Teixeira Mendes, *O Ano Sem Par* and Ch. de Rouvre, *L'Amoureuse Histoire d'Auguste Comte et de Clotilde de Vaux,* Chaps. IV–V.

[170] Teixeira Mendes, *A Pátria brasileira,* p. 45.

[171] *Ibid.,* pp. 49–50.

[172] *Ibid.,* p. 50.

[173] *Ibid.,* p. 51.

[174] *Ibid.,* p. 53.

[175] *Ibid.,* pp. 53–54.

[176] *Ibid.,* p. 54.

[177] After the fall of the Liberal party in 1868, the Republicans were joined by a personality of great political and social standing, who was to exercise a considerable influence on the decisions then made. This was Dr. Américo Brasiliense de Almeida Melo. Highly revered in the Liberal party, a man of great culture, he had been nominated president of Paraíba Province by the government of Zacarias de Goís in November, 1866. During the elections for the legislature held in 1867 and 1870, he was elected deputy for São Paulo. In 1867 he gave up the presidency of Paraíba to take his seat in parliament. But in March of the following year he was nominated president of the Province of Rio de Janeiro by the president of the Council. The fact that he was chosen president of the most important political area of the time, the traditional stronghold of the Conservative party, demonstrated the importance of the Paulista deputy and the confidence displayed in him by his fellow court politicians. Following the ministerial crisis of 1868, with the retirement of the Liberal cabinet and the dissolution of the Chamber of Deputies, he immediately handed in his resignation and, calmly and resolutely, he joined the radicals of his province. At the great banquet given in honor of José Bonifácio, Dr. Almeida Melo was seated between the guest of honor and Américo de Campos. Henceforth he was one of the most active and respected radicals of São Paulo. In the following year, two more new elements joined the vanguard of the Radical Club—the two young men from Itu, João Tibiriçá Piratininga and José Vasconcelos de Almeida Prado. Both were rural landowners, owning large numbers of slaves, but they had acquired in their frequent contacts with European life a mentality different from the mentality then prevalent among men of their class. They were democrats and wanted to see the Republican regime installed in Brazil as soon as possible. Almeida Prado, particularly, having recently returned from a two-year trip to the Old World, continually expounded the new ideas he had brought back, recommending the European books and political examples on which they were based." (José Maria dos Santos, *Os Republicanos Paulistas e a*

Abolição, pp. 96–97. Cf. *Cinquentenário da República* [Correio Paulistano, 1940], Chaps. III and XI.)

[178] Teixeira Mendes, *A Pátria brasileira,* p. 55.

[179] *Ibid.*

[180] *Ibid.*

[181] Cf. Afonso Celso, *Oito Anos de Parlamento,* pp. 146, 149–150, 153. Also: A. Ximeno de Villeroy, *op. cit.,* p. 36.

[182] Teixeira Mendes, *A Pátria brasileira,* p. 57.

[183] Cf. Primitivo Moacyr, *A Instrução e o Império,* III, 524.

[184] *Ibid.,* p. 532. Cf. Joaquim Norberto de Sousa Silva, *Criação de una Universidade no Império do Brasil.* "Inquiries made on behalf of His Excellency the Minister and Secretary of State of the Business of Empire, Baron Homen de Melo, by Joaquim Norberto de Sousa Silva, Chief of the Former Secretariat of the Empire and read at the Instituto Histórico during its session of December 5, 1884, by order of H.M. the Emperor."

[185] Miguel Lemos, 1st *Circular Anual,* Annex N. p. 97.

[186] *Ibid.* The project made provision for the university to be placed under the special protection of Dom Pedro II and was to be called: "Imperial Universidade Pedro II" (cf. Moacyr, *op. cit.,* III, 558).

[187] Miguel Lemos, 1st *Circular Anual,* Annex N, p. 97. The protest was also published in *Revue Occidentale,* Paris, March 1, 1881.

[188] Miguel Lemos, 1st *Circular Anual,* Annex N, p. 98. As for secondary education, the Positivists were always opposed to the transplantation of what they termed "the monstrous French baccalaureat system" which was so much to the taste of the Emperor (Miguel Lemos, 2d *Circular Anual,* p. 34). "Mais je ne saurai finir ce paragraphe sans dire que le puissant protecteur de cet entraînement irréfléchi et impolitique vers une imitation de la pédantocratie européenne, c'est l'empereur lui-même. Puisque je n'ai pas épargné le blâme a cette partie du public qui cherche à exploiter, à son profit les préjugés courants sur la science, il ne serait pas équitable d'oublier celui qui, quoique par des motifs plus honorables, encourage de tout son grand pouvoir cette déplorable singerie. Visant au titre de protecteur des sciences et même à celui de savant, notre empereur semble sacrifier souvent les véritable intérêts de notre patrie aux satisfactions puériles d'une vanité inquiète. Nous ne pouvons blâmer, à l'instar de beaucoup de démocrates et constitutionnels naifs, l'intervention personnelle et préponderante de l'empereur dans le direction des affaires publiques: nous savons qu'il n'y a et qu'il ne peut y avoir que des gouvernements personnels. Nous ne saurions blâmer que les mauvais gouvernements personnels" (*ibid.,* pp. 34–35). As for the proposed educational reforms, he wrote: "Chaque nouveau ministre de l'Empire qui arrive au pouvoir se croit obligé de recommencer, à sa manière l'oeuvre de son prédécesseur. Le désir sincère de faire quelque chose d'utile pour son pays n'est pas tout à fait exclu de cette ardeur réformatrice, mais étrangers par leur éducation è toute vue philosophique sur l'ensemble des sciences, nos hommes politiques se laissent conduire par la pédantocracie officielle qui pousse aveuglement à implanter chez nous le régime académique de l'Europe. Cette imitation irrationelle des institutions européenes est le grand danger des jeunes

patries américaines, car le plus souvent on cherche à importer comme un progrès ce qui est déjà ruiné en Europe" (p. 31).

[189] *Ibid.*

[190] *Ibid.*

[191] Teixeira Mendes, *A Universidade*, articles published in the *Gazeta de Notícias*, 1882; I used the book edition, published in 1903. This work, as the author indicates, must be supplemented and corrected by the reading of *A Política e o Regulamento das Escolas do Exército*, published in May, 1890.

[192] Teixeira Mendes, *A Universidade*, pp. 7–8.

[193] *Ibid.*, p. 8.

[194] *Ibid.*, p. 9.

[195] *Ibid.*

[196] *Ibid.*

[197] *Ibid.*, p. 10.

[198] *Ibid.*, p. 11.

[199] *Ibid.*, p. 14. In this section he added: "And it must be noted that the annulling of the present parliament is not the work of the Emperor, but the result of our historic antecedents, and, far from being an evil, it is all to the good. The destinies of nations have not been directed by parliaments, but by men like Henry IV, Richelieu, Frederick II, Danton, Pombal, and others, who made use of the elements they found, including assemblies. Parliamentarianism has hitherto been simply a dictatorship of mediocrities and intriguers; an instrument for every conceivable baseness in the hands of unscrupulous ministers; an obstacle to the public good, when the country has as leaders honest visionaries, men who take to heart the revolutionary fictions. Since parliament is not an end to be reckoned with, the government can proceed as though it did not exist, despite the rhetoric of the constitutional prattlers" (*ibid.*, pp. 14–15).

[200] *Ibid.*, p. 20.

[201] "Our efforts should go into extending as far as possible the influence of the family which will always be the primary educator, whether they like it or not. The conditions necessary to achieve this end, in a free regime, are as follows: (1) Monogamy and the sanctity of the conjugal bond, given civil sanction independent of any doctrine. This is indispensable to the dignity of woman and as a guaranty of spiritual freedom in addition to other factors. (2) Woman's liberation from practical chores to ensure her entire devotion to education. (3) Elevation of the feminine intellectual level to that generally attained by men, so that lack of harmony of opinion be not the cause of family discord, and to ensure the moral ascendancy of woman. No woman can today fail to see that her intellectual inferiority in relation to husband and sons is one of the strongest reasons for the break in the veneration due to her. If these three conditions are fulfilled, woman can take charge of her children's education until puberty; she will have sufficient time and education to do so. Furthermore, she may accompany him during the first stages of his public education. Primary schools and colleges can then be abolished" (*ibid.*, pp. 23–24).

[202] João Camilo de Oliveira Tôrres, *op. cit.*, p. 252.

203 Miguel Lemos, *Ódios Académicos*, p. 3.

204 Teixeira Mendes, *A Universidade*, p. 82.

205 Teixeira Mendes, *Benjamin Constant*, I, 245ff. See also: Miguel Lemos, 1st *Circular Anual*, p. 71, footnote.

206 Gruber, *op. cit.*, Part I, Chap. 2.

207 Miguel Lemos, 1st *Circular Anual*, p. 61. "He felt that in this way he could assure his personal independence without sacrificing any duties to the propagation of the doctrine and his priestly preparation. It was this sense of duty that prevented him from immediately accepting the proposal of certain Brazilian Positivists, who wished to take the initiative in reminding their brethren of their duty to support, according to the precepts of their faith, their spiritual chief. Before accepting this normal situation, he wished to allow time for Positivism to show proof of its correspondence to the urgent needs of our country and for the increase in the number of adherents to permit of fulfillment of his duty by the faithful. Now, as the action of Positivism increased among us, my position became increasingly incompatible with any practically dependent function, both because the business of administration and the demands of propaganda were taking up all my time and because, principally, it was only by becoming an employee of the industrial chiefs that our efforts for their regeneration and our civic attitude toward their blameworthy ventures would render impossible, morally and materially, such functions" (Circular dated December 3, 1881, in 1st *Circular Anual*, p. 62).

208 *Ibid.*, p. 61.

209 *Ibid.*

210 *Ibid.*

211 *Ibid.*, p. 63.

212 Cf. Auguste Comte, *Catecismo Positivista*, trans. Miguel Lemos, pp. 318–319. Auguste Comte, *op. cit.*, IV, 384.

213 Miguel Lemos, 1st *Circular Anual*, p. 63. The letter from Dr. Álvaro de Oliveira read as follows: "Rio, 22 de Bichat de 93 [December 24, 1881]. To My Illustrious Confrère, Sr. Miguel Lemos: I have only now found it possible to reply to your circular letter of 3d inst., received on the 6th. The delay has been the result of the gravity of the matter you raise. I did not want my reply to be affected by the surprise produced in me by this circular. After serious consideration, I have come to the conclusion that I should limit myself to declaring that I do not consider, as my confrère supposes, that it is my duty to contribute to the subsidy mentioned in your circular. Further: this new divergence has made me resolve to carry out the desire I have for some time entertained, of ceasing to be a member of the Positivist Society of Rio de Janeiro. Health and fraternity." [Signed] Álvaro Joaquim de Oliveira. (Apud Miguel Lemos, *op. cit.*, pp. 63–64, footnote.)

214 See Miguel Lemos, 1st *Circular Anual*, pp. 61–69.

215 "Sans revenir spécialement sur la question de la participation des positivistes au pouvoir politique, je vous engage à rèflechir davantage sur un tel sujet, car vous me paraissez être au point de vue logique, à ce sujet, dans une voie dangereuse. Il ne faut pas confondre les principes de la doctrine posi-

tiviste et les règles de sa morale avec les conseils donnés par Auguste Comte à un moment donné et qui n'ont qu'um simple caractère d'opportunité très susceptible de changer avec les temps et les lieux. Faute de tenir compte de cela et de bien distinguer la théorie de la pratique, le sacerdoce bien loin de conquérir l'adhésion publique restera sans action. Sa fonction est de se faire croire et non pas de s'imposer," wrote Pierre Lafitte in his letter to Miguel Lemos of June, 1883 (Miguel Lemos, *3ᵉ Circulaire Annuelle de l'Apostolat Positiviste du Brésil*, p. 17).

[216] *Ibid.*, p. 36.

[217] Miguel Lemos, 8th *Circular Anual* (1889), pp. 30–31.

[218] See letter from Benjamin Constant to Miguel Lemos in 1st *Circular Anual*, pp. 99–100.

[219] *Ibid.*, p. 101.

[220] The actual text reads as follows: "I know perfectly well that in your position as official teacher and public servant, we could only ask you for moral and material support. I never ask people for more than they can give in their situation; hence I shall never importune you with tasks that might embarrass you" (reply to Álvaro de Oliveira dated December 24, 1881, in *ibid.*, p. 68).

[221] Letter from Benjamin Constant to Miguel Lemos, *ibid.*

[222] Miguel Lemos, *2ᵉ Circulaire Annuelle de l'Apostolat Positiviste du Brésil* (1882). The introduction is dated April, 1884. I used the 2d (French) edition of the 2d *Circular Anual*.

[223] *Ibid.*, p. 8.

[224] *Ibid.* In 1878 the English group, led by Richard Congreve, the former Anglican priest, had broken with Lafitte. Even in the French group, Audiffrent and others had thought of asking Lafitte to give up the leadership of Positivism. Other Positivists belonging to the orthodox group were the amateur Frederick Harrison, George Eliot (Miss Mary Anne Evans), the famous English novelist; James Cotter Morrison, and others, who were not always sufficiently orthodox. (Cf. Gruber, *op. cit.*, Chap. III.)

[225] The circular for 1883 was published in July, 1885. I used the 2d edition published in French in May, 1908.

[226] Miguel Lemos, *Pour notre maître et pour notre foi—le positivisme et le sophiste Pierre Lafitte*, 2d ed. (1936). The epigraph for this work is from Canto XXXII of Dante's *Inferno*: "Alla tua onta, io portero de te vere novelle . . ."

[227] Cf. Auguste Comte, *Catecismo Positivista*, pp. 17 and 23.

[228] Miguel Lemos, Appendix A (*Circulaire Collective*) in *3ᵉ Circulaire Annuelle de l'Apostolat Positiviste du Brésil* (1883), pp. 103–112. The circular was signed by Miguel Lemos and the following: Teixeira Mendes, José Pereira de Araújo (artisan), José Mariano de Oliveira (agriculturist), Gabriel de Campos (medical student), Cipriano de Carvalho (engineer), Álvaro da Veiga (public servant), André Werneck (public servant), Augusto de Moura (medical student), Godofredo José Furtado (engineer and professor at the São Paulo Normal College), José Leão Perreira Souto (public servant), Calisto de Paula Sousa (engineer), Antônio da Silva Jardim (law-

yer and professor at the São Paulo Normal College), Sabastião Humel (public teacher), Américo Diamantino Lopes (geographer), Samuel Rodrigues de Almeida (engineering student), Bernardino Cândido de Carvalho (public servant), Benedito Vieira de Campos (engineering student), Luís de Brito (engineering student), Joaquim Bagúeira do Carmo Leal (doctor), Feliciano José Alves Gonzaga (public servant), A. C. Ferreira Paula (engineering student), Alfredo Coelho Barreto (professor at the Rio de Janeiro Normal College), Aníbal Falção and Joaquim de Ol. Marcondes, supported the circular although they did not sign it.

[229] Cf. 3d *Circular Anual,* Annex E, p. 119.

[230] João Pernetta, *Os Dois Apóstolos,* I, 53.

[231] Miguel Lemos, 3d *Circular Anual,* p. 1.

[232] *Ibid.,* p. 2. Godofredo Furtado had already refused the principalship of the São Paulo Normal College since the post was one of those generally given to persons trusted by the dominant political party (*ibid.,* p. 3).

[233] Letter from Pierre Lafitte to Miguel Lemos dated February 20, 1883, in *ibid.,* pp. 4–5.

[234] *Ibid.*

[235] *Ibid.,* p. 8.

[236] Letter to Lafitte dated March 24, 1883, in *ibid.,* p. 9.

[237] Miguel Lemos, 2d *Circular Anual,* pp. 9–10.

[238] Miguel Lemos, *O Positivismo e a Escravidão Moderna,* pp. 40–41.

[239] *Ibid.,* p. 41.

[240] *Ibid.*

[241] Cf. José Feliciano, *Les Habilités de M. Lemos: Épigraphe.*

[242] Miguel Lemos, 3d *Circular Anual,* p. 12.

[243] "Il faut bien que nous ayons, sous ce rapport une conduite bien nette, le grand débat qui préoccupe aujourd'hui le pays étant justement l'abolition de l'esclavage" (letter to Pierre Lafitte in Miguel Lemos, 2d *Circular Anual,* p. 13).

[244] Letter from Lafitte to Miguel Lemos dated June 8, 1883, in Miguel Lemos, 3d *Circular Anual,* p. 17.

[245] *Ibid.*

[246] *Ibid.,* p. 18.

[247] *Ibid.,* pp. 18–19.

[248] *Ibid.*

[249] Letter from Miguel Lemos to Lafitte (July 14, 1883) in *ibid.,* pp. 20–23.

[250] On this question of Lafitte's legacy, see Miguel Lemos, 3d *Circular Anual,* p. 169.

[251] "Extraits d'une lettre adressée à un positiviste français," dated November 12, 1883, in Miguel Lemos, *ibid.,* Doc. F., p. 162.

[252] *Ibid.* Refuting the opinion of a French Positivist who had pronounced judgment on the disagreeable consequences that would follow the break between the Brazilian and Parisian groups, even though he realized the defects of Lafitte's leadership, Miguel Lemos wrote: "My dear Sir: In your letter you depict in masterly manner the defects of the skeptical environ-

ment in which you find yourself, but permit me to say that although you describe it so well, you seem no less subject to its influence" (Miguel Lemos, *ibid.*, p. 162). He added, seeking to justify his attitude: "We are playing our normal role—reacting through the preponderance given by southern peoples to the moral point of view, against the deviations to which may succumb that skeptical environment, not yet entirely free from Voltaire" (*ibid.*, p. 165). "Lettres à M. le Docteur Robinet," in Miguel Lemos, *ibid.*, Doc. G, pp. 173ff.

²⁵³ *Ibid.*, pp. 25–26 and 103–112.

²⁵⁴ *Ibid.*, p. 26.

²⁵⁵ *Ibid.*, p. 29.

²⁵⁶ In his zeal, Congreve had soon broken away from the London Positivist group and later (1876) from Lafitte himself. Some French Positivists who supported his ideas thought of asking Lafitte to "abdicate" from his position as Comte's successor, and of placing Richard Congreve at the head of the Religion of Humanity. (Cf. Gruber, *op. cit.*, pp. 155–156.) Audiffrent broke away from Lafitte in 1877.

²⁵⁷ Miguel Lemos, 3d *Circular Anual*, pp. 42–77. (Cf. João Pernetta, *Os Dois Apóstolos*, I, 56–59.)

²⁵⁸ Cf. n. 216, above.

²⁵⁹ Cf. *Testament d'Auguste Comte*, 2d ed., pp. 154 and 172. "Dépourvu de venération et d'initiative, il ne sera jamais qu'un dilettante, ayant tout juste assez d'énergie pour gagner sa vie," Comte had said of Laffitte shortly before his death, according to Dr. Audiffrent. Cf. Miguel Lemos, 4th *Circular Anual* (1884), p. 7.

²⁶⁰ Miguel Lemos, *ibid.*, p. 75.

²⁶¹ In Miguel Lemos, 3d *Circular Anual*, Appendix A, p. 103.

²⁶² *Ibid.*, p. 107.

²⁶³ *Ibid.*, p. 106.

²⁶⁴ *Ibid.*, pp. 107–108.

²⁶⁵ *Ibid.*

²⁶⁶ *Ibid.*, p. 108.

²⁶⁷ *Ibid.*, p. 109.

²⁶⁸ *Ibid.*

²⁶⁹ Miguel Lemos, 4th *Circular Anual*, p. 97.

²⁷⁰ In Miguel Lemos, 3d *Circular Anual*, Doc. B., p. 123. Dr. Robinet ascribed the break to the lack of experience of the "American neophytes." He believed, however, that once time and experience had matured their "exaggerated faith and calmed their tempestuous ardor" they would return to the right path (*ibid.*, p. 121). Harrison interpreted the circular as an act of "puerile bigotry or Tartuffian hypocrisy" (p. 122), and E. S. Beesly, president of the Positivist Society of London, said: "Mr. Lafitte gave Mr. Lemos wise counsels that the latter should have followed instead of quoting texts as if the works of Auguste Comte were some sort of Bible" (p. 122).

²⁷¹ Miguel Lemos, "Positivisme et Lafittisme (réponse à la protestation lafittienne contre la Circulaire Collective du Centre Positiviste Brésilien)" in 3d *Circular Anual*, Doc. C., p. 138.

[272] *Ibid.*, p. 139.

[273] *Ibid.*, p. 141: "When one thinks that the new sect proclaiming its insurrection in the very house of the Master, that it took place in that sacred apartment in which each object recalls such venerable memories, that it was there that the rebels held their conventicle and uttered their blasphemies, one is convinced that the continuation of M. Lafitte at the head of the Parisian group, which is meant to serve as a link between all the other groups, is not only a disaster for the present and the future of our doctrine—it is a profanation" (*ibid.*, p. 141).

[274] *Ibid.*, p. 142.

[275] Jorge Lagarrigue, "Religion de l'Humanité" in Miguel Lemos, 3d *Circular Anual*, Doc. D., p. 148.

[276] Oliveira Viana, *O Ocaso do Império*, p. 123.

[277] It was likewise in 1883 that the Positivists protested for the first time against "sanitary despotism." Professor Domingos Freire, a professor of the Faculty of Medicine in charge of research into the causes of yellow fever, had claimed to have discovered in the earth of the grave of a victim of this disease a new microbe, *Cryptococcus xantogenicus*. (This discovery, incidentally, annoyed a number of the professor's medical colleagues.) As Miguel Lemos humorously said, the professor was to glide with his microbe into academic immortality. In the light of his "discovery," the professor recommended that cemeteries be removed to far beyond city limits, and that all corpses be cremated. The Positivists opposed this practice, which had been condemned by Comte. Another intervention by the Positivists in public affairs was on the question of slavery. They expressed themselves in favor of complete abolition with no compensation for the slave owners. On this occasion, Ribeiro de Mendonça published in the *Província de São Paulo* (now the *Estado de São Paulo*) an article ("A Diretoria do Positivismo no Brasil," 9th Year, No. 2550, September 19, 1883), criticizing Miguel Lemos and recommending abolition with compensation, supporting his case by referring to ideas expressed by Lafitte in the periodical *Politique Positive* (1872). In Miguel Lemos's reply, published in the 2d *Anual Circular*, Doc. E., he expressed himself entirely in favor of emancipation in the terms desired by the abolitionists.

The 1884 *Circular* was still almost entirely taken up with the question of the break with Laffitte. In it was announced the Feast of the Virgin Mother, which had always been recommended by Comte but which had never anywhere taken place.

[278] In 1886, when Dantas presented his project setting a five-year period for the complete abolition of slavery, the Positivists merely sent this minister a letter of support. When, at the same time, a commission was appointed to consider the reform of the educational system, with the strong possibility that it would recommend compulsory education, Miguel Lemos and Teixeira Mendes (who from this time on began to collaborate more actively with the Positivist executive) protested against this "fashionable panacea which constitutes a serious violation of spiritual freedom." Cf. A. *Obrigatoriedade e a Nova Reforma da Instrução Publicá* (1886), Miguel Lemos apud *Rapport*

pour l'Année 1886, p. 15. They wrote: "We declare that if such a monstrosity becomes the law, we prefer to suffer any legal persecution, including the imprisonment threatened for offenders, rather than allow our children to receive any education other than that approved by their mothers and ourselves." Temporal power, according to the teachings of the Master, should have no authority to interfere in these matters. It was also in this year that Sebastião Hummel, a public teacher of S. José dos Campos, who had joined the Republican Club in 1873, resigned from this club because the "sociocracy" proclaimed by Positivism differed from the "democracy" preached by the Republicans. The Master himself had said that a conservative takes a considerable risk when he aligns himself to the revolutionaries.

[279] Cf. Alexandre Zévaès, *Histoire de la III⁰ République,* pp. 258–261 and Chap. XII. Also: Adrien Dansette, *Le Boulangisme.*

[280] Cf. Zévaès, *op. cit.,* p. 259. This song, with music by Désormes and lyrics by Delormel and Garnier, enjoyed an enormous success at the time. The last stanza, typical of the Parisian spirit, goes:

> Ma soeur qui aim' les pompiers
> Aclam' ces fiers trompiers;
> Ma tendre épouse bat les mains
> Quand défilent les Saint-Cyriens;
> Ma belle-mere pouss' des cris
> En r'luquant les Spahis;
> Moi j'faisais qu'admirer
> Not'brav' générale Boulanger.

But anti-Boulangism also produced its songs, among them one by Jules Jouy:

> Maigres prolétaires,
> Modestes héros,
> Gare aux militaires,
> Aux "brav'généraux"!
> L'fusil, la giberne
> N'aiment pas les outils;
> L'peuple, à la caserne,
> N'eut jamais d'amis.
> Quand dans la ru' nous descendrons tout blêmes,
> Seuls nous nous battrons;
> Chassant les patrons,
> Dans les fournils nous f'rons not'pain nous-mêmes,
> Et pour le manger
> Nous nous pass'rons bien d'Boulanger.

(Zévaès, *op. cit.,* pp. 249–300.) Cf. M. Baumont, *L'Essor industriel et l'impérialisme colonial,* pp. 132–136.

[281] Miguel Lemos, 7th *Circular Anual,* pp. 5–6.

[282] Cf. Jorge Lagarrigue, *La Dictature republicaine d'après Auguste Comte* (with a letter to General Boulanger, pp. 3–6).

[283] Jean Jaurès, "L'Ideal de Justice" in *La Dépêche de Toulouse* (November 3, 1889), apud Zévàes, *op. cit.*, p. 329.

[284] João Camilo de Oliveira Tôrres, *op. cit.*, p. 84.

[285] João Pernetta, *Os Dois Apóstolos,* II, 43.

[286] Miguel Lemos, 8th *Circular Anual,* p. 26.

[287] *Ibid.*, p. 27. In Miguel Lemos's view, the imperial family was typical of the theocratic caste. But in Brazil, this caste had been grafted onto "a society that formed itself almost exclusively by the transplantation of the popular elements of an occidental nation at a time when the theological military regime was exhausted; the consequence was that this caste remained isolated and hence came its weakness. This weakness was aggravated by the miscegenation that characterizes our nation and the struggles between the people and the dynastic caste before and after independence. For all these reasons, it is clear that the monarchy, with us, could not be what it still is on the European continent, where the 'royal caste' is supported by the 'noble caste,' by tradition and the clergy. Thus, even in its weakened condition, the monarchy could only survive in Brazil while there was a privileged class exploiting another kind of caste—the slave caste. The slave owners naturally became the allies of the throne: one privilege protected the other" (Teixeira Mendes, "A Propósito da Agitação Republicana" in *Mistificação Democrática e a Regeneração Social,* p. 21).

[288] Miguel Lemos, 8th *Circular Anual,* p. 26.

[289] *Ibid.*, pp. 29–30.

[290] Miguel Lemos and Teixeira Mendes, *A Liberdade Espiritual e a Organização do Trabalho: Considerações Histórico-Filosóficas sôbre o Movimento Abolicionista.* (*Spiritual Freedom and the Organization of Labor: Historical and Philosophical Considerations on the Abolitionist Movement*), p. 5.

[291] *Ibid.*

[292] *Ibid.*, p. 21.

[293] *Ibid.*

[294] "It is our duty to express ourselves once more, albeit in passing, against the panacea of the small estate, which, together with European immigration, is usually preached as the real solution of our social problem. The favor found by this idea results above all from Western precedent and the struggle against the aristocracy, precedents which should not be imitated by other countries, on pain of going against the natural evolution of modern society which tends increasingly toward a concentration of wealth. A thorough examination of the subject cannot be undertaken within the limits of a footnote. We will limit ourselves to recalling the fact that the small estate has the serious drawback of creating a lower middle class—egoistical, mean, allied to the privileged classes in the exploitation of the worker, serving as an obstacle, by its interposition between the rich and the proletariat, to the establishment of the normal relations that must be established between these two groups. This was why Auguste Comte, in his manifesto to Tsar Nicholas I, concludes his meditations on the topic of the recent abolition of slave labor in Russia by

warning the Russian reformer against the dangerous imitation we have pointed out" (*ibid.*, p. 39, n. 4).

295 *Ibid.*, p. 22.

296 *Ibid.*, p. 23.

297 Auguste Comte, *Cours de philosophie positive* apud Roger Mauduit, *Auguste Comte et la science économique*, p. 209.

298 *Ibid.*, p. 221.

299 Oliveira Viana, *O Ocaso do Império*, p. 120.

300 Miguel Lemos and Teixeira Mendes, *A Liberdade Espiritual e a Organização do Trabalho*, p. 43, n. 6.

301 Ximeno de Villeroy, *op. cit.*, p. 165.

302 Teixeira Mendes, "Nota a Propósito da Abolição do Juramento Parlamentar" in *A Mistificação Democrática*, p. 13.

303 Teixeira Mendes, "A Propósito da Agitação Republicana" in *A Mistificação Democrática*, p. 19.

304 *Ibid.*, p. 20.

305 *Ibid.*, p. 27.

306 Some of Comte's principal exhortations were adopted, in a modified form, in the constitution of the State of Rio Grande do Sul (July 14). In 1940, C. Tôrres Gonçalves published a lecture in which he had compared certain aspects of the Constitution of July 14 and the Charter of 1937 (November 10) with the ideas of Auguste Comte. See Tôrres Gonçalves, *As Constituições de 14 de Julho e de 10 de Novembro*, p. 19; also, pp. 23, 24, 29, 31–32.

307 Teixeira Mendes, "A Propósito da Agitação Republicana" in *A Mistificação Democrática*, p. 28.

308 José Maria Bello, *História da República*, p. 31.

309 Afonso Celso, *Oito Anos de Parlamento*, p. 153.

310 Vicente Licínio Cardoso, "Benjamin Constant, o fundador da República" in *À Margem da História da República*, p. 301.

311 Celso, *op. cit.*, p. 146.

312 Bello, *op. cit.*, pp. 37–38.

313 Cardoso, *op. cit.*, pp. 301–302.

314 *Ibid.*

315 Geonísio de Mendonça, *Os Positivistas na Fundação da República*, p. 2.

316 Teixeira Mendes, *Benjamin Constant*, I, 359.

317 *Ibid.*, pp. 361–362.

318 Sérgio Buarque de Holanda, *Raízes do Brasil*, p. 120.

319 Teixeira Mendes, *Benjamin Constant*, I, 361–362.

320 Miguel Lemos, 9th *Circular Anual*, p. 7; see Annexes A and B. (Richard Congreve, *O Advento da República no Brasil*, pp. 69–71 and Juan Enrique Lagarrigue, *A Influência Positivista na Revolução brasileira*, pp. 73–74.)

321 Teixeira Mendes, *Benjamin Constant*, I, 361.

322 Cf. Zimeno de Villeroy, *op. cit.*, Chaps. 2, 3, and 4. Also Max Fleiuss, *op. cit.*, pp. 403–489 and Teixeira Mendes, *Benjamin Constant*, II, 209–239.

323 Miguel Lemos, 9th *Circular Anual*, p. 12.

324 *Ibid.*, pp. 7–8.

325 Max Leclerc, *Cartas do Brasil*, p. 90.

326 Miguel Lemos, 9th *Circular Anual*, p. 12.

327 *Ibid.* Cf. Teixeira Mendes, *Benjamin Constant*, I, 367.

328 Cf. Luís Viana Filho, *A Vida de Rui Barbosa*, p. 142 and João Mangabeira, *Rui, O Estadista da República*, p. 36.

329 Miguel Lemos, 9th *Circular Anual*, p. 14.

330 *Ibid.*, p. 13.

331 Manuel Bonfim, *O Brasil Nação*, II, 179.

332 George Friedmann, *Leibniz et Spinoza*, p. 17.

333 Sérgio Buarque de Holanda, *op. cit.*, p. 120.

334 Miguel Lemos and Teixeira Mendes, "Mensagem ao General Deodoro" in 9th *Circular Anual*, Annex C, pp. 75–78.

335 *Ibid.*, pp. 30–31.

336 Miguel Lemos, "Ao Povo e ao Govêrno da República" in 9th *Circular Anual*, Annex D, p. 79.

337 *Ibid.*, p. 80.

338 *Ibid.*

339 *Ibid.*, pp. 80–81.

340 Miguel Lemos, *Liberdade de Imprensa*; Teixeira Mendes, *Pela Federação*; Miguel Lemos and Teixeira Mendes, *A Política Positiva e a Grande Naturalização*; Teixeira Mendes, *A Incorporação do Proletariado na Sociedade Moderna.*

341 Teixeira Mendes, *A Bandeira Nacional* (2d ed.). Cf. Eduardo Prado, *A Bandeira Nacional*; Miguel Lemos, *A Questão da Bandeira* and Custódio José de Melo, *O Govêrno Provisório e a Revolução de 1893*, t. 2, I, 11–24. Cf. Miguel Lemos, 12th *Circular Anual*, pp. 36–37.

Comte's disciples managed to introduce into the national flag the motto "Order and Progress," which led to many protests at the time; they also managed to make a start on solving the problem of the separation of Church and state and managed to have the old forms of official correspondence ("May God keep Your Excellency") replaced by the formula "Health and Fraternity," although this reform lasted only a short time. They also succeeded in introducing the use of "citizen" and the use of the second person plural as a form of address [*vôs:* a more formal, archaic address than the common *vôcé*—Trans.]. These forms are still sometimes used today, although they are now somewhat on the decline.

In January, 1890, it was rumored in Europe that the new South American republic had adopted the Positivist calendar. When Rui, who had never had much sympathy for Positivism, heard of this rumor, he wrote in the following terms to the delegate of the Brazilian Treasury in London: "Give the lie to this rumor. It is absolute nonsense. No one has ever thought of such a thing, nor would anyone dare propose it to the government." (João Mangabeira, *Rui, o Estadista da República*, p. 43. Cf. Miguel Lemos, *Le Calendrier positiviste et M. le ministre des finances.*) The Positivists never forgave Rui for having said that Comte's calendar was nonsense.

342 Miguel Lemos, 9th *Circular Anual*, pp. 19–20.

³⁴³ Cf. the "Dispositions relating to the moral basis of the Positivist Apostolate in Brazil," which appear on all title pages of the Apostolate's circulars.

³⁴⁴ Teixeira Mendes, *Benjamin Constant,* I, 406–407. "We are convinced that he took a sincere interest in the cause of the proletariat, and it is beyond doubt that he was devoid of the majority—perhaps of all—of the bourgeoisocratic prejudices. One proof of this is that he did not hesitate to allow his family to mix with the poorer classes since, at the opera, he sat in the gallery seats usually sought only by members of the popular classes or by students (*ibid.,* p. 407).

³⁴⁵ Teixeira Mendes, *A Incorporação do Proletariado na Sociedade Moderna,* p. 5.

³⁴⁶ *Ibid.,* p. 6.

³⁴⁷ *Ibid.*

³⁴⁸ *Ibid.,* p. 7.

³⁴⁹ *Ibid.*

³⁵⁰ *Ibid.,* pp. 8–9.

³⁵¹ *Ibid.,* p. 10.

³⁵² *Ibid.,* p. 11.

³⁵³ The principal items of this draft labor law presented by Teixeira Mendes covered the abolition of task work, the institution of wages, with one part fixed and the other variable; a seven-hour day with free Sundays and holidays (including the holidays provided for in the workers' religions); the provision of two weeks' annual leave, and provision for it to be impossible to fire, without just motive and fair trial, a worker who had been employed for more than seven years. The whole of the fixed salary should be paid if the worker is sick and if he retires at the age of 63 or because he is incapacitated because of disablement. On the death of the worker, the widow (as long as she did not remarry and in accord with the Positivist theory of eternal widowhood) and children under 21 years of age should receive two-thirds of the worker's salary. Apprentices should only be indentured after the age of 14 and should remain in the factories only four hours on five days of the week, the apprenticeship to last until the age of 21. (Cf. Teixeira Mendes, *A Incorporação do Proletariado na Sociedade Moderna,* pp. 13–16.)

³⁵⁴ Rui Barbosa's Speech in the Federal Senate, November 16, 1904, apud Teixeira Mendes, *Uma Rectificação: A ditadura Republicana e o Positivismo,* p. 3. See Aurelino Leal, *História Constitucional do Brasil,* pp. 216–224.

³⁵⁵ Cf. Teixeira Mendes, *Uma Rectificação . . .* p. 4.

³⁵⁶ *Ibid.*

³⁵⁷ *Ibid.,* p. 5.

³⁵⁸ *Ibid.,* p. 6.

³⁵⁹ *Ibid.*

³⁶⁰ Miguel Lemos and Teixeira Mendes, *Bases de Uma Constituição Política Ditatorial Federativa para a República brasileira,* p. 1.

³⁶¹ *Ibid.*

³⁶² *Ibid.,* pp. 6–7.

³⁶³ José Veríssimo, *Estudos de Literatura brasileira,* 1st ser., p. 73.

³⁶⁴ "It seems that the monarchists were right when they opposed our prop-

aganda alleging that we were not prepared for the republic: the life of our republic seems to confirm their judgment, which had always seemed to me false" (letter from Prudente de Morais to Bernardino de Campos, dated August 22, 1894, in Silveira Peixoto, *A Tormenta que Prudente de Morais Venceu*, p. 122).

[365] Veríssimo, *op. cit.*, p. 57.

[366] Miguel Lemos, 10th *Circular Anual*, pp. 15–16.

[367] Aurelino Leal, *História Constitucional do Brasil*, p. 204.

[368] Miguel Lemos, 10th *Circular Anual*, p. 14 (cf. Annex B, p. 54).

[369] Cf. *Correio Paulistano*, January to June, 1890.

[370] *Ibid.*, March 22, 1890. This newspaper began to publish, on March 25, 1890, a series of replies from the most important people of the capital on the question of a "constitution without a constituent assembly." Among others, there are replies from Cerqueira César, Adolfo Pinto, Dr. Jaguaribe, João Monteiro, Godofredo Furtado, Macedo Soares, Alfredo Ellis, Paulo Bourroul, Pereira Barreto. The latter wrote: "Plebiscite is obvious and is in the logic of the political metaphysics now dominant. It flatters the vanity of the people and has in its favor its attraction for the majority: it imposes itself, therefore, in the name of the people. Observation and experience of our own past and that of other countries, however, shows that the plebiscite is simply a way of evading the truth of the matter, of parading before the unthinking masses a false accord between incompatible principles, and consequently it is no more than a superb instrument of corruption in the hands of despots" (*Correio Paulistano*, April 10, 1890). Cf. Cruz Costa, "A Confusão era Geral . . ." in *Jornal de São Paulo*, April 14, 1945 and "Positivismo e Constituição" in *Fôlhas da Manhã*, March 6, 1945.

[371] "Manifesto do Presidente da República aos Brasileiros" in Alm. Custódio José de Melo, *O Govêrno Provisório e a Revolução de 1893*, t. 1, I, 60.

[372] Miguel Lemos and Teixeira Mendes, *Representação ao Congresso Nacional*, p. 3. One of the defenders of Positivist ideas in the Constituent Assembly was Júlio de Castilhos, who was a member of the "Committee of 21." Among the other members were: João Pinheiro, José Higino, Ubaldino do Amaral, Amaro Cavalcanti, and Leopoldo de Balhões. Castilhos was defeated and voted separately—accentuating the importance attributed to federation by many Republicans. Otelo Rosa, *Júlio de Castilhos*, pp. 116–118.

[373] Miguel Lemos and Teixeira Mendes, *Representação . . .* , p. 4.

[374] *Ibid.*, p. 5.

[375] *Ibid.*, p. 6.

[376] *Ibid.*, p. 7.

[377] *Ibid.*

[378] *Ibid.*

[379] *Ibid.*

[380] *Ibid.*, p. 8.

[381] Miguel Lemos and Teixeira Mendes, *A Política Positiva e a Liberdade Bancária*, p. 3.

[382] Miguel Lemos and Teixeira Mendes, *Representação . . .* , p. 9.

[383] Miguel Lemos, 10th *Circular Anual*, p. 17.

384 Cf. João Mangabeira, *Rui, o Estadista da República*, pp. 44–45. Luís Viana Filho, *A Vida de Rui Barbosa*, pp. 140–142; A. B. Ramalho Ortigão, *A Moeda Circulante*, Chap. X.

385 Miguel Lemos, 10th *Circular Anual*, p. 18.

386 Miguel Lemos and Teixeira Mendes, *A Política Positiva e a Liberdade Bancária*, p. 7.

387 Auguste Comte, *Correspondance inédite*, 2d ser., p. 111, apud Roger Mauduit, *Auguste Comte et la science économique*, p. 75.

388 Miguel Lemos and Teixeira Mendes, *Representação* . . . , p. 10.

389 *Ibid.* It was the "financial question" that led to the dissidence between Positivism and the new republic. Rui Barbosa, author of the project creating the banks of issue henceforth became the constant target of Positivist criticism. "The author of this financial alchemy has lost nothing except the good opinion of the public. Having retired from the administration, together with his companions, for reasons that we do not wish to go into at this point, he is now a great banker and continues to make interminable speeches and write enormous reports to demonstrate his political and financial genius and his immaculate morality. In this respect, and without having especially in mind the former minister we refer to, we must confess that the eloquence of our political lawyers continues to have some devoted admirers; on the other hand, public good sense is beginning to free itself, thanks to painful and costly experiences confirmed by the growing penetration of Positivist influence, from the irresistible attraction exercised by the literary ignorance of our encyclopaedic bachelors" (Miguel Lemos, 10th *Circular Anual*, pp. 18–19).

390 Miguel Lemos and Teixeira Mendes, *Representação* . . . , p. 24.

391 *Ibid.*, p. 11.

392 *Ibid.*

393 *Ibid.*

394 *Ibid.*, p. 12.

395 *Ibid.*, pp. 13–14.

396 *Ibid.*, p. 13.

397 *Ibid.*, p. 24.

398 *Ibid.*, p. 14.

399 *Ibid.*, p. 26.

400 *Ibid.*, p. 14.

401 *Constituição Política do Estado do Rio Grande do Sul*, June 14, 1891 (Title IV, Art. 71, §5).

402 Miguel Lemos and Teixeira Mendes, *Representação* . . . , p. 26.

403 *Ibid.*, pp. 15–16.

404 The Positivists pleaded for the establishment of monogamy according to the Positivist conception; for testatory freedom and banking freedom. It is true that they did not achieve all their aims (testamentary liberty, the liberty of adoption and the liberty of banking), but they did achieve many amendments asked for (professional freedom, for instance, which in their opinion would result in the immediate abolition of academic privileges). (Cf. Miguel Lemos, 10th *Circular Anual*, p. 11, n. 2.) At the time of the first Republican Constituent Assembly, the Positivists were also fervent

defenders of the freedom of the Catholic Church. "Art. 5 of Decree No. 119A of January 7, 1890, drafted by Rui Barbosa, left in force the 'dead hand' legislation which weighed on the benefits of the Catholic clergy. This was directly opposed to the provisions of the initial project for a Law of Separation between Church and State, submitted to the provisional government on December 9, 1889, by Positivist Minister of Agriculture Demétrio Ribeiro," writes Ivan Lins (*Católicos e Positivistas*, p. 6). Felácio dos Santos, referring to the freedom of the Church in an article published in *O Jornal* on October 8, 1928, wrote: "As we know, thanks to the votes of the Positivists, the Catholic deputies managed to put through the freedom of the Church in the Constituent Assembly, which passed by only six votes" (apud Lins, *op. cit.*, p. 7). See also: Miguel Lemos, 10th *Circular Anual*, p. 17, n. 1.

[405] Miguel Lemos, *ibid.*, pp. 20–21.

[406] *Ibid.*

[407] Teixeira Mendes, *A Política Positiva e o Regulamento das Escolas do Exército*, p. 2.

[408] Cap. S. Sombra in *Diretrizes*, November 15, 1939, apud João Camilo de Oliveira Tôrres, *op. cit.*, p. 49.

[409] Oliveira Tôrres, *ibid.*

[410] Eduardo Prado, *Fastos da Ditadura Militar no Brasil*, p. 67.

[411] Teixeira Mendes, *A Política Positiva e o Regulamento das Escolas do Exército*, p. 1.

[412] Teixeira Mendes, *Benjamin Constant*, I, 348.

[413] Teixeira Mendes, *A Política Positiva . . .* , p. 1.

[414] Teixeira Mendes, *Benjamin Constant*, I, 348–349.

[415] Auguste Comte, *Système de politique positive*, IV, 416.

[416] Teixeira Mendes, *A Política Positiva . . .* , p. 34.

[417] *Ibid.*, p. 37.

[418] *Ibid.*, p. 38.

[419] *Ibid.*, p. 39. (Cf. Eduardo Prado, *op. cit.*, pp. 277ff.)

[420] *Ibid.*, p. 47.

[421] In addition to the "occasional articles" nearly always written by Miguel Lemos, the Positivist literature of propaganda and protest is abundant. In this period alone, the following works may be mentioned: Miguel Lemos, *A Liberdade Espiritual e o Exercício da Medicina*; J. Bagueira Leal, *O Regime Republicano e o livre Exercício da Medicina*, which deals with the freedom of practicing the medical profession. In 1891, there were protests against a project for the regulation of domestic work. Comte's disciples, who believed that any regulation of work was tyrannical, opposed this project (cf. Miguel Lemos, 10th *Circular Anual*, Annex F, p. 65). For their opposition to compulsory education proposed in the project of educational reform drafted by Ramiz Galvão, cf. Miguel Lemos and Teixeira Mendes, *A Obrigatoriedade do Ensino e o novo projeto de Reforma de Instrução Pública*. In their view, compulsory education, besides being one of the "fashionable panaceas," was "a despotic interference by the civil authorities in a realm outside their power, wounding to the most sacred prerogatives of parents" (cf. Miguel

Notes to Pages 82–175 355

Lemos, 10th *Circular Anual*, Annex F, p. 64). They also protested against the Code of Municipal Bylaws (cf. Miguel Lemos, *O Novo Código de Posturas Municipais*); against the imprisonment of "a reputedly false priest," an imprisonment demanded by the Vicar of Rio de Janeiro who was in this way making an attempt against civil liberty; against the persecution of fortune tellers, tramps, beggars, fetishists, and spiritualists; against the imprisonment of a priest who had preached an anti-Republican sermon; against the attack made on the newspaper *A Tribuna* (formerly the Viscount of Ouro Prêto's *Tribuna Liberal*); against the optional nature of the Holy Week celebrations; against the statute of Dom Pedro I, and so on. (Cf. Miguel Lemos, 10th *Circular Anual*, appendices and occasional articles published in 1891, *passim*.)

[422] Miguel Lemos, 11th *Circular Anual*, p. 7.

[423] In a letter to Hadery, Auguste Comte had written: "Our political advent requires the collaboration of public opinion, together with the worthy preparation of our own statesmen; power should be freely given to us by those in possession of it, when they realize that they have exhausted their resources against anarchy; any possibility of a violent rise to power is, for us, absurd and contrary to our principles. I in no way desired, nor even approved, the disturbances of 1830 and 1848, although I forced myself to make use of them after their consummation; if Positivists conduct themselves in this way, they will also foresee tempests, and will endeavor, in the first place, to avoid them, and finally to make use of them; but always considering themselves freely associated to the Western governments and never giving their support to any opposition—they will command the involuntary respect of the opposition and will never be considered the rivals to power of any political party" (Auguste Comte, *Correspondance inédite*, 2d ser., pp. 341–342).

[424] Miguel Lemos, *Artigos Episódicos*, p. 45.

[425] Minas Gerais and the State of Rio de Janeiro had promulgated their constitutions in the name of "Almighty God" (cf. Miguel Lemos, *ibid.*, pp. 35, 87).

[426] Miguel Lemos, 11th *Circular Anual*, p. 30.

[427] See Miguel Lemos and Teixeira Mendes, *A Última Crise: O Golpe de Estado de 3 de Novembre e a Revolução de 23 do Mesmo Mês*, pp. 11–14.

[428] *Ibid.*

[429] In his "Manifesto to the Brazilian People" ("Manifesto do Presidente da República aos Brasileiros"), Deodoro said: "Impassive, I witnessed the long gestation of this work [the transfer to the legislature of powers which he considered to be of the essence and nature of the executive], filled with dangers that piled up as reactionary ideas, lack of respect for national traditions, the spirit of abstruse philosophical sects, innovations, and Utopias began to penetrate this organism destined to serve the needs of practical good sense, defined by the great ideas of freedom, law, justice, and order" (apud Max Fleiuss, *História Administrativa do Brasil*, p. 456).

[430] Miguel Lemos, 11th *Circular Anual*, pp. 30–31.

[431] *Ibid.*, p. 31.

[432] Miguel Lemos and Teixeira Mendes, *A Última Crise . . .* , p. 4.

[433] *Ibid.*, p. 5.

[434] *Ibid.*, p. 9.

[435] *Ibid.*, p. 10.

[436] *Ibid.*

[437] *Ibid.*, p. 21.

[438] *Ibid.*, pp. 23–24.

[439] Richard Congreve, Annual Address at the Church of Humanity (1862) apud Miguel Lemos, 12th *Circular Anual*, p. 12.

[440] Miguel Lemos, 12th *Circular Anual*, p. 21.

[441] Teixeira Mendes, *Circular Anual*, 1903, p. 29.

[442] *Ibid.*, 1908, p. 42.

[443] It is worth transcribing the letters exchanged between the "Apostolate" and the Archbishopric of Rio de Janeiro. On December 13, 1892, Miguel Lemos addressed the following letter to the Bishop of Rio de Janeiro: "Our Master having recommended to his disciples that it was their duty to contribute to the free maintenance of the Catholic cult, once it had become separated from the state, in order to express in this way the homage we all owe to the immense services rendered to civilization by Catholicism and the services it continues to render in the realm of morals, I beg you to accept, with this intention in mind, the sum enclosed, a modest contribution which we wish henceforth to make annually for the purpose stated. Kindly accept our respectful greetings." In reply, Dom José Pereira de Sá Barros, the bishop who was removed from Rio de Janeiro in 1894 (cf. Miguel Lemos, 13th *Circular Anual*, pp. 28–32), wrote as follows: "Bishop's Palace: December 15, 1892. To Dr. Miguel Lemos. Illustrious Sir: We have received your communication dated 13th inst., in which you tell us that the Master of Positivism recommended that his disciples should contribute toward the free maintenance of the Catholic cult when it becomes separate from the state, as a homage universally due to the immense services rendered to civilization by Catholicism and the services it continues to render in the domain of morals, asking us, at the same time, to accept your offering, which you wish to continue to make annually, in the spirit intended. Without meaning to disregard the good intentions of this homage to Catholicism, which in the past civilized nations and which continues on the path of true morals, we wish respectfully to fulfill the duty of thanking you for your offer, with the declaration that we cannot accept it. You will, therefore, kindly permit us to return the generous amount you so kindly sent." (Miguel Lemos, 12th *Circular Anual*, pp. 79–80, Doc. J.)

[444] *Ibid.*, p. 52.

Notes to Chapter 6
(Pages 176–202)
Ideas during the Last Years of the Nineteenth Century

[1] Miguel Lemos, 13th *Circular Anual do Apostolado Positivista do Brasil,* p. 17.

[2] *Ibid.*

[3] Cf. *Diário Popular* of December 10, 1893, which reproduces Saldanha da Gama's "manifesto." Also *O Comércio de São Paulo* of December 12, 1893.

[4] Miguel Lemos, *op. cit.,* p. 18. He says that Saldanha had used an absurd expression in his "manifesto": "the alliance of sectarianism, militarism, and Jacobinism." He also says that "because of the bad effect produced by this document [the manifesto], the revolutionaries and their supporters tried to spread the rumor that it had been altered by the progovernment newspapers. But the official copy kept in the archives of the Villegagnon fortress confirmed the authenticity of the published text" (*ibid.,* p. 18, n. 22). Cf. Rocha Pombo, *História do Brasil,* X, 384 and Tobias Monteiro, "Introdução" in *O Presidente Campos Sales na Europa;* José Maria Bello in his *História da República* (p. 180) cites the following passage from the "manifesto": "Accepting the situation [revolt] imposed on me by my patriotism, I spurned secret plotting, taking full account of the responsibilities I assumed. I have openly allied myself to my brothers who, for the past year in the plains of Rio Grande do Sul and for the past three months in the bay of this capital, have been valiantly fighting for the liberation of the Brazilian homeland from militarism, aggravated by the alliance of sectarianism and the most unbridled Jacobinism."

[5] The Positivists were mistaken. Shortly afterward, Colonel Valadão, "the marshal's former secretary and confidant" was responsible for introducing into the Chamber of Deputies a proposal for the alteration of the national flag, as we have seen. As Tobias Monteiro says, Colonel Valadão was merely the spokesman, simply "a pseudonym for a person known only too well." (Cf. Tobias Monteiro, *O Presidente Campos Sales na Europa,* p. lii and Miguel Lemos, 13th *Circular Anual,* pp. 49, 52, and 76–77.)

[6] "História da Revolta de 6 de Setembro," published in *O Comércio de São Paulo,* p. 45. The authorship of this article is attributed to Alcindo Guarabara.

[7] *Ibid.*

[8] Cf. Bello, *op. cit.,* pp. 185–197. Also Joaquim Nabuco, *A Intervenção Estrangeira durante a Revolta de 1893.*

[9] Cf. Bello, *op. cit.,* p. 181.

[10] "Saldanha da Gama, who enjoyed exceptional prestige among his own class, remained aloof from intrigue after Deodoro's resignation, which he had worked so hard to avoid. He was absorbed in the administration of the

Naval School and, in his heart of hearts, was disgusted with the republican disorder, which offended his hierarchical and aristocratic concept of life and later led him to make the great error of supposing that the restoration of the monarchy might be possible." (Bello, *op. cit.*, pp. 169–170.) Cf. Tobias Monteiro, *Pesquisas e Depoimentos*, pp. 361 and 363.

[11] Bello, *op. cit.*, p. 168.

[12] *Ibid.*, p. 169.

[13] Apud Otelo Rosa, *Júlio de Castilhos*, pp. 158–159.

[14] Miguel Lemos, 13th *Circular Anual*, p. 65.

[15] *Ibid.*, pp. 67–68.

[16] *Ibid.*, p. 69.

[17] *Ibid.*

[18] *Ibid.*, p. 70.

[19] *Ibid.*, pp. 70–71.

[20] Monteiro, *op. cit.*, p. xxxiv.

[21] Miguel Lemos, *op. cit.*, p. 77. According to Henrique Alberto Carlos, the Positivist from Rio Grande do Sul who founded the Coöperative Club of Pôrto Alegre, "the people of Rio Grande prefer anything, even the monarchy, to the government of Júlio de Castilhos." It was Henrique Alberto Carlos who warned Miguel Lemos to abstain from making any "manifestation in favor of the Castilhos government," since otherwise he would alienate the sympathies of sincere Positivists living in Rio Grande. To this friendly warning, meant to shelter him from ill-feeling, Miguel Lemos once more gave a reply characteristic of his convictions. "The whole of Rio Grande, the whole of Brazil, the entire West, nay, the entire world could disagree with me, but while I remained convinced that I was faithfully following the teachings of Positivism, all their disagreement would have not the least effect on me. Besides, only someone whose common sense is disturbed by passion or vulgar prejudice could consider that in the appreciation of public matters your friends have greater ability than I, if the question is considered in the light of Positivist criteria." (Miguel Lemos, *op. cit.*, pp. 78–79.)

[22] João Pernetta, *Os Dois Apóstolos*, II, 4.

[23] Cf. Miguel Lemos and Teixeira Mendes, *A Secularização dos Cemitérios e o Privilégio Funerário*, which contains a number of works by the two Positivist leaders. See also: Miguel Lemos, 13th *Circular Anual*, pp. 28–31, and Annex C, pp. 57–58. Cf. João Cruz Costa, "O Positivismo na República" in *Revista de História*, Nos. 15–16 (1953).

[24] Cf. Pernetta, *op. cit.*, III, 4 and "Bases da Organização do Apostolado Positivista do Brasil," in 17th *Circular Anual*, p. 7.

[25] Miguel Lemos, 13th *Circular Anual*, p. 55.

[26] Oto Maria Carpeaux, "Notas sôbre o Destino do Positivismo," in *Rumo* (1943), I, 16.

[27] *Ibid.*, p. 12.

[28] Cf. H. Höffding, *Histoire de la philosophie moderne*, II, 275.

[29] Graça Aranha, *O Meu Próprio Romance*, p. 152.

[30] *Ibid.*, p. 154.

[31] Höffding, *op. cit.*, p. 304.

³² *Ibid.*

³³ *Ibid.*

³⁴ *Ibid.*

³⁵ "In romantic philosophy, the concept of evolution was equally predominant. The intimate connection of the particular with the whole was stressed and existence was conceived as a series of degrees, each of which expresses the substance of this world in progressively higher forms. The application of the concept of evolution was, however, purely ideal" (*ibid.*, pp. 456–57).

³⁶ W. R. Sorley, *A History of English Philosophy*, p. 267.

³⁷ *Ibid.*, p. 268.

³⁸ Clóvis Beviláqua, "Repurcussão do Pensamento Filosófico sôbre a Mentalidade brasileira" in *Esbocos e Fragmento*, p. 25.

³⁹ Sérgio Buarque de Holanda, *Raízes do Brasil*, p. 118.

⁴⁰ *Ibid.*

⁴¹ Konstantin Oesterreich, "Die deutsche Philosophie des XIX Jahrhunderts und der Gegenwart," in F. Ueberwegs, *Grundriss der Geschichte der Philosophie*, IV, 309.

⁴² "The urbanization of the Empire with the consequent change from rich plantation house to town house, and later even to cottage, the fragmentation of the slave quarters which became shanty towns, no longer for escaped Negroes in the heart of the jungle but for the free Negroes of the cities, this process, which constituted the Brazilian phenomenon of 1830 (and was later accentuated by the campaign for abolition), made it almost impossible to maintain the balance of the old days when the slave owners had enjoyed almost complete supremacy over all other elements of society, even over the viceroys and the bishops. Social status was beginning to be achieved on other grounds. It centred on Europe, but it was now a bourgeois Europe from whence new styles of life reached us, opposed to the old rural and patriarchal patterns: tea, cabinet government, beer, Clark's shoes, toast. Men's clothes became less colorful and more uniformly gray; there was a greater taste for the theater, which began to replace the church; the four-wheeled carriage, which began to replace the horse; the walking stick and parasol, which began to replace the swords of captain and sergeant-major worn by the former naval lords. And all these status symbols began to be considered the patent of a new aristocracy and a new nobility: the aristocracy of the town house, and the nobility of the doctors and bachelors. The new values were incarnated principally in the bachelor of law, whether or not he was the legitimate son of the sugar lord or plantation owner, the graduate who had studied in Europe—Coimbra, Montpellier, Paris, England, Germany—as the result of influence exerted by some more cosmopolitan Freemason relative. Sometimes the young men of the new urban middle class, sons and grandsons of pedlars, with the new status of their European education, returned on terms of social equality with the sons of the oldest and most powerful landed families." (Gilberto Freyre, *Sobrados e Mucambos*, pp. 302–303.) Cf. Humberto Bastos, *A Marcha do Capitalismo no Brasil*, pp. 211–12.

⁴³ The liberal professions in Brazil "enjoyed the same traditional prestige as in the motherland. In nearly all periods of Portuguese history, the bache-

lor's degree was almost as valuable as a letter of recommendation for the highest public posts." (Buarque de Holanda, *op. cit.*, pp. 116–17).

[44] Friedrich Engels, *Ludwig Feuerbach et la fin de la philosophie classique allemande*, p. 24.

[45] Georges Friedmann, *La Crise du progrès*, p. 247.

[46] Höffding, *op. cit.*, p. 523.

[47] August Messer, *La Filosofia en el Siglo XIX*, p. 170.

[48] Ernest Haeckel, professor at the University of Jena, developed the ideas of Darwin with such unusual audacity and dogmatism for scientific and university circles, that Darwin was led to write to his daring disciple in 1868, "your boldness makes me tremble."

[49] Messer, *op. cit.*, pp. 183–84.

[50] Cf. Sílvio Romero, *Outros Estados da Literatura Contemporânea*, p. 207 et seq.

[51] When Feijó was in Itu with the Fathers of the Patrocinate, he started a course in moral and rational philosophy (logic and ethics) using his own compendium, compiled from "authorities hitherto unknown in this country." (Octávio Tarquínio de Sousa, *Diogo Antônio Feijó*, p. 29.) In his work on Feijó, Dr. Egas reproduces the section of Feijó's *Noções Preliminares da Filosofia*, which contains a definition of Kant. (Eugénio Egas, *Diogo Feijó*, II, 25.) On the subject of Kant's impact in Brazil, see Clóvis Beviláqua, *Revista da Academia brasileira de Letras*, No. 83 (1929), pp. 5–14, and articles by Professors Laertes Ramos de Carvalho and Miguel Reale, published respectively in *O Estado da São Paulo* (June, July, and August, 1949) and *Fôlha da Manhã* (July, 1949). On the subject of Feijó and Kantism see Miguel Reale, *A Doutrina de Kant no Brasil*. Martin Francisco, who was a teacher of geometry and French also gave lessons on "eclectic philosophy, with vestiges of Kant," around 1830. (Aluísio de Almeida, "Aula de Retórica em São Paulo" in *Estado de São Paulo* of September 20, 1949.)

[52] Cf. João Ribeiro, "A Filosofia no Brasil" in *Revista do Brasil*, VI:22 (1917), 255.

[53] Cf. Almeida Magalhães, *Farias Brito e a Reação Espiritualista*.

[54] Buarque de Holanda, *op. cit.*, p. 113.

[55] Hermes Lima, *Tobias Barreto*, p. 1.

[56] "Impatient at finding himself shut up in the seminary, and full of homesickness and nostalgia, he created a scandal by playing a popular tune on the guitar, thereby breaking the silence that reigned in that household." (Lima, *op. cit.*, p. 5.)

[57] Graça Aranha, "Discurso na Academia brasileira," in *Revista da Academia brasileira* (January, 1911), p. 183.

[58] Omer Mont'Alegre, *Tobias Barreto*, p. 252.

[59] *Ibid.*, p. 254.

[60] Leonel Franca, S.J. *Noções de História da Filosofia*, p. 467.

[61] Tobias Barreto, *Obras Completas*, Vol. III: *Filosofia e Crítica*, p. 179.

[62] Tobias Barreto, *ibid.*, p. 117.

[63] "According to modern trends, credit for the philosophical reaction is usually given to Miguel Lemos and Teixeira Mendes in their Littréist period

from 1874 or 1875 onward, but in 1868 Tobias had published in the same spirit his vibrant criticism of the complex of metaphysical-Catholic doctrines personified by St. Thomas Aquinas and also his famous reply to Godofredo Autran, who had hastened to the defense of the old ideas under the title *Teologia e Teodiréia não São Ciências"* (Sílvio Romero, *Evolução da Literatura brasileira (Vista Sintética)*, p. 130–31). See also: Tobias Barreto, *Obras Completas*, Vol. II: *Polémicas*; in the article entitled "Crônica dos Disparates" the name of Auguste Comte is cited a number of times. Comte's influence on the northern group was short-lived. His categorical tone did not seem to suit Tobias's temperament. In the preface to the 1883 edition of *Estudos Alemães*, Tobias confessed himself "a restless spirit, who many times in his Jacob-like struggle against earth demons in the absence of heavenly angels, had to emerge, albeit victorious, not maimed, but sceptical."

[64] Tobias Barreto, *Estudos Alemães* (1883), preface.

[65] *Ibid.,* p. 3.

[66] *Ibid.*

[67] Considered as proved beyond a doubt is the claim to the priority of Tobias Barreto in the propagation of modern general criticism and, more specifically, in the criticism of philosophy. He has no priority in the propagation of the complex of ideas, intuitions, and ways of thinking and feeling, to which the name "Germanism" has, rightly or wrongly, been attributed. This honor has been claimed for Carlos de Koseritz, the illustrious German who lived and died in Rio Grande do Sul, having left an indelible imprint on the press of this state. However great may be our veneration for the remarkable author of *Roma perante O Século*, we cannot allow the triumph of views which he would have been the first to repudiate. It was generally known, and up to a short while ago often repeated as a censure and grave criticism, that the Germanist current had been introduced into our literature by Tobias Barreto, seconded in part by myself. Writers in Rio de Janeiro and journalists of the imperial court tried to be witty at the expense of this attempt, calling it the "Teuto-Sergipan School." In revenge, I nicknamed the opponents the "Gallo-Fluminense School." Tobias Barreto himself refers partly to this fact in his introduction to Estudos Alemães. He writes: "The school, if it deserve the name of school, which certain Rio de Janeiro writers have called the 'Teuto-Sergipan' school, with the clear intention of producing a comic effect by associating Germany with the native province of the two most tireless promoters of Germanism in Brazilian literature, not realizing that in this way they have conferred on them and on their province an immense honor, whose exact value only the future can estimate. Such a school still has to contend with the difficulties and embarrassments that years and years of struggle have not managed to remove." It was an idea everywhere known and repeated, notoriety for the creation of the expression "Teuto-Sergipana" being attributed to Carlos de Laet. Meanwhile in Rio Grande do Sul, an interesting article was published recently by a woman writer of this province; it concerns the literary personality of my late lamented friend, the illustrious journalist Carlos de Koseritz. The charming disciple of this sadly missed writer claims for him the honor of having created the Germanist

school. She does not value any more highly than I do the memory of Carlos de Koseritz, and no one is more ready than I to confer on that remarkable journalist the place he deserves in Brazilian literature. But there is no need to mount him on false legs in order to confer on him a title that is not, and never could be, his: he was not the creator of Germanism in Brazilian literature. This aspiration, for the time being, begins and ends with Tobias Barreto alone. I myself played a minor role, and in some senses an opposed one. (Sílvio Romero, *Evolução da Literatura brasileira*, pp. 115–117.)

[68] Sílvio Romero, *op. cit.*, pp. 120–21.

[69] Nietzsche, *Lettres choisies*, p. 295.

[70] Edmond Scherer, *Mélanges d 'histoire religieuse*, apud Virgilio de Sá Pereira, *Tobias Barreto*, pp. 85–86. Cf. O. Gerard, *Edmond Scherer, passim.*

[71] Sílvio Romero, *op. cit.*, p. 123. "Historic truth compels me to record that the celebrated Sergipan writer was preceded, albeit in a limited way, by two Brazilians who had for many years been enthusiasts of German literature and who, in articles written both in Portuguese and German, called the attention of the public to the science of this great nation. These two writers were Ernesto Ferreira França, who was a professor in the Faculty of São Paulo and Manuel Tomás Alves Nogueira, who was a lecturer at the Pedro II College. Both had been educated in Germany. To these names must be added that of Luís Antônio Vieira da Silva, who was a senator of the Empire. His work, however, was on a smaller scale. But these writers only touched on the subject incidentally, and on few occasions. For my own part, it was in Rio de Janeiro during 1863–1867, before my meeting with Tobias, that my enthusiasm for the German people was aroused, stimulated by the lessons of Dr. Francisco Primo de Sousa Aguiar, my geography and history master, who was also a celebrated teacher of certain branches of higher mathematics at the Military School." (Sílvio Romero, *op. cit.*, pp. 120–21.)

[72] Despite this, Tobias did not always extol the virtues of his "beloved Germany," as he called it. In *Questões Vigentes* he said: "I do not find German politics entirely to my taste. From this point of view, my beloved Germany is like a woman whose beauty is marred by enormous breasts" (*Obras Completas*, Vol. IX: *Questões Vigentes*, p. 42). He was also opposed to the scheme for German immigration supported by Taunay. (Cf. *Obras Completas*, "Cartas a Sílvio Romero" in Vol. X: *Varios Escritos*.)

[73] Leonel Franca, *op. cit.*, p. 468.

[74] Lima, *op. cit.*, p. 106.

[75] *Ibid.*, p. 107.

[76] Tobias Barreto, *Questões Vigentes*, pp. 47–48.

[77] "Nach Noirés's *Monismus*," writes Konstantin Oesterreich, "der vielfach nach Spinoza und Schopenhauer gebildet ist, kommen der Welt zwei einzige, ganz identische Eigenschaften zu, als innere und als äussere, Empfindung und Bewegung, aus welchen durch Entwicklung alle besonderen Daseinsformen hervorgegangen sind, aus welcher die Vernunft sich selbst wie alles Übrige herzuleiten berechtigt ist" (Oesterreich, *op. cit.*, p. 330). Ludwig Noiré (1829–1889), who became famous in Brazil and remained unknown in Europe, was professor at the Mainz Gymnasium in 1829. He

wrote a number of works, among them: *Die Welt als Entwicklung des Geistes* (1874), *Bausteine zu einer monistischen Weltanschauung* (1874). *Der monistische Gedanke: Konkordanz der Philosophien Schopenhauers, Darwins, R. Mayers und L. Geigers* (1875), *Das Werkzeug und seine Bedeutung für die Entwicklungsgeschichte der Menschheit* (1876), *Die Lehre Kants und der Ursprung der Vernunft* (1882). F. Ueberwegs, *Grundriss der Geschichte der Philosophie*, IV, 330.

[78] Tobias Barreto, *Questões Vigentes*, pp. 44–45.

[79] These ideas found an heir in the philosophy of Farias Brito. Cf. Farias Brito, *Finalidade do Mundo, passim.*

[80] Tobias Barreto, *Questões Vigentes*, p. 45.

[81] Tristão de Ataíde, *Estudos*, 1st ser., p. 381.

[82] *Ibid.*

[83] Tristão de Ataíde quotes a passage from Tobias in which the latter writes, "The society in which I live is certainly not strong enough to affect me; for my part, I am not strong enough to divert it from its path, to recreate it in my own image. Hence the eternal incompatibility between us, hence that tragic 'something' in my life, that would have made of me an unhappy misanthropist had not nature endowed me with an expansive temperament, a thousand times more disposed toward pleasure than toward pain." (Tobias Barreto, *Obras Completas*, Vol. IV: *Discursos*, p. 174 apud Tristão de Ataíde, *op. cit.*, p. 385.)

[84] Cf. Tobias Barreto, *Obras Completas*, "Cartas a Sílvio Romero" in Vol. X: *Varios Escritos.*

[85] Tristão de Ataíde, *op. cit.*, p. 389.

[86] Sílvio Romero himself gave the reply to those who considered him the new St. Paul to Tobias's Christ, when he wrote: "Tobias and I, who provided Brazil with an example of the most complete spiritual brotherhood, were two workmen, friendly but independent, who tried to work without any rivalry and without submission on the part of either; we worked in harmony, but independently." (Sílvio Romero, *Ensaio de Filosofia do Direito*, p. xx.) And again: "I am not prepared to allow my place in the intellectual history of Brazil to be purloined. Tobias influenced all who worked with him in the three phases of his life, through his ability to react, his critical intuition, his combative temperament, and not through any combination of fixed ideas, reduced to a system. I, for instance, who was always his great friend and admirer, had different ideas on the more serious doctrines." (Sílvio Romero, *Outros Estudos de Literatura Contemporânea*, p. 210.) In the same work, he writes: "He was in favor of 'Germanism' as something to be imitated by Brazilians; I only accepted the historical influence of the race and its critical spirit. In literature he preferred foreign subjects, I preferred national ones. . . . In philosophy, I was in favor of Herbert Spencer, having sought a sure path. Tobias did not admire this remarkable genius, to whom he opposed Haeckel and Noiré, having gone through Vacherot, Schopenhauer, and Hartmann" (pp. 210–211.).

[87] "The harsh and disillusioned temperament of Sílvio Romero has not yet allowed full justice to be done to his great work of literary construction.

The hatred and ill-will he aroused by the virulence of his criticism has not yet entirely disappeared. Many will not forgive him the rudeness with which he treated Machado de Assis, for instance. Others are irritated by his idolatry of Tobias Barreto. These two extremes—the severity toward Machado and the enthusiasm for Tobias—constitute, in the opinion of many, sufficient reason to doubt his impartiality and his criteria. He is considered by some to be simply a vigorous polemicist, somewhat rude in manner, of a limitless irreverence, disorderly and undisciplined, but no more. This is not so. All these judgments are wrong. Sílvio was more than a daring polemicist. He was a studious man, a tireless worker, a pioneer along little known paths, hacking away at the undergrowth of our ignorance, and, up to a point, he was also a renovator of the Brazilian intellect. It was he who gave to criticism the serious attitude which it has not yet lost, and he who gave to the study of literary history the nationalistic imprint which it has increasingly acquired. If he was not the first, although I believe he was, he was certainly the most important of those who looked to ethnography for elements with which to understand Brazilian spiritual life. No one has shown with greater warmth the importance of the role of poetry, folk tales, popular traditions, and folklore in the spiritual formation of Brazil. When he appeared, Romanticism reigned in literature. As a European importation, even in its cult of the American Indian, Romanticism drew from Sílvio the most vigorous attack right from the time of his earliest appearances in public life. His exalted patriotism could not tolerate the fact that our romantics, unlike the European, had made no attempt to resurrect the past in its most enduring aspects. He could not conceive that they had despised our old popular tunes and our old lyricism, with its epigrammatic vein." (Plínio Barreto, "Livros Novos" in *Estado de São Paulo,* April 30, 1938.)

[88] Almeida Magalhães, "Sílvio Romero" in *Estado de São Paulo,* August 17, 1938.

[89] Sílvio Romero, preface to Tobias Barreto, *Obras Completas,* Vol. II: *Polêmicas,* pp. xxii–xxiii.

[90] Sílvio Rabelo, *Itinerário de Sílvio Romero,* p. 126.

[91] *Ibid.* "Sa préoccupation essentielle," writes Deschoux of Brunschvicg's concept of philosophy, "semble avoir été de délivrer l'intellectualisme des systématisations arbitraires que en deformient l'esprit et en limitaient la portée. Toujours il s'est défendu d'avoir un système, d'opposer système à système." (Marcel Deschoux, *La Philosophie de Léon Brunschvicg,* p. 9.)

[92] Sílvio Rabelo, *op. cit.,* p. 127.

[93] Sílvio Romero, *O Evolucionismo e o Positivismo no Brasil,* p. 5.

[94] Cf. Léon Brunschvicg, *La Modalité du jugement,* p. 68. "Kant lui-même a entrevu la necessité logique de l'affirmation, et pourtant, it n'a pas voulu s'y résoudre explicitement. Il a donné une métode plutôt qu'il n'a pas laissé un système, et c'est par là que son oeuvre a été souverainement féconde comme l'avait été celle des Socrates et des Descartes" (*ibid.*). "L'intention d'établir la primauté de la raison sur l'expérience n'aboutit, trop souvent, qu'à mettre en relief le contraste entre le résultat et l'intention. C'est l'expérience qui va devant; la raison marche derrière comme elle peut et quand

elle peut." (Léon Brunschvicg, *L'Orientation du rationalisme*, apud Deschoux, *op. cit.*, p. 10.)

[95] Farias Brito, immediately after graduating as a lawyer, became prosecutor in Viçosa and later in Aquiraz. In 1888 he was invited to become government secretary by Caio Prado. After the proclamation of the republic, he was an opposition candidate for the Constituent Assembly, but was defeated in the election. In 1891, Farias Brito became secretary to the government of Ceará in the administration of General José Clarindo de Queirós who was shortly afterward deposed by Floriano. See Jônatas Serrano, *Farias Brito,* pp. 62f. Also, Laerte Ramos de Carvalho, *A Formação Filosofica de Farias Brito* (São Paulo: 1951).

[96] Some people have thought that Farias Brito's thinking was influenced by Spinoza. I fail to see a reason for such an affirmation. Berdyayev says that in all philosophers there is a trace of Spinoza's ideas. Farias Brito was certainly fascinated by the Jewish philosopher, but it is an exaggeration to say that he was a Spinozist. (*See* Cruz Costa, *A Filosofia no Brasil*, p. 104, and Sílvio Rabelo, *Farias Brito ou Uma Aventura do Espírito*, pp. 94f.)

[97] Cf. Jônatas Serrano, *op. cit.*, p. 81.

[98] "The end of philosophy is morality." (F. Brito, *A Finalidale do Mundo*, Part I, pp. 35, 40.)

[99] Sílvio Rabelo, *Farias Brito on Uma Aventura do Espírito*, p. 230.

[100] F. A. Lange, *Histoire du matérialisme*, Vols. II, IV, Chap. IV, *apud* Farias Brito, *A Finalidade do Mundo*, I, 5.

[101] Farias Brito, *op. cit.*, p. 8. "Faced by this somber spectacle, increasingly bitter doubts oppress the spirit of all thinkers, while the masses become filled with dread as though they foresaw the approach of some danger threatening to engulf civilization! We feel that for everyone the ground shifts under his feet. Despite this, pursuing their headlong careers from moment to moment, the triumphant turn to the multitude, crying: 'Fear not. This is but the weariness of civilization, this is but the sound of civilization in action.' But confusion grows greater, the number of the unhappy is legion, and everywhere the hurricane of revolution begins to swell with growing violence. And in this terrifying confusion, when self-interest becomes the only criterion of action, when corruption like an avalanche is swallowing up all in its insatiable path, what matters to each individual is to survive, and each man for himself becomes the counsel of experience in this veritable shipwreck of humanity. The survival of the fittest leads to the progress of the whole—this is the application to society of the law of natural selection, the basic concept of Darwinism. But if the end is survival, the means becomes of little importance; hence it is not to be wondered at that in the breast of contemporary civilization, in protest against the contrast between the triumph of some and the misery of others—the latter in the great majority—there should emerge, like the hysteria of despair, this monstrosity of propaganda through accomplished fact, this incomprehensible madness to which the name of 'anarchism' is given." (Farias Brito, *A Finalidade do Mundo*, Vol. II: *A Filosofia Moderna,*" pp. 20–51. Cf. Jônatas Serrano, *op. cit.*, pp. 146–47.)

[102] Farias Brito published the following philosophical works: *A Finalidade*

do Mundo (3 vols. 1895–1899 and 1905); *A Verdade como Regra das Ações* (1905); *A Base Física do Espírito* (1912); and *O Mundo Interior* (1914). The first was published in Ceará; the second in Belém and the last two in Rio de Janeiro.

[103] Farias Brito, *A Finalidade do Mundo,* III, 3.

[104] For Farias Brito, "the anarchy of the modern world would become more and more profound if the Positivist religion were of a kind to influence the destiny of humanity. The inanity of this so-called religion is proved by the isolation to which it has been reduced, and, if one still sought a concrete proof of its absurdity, one need only consider the detestable influence it somehow managed to exercise on our country after the establishment of the republic." (Farias Brito, *A Finalidade do Mundo,* II, 23.) See also: Jackson de Figueiredo, "Da Crítica do Positivismo na Obra de Farias Brito" in *Algumas Reflexões sôbre a Filosofia de Farias Brito,* pp. 91–163, and Gilberto Freyre, *Perfil de Euclides e Outros Perfis,* p. 158.

[105] Farias Brito, *A Finalidade do Mundo,* I, 18. See Jackson de Figueiredo, *Algumas Reflexões . . . ,* p. 225.

[106] "The only persons interested in contemporary anarchy, which is the sole fountainhead of their pretensions and their ephemeral successes, are those who had thought that Positivism was mere philosophical dilettantism having no real effect on private and public conduct, those who had ingenuously believed that the new synthesis was merely a fashionable formula and would permit the same old habits and pretensions to be retained—all those who initially applauded the doctrine ('incurable rhetoricians, aspirants to some little glory in the literary or scientific world') and became steadfast enemies of Positivism when they realized that this doctrine aimed at an effective regeneration, in the name of a system that would discipline the intelligence and the personality for the ultimate preponderance of the social good. . . . The progress of the doctrine had nothing to fear, however, from this hostile minority, whose moral significance is equaled only by their intellectual nullity." (Miguel Lemos, 11th *Circular Anual* [1882], pp. 13–14.)

[107] Farias Brito, *Finalidade do Mundo,* II, 20.

[108] *Ibid.*

[109] João Ribeiro, "A Filosofia no Brasil" in *Revista do Brasil,* VI: 22 (1917), 255. João Ribeiro is right when he says that Farias Brito was an "irresolute and unbelieving spiritualist" who "took the path of faith." Farias Brito wrote: "All current religions are dead: they are kept up merely as a tribute to the traditions of the past, but are no longer alive in the minds of the masses, nor do they have the strength to make peace among nations. Nevertheless, with the decisive energy of a profound and invincible conviction, I maintain that religion is the first and most important of all public needs, since without religion there can be no stability, no order in society. The conclusion I reach is this: a new religion must be created, otherwise contemporary society cannot be preserved and will inevitably dissolve and die." (*Finalidade do Mundo,* I, 121.) See also: Farias Brito, *O Mundo Interior,* p. 102; Leonel Franca, *op. cit.,* pp. 518–519; Luís Delgado apud Sílvio Rabelo, *Farias Brito ou Uma Aventura do Espírito,* pp. 217–218.

[110] Cf. "Carta de Farias Brito," in Jackson de Figueiredo, *op. cit.*, pp. 225–226.

[111] Freyre, "Um Mestre sem Discípulos" in *Perfil de Euclides e Outros Perfis*, p. 156, and "Carta de Farias Brito," in Figueiredo, *op. cit.*, pp. 216–217.

[112] Cf. Figueiredo, *op. cit.*, pp. 167–186 and 189–226; Almeida Magalhães, *Farias Brito e a Reação Espiritualista*, p. 4.

[113] Farias Brito, *A Base Física do Espírito*, p. 60. Many of Spencer's admirers became students of mathematics, and Spencer—who was an engineer —had many disciples among engineers in Brazil. In August, 1889, Farias Brito left for Rio de Janeiro, intending to matriculate at the Polytechnic school, not because he wished to acquire an engineering diploma but simply because he wanted to make a thorough study of the general part of the engineering course, in preparation for further development of certain ideas he hoped to pursue, more directly related to mathematics and particularly to mechanics. Cf. Farias Brito, *Finalidade do Mundo*, I, 1.

[114] Farias Brito, *A Base Física do Espírito*, p. 61.

[115] *Ibid.*, pp. 212–215.

[116] Tasso da Silveira, "A Consciencia brasileira" in *À Margem da História da República*, p. 232. Vítor says that Farias Brito's work "in a general sense corresponds curiously to the spiritual tendencies of our country." (Nestor Vítor, *Farias Brito*, p. 91.)

[117] Tasso da Silveira, *op. cit.*, pp. 232–233. Italics mine.

[118] Sílvio Rabelo, *Farias Brito ou Uma Aventura do Espírito*, p. 230.

[119] *Ibid.*, p. 229.

[120] "Farias Brito expresses in a moving way the most anguished phase in human thought at the dawn of the twentieth century. His work, as a whole, gives us the impression of a navigator sailing on tempestuous seas who has realized that all the sailing charts are covered with amendments, erasures, and troubling alterations, and so useless as guides for steering the ship to safety. . . . Farias Brito's work must be made known to all Brazilians. It marks the end of one age and the beginning of another; it marks the end of one philosophical concept and the dawn of a new philosophy. It establishes the limits between scientific experimentalism and that zone which cannot be penetrated by laboratory research, being comprehensible only through contemplation and the interpretation of the human spirit itself. Farias Brito was not merely the greatest Brazilian thinker and philosopher; he was the greatest in the Americas, and one of the most important figures of his time." Plínio Salgado, "Farias Brito" in *Cadernos da Hora Presente*, No. 4 (September, 1939), pp. 191–92.

[121] Freyre, *Perfil de Euclides e Outros Perfis*, p. 155.

[122] Almeida Magalhães, "É Preciso Reeditar Farias Brito," in *Cadernas da Hora Presente*, I (May, 1939), 60. "In personal relationships Farias Brito was enchantingly simple. His manner of speech was slow and precise, underlined by a slight smile in which was patent the infinite goodness of his soul." (Testimony of Arnaldo D. Vieira in Jônatas Serrano, *op. cit.*, p. 308.)

[123] Freyre, *op. cit.*

[124] "Carta de Farias Brito a Jackson de Figueiredo," published in O País on November 12, 1915, and reproduced in Jackson de Figueiredo's Albumas . . . , pp. 225–226.

[125] Ibid. Italics mine.

[126] Freyre, op. cit., p. 158.

[127] In the works, published after his death in Revista Latina (August, 1914), we read the melancholy confession: "Perhaps this is why I only pose questions and find no solutions, guided only by the constantly trembling and uncertain light of reason," apud introduction by Barreto Filho in O Mundo Interior," p. xi.

Notes to Chapter 7
(Pages 205–271)
Ideas in the Twentieth Century

[1] A few months before independence, a newspaper of the period had written: "If the prince departed it would not be surprising if a Puyrredon, an Artiga, a Bolívar, or a San Martín were to be born in our midst, or if some imperfect system of federation were to be devised, bringing in its train disorder and anarchy." (Octávio Tarquinio de Sousa, A Vida de Dom Pedro I, I, 345.) "Among those in authority," writes Tarquinio de Sousa later in his book, "it was completely agreed that circumstances demanded a constitutional monarchy with Dom Pedro at its head. This opinion was shared even by the more radical elements, who in their hearts only accepted him as a temporary expedient, as a solution for the moment, disguised in the phrase 'Dom Pedro I without II,' which appears in Soares Lisboa's journal" (ibid., II, 450).

[2] Costa Pôrto, Pinheiro Machado e Seu Tempo, p. 81.

[3] Evaristo de Morais, Da Monarquia para a República, p. 13.

[4] Oliveira Viana, O Ocaso do Império, p. 17.

[5] José Maria dos Santos, A Política Geral do Brasil, p. 125.

[6] Ibid., p. 203.

[7] Ibid., p. 204.

[8] José Maria Bello, História da República, p. 55. This work had already gone to press when the Brazilian translation of George C. A. Boehrer's book, From Monarchy to Republic appeared.

[9] "I have not the honor to belong to the group of historical republicans, I am one of the republicans of the moment." Apud Luís Delgado, Rui Barbosa, p. 13.

[10] "The republicans did not succeed in formulating a program of ideas more progressive than the liberal trends of the monarchy. To make up for the lack of a program of ideas, they devised a program of administration for a large estate. They began by saying that the best system for a new and poten-

tially great country like Brazil, with its tremendous natural resources, was the system which would assure a strong government able to promote the country's greatest material development without the enervating and procrastinating encumbrance of parliamentary debate. The first historical republican to orient himself in this direction was Dr. Luís Barbosa da Silva. In 1871 on his return from a quick trip to the United States, he adopted the pseudonym 'Theodore Parker' for the publication of articles in the newspaper *A República* professing these views. His style became popular. In 1875 our press was full of articles signed by symbolic and topical names such as Hamilton, Madison, or Jefferson. In the uncertainty of conviction and doctrines, it was inevitable that propagandists should end up much unpreoccupied with the moral aspect of their attitudes. In their rivalry for adherents the essential aim was to please the senses and flatter the more immediate passions. To make the republic seem desirable they did not waste time considering it as a system or a mechanism for the function of liberty. They merely made the vague and more or less delirious promise that a golden age was on the way, in which we would equal in wealth the North Americans simply by adopting their political customs." (Maria dos Santos, *op. cit.,* pp. 205–206.)

[11] Dunschee de Abranches, *Atas e Atos do Governo Provisório,* p. 30.

[12] Bello, *História da República* (2d ed.), p. 86.

[13] Rui Barbosa, speech delivered in the Senate, May 30, 1911, apud Luís Delgado, *Rui Barbosa,* p. 13. "The Brazilian monarchy, by maintaining the hereditary nature of the supreme leadership of public power and by cultivating anarchy in its parliamentary practices, was doubly condemned." (Maria dos Santos, *op. cit.,* p. 215.)

[14] Cf. Rui Barbosa, speech cited, apud Luís Delgado, *op. cit.,* p. 14.

[15] Batista Pereira, "Diretrizes de Rui Barbosa" apud Delgado, *op. cit.,* p. 66.

[16] Delgado, *op. cit.,* p. 67.

[17] Fernando de Azevedo, *Na Batalha do Humanismo,* p. 117.

[18] Cf. Luís Viana Filho, *A Vida de Rui Barbosa,* p. 289.

[19] Azevedo, *op. cit.,* p. 121.

[20] Bello, *op. cit.,* p. 57.

[21] Delgado, *op. cit.,* p. 258.

[22] Bello, *loc. cit.*

[23] Apud Viana Filho, *op. cit.,* pp. 279–280. "Some have said that the case of the translator of *O Papa e o Concílio* is another instance of our horror of metaphysics," writes Professor Reale. "Everything indicates the need for a revision which does not aim to establish definitive conclusions, all the more so since it was not possible to lay hands on complete bibliographical details. . . . I have never accepted the theory of Rui's complete indifference to problems of a philosophical order, although all evidence points to the fact that his permanent preoccupations were centered on questions of another order, questions related to concrete existence, or more properly to human coexistence fulfilling the need for freedom. Far be it from me, then, to attempt to present him as a philosopher or a thinker." (Miguel Reale, "Posição de Rui Barbosa no Mundo da Filosofia" in *1° Congresso Brasileiro de Filosofia,* I, 52.)

[24] Rui Barbosa, speech in honor of Anatole France, apud Delgado, *op. cit.*, p. 259.

[25] Roger Daval, *Histoire des idées en France*, p. 6.

[26] Gilberto Freyre, "O Periodo Republicano" in *Estado de São Paulo* of September 30, 1943.

[27] Cf. João Mangabeira, *O Estadista da República*, pp. 30–32.

[28] Cf. João Ribeiro, *História do Brasil*, 12th ed., p. 315.

[29] Bello, *op. cit.*, p. 86. Already during the Empire, Republican propaganda had presented the United States republic as the model to be copied. In 1869 Luís Gama's slogan was: "An American Brazil, and the lands of the Southern Cross free of king and slave." (Cf. Maria dos Santos, *op. cit.*, p. 208.) Against this imitation of the North American model, against the pro-North American tendencies of the new republic's politicians, Eduardo Prado published his book *A Ilusão Americana*, which was confiscated by the government and which, perhaps for this very reason, excited a good deal of curiosity and attention. It devolved upon a monarchist, Joaquim Nabuco, to work, at a later date, for a better understanding between Brazil and the United States.

[30] Cf. João Cruz Costa, "O Positivismo na República" in *Revista de História,* Nos. 15 and 16 (1953).

[31] Professor Paul Arbousse-Bastide, who defended an interesting thesis on Positivism in Brazil (*Le Positivisme politique et religieux au Brésil*) communicated to me part of an unpublished series of letters from Miguel Lemos to Teixeira Mendes written shortly before the latter's conversion. These letters are dated 1879. In one of them the following statements appear: "Let us forget about 'democracies' and abandon these prejudices worthy of the last century. The proper nature of the revolutionary school is precisely its tendency to break historic continuity by the negation of the past. Let us be Positivists." In another, dated "4 Frederick 91" (November 8, 1879), Miguel Lemos says: "We Positivists reject the democratic doctrine of the sudden inspiration of the masses."

[32] Cf. Maria Bello, *op. cit.*, p. 178.

[33] Viana Filho, *op. cit.*, p. 3.

[34] Maria Bello, *op. cit.*, p. 57.

[35] Maria dos Santos, *op. cit.*, p. 224.

[36] Freyre, "O Periodo Republicano" in *O Estado de São Paulo*, October 9, 1943.

[37] *Ibid.*

[38] Sant'Ana Dionísio, *A Não Cooperação da Intelligência ibérica na Criação da Ciência*, pp. 37–38.

[39] Maria Bello, *op. cit.*, p. 12. Professor Miguel Reale's opinion as to Rui's position is significant: "During half a century of intense cultural activity, in direct contact with the most varied human dramas, although there was one fundamental leitmotiv in his life in the realm of *ideas,* he did not ignore the successive appeals of time, and abandoned old ideas for new ones, or repudiated systems and tools of action when they seemed no longer adequate for achieving the desired ends. This capacity for adaptation to historical events, which certain of his enemies decried, and the adherence to political life al-

ready mentioned, are indications of a pragmatic tendency, not always compatible with pure philosophical speculation." (Reale, *op. cit.*, p. 53.)

40 Clóvis Beviláqua, *Esboços e Fragmentos*, p. 25.

41 Delgado, *op. cit.*, p. 67.

42 Reale, *op. cit.*, p. 52.

43 *Ibid.*

44 Joaquim de Carvalho, *Estudos sôbre a Cultura Portuguêsa no Século XVI*, p. 29.

45 Sérgio Buarque de Holanda, *Raízes do Brasil*, 2d ed., pp. 31–32.

46 Max Leclerc, *Cartas do Brasil*, trans. by Sérgio Milliet, p. 17.

47 Maria dos Santos, *op. cit.*, p. 224.

48 Leclerc, *op. cit.*, p. 9.

49 *Ibid.*, pp. 7–8. Cf. L. C. A. Knowles, *O Desenvolvimento Econômico durante o Século XIX*, pp. 179–195.

50 Afonso Arinos de Mello Franco, *Desenvolvimento da Civilização Material no Brasil*, pp. 132–33.

51 Cf. Fernando Carneiro, "História da Imigração no Brasil: Uma interpratação" in *Boletim Geográfico do Instituto brasileiro de Geografia e Estatística*, No. 69, *passim*.

52 Prado Júnior, *História Econômica do Brasil*, pp. 270–271.

53 Maurice Baumont, *L'Essor industriel et l'imperialisme colonial*, p. 2.

54 Cf. Maria Bello, *op. cit.*, p. 73.

55 The penetration of capital into Brazil is a long and important story which still remains to be told. With the competence everyone acknowledges, Prado Júnior gave an outline of the subject in the last two chapters of his book on the economic history of Brazil, pp. 281–293. See also: Humberto Bastos, *A Marcha do Capitalismo no Brasil* and *A Economia brasileira e o Mundo Moderno*. Also J. F. Normano, *Evolução Econômica do Brasil*. The reports of the minister of finance are likewise of considerable importance for an understanding of the history of the republic. I have made use of some information given me by my friend Guilherme dos Santos Deveza, one of the most competent experts on the subject. See also: Dorival Teixeira Vieira, *A Evolução do Sistema Monetário brasileiro* and Antônio Carlos Ribeiro de Andrada, *Os Bancos de Emissão no Brasil*.

56 Maria Bello, *op. cit.*

57 Cf. Benedito Mergulhão, *A General Café na Revolução Branca de 37.*

58 José Maria Bello, *Panorama do Brasil*, p. 118.

59 During the ministry of João Alfredo a system was devised of issuing bank notes backed by legal tender notes exchangeable for gold. This system was followed by the last cabinet of the monarchy under the leadership of the Viscount of Ouro Prêto, who drew up an agreement with the "National Bank of Brazil for the gradual replacement of government bills by legal tender notes convertible in gold, this facility being extended to another Rio bank, which immediately made use of it and to a bank in São Paulo which issued only small sums of money." (Cf. Maria Bello, *História da República*, p. 90.) Bello also says that the stability of the exchange rate maintained by the imperial government (which remained at par) was the result of an inflow

of gold owing to the 1887 foreign loan and to the inversion of foreign capital after May 13. There was, in fact, no genuine economic prosperity. Nevertheless foreign loans and the influx of foreign capital created a climate of optimism from which the republic was to benefit. But, because of the lack of a genuine foundation, disaster soon followed. Thus the "wave of inflation that had started with the Ouro Prêto Ministry, grew apace, causing havoc on the stock exchange. The most extraordinary enterprises, with the most incredible aims, were daily incorporated with the guaranty of government interest. The fever of fabulous business activity that had afflicted other countries, especially the United States and the Argentine—the two nearest models —threw Brazilian markets into a frenzy, the Rio market above all" (*ibid.*, pp. 91–92.) Cf. Humberto Bastos, *A Economia brasileira e o Mundo Moderno*, pp. 172–73.

[60] Prado Júnior, *op. cit.*, p. 230.

[61] *Ibid.*, p. 231.

[62] Maria Bello, *Panorama do Brasil*, p. 119. Cf. Rui Barbosa, *Finanças e Política da República*.

[63] San Tiago Dantas, *Dois Momentos de Rui Barbosa*, p. 38.

[64] Humberto Bastos, *Rui, Ministro da Independência Econômica do Brasil*, p. 67.

[65] Humberto Bastos, *A Economia brasileira e o Mundo Moderno*, p. 67.

[66] Cf. "Retrospecto Comercial" in *Jornal do Comércio* for 1891.

[67] Machado de Assis, *Esaú e Jacó*, pp. 228–229. Cf. Roberto Simonsen, *A Evolução Industrial do Brasil*, pp. 24–25. It is interesting to note some of the names of the banks opened at this time. Mobilizing Bank, Guaranteed Credit Bank, Impulsive Bank, Sporting Bank, Carriers' Union Bank, Petite Banque of the United States of Brazil, Sportmans [sic] Bank, Brazilian Theatrical Bank, Life-long Bank of Brazil, Turf Bank and so on. (Cf. "Retrospecto Comercial" in *Jornal do Comércio* for 1891.) Referring to the Baron de Lucena's management of the Treasury, as minister of finance, Simonsen writes: "His Excellency's policy is still so vivid in the memory that it would be cruel to do more than refer to it in passing. . . . The minister's articles of faith were: a larger issue of paper money and the alienation of the Central Railroad. When Congress showed its opposition to these ideas, it was simply dissolved, an action that has given rise to the nickname 'coup de bourse' for this particular coup d'état."

[68] Dantas, *op. cit.*

[69] Simonsen, *A Evolução* . . . , p. 19.

[70] Tristão de Ataíde, "Política e Letras" in *À Margem da História da República*, p. 252. In Tristão de Ataíde's opinion there were four new factors contributing to the republican transformation in Brazil. These were: "The popular factor in Rio Grande, through its adventurous and anarchistic instincts; the economic factor in São Paulo, through its development of individual initiative; the political factor in Rio, through the growing oscillation of political currents . . . and the intellectual factor in Recife, through its opposition to ideas and sentiments which had, after all, been the essence of the Empire's moral features" (*ibid.*, p. 253). This presentation of the Bra-

zilian scene seems to me somewhat schematic and therefore insufficient. I must point out, however, that this was written by the illustrious Brazilian thinker in 1924. It nevertheless contains suggestive elements for the comprehension of some aspects of the history of the Republican regime in Brazil.

71 Tristão de Ataíde, *Contribução à História do Modernismo*, pp. 244–245.

72 Fernando de Azevedo, *Princípios de Sociologia*, p. 313.

73 In 1898 Estelita Tapajós published in São Paulo *Ensaios de Filosofia e Ciência*. Tapajós is an extreme representative of evolutionist monism. "Truth," he says in the first few pages of his work, "does not issue from the lips of Krishna, Christ, Brahma or Jehovah—disturbing visions of terror or awe, the deification of vain and impalpable shadows, endowed with life through faith which is the theological form of ignorance—but from scientific investigation, in the slow evolution of the organic progress, the fixation in the cerebral cells, as a permanently stable acquisition, the different stages of the ego born of external phenomena transmittable in space and time through palingenetic evolution" (pp. 4–5). He claims that his book is "in our environment, a small protest in the name of the science we venerate against the pseudo-science with which the 'apostles' of a detestable orthodoxy ingenuously try to impose themselves on us, and it is a faint cry in the midst of the morbid debilitation of Brazilian thought. It seems to me, in my possibly strange ingenuity, a duty" (p. 7). Everywhere "groups are formed, swarming with disciples as damp caverns swarm with lesser mushrooms, the Catholic party, spiritualism, Comtism, and, in politics, science, art, and administration, everywhere in fact, representatives of these groups are sprouting up and trying to impose the ideas arising from the condition of their spirits which are atrophied with regard to the scientific vision by their faith, or crystallized in time by their Master's voice" (p. 8). What does all this mean? Tapajós provides a "universal explanation" through science, or rather through the "law of limitless adaptation," the organic basis of all biological progress, whether individually or in collective groups, in the different stages of historical evolution. Whenever collective groups lose this balanced capacity for adaptation, progress comes to a halt, and a degenerative process starts . . . This, in Tapajós's opinion, explains the "deplorable mental functioning of our middle and upper classes" (p. 9). This nation's mind, in relation to the development of human progress, is a case of quiescence or retrogression . . . How can we remedy this ill? Only two conditions can cure or change the "nation's mind" . . . "education, and immigration from the old races of Europe. The first acts directly as an element of culture which is the metamorphic ontogenesis of the people . . . The second force is the great human regenerating force" (pp. 10–11). I agree with Leonel Franca when he says that Tapajós "offers another example of the fascination exercised by error on minds unequipped by profound philosophical studies, when it presents itself under the assumed label of modern science, of the latest scientific trends." (Leonel Franca, *Noções de História de Filosofia*, p. 494.) These cases are frequent, and unfortunately they still crop up today, decked out in language as pompous as it is hollow. In his study on "the type and the decadence of the cycle of European civilization" that constitutes the final

chapter of his work, Tapajós, having established the "principles, laws and facts" (all according to his Haeckelian concepts) examines the problem of European civilization. "At the moment three of these great collective entities confront and are indistinguishable from one another: the Asiatic cycle, the European cycle, and the American cycle, that is: a social organism in the throes of decomposition, one that is entering on this phase, and a third that is beginning to exercise its youthful audacity" (p. 150). Tapajós dwells on the "European cycle." What problems have been solved by European civilization? he asks. None. "Witness the industrial plethora which strangles and stupefies its workmen, Socialism—the cry of the miserable and the oppressed —nihilism, anarchism, the strikes, the terrible poverty, finally the dark storm clouds made up of all the disillusionments of those who suffer and go hungry, which are speedily rising and gathering on the European social horizon, heavy and brooding, striking terror into all hearts" (p. 164). If this is the internal situation of the European cycle, its external action (naturally dictated by the internal situation) is applied in America and Asia. It is the law of the strongest, a law administered by "diplomatic astuteness, or by steel cannon, because at all costs the blood-thirsty leopards, eagles, and dragons of European imperialism must be fed" (p. 165). Had Europe solved the scientific problem? "No, says Brunetière: science is bankrupt. Yes, the official science taught in schools, the analytical science of phenomena in which German myopia, French madness, and the splenetic seriousness of John Bull are becoming increasingly disoriented; this false science . . . which goes with the absolute dominion of your cycle by its nutritive material power, a monster which stops us from flying high into the realms of pure nonegoistical intelligence" (p. 165). No more is needed to reveal the existence, in Tapajós, of the "morbid debilitation" he claimed to have distinguished in Brazilian thinking. . . . I was unable to obtain his other book, *A Psicofisiologia da Percepção;* nor could I find Trajano de Moura's work *O Homem Americano,* which Sílvio Romero says was completely inspired by evolutionist ideas. At the same time, Fausto Cardoso published a book of essays entitled *Taxinomia Social* (Rio de Janeiro: 1898). A disciple of Tobias Barreto, an evolutionist like Estelita Tapajós, he shows no originality. He follows "Haeckelian principles" which "present history as a summary repetition of organic history" (p. 3 of *Taxinomia Social*). This was the period in which Gustave le Bon, Lilienfeld, Novikov, and Renan were the fashionable authors among Brazilian intellectuals. There are some interesting pages in Fausto Cardoso's work. He had already published a book based on similar ideas in 1894: *Concepção Monística do Universo: Introdução no Cosmos do Direito e da Moral* with a preface by Graça Aranha, in which the influence of Tobias Barreto and the writers followed by Tobias, such as Edward Hartmann, Lange, Buckle, and Ihering is easily discernible.

[74] W. R. Sorley, *History of English Philosophy,* pp. 268–69.

[75] I. M. Bochenski, *La Philosophie contemporaine en Europe,* p. 20.

[76] Cf. *ibid.,* p. 21.

[77] Paul Hazard, *La Pensée Européenne au XVIIIᵉ siècle,* I, 1.

[78] Léon Brunschvicg, *Les Progrès de la conscience dans la philosophie occidentale*, I, 489f.

[79] Cf. *Journal de Psychologie* (1924), p. 907.

[80] Azevedo, *Princípios* . . . , pp. 313–314.

[81] I believe that it was for this reason that Mário de Andrade wrote: "Sociology is the art of rapidly saving Brazil." (*O Emphalhador de Passarinho*, p. 36.)

[82] Sílvio Romero, *Outros Estudos de Literatura Contemporânea*, p. 45.

[83] Oliveira Viana, "O Idealismo da Constituição" in *À Margem da História da República*, p. 139.

[84] *Ibid.*, p. 142. As for solidarity of opinion, the truth is that even on the eve of the republic there were disagreements, such as the argument that divided Silva Jardim and Quintino Bocaiúva. Cf. Silva Jardim, *A Situação Republicana: A Questão da Chefia do Partido*.

[85] Oliveira Viana, *op. cit.*

[86] Agenor de Roure, *A Constituinte Republicana*, I, 16.

[87] Lúcio Pestana, *Memórias de um Histórico*, I, 161.

[88] Roure, *op. cit.*, pp. 6–7.

[89] Luís Viana Filho, *A Vida de Rui Barbosa*, pp. 149–50. "The republic was the natural element of the younger generation, the Jacobins in their red waistcoats, the Democrats who treated *The Federalist* as a Bible, and the Positivists for whom Auguste Comte was a demigod. Among them was Epitácio Pessoa, an eloquent orator who had been preceded by his fame, Lauro Müller, said to be 'a fox girded with a sword,' Barbosa Lima, a military man who knew more of law than of strategy; and Pinheiro Machado, the boy who had run away from Military School to fight on the battlefields of Paraguay. They thought of sharing the honors of the new republics, but did not quite know how to do it. There was, however, no difficulty in dreaming up schemes" (*ibid.*, p. 150). The Viscount of Sabóia (Vicente Cândido Figueira de Sabóia) wrote, under the pseudonym "Testis," a curious and bitter appreciation of Republican politics (*Traços da Política Republicana no Brasil*, 1897); the Viscount of Sabóia who, as we shall see, also concerned himself with philosophical subjects, was a "restorer," and did not hesitate to say in 1897 that the republic was composed of "thieves, bandits, and assassins" (p. 135).

[90] "They all wanted to speak, and if there had not been bridles on loquacity, we might still today be planning the Constitution" (Roure, *op. cit.*, p. 17).

[91] Roure, *op. cit.*

[92] Under the pseudonym "Wolsey," Aristídes César Spinola Zama, a Bahian delegate, wrote *Um Capítulo da História Contemporânea* (1893), in which he attacked Rui and Quintino, alleging that "the elections of November 15, 1890 were a flagrant scandal" (p. 14). It is true that the Cesário Alvim regulation provided an opportunity for the "assault on the ballot boxes" referred to by Zama, but it is likewise true that it was "as compressive of the true results of the elections as the electoral laws of the monarchy." (José Maria Bello, *op. cit.*, pp. 100–101.)

[93] Américo Werneck, *Erros e Vícios da Organização Republicana*, p. 14.

[94] Pestana, *op. cit.*

[95] Oliveira Viana, *op. cit.*, p. 141. "They could have given us a beautiful edifice solidly built and perfect, made of the purest national masonry, but they gave us instead an enormous federative shack, improvised and tacked together with strips of positive philosophy and beams of American pine," writes Oliveira Viana in *O Idealismo na Evolução Política no Império e na República*, pp. 79–80.

[96] *Ibid.*

[97] Roure, *op. cit.*

[98] *Ibid.*

[99] Oliveira Viana, *op. cit.*, p. 157.

[100] *Ibid.*, p. 159.

[101] One of the problems that troubled the Assembly was the ultrafederalism of certain delegates influenced by Comte's ideas or by the example of the United States. Some would not have hesitated to transform the country into a veritable confederation of small nations. "Rui Barbosa had to organize the resistance against what he himself called the 'morbid overexcitement or uncontrolled and unhealthy appetite for federalism,'" writes Maria Bello. "The radical federalists were particularly prominent among the Rio Grande delegation led by Júlio de Castilhos and more or less influenced by Comtian Positivism; but they were joined by deputies from the other states, some of them well-known, for instance, João Barbalho of Pernambuco, Campos Salles of São Paulo and Leopoldo de Bulhões of Goiás. Some wanted to prevent the existence of a permanent national army; others to empower the different states to maintain naval forces. . . . For the ultrafederalists, most of whom were Jeffersonian, the States were the reality and the Union the fiction, and as such it should be limited, in João Barbalho's words, to the bare essentials for survival" (Maria Bello, *História da República*, pp. 101–102). Cf. also Roure, *op. cit.*, Vol. I, Part I.; A. C. de Salles Júnior, *O Idealismo Republicano de Campos Salles*, Chap. VI; Augusto de Bulhões, *Leopoldo de Bulhões*, Chaps. IV and V.

[102] "The military rebellion, which by nightfall had become a government, made sure that by the following morning it would be the republic itself." (José Maria dos Santos, *A Política Geral do Brasil*, p. 217.)

[103] Maria dos Santos, *op. cit.*, p. 189.

[104] Cap. S. Sombra in *Diretrizes*, November 15, 1939, apud João Camilo de Oliveira Tôrres, *O Positivismo no Brasil*, p. 49.

[105] João Cruz Costa, "O Positivismo no República" in *Revista de Historia*, part 2 (cited in n. 30).

[106] Eduardo Prado, *Fastos da Ditadura Militar no Brasil*, p. 67.

[107] Evaristo de Morais, *Da Monarquia para a República*, p. 75.

[108] Antônio Cândido de Mello e Sousa, *Introdução ao Método Crítico de Sílvio Romero*, p. 187.

[109] Dantas, *op. cit.*, pp. 17–18.

[110] Oliveira Viana, *O Ocaso do Império*, pp. 131–132.

[111] Capistrano de Abreu, *Ensaios e Estudos*, 3d ser., p. 129.

[112] Elpídio de Mesquita, *Dois Regimes* apud A. Sodré, *A Gênese da Desordem*, p. 23.

[113] José Américo de Almeida, *Ocasos de Sangue*, p. 22.

[114] Américo Werneck, *Erros e Vícios da Organização Republicana*, p. 14.

[115] Leontina Licínio Cardoso, *Licínio Cardoso, Seu Pensamento, Sua Obra, Sua Vida*, p. 22.

[116] Dantas, *op. cit.*, p. 18.

[117] João do Rio, *O Momento Literário*. This book contains important contributions by Olavo Bilac and Coelho Neto, letters written by João Ribeiro, Clóvis Bevilácqua, Sílvio Romero, Raimundo Correa, Medeiros e Albuquerque, Curvello de Mendonça, Nestor Vítor, Artur Orlando, Sousa Bandiera, Inglês de Sousa, Afonso Celso, and others.

[118] Bevilácqua, *op. cit.*, p. 24.

[119] Maria Bello, *op. cit.*, p. 103.

[120] *Ibid.*, p. 112. "Floriano was for a long time, and still is, the symbol of the authentic nation of the immense and untamed interior, the *sertão*, as opposed to the artificial nation of the cities nourished by the Empire and considered untouchable by the bachelors and journalists of the provisional government" (*ibid.*, pp. 113–114).

[121] Euclides da Cunha, *Contrastes e Confrontos*, pp. 239–248.

[122] César Zama (Wolsey), *Um Capítulo da História Contemporânea*, p. 16.

[123] Maria Bello, *op. cit.*, p. 13. Cf. Wenceslau Escobar, *Apontamentos para a História da Revolução rio-grandense, de 1893*.

[124] Maria Bello, *op. cit.*, p. 13.

[125] Tristão de Ataíde, "Política e Letras" in *À Margem da História da República*, p. 255.

[126] Costa Pôrto, *Pinheiro Machado e seu Tempo*, p. xxvii.

[127] Tristão de Ataíde, *op. cit.*, p. 256.

[128] *Ibid.*

[129] *Ibid.*

[130] *Ibid.*, p. 257.

[131] *Ibid.*, p. 258.

[132] *Ibid.*

[133] *Ibid.*

[134] Costa Pôrto, *op. cit.*, p. 60.

[135] *Ibid.* Cf. also Vítor Nunes Leal, *Coronelismo, Enxada e Voto*; Orlando de Carvalho, *Política do Município*; Afonso Arinos, *História e Teoria do Partido Político no Direito Constitucional brasileiro*; Prado Júnior, *Evolução Política do Brasil*; Octávio Tarquínio de Sousa, "Aspectos Econômicos das Lutas Políticas no Tempo do Império" in *Digesto Econômico*, No. 43 (1948).

[136] Caio Prado Júnior, *Formação do Brasil Contemporâneo*, pp. 6–7.

[137] Costa Pôrto, *op. cit.*, p. 81.

[138] Cf. Silveira Peixoto, *A Tormenta que Prudente de Morais Venceu*. See also the important reports of the Ministers of Finance Bernardino de Campos (1898 and Joaquim Murtinho (1900).

[139] Cf. Cruz Costa, *op. cit.*

[140] *Ibid.*, pp. 124–131.

¹⁴¹ Although Rui Barbosa had already proposed, in 1882, the creation of a chair of sociology, it was only with Benjamin Constant's reform that a course of "sociology and morals" was included in the final year of the secondary-school curriculum (cf. Azevedo, *Princípios* . . . , pp. 305, 315).

¹⁴² Capistrano de Abreu, *Ensaios e Estudos,* 1st ser., pp. 61–107.

¹⁴³ Léon Brunschvicg, "Histoire et Philosophie" in *Écrits philosophiques,* II, 138.

¹⁴⁴ Gilberto Freyre, *Perfil de Euclides e Outros Perfis,* p. 26.

¹⁴⁵ Alcântara Machado, *Vida e Morte do Bandeirante,* p. 245.

¹⁴⁶ This was the period when "Afonso Arinos, in describing scenes of the backlands of Minas Gerais, was unable to identify himself with the most un-European aspects of the landscape and life of the backlanders, and showed for them merely the same sympathy as Eduardo Prado or the Viscount of Taunay" (Freyre, *op. cit.,* p. 23).

¹⁴⁷ *Ibid.,* p. 22.

¹⁴⁸ *Ibid.,* p. 26.

¹⁴⁹ Euclides da Cunha, *Os Sertões,* p. 205.

¹⁵⁰ "The new generation continues to indulge in literature out of sheer dilettantism, without any ideals, with no defined and civilizing ideal, for the most part merely copying foreign authors in a poor and imperfect style" (Capistrano de Abreu, *Cartas Literárias da Gazeta de Notícias,* [November, 1893] apud Tristão de Ataíde, *op. cit.,* p. 280, n. 1).

¹⁵¹ Vicente de Sousa, who was a doctor of medicine, taught philosophy and Latin at the Pedro II College for a number of years. His book, *Curso de Lógica,* was based on the compendia of Rabier and Worms, corrected here and there by Alfred Weber's *History of Philosophy,* and it is completely un-original. Franca who criticizes Vicente de Sousa devotes little more than a page to his work (Leonel Franca, *Noções de História da Filosofia,* VII, 464–465).

¹⁵² In a letter to Oliveira Lima written in 1908, he said: "In any case if, in the course of this year, I don't make tracks again for the desert, I shall have to do something with my life so that my children will not have to pay the penalty of all my improvidence" (cf. Francisco Venâncio Filho, *A Glória de Euclides da Cunha,* p. 52).

¹⁵³ Eloy Pontes, *A Vida Dramática de Euclides da Cunha,* p. 267.

¹⁵⁴ Letter to Oliveira Lima (May 5, 1909) from the archives of the Lima Library apud Sílvio Rabelo, *Euclides da Cunha,* p. 438.

¹⁵⁵ *Ibid.,* p. 439.

¹⁵⁶ Letter to Oliveira Lima cited in n. 154.

¹⁵⁷ Pedro Calmon, *História Social do Brasil: A Época Republicana,* III, 71.

¹⁵⁸ In a letter to Bernardino de Campos, Prudente de Morais wrote: "I know that the Jacobins hate me—and they grow daily more arrogant in proportion to the encouragement they get from their leaders, Generals Quintino and Glicério—and as soon as they feel strong enough to replace me by some 'general' who will carry out the strong policy of the marshal, they will not put it off for a single day. But until this day arrives, I will continue on the path set out in my administrative program, which is that of the Federal

Republican party, whose leaders have caused me great difficulties and embarrassments, calling themselves my 'friends'! My dearest wish is to be free of this hell and, for the rest of my life, to take care of my ruined health and occupy myself exclusively with my family. I grow increasingly sick of politics and politicians." (Letter dated January 10, 1896, in Cândido Motta Filho, *Uma Grande Vida*, pp. 271–272. Cf. Luís Martins, *O Patriarca e o Bachanel, passim.*)

159 Prado Júnior, *História Econômica do Brasil*, p. 235. Cf. Pandiá Calógeras, *Formação Histórica do Brasil*, pp. 444–445. Nuno Pinheiro, "Finanças Nacionais," in *À Margem da História da República*, pp. 111–136.

160 Costa Pôrto, *op. cit.*, pp. 102–103.

161 Afonso Arinos de Mello Franco, *História e Teoria do Partido Político no Direito Constitucional brasileiro*, p. 62. Another historical Republican, João Pinheiro—one of the most endearing and honest figures of the first Republican generation, said of the problem of parties: "There have been many attempts, in the Republican régime, to create parties, but hitherto not a single party has been formed that has managed to attract any considerable support of opinion. . . . The kind of partisanship that led to the fall of the monarchy in the face of national indifference must be banished in the republic, which needs to heal the grave wound that afflicts us" (João Pinheiro, "Plataforma" in Augusto Franco, *Dr. João Pinheiro, Ensaio Biográfico e Político*, p. 87 apud Afonso Arinos de Mello Franco, *op. cit.*, p. 62.) In one of his manifestos, João Pinheiro once said: "The chief duty of the governments of new countries is, first and foremost, to concern itself with their material progress and the development of their resources" (apud Paulo Tamm, *João Pinheiro*, p. 132). In a letter to a friend, in which he refers to his political ideals including the remnants of his Positivist youth in São Paulo, João Pinheiro said that his intentions were: "to suppress the political intrigues of the municipalities, to provoke healthy competition in the country's activities by providing industrial and agricultural prizes; to ensure at least an internal market for Brazilian products; to create technical education as a countermeasure to the influence of the noxious graduate bachelors, who were the source of all ills, to link, in this way, the republic to the destiny of the conservative classes, incorporating the proletariat, setting a value upon national labor—which meant a rise in wages—in short, coping with the Brazilian economic problem which is at one and the same time the social problem and its political mission" (Tamm, *op. cit.*, p. 114). Cf. also Caio Nélson de Senna, *João Pinheiro da Silva, passim.*

162 Campos Salles, *Da Propaganda à Presidência*, pp. 225–226.

163 *Ibid.*, pp. 227–228.

164 Maria dos Santos, *op. cit.*, p. 215.

165 "Other noteworthy Republicans such as Carlos Peixoto and David Campista, could also be cited for their opinions against national parties. There were, however, exceptions to this rule. Some Rio Grande politicians such as Assis Brasil, who became famous for his premature defense of proportional representation, and Pedro Moacyr, heir to the traditions of Silveira Martins, defended the party system in this anti-party-system Republic"

(Afonso Arinos de Mello Franco, *op. cit.*, pp. 63–64). "Although there are no divergent currents in the spirit of national politics which would naturally canalize themselves into parties of a definitive and permanent nature, opinion could always group itself around important theses related to the practice of the same system of principles" (*ibid.*).

[166] Costa Pôrto, *op. cit.*, p. 105.

[167] Maria Bello, *op. cit.*, p. 216.

[168] Sertório de Castro, *A República que a Revolução Destruiu*, p. 161.

[169] *Ibid.*, p. 163. The "Dissidência Paulista" or the disagreement of the São Paulo group resulted from this meeting. The leader of the group was Júlio de Mesquita and it was composed of Prudente de Morais, Cerqueira César, Manuel de Morais Barros, Cesário Bastos, Carlos Guimarães, Cunha Canto, Francisco Alves dos Santos, and others (cf. *ibid.*, p. 164).

[170] Maria Bello, *op. cit.*, pp. 216–217.

[171] Sertório de Castro, *op. cit.*, p. 169.

[172] Pedro Calmon, *op. cit.*, p. 97.

[173] *Ibid.*, p. 98.

[174] Rui Barbosa, "O Artigo 6, No. 3" in *Discursos Parlamentares*, apud Pedro Calmon, *op. cit.*, pp. 99–100.

[175] Pedro Calmon, *ibid.*, p. 232.

[176] Campos Salles, *op. cit.*, p. 365.

[177] *Ibid.*, pp. 316–317.

[178] "Rodrigues Alves really embodied, at the time, one of the finest types of political leader: discreet, calm, liberal and sincere, more attentive to the reality of things than to doctrines . . ." (cf. Maria Bello, *op. cit.*, p. 224).

[179] Pedro Calmon, *op. cit.*, p. 246.

[180] Fernando Carneiro, "História da Imigração no Brasil" in *Boletim Geográfico*, No. 69 (1948), p. 1029.

[181] Prado Júnior, *História Econômica do Brasil*, p. 222. See also Chaps. 22 and 23 of this work.

[182] Baumont, *op. cit.*, p. 286.

[183] Certório de Castro, *op. cit.*, p. 217.

[184] João Pinheiro da Silva—son of a Neopolitan immigrant, Giuseppe Pignataro, who had Brazilianized his name on disembarking to José Pinheiro da Silva—was, in the words of Pedro Calmon, "the Castilhos of Central Brazil." Like Castilhos, he was strongly influenced by Positivist ideas, both in Ouro Prêto and in São Paulo where he graduated in law and where he taught for a period at the Normal College. He was one of the first politicians to call attention to "national realities" which, "ten years later, was all the fashion" (cf. Pedro Calmon, *op. cit.*, p. 259, and Paulo Tamm, *João Pinheiro*, pp. 7–9).

[185] Pedro Calmon, *op. cit.*, p. 259.

[186] Cf. Sertório de Castro, *op. cit.*, Chap. XII; João Mangabeira, *Rui, O Estadista de República*, pp. 111–130.

[187] Pedro Calmon, *op. cit.*, p. 262.

[188] Américo Palha, *História da Vida de Rui Barbosa*, pp. 70, 72–73.

[189] Pedro Calmon, *op. cit.*, p. 264.

[190] Cf. Lúcia Miguel Pereira, *Machado de Assis*; José Osório de Oliveira, *História Breve da Literatura brasileira*; and Ronald de Carvalho, *Pequena História da Literatura brasileira.*

[191] Osório de Oliveira, *op. cit.*, p. 81.

[192] Astrogildo Pereira, *Interpretações,* pp. 49–145.

[193] The curious work entitled *O Problema Operário no Brasil* (*The Problem of the Worker in Brazil*) was published in 1901. In it, Marx and Malon are quoted, albeit in a somewhat confused way. Euclides da Cunha in *Contrastes e Confrontos* refers to Karl Marx. Lima Barreto also refers to Marx a number of times.

[194] Cf. Fernando de Azevedo, *A Cultura brasileira*, Part II, Chap. IV.

[195] Pedro Calmon, *op. cit.*, p. 283.

[196] Maria Bello, *op. cit.*, p. 290.

[197] *Ibid.*

[198] *Ibid.*, pp. 290–291. The star of the great leader was beginning to set. "He did not break with the government: he attempted to keep up the appearance of his position as the 'censor' of the regime and the moral leader of politics. He was postponing his revenge for a better opportunity during the difficulties of the coming presidential succession. In 1915, he was a *condottiere* presumed to be on leave, keeping a watchful eye on political currents" (Pedro Calmon, *op. cit.*, p. 285). In September, 1915, Pinheiro was assassinated by an enraged fanatic obsessed with Pinheiro's unpopularity.

[199] Theodore Roosevelt declared that the war signified "disillusionment and warning" (cf. "America and the World War" apud Pedro Calmon, *op. cit.*, p. 289).

[200] *Ibid.*

[201] Cf. Paulo Egídio, *Contribuição para a História Filosófica da Sociologia.* This work was published in São Paulo in 1899, and cites Stuart Mill, Buckle, Quetelet, Espinas, and René Worms. Cf. Beviláqua, *op. cit.*, p. 277.

[202] Farias Brito in *O Mundo Interior* (1914) shows a certain Bergsonian influence (cf. Barreto Filho, introduction to the 2d ed. of *O Mundo Interior*, p. xxx). He did not, however, escape from the naturalistic influences of his youth. The work of the Viscount de Sabóia, *A Vida Psíquica do Homem: Ensaio sôbre o Materialismo e o espiritualismo*, which appeared in 1903, is a curious study in which the author, who was professor of surgery at the Rio de Janeiro Faculty of Medicine, undertook a kind of defense of a confused scientific spiritualism. He criticizes the Positivists (p. 30) and those who "attempt to please both republicans and monarchists" as was the case with Father Júlio Maria (p. 136) and cites Ribot, Mach, Fouillée, and James. It is, however, difficult to discover, in so extreme a defender of spiritualism, the real—or truly assimilated—influence of any spiritualist philosopher. Among the neo-Thomists or, to follow Leonel Franca's distinction (*Noções de História da Filosofia*, p. 434) among the writers inspired by Scholastic philosophy, we must distinguish Monsignor C. Sentroul, with his *Tratado de Lógica,* which shows no originality and reveals nothing characteristic of the country except the syllabus for logic then used in the São Paulo Faculty of Law. Sentroul was a Belgian Benedictine who taught in São Paulo for

some time. His book, for our purposes, reveals one interesting fact: that the "Faculdade Livre de Filosofia e Letras" (St. Benedict's) was founded in 1908. This date is important, since it provides us with a point of departure for the study of the current of ideas related to Thomism in Brazil. At this period the teaching of Positive philosophy still flourished in Rio de Janeiro. The book on philosophy (*Breve Curso de Filosofia para Uso da Mocidade*) prepared by Father Francisco M. Terlizzi and printed in Rome, is also devoid of interest for the history of ideas in Brazil. It is not well written and, as Leonel Franca says (*ibid.*) "one feels the lack of a more intimate contact with the experimental sciences and modern philosophical systems." The *Sinopse de Lógica* written by Cardinal Arcoverde and published by Monsignor Fernando Rangel in 1918, is a more interesting work. It summarizes the lessons given by the cardinal when he was a canon at Olinda Cathedral and a teacher in the local seminary.

[203] Farias Brito, *A Finalidade do Mundo* (Part II: *A Filosofia Moderna*), p. 307. In the introduction to his book *A Teoria do Conhecimento de Kant*, Januário Lucas Gaffrée wrote: "In Brazil the study of philosophy, when it goes beyond mere dilettantism, is completely neglected and, we might add, regarded with disfavor" (p. 1). Gaffrée's work has no noteworthy features. It merely indicates the presence of a Kantian commentator in Brazil in 1909. In 1929, Clóvis Beviláqua wrote a short article on Kant's doctrines in Brazil, where he demonstrates the influence of Kant on Tobias Barreto, Farias Brito, and Lucas Gaffrée ("Doutrina de Kant no Brasil" in *Revista da Academia brasileira de Letras*, XXI, 5–14.)

[204] José Veríssimo, *Letras e Literatos*, pp. 42–43.

[205] *Ibid.*, p. 152.

[206] *Ibid.*, p. 153.

[207] Maria Bello, *História da República*, p. 301.

[208] Tristão de Ataíde, *Primeiros Estudos*, p. 63. Complete works of Alceu de Amoroso Lima (*Tristão de Ataíde*), I.

[209] Maria Bello, *op. cit.*, p. 302.

[210] Euclides da Cunha, *Contrastes e Confrontos*, pp. 140–141.

[211] Alvaro Moreyra, *O Brasil continua . . .*, p. 82. Someone said of Alberto Tôrres that he was the "ardent formulator of a synthesis of the objective truths concerning Brazilian social and political life" and that he would survive as "the pedagogue of the coming generations" (A. Sabóia Lima, *Alberto Tôrres e a Sua Obra*, p. vii). "Unfortunately," writes Sabóia Lima, "Alberto Tôrres died tormented and embittered by the indifference with which his sincere and patriotic words were received by the new administrators and legislators. His voice was lost in the same wilderness that swallowed up the echoes of the powerful and brilliant words of Euclides da Cunha and the sincere and patriotic words of Sílvio Romero, the three greatest thinkers that Brazil has ever produced" (*ibid.*, p. viii).

[212] *Ibid.*, p. 20.

[213] Alberto Tôrres, *Le Problème mondial*, p. xvii.

[214] *Ibid.*, p. 5.

[215] Cf. Alberto Tôrres, "Preparemo-nos" in *A Noite* (January 17, 1916);

"Salve-se quem puder" in *Tribuna* (May 3, 1916); "Portugal e a Guerra" in *A Noite* (March 3, 1916), and "A Guerra" in *A Noite* (March 20, 1916), apud Alcídes Gentil, *As Idéias de Alberto Tôrres*, p. 142.

216 In an article written for the *Estado de São Paulo* (December 22, 1915) entitled "A Defesa Nacional e o Serviço Militar Obrigatório," he wrote: "Russia figures in the European conflagration as an incoercible whirlpool of future disturbances," apud Alcídes Gentil, *op. cit.*, p. 142.

217 Alberto Tôrres, *O Problema Nacional brasileiro*, p. ix.

218 *Ibid.*

219 *Ibid.*, p. x.

220 *Ibid.*, p. xi. Tôrres cited Woodrow Wilson's speech alluding sympathetically to the economic emancipation of the South American countries (*ibid.*, pp. xii–xiii).

221 *Ibid.*, p. xvi.

222 "Tôrres spoke easily with a colorful, vibrant, and almost uncontrolled and uncontrollable flow of speech. He spoke in a loud voice and in an oratorical tone as if he were in a state of chronic exaltation" (Oliveira Viana, "A Guisa de Prefácio" in Alcídes Gentil, *op. cit.*, p. ii).

223 Tôrres, *op. cit.*, p. 8.

224 Plinio Barreto, "Livros Novos" in *Estado de São Paulo*.

225 "I have endeavored to study the life and work of Alberto Tôrres," writes Sabóia Lima, "without any critical spirit, in fact with the sole aim of studying his life; and briefly analyzing his ideas" (*op. cit.*, p. v).

226 Geraldo de Silos, "Pensador da Nova Geração" in *Cadernos da Hora Presente* (October, 1939), p. 138. This number bore the sad stamp of the time, reading "This number has been passed by the censor . . ."

227 Oliveira Viana, in Alcídes Gentil, *op. cit.*, p. 9.

228 "The October Revolution had no program of reforms to be undertaken. Having originated in an electoral struggle for power, it could not go beyond a straight political change, a mere matter of form, as the only possibility in the circumstances (Alcindo Sodré, *A Gênese da Desordem*, p. 116).

229 Apud Geraldo de Silos, "Meia Hora com Miguel Reale" in *Cadernos da Hora Presente* (June, 1940), p. 158.

230 *Ibid.*, p. 159.

231 *Ibid.*

232 Cf. Miguel Reale, *O Estado Moderno*, pp. 9, 176, 240.

233 Gilberto Freyre, "O Período Republicano" in *Estado de São Paulo* of October 7, 1943. Freyre writes: "Among the critics of the predominating practices were disciples of Alberto Tôrres, enthusiasts of Euclides da Cunha, readers of Sílvio Romero . . . At the same time there were people who, harking back to Methuselah, cast languidly oriental eyes towards the parliamentary solution: 'What Brazil needs is more parliamentarianism,' sighed these malcontents—somewhat hypocritical malcontents, who were at the same time in favor of greater autonomy for the states in view of the 'abuses' practiced by the central authority. Some of these false malcontents—let us observe in passing—ended by becoming fascists, integralists, or partisans of violent dictatorships."

[234] Bello, *op. cit.*, p. 312.

[235] *Ibid.*, p. 313.

[236] Cf. Cruz Costa, "Os Positivistas e as Greves" from "O Positivismo na República," in *Revisita de História*, No. 15, p. 127, n. 6. On the 1917 strike, see: *O Comércio de São Paulo* for May 15 and June 1, 1906. Also: Antônio dos Santos Figueiredo, *A Evolução do Estado no Brasil* and Ivan Subirof (Nereu Rangel Pestana), *A Oligarquia Paulista*.

[237] Cf. Francisco de Assis Barbosa, *A Vida de Lima Barreto*, p. 249.

[238] Cf. Afonso Arinos de Mello Franco, *op. cit.*, pp. 114–115.

[239] *Ibid.*, p. 115.

[240] Barbosa Lima Sobrinho, *A Verdade sôbre a Revolução de Outobro*, p. 1.

[241] *Ibid.*, pp. 1–2.

[242] *Ibid.*, pp. 2–3.

[243] Sertório de Castro, *op. cit.*, p. 62.

[244] *Ibid.*, pp. 63–64.

[245] Bello, *op. cit.*, p. 324.

[246] Cf. Lourenço Moreira Lima, *A Coluna Prestes*; João Alberto Lins de Barros, *Memórias de Um Revolucionário*; Ítalo Landucci, *Cenas e Episódios da Coluna Prestes e da Revolução de 1924*; João Lima, *Figuras da República Velha*; J. Nunes de Carvalho, *A Revolução no Brasil*.

[247] Cf. Jorge Amado, *Vida de Luís Carlos Prestes: O Cavaleiro da Esperança*.

[248] Caio Prado Júnior, preface in Lourenço Moreira Lima, *op. cit.*, p. 15.

[249] Mário de Andrade, *O Movimento Modernista*, p. 13.

[250] Andrade Muricy, *A Nova Literatura brasileira*, p. 7.

[251] Mário de Andrade, *op. cit.*, p. 14.

[252] Menotti del Picchia, "Modernismo" in *A Gazeta* of October 12, 1954.

[253] *Ibid.*

[254] Mário de Andrade, *O Empalhador de Passarinho*, p. 162.

[255] *Ibid.*, p. 159. "Who originally had the idea for the 'Week of Modern Art'? I, for one, don't know, and have never known, all I can say is that it wasn't me. The movement, gradually spreading, became a permanent public scandal. We had already held a public poetry reading in Rio de Janeiro; and an important session had been held at the house of Ronald de Carvalho, where Ribeiro Couto and Renato de Almeida were present in an atmosphere of general sympathy. Manuel Bandeira gave his consent to the publication of *Paulicéia Desvairada*. Bandeira had published his first free verse poems in *Carnaval* in 1919. And then Graça Aranha, already famous and bringing with him from Europe his *Estética da Vida*, arrived in São Paulo to meet us and to group us around his philosophy. We used to laugh at his *Estética da Vida* which still attacked certain modern Europeans whom we admired, but we were frankly impressed by Graça Aranha himself. And someone threw out the idea of organizing a 'Week of Modern Art' with an exhibition of plastic arts and offering concerts, readings, and explanatory lectures. Was it Graça Aranha himself? Was it Di Cavalcanti? . . . What mattered was the actual organization of the 'Week,' which, apart from its audacity was a pretty expensive undertaking. And the real spirit behind the 'Week of

Modern Art' was Paulo Prado." (Cf. Mário de Andrade, *O Movimento Modernista*, pp. 22–23.)

[256] "It is generally accepted, and quite rightly, that modernism, as a dominant and creative state of mind, lasted just under ten years, having come to an end in 1930 with the political revolutions and literary pacification" (Mário de Andrade, *O Movimento Modernista*, p. 161).

[257] *Ibid.*

[258] *Ibid.*, p. 27.

[259] *Ibid.*, pp. 28–29.

[260] *Ibid.*, p. 30.

[261] Nélson Werneck Sodré, *Orientação do Pensamento brasileiro*, p. 14.

[262] Mário de Andrade, *op. cit.*, p. 42.

[263] Mário de Andrade, *Aspectos da Literatura brasileira*, p. 238.

[264] Mário de Andrade, *O Movimento Modernista*, p. 80.

[265] João Alphonsus de Guimarães, "A Deriva" in Edgar Cavalheiro, *Testamento do Uma Geração*, p. 147.

[266] Graça Aranha, *O Meu Próprio Romance*, p. 149.

[267] *Ibid.*, p. 151. "The lesson of Tobias Barreto was to think fearlessly, to think for oneself, free of authorities and canons. His principal action was destructive. Naturally. There is always a lot to destroy in Brazil. But while his criticism destroyed, new perspectives for culture emerged, new foundations were laid for the intellect. To realize what effect Tobias Barreto had, it is sufficient to consider the state of legal studies before and after his contribution. We left the discipline of Brás Florentino, Ribas, Justino, for the lessons of emancipated masters. The Brazilian Civil Code, worked out by Clóvis Beviláqua, is affiliated to Tobias Barreto's inspiration" (pp. 151–152). Clóvis Beviláqua, a jurist rather than a philosopher, was also a product of the influence of the Recife school. "The gentle Clóvis is the saint of Brazilian evolutionism" (Gomez Robledo, *La Filosofia en el Brasil*, p. 115). Clóvis was influenced by Tobias but "is no longer his disciple in the strict sense of the word" (cf. Araripe Júnior, introduction to Clóvis Beviláqua's book, *Esboços e Fragmentos*, p. xlv). In 1899, Clóvis Beviláqua undertook a calm and serene study of philosophical vicissitudes in Brazil (*Esboços e Fragmentos*). It is in this work that we find the sentence that has so much impressed me and that I believe to be true, even today, of the direction of philosophy in Brazil: "If we are some day to make a philosophical contribution of significance, I am convinced that it will not emerge from the heights of metaphysics." One can see in his work the traces of Positivist influence, as when he attributes the benign nature of Brazilian law to the influence of the gentleness of the Negro race in our culture.

[268] Cf. Agripino Grieco, *Evolução da Prosa brasileira*, p. 116, and Olivio Montenegro, *O Romance brasileiro*, pp. 125–126.

[269] Guilherme Francovich, *Filósofos brasileiros*, p. 126.

[270] Graça Aranha, *O Espírito Moderno*, p. 49.

[271] *Ibid.*, p. 58.

[272] *Ibid.*, p. 50.

[273] *Ibid.*, pp. 60–61.

[274] Aníbal Sanchez Reulet, *La Filosofia latino-americana Contemporânea,* p. 141.

[275] Fausto Cardoso, *A Concepção Monista do Universo,* pp. ix-xxxvii.

[276] Graça Aranha, *op. cit.,* p. ix.

[277] *Ibid.,* pp. xiv–xv.

[278] Graça Aranha, *A Estética da Vida,* p. 16.

[279] *Ibid.,* p. 29.

[280] *Ibid.,* p. 86.

[281] ". . . the bird which for me symbolizes our land. It is tall, has thick legs and folded wings, and spends its days with one leg crossed over the other, sad, sad, with a meek and vile sadness: you know it well, I am convinced. The image of the *jaburu* is ever present in my mind when the train skims over the endless coffee plantations, pressing down the purple soil that feeds them." (Letter from Capistrano de Abreu to João Lúcio de Azevedo in *Correspondência de Capistrano de Abreu* [ed. José Honório Rodrigues], II, 21.)

[282] Cf. Graça Aranha, *op. cit.,* pp. 87–89.

[283] *Ibid.,* pp. 92–93.

[284] Sebastião da Rocha Pitta, *História da América Portuguêsa,* p. 1.

[285] Graça Aranha, *op. cit.,* p. 95.

[286] *Ibid.,* p. 109.

[287] *Ibid.,* p. 166.

[288] *Ibid.,* p. 168.

[289] *Ibid.,* p. 170. "One cannot say that the writers who, shortly after Graça Aranha, and with less distinction, began to write socialist novels, were his disciples or imitators. Graça Aranha was undeniably the first to introduce into literature the social problems which were then beginning to have repercussions in Brazil. These repercussions of the European struggle to achieve a new organization of society were not very strong, but they did occur. A group of intellectuals sided with the workers who were beginning to organize themselves; perhaps, in a country almost without industries, they were in fact initiators of the movement; there was also an attempt to create a People's University where, among others, Fábio Luz, Rocha Pombo, and Pedro do Couto, taught. These intellectuals, together with Curvello de Mendonça, wanted literature to serve a cause, and for this reason were more or less openly hostile toward Machado de Assis." (Lúcia Miguel Pereira, *História da Literatura brasileira,* XII, 238–239.)

[290] Apud Nestor Vítor, *Os de Hoje,* p. 28.

[291] Jackson de Figueiredo was for a time a pupil at the American College run by the Evangelist minister, W. E. Finley. In 1904 or 1905 he was matriculated at the "Ateneu Sergipano." (Cf. Olegário Silva, "Infância e Adolescência" in *In Memoriam,* p. 59.)

[292] Jackson de Figueiredo, *Algumas Reflexões sôbre a Filosofia de Farias Brito,* p. 15.

[293] Olegário Silva, *op. cit.,* p. 66.

[294] Jonathas Serrano, "O Nosso Jackson" in *In Memoriam,* p. 286.

[295] Cf. Antônio Gomez Robledo, *La Filosofia en el Brasil,* p. 162.

[296] Jackson de Figueiredo, *Correspondência,* p. 283.

[297] Jonathas Serrano, *op. cit.,* p. 288.

[298] Jackson de Figueiredo, *Algumas Reflexões* . . . , p. 18.

[299] Hamilton Nogueira, *Jackson de Figueiredo,* p. 59.

[300] Alexandre Correia, "O Filósofo" in *In Memoriam,* p. 91.

[301] Sérgio Buarque de Holanda, "Indicação" in *In Memoriam,* p. 148.

[302] Nestor Vítor, "Jackson de Figueiredo" in *In Memoriam,* p. 229.

[303] Virgilio de Mello Franco, "Jackson de Figueiredo" in *In Memoriam,* pp. 297–298.

[304] *Ibid.,* p. 298.

[305] *Ibid.,* p. 299.

[306] Leonel Franca, "Jackson de Figueiredo" in *In Memoriam,* p. 306.

[307] Jackson de Figueiredo, *Pascal e a Inquietação Moderna,* p. 9.

[308] Jonathas Serrano, *op. cit.,* p. 294.

[309] Jackson de Figueiredo, *Algumas Reflexões* . . . , p. 16.

[310] *Ibid.*

[311] Tristão de Ataíde, "Seu Lugar" in *In Memoriam,* p. 558.

[312] Alexandre Correia, *op. cit.,* p. 90.

[313] Jonathas Serrano, *op. cit.,* p. 294.

[314] Ronald de Carvalho, "O Realista" in *In Memoriam,* p. 140.

[315] Augusto Frederico Schmidt, "Meu Depoimento" in *In Memoriam,* p. 145.

[316] Jackson de Figueiredo, *Do Nacionalismo na Hora Presente,* apud Contreiras Rodrigues, "O Sociólogo" in *In Memoriam,* p. 108.

[317] Jackson de Figueiredo, "Inéditos" in *In Memoriam,* p. 4.

[318] Cf. Mário de Andrade, "Tristão de Ataíde" in *Aspectos da Literatura brasileira,* pp. 15–40.

[319] Carlos Malheiro Dias, *Pensadores brasileiros,* pp. 7–8.

[320] In his work, *Letras Mineiras,* Eduardo Frieiro, whom I consider one of the best Brazilian critics, examines the problem of *sertanismo* in relation to Mário Matos's study of Afonso Arinos: *O Último Bandeirante.* He feels that the *sertanismo* of some of our writers is "tinged with the colors of time." This fashionable sentiment, he says, dates from the second half of the nineteenth century, from the *Volkgeist* which in Latin America corresponded to the desire for liberation from the "cultural yoke of Europe." "Reacting against the cosmopolitan spirit of the urban centers, which they mistakenly believed to be the cause of a depersonalization, the nativists turned toward life on the plantations and the soul of the interior." Hence an exaggeration: their supposition that "life in the *sertão* is more typical and more representative than that of the cities." In Frieiro's opinion, Euclides da Cunha's book *Os Sertões* was a great and unique work. "The rest were merely the literature of imitators and descendants." "Our regionalist writers all suffer from the same weakness: they record only the external details of what they see and observe; the only element with which they compose is the picturesque and the decorative; they give us only the outer shape of things, but fail to penetrate to the essence. Incapable of real communication with the human reality, they stylize the *sertanejo,* or backlander, depicting him as invariably strong, honorable,

brave, and manly. In this way, the poetic successor to Rousseau's noble savage has been concocted, romanticized by our "Indianists" (cf. Eduardo Frieiro, *Letras Mineiras*, pp. 193–202).

321 "When Capistrano de Abreu appeared in Brazilian historiography, its interest was centered particularly on the coastal communities. He saw the sertão and the paths to the interior as a process of incorporation and expansion of our western frontier; it was a new field, an original method of investigation and interpretation of Brazil's colonial formation. The sertão and the paths opened up by the *bandeirantes* are a factor in the creation of Brazilian life" (José Honório Rodrigues, "Capistrano de Abreu e a Historiografia" in *Correspondência de Capistrano de Abreu*, p. liii). In the *Capítulos de História Colonial*, it is the people "castrated and bled, bled and castrated," as Capistrano says, that is "the central character" (cf. *ibid.*, pp. xlvi–xlix).

322 Afonso Arinos, *Lendas e Tradições brasileiras*, pp. 29–30.

323 Ronaldo de Carvalho, *Estudos brasileiros*, 1st ser., p. 63.

324 Eduardo Frieiro, *A Ilusão Literária*, p. 59.

325 *Ibid.*, p. 67.

326 *Ibid.*, p. 69.

327 José Osório de Oliveira, *História Breve da Literatura brasileira*, p. 113. "The man of letters in Brazil," writes Osório de Oliveira further on [liberated from the intellectual European prejudice] "is, in a way, on equal terms with the people; he often shares their tastes, sentiments and ideas, he follows or adopts many of their customs and practices. This is simply because social culture in Brazil is stronger than the culture we call intellectual to distinguish it from the living culture of the people, the culture synonymous with human experience" (*ibid.*, p. 119).

328 Nélson Werneck Sodré, *Orientações do Pensamento brasileiro*, p. 100.

329 *Ibid.*

330 Vicente Licínio Cardoso, *À Margem da História do Brasil*, p. 72.

331 Vicente Licínio Cardoso, "Benjamin Constant, o Fundador da República" in *À Margem . . .* , p. 294.

332 Alcides Bezerra, cited in Azevedo Amaral's "Preface" to the 2d ed. of Cardoso's *Filosofia da Arte*, pp. 11–12.

333 Vicente Licínio Cardoso, preface to the 1st ed. of *Filosofia da Arte*, p. 9.

334 Vicente Licínio Cardoso, *Figuras e Conceitos*, pp. 134–135.

335 Azevedo Amaral, preface to the 2d ed. of *Filosofia da Arte*, p. 20.

336 Ronald de Carvalho's first series of *Estudos brasileiros* was published in 1924. In this work he studies the bases of the nation—literature, art and the Brazilian psyche—expressing in this way a preoccupation which seems common to the generation of intellectuals born after the advent of the republic. In the second series of *Estudos brasileiros* (1931), Ronald de Carvalho examines the work of some of his contemporaries, and studies the theory of the novel (pp. 155–165) and modern aesthetics (pp. 181–203). The third volume of the series (1931) is almost entirely devoted to historical studies of Brazilian diplomacy in South America. The first edition of his *Pequena História de Literatura brasileira* was published in 1919. I believe this work is now in its fifth edition. "Endowed with a well-formed spirit,

he brought to Brazilian letters the almost scandalous novelty of possessing style and being an artist, even in dealing with subjects of a professional nature" (Agripino Grieco, *Evolução da Prosa brasileira*, p. 243).

[337] Cf. *Correspondência de Capistrano de Abreu*, II, 386–486.

[338] Paulo Prado, *O Retrato do Brasil*, p. 10.

[339] *Ibid.*, pp. 213–216.

[340] Nélson Werneck Sodré, *Orientação do Pensamento brasileiro*, p. 66.

[341] *Ibid.*

[342] *Ibid.*, p. 67.

[343] Oliveira Viana, *Populações Meridionais do Brasil*, I, x (3d ed.).

[344] Manuel Bonfim, *O Brasil na História*, p. 7.

[345] Nélson Werneck Sodré, *op. cit.*, p. 84.

[346] Azevedo Amaral, *O Estado Autoritário e a Realidade Nacional*, p. 7.

[347] Nélson Werneck Sodré, *op. cit.*, p. 13.

[348] *Ibid.*, p. 14.

[349] The most interesting studies on this subject are: Barbosa Lima Sobrinho, *A Verdade sôbre a Revolução de Outubro* (São Paulo: 1933); Sertório de Castro, *A República que a Revolução Destruiu* (Rio de Janeiro: 1932); Sertório de Castro, *Política és Mulher* (Rio de Janeiro: 1933); Virgílio de Mello Franco, *Outobro, 1930* (Rio de Janeiro: 1931); Maurício de Lacerda, *A 2ª República* (Rio de Janeiro: 1931); Hamilton Barata, *O Assalto de 1930* (Rio de Janeiro: 1932); Virgílio Santa Rosa, *O Sentido do Tenentismo* (Rio de Janeiro: n.d.); Alcindo Sodré, *A Gênese da Desordem* (Rio de Janeiro: 1953); Martins de Almeida, *Brasil Errado*, 2d ed. (Rio de Janeiro: 1953); Hermes Lima, *Problemas do Nosso Tempo* (São Paulo: 1935); Paulo Duarte, *Agoro Nós* (São Paulo: 1927); Paulo Duarte, *Que é Que Há?* (São Paulo: 1931); José Carlos de Macedo Soares, *Justiça* (Paris: 1925).

[350] *O Caso de São Paulo* (São Paulo: 1931); Menotti del Picchia, *A Revolução Paulista* (São Paulo: 1932); Herculano C. e Silva, *A Revolução Constitucionalista* (Rio de Janeiro: 1932); João Neves, *Acuso* (Rio de Janeiro: 1933); Manoel Osório, *A Guerra de São Paulo* (São Paulo: 1932); Paulo Duarte, *Palmares pelo Avêsso* (São Paulo: 1947); Euclides de Figueiredo, *História da Revolução Constitucionalista* (São Paulo: 1954).

[351] Plínio Salgado, *Palavra Nova de Tempos Novos* (Rio de Janeiro: 1936); *A Quarta Humanidade*, 2d ed. (Rio de Janeiro: 1936); *O Que é o Integralismo* (Rio de Janeiro: 1937); *Psicologia da Revolução*, 4th ed. (Rio de Janeiro: 1953); *Extremismo e Democracia* (São Paulo: n.d.); *Madrugada do Espírito* (São Paulo: n.d.); *Espírito da Burguesia*, 2d ed. (Rio de Janeiro: 1951).

Miguel Reale, *A.B.C. do Integralismo* (São Paulo: 1937); *O Estado Moderno* (Rio de Janeiro: 1934); *O Capitalismo Internacional* (Rio de Janeiro: 1935); *Formação da Política Burguesa* (Rio de Janeiro: 1934).

Gustavo Barroso, *Integralismo de Norte a Sul* (Rio de Janeiro: 1934); *Brasil-Colônia de Banqueiros* (Rio de Janeiro: 1934); *A Sinagoga Paulista*, 2d ed. (Rio de Janeiro: 1937); *Integralismo e Catolicismo* (Rio de Janeiro: 1937).

Octavio de Faria, *Machiavel e o Brasil* (Rio de Janeiro: n.d.).

³⁵² Lourenço Moreira Lima, *A Coluna Prestes* (São Paulo: 1945). Ítalo Landucci, *Cenas e Episódios da Coluna Prestes* (São Paulo: 1952). Jorge Amado, *Vida de Luís Carlos Prestes, O Cavaleiro da Esperança* (São Paulo: n.d.; Argentine ed., Buenos Aires: 1942). Luís Carlos Prestes, *O Problema da Terra e a Constituição de 1946* (Rio de Janeiro: 1946); *Organizar o Povo para a Democracia* (Rio de Janeiro: 1945); *União Nacional para a Democracia e o Progresso* (Rio de Janeiro: 1945).

³⁵³ Francisco de Campos, *O Stado Nacional: Sua Estrutura, Seu Conteúdo Ideológico* (Rio de Janeiro: 1940); Bezerra de Freitas, *Fisionomia e Estrutura do Estado Novo* (Rio de Janeiro: 1941); André Carrazzoni, *Getúlio Vargas* (Rio de Janeiro: 1939); Paul Frischauer, *Presidente Vargas* (São Paulo: 1943).

³⁵⁴ Marshal J. B. Mascarenhas de Morais, *A F.E.B. pelo Seu Comandante* (São Paulo: 1947); *Depoimento de Oficiais da Reserva sôbre a F.E.B.* (São Paulo: 1949).

³⁵⁵ Armando Pacheco, *Getúlio me disse . . .* (Rio de Janeiro: 1949); Wellington Brandão, *Quarta República* (Rio de Janeiro: 1951); Adyr Fontes Sette, *A Verdade sôbre a Deposição de Getúlio Vargas* (Juiz de Fora: 1947).

³⁵⁶ Armando de Salles Oliveira, *Diagrama de Uma Situação Política* (São Paulo: 1945); Osório Borba, *Sombras no Túnel* (Rio de Janeiro: 1946); Virgílio de Mello Franco, *A Campanha da U.D.N.* (Rio de Janeiro: 1946).

³⁵⁷ These two surveys, we must note, were undertaken during the dictatorship of the *Estado Novo* when censorship was in force. They must therefore be examined with due care. Despite this, they include useful information for the historians and critics of the future.

³⁵⁸ Antônio Cândido de Mello e Sousa, in Mário Neme, *Plataforma da Nova Geração*, p. 31.

³⁵⁹ Mário Schenberg in Mário Neme, *op. cit.*, p. 114.

³⁶⁰ Vicente Licínio Cardoso, *À Margem da História do Brasil*, p. 77.

NOTES TO CHAPTER 8
(Pages 272–277)
Conclusions

¹ Ralph Barton Perry, "Is there a North-American Philosophy?" in *Philosophy and Phenomenological Research*, IX: 3 (March, 1949), 368.

² *Ibid.*

³ Arnold J. Toynbee, *A Study of History*, p. 3.

⁴ Herbert W. Schneider, "La Emigración de las Ideas hacia America" in *Filosofia y Letras*, No. 8, p. 411.

⁵ Francisco Romero, "Influencia del Descobrimento de America en las Ideas Generales," *Humanidades*, XXIX, 11 (separate).

⁶ Joaquim de Carvalho, *Estudos sôbre a História Portuguêsa, no Século*

XVI, p. 39, and Vieira de Almeida, "A Dispersão do Pensamento Filosófico Português" in *Revista da Faculdade de Letras de Lisboa*, IX, 176.

[7] João de Barros, *Pequena História da Poesia Portuguêsa*, pp. 40–41 and 96.

[8] Antônio Cândido de Mello e Sousa, *O Método Crítico de Sílvio Romero*, p. 180.

[9] Cf. Risieri Frondizi, "Hay Una Filosofia ibero-americana?" in *Realidad*, No. 8 (1948), p. 9.

[10] Alberdi, *Obras Póstumas*, XV, 603, apud Frondizi, *op. cit.*, p. 9.

[11] Tristão de Ataíde, *Contribuição à História do Romantismo*, I, 244–245.

[12] Andrade Muricy, *A Nova Literatura brasileira*, p. 353.

[13] João Frederico Normano, *Evolução Económica do Brasil*, p. xvii.

[14] Alfonso Reyes, *Última Tule*, pp. 107–108.

BIBLIOGRAPHY

Bibliography

Abranches, Dunschee de, "Memórias de um Histórico," in *Jornal do Brasil*. Rio de Janeiro, 1896.

———. *Actas e Actos do Governo Provisorio*. Rio de Janeiro, Imp. Nacional, 1907.

Afonso Celso de Assis Figueiredo, *Oito Anos de Parlamento,* new ed. São Paulo, Melhoramentos, n.d.

Afonso Ruy, *A Primeira Revolução Social Brasileira*, 2d ed. Salvador, Beneditina, 1951.

Alcântara Machado, Antônio de, *Gonçalves de Magalhães ou o Romântico Arrependido*. São Paulo, Saraiva, 1936.

———. *Vida e Morte do Bandeirante*, 2d ed. São Paulo, 1930.

Alfaric, P. *Laroumiguière et son école*. Paris, Belles Lettres, 1929.

Almeida, Aluísio, *A Revolução Liberal de 1842*. Rio de Janeiro, José Olympio, 1944.

Almeida, Fortunato de, "O Seculo XVI: Aspectos Gerais–A Sociedade, o Rei" in *Hist. da Lit. Portuguêsa*, ed. Albino Forjaz de Sampaio. Lisbon, Aillaud-Bertrand, n.d. Vol. I.

Almeida, José Américo de, *Ocasos de Sangue*. Rio de Janeiro, José Olympio, 1954.

Almeida Magalhães, Bruno de, "Farias Brito e a Reação Espiritualista," in *Revista dos Tribunais*. Rio de Janeiro, 1918.

———. "Sílvio Romero," *Estado de São Paulo*. August, 1938.

Altamira, Rafael, *Historia de la Civilización Española.* Madrid, Espasa-Calpe, 1932.

Alves, José Luiz, "Os Claustros e o Clero no Brasil," in *Revista do Inst. Hist. e Geogr. Brasileiro,* Vol. LVII. Rio de Janeiro, 1894.

Amado, Jorge, *A Vida de Luís Carlos Prestes,* São Paulo, Martins, n.d.

Andrade, A. A. *Vernei e a Filosofia Portuguêsa.* Braga, Cruz, 1946.

Andrade, Mário de, *Aspectos da Literatura Brasileira.* Rio de Janeiro, Americ., 1943.

———. *O Movimento Modernista.* Rio de Janeiro, C. E. B., 1942.

———. *O Empalhador de Passarinho.* São Paulo, Martins, n.d.

Andrade Muricy, José Cândido de, *A Nova Literatura Brasileira.* Pôrto Alegre, Globo, 1936.

Araguaia, Visconde de [Domingos José Gonçalves de Magalhães]. *A Alma e o Cérebro.* Rio de Janeiro, Garnier, 1865.

———. *Comentários e Pensamentos.* Rio de Janeiro, Garnier, 1880.

———. *Os Fatos do Espírito Humano.* 2d ed. Rio de Janeiro, Garnier, 1865.

Araújo, Oscar, *L'Idée républicaine au Brésil.* Paris, Perrin, 1893.

Arciniegas, Germán, *America, tierra firme.* Buenos Aires, Losada, 1944.

Arcoverde, Cardeal, *Sinopse de Lógica.* Petrópolis, Vozes de Petrópolis, 1918.

Ardao, A. *La Filosofia pre-universitaria en el Uruguay.* Montevideo, Garcia, 1945.

Ataíde, Tristão de, "Política e Letras," in *À Margem da História da República,* Anuário do Brasil, Rio de Janeiro, 1924.

———. *Estudos,* 1st ser. Rio de Janeiro, 1927.

———. *Contribuição a História do Modernismo.* Rio de Janeiro, José Olympio, 1939.

Azevedo, Fernando de, *A Cultura Brasileira.* 2d ed. São Paulo, Edit. Nacional, 1944.

———. *Canaviais e Engenhos na Vida Política do Brasil,* Rio de Janeiro, Inst. do Açúcar e Álcool, 1948.

———. *Na Batalha do Humanismo.* São Paulo, Melhoramentos, 1952.

———. *Princípios de Sociologia.* 5th ed. São Paulo, Melhoramentos, 1951.

Azevedo, João Lúcio de, *Épocas de Portugal Econômico.* Lisbon, Clas., 1929.

———. *O Marquês de Pombal e a sua Época.* 2d ed. Rio de Janeiro, Anuário do Brasil, 1922.

Barbosa Lima (sobrinho), Alexandre José, *A Verdade sôbre a Revolução de Outubro.* São Paulo, Unitas, 1933.

Barbosa Machado, Diogo, *Biblioteca Lusitana.* 2d ed. Lisbon, Associação dos Arqueólogos Portuguêses, 1930.

Barbosa, Rui, *Cartas de Inglaterra*. 2d ed. São Paulo, Saraiva, 1929.

Barcellos, M. *Evolução Constitucional do Brasil*. Rio de Janeiro, Imp. Nacional, 1933.

Barreto, Paulo, *O Momento Literário*. Rio de Janeiro, Garnier, n.d.

Barreto, Plínio, "Livros Novos," in *Estado de São Paulo*, April, 1938.

Barros, João de, *Pequena História da Poesia Portuguêsa*. Lisbon, Cosmos, 1941.

Barros, João Alberto Lins de, *Memórias de um Revolucionário*. Rio de Janeiro, Civ. Bras., 1954.

Bastos, Humberto, *A Economia Brasileira e o Mundo Moderno*. São Paulo, Martins, 1948.

———. *A Marcha do Capitalismo no Brasil*. São Paulo, Martins, 1944.

———. *Rui Barbosa, Ministro da Independência Econômica do Brasil*. Rio de Janeiro, Casa de Rui Barbosa, 1949.

Batista Pereira, Antônio, *Pelo Brasil Maior*. São Paulo, Edit. Nacional, 1934.

Baumont, M. *L'Essor industriel et l'impérialisme colonial (1878–1904)*. Paris, Alcan, 1937.

Bell, A. F. Aubrey, *A literatura Portuguêsa*, trans. by A. de Campos and B. Cunha, Coimbra, Imprensa de Universidade, 1931.

Bello, José Maria, *História da República*. Rio de Janeiro, Civilização Edit., 1940.

———. *História da República*. 4th ed. Rio de Janeiro, Organização Simões, 1952.

———. *Panorama do Brasil*. Rio de Janeiro, José Olympio, 1936.

Besouchet, Lídia, *José Maria Paranhos, Visconde do Rio Branco*. Rio de Janeiro, Zélio Valverde, 1945.

———. *Mauá e o seu tempo*. São Paulo, Anchieta, 1942.

Beviláqua, Clóvis, *Esboços e Fragmentos*. Rio de Janeiro, Laemert, 1899.

Bezerra, Alcides, *Achegas à História da Filosofia*. Rio de Janeiro, Graf. Arquivo Nacional, 1936.

Bochenski, I. M. *La Philosophie contemporaine en Europe*. Paris, Payot, 1951.

Bonfim, M. *O Brasil Nação*. Rio de Janeiro, Francisco Alves, 1928.

Bouillier, Francisque, *Histoire de la philosophie cartésienne*. Paris, Delagrave, 1868.

Bourgeois, E. *Manuel historique de politique etrangère*. 9th ed. Paris, Belin, 1931.

Braga, Teodoro, *História da Universidade de Coimbra*. Lisbon, Academia Real das Ciências, 1892.

Brandão, Mário, *O Colégio das Artes*. Coimbra, Imprensa da Universidade, 1924.

Brasiliense, Américo, *Os Programas dos Partidos e o Segundo Império.* São Paulo, Jorge Seckler, 1878.

Brehier, Émile, *La Philosophie et son passé,* Paris, Presses Universitaires de France, 1940.

——. *Histoire de la philosophie.* Paris, Alcan, 1932.

Brunschvicg, Léon, "Finesse et géometrie," in *L'Évolution de la physique et la philosophie.* Paris, Alcan, 1935.

——. *La Modalité du jugement.* Paris, Alcan, 1897.

——. *Le Progrès de la conscience dans la philosophie occidentale.* Paris, Alcan, 1927.

——. *Écrits philosophiques.* Paris, Presses Universitaires de France, 1954.

Buarque de Holanda, Sérgio, *Cobra de Vidro.* São Paulo, Martins, 1944.

——. *Monções.* Rio de Janeiro, C. E. B., 1945.

——. "Prefácio Literário," in *Obras Completas* of D. J. G. de Magalhães, Vol. II. Rio de Janeiro, Ministerio da Educação, 1939.

——. *Ráies do Brasil.* 1st ed. Rio de Janeiro, José Olympio, 1936; 2d ed., 1948.

Cabral de Moncada, L. *Um "iluminista" Português do Século XVIII: Luís Antônio Vernei.* São Paulo, Saraiva, 1941.

Calógeras, João Pandiá, *A Formação Histórica do Brasil.* Rio de Janeiro, Pimenta de Melo, n.d.

——. "O Brasil em 1840," in *Revista do Instituto Hist. e Geogr. Brasileiro,* Tome 98, Vol. 152. Rio de Janeiro, Imp. Nacional, 1927.

——. *Os Jesuítas e o Ensino,* Rio de Janeiro, Imp. Nacional, 1911.

Canabrava, A. P. "Máquinas Agrícalas," in *O Estado de São Paolo,* July, 1949.

Capistrano de Abreu, João, *Estudos,* 1st ser. Rio de Janeiro, Briguiet, 1931.

——. *Estudos,* 2d ser. Rio de Janeiro, Briguiet, 1932.

——. *Estudos,* 3d ser. Rio de Janeiro, Briguiet, 1938.

——. *Correspondência de Capistrano de Abreu.* Rio de Janeiro, Inst. Nacional do Livro, 1954.

——. *Capítulos de História Colonial,* 4th ed. Rio de Janeiro, Briguiet, 1954.

Cardoso, Fausto, *Concepção Monística do Universo.* Rio de Janeiro, Laemmert, 1894.

——. *Taxinomia Social.* Rio de Janeiro, Morais, 1898.

Cardoso, Leontina L. *Licínio Cardoso—seu pensamento, sua obra, sua vida.* Rio de Janeiro, Valverde, 1944.

Cardoso, V. Licínio, *Vultos e Idéias.* Rio de Janeiro, Anuário do Brasil, 1924.

——. *Figuras e Conceitos,* Rio de Janeiro, Anuário do Brasil, 1924.

————. *Pensamentos Brasileiros.* Rio de Janeiro, Anuário do Brasil, 1924.

————. *Pensamentos Americanos.* Rio de Janeiro, Minerva, 1937.

————. *A Filosofia da Arte.* 2d ed. Rio de Janeiro, José Olympio, 1935.

————. *À Margem da História do Brasil.* São Paulo, Edit. Nacional, 1933.

Carneiro, F. "História da Imigração do Brasil, uma Interpretação," in *Boletim Geográfico, do Inst. Bras. de Geografia e Estatística,* no. 69, 1948.

Carpeaux, Oto Maria, "Notas Sôbre o Destino do Positivismo," in *Rumo,* Ann. I, Vol. I., Rio de Janeiro, 1943.

Carqueja, Bento, *O Capitalismo Moderno e as suas Origens em Portugal.* Pôrto, Lelo, 1908.

Carvalho, Joaquim de, "A Cultura Filosófica e Científica," in *História de Portugal,* ed. Damião Peres, Vol. IV. Barcelos, Portucalense, 1932.

————. *Desenvolvimento da Filosofia em Portugal durante a Idade Média.* Coimbra, Imprensa da Universidade, 1927.

————. *Estudos Sôbre a Cultura Portuguêsa do Século XVI,* Coimbra, Imprensa da Universidade, 1947.

————. "A Teoria da Verdade e do Êrro nas 'Disputationes Metaphysicae' " by F. Suarez, in *Revista da Universidade de Coimbra,* Vol. 6. Coimbra, Imprensa da Universidade de Coimbra, 1917.

Carvalho, Ronald, *Pequena História da Literatura Brasileira.* 3d ed. Rio de Janeiro, Briguiet, 1925.

————. *Estudos Brasileiros,* 1st ser. Rio de Janeiro, Anuário do Brasil, 1924.

————. *Estudos Brasileiros,* 2d ser. Rio de Janeiro, Briguiet, 1931.

————. *Estudos Brasileiros,* 3d ser. Rio de Janeiro, Briguiet, 1931.

Carvillo, M. "Francisco Suarez," in *Jornadas,* No. 43. México, Colégio do México, n.d.

Castello, José Aderaldo, *"A Polêmica sôbre a "Confederação dos Tamoios,"* in Bulletin II of the Faculty of Philosophy, Sciences, and Letters, University of São Paulo, 1953.

Castro, D. João de, *Tratado da Sphaera,* . . . , pref. e notas por A. Fontoura da Costa. Lisbon, Divisão de Publicaçoes Biblioteca Agência Geral das Colonias, 1940.

Castro, Sertório, *A República que a Revolução destruiu,* Rio de Janeiro, Bastos, 1932.

Castro, Tito Lívio, *A Mulher e a Sociogenia.* Rio de Janeiro, Alves, n.d.

————. *Questões e Problemas,* São Paulo, 1913.

Castro, Viveiros de, "A Questão Religiosa," in *Contribuições para a Biografia de D. Pedro II, Revista do Inst. Hist. e Geogr. Brasileiro,* (Part I, special no.). Rio de Janeiro, Imp. Nacional, 1925.

Cavalheiro, Edgard, *Testamento de uma Geração*. Pôrto Alegre, Globo, 1944.

Ceñal, Ramon, S.J., "Juan Caramuel, su epistolario con Anastasio Kircher, S.J.," in *Revista de Filosofia*, No. 44. Madrid, 1953.

———. "La Filosofia de Emmanuel Maignon," in *Revista de Filosofia*, No. 48. Madrid, 1954.

Cidade, H. *Ensaio sôbre a Crise Mental do séc. XVIII*. Coimbra, Imprensa da Universidade, 1929.

———. "A Literatura: O Seiscentismo," in *História de Portugal*, ed. Damião Peres, Vol. VII. Barcelos, Portucalense, 1934.

———. *A Literatura Portuguesa e a Expansão Ultramarina*, Vol. I. (Fifteenth and Sixteenth Centuries.) Lisbon, Divisão de Publicações Biblioteca Agência Geral das Colonias, 1943.

———. *Licões sôbre a Cultura e Literatura Portuguêsas*, Coimbra, Coimbra Ed., 1933–1939.

Comte, Auguste, *Apêlo aos Concervadores*. Trans. by Miguel Lemos. Rio de Janeiro, Templo da Humanidade, 1899.

———. Correspondance inédite. Paris, Siège de la Societé Positiviste, 1903.

———. *Lettres à Valat*. Paris, Dunod, 1870.

———. *Manifesto Inicial da Sociedade Positivista de Paris*. Trans. by Miguel Lemos. Rio de Janeiro, Posit. do Brasil, 1900.

———. *Cours de philosophie positive*. 6th ed. Paris, Alfred Costes, 1934.

———. *Système de politique positive*. Paris, Mathias, 1851.

———. *Testament*. 2d ed. Exec. Testamentaire d'Auguste Comte, Paris, 1896.

Constituicão Politica do Estado do Rio Grande do Sul. 2d ed. Pôrto Alegre, Echenique & Irmão, 1891.

Correio Paulistano. Cinqüentenario da República. São Paulo, Edição do Correio Paulistano, 1940.

Cortezão, Jaime, "Influência dos Descobrimentos dos Portuguêses na História da Civilização," in *História de Portugal*, ed. Damião Peres. Vol. II. Barcelos, Portucalense, 1932.

———. *Teoria Geral dos Descobrimentos Portuguêses*. Lisbon, Seara Nova, 1940.

Costa, Craveiro, *O Visconde de Sinimbu*. São Paulo, Comp. Edit. Nacional, 1937.

Costa, D. Antônio da, *História da Instrução Popular em Portugal*. 2d ed. Pôrto, Figuerinhas, 1900.

Costa, Pôrto, *Pinheiro Machado e o seu tempo*. Rio de Janeiro, José Olympio, 1951.

Costa Marques, D. *Duarte, Leal Conselheiro*. Lisbon, Classica, 1942.

Croce, Benedetto, "Antihistoricisme," in *Revue de Métaphysique et de Morale,* Paris, Colin, 1931.

———. *Il Carattere della Filosofia Moderna.* 2d ed. Bari, Laterza, 1945.

Cruz Costa, João, "Ensaio sôbre a Vida e a Obra do Filósofo Francisco Sanchez," in Bulletin XXIX, of the Faculty of Philosophy, Sciences, and Letters, University of São Paulo, 1942.

———. "O Pensamento Brasileiro," in Bulletin LXVII, of the Faculty of Philosophy, Sciences, and Letters, University of São Paulo, 1946.

———. *A Filosofia no Brasil.* Pôrto Alegre, Globo, 1945.

———. "A Situação da Filosofia no Brasil e em outros paises da América," in *A Medicina Moderna,* Vol. I, No. 2. São Paolo, 1948.

———. "Sentido da Filosofia," in *Kriterion,* Nos. 7, 8. Belo Horizonte, 1949.

———. *O Desenvolvimento da Filosofia no Brasil no séc. XIX e a Evolução Histórica Nacional.* São Paulo, Magalhães, 1950.

———. "O Positivismo na República," in *Revista de História,* Nos. 15, 16. São Paulo, 1953.

Cunha, Euclides da, *Canudos.* Rio de Janeiro, José Olympio, 1939.

———. *À Margem da História.* Pôrto, Lelo, 1913.

———. *Os Sertões.* 5th ed. Rio de Janeiro, Francisco Alves, 1914.

Dansette, Adrien, *Le Boulangisme.* Paris, Fayard, 1946.

Dantas, San Tiago, *Dois Momentos de Rui Barbosa.* Rio de Janeiro, Casa de Rui Barbosa, 1951.

Daval, R. *Histoire des idées en France.* Paris, P.U.F., 1953.

Delboux, Luís Gonzaga da Silveira, *O Padre Leonel Franca,* S.J. Rio de Janeiro, Agir, 1953.

Delgado, Luís, *Rui Barbosa.* Rio de Janeiro, José Olympio, 1945.

Delpech, Adrien, "Da Influência Estrangeira cm nossas letras," in *Anais do Congresso Internacional de História da América,* in *Revista do Inst. Hist. e Geogr. Brasileiro,* Vol. IX. Rio de Janeiro, Imp. Nacional, 1930.

Deschoux, M. *La Philosophie de Léon Brunschvicg.* Paris, Presses Universitaires de France, 1949.

Dias, Carlos M. *Pensadores Brasileiros.* Lisbon, Bertrand, n.d.

Dilthey, Wilhelm, *El Mundo Historico.* México, Fondo de Cultura Economica, 1944.

Dornas, João (filho), *O Padroado e a Igreja no Brasil.* São Paulo, Edit. Nacional, n.d.

———. *Silva Jardim.* São Paulo, Edit. Nacional, n.d.

———. *Apontamentos para a história de República.* Curitiba, Guaira, 1941.

Duque Estrada, Osório, *A Abolição.* Rio de Janeiro, Ribeiro e Maurilo, 1918.

Egídio, Paulo, *Contribuição para a história filosófica da Sociologia*. São Paulo, 1899.

Ellis, Alfredo (júnior). *O Bandeirismo Paulista e o Recuo do Meridiano*. São Paulo, Piratininga, n.d.

———. *Os Primeiros Troncos Paulistas e o Cruzamento Euro-Americano*. São Paulo, Edit. Nacional, 1936.

———. *Raca de Gigantes*. São Paulo, Helios, 1926.

Engels, Fred, "Ludwig Feuerbach et la fin de la philosophie classique allemande," in *Études philosophiques*. Paris, Sociales, 1947.

Etcheverry, A. *L'Idéalisme français contemporain*. Paris, Alcan, 1934.

Farias Brito Raimundo de, *A Base Físcia do Espírito*. Rio de Janeiro, Francisco Alves, 1912.

———. *Finalidade do Mundo (I)*. Fortaleza, Universal, 1894.

———. *Finalidade do Mundo (II)*. Fortaleza, Universal, 1899.

———. *O Mundo Interior*. Rio de Janeiro, Rev. dos Tribunais, 1914.

Febvre, Lucien, Preface to *Maîtres et esclaves* (French translation of Gilberto Freyre's *Casa-Grande e Sensala*). Paris, Gallimard, 1952.

Feliciano, José, *Les Habilités de Mr. Lemos*. São Paulo, 1899.

Ferreira, Joaquim, *O Verdadeiro Método de Estudar, por Luís Antônio Vernei*. Pôrto, Barreira, n.d.

Ferreira França, Eduardo, *Investigações de Psicologia*. Bahia, Pedrosa, 1854.

Figueiredo, Fidelino de, *Estudos de Literatura*. 4th series. Lisbon, Portugália, n.d.

Figueiredo, Jackson de, *Algumas Reflexões sôbre a Filosofia de Farias Brito*. Rio de Janeiro, Rev. dos Tribunais, 1916.

———. *Pascal e a Inquietação Moderna*. Rio de Janeiro, Anuário do Brasil, 1922.

———. *In Memoriam*. Rio de Janeiro, Centro D. Vital, 1929.

———. *Correspondência*. 3d ed. Rio de Janeiro, Agir, 1946.

Fiorentino, F. *Compendio di Storia della Filosofia*. Florence, Vallecchi, n.d.

Fleiuss, Max, *Hist. Administrativa do Brasil*. 2d ed. São Paulo, Melhoramentos, n.d.

Franca, S.J., Leonel, *Noções de História da Filosofia*. 9th ed. São Paulo, Edit. Nacional, 1943.

———. *Noções de História da Filosofia*. 2d ed. Rio de Janeiro, Pimenta de Melo, 1928.

France, Anatole, *Oeuvres complètes*. Paris, Calman-Levy, 1928. Vol. XVII.

Francovich, Guillermo, *La Filosofia en Bolivia*. Buenos Aires, Losada, 1943.

———. *Filósofos Brasileños*. Rio de Janeiro, 1939.

————. *El Pensamiento Universitario de Charcas.* Universidade de Sucre, 1948.

————. *Filósofos Brasileiros.* Trans. by I. Strenger. Preface by Cruz Costa. São Paulo, Flama, 1947.

Freyre, Gilberto, *Casa Grande e Senzala.* 4th ed. Rio de Janeiro, José Olympio, 1943.

————. *Interpretación del Brasil.* México, Fondo de Cultura Economica, 1945.

————. *O Mundo que o português criou.* Rio de Janeiro, José Olympio, 1940.

————. *Perfil de Euclides e outros Perfis.* Rio de Janeiro, José Olympio, 1944.

————. *Sobrados e Mucambos.* São Paulo, Edit. Nacional, 1936; 2d ed., Rio de Janeiro, José Olympio, 1951.

————. *Interpretação do Brasil.* Rio de Janeiro, José Olympio, 1947.

————. *Inglêses no Brasil.* Rio de Janeiro, José Olympio, 1948.

Friedman, G. *La Crise du progrès.* Paris, Gallimard, 1936.

————. *Leibniz et Spinoza.* Paris, Gallimard, 1946.

Frieiro, Eduardo, *A Ilusão Literária.* Belo Horionte, Bluhm, 1941.

————. *Letras Mineiras.* Belo Horizonte, Amigos do Livro, 1937.

————. *O Diabo na Livraria do Cônego.* Belo Horizonte, Cultura Brasileira, 1945.

Frondizi, Risieri, "Hay una Filosofia ibero-americana?" *Sep. de Realidad,* No. 8. Buenos Aires, 1948.

Gaffrée, Joaquim Lucas, "A Teoria do Conhecimento de Kant," in *Jornal do Comércio.* Rio de Janeiro, 1909.

Gaos, José, "El Pensamiento Hispanoamericano," *Jornadas,* No. 12. Mexico, Colégio de Mexico, n.d.

Garcia, Rodolfo, *Primeira Visitação do Santo Ofício às Partes do Brasil.* São Paulo, 1929.

Gentil, Alcides, *Idéias de Alberto Tôrres.* 3d ed. São Paulo, Edit. Nacional, 1938.

Gois, Damião de, *Lisboa de Quinhentos.* Trans. by R. Machado. Lisbon, A. Machado, 1937.

Gomez Robledo, Antonio, *La Filosofia en el Brasil.* México, Imprensa Universitaria, 1946.

Gonçalves Cerejeira, Cardeal, "Clenardo," in *O Humanismo em Portugal.* Coimbra, 1926.

Gouhier, Henri, *Le Jeunesse d'Auguste Comte et la formation du positivisme.* Paris, Vrin, 1933, 1936, 1941.

————. *La Vie d'Auguste Comte.* 7th ed. Paris, Gallimard, 1931.

Graça Aranha, José Pereira da, *O meu próprio Romance.* São Paulo, Edit. Nacional, 1931.

———. *Canaã*. 8th ed. Rio de Janeiro, Garnier, n.d.

———. *A Estética da Vida*. Rio de Janeiro, Garnier, n.d.

———. *O Espírito Moderno*. 2d ed. São Paulo, Edit. Nacional, n.d.

Greard, O. *Edmond Scherer*. 2d ed. Paris, Hachette,1891.

Grieco, Agripino, *Evolução da Prosa Brasileira*. Rio de Janeiro, Ariel, 1933.

Gruber, R. P. *Le Positivisme depuis Comte jusqu'à nos jours*. Paris, Letheilleux, 1893.

Hauser, H. *La Modernité du XVIᵉ siècle*. Paris, Alcan, 1930.

Hawkins, Richmond Laurin, *Auguste Comte and the United States*. Cambridge, Harvard University Press, 1936.

———. *Positivism in the United States*. Cambridge, Harvard University Press, 1938.

Hazard, Paul, *La Pensée européenne au XVIIIᵉ siècle*. Paris, Boivin, 1946.

Herculano, Alexandre, *História de Portugal*. 8th ed. Lisbon, Aillaud, Bertrand, n.d.

Hoffding, H. *Histoire de la philosophie moderne*. 3d ed. Paris, Alcan, 1924.

Hubert, R. *Histoire de la pédagogie*. Paris, Presses Universitaires de France, 1949.

Ingenieros, José, *La Cultura Filosofica en España*. Coleción Cervantes, 1916.

———. *Evolución de las Ideas Argentinas*. Buenos Aires, Rosso y Cia, 1918.

Janet, Paul and Gabriel Seailles, *Histoire de la philosophie*. 12th ed. Paris, Delagrave, 1921.

Knowles, L. C. A. *O Desenvolvimento Econômico durante o século XIX*. Coimbra, 1947.

Konstantin Oesterreich, T. "Der Wiederaufstieg der Philosophie (seit 1870)," in Ueberwegs, *Grundriss der Geschichte der Philosophie*. Berlin, Mittler, 1924. Vol. IV.

———. "Die Deutsche Philosophie des XIX Jahrhunderts und der Gegenwart," in *Uberwegs, Grundriss der Geschichte der Philosophie*. Berlin, Mittler, 1924. Vol. IV.

———. "Die Entwicklungslehre und der Monismus," in Ueberwegs, *Grundriss der Geschichte der Philosophie*. Berlin, Mittler, 1924. Vol. IV.

Korn, Alejandro, *Obras Completas*. Buenos Aires, Claridad, 1949.

Lacerda, Gustavo, *O Problema Operário no Brasil*. Rio de Janeiro, 1901.

Lacerda, Maurício, *Segunda República*. 3d ed. Rio de Janeiro, Freitos Bastos, 1931.

Lagarrigue, Jorge, *La Dictature republicaine d'après Auguste Comte.* Rio de Janeiro, Fond. Typ. "Auguste Comte," 1934.

Lalande, A. *Vocabulaire technique et critique de la philosophie.* Paris, Alcan, 1928.

Lange, F. A. *Histoire du matérialisme.* Trans. by Alfred Costes. Paris, 1921.

Leal, Aurelino, *História Constitucional do Brasil.* Rio de Janeiro, Imp. Nacional, 1915.

Leclerc, Max, *Cartas do Brasil.* Trans. by S. Milliet. São Paulo, Edit. Nacional, 1942.

Leite, S.J., Serafim, *Historia da Companhia de Jesus no Brasil.* Rio de Janeiro, Liv. Portugália e Civ. Brasileira, 1938.

Lemos, Miguel, *Artigos Episódicos* (1891). Rio de Janeiro, Templo da Humanidade, 1892.

————. *Le Calendrier positive et M. le ministre des finances.* Rio de Janeiro, Temple de l'Humanité, 1890.

————. *1ª Circular Anual do Apostolado Positivista do Brasil* (1881). 2d ed. Rio de Janeiro, Temple da Humanidade, 1900.

————. *IIIᵉ Circulaire annuelle de l'apostolat positiviste du Brésil.* Rio de Janeiro, Temple de l'Humanité, 1908.

————. *IVᵉ Circulaire annuelle de l'apostolat positiviste du Brésil* (1884). 2d. ed. Rio de Janeiro, Temple de l'Humanité, 1895.

————. *VIIIᵉ Circulaire annuelle de l'apostolat positiviste du Brésil,* 1887. Rio de Janeiro, Temple de l'Humanité, 1898.

————. *9th Circular Anual do Apostolado Positivista do Brasil* (1889). Rio de Janeiro, Templo da Humanidade, 1891.

————. *10th Circular Anual do Apostolado Positivista do Brasil* (1890). Rio de Janeiro, Templo da Humanidade, 1892.

————. *12th Circular Anual do Apostolado Positivista do Brasil* (1892). Rio de Janeiro, Templo da Humanidade, 1894.

————. *13th Circular Anual do Apostolado Positivista do Brasil* (1893). Rio de Janeiro, Templo da Humanidade, 1894.

————. *17th Circular Anual do Apostolado Positivista do Brasil* (1897). Rio de Janeiro, Templo da Humanidade, 1899.

————. *Imigração chinesa.* 2d ed. Rio de Janeiro, Templo da Humanidade, 1927.

————. *Liberdade de Imprensa.* 2d ed. Rio de Janeiro, Jornal do Comerico, 1936.

————. *O Livre Exercício da Medicina.* Rio de Janeiro, Templo da Humanidade, 1890.

————. *Louis de Camoens.* Paris, Au Siège central du positivisme, 1880.

————. *Pela Liberdade Espiritual.* Rio de Janeiro, Templo da Humanidade, n.d.

————. *O Positivismo e a Escravidão Moderna*. 2d ed. Rio de Janeiro, Templo da Humanidade, 1934.

————. *Pour notre maître et notre foi: Le positivisme et le sophiste Pierre Lafitte*. 2d ed. Rio de Janeiro, Temple de L'Humanité, 1936.

————. *Ao Povo e ao Govêrno da República, Indicações Urgentes*. Rio de Janeiro, Central, 1889.

————. *A Questão da Bandeira*. Rio de Janeiro, Templo da Humanidade, 1894.

————. *Rapport pour l'année 1866*. 2d ed. Rio de Janeiro, Temple de l'Humanité, 1936.

Lemos, Miguel, and T. Mendes, *Bases de uma Constituição Política Ditatorial Federative para a República Brasileira*. 2d ed. Rio de Janeiro, Templo da Humanidade, 1934.

————. *A Liberdade Espiritual e a Organização do Trabalho*. 2d ed. Rio de Janeiro, Templo da Humanidade, 1902.

————. *Mensagem ao General Deodoro*. Rio de Janeiro, Apostolato Positivista do Brasil, 1889.

————. *A Nossa Iniciação no Positivismo*. Rio de Janeiro, Templa da Humanidade, 1889.

————. *A Política Positiva e a Grande Naturaliação*. 2d ed. Rio de Janeiro, Templo da Humanidade, 1935.

————. *Representação ao Congresso Nacional*. 2d ed. Rio de Janeiro, Templo da Humanidade, 1935.

————. *A Última Crise*. Rio de Janeiro, Templo da Humanidade, 1891.

Lenoir, Raymond, *Condillac*. Paris, Alcan, 1924.

Leonard, E. G., "L'Église presbytérienne du Brésil et ses expériences ecclésiastiques," in *Études Évangéliques*. Aix-en-Provence, 1949.

Levy-Bruhl, Lucien, *La Philosophie d'Auguste Comte*. 6th ed. Paris, Alcan, n.d.

Lima, Hermes, *Tobias Barreto*. São Paulo, Edit. Nacional, 1939.

————. "O Positivismo e a República," in *Revista do Brasil*, Vol. II, No. 17. November, 1939.

Lins, Ivan, "Augusto Comte e o Liberalismo Econômico," in *Digesto Econômico*. São Paulo, 1949.

————. *Católicos e Positivistas*. Rio de Janeiro, 1937.

Lipparoni, Gregorio, *A Filosofia conforme a mente de S. Tomás de Aquino, exposta por Antônio Rosmini em harmonia com a religião*. Rio de Janeiro, Imprensa Industrial de João Paulo Ferreira Dias, 1880.

Lopes Praça, J. J. *História da Filosofia em Portugal*. Coimbra, Imp. Literária, 1868.

Lyra, Heitor, *História de D. Pedro II*. São Paulo, Edit. Nacional, 1938.

Macedo, Newton de, "A Renovação das Idéias e das Instituições de Cultura," in *História de Portugal*, ed. Damião Peres, Vol. VI. Barcelos, Portucalense, 1934.

Macedo Costa, D. Antônio de, *O Barão de Penedo e a sua Missão a Roma*. Rio de Janeiro, Leuzinger e Filhos, 1888.

————. *Direito contra o Direito*. Pôrto, Liv. Internacional, 1875.

————. *Processo e Julgamento do Bispo do Pará*. Rio de Janeiro, Teatral e Comercial, 1874.

Machado de Assis, Joaquim Maria, *Esaú e Jacó*. Rio de Janeiro, Garnier, n.d.

Madre de Deus, Frei Gaspar da, *Memórias para a Capitania de S. Vicente . . .* , ed. Afonso E. Taunay. São Paulo, Weizflog Irmãos, 1920.

Madureira, J. M. "A liberdade dos índios e a Companhia de Jesus," in *Revista do Inst. Hist. e Geogr. Brasileiro*, (Congresso Hist. da América), Tome IV. Rio de Janeiro, Imp. Nacional, 1927.

Magalhães, Basilio de, *Estudos de História do Brasil*. São Paulo, Edit. Nacional, 1940.

Magalhães Godinho, V. *História Econômica e Social da Expansão Portuguesa*, Lisbon, Terra, 1947.

Mangabeira, João, *Rui, o Estadista da República*. São Paulo, Martins, 1946.

Maria, Father Júlio, "A Religião," in *O Livro do Centenário (1500–1900)*, Rio de Janeiro, Imp. Nacional, 1900. Vol. I.

Maritain, Jacques, *Humanismo Integral*. São Paulo, Editôra Nacional, 1941.

Martin, Luís, *O Patriarca e o Bacharel*. São Paulo, Martins, n.d.

Mauduit, R. *Auguste Comte et la science économique*. Paris, Alcan, 1929.

Maugüé, J. "O Ensino da Filosofia—Suas Diretrizes," in *Annuário da Faculdade de Filosofia, Ciências e Letras, 1934–1935*. São Paulo, 1937.

Mawe, John, *Viagens ao Interior do Brasil*. Rio de Janeiro, Zélio Valverde, 1944.

Mayer, J. P. *Trajectoria del Pensamiento Politico*. Mexico, Fondo de Cultura Economica, 1943.

Meinecke, Friedrich, *El Historicismo y su Genesis*. Mexico, Fondo de Cultura Economica, 1943.

Melo Custódio, José de, *O Governo Provisório e a Revolução de 1893*. São Paulo, Edit. Nacional, 1938.

Melo Franco, Afonso Arinos de, *Conceito de Civilização Brasileira*. São Paulo, Edit. Nacional, 1936.

————. *O Índio Brasileiro e a Revolução Francesa*. Rio de Janeiro, José Olympio, 1937.

————. *Terra do Brasil.* São Paulo, Edit. Nacional, 1939.

————. *Desenvolvimento da Civilização Material no Brasil.* Rio de Janeiro, Serv. do Patrimônio Hist. e Art. Nacional, 1944.

————. *História e Teoria do Partido Político no Direito Constitucional Brasileiro.* Rio de Janeiro, 1948.

Melo Franco, Virgílio A. *Outubro de 1930.* 4th ed. Rio de Janeiro, Schmidt, 1931.

Melo e Sousa, Antonio Cândido de, "Introdução ao Método Crítico de Sílvio Romero." (Doctoral dissertation.) São Paulo, 1945.

Mendonça, Carlos Sussekind, *Sílvio Romero, sua Formação Intelectual.* São Paulo, Edit. Nacional, 1938.

Mendonça, Geonísio, *Os Positivistas na República.* Rio de Janeiro, n.d.

Mendonça, Renato, *O Barão de Penedo e a sua Época.* São Paulo, Edit. Nacional, 1942.

Mendonça, Salvador, *Trabalhadores Asiáticos.* New York, "Nova Mundo," 1879.

Mont'Alegre, Omer, *Tobias Barreto,* Rio de Janeiro, Vecchi, 1939.

Mont'Alverne, Francisco, *Compêndio de Filosofia.* Rio de Janeiro, Nacional, 1859.

Menendez y Pelayo, *História de los Heterodoxos Españoles,* Buenos Aires, Emecé, 1945.

Mergulhão, Benedito, *O General Café na Revolução Branca de 1937.* Rio de Janeiro, Pongetti, 1943.

Mesquita, Júlio de (filho), *Ensaios Sul-Americanos.* São Paulo, Martins, 1946.

Messer, August, *La Filosofia en el Siglo XIX.* Madrid, Revista de Occidente, 1926.

Meunier, René, *Introduction à la sociologie.* Paris, Alcan, 1929.

Milliet, Sérgio, *O Roteiro do Café a outros Ensaios.* São Paulo, Dept. de Cultura, 1941.

Moacyr, Primitivo, *A Instrução e o Império.* São Paulo, 1936.

Mondolfo, Rodolfo, *En los Origenes de la Filosofia de la Cultura.* Buenos Aires, 1942.

Moniz, Egas, *Ao lado da Medicina.* Lisbon, Bertrand, 1940.

Monteiro Lobato, J. B. *A Barca de Gleyre.* São Paulo, Edit. Nacional, 1944.

Montesquieu, L. *Le Système politique d'Auguste Comte.* Paris, Lib. Nationale, n.d.

Morais, Evaristo de, *Da Monarquia para a República.* Rio de Janeiro, Atena, n.d.

————. *A Escravidão Africana no Brasil.* São Paulo, Edit. Nacional, 1933.

Moreira Lima L. *A Coluna Prestes.* São Paulo, Brasiliense, 1945.

Morazé, Charles, *Trois essais sur histoire et culture*. Paris, Colin, 1948.

Morus, Campanella, Bacon, *Utopias del Renascimiento*. Coimbra, Imprensa da Universidade, 1872.

Motta, Cândido (filho), *Uma Grande Vida*. São Paulo, Politica, 1931.

Motta Veiga, M. E. da, *Esbôço Histórico-Literário da Faculdade de Teologia da Universidade de Coimbra*. Coimbra, Imprensa da Universidade, 1872.

Nabuco, Joaquim, *Um Estadisto do Império*. Rio de Janeiro, Garnier, n.d.

———. *A Intervenção Estrangeira durante a Revolta*. São Paulo, Edit. Nacional, 1939.

———. *A minha formação*. Rio de Janeiro, Garnier, 1900.

Neme, Mário, *Plataforma da Nova Geração*. Pôrto Alegre, Globo, 1945.

Nietzsche, *Lettres choisies*. Paris, Stock, 1931.

Nobiling, O. *As Cantigas de D. João Garcia de Guilhade*. Erlangen, Jung & Sohn, 1907.

Nogueira, Hamilton, *Jackson de Figueiredo*. Rio de Janeiro, Terra de Sol, n.d.

Normano, J. F. *Evolução Econômica do Brasil*. São Paulo, Edit. Nacional, 1939.

Oesterreich. *See* Konstantin.

Oliveira Franca, E. "O Poder Real em Portugal e as Origens do Absolutismo," in Bulletin LXVIII of the Faculty of Philosophy, Sciences, and Letters, University of São Paulo, 1946.

———. "A Ocupação Econômica do Brasil pelos Europeus," in *Paralelos*, Nos. 4, 5, February–June. São Paulo, 1947.

Oliveira, José Osório de, *Breve História da Literatura Brasileira*. Lisbon, Inquérito, 1939.

———. *Ensaístas Brasileiros*. Lisbon, Bertrand, n.d.

Oliveira Lima, Manoel de, *O Império Brasileiro*. São Paulo, Melhoramentos, n.d.

———. *D. João VI no Brasil*. 1st ed. Rio de Janeiro, Jornal do Comércio, 1908.

Oliveira Martins, J. P. *Os Filhos de D. João I*. 5th ed. Lisbon, A. M. Pereira, 1926.

———. *História da Civilização Ibérica*. 6th ed. Lisbon, A. M. Pereira, 1918.

Oliveira Tôrres, João Camilo de, *O Positivismo no Brasil*. Petrópolis, Vozes, 1943.

Oliveira Viana, F. J. de, *O Ocaso do Império*. São Paulo, Melhoramentos, n.d.

———. *O Idealismo na Evolução Política do Império e da República*. São Paulo, 1922.

————. *Populações Meridionais do Brasil.* 3d ed. São Paulo, Edit. Nacional, 1933.

————. *Evolução do Povo Brasileiro.* São Paulo, Monteiro Lobato, n.d.

Ottoni, C. B. *O advento da República no Brasil.* Rio de Janeiro, Perseverança, 1890.

Pacheco Pereira, Duarte, *Esmeraldo de Situ Orbis.* Lisbon, Sociedade de Geografia de Lisboa, 1905.

Palha, Américo, *História da Vida de Rui Barbosa.* Rio de Janeiro, Casa de Rui Barbosa, 1954.

Peabody, A. P. *The Positive Philosophy.* Boston, Gould and Lincoln, 1867.

Perdigão Malheiros, Agostinho Marques, *A Escravidão no Brasil.* São Paulo, Cultura, 1944.

Pereira, Lúcia Miguel, *Machado de Assis.* São Paulo, Edit. Nacional, 1936. Vol. XII.

————. *História da Lit. Brasileira.* Rio de Janeiro, José Olympio, 1950.

Pereira Barreto, Luís, *O seculo XX sob o ponto de vista brasileiro.* São Paulo, "O Estado de São Paulo," 1901.

————. *Positivismo e Teologia.* São Paulo, Popular de Abílio A. S. Marques, 1880.

————. *As Três Filosofias (Part I): Filosofia Teológica.* Rio de Janeiro, Laemmert, 1874.

————. *As Três Filosofias (Part II): A Filosofia Metafísica.* Jacareí, Comercial, 1876.

Pereira da Silva, João Nanoce, *História do Brasil durante a minoridade de D. Pedro II.* 2d ed. Rio de Janeiro, Garnier, n.d.

Pernetta, João, *Os Dois Apóstolos.* Curitiba, 1927, 1928, 1929.

Perry, R. B. "Is There a North American Philosophy?" in *Philosophy and Phenomenological Research,* Vol. X, No. 3 (March, 1949).

Picanco, M. *Clóvis Beviláqua.* Rio de Janeiro, Educadora, 1936.

Picard, Roger, *Le Romantisme social.* New York, Brentano, 1944.

Picavet, F. *Les Idéologues.* Paris, Alcan, 1891.

————. *Histoire générale et comparée des philosophies médievales.* Paris, Alcan, 1907.

Pinheiro, Nuno, "Financas Nacionais," in *À Margem da História da República.* Rio de Janeiro, Anuário do Brasil, 1924.

Pinheiro Chagas, Paulo, *Teófilo Ottoni, o ministro do povo.* Rio de Janeiro, Valverde, 1943.

Pinheiro Ferreira, Silvestre, "Memórias Políticas sôbre os abusos gerais e o modo de os reformar e prevenir a revolução popular," in *Revista do Instituto Histórico e Geográfico Brasileiro,* Vol. XLVIII. Rio de Janeiro, 1884.

————. *Noções Elementares de Filosofia e sua aplicação às ciências morais e políticas*. Paris, Rey et Gravier, 1839.

————. *Preleções Philosophicas sôbre a Theórica do discurso e da Linguagem, a Esthetica, a Diceosyna e a Cosmologia*. Rio de Janeiro, Imprensa Régia, 1813.

Pires, Homero, *Junqueira Freire*. Rio de Janeiro, Edição da Ordem, 1929.

Pontes, Eloy, *A Vida Dramática de Euclides da Cunha*. Rio de Janeiro, José Olympio, n.d.

Prado, Caio (júnior), *Evolução Politica do Brasil*. São Paulo, 1933.

————. *Formação do Brasil Contemporaneo*. São Paulo, Martins, 1942.

————. *História Econômica do Brasil*. São Paulo, Edit. Brasiliense, 1945.

————. *Evolução Politica do Brasil*. 2d ed. São Paulo, Brasiliense, 1953.

Prado, Eduardo da Silva, *A Bandeira Nacional*. 2d ed. São Paulo, 1921.

————. "O Catolicismo, a Companhia de Jesus e a colonizaçã do Brasil," in *III Centenário do Venerável José de Anchieta*. Lisbon, Aillaud, 1900.

————. "Fastos da Ditadura Militar no Brasil," in *Revista de Portugal*, December, 1889–June, 1890 [2d ed. São Paulo, 1902].

————. "Imigration," in *Le Brésil* by M. F. J. de Sant'Anna Nery. Paris, Delagrave, 1889.

Prado, Paulo da Silva, *Paulística*. 1st ed. São Paulo, Gráfica Editôra Monteiro Lobato, 1925; 2d ed. Rio de Janeiro, Ariel, 1934.

————. *Retrato do Brasil*. São Paulo, Duprat, 1928.

Prenant, Lucy, "Marx et Comte," in *A la lumière du marxisme*, Vol. II. Paris, Sociales Internacionales, 1937.

Quental, Antero de, "Causas da Decadência dos Povos Peninsulares nos últimos três séculos," in *Prosas*, Coimbra, Imprensa da Universidade, 1926. Vol. II.

Querino Ribeiro, José, "A 'Memória' de Martim Francisco sôbre a Reforma dos estudos na Capitania de São Paulo." Bulletin LIII of the Faculty of Philosophy, Sciences, and Letters, University of São Paulo, 1945.

Quintas, Amaro, *Um Intérprete da Revolução Praieira*. Recife, Imp. Oficial, 1948.

————. *Consideraçoes sobre a Revolução Praieira*, separate of the *Revista do Arq. Público*, ano III, Vol V. Recife, Imp. Oficial, 1949.

Rabelo, Sílvio, *Euclides da Cunha*. Rio de Janeiro, C. E. B., 1948.

————. *Farias Brito ou Uma Aventura do Espírito*. Rio de Janeiro, José Olympio, 1941.

————. *Itinerário de Sílvio Romero*. Rio de Janeiro, José Olympio, 1944.

Ramalho Ortigão, A. B. *A moeda circulante*. Rio de Janeiro, Leite, 1912.

———. "Surto do Cooperativismo, etc.," in Contribuições para a Biografia de D. Pedro II (Part I) of the Revista do Inst. Hist. e Geogr Brasileiro. Rio de Janeiro, Imp. Nacional, 1925.

Ramos, Samuel, História de la Filosofía en México. México, Imprenta Universitaria, 1943.

Ramos Carvalho, Laerte, "A lógica de Mont'Alverne," in Bulletin LXVI, of the Faculty of Philosophy, Sciences, and Letters, University of São Paulo, 1946.

———. "Feijó e o Kantismo," in Estado de São Paulo, 1949.

———. A Formação Filosófica de Farias Brito. São Paulo, 1951.

Raposo de Almeida, José Maria, "Origens do Colégio Pedro II," in Rev. do Inst. Hist. e Geogr. Brasileiro, Vol. XIX. Rio de Janeiro, Imp. Nacional, 1898.

Ravaisson, Félix, La Philosophie en France au XIXe siècle. 2d ed. Paris, Hachette, 1885.

Reale, Miguel, A Doutrina de Kant no Brasil. São Paulo, 1949.

———. "Feijó e o Kantismo," in Fôlha da Manhã. 1949.

———. "Posição de Rui Barbosa no mundo da Filosofia," in Anais do I Congresso Brasileiro de Filosofia. São Paulo, 1950.

Reik, Theodor, Treinta anos con Freud. Buenos Aires, Iman, 1943.

Reyes, Alfonso, Última Tule. México, Imprenta Universitaria, 1942.

Rezende, José Severino de, Eduardo Prado. São Paulo, Falcone, n.d.

Ribeiro, Álvaro. O Problema da Filosofia Portuguêsa. Lisbon, Inquérito, 1943.

Ribeiro, João, "A Filosofia no Brasil," in Revista do Brasil, No. 22, An. II, Vol. VI. 1917.

———. História do Brasil. 12th ed. Rio de Janeiro, Alves, 1929.

———. Crítica: Os Modernos. Rio de Janeiro, Brasileira de Letras, 1952.

Ribeiro, José Silvestre, História dos Estabelecimentos Científicos Literários e Artísticos de Portugal. Lisbon, Academia Real das Ciências, 1874.

Ribeiro de Andrada, Antônio Carlos, Os Bancos de Emissão no Brasil.

Rocha Pitta, Sebastião, História da América Portuguêsa. 2d ed. Lisbon, Francisco A. da Silva, 1880.

Rocha Pombo, José Francisco da, História do Brasil. Rio de Janeiro, Aguila, n.d. Vol. X.

Rodrigues, Milton Camargo da Silva, Educação Comparada. São Paulo, Edit. Nacional, 1938.

Rodrigues de Brito, J. A Economia Brasileira no Alvorescer do Século XIX. Salvador, Bahia, Progresso, n.d.

Rodrigues Lapa, Dom Duarte e os Prosadores da Casa de Aviz. Lisbon, Seara Nova, 1940.

————. *Das Origens da Poesia Lírica em Portugal na Idade Média.* Lisbon, Seara Nova, 1929.

Romero, Francisco, *Filosofia de la Persona.* Buenos Aires, Losada, 1944.

————. *Influencia del Descubrimiento de America en las Ideas Generales.* Buenos Aires, Lopez, 1944.

Romero, Sílvio, *Ensaio de Filosofia de Direito.* 2d ed. Rio de Janeiro, Alves, 1908.

————. *Novos estudos de Literatura Contemporânea.* Rio de Janeiro, Garnier, n.d.

————. *Evolução da Literatura Brasileira.* Campanha, 1905.

————. *O Evolucionismo e o Positivismo no Brasil.* 2d ed. Rio de Janeiro, Alves, 1895.

————. "Explicações Indispensáveis," preface in Tobias Barreto, *Vários Escritos.* 1st ed. Rio de Janeiro, Laemmert, 1900.

————. *A Filosofia no Brasil.* Pôrto Alegre, Deutsche Zeitung, 1878.

————. *História da Literatura Brasileira.* 2d ed. Rio de Janeiro, Garnier, 1902; 3d ed. Rio de Janeiro, José Olympio, 1943.

————. "A Prioridade de Pernambuco no movimento espiritual brasileiro," in *Revista Brasileira.* Rio de Janeiro, 1879.

————. *Outros Estudos de Literatura Contemporânea.* Lisbon, A Editôra, 1905.

————. *Zeverissimações Ineptas da Crítica.* Pôrto, "Comércio do Pôrto," 1909.

Rosa, Otelo, *Júlio de Castilhos.* Pôrto Alegre, Globo, 1928.

Roure, Agenor, *A Constituinte Republicana.* Rio de Janeiro, Imp. Nacional, 1920.

Rouvre, Ch. *L'Amoureuse histoire d'Auguste Comte et de Clotilde de Vaux.* Paris, Calman-Levy, 1920.

————. *A Vida Psíquica do Homem.* Rio de Janeiro, Laemmert, 1903.

Sá Pereira, Virgílio de, *Tobias Barreto.* Rio de Janeiro, Rev. dos Tribunais, 1917.

Sabóia, Barão Visconde de, *Traços da Política Republicana no Brasil.* Rio de Janeiro, 1897.

Sabóia, Lima A. *Alberto Tôrres e a sua Obra.* Rio de Janeiro, Labor, n.d.

Sacramento Blake, Augusto Vitorino Alves do *Dicionário Bibliográfico Brasileiro.* Rio de Janeiro, Imp. Nacional, 1883.

Saitta, Giuseppe, *Le Origini del neo-tomismo nel secolo XIX.* Bari, Laterza, 1912.

————. *La Scolastica del Secolo XVI e la Politica dei Gesuiti.* Turin, Bocca, 1911.

Salgado, A. (júnior), *O Verdadeiro Método de Estudar,* of Luís Antônio Verney, Lisbon, Sá da Costa, 1949–1952. 4 vols.

Salles, Campos, *Da Propaganda à Presidência.* São Paulo, 1908.

Sanchez-Reulet, Anibal, *La Filosofia Latinoamericana Contemporanea.* Washington, D.C., Panamerican Union, 1949.

Sant'Ana, Dionisio, *A não cooperação da inteligência ibérica na ciração das ciências.* Lisbon, Seara Nova, 1941.

Santos, Delfim, "Silvestre Pinheiro Ferreira," in *Perspectivas da Literatura Portuguêsa do século XIX.* Lisbon, Atica, 1947. Vol. I.

Santos, José Maria dos, *A Política Geral no Brasil.* São Paulo, Magalhães, 1930.

Santos Werneck, A. L. *O Positivismo Republicano na Academia.* São Paulo, Seckler, 1880.

Schneider, Herbert. *A History of American Philosophy.* New York, Columbia University Press, 1947.

Sée, Henri, *Les Origines du capitalisme moderne.* Paris, Colin, 1930.

Seillière, E. *Auguste Comte.* Paris, Alcan, 1924.

———. *Le Romantisme.* Paris, Stock, 1925.

Senna, Caio Nélson de, *João Pinheiro da Silva.* Belo Horizonte, 1941.

Sentroul, Mons. C. *Tratodo de Lógica.* 2d ed. Rio de Janeiro, Alves, 1912.

Sérgio, Antônio, *Antologia dos Economistas Portuguêses,* Lisbon, Biblioteca Nacional, 1924.

———. Art. sôbre o trabalho do Dr. Murias: "O Seiscentismo em Portugal," in *Lusitânia.* 1924.

———. *História de Portugal.* Barcelona, Editorial Labor, 1929.

———. "O reino cadaveroso ou o problema da Cultura em Portugal," in *Ensaios,* Vol. II. Lisbon, Seara Nova, 1929.

Serrano, Jonathas, *Farias Brito.* Comp. Edit. Nacional, 1939.

Silva, Inocêncio F. da, *Dicionário Bibliográfico.* Lisbon, Imp. Nacional, 1862.

Silva Bastos, J. T. *História da Censura Intelectual em Portugal.* Coimbra, Imprensa da Universidade, 1926.

Silva Jardim, Antônio, *Salvação da Patria.* Santos, "Diário de Santos," 1888.

———. *A República no Brasil.* Rio de Janeiro, Montalverne, 1889.

———. *Pela República contra a Monarquia.* Rio de Janeiro, "Gazeta de Notícias," 1889.

Silveira, Tasso Azevedo da, "A Consciência Brasileira," in *À Margem da História da República.* Rio de Janeiro, Anuário do Brasil, 1924.

Silveira Peixoto, *A Tormenta que Prudente de Morais Venceu.* Curitiba, Editôra Guaira, 1942.

Simões de Paula, E. *Marrocos e as suas relações com a Ibéria na antiguidade.* São Paulo, 1946.

Simon, Jules, *Victor Cousin.* 4th ed. Paris, Hachette, 1910.

Simonsen, Roberto, *História Econômica do Brasil*. São Paulo, Edit. Nacional, 1937.

———. *A Evolução Industrial do Brasil*. São Paulo, 1939.

Sodré, Alcino, *A Gênese da Desordem*. Rio de Janeiro, Bras, n.d.

Solana, Marcial, *História de la Filosofia Española* (*Epoca del Renacimiento*). Madrid, Associacion Española para el Progreso de las Ciencias, 1941.

Sorley, W. R. *History of English Philosophy*. Cambridge University Press, 1920.

Sousa, José Soriano de, *Compêndio de Filosofia ordenado segundo os princípios e o método do Doutor Angélico S. Tomás de Aquino*. Recife, Renascença, 1867.

Sousa Bandeira, A. H. de, "Rosmini e a Sociedade Brasileira," in *Revista Brasileira*, VIII. 1881.

Sousa Silva, Joaquim Norbeto de, "Criação de uma Universidade no Império do Brasil," in *Revista do Inst. Hist. e Geog. Brasileiro*, Vol. LI. Rio de Janeiro, Garnier, 1875.

Spuller, E. *Royer-Collard*. Paris, Hachette, 1895.

Strowski, Fortunat, *Montaigne*, Paris, Alcan, 1906.

Taine, H. *Les Philosophes classiques du XIXe siècle en France*. 6th ed. Paris, Hachette, 1888.

Tamm, Paulo, *João Pinheiro*. Belo Horizonte, 1947.

Tarquínio de Sousa, Octavio, *Vida de D. Pedro I*. Rio de Janeiro, José Olympio, 1953.

———. *José Bonifácio*. Rio de Janeiro, José Olympio, 1945.

———. *O Pensamento Vivo de José Bonifácio*. São Paulo, Martins, 1944.

———. "Frades e Professôres," in *O estado de São Paulo*. 1947.

Teixeira Mendes, Raimundo, *O Ano sem Par*. Rio de Janeiro, Templo da Humanidade, 1900.

———. "Apontamentos para a solução do problema social no Brasil," in *O Positivismo e a Escravidão Moderna*. 2d ed. Rio de Janeiro, Templo da Humanidade, 1934.

———. *A Bandeira Nacional*. 2d ed. Rio de Janeiro, Templo da Humanidade, 1921.

———. *Benjamin Constant*. 2d ed. Rio de Janeiro, Templo da Humanidade, 1913.

———. *Benjamin Constant*. Edição Comemorativa. Rio de Janeiro, Imprensa Nacional, 1936.

———. *Circular Anual* (1908). Rio de Janeiro, Templo da Humanidade, 1904.

———. *Circular Anual* (1908). Rio de Janeiro, Templo da Humanidade, 1909.

————. *A Incorporação do Proletariado na Sociedade Moderna.* 2d ed. Rio de Janeiro, Templo da Humanidade, 1908.

————. *A Mistificação Democrática e a Regeneração Social.* Rio de Janeiro, Templo da Humanidade, 1906.

————. *A Pátria Brasileira*, 2d ed. Rio de Janeiro, Templo da Humanidade, 1902.

————. *Resumo Cronológico da Evolução do Positivismo no Brasil.* Rio de Janeiro, Templo da Humanidade, 1930.

————. *Uma Retificação: a ditadura republicana e o positivismo.* 2d ed. Rio de Janeiro, Templo da Humanidade, 1933.

————. *A Universidade.* 2d ed. Rio de Janeiro, Templo da Humanidade, 1903.

————. *A Verdadeira Política Republicana e a Incorporação do Proletariado na Sociedade Moderne (I).* Rio de Janeiro, Templo da Humanidade, 1912.

————. *A Verdadeira Política Republicana e a Incorporação do Proletariado na Sociedade Moderna (III).* Rio de Janeiro, Templo da Humanidade, 1914.

Teixeira de Sousa, *Calderón de la Barca.* 2d ed. Rio de Janeiro, Templo da Humanidade, 1936.

Thomas, Lothar, *Contribuição para a História da Filosofia Portuguêsa.* Lisbon, Liv. Clássica Ed., 1944.

Tobias Barreto de Meneses, *Estudos Alemães.* Recife, Central, 1883.

————. *Obras Completas, Polêmicas,* Vol. II. Edição do Estado de Sergipe, 1926.

————. *Obras Completas,* Vol. IX: *Questões Vigentes.* Edição do Estado de Sergipe, 1926.

————. *Obras Completas,* Vol. X: *Vários Escritos.* Edição do Estado de Sergipe, 1926.

Tobias Monteiro, *História do Império (A Elaboração da Independência).* Rio de Janeiro, Briguiet, 1927.

————. *Pesquisas e Depoimentos.* Rio de Janeiro, Alves, 1913.

————. *O Presidente Campos Sales na Europa.* Rio de Janeiro, Briguiet, 1928.

————. "A Tolerância do Imperador." in *Contribuições para a Biografia de Pedro II, Revista do Inst. Hist. e Geogr. Brasileiro,* Vol. 152, tome 98. Rio de Janeiro, Imp. Nacional, 1927.

Tôrres, Alberto. *Le Problème mondial.* Rio de Janeiro, Imp. Nacional, 1913.

————. *A Organização Nacional.* Rio de Janeiro, Imp. Nacional, 1914.

————. *O Problema Nacional.* Rio de Janeiro, Imp. Nacional, 1914.

————. *Fontes de Vida no Brasil.* Rio de Janeiro, 1915.

Torres Gonçalves, C. *As Constituições de 14 do Julho e de 10 de novembro*. Rio de Janeiro, Jornal do Comércio, 1940.

Townsend, H. G. *On the History of Philosophy*. University of California Publications in Philosophy, vol. 16, no. 8. Berkeley, University of California Press, 1946.

———. *Philosophical Ideas in the United States*. New York, American Book Company, 1934.

Unamuno, Miguel de, *Del sentimiento Tragico de la Vida*. Madrid, Renascimiento, n.d.

Venâncio, Francisco (filho), *A Glória de Euclides da Cunha*. São Paulo, Edit. Nacional, 1940.

Veríssimo, José, Dias de Mattos, *Estudos de Literatura Brasileira*. 1st. ser. Rio de Janeiro, Garnier, 1901–1907. 6 vols.

———. *História da Literatura Brasileira*. Rio de Janeiro, Alves, 1916.

Viana, Luís (filho), *A Sabinada*. Rio de Janeiro, José Olympio, 1938.

———. *A Vida de Rui Barbosa*. São Paulo, Edit. Nacional, 1941.

Viana Moog, Cladomir, *Uma Interpretação da Literatura Brasileira*. Rio de Janeiro, C. E. D., 1943.

Villeroy, A. Ximeno de, *Benjamin Constant e a Política Republicana*. Rio de Janeiro, 1916.

Vitier, M. *La Filosofia en Cuba*. México, Fondo do Cultura Economica, 1948.

Vitor, Nestor, *Farias Brito*. Rio de Janeiro, Revista dos Tribunais, 1917.

Weber, Alfred, *Histoire de la philosophie européenne*. 9th ed. Paris, Fischbacher, 1925.

Weber, Max, *Historia Economica General*. México, Fondo de Cultura Economica, 1942.

Webster, C. K. *Gran Bretanha y la Independencia de la America Latina*. Buenos Aires, Kraft, 1944.

Werneck, Américo, *Erros e Vícios da Organização Republicana*. Petrópolis, "Correio de Petrópolis," 1893.

Werneck Sodré, Nélson, *Formação da Sociedade Brasileira*. Rio de Janeiro, José Olympio, 1944.

———. *História da Literatura Brasileira*. 2d ed. Rio de Janeiro, José Olympio, 1940.

———. "O Tratado de Methuen," in *Digesto Econômico*, June, 1949.

Wulf, Maurice de, *Histoire de la philosophie médievale*. 5th ed. Paris, Alcan, 1925.

Zama, César, *Um Capítulo de História Contemporânea*. 1893.

Zea, Leopoldo, "Antecedentes Historicistas en Hispanoamerica," in *Filosofia y Letras*, no. 28 (Oct.–Dec., 1947). Mexico.

———. *El Positivismo en México*. Mexico, Colegio de México, 1943.

————. *Ensayos sóbre la Filosofia en la Historia.* México, Editorial Stylo, 1948.
Zevaès, Alexandre, *Histoire de la troisième republique.* Paris, Anquetil, 1926.

Newspapers

Correio da Manhã. Rio de Janeiro.
Correio Paulistano. São Paulo.
Diário Popular. São Paulo.
Estado de São Paulo.
Fôlha da Manhã. São Paulo.
Jornal do Comércio.
Jornal de São Paulo.
País. Rio de Janeiro.
Província de São Paulo.

Periodicals

Cadernos da Hora Presente. São Paulo.
Filosofia y Letras. Mexico City.
Kriterion. Belo Horizonte.
A Medicina Moderna. São Paulo.
Revista do Brasil. Rio de Janeiro.
Revista de História. São Paulo.
Revue de Métaphysique et de Morale. Paris.

INDEX

Index